J. ALBERTO SOGGIN

INTRODUCTION TO THE OLD TESTAMENT

THE OLD TESTAMENT LIBRARY

General Editors

J. ALBERTO SOGGIN

INTRODUCTION
TO THE
OLD TESTAMENT

FROM ITS ORIGINS TO THE CLOSING
OF THE ALEXANDRIAN CANON

THE WESTMINSTER PRESS
PHILADELPHIA

Translated by John Bowden from the Italian
Introduzione all'Antico Testamento
second revised and updated edition,
© Paideia Editrice, Brescia 1974,
with additional revisions by the author.
The bibliography has been completely revised
for English-speaking readers by R. J. Coggins.

Translation © SCM Press Ltd. 1976

Published by The Westminster Press®

Philadelphia, Pennsylvania

PRINTED IN THE UNITED STATES OF AMERICA

Library of Congress Cataloging in Publication Data

Soggin, J   Alberto.
  Introduction to the Old Testament, from its origins
to the closing of the Alexandrian canon.

  Translation of the 2d rev. and updated ed. of
Introduzione all'Antico Testamento.
  Bibliography: p.
  Includes index.
  1. Bible. O.T. — Introductions. I. Title.
BS475.2.S613   221.6'6   -76-20650
ISBN 0-664-21339-1

To my wife

CONTENTS

IV   DESCRIPTIONS OF THE OLD TESTAMENT

V   MYTH, LEGEND AND HISTORY

VI   THE PRE-LITERARY DEVELOPMENT OF THE BIBLICAL MATERIAL

PART TWO

THE PENTATEUCH AND THE FORMER PROPHETS

I   THE PENTATEUCH

II   THE INDIVIDUAL SOURCES: THE 'YAHWIST' AND THE 'ELOHIST'

PART THREE

THE PRE-EXILIC PROPHETS

PART FOUR

THE EXILIC AND POST-EXILIC PROPHETS

PART FIVE

THE WRITINGS

PART SIX

THE DEUTERO–CANONICAL BOOKS

APPENDIX I: PALESTINIAN INSCRIPTIONS FROM THE FIRST HALF OF THE FIRST MILLENIUM

APPENDIX II: PAPYRI FROM THE FIRST CENTURIES AFTER THE EXILE

PREFACE TO THE FIRST EDITION

This work sets out to present to a wider audience material which is usually difficult to find because of the specialized character of the books which deal with it. Too often it happens that people with a good general education do not feel drawn to a critical study of the Old Testament, or that students of the arts, theology and sometimes law fail to specialize in the subject because of the lack of a work which familiarizes them with its literary problems and shows them, where possible, assured solutions without discouraging them by its size and the difficulty of understanding it.

Moreover, since Hebrew language and literature have traditionally been the gateway to all Semitic studies (this is not the place to ask with what justification), who knows whether presenting the biblical literature in an accessible form might not succeed in introducing an increasing number of students not only to the Old Testament but also to the wider context of Semitic languages and literature to which the Old Testament belongs? This discipline has made brilliant progress over recent years and is a worthy heir to a tradition of study which has never been interrupted.

Consequently, only a selected bibliography is given, and it has been necessary to limit it to essential reading. Such a choice inevitably runs the risk of being subjective, and is therefore open to fundamental criticism. On the other hand, the works of R. H. Pfeiffer, [2]1948, and O. Eissfeldt, 1965, which are cited in the bibliography, provide almost complete information.

A work like this runs the risk of not being theological enough for the theologian and being too theological for the rest. At this point some more precise remarks may be of help to the latter group. From whatever point of view we may wish to study the Old Testament, it is necessary to remember that it has always been handed down as holy scripture, first by Israel, then by Israel and the church; consequently it has been used in liturgy and in public and private devotion since time immemorial. We only have the Old Testament at all because it is sacred book, and its transmission has been a complex one. The study of biblical theology is not, therefore, just an activity reserved for theologians or for the faithful in general; it is an essential means of understanding the texts themselves. To ignore this distinctive character of biblical literature would be *a priori* to rob it of its essential content, abandoning the empathy which Dilthey came to consider a necessary condition for understanding every form of culture. Anyone who studies the Old Testament, whether or not he has a personal faith, will constantly have to come to terms with the theological element in it if he wishes to understand what he is reading. The theologian, on the other hand, should not expect in a work like this expressions of confessional stances which are not relevant to the subject matter: what we propose is as objective a study as possible of the texts, their history, their content and their development.

I have not referred to other *Introductions* and commentaries unless this has been inevitable. In fact, however, the present book presupposes their existence. As the principal *Introductions* are listed in the bibliography, it will not be difficult for anyone who wishes to find the relevant passages. The *Introduction* to which I am most indebted is that of A. Weiser, 1961. I have avoided citing biblical passages except where proper understanding of them depends on the way in which they are translated. Any reader who is not conversant with the original should therefore refer to a good translation. Need anyone be reminded that the Old Testament is meant to be read, from the moment when studies begin? Or, to put the question more pointedly: who would dare to study any kind of literature without constant attention to the text?

I am indebted to my students in Buenos Aires, Rome and Princeton who have seen this work grow through my lectures. I have received a great deal of stimulation from them, and they have often called my attention to many problems which otherwise would have at least partly escaped me. Moreover, it is through animated discussion with them that this work came to be written.

Lastly, my grateful thanks go to Dr Marcella Ravà, who with indefatigable care supervised the preparation of the manuscript for the publisher.

Rome
November 1967

PREFACE TO THE SECOND EDITION

It has taken only a few years (considering the nature of the work) for the first edition of this *Introduction* to be sold out. The reader who is familiar with it will note that in the second edition not only have a number of errors and inadequate or misleading statements been corrected, but in a number of points what was written in the first edition has been modified or amplified. Most radical changes have been made in the sections dealing with the Pentateuch, following a course held at the Pontifical Biblical Institute in Rome in the second semester of the academic year 1970–71. The sections dealing with the prophets and wisdom have each been expanded by an introduction aimed at giving the reader information about the problems associated with them; the material on the prophets was used in another course held at the Pontifical Biblical Institute in the second semester of the academic year 1972–73. The present volume is thus truly a second edition and not simply a revised and updated reprint of the first edition. As such, it served as the basis for a course on Hebrew literature in the biblical period, held in the University of Rome in the academic year 1972–73. The chronological charts at the end of the book have been enlarged; the chronology worked out by W. F. Albright and his disciples has been supplemented with that of J. Begrich, recently brought up to date by A. Jepsen, for reasons which will be given later; the problem of the chronology of the pre-exilic period of the Old Testament is so complex that a satisfactory solution is extremely improbable. The bibliographies have been brought up to date, where possible up to 1972, but some important items will certainly have been omitted.

From what has been said, the reader will have inferred that the present work has grown out of courses of lectures; it maintains a number of their characteristics. This was inevitable, even if the presentation may sometimes prove inconvenient as a result. In any case, I would like to thank those who have received the first edition of this work favourably, and especially those who produced criticisms and suggestions; where I have considered them to be well-founded, I have incorporated them in the second edition.

Once more, the patient and rigorous work of Dr Marcella Ravà has been of immense help. I am again deeply grateful.

Rome
January 1973

PREFACE TO THE ENGLISH EDITION

This English edition of the *Introduction* is based on the second Italian edition. It has been possible, however, to update certain parts of the original and to correct several slips, some of which were noted by a colleague in the Waldensian School at Rome, M. Sinigaglia. The bibliography has been brought up to 1974–75. Only in the chapter on Deutero–Isaiah have some major changes been introduced; on the whole, however, the text is that of the Italian edition.

The author acknowledges the friendly and helpful reviews by É. Lipiński, *VT* 25, 1975, 538–61; G. Garbini, *AION* 35, 1975, 139–44; M. Treves, *Bollettino dell' Amicizia ebraico-cristiana* 10, 1975, 55–9; A. A. DiLella, *CBQ* 37, 1975, 426f.; and G. Ravasi, *La Scuola cattolica* 102, 1975, 664f. A large number of their suggestions have been incorporated into the translation, as far as this was possible and did not contradict the author's opinions, based on his own scholarship.

Rome   J.A.S.
Autumn 1975

ABBREVIATIONS

A	Greek translation by Aquila
AASOR	*Annual of the American Schools of Oriental Research*, New Haven
AB	Anchor Bible, New York
AION	*Annali dell'Istituto Orientale di Napoli*
ALUOS	*Annual of the Leeds University Oriental Society*
ANEP	J. B. Pritchard (ed.), *The Ancient Near East in Pictures*, Princeton ²1969
ANET	J. B. Pritchard (ed.), *Ancient Near Eastern Texts relating to the Old Testament*, Princeton ³1969
AO	Archiv für Orientforschung, Graz
ArOr	*Archiv Orientální*, Prague
ASTI	*Annual of the Swedish Theological Institute*, Jerusalem/Leiden
ATD	Das Alte Testament Deutsch, Göttingen
Aug	*Augustinianum*, Rome
BA	*The Biblical Archaeologist*, New Haven
BASOR	*Bulletin of the American Schools of Oriental Research*, New Haven
BeO	*Bibbia e Oriente*, Fossano (Cuneo)
BH³	*Biblia Hebraica*, ed. R. Kittel, Stuttgart ³1937
BHS	*Biblia Hebraica Stuttgartensia*, Stuttgart 1968ff. = *BH⁴*
Bibl	*Biblica*, Rome
BiblRes	*Biblical Research*, Chicago
BJRL	*Bulletin of the John Rylands Library*, Manchester
BK	Biblischer Kommentar, Neukirchen
BTB	*Bulletin of Biblical Theology*, Rome
BZ	*Biblische Zeitschrift*, Paderborn
BZAW	Beiheft zur *ZAW*
CAT	Commentaire de l'Ancien Testament, Neuchâtel
CBQ	*The Catholic Biblical Quarterly*, Washington
Denzinger	H. Denzinger and G. Bannwart, *Enchiridion Symbolorum*, Barcelona ²⁸1952

EB	Études Bibliques, Paris
EphThLov	*Ephemerides Theologicae Lovanienses*, Louvain
EstBibl	*Estudios Bíblicos*, Madrid
ET	English translation
EvTh	*Evangelische Theologie*, Munich
ExpT	*The Expository Times*, Edinburgh
FRLANT	Forschungen zur Religion und Literatur des Alten und Neuen Testaments, Göttingen
HAT	Handbuch zum Alten Testament, Tübingen
HKAT	Handkommentar zum Alten Testament, Göttingen
HTR	*Harvard Theological Review*, Cambridge, Mass.
HUCA	*The Hebrew Union College Annual*, Cincinnati
ICC	International Critical Commentary, Edinburgh
IEJ	*Israel Exploration Journal*, Jerusalem
Interpretation	*Interpretation*, Richmond, Virginia
JAAR	*Journal of the American Academy of Religion*, Boston, Mass. (formerly *JBR*)
JAOS	*Journal of the American Oriental Society*, New Haven
JB	La Bible de Jérusalem, Paris
JBL	*Journal of Biblical Literature*, New Haven
JBR	*Journal of Bible and Religion*, Philadelphia (now *JAAR*)
JJS	*Journal of Jewish Studies*, London
JNES	*Journal of Near Eastern Studies*, Chicago
JPOS	*Journal of the Palestine Oriental Society*, Jerusalem
JSS	*Journal of Semitic Studies*, Manchester
JTS	*Journal of Theological Studies*, Oxford
KAI	H. Donner and W. Röllig, *Kanaanäische und aramäische Inschriften*, 3 vols., Wiesbaden [3]1966–70
KAT	Kommentar zum Alten Testament, Leipzig
KHC	Kurzer Hand-Commentar zum Alten Testament, Tübingen
KuD	*Kerygma und Dogma*, Göttingen
LXX	Septuagint
MIO	*Mitteilungen des Instituts für Orientforschung*, Berlin
MT	Massoretic text
NCB	New Century Bible, London
NRT	*Nouvelle Revue Théologique*, Tournai
NS	New series
Or	*Orientalia*, Rome
OrAnt	*Oriens Antiquus*, Rome
OTL	Old Testament Library, London
OTS	*Oudtestamentische Studiën*, Leiden

PEQ	*Palestine Exploration Quarterly*, London
PG	J.-P. Migne, Patrologia Graeca, Paris
PL	J.-P. Migne, Patrologia Latina, Paris
RB	*Revue Biblique*, Jerusalem/Paris
RBibl	*Rivista Biblica*, Brescia
RGG	*Die Religion in Geschichte und Gegenwart*, 7 vols., Tübingen ³1957–64
RHPR	*Revue d'Histoire et de Philosophie Religieuses*, Strasbourg
RHR	*Revue de l'Histoire des Religions*, Paris
RSLR	*Rivista di Storia e di Letteratura Religiosa*, Turin
RTP	*Revue de Theologie et de Philosophie*, Lausanne
RSO	*Rivista degli Studi Orientali*, Rome
SacBib	Sacra Bibbia, Turin
SB	Sources Bibliques, Paris
SBT	Studies in Biblical Theology, London
SEÅ	*Svensk Exegetisk Årsbok*, Lund
SMSR	*Studi e Materiali di Storia delle Religioni*, Rome
StTh	*Studia Theologica*, Lund
SVT	Supplements to *Vetus Testamentum*, Leiden
Syr	Syriac translation
T	Targum, Aramaic paraphrase
THAT	*Theologisches Handwörterbuch zum Alten Testament*, ed. E. Jenni and C. Westermann, 2 vols., Munich 1971–5
TLZ	*Theologische Literaturzeitung*, Leipzig
TR	*Theologische Rundschau*, Tübingen
TWAT	*Theologisches Wörterbuch zum Alten Testament*, ed. G. J. Botterweck and H. Ringgren, Munich 1970ff.
TZ	*Theologische Zeitschrift*, Basle
UF	*Ugaritforschungen*, Münster
V	Vulgate, Latin translation
VetLat	Vetus Latina, Latin translation
VT	*Vetus Testamentum*, Leiden
WissZ	*Wissenschaftliche Zeitschrift*
WMANT	Wissenschaftliche Monographien zum Alten und Neuen Testament, Neukirchen
ZAW	*Zeitschrift für die alttestamentliche Wissenschaft*, Giessen/Berlin
ZBK	Zürcher Bibelkommentare, Zurich
ZDPV	*Zeitschrift des Deutschen Palästinavereins*, Wiesbaden
ZTK	*Zeitschrift für Theologie und Kirche*, Tübingen
Θ	Greek translation by Theodotion
Σ	Greek translation by Symmachus

PREFACE TO THE BIBLIOGRAPHIES

In preparing the bibliographies for this English translation the attempt has been made to keep two basic principles in mind. First, since Professor Soggin has used the bibliographies in the original as major supports and illustrations of his argument, it has seemed important to retain in full material that came into this category. Scholars will thus be more readily enabled to consider the implications of the discussion, and may also be glad to have references to Italian material in particular which is not always included in the standard bibliographical aids. Secondly, the needs of the general reader have led to the inclusion of additional material in English, especially of commentaries on individual books. In all cases English versions of books and articles have been cited where they were known to exist.

King's College, London
February 1976   R. J. COGGINS

GENERAL BIBLIOGRAPHY

1. Introductions to the Old Testament

G. W. Anderson, *A Critical Introduction to the Old Testament*, London 1959 (popular)

G. L. Archer, *A Survey of Old Testament Introduction*, Chicago [2]1971 (emphasizes conservative Protestant ['fundamentalist'] views)

T. Ballarini (ed.), *Introduzione alla Bibbia*, Turin I, 1965; II.1, 1969; II.2, 1971 (Roman Catholic)

A. Bentzen, *Introduction to the Old Testament*, Copenhagen [3]1957 (valuable introduction to the methods of the Scandinavian school)

J. A. Bewer, *The Literature of the Old Testament*, New York [3]1962, ed. E. G. Kraeling

U. Cassuto, 'La letteratura ebraica antica', in *Le Civiltà dell'Oriente*, ed. G. Tucci, II, Rome 1957, 151–89 (modern Jewish presentation)

H. Cazelles, *Introduction critique à l'Ancien Testament*, Paris 1973 (based on the earlier work by Robert and Feuillet)

O. Eissfeldt, *The Old Testament: an Introduction*, ET Oxford 1965 (very detailed, with full bibliography)

G. Fohrer, *Introduction to the Old Testament*, ET London 1968 (revision of the earlier work by Sellin)

R. K. Harrison, *Introduction to the Old Testament*, Grand Rapids 1969 (conservative Protestant viewpoint)

O. Kaiser, *Introduction to the Old Testament, a Presentation of its Results and Problems*, ET Oxford 1975

A. Lods, *Histoire de la Littérature hébraique et juive*, Paris 1950 (ed. after the death of the author by A. Parrot) (critical standpoint now rather outdated)

R. Mayer, *Einleitung in das Alte Testament*, Munich I, 1965; II, 1967

F. Michelini Tocci, *La letteratura ebraica*, Florence 1970 (deals with all Hebrew literature down to the establishment of the State of Israel)

R. H. Pfeiffer, *Introduction to the Old Testament*, New York [2]1948 (very full; old-fashioned critical standpoint)

R. Rendtroff, *Das Werden des Alten Testaments*, Neukirchen [2]1965 (popular)

G. Rinaldi, *La letteratura ebraica biblica*, Turin 1954 (Roman Catholic)

A. Robert and A. Feuillet, *Introduction to the Old Testament*, ET New York 1968 (Roman Catholic; see also above under Cazelles)

H. H. Rowley, *The Growth of the Old Testament*, London 1950 (popular)

E. Sellin-L. Rost, *Einleitung in das Alte Testament*, Heidelberg [9]1959 (see also above under Fohrer)

A. Weiser, *Introduction to the Old Testament*, ET London 1961

2. *Commentaries on the complete Old Testament*

(a) *Multi-volume*
The Broadman Bible Commentary, 12 vols.; Nashville and London 1969ff.
The Interpreter's Bible, 12 vols.; New York and Nashville 1951–57
La Bible de Jérusalem, Paris 1948ff.

(b) *One-volume*
The Interpreter's One-Volume Commentary, Nashville, New York and London 1971
The Jerome Bible Commentary, Englewood Cliffs and London 1969
Peake's Commentary on the Bible, revised edition by M. Black and H. H. Rowley, London 1962
See also the bibliographies on individual biblical books.

3. *Encyclopaedias and Biblical Dictionaries*

Bibel-Lexikon, edited by H. Haag, Einsiedeln 1968
Biblisch-historisches Handwörterbuch, ed. B. Reicke and L. Rost, 4 vols., Göttingen 1962–74
Enciclopedia della Bibbia, 6 vols., Turin 1969–71
The Interpreter's Dictionary of the Bible, 4 vols., New York and Nashville 1962
Encyclopaedia Judaica 16 vols., Jerusalem 1971–2
Die Religion in Geschichte und Gegenwart, 7 vols., Tübingen [3]1957–65
Supplément au Dictionnaire de la Bible (9 vols. have so far appeared), Paris 1928–

4. *Histories of Israel*

W. F. Albright, *From the Stone Age to Christianity*, Baltimore [2]1957
J. Bright, *A History of Israel*, London [2]1972
S. Herrmann, *A History of Israel in Old Testament Times*, ET London 1975
M. Noth, *The History of Israel*, ET London [2]1960
R. de Vaux, *Histoire ancienne d'Israël*, 2 vols., Paris 1971–3 (to the Judges period only)

5. History and Thought of the Ancient Near East

The Cambridge Ancient History, ³1970–   (Vols. 1–2, in two parts each, 1970–5)

L. J. Delaporte, *Le Proche-Orient asiatique*, Paris ³1948

H. Frankfort et al., *The Intellectual Adventure of Ancient Man*, Chicago 1946

P. Garelli, *Le Proche-Orient asiatique*, Paris 1969

M. Liverani, *Introduzione alla storia dell'Asia Anteriore antica*, Rome 1963

S. Moscati, *The Semites in Ancient History*, Cardiff 1959

H. Ringgren, *Religions of the Ancient Near East*, ET London 1973

H. W. F. Saggs, *The Greatness that was Babylon*, London 1962

A. Scharff and A. Moortgat, *Ägypten und Vorderasien im Altertum*, Munich 1950

H. Schmökel (ed.), *Kulturgeschichte des Alten Orient*, Stuttgart 1961

6. History of Critical Study of the Bible

Cambridge History of the Bible, 3 vols., 1963–70

L. Diestel, *Geschichte des Alten Testaments in der christlichen Kirche*, Halle 1869, reprinted Berlin 1976

E. G. Kraeling, *The Old Testament since the Reformation*, London 1955

H.-J. Kraus, *Geschichte der historisch-kritischen Erforschung des Alten Testaments*, Neukirchen ²1969

7. Israelite Religion

W. Eichrodt, *Religionsgeschichte Israels*, Berne 1969

G. Fohrer, *History of Israelite Religion*, ET Nashville and London 1973

A. Penna, *La Religione di Israele*, Brescia 1958

H. Ringgren, *Israelite Religion*, ET London 1966

W. H. Schmidt, *Alttestamentlicher Glaube und seine Umwelt*, Neukirchen 1968

T. C. Vriezen, *The Religion of Ancient Israel*, ET London 1967

8. Life and Customs of Israel

J. Pedersen, *Israel, its Life and Culture*, Copenhagen, vols. 1–2, 1926, vols. 3–4, 1940

R. de Vaux, *Ancient Israel*, ET London 1961

9. Collections of Near Eastern Texts

W. Beyerlin, *Religionsgeschichtliches Textbuch zum Alten Testament*, ATD, 1975 (ET in preparation)

H. Donner and W. Röllig, *Kanaanäische und Aramäische Inschriften*, 3 vols., Wiesbaden [2]1966–9

K. Galling, *Textbuch zur Geschichte Israels*, Tübingen [2]1968

J. C. L. Gibson, *Textbook of Syrian Semitic Inscriptions*, 2 vols., Oxford 1971, 1975

F. Michaeli, *Textes de la Bible et de l'ancien Orient*, Neuchâtel 1961

J. B. Pritchard (ed.), *The Ancient Near East: an Anthology of Texts and Pictures*, Princeton [3]1969 (see also *ANET* and *ANEP* in the list of abbreviations; the work listed here is a selection from the larger works)

D. Winton Thomas (ed.), *Documents from Old Testament Times*, London 1958

10. *Bibliographical Aids for Old Testament Study*

Elenchus Bibliographicus Biblicus (annual supplement to *Biblica*); the annual *Book List* of the British Society for Old Testament Study, with collected volumes of past issues available; *Internationale Zeitschriftenschau für Bibelwissenschaft und Grenzgebiete*. The journals devoted to Old Testament study (see list of abbreviations) also contain periodic bibliographical discussion.

J. ALBERTO SOGGIN

INTRODUCTION TO THE OLD TESTAMENT

PART ONE

THE OLD TESTAMENT:
HISTORY AND GENERAL PROBLEMS

I

INTRODUCTION TO THE OLD TESTAMENT

§1. *Description and definition*

The term 'Introduction', Greek *eisagōgē*, Latin *introductio*, was used for the first time by the Antiochene monk Adrianus, who died about AD 440. Only in the eighteenth century, however, from the works of the German scholar J. D. Michaelis on, does it appear as a synonym for the science which studies the biblical literature from a historico-critical and literary perspective, and from there it has passed into the current terminology of theology and arts faculties.

Introduction to the Old Testament as a discipline, though, really began very early, sometimes with the composition of the biblical texts themselves: the redactors (editors), and more rarely the authors, of the books of the Bible felt it necessary to preface the material they had collected with certain explanations intended to make this material easier to understand and to put it in its proper historical and ideological context. Thus we have the well-known superscriptions to the Psalms (our modern translations often do not include them in the numbering of verses because of their obviously redactional character), which attempt to connect the compositions in question with people and events in the history of Israel or to relate them to particular liturgical situations. There are also superscriptions to passages contained in the prophetic books and in the wisdom literature which usually seek to indicate an author and sometimes a particular historical situation; some of them perhaps go back to the prophets themselves or to their immediate disciples, who recorded them from the lips of their masters. The most convincing example is the well-known opening of Isa.6.1: 'In the year that King Uzziah died I saw the Lord', i.e. about 742 BC. By contrast, other superscriptions in the prophetic books or the wisdom literature are clearly the work of later redactors: these are immediately recognizable for what they are in their context; see, for example, the words with which the book of

Jeremiah begins. Notwithstanding their different characteristics, these superscriptions have in common an awareness that it is impossible to understand the attitudes of people or schools of thought, and therefore the writings that derive from them, without knowing the events which have influenced them in whole or in part. For example, inadequate knowledge of Canaanite religion would constitute a most serious obstacle to understanding the message of the prophets, who were engaged in a continuous struggle against the religious syncretism of their time; nor could we understand properly their comments on society if we did not know the economic and social conditions which they were attacking.

We have, then, in the Old Testament itself a number of what have rightly been called 'introductory notes', a few of which derive directly or indirectly from the authors of the Old Testament writings; others, the majority, have been introduced by redactors to whom we owe the final editing of the books. The latter notes in particular are easily recognizable from their context.

Rabbinic literature continued along these lines and from it we can sometimes derive 'introductory notes' which are particularly important because they are based on trustworthy tradition; at other times we have material based on traditions which cannot be verified and are often improbable, occasionally governed by the demands of teaching or instruction; they are interesting for the history of exegesis, but not for understanding the passages to which they refer.

Introduction is not, however, a typical discipline of biblical literature. It becomes necessary whenever the reader (in our case the reader of today) has no immediate and direct contact with the milieu from which a certain type of literature derives. This can happen because of a distant geographical setting (for example, as with more modern literature which comes from a remote area and therefore speaks of alien customs and institutions in an alien language); it can also happen because of a significant distance in time between the reader and the events narrated, even if they are geographically close to him (for example, Greek and Latin classical literature, mediaeval and Renaissance literature in the West). In the case of the Old Testament and all the literature of the ancient Near East the reader finds himself at a considerable remove in both geographical setting and chronological context; the modern reader, especially the Westerner, meets peoples (and therefore literature, customs, institutions and patterns of thought) with which he has little or nothing in common. We shall certainly be right in supposing that anyone who does not have an advanced and specialist education will be largely ignorant of the historical, political, economic, social and religious facts to which the texts refer. In addition, there is the problem of language, an obstacle to a direct knowledge of the sources which is usually difficult to surmount. Finally, there is a problem peculiar to the biblical texts; when considering a work which for thousands of years has been the sacred scripture of Judaism and Christianity, and still is, it is all too easy for the Western reader, who has grown up within the Judaeo-Christian tradition, to have assimilated unconsciously a theological and ecclesiastical tradition which will not fail to make its weight felt in any explanation of the texts. Without one noticing it, centuries of exegesis loaded with preconceptions can lead either to uncritical acceptance of certain unproved assertions or, paradoxically, to an equally uncritical rejection of particular positions simply because they have traditionally been sustained within the sphere of the religious community. The need for a science of introduction which offers a critical view of the biblical literature must therefore be obvious to anyone.

I propose the following definition of the subject; we may term that discipline Introduction to the Old (or the New) Testament which sets out to present, where possible, the information needed to identify the authors of a text, its literary genre, the milieu from which it derives and so on, making it comprehensible against the background of the events and the problems which have shaped it. As can be seen, this definition is more descriptive than systematic, but it should contain the essence of the problem. The task is much more difficult than it might seem at first sight, especially in the context of Semitic literature, as we shall see in the course of our examination.

While there has never been a time when the reader of the Bible has not felt the need for information about the circumstances which accompanied and often governed the origins of a particular text, whether he is concerned with it as scripture or as history, we must remember that (leaving aside the Antiochene school and Jerome) up to the Renaissance the Christian church was not very interested in establishing in an independent and original form the circumstances in which the sacred books had their origin, being content to accept the traditional views of them handed down by the synagogue. Allegorical exegesis, very soon practised on a large scale in the medieval church, avoided problems by means of that special form of unhistorical sublimation which is its hallmark; consequently the problem of the difference between the reality presented in the texts and the traditional interpretation of them did not arise before humanistic exegesis at the beginning of the sixteenth century. Another reason for this was that Hebrew was practically unknown to scholars (with the notable exceptions of Jerome and, much later, of Nicholas of Lyra) and the Bible was read in its Latin version. It was humanism, with its principle of a return to the sources, which first laid the foundations for scientific and critical Introduction, while the acceptance of this principle on the part of the Protestant Reformation in the sixteenth century can be said to have constituted the decisive step in this direction in ecclesiastical circles. Nevertheless, if we leave aside the theses defended by Carlstadt in Wittenberg in 1520, the first attempt at historico-critical Introduction paradoxically grew out of the Catholicism of the Counter-Reformation rather than out of Protestantism. The first modern Introduction was the work of the Oratorian Richard Simon, *Histoire Critique du Vieux Testament*, Paris 1678, though it was not accepted by the Catholic church and the author had to leave his order. It was only about the middle of the eighteenth century, during the Enlightenment, that Introduction succeeded in freeing itself from ecclesiastical and dogmatic presuppositions and becoming an independent critical science. This connection with the Enlightenment, and thus with an approach to problems which was *a priori* rationalistic, was then to prove a heavy burden for Introduction over about a century and a half. It had yet to free itself from preconceived ideas, for in fact ecclesiastical dogma was quickly replaced by the dominant philosophy of each particular period: idealism in its Kantian or Hegelian forms, evolutionism, historicism and so on. Old Testament scholarship here was also involved in the question of its proper relationship with the church, since it was deeply committed to the work of training the clergy, at least within the setting of faculties of theology.

However, despite some contingent difficulties, it cannot be said that Introduction suffered from the change. Philosophical doctrines could be attacked and often refuted, while this was not an easy matter with Catholic or orthodox Protestant ecclesiastical doctrines; besides, the philosophical theories in question did not necessarily have a preconceived idea about the origin and development of the books of the Bible. Thus it was possible, at least in the so-called 'Protestant' countries, to initiate a fruitful collaboration between the faculties of theology and philosophy, without the development of the divisions which we usually find in 'Catholic' or 'Orthodox' countries, and even in large sectors of Judaism. At the same time, however, this collaboration often brought the theological faculties into more or less open conflict with the churches who depended on them for their ministers, and this conflict has not been entirely overcome even today.

The new situation of ideological liberty which Introduction encountered coincided with the ongoing rediscovery of the world of the ancient Near East. From Napoleon's expedition to Egypt onwards, with the discovery of the Rosetta stone which provided the key for the deciphering of its two scripts and of the Egyptian language (1798), through the nineteenth century and into the first half of the twentieth, there was a rediscovery of the world in which the men of the Old Testament had lived and against which they often struggled. Practices and customs, religious, political, judicial and social institutions, people and places previously unknown, or known only vaguely, began to take shape. Perhaps more important still, their languages came to be understood. This restored a proper historical basis and a setting in a wider historical context for texts which hitherto had almost always been read only in a church setting. It also often eliminated fictitious themes and explanations which had been created by the traditions of synagogue and church.

Anyone beginning the study of Old Testament Introduction today no sooner takes his first steps into the complex material than he finds himself face to face with a problem which the biblical literature has in common with other literature of the ancient Near East; sometimes, indeed, he finds himself in an even more difficult position. On the one hand, many texts are anonymous or even pseudonymous (that is, they have been attributed either by their authors or by tradition to famous figures of the past); on the other, there are no objective elements which help to establish a date. Dating is therefore often arrived at by subjective criteria and thus is destined to vary from generation to generation following changes and developments of different techniques. There are some cases in which particular explanations are no more than the product of exegetical 'fashion', a term which should not surprise the reader: even in Oriental studies, of which Introduction to the Old Testament is an integral part, it may happen that a discovery of source material or of a new method comes to be generalized improperly and considered as the key which will open every door. A 'fashion' then tends to develop, dressing a variety of features in a uniform garb which is inappropriate for them. One obvious and undoubted example of this will be discussed in connection with the dating of the Psalms (cf. Part Five, ch. I, §5): some compositions (e.g. Ps. 2) which up to a few decades ago were regarded as works from the time of the Maccabees (first half of the second century BC) are now regarded by all but a few authors who are inexplicably wedded to outdated positions as texts connected with the person and ceremonial of the king (his coronation, his marriage, his departure for war, his functions in the cult, and so on). Ignoring for the moment the possibility of later revision, these are therefore certainly earlier than the exile in 587 BC and the fall of the monarchy in Judah: some of them even contain Canaanite material which was taken over and adapted by Israel along with the institution of the monarchy. Instances like this are relatively frequent in Introduction to the Old Testament because of the lack of objective material for dating in so many cases, especially in the older texts and in those with a poetic form. In such situations one obviously cannot blame scholars who have allowed themselves to be carried away by the dominant view of their time; this is the consequence of the very nature of the texts, which often lend themselves all too easily to different interpretations, sometimes in marked contrast to one another. Moreover, it is for this reason that, notwithstanding the recent authoritative attempt by A. Lods to write a history of Hebrew literature in full awareness of the problems raised by such a venture, it is impossible to draw up such a history on the models of histories of classical or modern literature. However, if by a history of literature we mean a history first of oral traditions and then of written traditions and the literary genres recurring in them, we shall avoid this difficulty (for the concept of 'literary genre' see ch. VI, §3 below). Instead of applying an alien method to the texts we shall be using one which is also valid for the other writings from the ancient Near East, avoiding criteria derived from Western literature which are inapplicable to the works with which we are concerned.

§2. *The scope and limitations of Introduction*

The anonymity of large parts of the Old Testament and the difficulty of dating them means that the problems for Introduction to the Old Testament are very special ones, and extremely few analogies are known to us from Western literature. The scholar must therefore seek comparative material from the ancient Near East, breaking away from the classical schemes which are still dominant, at least in the West.

First of all we must try to define the chronological boundaries of the material with which we are concerned. By general consent Old Testament literature begins towards the twelfth century BC with the Song of Deborah in Judg. 5 (cf. below, Part Two, ch. VII, §3) and, if we count the pseudepigraphical books of late Judaism and the Qumran writings, goes down to the period when there was a fundamental split at the heart of Judaism: the birth of the Christian church during the second half of the first century AD. There is also good reason for Introduction to the New Testament, although, to be strictly logical, the New Testament too by no means lies outside the literáry tradition of Israel. This means that Introduction to the Old Testament is concerned with the proto- and deutero-canonical writings, with the pseudepigraphical and apocalyptic writings of late Judaism, and finally with those of the sect of Qumran. The present work will deal only with the proto- and deutero-canonical writings (for a definition of these terms see ch. II below).

In the course of our study we shall seek to identify, where possible, the authors of individual books or of smaller literary units, isolating passages which are certainly inauthentic and seeking to understand why they appear in their present context; we shall examine the literary genres of each unit, studying the traditions which preceded them and the environment which influenced them. In particular, we shall seek to discover a definite setting in everyday life: politics, cult, controversy, etc. We shall see the message that the author, anonymous or even pseudonymous, wished to give to the men of his age and how this message was understood (or sometimes misunderstood) by posterity. In an attempt to achieve these somewhat ambitious aims we shall make use of a number of auxiliary disciplines: linguistics and comparative philology (especially Hebrew and biblical Aramaic, and then the western Semitic languages: Ugaritic, Phoenician, Moabitic and Aramaic; and also the Greek and Latin of the principal ancient translations), the history of religions, especially of the religions of western Asia, and much else besides.

As we indicated at the beginning of this chapter, the course taken by Introduction to the Old Testament for about two centuries has never been the monopoly of a single faculty, that of theology; through history, linguistics and comparative philology the material has come to be an integral part of the subject-matter of the arts faculty. The difference between the two faculties is not over material or method, but rather concerns the ultimate decision between faith and unbelief. For example, the fact that the Christian theologian is convinced that he finds Christ foretold in the writings of the Old Testament (cf. John 5.39) or that the Jewish believer discovers here the revelation and the promise of God for his people, and the divine law, should not in any way prejudice critical and historical study of the texts, which is needed if faith is not to be reduced to the level of ideological prejudice. The fact that the texts of the Old Testament have an authoritative character for the believer, whether Jew or Christian, which they evidently do not have for the unbeliever, should not prevent the former from achieving a proper objectivity. On the contrary, it should compel him to listen humbly to what they say. This is not a paradox. He should therefore make as calm an examination of the text as possible, taking care not to read into it what is not there. Thus the criterion of scientific objectivity applies first of all to the believer, if he wishes to hear the word of the Lord instead of his own, and if he wishes to have a dialogue with his Lord instead of a monologue with himself and his own opinions. At the same time, it is right that the scholar who is not a believer should be asked to apply the same objectivity to the text of the Bible as to any other oriental text.

This attitude of historical and critical objectivity has come to be accepted in theological faculties over about two centuries; it should not therefore surprise the believer, much less scandalize him: its aim is a better understanding of the texts, while at the same time it opens the door to all kinds of collaboration, encounter and even constructive polemic with other faculties, especially arts and philosophy faculties.

BIBLIOGRAPHY

§1. For the figure of Richard Simon cf. J. Steinmann, *Richard Simon et les origines de l'exégèse biblique*, Bruges 1960. For the widespread and somewhat disconcerting lack of knowledge of Hebrew and thus of the original text of the Old Testament in western medieval Christianity down to the beginning of the sixteenth century, cf. M. Thiel, 'Grundlagen und Gestalt der Hebräischkenntnisse des frühen Mittelalters', *Studi Medievali*, 10, 3, Turin 1969, 9–212. See also the summary articles, with bibliographies in the *Cambridge History of the Bible*.

§2. The possibility of writing a history of Hebrew literature has been examined with negative results by M. Noth, *A History of Pentateuchal Traditions*, ET Englewood Cliffs 1972.

III

THE CANON OF THE OLD TESTAMENT

§1. *Traditions about the Palestinian canon*

The term 'canon' is almost certainly of Semitic origin: it probably derives from the Akkadian *qanū*, Hebrew *qāneh*, which means 'measuring rod'; in Greek we have the term *kanōn*, which generally means 'measure' and in philosophy 'norm'. Philo of Alexandria seems to have been the first to use the term to indicate the collection of books normative for faith, in contrast to other works which may be useful for edification but are not considered normative in the above-mentioned sense.

We have two traditions about the formation of the Palestinian canon and the criteria according to which books were included in it; they come from the end of the first century AD and are a report by Flavius Josephus and a passage preserved in the pseudepigraphical IV Ezra.

(*a*) Flavius Josephus, *Contra Apionem* 1.8, lists the following qualifications needed by a book for it to become part of the canon as conceived by the Pharisaic movement:

(i) It had to have been composed during the period between Moses and Ezra; in other words, a *terminus ad quem* was set for the composition of books which were divinely inspired and therefore eligible to enter the canon with the reign of Artaxerxes I of Persia, in the fifth century BC.

(ii) It had to have a certain objective sacred quality which differentiated it from all other non-sacred books. In consequence of this principle, anyone who approached the sacred book had to undergo certain rites, in the same way as with certain priestly functions.

(iii) It had to be included in the number of the twenty-two books listed by Josephus. According to present-day reckoning, these books amount to thirty-eight; the reason is that Josephus' figure is arrived at by a different calculation and excludes the Song of Songs (cf. below, Part Five, ch. VI, §2).

The untouchability and hence the immutability of a text derived from these qualifications.

(b) The tradition preserved in IV Ezra 14.18ff. tells how Ezra dictated to assistants all the writings which had been lost during the siege and destruction of Jerusalem in 587 BC. He did this about thirty years afterwards, i.e. about 557, following a divine vision which commanded him to act in this way. It should be noted how this chronology antedates the real chronology by about a century (cf. below Part Five, ch. X, §3). In this way Ezra is made to have written the twenty-four canonical books (this figure does not differ much from the one given by Josephus and is probably arrived at by an analogous procedure) and in addition seventy secret books intended only for the wise. If this last note has any historical basis, it may refer to the composition of the apocalyptic and pseudepigraphical books, only some of which have come down to us.

We are not in a position to pronounce on the normative value of these two traditions in Judaism at the end of the first century, and in any case they do not seem to have any historical foundation; they do, however, agree in one detail about which we might be more positive, and which therefore seems to be of some importance: the time of Ezra was the lower chronological limit for a canonical book. Anything written later (and Josephus recognizes the existence of important Hebrew literature after this era, though it had no sacred character because the gift of prophecy had ceased), was *ipso facto* excluded from the canon, even if the work was of such notable spiritual character as I Maccabees or Ecclesiasticus (cf. Part Six), simply because it could not have been composed within the dates fixed.

The theory that the canon was closed at the time of Ezra was accepted uncritically down to the eighteenth century, but its only historical foundation is that it expresses the intention of those who decided whether a book was canonical or not. In the first place, it in fact conflicts with the contents of certain books or literary units which are certainly later than the period of Ezra but have nevertheless become part of the canon; it does not explain why the only part of the canon accepted by the Samaritans was the Pentateuch, since the canon of the Hebrew Bible would have been completed by the time of the schism; furthermore, it leaves unexplained the origins of the Alexandrian canon (or, as some would have it, collection), which contains a much larger number of books than the Palestinian canon and additions to the canonical books of the latter. In reality the

process which led to the creation of the canon was remarkably complex and extended over a lengthy period; in any case it was not the
product of decisions, much less of direct dictation.

We have noted that the criterion adopted, namely that a book
should not have been written after the time of Ezra, conflicts with the
fact that later sections found their way into the canon, and we have
seen that this criterion was really more an intention of the compilers
than an actual fact. The same is true of the New Testament canon:
here too the books were chosen according to a criterion, that of
apostolicity: books later than the apostolic age should not therefore
have been included. Here too, however, works which were certainly
later found their way into the canon. The intention is thus combined
with a notable lack of information; in other words, if Introduction to
the Old Testament then had had all the information available today,
either the canon would have been different or other criteria for
inclusion would have been used.

§2. *Information about the Palestinian canon known to us*

The traditional divisions of the Hebrew Bible give us useful directions
for following the origin and development of the Palestinian canon.
The Hebrew Bible is divided into three parts: the Pentateuch (Hebrew *tōrāh* = 'instruction', then synonymous with 'law'); the
prophets (Hebrew *nᵉbîʾîm*; at that time divided into the former
prophets, Hebrew *rîʾšōnîm*, i.e. the historical books of Joshua, Judges,
Samuel and Kings, and the latter prophets, Hebrew *ʾaḥᵃrōnîm*, comprising all the prophets except Daniel, which Israel rightly did not
put in this category); and finally the writings (Hebrew *kᵉtūbîm* =
'written', comprising the rest). This collection is only called 'holy
scripture' in II Macc. 8.23, in the second half of the second century
BC, but, as often happens in cases like this, the idea is much older:
whatever has been communicated by God to man through Moses, the
prophets and other inspired authors has authority independently of
the expressions used.

In any case, and here we note a difference between earlier and
more recent times, all this material, whether oral or written (for the
problem of oral tradition see ch. VI, §2 below), seems to have
circulated in the Jewish community with remarkable freedom. The
community used it for liturgical purposes and for instruction, and did
not hesitate to adapt it continually to every changing need. This

seems to have been the situation up to the recognition and the closing of the canon, and here we have the explanation of the material added to the ancient texts at a later date. But we do not have any indication that this fixing of the tradition and closing of the canon took place before the end of the first century or the beginning of the second century AD; before this period material, even material considered 'holy scripture', had a somewhat fluid character, and it was only after the catastrophes which befell Judaism in AD 70 and AD 134 that it became necessary to give scripture a fixed form because of the dispersion of the community and hence the danger that the tradition might become corrupt or be lost.

We shall now examine in detail the three or four parts into which the Hebrew Old Testament is traditionally divided.

(a) The Pentateuch. This is the collection which enjoyed the greatest canonical authority in Israel and has always been the standard by which the canonicity of the other writings has been assessed. It has also been accepted from time immemorial with the same status by the Samaritans; they have their own version of it which has a number of variants from the Jewish Pentateuch (see further §6). This may be taken to indicate that at the time when the schism between Jews and Samaritans took place, an event the date of which cannot be determined with any certainty, but which cannot be after the end of the fourth century BC, the Pentateuch must have been virtually complete in its present form and must have had indisputable canonical authority. On the other hand, passages like Ezek. 40–48 and the fact that the final redaction of the Pentateuch was made on the basis of the source P (cf. further Part Two, ch. IV, §5) demonstrate that the final redaction must have taken place in the early post-exilic period, regardless – as is logical – of the dating of the individual traditions contained in it. This period is near to the time of Ezra and Nehemiah (middle of the fifth century BC, cf. Part Five, ch. X, though the date is only an approximate one) and their reforms, which probably laid the foundation for the final split between Jews and Samaritans. As can be seen, here, too, the difficulties presented by the texts and the impossibility of establishing certain dates allow us to put forward only hypothetical solutions.

(b) The earlier parts of the former prophets are composed of material contemporary with or a little later than the earliest sources of the Pentateuch, with which up to a few years ago they were wrongly connected (cf. Part Two, ch. II), but the latest authentic passages cannot be earlier than the events described in II Kings 25.27–30 (c. 561 BC). This material, which does not therefore reach beyond the first twenty-five years of the second exile in Babylon, has been re-worked by a school known, as we shall see (Part Two, ch. VI, §1), as the 'Deuteronomistic' school because it makes use of the directives given in the fifth and last book of the Pentateuch as criteria for the revision of the ancient traditions. The work of this school took place immediately before and then during the exile, perhaps in two stages; it was certainly not before nor much after the sixth century BC. The differences between this work and that of the Chronicler (beginning of the fourth century BC, cf. Part Five, ch. IX), which largely draws on the same sources, may be a sign that the 'Deuteronomistic' work was also finished at this time and enjoyed canonical authority. It was not accepted by the Samaritans, which might indicate that it was brought to a conclusion after the schism; but the reason for this may also be that the whole work is oriented on the centralization of the cult in Jerusalem which was brought about under King Josiah in 622–21, a position which the Samaritans rejected and still reject even today. The two explanations are not mutually exclusive.

(c) The latter prophets, sometimes wrongly called the 'writing prophets' because in contrast to the earlier prophets we possess books to which they have given their name, derive their canonical authority from the fact that their words are presented as messages which the God of Israel reveals to his people by means of them. We may recall that Josephus set the time of the closing of the canon in the period of Ezra because from then on there were no more prophets (see §1 above). It is possible that originally there was a larger collection: prophets like Elijah and Elisha (I Kings 17–II Kings 10, ninth century BC) were well known, and the former came to be celebrated, especially in late Judaism, as the precursor of the Messiah (on the basis of Mal. 3.23, EVV 4.5), a function which believing and practising Jews still believe him to have. Very few of the sayings of these two prophets have, however, been preserved. A prophet like Micaiah ben Imlah (I Kings 22.10ff., from the same period) may also have spoken more words than the few of his which have been transmitted. Here, too, however, we can do no more than guess: the fact is that the texts restrict themselves to reporting a few words and a number of episodes from the lives of these figures.

The prophets were essentially preachers and not writers. Their sayings were rarely fixed in writing on their own initiative; their books are generally the work of disciples and schools which formed around them. Isaiah 8.16ff. makes explicit mention of the master's disciples, while in Jer. 36 we are given the name of the prophet's secretary; this chapter is the first to state explicitly that a sizeable collection of prophetic sayings had been put in writing. We do not, however, have the least indication when any single prophetic book was finished: we know, rather, that often other oracles which could be either centuries later, or even from the same period but written by different authors, were interpolated in or added to the authentic words of particular prophets. At times the problem becomes so complex that there are scholars who would prefer to give up any effort to identify the authentic sayings of the various prophets. In certain cases it is possible to explain the phenomenon by the hypothesis that the school founded by a prophet continued his work for a long time afterwards and that the writings stemming from it circulated under the name of the prophet in question, which was then the name of the school (for example in the case of Isaiah); in other cases, however, the phenomenon is inexplicable.

Even here, however, we have a fixed date, although it is relatively late: the deutero-canonical book of Ecclesiasticus, 48.22–49.12 (beginning of the second century BC, cf. Part Six, ch. V below), knows the three major prophets (it will be remembered that the Hebrew Bible does not consider Daniel to be a prophet) and the twelve minor prophets, with whom, a little later, towards the end of the third century BC, the collection was thought to be closed. It was then probably considered canonical.

(d) The 'Writings' have always been the part of the Hebrew Bible which has enjoyed the least authority in Israel. The Psalms are the exception to this. Some of the books which belong here have now been recognized to be late (e.g. Daniel); others were included only after laborious discussions (e.g. the Song of Songs, Esther, etc.). However, among the Psalms and in Proverbs there is no lack of texts belonging to the earliest traditions of Israel, perhaps going back to the Canaanite period (e.g. Pss. 29 and 68); these passed over to Israel after some alterations in a monotheistic direction which can be clearly recognized by the attentive reader.

§3. The Alexandrian canon

Alexandrian Judaism did not accept the chronological limitatio n imposed by Palestinian Judaism on the canon, and admitted to the canonical writings works which can be dated up to the last years of the first millennium BC. It is not easy to determine the character of the canon of this collection: it is possible, for example, to suppose that the Jews of Alexandria simply wanted to collect together all the books used in worship without raising the problem of their normative character for faith. It is no coincidence, however, that the Greek translation, the Septuagint (LXX: see further §6), which contains a number of books missing from the Hebrew Bible, was acquiring increasing authority to the point of being considered inspired and being adopted by the Christian church. In any case its influence was limited to Hellenistic Judaism, from which it then passed over to the church, the community of which was initially founded in the milieu of the Hellenistic synagogue outside Palestine and often had a very scanty knowledge of Hebrew and Aramaic. Then, as the church spread gradually first into the Hellenistic and then into the Roman world, it is not surprising that the Septuagint found increasing acceptance. The Jews meanwhile showed considerable reserve towards it, and with it to those books and additions which had not found their way into the Palestinian canon. Even today, moreover, the status of the books in the Alexandrian canon is a matter of controversy among the various Christian churches: the Roman Catholic Church accepted the canonicity of the greater part of the Alexandrian canon after the Council of Trent (but not all: it excluded III Ezra and III Maccabees); some Eastern Orthodox churches maintain an equivocal attitude, while others include different books in their canon; the Protestant and Anglican churches have generally rejected their canonicity, for the most part merely according them the status of books for edification; thus up to the first decades of the nineteenth century they could often be found printed in an appendix to some Protestant editions of the Bible. The problem is rather like that of ecclesiastical Byzantinism, since while the books in question fill a chronological void of some centuries (for the Christian church, there would otherwise be no valid traces of Israelite belief between the fourth century BC and the first century AD), they do not add to or detract from any doctrine of scripture (except for abuses in exegesis) and should not therefore be a matter of controversy. All the Christian translations have kept the order of the Greek Bible.

We shall deal with the Alexandrian canon in Part Six of this book. In view of its problematical character, I have chosen to use the term 'deutero-canonical books', which is historically more neutral and correct, instead of 'apocrypha', often used in Protestantism, which is polemical and historically inexact.

§4. *The closing of the Palestinian canon*

The closing of the Palestinian canon is, then, to be sought in the last years of the first century and the first of the second century AD. Jewish traditions mention assemblies (in the West sometimes called 'synods') which met, one at Jerusalem towards AD 65, i.e. before the first destruction of the capital in AD 70, and another at Jabneh (Greek Jamnia) towards 90, i.e. before the last rebellion of Bar Cochba in 132–135. Among the other important matters discussed it seems that these assemblies decided on the inclusion or rejection of a number of controversial books: Song of Songs, Esther and Ecclesiastes; their inclusion thus took place at a late date and was not without opposition. Among the books discussed was also the book of Ezekiel, the last part of which, chs. 40–48, differs in some of its contents from the Pentateuch which, as we have seen, was considered the touchstone for judging the canonicity of a book. Whole books like that of Daniel, and sections like Isa. 24–27 and Zech. 12–14, although later than the time of Ezra, were retained because they were attributed to authors before the terminus in question.

We may, then, affirm that the Hebrew Bible as we now have it was complete at the end of the first century BC, at least in its consonantal text (the western and southern Semitic languages were originally written without vowels, and the latter were added, as we shall see, at a later stage). On the basis of the two manuscripts of Isaiah and other texts discovered in the Qumran caves it is possible to date this situation back about two centuries (or perhaps a little more), with a few important exceptions to which we shall return in due course.

§5. *The Hebrew Bible: the text*

So far we have been occupied with the divisions of the Hebrew Bible and with the canon (§2 above); we shall now turn our attention to the text. In addition to this we shall also consider the two most celebrated translations, the Greek of the LXX and the Latin of Jerome.

The Hebrew text now in our possession has one special peculiarity: notwithstanding its considerable age, it comes to us in relatively late manuscripts which are therefore far removed in time from the originals (sometimes by more than a thousand years). The earliest ancient codex of the complete Hebrew Bible, which has served as the basis for the text of *Biblia Hebraica*, ed. R. Kittel, Stuttgart [3]1937, and the *Biblia Hebraica Stuttgartensia* supervised by K. Elliger and W. Rudolph, the publication of which began in 1968 (to date twelve fascicles have been published), is the Codex Leningradensis (coll. B 19^a of the Leningrad Public Library), dated according to the colophon in AD 1008. Another virtually complete codex serves as the basis for the edition of the Hebrew University Bible Project: this is the Aleppo Codex from the beginning of the tenth century, which is now in Israel. We also have some earlier codices containing parts of the Bible: the Codex Cairensis of 895 and a codex recently discovered in the collection of the Institute for Asiatic Peoples in Leningrad, from 847, both containing only the prophets. As can be seen, none of these manuscripts is earlier than the ninth century AD. This explains the importance of writings like those at Qumran, which take us back about a thousand years, or of a translation like the Greek of the Septuagint, a little earlier.

The reasons for this apparently disconcerting phenomenon are to be sought in the work of textual criticism and the re-editing of the canonical text of the Old Testament which took place during the second half of the first millennium AD through the work of the scholars who are known as Massoretes (from the Hebrew *massōret* = 'tradition').

As we have seen, the consonantal text on which they worked was practically complete at the end of the first century AD, and indeed probably earlier. The Massoretes were in the first place concerned to revise the text and in the case of textual variants to choose the readings which they considered to be most authoritative: they introduced a unitary orthography (their attempts did not always succeed with the coherence that we might expect) which is often better than the somewhat extravagant system existing at the end of the first millennium BC and the beginning of the first millennium AD. In their system, vowels which were long by nature (that is, those which were not the contingent product of inflections of the root) came to be represented in writing by their nearest consonants: *y* for the sounds *ē/ī*, *w* for the sounds *ō/ū*, *h* for final *ā*. These are the vowels which some modern grammarians represent with a circumflex accent. In this way, all the more or less precarious systems of representing vowels by means of other consonants (e.g. by *'aleph* and *'ayin*), partially attested also in late Phoenician and Punic, came to be eliminated. The most important work to have been completed by the Massoretes was, however, without doubt that of stabilizing the traditional pronunciation of every word by means of the addition of diacritical signs equivalent to the vowels which the above-mentioned system did not express; and although we cannot affirm with any certainty (or rather, although there are fundamental objections to asserting) that this system always maintained the original sounds, it preserved Hebrew from irremediable confusion with the pronunciation of similar languages, especially Aramaic and Syriac, and later Arabic.

There were various Massoretic schools: the eastern school, which grew up among the Israelites living in Babylon, and the western school, originating in Palestine, out of which developed the school of Tiberias, which soon achieved the greatest authority. Although the system of this last group was the most complicated, it took precedence over all the rest, to such a degree that it is still used today in Hebrew Bibles. From the numerous fragments of the other schools which have come down to us, we know, however, that there were sometimes notable differences in the pronunciation of the same words among various schools, and this fact is confirmed, albeit in an indirect way, by the Greek and Latin translations of proper names or by fragments of the second column of Origen's Hexapla. Here, too, then the tradition appears long and complex, and it is far from certain that the Massoretes always made the best choices.

In any case, from the end of the work of the Massoretes down to the present day the text of the Hebrew Bible has remained the same, even if some medieval manuscripts have retained readings which appear either in fragments of the eastern Massoretes or in translations or transcriptions into western languages.

One important category of variants is represented by quotations of the Greek Old Testament in the New Testament; the majority of these repeat the text of the Septuagint, though there are some of them which do not correspond to any Greek version known to us, but differ from the Hebrew text which we have received. It is possible that there were other Greek versions which have not come down to us, but which were used by the writers of the New Testament, unless the quotations are just approximations or have been made from memory.

The Massoretes of Tiberias did not have the last word on the pronunciation of Hebrew, although their system soon became dominant. Even now, there are three established ways of pronouncing Hebrew: among the Jews of eastern Europe a long *a* is pronounced like *o*, final *t* like *s*, and so on; among Jews of Spanish origin, until a few years ago dispersed throughout North Africa and the Near East and in some Balkan countries and Italy, we have the pronunciation generally accepted in universities, from which the modern Israeli pronunciation derives. The first is called Ashkenazi, the second Sephardic. A third pronunciation is that of the Jews of the Yemen, which offers the whole range of gutturals and dentals attested in Arabic; it is difficult to establish whether they have maintained the original pronunciation of Hebrew or whether they have adapted it to the pronunciation of the neighbouring Arab population. In any case, the extermination of large numbers of Eastern European Jews and the immigration of Yemeni Jews into Israel has condemned the first and the third modes of pronunciation to oblivion in favour of the second. At all events, these pronunciations are an important indication that the unifying work of the Massoretes never succeeded in overcoming the traditional differences in pronunciation.

As a result, it is not surprising that today there are scholars who talk of two original Hebrew dialects, the southern (which then became the sacred language), and the northern with a remarkable affinity to Moabitic and Phoenician/Punic, and who think even in terms of two recensions of the Hebrew text, the southern recension taking place in Israel and the northern being attested in the Samaritan writings. These are evidently no more than hypotheses, but they are a very good explanation of the differences of orthography and pronunciation existing in the Massoretic text, notwithstanding the work of unification completed by its editors: sometimes a phonetic tradition may have been deeply rooted, and not even the Massoretes were either able or willing to supplant it.

§6. *The Greek translations*

The attention of scholars had long been directed towards the ancient translations of the Hebrew texts, given their considerable age in comparison with the Massoretic text, and from the publication of the *Biblia polyglotta Complutensis*, edited by Cardinal F. Ximénez de Cisneros between 1514 and 1517 in Alcalá (Complutensian Polyglot), onwards, numerous editions, more or less critical, have sought to compare the Hebrew text with the ancient translations. The aim of this work has always been essentially that of getting back, where possible, to a textual tradition earlier than that of the Massoretes. Among these translations, the earliest and therefore the most authoritative is that of the Septuagint.

(a) The Septuagint translation is so called because according to a pseudepigraphic Jewish writing composed in Greek towards 100 BC, the Letter of Aristeas, the work originated from the labours of 72 scholars, invited by Ptolemy II Philadelphus of Alexandria to make a Greek translation of the Pentateuch for the library at Alexandria.

They were lodged on the island of Pharos so that they could be free to work without interruption, and had all the material they needed at their disposal; they worked no more than nine hours a day and attempted by constant comparison to arrive at a uniform text (Arist. §302). This version of the facts is not intrinsically improbable, as has recently been argued in authoritative fashion by L. Rost. It later came to be elaborated with legendary elements: after intensive labour, each in utter solitude, the translators arrived at an identical translation without copying each other's work. This version of the facts was evidently meant to prove the inspired character of the translation in question, and the argument is indirectly supported by the author of the Letter of Aristeas, when towards the end (§311) he states that anyone who altered the text in any way, either by addition or by subtraction, was to be cursed – a formula used exclusively for works considered to be divinely inspired.

Thus the Letter puts the Greek translation of the Pentateuch at the end of the first half of the third century BC, but does not explain how all the translations of the other writings of the Old Testament were added and how what we have called the Alexandrian canon (see §3 above) was formed; nor does it explain how there are sometimes re-markable differences in the methods of translation between one book and another, differences which range from an exact (sometimes literal) translation into a tolerable Greek to free translation or stilted Greek. It also leaves unexplained the differences between the Massoretic text and that of the LXX in some cases: for example in the books of Samuel, in which the text of LXX Codex B (Vaticanus) is better than the Massoretic text; a Hebrew original, unfortunately extremely fragmentary, has recently been discovered in the Qumran caves (4Q Sam^{a-b}). Moreover, the note in the Letter of Aristeas com-pletely ignores the situation in the Greek-speaking Jewish community, which always found difficulty with Hebrew: the need for a translation must have been particularly felt; the tendency to consider the transla-tion in question inspired can only be sought, in fact, in the Jewish community of the Diaspora and obviously not among the authorities of the library of Alexandria. Thus we have two theories, which are not necessarily contradictory, on the origin of the translation.

The Pentateuch is obviously the most carefully treated part of the Septuagint; it is elsewhere that we come up against the difficulties which have been indicated.

One of the problems in modern study of the translation is the lack of a complete critical edition. Two editions are in course of publica-tion: the Cambridge Septuagint (edited by A. Brooke, N. McLean and H. St J. Thackeray, I,1 [1906] – III,1 [1940]; it covers the historical books and came to a premature conclusion in 1940) and the Göttingen Septuagint (supervised by J. Ziegler, which has been publishing the other parts from 1926 on). The problem for the scholar is that the criteria underlying the approaches of the two works are different, so that they cannot be considered complementary. Handier editions, at a much more reasonable price, are those edited by H. B. Swete, *The Old Testament in Greek* (3 vols.), Cambridge 1894ff., and by A. Rahlfs, *Septuaginta* (2 vols.), Stuttgart 1935. The experts often prefer the former.

(b) In this situation it is not surprising that the Jews felt the need of other translations, especially as the Christian church often made use of the imperfections of the LXX for apologetic and polemical purposes: these translations were primarily meant to be more faithful to the Hebrew text. We know of three of them, those of Aquila (A), Symmachus (Σ) and Theodotion (Θ). The three authors are unknown; Symmachus seems to have been an exponent of Ebionite Jewish Christianity and thus would be midway between the primitive church and Judaism. It is interesting to note Aquila's method: to avoid errors he tried to be as literal as possible in his translation and chose, where possible, terms which had the same etymology as their Hebrew equivalents. Moreover, there had to be a Greek term to correspond to every Hebrew one. Needless to say, the results are always absurd and sometimes misleading. The fact remains that these three translations did not succeed in taking the place of the LXX, and they remain in an extremely fragmentary form.

A critical edition of the fragments of the Hexapla was made by F. Field, *Hexaplorum quae supersunt . . . fragmenta* (2 vols.), Oxford 1875, reprinted Hildesheim 1964.

§7. *The Samaritan Pentateuch*

The Samaritan Pentateuch is a unique example of a section of the Hebrew Bible which has evolved in a form independent of the Massoretes, among the Samaritan community. It has about 6000 variants from the Massoretic text, but most of them are only orthographic. In about 1900 cases the Samaritan text agrees with the text of the LXX against the Massoretic text; other variants are the product of the theological position of the sect: for example, in Exod. 20.17, at the end of the Decalogue, a commandment has been added which requires the building of a sanctuary on Mount Gerizim, above

Nablus, which is still the sacred mountain of the Samaritans. The choice of the place where Yahweh will make his name to dwell is often indicated in the past tense and therefore refers to Gerizim, an echo of the old polemic between Jews and Samaritans which was still acute in the New Testament period, cf. John 4. The name is, in fact, given in at least one case, Deut. 27.5–7, in which the reading 'Gerizim' of the Samaritan Pentateuch, confirmed by Σ and the Old Latin, seems to be preferable to that of the Massoretic text, which has 'Ebal', the other mountain standing above Nablus. A critical edition based on more recent research is in preparation; for the moment the edition by A. von Gall, *Der hebräische Pentateuch der Samaritaner*, Giessen 1914–18, reprinted Berlin 1960, is adequate.

§8. *Aramaic paraphrases and translations*

(a) In the last centuries of the first millennium BC, Hebrew became less and less a spoken language and more and more a sacred language, or at best an academic language; it therefore became increasingly more incomprehensible to large areas of the population who either spoke in dialect forms or used Aramaic. Aramaic paraphrases of the biblical text began to arise during synagogue worship, especially during public readings; these translations differed in quality, in method and in scope. Sometimes they were literal, sometimes free and sometimes they were paraphrases which not only translated the original, but also interpreted it. They were given the name *targūmīm*, in the singular *targūm* = 'translation'. Given the origin of these writings, the variety of the materials circulating under the name *targūmīm* is not surprising; the Samaritans also found themselves in a similar position to the Jews over language, and the Qumran sect had its own *targūmīm*. Here, too, however, we should also notice the tendency in time to concentrate on an official text: the text now printed is close to the Hebrew text in rabbinic Bibles and is not earlier than the fifth century AD. The Targum of the Pentateuch came to be attributed, probably wrongly, to Aquila, and is called the Targum Onkelos; that of the prophets is attributed to Theodotion and called the Targum Jonathan, the Hebrew translation of this name. A critical edition, published under the editorship of A. Sperber, *The Bible in Aramaic*, Vols. I–IV, Leiden 1959–73, has been interrupted by the editor's untimely death.

(b) An earlier Syriac translation of the Old Testament than the classic text, the Peshitto = 'the simple', has been attested, but we know little about it; some authors even argue that it is of Christian origin. There is still no critical edition of the Peshitto, which makes it difficult to study. In the Pentateuch and, it seems, Isaiah, it shows strong Targumic influence, which is not surprising in view of the close relationship between Syriac and Aramaic. This appears to prove the Jewish origin of the work, at least in its original form, but does not rule out the possibility of later Christian revisions. We sometimes find readings corresponding to those in the Septuagint, in contrast to the Massoretic text, but the problem is whether these are authentic variants or corruptions which have entered the two texts. A critical edition is being prepared in Holland under the editorship of P. A. H. de Boer and W. Baars.

§9. *Latin translations*

(*a*) Fragments of a Latin translation prior to the Vulgate, called the *Vetus Latina* or *Vetus Itala*, have been transmitted through fragments of manuscripts, liturgical works and patristic texts. The work is strongly influenced by the Septuagint translation, so much so as to arouse the suspicion that it was not made from the Hebrew text but from the Greek; nothing definite can, however, be said before the appearance of a large part at least of the critical edition which is in preparation at the Abbey of Beuron, under the editorship of B. Fischer. So far, an introductory volume and Genesis have appeared.

(*b*) Much more important, not least because of the position it attained in the West and hence in medieval philosophy, is the translation which derives from the work of Jerome, commonly called the Vulgate (V) because it was in common use in the West from the seventh century on. The original translation by Jerome was preceded by a number of introductory studies and revisions of existing material and was finished between 390 and 405. Its importance still lies in the fact that it was made on the basis of Hebrew and Aramaic texts, often in contrast to that of the LXX. This did not fail to arouse hostility among illustrious contemporaries like Augustine. The translation was then revised a number of times in successive centuries. Jerome did not hesitate to enlist the help of Jewish scholars, so that his work is also important from a technical and critical point of view; also important are the introductions to and commentaries on individual books, the first example of scientific and critical biblical exegesis known to us in history. From the time of the Council of Trent (session of 8 April 1546, Denzinger 785ff.) it became the official text of the Roman Catholic Church; in Protestantism, however, it has often been attacked because of some textual variants assembled by Catholicism to sustain certain of its dogmatic positions. It is obvious, however, that the author cannot be considered responsible for this official situation, just as the translators of the LXX are not responsible for the semi-official position which has been conferred upon it by the Greek-speaking Orthodox church after more than a millennium and a half of use.

A critical edition of the Vulgate has been in the course of publication under the editorship of the Benedictine order since 1926, and to date more than half the Old Testament has already appeared (Jeremiah, 1972). A more recent concise edition, also produced by the same order, is that of R. Weber, *Biblia sacra juxta Vulgatam versionem*, Stuttgart 1969.

BIBLIOGRAPHY

§1–2. General introduction to the Hebrew text and its problems, together with the ancient versions: B. J. Roberts, *The Old Testament Text and Versions*, Cardiff 1951; M. Noth, *The Old Testament World*, ET London 1966 (esp. Part Four); E. Würthwein, *The Text of the Old Testament*, ET Oxford 1957 (a revised fourth edition of the German original, *Der Text des Alten Testaments*, has been published, Stuttgart 1973); P. Sacchi, 'Rassegna di studi di storia del testo del Vecchio Testamento ebraico', *RSLR* 2, 1966, 257–324; id., 'Per una edizione critica del testo dell'Antico Testamento', *OrAnt* 9, 1970, 221–33.

§4. For the 'synod' of Jabneh and the school which was at work in the locality, see K. H. Rengstorf, 'Der Glanz von Jabne', in *Festschrift W. Caskel*, Leiden 1968, 233–44.

§5. For the Massoretic text, cf. C. D. Ginsburg, *Introduction to the Massoretico-Critical Edition of the Hebrew Bible*, London 1897 (reprinted New York 1966); P. E. Kahle, *The Cairo Geniza*, Oxford ²1959; G. É. Weil, *Élie Lévita, humaniste et massorète*, Leiden 1963; R. Edelmann, 'Soferim – Massoretes, "Massoretes" – Nakdanim', in *In Memoriam Paul Kahle*, BZAW 103, 1968, 116–23. A communication was scheduled by K. Starkova at the Sixth Congress of the International Organization for the Study of the Old Testament, Rome 1968, on the Leningrad manuscript containing the prophets; unfortunately the author was prevented from giving the paper. One fascicle of the Hebrew University Bible Project, which is under the editorship of M. H. Goshen-Gottstein, C. Rabin and S. Talmon, has so far appeared: *The Book of Isaiah*, II, Jerusalem 1975.

The thesis of the double recension of the Hebrew text has been maintained by W. F. Albright, 'Jethro, Hobab and Reuel in early Hebrew Tradition', *CBQ* 25, 1963, 1–11; and W. F. Albright and D. N. Freedman, 'The Continuing Revolution in Biblical Research', *JBR* 31, 1963, 110–13.

§6. The text of the Letter of Aristeas is published in an appendix to H. B. Swete, *Introduction to the Old Testament in Greek*, Cambridge ²1914, and in A. Pelletier, *Lettre d'Aristée à Philocrate*, Sources chrétiennes 89, Paris 1962; see also Pelletier, *Flavius Josèphe adaptateur de la 'Lettre d'Aristée*, Paris 1962; D. W. Gooding, 'Aristeas and Septuagint Origins, a Review of Recent Studies', *VT* 13, 1963; D. Barthélemy, 'L'Ancien Testament a mûri à Alexandrie', *TZ* 21, 1965, 358–70. L. Rost, *Vermutungen über den Anlass für griechischen Übersetzung der Tora*, Zürich 1970, has put forward the theory that the LXX translation was made as the result of an official commission, in the peculiar legal situation which the Jews enjoyed in Alexandria. Cf. also R. Hanhart, 'Die Septuaginta als Problem der Textgeschichte, der Forschungsgeschichte und der Theologie', *SVT* 22, 1972, 185–200, and P. Walters and D. W. Gooding, *The Text of the Septuagint*, Cambridge 1973. For the relation between LXX, the Qumran texts and MT see R. W. Klein, *Textual Criticism of the Old Testament*, Philadelphia 1974.

For those Qumran fragments which presuppose a text similar to that underlying LXX cf. F. M. Cross, Jr., 'A New Qumran Biblical Fragment related to the original Hebrew underlying the Septuagint', *BASOR* 132, 1953, 15–26; id., 'The Oldest Manuscripts from Qumran', *JBL* 74, 1955, 147–72, esp. 165ff. The critical edition of these fragments together with those of a third, more complete manuscript, is now in course of publication (oral communication from F. M. Cross). There are analogous problems with the fragments of Exodus, Deuteronomy and Jeremiah, cf. id., *The Ancient Library of Qumran*, London 1958, esp. 135 n. 30, 137 n. 31, 139 n. 38.

For the translation of LXX in general cf. also P. Sacchi, 'Il testo dei LXX nella sua problematica più recente', *Atene e Roma*, NS 9, 1964, 145–58; J. W. Wevers, 'Septuaginta Forschungen seit 1954', *TR* 33, 1968, 18–76; C. Rabin, 'The Translation Process and the Character of the Septuagint', *Textus* 6, Jerusalem 1968, 1–26; G. B. Caird, 'Toward a Lexicon of the Septuagint', *JTS* NS 19, 1968, 453–75; S. Jellicoe, *The Septuagint and Modern Study*, Oxford 1968 (with extensive bibliography).

§7. For the Samaritan Pentateuch, cf. P. Sacchi, 'Studi Samaritani I', *RSLR* 5, 1969, 413–40, esp. 432ff.

§8. Fragments of a Syro-Palestinian targum have recently been collected by M. H. Goshen-Gottstein, *The Bible in the Syropalestinian Version*, Pt. 1, Jerusalem 1973. A manuscript of the complete Pentateuch in the Palestinian targum (contained in MS Neophiti I in the Vatican Library) is in course of publication; cf. A. Díez Macho, *Neophyti I Targum Palestinense MS de la Biblioteca Vaticana*, Barcelona 1968– .

§9. Even a partial bibliography on Jerome and the Vulgate cannot be given here; cf. the relevant articles in the dictionaries and encyclopaedias listed in the general bibliography. On Jerome's knowledge of Hebrew and his exegetical methods, cf. J. Barr, 'St Jerome's Appreciation of Hebrew', *BJRL* 49, 1966–7, 281–302. For the polemic aroused by Jerome's work, cf. J. Jouassard, 'Réflexions sur la position de Saint Augustin relativement aux Septante dans sa discussion avec Saint Jérôme', *Revue des Études Augustiniennes* 2, Paris 1956, 93–9.

BIBLICAL CRITICISM

§1. *Introduction*

The problems which we have sought to outline in an elementary and simplified form indicate the sometimes extremely complicated factors underlying the process which led to the formation of the texts that make up the Old Testament. Any careful reader of the Bible cannot fail to notice their existence from time to time, but they trouble the scholar and especially the translator constantly. To give a few examples: what if a scholar happens to notice a significant difference between the Massoretic text on the one hand and, say, a Qumran text or an ancient translation on the other? If the Hebrew text is perfectly clear, the difference may simply have arisen from an error in copying, orthography or dictation. There are, however, frequent instances when there is a genuine textual variant, sometimes preferable to the traditional Hebrew text, which is evidently corrupt and sometimes incomprehensible in particular passages. We have already come across the case of LXX codex B in the books of Samuel, the readings of which have now in part been confirmed by Hebrew fragments discovered at Qumran. The text of this codex, as is well known, is better than the Massoretic text. This sort of situation, which is much more common than might be supposed, compels the scholar generally, and especially the commentator and the translator, to make a choice; he must necessarily prefer the better text and reject the less reliable one, even if this means a correction to the Hebrew text on the basis of the material indicated.

Now there are some well-tried rules in the field of classical philology which can easily be applied not only to the biblical text but also to oriental texts in general:

(*a*) Prudence and circumspection must come first: literary criticism is not, and never will be, the place for the exercise of individual inspiration.

(b) There must be a fundamental examination of the relative value of variants and the traditional text; the importance of a text is not always established by its antiquity, but often by the authority of a tradition, even if chronologically it is relatively late. In our case, a reading attested in a fragment from Qumran or presupposed by a translation in the LXX is not necessarily better than a different reading in the Massoretic text, even if strictly speaking it is earlier; in biblical criticism, rather, the tendency today is in any case to give precedence to the Massoretic text.

(c) In any comparison between a shorter and a longer text the shorter text must always be presumed to be the authentic one. In fact, it was easy for sacred texts in particular to attract explanations and comments which could easily enter the text during the transmission of a manuscript; to take something away from the text would be more difficult because it would be blasphemy, although we do have omissions through mistakes in transmission.

(d) The more difficult text, and not the easier one, is always more likely to be the authentic one; interventions in the text tend to simplify it rather than to make it more complicated.

These two last principles are called the *lectio brevior* and the *lectio difficilior* respectively.

§2. *Biblical criticism*

We have come to mention the term 'biblical criticism' almost spontaneously. As is well-known, 'criticism' comes from the Greek *krinein*, the original meaning of which is 'separate', 'distinguish', and then 'judge'. This is the sense of our term 'criticism'. Now because the believer, Jewish or Christian, sees the text as having a sacred and therefore authoritative character, he should be able to accept biblical criticism without difficulty in so far as it sets out to present a text which is as close as possible to the original. However, precisely the opposite has happened: among conservative Jews, Protestants and Catholics biblical criticism has often been received with mistrust, as though the discipline set out arrogantly, and therefore impiously, to put itself above the text to judge it and to 'criticize' it. Such an interpretation of the functions of criticism shows a complete lack of familiarity with the concept, which besides is also valid in music and the arts, and it cannot therefore be taken seriously. Moreover, conservative but educated religious circles do accept the principle of literary criticism applied to the Bible, to a greater or lesser degree

depending on the case in question; it is not in fact a matter of setting
oneself above the text, of 'judging' it, but simply of making use of well-
tried methods to restore the text as far as possible to the original form
from which it has been removed by centuries and even millennia of a
transmission which was first oral and then continued through manuscripts. Nor is there any need to go to the opposite extreme: to believe
that biblical criticism provides the solution to the majority of the
problems inherent in the texts. This too is an emotional position like
its opposite, a position which forgets that the synagogue and the
church have read the texts in question for millennia without criticism
and have succeeded in capturing the essential part of the message
without its help. Thus today we accept biblical criticism simply as
one of the many instruments which science puts at our disposal, as
biblical scholars, without either unjustified pessimism or exaggerated
enthusiasm – and we make use of it with gratitude, and at the same
time with freedom.

To understand how it is possible that a text can present sometimes
quite notable differences between one manuscript and another, it is
enough to remember how a book came into being before the invention of printing. In a modern edition of a work the author reads
proofs at least once, so that, leaving a minimal margin for errors and
omissions which escaped the proof-corrector or the printer, we may
believe the book to accord completely with the text as he produced it.
But this has happened only since the invention of printing. Up to the
middle of the fifteenth century the scholar either copied the manuscripts which he needed personally, or had copies made for him; the
bookseller had the books he sold either copied by or dictated to his
amanuenses. The works produced by this method were few and therefore extremely expensive; anyone who was writing from dictation or
copying from elsewhere in a more or less mechanical fashion could
easily make mistakes or misunderstand whole phrases or rare words.
In this way, mistakes entered the text, and this danger naturally increased the more the editions of the same work grew in number. The
scholar who copied a text for his own use was less likely to make a
mistake; but even he might be distracted, or might have to work
hurriedly on a book that was only available for a limited period of
time. Sometimes he may have had a tendency to 'correct' what
seemed to him to be 'errors' in the text or to explain difficult passages
(or those he considered difficult) by marginal notes; these notes could
easily be introduced into the body of the text by a later copyist.

This general situation will also have applied to the texts of the Old
Testament with one important qualification: in the last centuries of

the first millennium BC and then especially with the closing of the canon, increasing attention began to be paid to the copying of the sacred texts and to their transmission which excluded almost all errors. Manuscripts which contained what was considered an excessive number of mistakes or which had become illegible through use were taken out of circulation. Before this period, however, even the biblical texts were exposed to the dangers which beset any text transmitted in manuscript form. To begin with, there was no punctuation, which made it possible for the syntax of a sentence to be misunderstood; often so-called *scriptio continua* was used, a form of writing which left no space between one word and another and which encouraged erroneous divisions between individual words. It is not surprising, therefore, that purely mechanical errors of the kind that are well known today to anyone who uses a typewriter found their way even into the text of the Bible. If we add to that the fact that conflicts between different textual traditions were also to be encountered (we may recall the example of the books of Samuel), we can see that we must reckon with the existence of errors, omissions and confusions even in the Old Testament.

The following mechanical errors arise simply from distraction during dictation or the copying of texts:

(*a*) Haplography, that is, the failure to repeat a syllable or a word that should have been written twice. Thus if we were to want to write 'he used no notes' and left out the first or the second syllable 'no', we would have a comprehensible text but one which would not only fail to reflect the author's intention but even give the opposite sense. However, the literary critic would immediately know how to restore the original form of the text. Another mistake is the opposite of this and is called dittography.

(*b*) Dittography is the repetition of a word or a syllable which should only be written once. If in the phrase 'He used notes' the syllable 'no' is repeated, once again we have a comprehensible text, but an inexact one: again, the expert in literary criticism would know how to restore the original form.

(*c*) A third mechanical error which is more frequent in copying than in writing from dictation is homoioteleuton. Here the whole of a phrase lying between two occurrences of the same word or of similar words is omitted because the eye of the copyist jumps directly from the first word to the second. This error can easily be recognized, but it is difficult to correct without the help of a parallel text or a translation. We have a number of obvious examples in the Old Testament in which the mistake can only be corrected by recourse to an ancient version. In Josh. 15.59, part of the list of cities enumerated has been omitted, and can only be replaced with the help of the LXX (the omission occurs between two similar phrases); in I Kings 19.2 we have the following text (the phrase omitted is replaced within square brackets): 'Then Jezebel sent a messenger with the following message: "[If you are Elijah, I am Jezebel, but] so may God do . . ."' (corrected on the basis of the text of LXX and V); there is another instance in II Kings 23.16: 'According to the word of Yahweh which the man of God proclaimed [, when Jeroboam was standing by the altar at the time of the feast. As he looked around, Josiah caught sight of the tomb of the man of God] who had foretold these things . . .' (corrected on the basis of LXX). In the second example the Massoretic text, which in the preceding verse explicitly makes reference to the tomb of the prophet in question, is obscure and indeed tautological without the insertion from LXX, which allows us to restore the original text; the reason for the omission is clearly that the eye of the copyist jumped from the first 'man of God' to the second, omitting the intervening phrase. It seems to go without saying that it is necessary to restore the authentic form simply to be faithful to the text, without uselessly tearing one's hair trying to make out the sense of what is simply a corrupt reading.

§3. Textual criticism or 'lower criticism'

Textual criticism or 'lower criticism' is the name of the discipline which sets out to restore, as far as possible, the original form of a text. It therefore works essentially with grammar, syntax and philology, comparing the text with ancient manuscripts and versions. It is required whenever there is uncertainty whether the text that we have corresponds to that intended by the author, which is almost always the case before the invention of printing. In the course of the first two sections we have discussed some of its principal elements.

In the Old Testament field, the tendency of scholars at the end of the last century and at the beginning of this was to mistrust the Massoretic text because of the late date of the manuscripts which have been preserved, and to prefer earlier translations, above all the LXX. In every critical commentary up to the 1930s, therefore, it is easy to find in doubtful or controversial cases a pronounced preference on the part of scholars for the readings of the LXX rather than the Hebrew text. This is, of course, a choice which can rebound against the person who makes it: if the Massoretic text showed a higher incidence of errors or omissions than can be found in the LXX translation, could this not be a sign, applying the criteria of the *lectio brevior* and the *lectio difficilior*, of an accurate transmission, as no one has dared to correct errors or evident omissions? In this connection one might well recall Jesus' saying in Matt. 5.18 and Luke 16.17 according to which not a *yod* (or a stroke) of the law will be lost, an all too evident reference to the care taken over the transmission of texts in the first century AD.

Literary criticism today tends to be much more prudent about the traditional Hebrew text than it was some decades ago. It is not that scholars fail to recognize errors of various kinds (we have enumerated some quite glaring ones), nor that it is impossible that in certain cases a parallel text or translation may have preserved a more accurate textual tradition; it is the fundamental attitude to the Massoretic text that has changed. The starting-point for the scholar today will always be only the Hebrew text, which is accorded a remarkable authority on almost all sides. As we have seen, this does not exclude some blemishes of notable proportions. But it has been recognized that these rarely prejudice the sense of passages which are historically or theologically important.

§4. *Historical criticism or 'higher criticism'*

Once the scholar has arrived at a text which, within the limits of possibility, is as near as possible to the original, a second stage of his work begins; we can compare it with that of the engineer who is building a bridge between the two banks of a river, with the reader on one bank and the text to be examined on the other. The wider and deeper the river bed to be crossed, that is, the greater the chronological and ideological distance which divides us from the times and the setting in which the author of the texts lived or in which the texts, if they are anonymous, came to be written, the more difficult will be the work. In this phase of research the scholar investigates the formal aspects of the text, its contents and hence its literary genre; he determines, where possible, the author or at least the period in which it was written, and seeks to discover whether it was used in particular situations in the life of the people: the cult and possibly the particular occasion, the protocol of the court, the wisdom schools, public or private prayer, etc. In this way he discovers data which are indispensable for a proper understanding of the text in question. For example, no scholar can be indifferent to the fact that some of the oracles contained in the first chapter of Isaiah were pronounced during the course of Sennacherib's expedition against Judah and Syria–Palestine in general in 701 BC; or that Exod. 1–15 were probably part of the paschal liturgy in the pre-exilic period; or again that the creation narrative in Gen. 1.1–2.4a probably belonged to the liturgy of the New Year Festival, and that this is also probably true of the complex narrative in Exod. 19–34 which records how the Torah was given to Israel. In this last case the possibility must seriously be considered that the liturgy in question relates to the 'Feast of Weeks', that is, Pentecost. It is not always easy to obtain certain information: in these last lines we have used the word 'probably' three times; too often the elements at our disposal are fragmentary or of doubtful value, so that we find ourselves compelled to work with conjectures and hypotheses.

However, there should be no doubt as to the necessity to clarify as far as possible the occasion and the milieu in which certain texts came into being: for example, a memorable saying is attributed to one of Leonidas' three hundred Spartans, that if the Persians had so many arrows that they obscured the sun, he and his comrades could fight in the shade (Herodotus VII, 226). But what use would this be if we did not know the circumstances in which it was pronounced? This, then, in the principal concern of literary criticism, which forms the greater part of the discipline of Introduction.

BIBLIOGRAPHY

§1–2. For literary criticism in general cf. the by now classic manuals of P. Maas, *Textual Criticism*, ET Oxford 1958, and G. Pasquali, *Storia della tradizione e critica del testo*, Florence ²1952. These works are primarily concerned with classical literature (to which LXX and V in any case belong) but the fundamental problems and the proposed solutions are also essentially valid for the Hebrew text. Pasquali, 241ff., gives a series of examples in which readings attested by the Greek papyri reflect a more genuine tradition than the later Alexandrian one; and, 261ff., examples of the opposite tendency, where the readings of the *textus receptus* are better than those of the much older papyri. The same criterion holds good in both the classical and the biblical worlds: the antiquity of a manuscript does not by itself guarantee, and certainly cannot prove, that it contains a better reading. For the Massoretic text, cf. bibliography to ch. II, §§1–2, and also D. R. Ap-Thomas, *A Primer of Old Testament Text Criticism*, Oxford ²1964, and H. Barth and O. H. Steck, *Exegese des Alten Testaments; Leitfaden der Methodik*, Neukirchen ²1971.

§3. For the scope and limits of literary criticism as applied to the Old

Testament cf. H.-J. Stoebe, 'Grenzen der Literarkritik im Alten Testament', *TZ* 18, 1962, 385–400, and J. Coppens, 'La Critique Textuelle de l'Ancien Testament', *EphThLov* 36, 1960, 464–77. What is now a classic work, Friedrich Delitzsch, *Die Lese- und Schreibfehler im Alten Testament*, Berlin 1920, has listed the orthographical and mechanical errors found in the Massoretic text. The work must, however, be used with caution, since what are in fact recognizable today in the light of better knowledge of Hebrew and cognate languages as archaic or unusual forms may have been listed as errors.

§4. For literary criticism, cf. O. Cullmann, 'The Necessity and Function of Higher Criticism', *Student World* 42, 1949, 117–33; H. Ringgren, 'Literarkritik, Formgeschichte, Überlieferungsgeschichte', *TLZ* 91, 1966, 641–50; and A. Nitschke, 'Historische Wissenschaft und Bibelwissenschaft', *EvTh* 27, 1967, 225–36. For 'popular' but very well presented explanations of basic problems, cf. D. Michel, *Israels Glaube im Wandel*, Berlin 1968, chs. I–II.

IV

DESCRIPTIONS OF THE OLD TESTAMENT

§1. *The Old Testament as a history book*

What kind of a book is the Old Testament? Or better, what kind of book does the Old Testament consider itself to be? The answers to these questions can vary depending on the standpoint or the aims of the questioner and the person to whom he puts his question. For example, there is no doubt that the Old Testament is, *inter alia*, the fundamental document for the religion of Israel during the first three quarters of the first millennium BC, or that an ethnologist or sociologist might consider it the principal source for a study of ancient Israel from these particular perspectives. For the comparative philologist it will be the principal source for the Hebrew language in the period mentioned. Similar examples could be multiplied. But one reply which should be obvious and should satisfy any questioner is a simpler one: the Old Testament is a collection of books which for the most part lay claim to being history books. In other words, the Old Testament professes a very special interest in the history of a specific people in the ancient Near East, the Hebrews. This interest is not, however, historiographical in the strict sense of the word: the Old Testament believes itself to be concerned with the history of a people to whom God has spoken and through whom he has acted, and, of course in a more indirect way, with those people with whom Israel came in contact and who thus contributed to the formation of its history.

This statement does not apply only to the historical books proper; it can also be verified for the greater part of the prophetic books, continually in dialogue as they are with people in a particular situation, and for a considerable part of the Psalms, even if it is often a difficult undertaking to discover the events underlying their rather nebulous allusions. The one exception is the wisdom literature, which prefers to express universal truths which are always valid and therefore detached from historical problems. Writers of very different tendencies agree on this point: in 1946, H. W. Robinson wrote that 'The Old Testament is formally a history into which other forms of literature have been incorporated', while Bultmann affirmed in 1949 that 'History is the major theme of the Old Testament literature.' Thus we can see, for example, that collections of legal material in the Pentateuch or in Ezekiel have been inserted respectively either into the account of the journey through the wilderness during the exodus or into the context of the promise of a speedy restoration of the community which was largely destroyed or deported during the events of 587 BC.

Of course, to speak of 'history' introduces some extremely complex problems concerning the value of a term which is so controversial today in a philosophical context. The problems involved are impossible to deal with here. We shall therefore content ourselves with saying that the historical character of the greater part of the biblical texts is not constant, as every reader knows: in some cases it does not go beyond the intentions of the authors or those who transmitted certain stories. The authors or transmitters of the primal stories in Gen. 1–11 clearly located them in time and space and therefore regarded them as history, difficult though it may be to recognize this characterization in the context of modern historiography. The historical character of the patriarchal narratives is different again. Recent discoveries from the ancient Near East have made it probable that they are substantially historical, but do not enable us to identify the people involved or to synchronize them with persons or events otherwise known to us. One type of historiography which is almost modern has in the past been recognized in the so-called 'succession narrative' (to the throne of David) in II Sam. 9–20 (perhaps preceded by 21.1–14) and I Kings 1–2, but a more accurate analysis of the sections oblige us to revise considerably such a sweeping affirmation. Certain prophetic legends do refer to historical figures and have been collected in contexts whose historicity is beyond question, but it is quite impossible to verify them in a historical context and they often contain very improbable elements (e.g. II Kings 4). Elsewhere we are dealing more with a theology of history: the motive power behind this history is the God of Israel, its sovereign, who in his wisdom rewards the righteous and punishes the wicked, either on an individual or on a collective basis. Here we can recognize a series of details which make Israelite thought a precursor of the philosophy of history in that it is clearly in search of a principle which unifi , certain events and around which particular events crystallize. In other words, Israel has already gone far beyond a mere chronicle which narrates facts as such. Israel begins from its present situation and seeks in the past the cause of that situation, choosing only those events and those figures which it considers relevant. In this way there develops a consciousness which, leaving aside the brief episode of the historical prologues to the Hittite treaties in the second half of the second millennium BC, is without parallel in antiquity in either East or West. The faith of Israel is thus clearly centred on history, not on chronicle, and still less, as we shall see, on myth (ch. V, §1 below).

This explains why, contrary to what we might expect in a book which is essentially an expression of the faith of Israel, the Old Testament, like the New, contains very few doctrinal propositions. Accustomed as we are to exact dogmatic formulations, at least in the Western tradition, first from the Hellenistic world and then from the Middle Ages and the baroque era, we are surprised not to find anything similar in the biblical world. Some have sought to see this peculiarity as a typical element of Semitic mentality, which they understand to be more inclined to proclamation than to reasoning in a systematic form, more ready for dynamic descriptive concepts, in action, than for more or less objective accounts, in a static form. But the historical approach adopted by the faith of Israel from the very beginning would be a better explanation. Israelite belief is not so much interested in definitions as in history, and it is therefore in history, that is in action, that Israel gained its religious experience. God is not therefore defined in formulae of a catechetical kind, but is confessed for what he has done. 'I am Yahweh your God, who brought you out of the land of Egypt, out of the house of bondage . . .' (Exod. 20.1); and if the New Testament says at one point that 'God is love' (I John 4.8), it is not so much giving a systematic definition which would in any case be rather vague, as drawing the conclusions of the affirmation which is contained in the Fourth Gospel, 'God so loved the world that he gave his only Son' (John 3.16). In other words, even where we seem to have a definition of a doctrinal kind, we really have a connection with an element which is firmly associated with a historical fact. This happens throughout the New Testament. When Hebrews 11.1ff. gives a rather complex definition of faith, it does so only in conjunction with the presentation of a series of examples which show how faith has operated in the past. None of the more doctrinal passages in the writings of Paul could be understood without the presence of two inescapable historical facts: the crucifixion of Jesus and the apostolic testimony to his resurrection. The choice of examples from the New Testament rather than the Old was deliberate, to show that even in a period when there were continuous contacts with Hellenistic philosophy, which led to abstraction and spiritualization, this form of thinking continued unchanged. As H. W. Robinson said, God did not reveal himself of old in doctrine, but acted primarily in history and secondarily in man and in nature, while Bultmann, who was quoted earlier, was continuing a discussion in which he pointed out that whereas most Greek philosophy sees nature with its order and its laws (concepts of which Israel seems to be ignorant) as constituting the primary source of revelation, in Israel, nature, when it appears in this function, does so only in its less attractive and catastrophic forms: storms, earthquakes and so on. These are the phenomena which have historical relevance and not others. Such an attitude towards natural revelation is certainly negative, but it did not prevent the Israelite believer from showing due wonder and astonishment when confronted with all the marvels of creation, cf. Pss. 8; 19; 104, etc.

The student of Israelite religion will sometimes find himself confronted with the problem of translating these historical and descriptive forms in which the Old Testament is expressed into categories comprehensible to modern man, and in this work Introduction to the Old Testament provides him with his principal tools.

§ 2. For the synagogue and the church the Bible is still the inspired Word of God

This is one of the few points where the course which the arts and theology have so far covered together divides, and we enter, however briefly, the area of the ultimate decision between belief and unbelief.

The Old Testament does not affirm explicitly the inspired character of the writings which comprise it, and the New Testament reaches this point only in the final phase of its redaction (cf. II Tim. 3.16; II Peter 1.20f.). The late character of these affirmations indicates that the primitive church, still solidly anchored in Hebrew tradition, did not even raise the problem. What God had said and done through men and the events which had been singled out for this purpose had normative value. This also means that the concept which later the primitive church felt the need to define in a more or less systematic form (even if it did not specify what in particular made up inspiration, which is by no means an obvious matter), was also implicitly present in an earlier age.

(a) In Protestant orthodoxy between the sixteenth and the eighteenth centuries, in conservative currents within Catholicism and also in Judaism, the concept of inspiration has been understood as special divine aid granted to the biblical authors by which they were to be kept free from doctrinal and factual error; in this way the normative character of the books in question was justified. This is not the place for the history of a theory which is so complex and controversial: even now it exists in a remarkable number of variants and shades of meaning, and there is an apologetic of doubtful effectiveness based on this very presupposition. It is difficult, therefore, to establish a common denominator between the different concepts of what is sometimes called 'verbal' inspiration, given the differences of culture and social class that exist between the various churches and sects which maintain it. In any case, one element appears with some constancy: the Holy Spirit intervened directly in the production of the sacred writings and in particular in the work of their authors, protecting them from error. A contemporary Protestant author who belongs to one of the theologically more progressive of these groups can still say that God has supervised the choice of every word in the sacred book so that it can be said to be entirely the word of God, without the addition of human errors. However, the same author rejects mechanistic caricatures of the concept, expressions like 'dictated' by the Spirit and similar formulations.

Still, leaving aside the static concept of truth and error which underlies this kind of definition, the problem cannot be defined in terms of truth against error, where inspiration creates the first by excluding the second, which is left to human reason: this is a crudely antihistorical way of stating the problem. Scientific opinions are valid until later discoveries or the perfection of existing methods supersede them, and this applies to all sciences, the humanities as well as the natural sciences. Thus certain statements in the Bible about astronomy, geography, human or animal medicine can hardly be considered 'true' in the present state of the relevant sciences: on the contrary, the geocentric character of the pre-Copernican and indeed pre-Ptolemaean world (Gen. 1.1ff.; Josh. 10.12ff.), the flatness of the earth which therefore has 'ends' (Acts 1.8; 13.47), the zoological affirmation that the rock badger and the hare 'chew the cud' (Lev. 11.5f.), or the astronomical statement that the universe is organized into three successive layers (cf. the creed, in which one 'ascends' to heaven but 'descends' to hell), and so on, are statements which do not seem so much to fall into the categories of true and false as into those of modern and old-fashioned. For this reason it is impossible to speak of 'inspiration' in connection with this kind of affirmation, since the texts have been composed at particular times, in clearly established ideological contexts which have now been superseded. In the same way, many of our affirmations will be superseded in the future (we are thinking only of the advances in natural science, often unknown to the public, from the beginning of the century up to the present day with the discovery of the theory of relativity or the quantum theory). Terms like truth and error are therefore inadequate to express such a complex reality. Furthermore, the opinions in question constitute the common heritage of all the ancient Near East and some of the West, without containing any of the elements which are typical of Israelite faith. Thus an erroneous apologetic attitude has led the church and the synagogue all too often into useless conflicts with the natural sciences.

A church which takes the incarnation seriously should admit that holy scripture takes human form in particular historical and ideological contexts and should not attempt to reconcile irreconcilable elements.

(b) By contrast, liberal Protestant theology, in many questions followed at the beginning of the century by Roman Catholic modernism and Jewish groups of similar tendencies, has always professed the utmost openness to natural science and the humanities. Concepts which have been regarded as outdated have been left on one side, and alternative positions have developed with terms which have not always been clearly defined, like 'ethical monotheism', 'universalism', 'moral law' in opposition to 'national God', 'ethnic particularism', 'ceremonial law' etc., without any concern for the meaning of these expressions or for their adequacy in describing an extremely complex reality like that of the belief of the Old and New Testaments. Moreover, the normative character of the Bible has only been accepted in so far as it conforms to certain ethical and scientific canons of a particular age: scripture is no longer scripture, but a source of inspiration, a (temporary) culmination in a process of evolution which is still under way.

(c) As is often the case, neither side is right. The truth lies midway between. Both positions are the consequence of the same form of rationalism according to which only what is verifiable or acceptable in the scientific sense is 'true'. Thus the conservative who wishes to safeguard the authority of the Bible has to demonstrate that there is no apparent divergence between science and faith, while the 'liberal' feels obliged to suppress the parts in which the divergence is to be found. However, as we have seen, it is not a question of accusing of 'falsehood' a scientific statement made two or three thousand years ago, but rather of accepting the obvious fact of its antiquity. The inadequacy of these formulations never prejudices the validity of the message of the Bible, just as the scientific affirmations of today, which will seem equally inadequate tomorrow, should not condition the truth of our faith. To ask the astronauts, if only in jest, whether they have seen God and the angels is an anti-historical mistake of a certain popular kind of Marxism.

With this proviso, we can now understand what the Old Testament means by inspiration, a concept which, as we have seen, is neither formulated nor described in the Old Testament itself.

(d) Given this absence of formulations, the most adequate way of attempting to describe the concept of inspiration in the Old Testament is probably that of asking: in what way does the biblical narrative differ from other narratives of the same literary genre among neighbouring peoples? As an example we might take the story of the exodus and the conquest of Palestine, events which have been fixed hypothetically, though by the general consent of scholars, in the course of the thirteenth century BC. We shall deliberately leave on one side the complicated problems connected with their historicity and their complex details, and concentrate on the distinctive elements. We immediately notice that it is possible to narrate these events in a completely secular way: a semi-nomadic people, settled for centuries in Egypt in the eastern region of the delta, is suddenly considered to be a danger because it is growing in numbers and economic strength. Moreover, because it is close to the frontier, it can make common cause with other peoples of the same extraction who are hostile to Egypt. A series of natural catastrophes makes it possible for the people to escape their oppressors. After a long march across the desert the fugitives succeed in reaching Canaan, having been re-inforced along the way by similar groups. Palestine is in a state of political and economic decadence: Egyptian authority has become purely nominal in most cases (that is, with the exception of certain strongholds like Beth-shean, Gezer, etc.), and now counts for almost nothing. By means of a skilful system of alliances through which the invaders succeeded in dividing the enemy (e.g. Gibeon, Josh.9), the ancestors of Israel were able to settle first in the less populated zones, while their ranks were swelled by all those who were discontented with the semi-feudal regime by which the city-states of the region were governed. Then, under David and Solomon at the beginning of the first millennium BC, the invaders were able to conquer the city states which were still resisting.

As can be seen, this interpretation is completely free from all theological and religious elements; it is not false to the biblical text, but merely incomplete. The Old Testament sees in these facts much more than one of the many migrations of peoples which took place at the end of the second millennium BC; it sees here the divine action in history for the salvation of a fallen humanity, by means of the election of a people and the fulfilment of the divine promises towards them. This capacity for discerning the divine plan within history beyond events is what distinguishes a 'sacred' author in the Old Testament from any other kind of writer, just as it distinguishes the believing hearer or reader (who accepts this interpretation of events) from any other kind of hearer or reader. What applies to the text also applies here: ascertaining the nature of the facts is the same for both the believer and the non-believer, and consequently it would be absurd to want to speak of infallibility in the field of history any more than in that of natural science. History, too, progresses and this is why the reconstruction of the exodus and the conquest which we have just given would no longer be accepted today by any historian, whether he was a believer or not. At the same time, however, the believer can accept the message we have indicated above, since this is not founded on the detailed verification of the events in question but on their general outline: there is no reason to doubt that ancestors of Israel were in Egypt and that they left there and conquered Canaan.

We can see, then, how stories which were originally rich in legendary and sometimes mythical elements, whose primary scope must have been to glorify ancestors on a tribal or national level, have been transformed by the biblical narrators into testimonies to the redeeming work of God.

BIBLIOGRAPHY

§1. The quotations are taken from the posthumous work of H. W. Robinson, *Inspiration and Revelation in the Old Testament*, Oxford 1946, 123, and R. Bultmann, *Primitive Christianity in its Contemporary Setting*, ET London 1960, 22, cf. 18; cf. more recently N. Lohfink, 'Théologie de l'histoire dans l'ancien Israël', *Archivio di Filosofia*, Rome 1971.2, 189–99, and N. W. Porteous, 'Old Testament and History', *ASTI* 8, 1972, 21–77. The views expressed in these works have also been widely criticized; cf. G. Fohrer, *Theologische Grundstrukturen des Alten Testaments*, Berlin 1972, 42ff., where he indicates not only the ambiguity of the term 'history' but also its inapplicability to certain Psalms, the wisdom literature, and the concept of *tōrāh* (usually translated 'law') as it developed within Judaism as something valid beyond time and history.

For the Hittite treaties cf. A. Malamat, 'Doctrines of Causality in Hittite and Biblical Historiography: a Parallel', *VT* 5, 1955, 1–12; H. Gese, 'The Idea of History in the Ancient Near East and the Old Testament', *Journal for Theology and the Church* 1, New York 1965, 49–64. To assert that in the Old Testament revelation takes place *in* rather than *through* history is clearly not to assert that other people did not have similar experiences; cf. in this respect B. Albrektson, *History and the Gods*, Lund 1967: all the peoples of the ancient world, both East and West, saw in war, pestilence or earthquake the hand of the God who judged human sin. The qualifying element is the organic character of the biblical history, in which we can see a coherent attempt to eliminate myth.

§2. The concept of verbal inspiration, which in Protestantism goes back to Matthias Flaccius Illyricus, is here based on statements by R. L. Harris, *Inspiration and Canonicity of the Bible*, Grand Rapids 1957, 20. This theory underlies the introduction by G. L. Archer (cf. general bibliography), and has been criticized as 'docetic' by O. Cullmann, art. cit. (cf. bibliography to ch. III, §4), 125. Karl Barth, *Church Dogmatics* III. 1, ET Edinburgh 1958, 81ff., has maintained that both conservative and liberal positions derive from the rationalism of the Enlightenment. For all the problems and their semantic and hermeneutic ramifications, cf. L. Alonso Schökel, *The Inspired Word*, ET New York 1965.

V

MYTH, LEGEND AND HISTORY

In the previous chapter (and here we can rejoin those interested in the Old Testament from a humanistic perspective) we spoke of history-writing of different kinds in which there are variants between the authors and transmitters of the biblical tradition, though all alike are concerned with writing history. At this point it is necessary to give the reader a number of definitions which are aimed at distinguishing between the different literary genres. The categories are myth, saga and legend; fable and fairy tale; and finally historiography proper. All these genres are present in greater or lesser degree in the Old Testament.

§1. *Myth*

Myth is a narrative literary genre which appears in one form or another in all the religions outside the Judaeo-Christian tradition. In biblical studies, and often in ancient Near Eastern studies, the theme of the genre is the deeds of gods or heroes, deeds which are independent of any historical or geographical or chronological context because they are usually, at least in their origin, bound up with the cyclical pattern of nature and its fertility (H. Gunkel). Through myth man participates in the cult in an active way, in the timeless mysteries of birth, life and death, and knows the universe as an eternal image of the sacred alternation of light and darkness (E. Haller).

At this point it will be easy to see that myth is therefore the opposite of history: it is cyclical where history is linear; it takes place outside, or perhaps better, above time and space, where history is deeply and ineradicably rooted in them; it deals with gods and heroes, but history has as protagonists human beings like ourselves, although in ancient history there is often an obvious tendency to choose the actions of kings and not of commoners. It would, however, be completely wrong to affirm that myth belongs to the world of fantasy, whether religious or not; it is still less accurate to say that myth belongs to the world of fable. Myth belongs, rather, to the world of the cult, as we indicated earlier; that is, it provides the *hieros logos* of a rite or a sanctuary and the theme for the liturgical action which the cult sets out to repeat, by actualizing a primordial event for the benefit of those who take part, the community. At this point we could discuss whether myth precedes, and therefore creates, the liturgy in question or whether it is merely the narrative expression of an already existing liturgy of which it is therefore the product. This is a problem which, given the considerable antiquity of the two, would be very difficult to resolve. It is also difficult to say with certainty whether or not a real religious experience lies at the heart of myth.

In any case, there are important limits to be set to the possible historicity of the narrative: these arise from the supra-historical character of the myth itself. That does not mean, however, that a myth is incapable of realizing relevant historical facts, for example in the social sphere (one may remember the caste system in India or the position of women in certain religious contexts, etc.), and also in politics (see the importance that augurs and soothsayers had throughout the ancient world, in East and West). From the point of view of its specific consequences, then, myth is quite capable of producing historically relevant effects. It is also possible that a mythical narrative may have effectively retained the memory of real religious experiences, but for the reasons mentioned it is difficult, and usually impossible, to verify this. As a general rule it would not be rash to say that the connection of myth with the cycles of nature and with the fertility of the soil, which is particularly evident in myths like that of Persephone (to give a well-known example), robs it of any specific historical or geographical reference: the myth of Persephone happens everywhere and nowhere, eternally and therefore never.

Now it is a characteristic feature of the biblical writers that because of their historical mentality, for all the limitations indicated, they have eliminated myth from their texts where possible. Obvious survivals of myth remain, but these are survivals: there are many poetical passages which show how Israel too must have had a remarkably developed mythology in the first centuries of her existence, though we can no longer establish whether it was original or acquired. These are myths which speak of the struggle of God the creator and preserver of the world against chaos, of sacred or semi-sacred marriages. But the interesting thing is that in almost every case we have quotations incorporated in quite different contexts, just as a Greek philosopher might cite an ancient text, or just as we might introduce a quotation ourselves, without these texts having the slightest relevance on the historical and religious plane. On the contrary, as we have seen, Israel does not even know the concept of a 'sacred' history, the theatre of the divine action; it simply knows of 'history', the context in which both God and men are at work.

Both the Old Testament and the New have often followed a deliberate and coherent practice of demythologization in connection with myth. Ancient mythical themes have been taken and inserted into a historical context, thus becoming simply illustrations to the text and at the same time losing their supra-historical character. The myth of marriages between the gods, which in the Canaanite world came to be represented in the cult under the form of the union between the king or a priest and a priestess, became in Israel the marriage between Yahweh and his people Israel, a theme beloved of the prophets Hosea, Jeremiah and Ezekiel. Granted, this theme is still mythical, but in this respect it is possible to assign an origin, a date, a locality: the experience at Sinai, which reduces the mythical character of the theme to the unavoidable minimum. A myth of giants who try to scale heaven is in fact used as an illustration of the arrogance of the king of Babylon and its consequences in Isa. 14; the myth of the original god-man, which in Gen. 2–3 is reduced to a minimum, reappears in Ezek. 28 as an example of the pride and the punishment of the king of Tyre. The death and resurrection of some gods connected with fertility (Baal, Adonis, etc.) is replaced in the New Testament by the unique event of the death and resurrection of Jesus, but this took place in Jerusalem 'under Pontius Pilate' between 30 and 33 and is therefore stripped of the chief elements which characterize myth, even if it is the basis of Christian worship, with lasting effects. An ancient myth which spoke of the struggle against chaos has now been inserted into the text of Isa. 51.9ff., where chaos has become the image of the enemies of God and Israel, in the form first of Egypt and then of Babylon towards the end of the sixth century BC. The mythical mountain of the gods, Zaphon, situated in the extreme north of Syria, has come to provide the terminology for describing Zion: in Ps. 48.2 Zion is said to be 'in the far north', a description which is certainly hyperbole if it is thought only to report the fact that Zion is some tens of metres north of the city of David. We do, however, know the origins and the date of the foundation of the sanctuary of Zion, which was under David and Solomon during the first half of the tenth century BC; its origins are thus quite unmythical, even if part of the terminology applying to the Syro-Palestinian Olympus has come to embellish the traditional description of the Jerusalem sanctuary.

This dominant tendency does not mean, however, that myth has been completely eliminated: this does not happen in the mentality of an era from one century to another. Thus in Gen. 6.1–4 we have a myth which was originally meant to narrate the origin of a generation of giants and heroes, offspring of the marriage of divine beings and women. But from the point of view of modern philosophy any attempt to distinguish between transcendence and immanence, between God and man, could be considered mythical. Now in this last case we reach the limit beyond which we cannot proceed without at least the partial use of a language which others could consider mythical.

It is, however, important that the faith of Israel laid the foundations for a separation between faith and myth, that the universe and nature have been so to speak secularized, robbed of any divine immanence and made accessible to scientific investigation. This happened in times which proved incapable of assimilating the consequences, with the result that Jews and Christians soon reverted to the world of myth from which the Old Testament should have been excluded for ever. However, that is another question and it is hard to blame the biblical authors for the fact.

§2. Legend and saga

The term 'legend' may meet with negative reactions from those who are accustomed to the way in which it is used in everyday language, where it is equivalent to a more or less fantastic story (in current understanding, 'legendary' describes an incredible episode), or to the use made of it by medieval hagiographers, among whom it serves essentially to refer to edifying episodes drawn from the lives of the saints. In ethnology and the history of religion, however, the use of the word is more positive: the legend is the record of a fact which really happened, of an experience really undergone or of a person who really existed, but in a prehistoric era, from which we possess only traditional material of a popular type. The saga is similar, but presents more than the individual. Here the tribe, the clan, appear in the figures of their protagonists. Consequently the two genres tend to become intermingled and coalesce. In legend and saga, then, we have the historiography of peoples who have not yet reached the stage of mature history-writing and who therefore lack the capacity for synthesis and choice which is to be found among those who have arrived historically at a certain level of maturity. The two phases, that of the man who has remained at the point of legend and that of the man who has reached the level of mature history writing, can even coexist peacefully in the same people: in mountainous or rural areas there can exist a legendary historiography with a unique relationship between the present and the past. In fact – and we do not believe that this is a case of digressing from the argument – such maturity is the product of a series of historical and political, cultural and economic coefficients which create the consciousness of a critical examination of a people's past as a condition, a presupposition, for particular present situations.

We have various obvious examples of legendary narrative in the Old Testament: in Exod. 1 the name of the Pharaoh of the oppression and the exodus is never mentioned (indeed no Pharaoh is named in the Old Testament before the end of the tenth century BC), but we do have a careful reference on the basis of a tradition which is certainly trustworthy to the names of two brave midwives who by their resistance nullified the unjust decree of the Pharaoh aimed at the extermination of the newborn Israelites in Egypt. Now if an interest in these midwives is quite understandable on the level of popular tradition, it is completely absent on the historical level, while the silence over the name of the Pharaoh makes it impossible to determine with certainty the date of the oppression and the exodus. The patriarchs, too, seem to move in a world populated by only a few phantoms; otherwise it is ethnically void. There is not a single name which allows us to establish any synchronism between their persons and facts contemporaneous to them, and we know a great deal about the latter. The unique episode which seeks to put Abraham in the context of international events appears in Gen. 14, but at this very point there are so many insoluble problems that the chapter might as well not be there. Fortunately, in connection with the patriarchs we have evidence of a series of laws, customs and practices which have parallels in Mesopotamia from the end of the first half of the second millennium BC, and on the basis of these the patriarchs are usually dated in this period.

These are examples which prompt reflection and suggest a conclusion: Israel achieved mature historiography at the beginning of the period of the monarchy, that is, during the first decades of the tenth century BC; before this period, with few exceptions, the sources are inadequate for establishing relevant historical details (names of Pharaohs or of other people of some pre-eminence), but we find the

names of midwives, nurses and similar people, all moving within a
domestic milieu. Already in the eleventh century, however, we have
the first hints of a new maturity: interest begins to shift from the
anecdote to the relevant historical details, and an example can be
found in the more ancient verses of Judg.9. From the time of David
and Solomon onwards, we see that in court circles there are not only
traces of remarkably developed annals (we only have notes of them,
the texts have been lost), but organic history-writings are beginning
to take shape. A now classic example has been recognized in the so-
called 'history of the succession to the throne of David' (II Sam.21.1–
14 + chs.9–20 and I Kings 1;2), mentioned above. Here, alongside
the presence of legendary elements or even fantasies which have been
recognized in recent years, we have an attempt to see the development of the reign of David along certain organic lines, which investigates causes and effects. Legend has continued to exist at the
same time, being particularly concerned with people the memory of
whom may have been especially vivid in popular tradition: prophets
like Elijah and Elisha in the second half of the ninth century BC. In
late Judaism the genre underwent a change: narratives develop about
the important figures of antiquity, which are nearer to fairy-tale than
to legend, even if they look like legends.

Now as has already been indicated, Israel was much in advance of
the other peoples of either East or West in this area. It too, however,
like them, had to grow laboriously to maturity in this respect.

The fundamental difference between legend and myth is this: the
former has its setting in a real historical experience and develops in
time and space; its protagonists are historical (or presumably historical) people and not gods or heroes. Sometimes it is at least theo-
retically possible to go back from the text of the legend to the
experience which underlies it, even if this rarely happens in practice.
In the classical world we have some remarkable analogies in this
respect: the legend of the Iliad takes us back to the Mycenaean and
Aegean world, that is, many centuries before the final 'Homeric'
redaction; but in the Odyssey the situation is already more complex
because of the variety and intricacy of the traditions, only held together by the figure of the hero. In the same way we can now go back
from the legends of the patriarchs to the world to which they belong,
as we have just indicated. If we accept a remarkably widespread
hypothesis, this is the world of the semi-nomadic Western Semites to
be found between the eighteenth and the seventeenth century BC in
the region of the Western Mesopotamian city state of Mari on the
Euphrates: analogous material in the legal field has connections with

the practices attested in the city-state of Nuzi in northern Mesopotamia. But we need also to recognize that at this point our knowledge ends and that the questions which remain unanswered are more than the results: centuries of oral tradition in a milieu without real historical interest have ended by distorting beyond remedy the original form of this material.

One particular type of legend is the so-called aetiological legend, from the Greek *aitia* = 'cause': this sets out to explain to an audience the origins of a name, a custom or a rite, sometimes a feature connected with a natural element. Gen. 32.32 is a typical example: the custom of not eating a certain part of the thigh of an animal is connected with the episode of the struggle of Jacob with the angel; there are numerous etymological aetiologies, i.e. aetiologies which explain a name. These last-mentioned rarely have a true historical foundation, but are based on popular etymologies of the names in question, and usually have no value in the linguistic sphere.

§3. Fable and fairy-tale

The fable is a narrative literary genre in which the protagonists are usually animals or plants, and only rarely humans: it normally ends with a lesson, a 'moral', which is its evident purpose. By definition, then, the fable is an ahistorical literary genre and does not have any pretensions in that direction, even if on a purely theoretical plane the narrative part could contain historical elements when dealing with people. To arrive at the lesson, the final 'moral', 'a situation is made concrete', as the German historian of religion, A. Bertholet, put it, and in this sense the fable is distinct from the parable, even if it is not always easy to distinguish the two genres in practice. We have at least two examples of the fable in the Old Testament, Judg. 9.8ff. and II Kings 14.9, though it is not easy to discover the moral in the first case. Given the fictitious character of the contents, the fable does not present problems for the historian.

The fable was given its classical form first in Greece by Aesop, then in Rome by Phaedrus, and finally in France by Jean de La Fontaine.

The fairy-tale or *Novelle* is similar to the fable, and develops out of a delight in story-telling, what the Germans call *Lust zum Fabulieren*. The fairy-tale mixes men and animals, the sacred and the profane, and can also include famous historical people, though in obviously fictitious contexts. In it the narrative part does not move towards a moral, while the conflicts and the tensions which it contains are not resolved by struggle or compromise, but through the intervention of figures with marked miraculous characteristics similar to the ancient *deus ex machina*, who authoritatively arrange everything to the great satisfaction of all. Late Judaism knows a series of rabbinic tales about famous people in the history of Israel, David, Solomon, Elijah, etc., which are between history and fable: well-known collections of fairy-tales are those by the brothers Grimm in Germany, by 'Mother Goose' in France and by L. Capuana in Italy, all in the past century. No fairy-tales exist in their pure state in the Old Testament, although there is no lack of themes which we might characterize in this way: Joseph who from the deepest humiliation achieves the highest office by virtue of his moral character; Saul who sets out to look for lost animals and finds a kingdom. The story of Joseph is typical because everything is attributed to divine providence and there is no criticism of the injustice with which the story begins.

§4. *Legend and historiography*

We indicated earlier the problems of the relationship between legend and historiography and showed how legend could sometimes provide very important historiographical material. This raises a problem which indubitably deserves to be looked at in more detail and which we cannot leave without having posed it properly. For example, consider the mere fact that legend has its roots in real historical experience but has emerged from a people who have not reached such historical maturity that they would automatically put it in the category of popular tradition. This results in a markedly dialectical and sometimes ambiguous relationship between it and the historian who makes use of it.

The Enlightenment and the rationalism which developed from it made a notable contribution towards demonstrating the ambiguity of this kind of relationship, and the same is true for historicism and positivism at the end of the last century and the beginning of this. All these approaches accepted the principle that we should take into account only material which could be verified in a historico-critical setting, that is, official documents, contemporary testimony, archive material; but it is obvious that in this way the chronological limit at which historiography begins to operate is notably later and that a considerable amount of material which, if carefully studied, could provide valuable information for the researcher, is discarded *a priori*, on principle. This was understood by romantic historiography, which sought to discover what it called the 'soul of the people', and which was ready to resort to intuition when material for critical research was lacking. On the other hand, this recourse to intuition and therefore to subjective fantasy has been a serious disadvantage for romantic historiography, and in many cases has prejudiced scientific credibility; the reader will be familar with the idyllic or violent reconstructions of medieval European life written in this vein. It is thus no surprise that this kind of historiography has involuntarily contributed to a devaluation of legend as a historical source.

We are only repeating findings which are now well-known if we assert that historiography can only exist if a number of conditions are fulfilled which include: (*a*) the existence of sources and (*b*) their adequacy in a critical sense. For legend, the first of these elements does not present any problems: there are as many legends as one could desire; it is the second condition which presents often insurmountable difficulties. Although the material is abundant, it is rarely adequate, even if, at least in theory, it should be possible to go back from it to facts and people. In practice, however, given the popular character of the traditions in question and hence the uncritical way in which they have been collected and transmitted, the possibility of going back to the events and persons involved is often virtually non-existent, unless we have other more reliable sources which permit of valid comparisons. The patriarchal narratives would remain in the limbo of conjecture had the texts found in the Mesopotamian city-states of Mari and Nuzi not furnished material by which to verify them; we would know virtually nothing about the character of the traditions contained in the Iliad had H. Schliemann in the second half of the last century not carried out his famous investigations and had their results not been continually perfected and largely corrected by his successors; the decipherment of Linear B writing in the 1950s then opened up the possibility of connections with the Mycenaean-Aegean world, by offering yet other material. In other words, it is often possible to go back from legends to the people and events of which they speak, but this usually happens only when we have some possibility of comparison with other more reliable literary material: at Mari and Nuzi, for example, archive material has been found, a series of texts of which the historian can make direct use.

In the light of these texts, various elements in the patriarchal narratives unexpectedly begin to make sense. It had already been noted that patriarchal nomenclature no longer appeared in Israel after the beginning of the monarchy, whereas a series of practices and customs seemed not only strange, but also unparalleled in earlier times. However, remarkable parallels to the nomenclature have been found in western Semitic onomastica from the region of the city-state of Mari, while the city of Nuzi and its laws has provided the key for a series of explanations of practices and customs. We cite only a few instances.

Where a man died without heirs, his steward would officially become the heir to his property, cf. the lament of Abraham in Gen. 15.2f.; when a wife did not have children, she was permitted to give her husband one of her female slaves to bear 'on her knees' a son who would be considered quite legitimate in every respect. If the legitimate wife then had a son, the first son would lose his character as firstborn, though the father would not be able to drive him and his mother away: cf. Gen. 16.3ff.; 30.1ff. In 21.10ff. Sarah asks Abraham to send away Hagar and Ishmael, and Abraham's reluctance is overcome only by a divine ordinance to this effect. This is probably a reminiscence of the prohibition against sending the female slave and her child away when the legitimate wife later had a son of her own. Now, for all the problems which parallels of this sort present to the scholar and hence the difficulty of establishing the existence of relationships with any degree of certainty, we need to recognize that nevertheless the legendary tradition of the Bible has preserved the memory of laws and traditions which really existed, a fact that is all the more remarkable since the laws and the institutions are no longer attested in the historical period. However, without the comparative material indicated above, such a conclusion would have been impossible. For the rest, we must recognize that very little of this kind of material has been made available to the historian, despite some notable efforts at research. We have therefore sketched out only a few examples here, not the limits of possible discoveries.

BIBLIOGRAPHY

§1. For myth, its nature and its possible historicity cf. the classical study by R. Pettazzoni, 'The Truth of Myth', in *Essays on the History of Religions*, Leiden 1954, 11–23; M. Marconi, 'Mita e verità scientifica', *SMSR* 32, 1961, 99–106; U. Bianchi, 'Religione, mito e storia', *Atti del XV Convegno del Centro di Studi Filosofici tra Professore Universitare, Gallarate 1960*, Brescia 1961, 302–15; and F. Festorazzi, *La Bibbia e il problema delle origini*, Brescia ²1967, 167ff. For myth in the Old Testament, cf. G. Hartlich and W. Sachs, *Der Ursprung des Mythosbegriffes in der modernen Bibelwissenschaft*, Tübingen 1952; B. S. Childs, *Myth and Reality in the Old Testament*, SBT 27, 1960; W. H. Schmidt, 'Mythos im Alten Testament', *EvTh* 27, 1967, 237–54;

J. Garcia Trapiello, 'Mito y culto en el Antiguo Testamento', *Angelicum* 44, Rome 1967, 449–77; T. H. Gaster, 'Myth and Story', *Numen* 1, Leiden 1954, 184–212; and J. W. Rogerson, *Myth in Old Testament Interpretation*, BZAW 134, 1974. H. Cancik, *Mythische und historische Wahrheit*, Stuttgart 1970, gives a view from the field of classical history and literature.

§2. G. von Rad, 'The Beginnings of Historical Writing in Ancient Israel', in *The Problem of the Hexateuch and other Essays*, ET Edinburgh 1966, 166–204. The remarks of E. Meyer, *Geschichte des Altertums*, II. 1, Munich [2]1928, are still valid for the problem of mature history writing. For the situation in prehistoric Greece, cf. A. Lesky, *Geschichte der griechischen Literatur*, Bern 1957–8, 86ff. We also find a remarkable phenomenon of demythologization in ancient Rome; cf. D. Sabbattucci, 'Mito e demitizzazione nell' antica Roma', *Religioni e Civiltà* 1 (= *SMSR* NS 1), Rome 1972, 539–89; this is a phenomenon which took place a few centuries later than that attested in Israel. It is not possible here to investigate whether this process gave rise to historiography, and, if so, when.

For aetiological legend cf. B. O. Long, *The Problem of Etiological Narrative in the Old Testament*, BZAW 108, 1968, with bibliography; F. Golka, 'Zur Erforschung der Ätiologien im Alten Testament,' *VT* 20, 1970, 90–8; and L. Sabourin, 'Biblical Etiologies', *BTB* 2, 1972, 199–205.

§3. For the fable, cf. A. Bertholet (ed.), *Wörterbuch der Religionen*, Stuttgart 1952, s.v. 'Fabel'; for the fairytale the classic work is H. Gunkel, *Das Märchen im Alten Testament*, Tübingen 1917; cf. also E. Haller, 'Märchen und Zeugnis', in H. W. Wolff (ed.), *Probleme biblischer Theologie: G. von Rad zum 70. Geburtstag*, Munich 1971, 108–15. M. Liverani, 'Partire sul carro, per il deserto', *AION* 32, 1972, 403–15, has pointed out that fairytale elements are often inserted in historical narratives throughout the ancient Near East, and that they often serve to legitimate the succession of an important figure who has received office in an irregular fashion; cf. in the Old Testament the stories of Joseph, Saul and David.

§4. For Schliemann and Troy, cf. H. Schliemann, *Kein Troja ohne Homer*, ed. W. Schmied, Nuremberg 1960; or Robert Payne, *The Gold of Troy*, London 1959 (both useful popular introductions). For comparisons between the patriarchal narratives and the Mesopotamian texts of the second millennium BC cf. J. van Seters, 'Jacob's Marriages and Ancient Eastern Customs', *HTR* 62, 1969, 377–95, which stresses the very limited nature of the comparison. For a criticism of those views which stress the historical character of the patriarchal stories cf. T. L. Thompson, *The Historicity of the Patriarchal Narratives*, BZAW 133, 1974.

Terminology. R. M. Hals, 'Legend: a Case Study in Form-Critical Terminology', *CBQ* 34, 1972, 166–76, rightly points out that terminology is remarkably confused and tends to become even more so with translation from one language to another (e.g. the difference between German *Sage* and Scandinavian *saga*: on this cf. also P. Gibert, 'Légende ou Saga', *VT* 24, 1974, 411–20). Problems of this kind have to be tackled in the context of each particular language.

VI

THE PRE-LITERARY DEVELOPMENT OF THE
BIBLICAL MATERIAL

§1. *1200–900 BC and the importance of the period for the formation of
the earlier writings*

As anyone concerned with Oriental studies well knows, the people of
Israel are an inseparable part of the wider context of the peoples of
the ancient Near East, and especially of the western Semites. This is
true ethnically, linguistically, historically and culturally; it is also
true, within certain limits, of Israelite religion, a field in which Israel
represents the exception rather than the rule. Israel's position becomes
understandable only against the above-mentioned background.

The relationship between the people of Israel and their neighbours
is almost comparable to that existing today among people of the same
stock: neo-Latins, Germans, Slavs and Anglo-Saxons. The difference
is that with the non-Aramaean peoples of Syria-Palestine the relationship is even closer, whether linguistically (in the first millennium
BC, Phoenician, Hebrew and Moabitic are variants of the same language rather than three different languages) or on the general level of
civilization, with the exception (already mentioned) of religion. The
rediscovery of the civilization of the city-state of Ugarit, situated on
the Mediterranean coast in northern Syria, a few miles north of
Laodicea (the modern Latakia), which began in 1929 (excavations
are still in process), has merely confirmed this state of affairs, already
known for some decades previously, although to be exact Ugarit is a
peripheral phenomenon in the area. At least once, the Israelites call
their language the 'language of Canaan' (Isa. 19.18), and this is not
surprising, given that it seems evident that the conquerors would have
adopted the language of the region which they occupied, for the most
part abandoning the language which they spoke earlier. The biblical
tradition describes the ancestors of Israel as 'wandering Aramaeans'
(Deut. 26.5), and although it is impossible to ascertain the historical

value of this note, it shows that Israel itself was conscious of the way in which their passage from a semi-nomadic to a sedentary state represented a break for the people, and even for their language. Just as the Romanized barbarians learnt Latin in the countries of the Roman empire which they had conquered, albeit at the expense of the original perfection of the language, so the Israelite invaders adopted in Canaan the language of the country, and with it that country's literary forms. It is not surprising, therefore, that the earliest Israelite poetry, for example in Gen. 49; Exod. 15; Num. 23–24; Deut. 32–33; Judg. 5; I Sam. 2; II Sam. 1.19ff.; 23.1–7; Pss. 29; 68; etc., presents problems which scholars believe can best be resolved by recourse to the hypothesis that here we have Canaanite poetry, and by treating it as though it were Ugaritic texts. The outlines of this study have been marked out since the last years of the Second World War by the American scholar W. F. Albright and his followers, though the method is far from having won unanimous approval.

On the other hand, a people with an inferior civilization occupying a more developed country accepts not only the language, along with certain customs and techniques of the country which it occupies, but also a new form of mind; this is a problem which arises in even more radical forms when the invading people is made up of nomads or semi-nomads finally settling down. The techniques of agriculture and construction, political and social structures and modes of thought, are often adopted by the conqueror simply because otherwise he has nothing of this sort. Often religion, too, comes to be taken over in a similar way. Here, however, the Israelites, like the Arab invaders centuries later, did not allow themselves to be assimilated, but maintained their independence (apart from occasional backslidings, often caused by contingent political factors).

It was only during the last centuries of the second millennium BC, when this process started, that the first oral cycles of legends, the first epics, began to take shape in Israel and to be assembled in larger or smaller collections. Material imported from the desert, sometimes confined to a single clan or tribe, began this formative process, which led to what we now possess. For example, the traditions about Abraham, Isaac and Jacob may then have been collected into a single cycle of patriarchal traditions with the addition of the story of Joseph; the material would have been put in a chronological setting which sometimes extended down to the time of the collector or transmitter. We know nothing of the criteria which governed this work, but some scholars have authoritatively suggested that, following a practice well attested in the ancient Near East, the sanctuaries were the places where this development took place. Since we are now talking of the happenings which even antedate the origins of the earliest writings of the Old Testament, it will be useful to look first at the rather later stages.

§2. *Oral tradition*

Over the preceding pages we have often used the term 'tradition'. We must now justify this choice of terminology, since it is by no means obvious.

It is well known that among all peoples oral tradition has preceded the written redaction of ancient texts, sometimes by centuries. This phenomenon does not seem strange to the modern reader, especially in the West: the love which people, especially in ancient times, show for immediate contact with affairs and people of the past is familiar, and this contact seems to many people even today to be a better guarantee of an uninterrupted chain of tradition than a written document.

We now know that the classical 'Homeric' literature stands at the end of a long chain of bards and poets and therefore that the Iliad and the Odyssey came to be written down at a relatively late stage after the events which they describe. This did not happen because the Mycenaean-Aegean world was ignorant of writing: the great discoveries of texts in Crete, on other islands and on the mainland, show the opposite; but writing served principally for the compilation of archives and inventories, that is, for administrative documents, and not for the transmission of literary texts. We still find the same situation millennia later in the early church, where the community preferred to hear the words of Jesus directly from the mouths of the apostles or indirectly from those of their disciples, rather than reading it in a 'scripture'. The need to put down traditional material in writing usually arises in moments of crisis: for Israel in the time of the exile of 587 or a little earlier, when the catastrophe was already beginning to loom; for the church during the persecutions or when heresy threatened to corrupt pure doctrine; for Israel again at a later stage, after the catastrophes of AD 70 and 135, when tradition which until then had been oral was set down in written documents. The period from 1200 to 900 BC was one of these times of crisis: the semi-nomadic people was settling in Palestine, the monarchy was coming into being, confronting them with an institutional change of the kind which was often to be the occasion for a profound crisis during the history of Israel; other nations with their own traditions were entering the country, to become part of the group 'Israel'. In addition, the court had need of annals, and we can also postulate the same kind of documents for the temple, on the basis of what is known elsewhere in the ancient Near East. In time the various traditions began to acquire a remarkable degree of fixity, so that with written redaction the means of transmission changed but not the content.

We can be sure that writing was known in the earliest period of Israel's settlement in Canaan: Judg.8.14 asserts this explicitly. It is therefore by no means strange that administrative acts, legal texts, religious documents (e.g. the clauses of the law which regulated the obligations of the people towards their God) came to be put down in writing; but even in Israel, as among the peoples by whom it was surrounded, the tendency was to maintain the literary tradition and the religious epics in oral form, all the more since transmission among the various sanctuaries must have been a sufficient guarantee that they would be preserved.

This principle appears clearly in the city-states which have already been mentioned: the Mesopotamian state of Mari in the eighteenth and seventeenth centuries, and the Syrian state of Ugarit from the fourteenth to the twelfth centuries. The letters sent by their rulers are directed, paradoxically, not to their addressees but to the messenger who delivered them. They follow more or less this pattern: 'To . . . (name of addressee) say: "This is the message . . . (name of the sender) your servant . . .", or, "Message of . . . to . . . ; say thus . . ." This would not be so important if we did not have an evident parallel in the Old Testament from the second half of the eighth century BC in II Kings 19.10ff., where the text of the message of Sennacherib is communicated to king Hezekiah of Judah orally by the messenger: the king reads it and then 'spreads it before Yahweh'; in other words, puts it in the temple archives, which seem also to have been political archives, a practice attested to the smallest details in the above-mentioned city-states.

We do have a very wide selection of Mesopotamian literature, but we owe it only to the fact that one of the last kings of Assyria, Asshurbanipal, diligently collected through his amanuenses and deposited in a library a large part of the Mesopotamian literature known in his day. This was then rediscovered in the course of excavations. The Ugaritic literature, on the other hand, was found in the temple archives and was discovered by archaeologists at a very early stage.

If we turn to the Old Testament prophets, we discover only three cases of writing: Isa.8.1, which is irrelevant because of the brevity of the text; Hab. 2.2, where we do not known exactly what was written; and finally Jer. 36, where we have the first and only note on the compilation of a writing of any length. It is, however, significant that when the first document was destroyed by the king, Jeremiah had no difficulty in dictating a second enlarged edition to his amanuensis Baruch (36.32): he knew the text (and more) off by heart.

Such a love of oral tradition and of the memory which naturally goes with it has been maintained in the East down to the present day: even an uneducated but practising Arab will easily know the Koran off by heart, and before the Nazi extermination of the Jews in Eastern Europe it was easy to find people, often in menial occupations, who knew off by heart not only the whole of the Old Testament but a large part of the Talmud!

All this has been well known for a long time, but it needed the analyses of H. Gunkel to bring out the logical consequences for understanding the origin of Hebrew literature. It was Gunkel who in his commentary on Genesis (which appeared in a first edition in 1901 and in the third definitive edition in 1910) for the first time indicated the value of oral tradition not only as a formative element in the primitive tradition of Israel but also as an explanation of certain variants in the texts and certain variant texts. This element was then developed in central Europe, especially in Germany, by his pupils M. Noth and G. von Rad, but has been taken to the greatest lengths in Sweden, first by the historian of religion H. S. Nyberg, then by his contemporaries G. Widengren and I. Engnell. The last-mentioned in particular rejected sharply all 'literary' explanations of the origins and transmission of Israelite literature as 'modern European interpretation' which was therefore quite inadequate for explaining a literature which developed on such different premises. We shall see the details of his argument in Part Two, Ch. I, §7.

Had it not been for oral tradition, the literature of Israel would have hardly been able to survive the catastrophes of 587 BC and AD 70, not to mention the other precarious situations which came upon the country. It does not, in fact, take much to imagine how the majority of manuscripts would be lost or have become irremediably damaged in the pillaging and burning which followed, while the exiles would have been able to carry little or nothing with them. A literature which was exclusively committed to written texts could not have survived. As it was, however, most of this literature could be reconstructed because it had been zealously kept in the minds of those responsible for it, even if the material thus passed through a complex process of redaction.

Oral tradition, then, first preceded written tradition and then continued parallel to it, so that each exercised a kind of constant control on the other.

§3. *The literary genres*

Oral tradition tends to divide into complexes of identical form and similar content, called 'literary genres'. Compositions belong to the same literary genre which display certain characteristic constants of form (choice of vocabulary, style, etc.), content, or setting in life (the cult, the protocol of the court, the prophetic or wisdom schools) and therefore have a common raison d'être. To give a modern example: we speak today of a thriller, of epic poetry, of a leading article, a review; each of these genres has its own particular language which is easily recognizable, a similar theme and, in the case of poetry, a consistent metre. Today there are evidently notable differences of style caused by the personal character of individual authors, but this is something that, as we have seen, is not to be found in the ancient East.

Any reader of the Bible is well aware how certain formulae tend to be repeated at various times and in different books: the style of the description of a battle in the books of Judges or Samuel is not noticeably different from that to be found about a millennium later in the books of Maccabees; certain formulae are repeated constantly in poetry, from the earliest texts, e.g. Exod. 15, to the latest, e.g. the songs at the beginning of the gospel of Luke. A similar problem also arises in the case of early classical literature, for example the poems of 'Homer' and Hesiod, as well as in the rest of the literature of the ancient Near East, so that what we discover is by no means peculiar to Israel.

A first fundamental division is that between poetry and prose. The former precedes the latter, just as even today the popular ballad singer tends to use poetic forms or rhythmic prose rather than narratives in prose; moreover, the epic, which is always in poetry, precedes every kind of prose narrative, not least because it can be more easily memorized, a factor which, as we have seen, is important in the context of oral tradition.

Now one of the most remarkable differences between the literature of the ancient Near East and, first, classical and medieval literature and then modern literature, is, as we have seen, its anonymity (or even pseudonymity); in consequence there is a complete lack of any tendency towards creative originality, which is typical in the West. Rather, the opposite happens: we find the use of literary genres and therefore formulae, which are stabilized over centuries and sometimes millennia. The true poet is not the one who creates, but the one who uses the traditional literary genres with ability and in constantly new combinations. This again is a situation which it is difficult for modern man to understand, but which is well known to those concerned with Near Eastern or Far Eastern studies. The person of the author thus falls completely into second place and tends to disappear, which explains the anonymity of such a large number of biblical and oriental writings. The fact that late Hebrew tradition tried to identify the authors of certain books or complexes of books, sometimes attributing them to a fictitious author, makes no difference to this pattern, which in practice continues right through the New Testament period (first century AD).

This situation presents the historian of literature with insurmountable obstacles: he is usually confronted with formulae which are thousands of years old and originate with, or at least are attested among, neighbouring people from an even earlier date. A composition which in itself is late can hide its origin by using ancient formulae, and it is only possible sometimes, and not always, to date the text in question on the basis of certain indications.

If, for example, we did not know that the compositions contained at the beginning of the gospel of Luke were attributed to people closely connected with the birth of Jesus, but had them outside their actual context, and they were in Hebrew, we would be hardly aware, if at all, of their late origin. We cannot in fact exclude *a priori* the possibility that they *are* early: indeed, it is probable that the people in question recited ancient liturgical compositions intended for a joyful event and therefore that the whole of the scene is simply part of a rite.

Of the literary genres in poetry, the priests in particular cultivated the psalm. This does not, of course, exclude the possibility that the laity also recited psalms when the ritual provided for it. The tradition which assigns a certain number of the psalms to David seems to presuppose that the laity could also compose them. We find a special genre among the prophets, the oracle in poetry which interprets past history, whether recent or remote, or announces events in the imminent future. They handed down this material to posterity by making use of their disciples and amanuenses (see Isa. 8.16 and Jer. 36), which have already been mentioned. Num. 21.27 knows of people called *hammōšᵉlim*, a term which indicates those who pronounced the oracle known as the *māšāl*, and is generally translated by an expression like 'gnomic poets'. They were later intimately connected with Israelite wisdom; in an early period they may have been regarded as a kind of ballad-singer (see RSV). The genre of the funeral lament is often applied in the Old Testament in a sardonic manner to persons or peoples who have fallen under the divine judgment (cf. Amos 5.1–16 and Jer.9.17). Legal forms, on the other hand, are typically in prose, and were preserved and handed down among the sanctuaries, if we can apply to Israel well-attested instances from elsewhere in the Near East.

Gunkel also tried to trace the evolution of literary genres, from more simple primitive forms to more complex and developed forms: the shorter and purer forms were taken to be primary and the longer ones, often composed of several literary genres, were taken to be secondary. This is the weakness of his theory. Long and complex forms are to be found throughout the ancient Near East and also in the Old Testament, in passages which are certainly very ancient, like Judg.5 and II Sam.1.19ff.

In the present form of its writings the Old Testament often gives the names of authors who are traditionally connected with the formation of certain groups of books, individual books or sections. Many psalms are attributed to David; part of Proverbs and probably Ecclesiastes to Solomon; a tradition which is now thousands of years old tacitly assigns the Pentateuch to Moses; and all the prophetic books are explicitly attributed to the authors whose names they bear. This seems in sharp contrast to the statement made a few pages earlier that the greater part of the Old Testament is anonymous or pseudonymous. Now without wishing to anticipate here the detailed discussion which will be given later, it may be enough to assert that almost all these attributions are later and almost always artificial. We come nearest to reality in the attribution of the prophetic books, but here too there are countless problems, so that we should probably consider even large parts of the prophetic books to be pseudonymous. There is no lack of books which are not attributed to any author: the 'former prophets', Chronicles, Job, the anonymous psalms and proverbs, and Daniel.

We have remarked that the majority of the literary genres attested in the Old Testament are known in other Semitic literature in the ancient Near East. Given this, it is not surprising to find in the Old Testament compositions reshaped along the lines of other oriental, non-biblical patterns. Ps.104 follows the imagery and perhaps the model of a hymn to the sun from the time of the Pharaoh Akhenatun; Prov.22.17ff. follows sometimes word for word a tractate of the

Egyptian sage Amenemope who lived at the beginning of the first millennium BC; some themes in the story of Joseph have remarkable analogies in the Egyptian story of the Two Brothers, whereas the whole of the wisdom literature generally has strong contacts, even in fundamental matters, with Semitic and non-Semitic Eastern wisdom, from Sumerian times on.

The importance of these facts should not be overestimated; if Israel had lived in a watertight compartment, removed from contacts with other peoples, the originality of Israelite faith would not surprise anyone. But it is precisely its continual contact with the whole of the world of ancient Eastern civilization which makes this independence on the religious plane a unique historical phenomenon. The peoples with whom Israel had to do were almost always more civilized, technically and scientifically more advanced, and it would therefore have seemed logical that the less advanced group would be absorbed by the more advanced. This happened elsewhere on a very wide scale, but not in the religious field, although, as we shall have occasion to see, conflicts in this area were by no means lacking. Then in the post-exilic period this same people, deprived of political independence (with the exception of a brief interregnum by the Maccabees which lasted about a century), autonomous only in the smallest matters, always culturally inferior to the Hellenistic world and very conscious of its inferiority, moved over to the offensive and converted thousands of Gentiles to its beliefs. These are elements which only the richness of the contacts with the surrounding world allows us to appreciate to the full.

§4. *Literary genres in poetry*

Discussion of the nature and especially the metre of Hebrew poetry, as of western Semitic poetry in general, is not only far from being exhausted, but has yet to be correctly framed. Biblical criticism has yet to discover the key to Hebrew metre, with the exception of very few instances, e.g. that of the lament. There are many reasons for this phenomenon. First of all, the revision of texts over the centuries and then the difficulty, and often the impossibility, of distinguishing the authentic parts from additions, make it impossible to determine individual verses exactly; secondly, the vocalization is that traditionally fixed by the Massoretes and necessarily represents a late stage: we cannot know the original vocalization of the texts, the licence allowed, and so on. There are even sound reasons for supposing that as early as the Hellenistic period Hebrew metre was no longer known; otherwise certain additions would be inexplicable.

The most valid criterion for distinguishing poetry from prose remains that discovered by the Anglican bishop Robert Lowth in 1753 and called by him *parallelismus membrorum*, an element which has its clear parallels in other Semitic literature and also in Egyptian literature; it was rejected in the West because of its repetitive and hence aesthetically unacceptable character. It poses a complex problem for any translator, bound as he is on the one hand to be faithful to the text which he is translating and on the other to reproduce it in a correct and acceptable form in the language into which he is translating.

The basic characteristic of parallelism is that what is affirmed or denied in the first member is confirmed in the second with an analogous affirmation expressed in a different way. When there are several verses, the process is repeated in each. Depending on the manner in which the repetition is made we have the following varieties:

(a) *Synonymous parallelism*, in which the concept expressed in the first line is repeated in the second with different words or concepts which are more or less equivalent (cf. Num. 21.28; Ps. 2.1–4; Prov. 9.10, etc.);

(b) *Antithetical parallelism*, in which the concept expressed in the first line is reinforced in the second by means of the introduction of an opposed concept which is negatived (cf. Prov. 10.1 or 11.1);

(c) *Synthetic parallelism*, in which the second member complements the first (cf. Ps. 1.1–3);

(d) *Climactic parallelism*, discovered only recently on the basis of Ugaritic poetry, in which the second member and possibly those following reinforce the theme by comparisons with what was affirmed first (cf. Amos 1.3ff.: 'For three transgressions of Damascus and for four', i.e. 'For the innumerable transgressions of Damascus', or Prov. 6.16: 'There are six things which Yahweh hates, seven which are an abomination to him ...', i.e. 'There are innumerable ...').

The problem whether there can be poetry without parallelism or whether parallelism can also be found in prose has not yet been resolved in a satisfactory way.

A first distinction which modern readers are inclined to make in this context is between secular poetry and religious poetry. In view of the character of the Old Testament, we would not expect to find a great deal of the former, and it should be relatively easy to identify.

(i) There are indeed many passages in which various scholars have claimed to recognize texts of secular poetry, but as will be seen, the character of these compositions is at least doubtful. Let us list them briefly. In Neh. 4.10 a song of unskilled labourers seems to have been handed down, and in Num. 21.17 a well-diggers' song. Isa. 16.9f.; Jer. 25.30; 48.33 refer to harvest songs without giving the words, while Judg. 9.27 and Isa. 9.3 also allude to the joy which accompanies this occasion. Unlike modern Western peoples, then, Israel will have been a people which was often ready to express its sentiments in song. As we have seen, however, there are fundamental doubts about the secular character of these songs: the first of those mentioned could be the echo of a lament which the poor oppressed labourers were making to God; the second, with its mention of sceptres and staves involved in the activity, could refer to the work of those who make water spring up in the desert (Moses would be a famous precursor here, cf. Exod. 17.6 and Num. 20.11, so that the diggers in question would be referring to his example and his person). Moreover, from what we know of the religious world of Canaan and of the Israelite syncretism which is closely connected with it, the likely explanation of the harvest and vintage songs would seem to be that they were songs of an orgiastic type, to ensure fertility, in origin dedicated to the relevant pagan deities. They will then have come over to Israel in a weaker and perhaps distorted form. The epithet 'secular' cannot obviously be applied in any of these cases, at least in our sense of the word. There are also war songs, banqueting songs and watchmen's songs: fragments of the taunt-song against Moab which is probably very ancient have been preserved in Num. 21.27–30; the satire on the aging prostitute who goes around offering her favours in vain (Isa. 23.16, in doubtful taste by modern standards) is now applied to the city of Tyre, a form of historicization similar to what we have seen practised in the case of ancient mythical texts (cf. ch. V, §1 above). Isa. 22.13 records a fragment of a banqueting song which is again quoted in the New Testament period in I Cor. 15.32 and survives with variants in the medieval *Gaudeamus igitur*, see also Isa. 56.12 and Song of Songs 5.1. Here too, however, the secular character of many of these songs is open to doubt; the taunt-song on the prostitute, applied to Tyre, would not make sense unless it was a variant of the curse which is intended to produce negative effects on the person at whom it is directed. We must take seriously the possibility that the others are secular songs, but they can hardly be said to be numerous. In Isa. 21.11f. we have a fragment of a song to a night-watchman, which is also perhaps secular, but what it means is doubtful because of the obscurity of the text.

To the modern reader, nothing might seem more secular than a wedding song, and we have a notable example of one in the Old

Testament in the Song of Songs. However, the problem is more complex than that, and without wanting to anticipate what we shall be discussing in greater detail later (cf. Part Five, ch. VI), it is necessary to make the following points. Marriage has a more or less sacral character in every civilization, if we leave aside the modern secular Western world, and it has never been a purely secular institution; thus even the marriage song can be considered essentially sacred, without resorting to later mystical and allegorical interpretations. Given the importance of wedding feasts throughout the Near East, ancient and modern, there must have been many of these songs; the length of weddings will have been a contributory factor. According to Gen. 29.27ff. one lasted seven days. We can see why Jesus often referred to weddings in his parables. However, apart from the Song of Songs, virtually none of these songs has been preserved. Funeral songs were also frequent; they were often sung by professional singers during funerals (Jer. 9.17) and otherwise by relatives or friends of the dead person. We have examples of a funeral song sung by friends in David's elegy in II Sam. 2.19ff.; 3.33. Of course these are not secular, but religious songs, even if their religion is often not very orthodox; in fact they go back to celebrations of the death of the god of nature, a periodical death which is followed by resurrection, but which in the meantime is lamented in ritual. The lament for the death of Tammuz in Ezek. 8.14 explicitly indicates that these practices will have been known to the Hebrew community at the end of the sixth century BC. In Israel, such funeral myths rapidly disappeared in more mature theological settings, being confined to the milieu of the underground religion of popular piety, especially in connection with the dead. Even here, however, there is a clear tendency to demythologize and to historicize (Amos 5.1ff.; cf. Jer. 9.17ff.; Ezek. 19; 26.16–18; 27.3–9; Nahum 3.7). In the first instance the lament is on the fall and death of Israel, and in such cases it is not always easy to distinguish between a funeral song proper and a bitter taunt. The same literary genre appears in the book of Lamentations, a work which is certainly not secular.

We also have war songs, but given the sacral character conferred on war by ancient religious feeling, an element which was inherited centuries later by Islam, even here it is impossible to talk of secular poetry. In the Old Testament we have one almost complete composition of this kind, Judg. 5, and important fragments in Josh. 10.12f. and perhaps in the difficult text Ezek. 17.9ff. (cf. also II Kings 13.17). We should probably also include in this category the blessings and curses pronounced on occasions of war or battle (Num. 23; 24; Ps.

68.1; I Sam. 17.8, 10, 43f., etc.). Here, too, everything already suggests that we should think of religious texts and not yet of secular poetry.

Finally, we must consider briefly a special literary genre with which we shall be concerned in detail as we go on to examine the texts: the last words of famous people from ancient Israel, eponymous heroes, and so on, in which these delivered to their hearers brief words of blessing or cursing or sayings connected with their life in other ways. The most important examples are to be found in Gen. 49; Deut. 33; II Sam. 23.1–7, etc., cf. also Gen. 9.25ff. In the first two cases the songs presuppose certain political situations which are quite clear and are evidently later than the speaker. The intention is to give an aetiological explanation of these situations. Often the material is very old and probably originates in the context of the groups to which it refers. The oracles of Balaam in Num. 23; 24 are similar. While these songs might originally have been secular epics, they certainly are not in their present context.

Consequently it is easy to end this brief review by pointing out that there are extremely few really secular songs – perhaps only the banqueting songs. Not all the compositions in question have been handed down to us: one example is that of a Book of the Lamentations of Jeremiah which is attested in II Chron. 35.25 and was composed on the occasion of the death of king Josiah at Megiddo in 609 BC. This, however, has nothing to do with Lamentations, which bears the same name, even if this latter book is traditionally attributed to the prophet. No traces of the former book remain. Other works which have disappeared are a Book of the Wars of Yahweh and a Book of the Upright or of Jashar, the first of which is attested in Num. 21.14 and the second in Josh. 10.13; II Sam. 1.18. A Book of Song is attested in the LXX translation in I Kings 8.13 (v. 53 in the LXX numbering) and it is possible that this is the same work (the metathesis of *yšr* and *šyr*). It was probably an ancient collection which was fundamentally epic, a kind of ancient Hebrew Iliad.

In all these cases, given that the subject of the song is Yahweh or that it is addressed to him, we certainly have religious compositions.

(ii) Religious poetry is made up for the most part of the Psalms, but there are indications of it right through the Old Testament from Gen. 49 on, especially in the prophets and the wisdom literature, and also in the pseudepigraphical literature, in the Qumran texts and in the New Testament. Here the everyday setting is evidently the cult, in which Yahweh was celebrated; we have seen some examples of less orthodox religious poetry. From the reform of King Josiah (622/621

BC) onwards, the sanctuary was certainly that of Jerusalem, but we should first allow the possibility that the compositions in question were also used in the liturgy of other sanctuaries.

Because of the abundance of religious poetry contained in the Old Testament (and as has been said, this is what we would expect in a book of this kind) we can, finally, begin to classify it in literary genres, though a number of the details will be reserved for our discussion of the psalms (Part Five, ch. I below). First we have the *hymn*, a composition primarily in honour of Yahweh, but secondarily used also for elements closely connected with him in the invitation *hal^elū-yāh*, that is, 'Praise Yah', from which is derived the Alleluia of Christian liturgy. This and the lament are probably the literary genres which are best represented. These compositions are also directed to other recipients: there are songs in honour of Zion, in which God is celebrated through praise of the sanctuary which he has chosen (Pss. 46; 48; 76.1ff.); one variant which has a special theme is made up of the hymns for the enthronement of Yahweh, which were perhaps connected with a feast in which his eternal kingship was celebrated. This feast was probably observed every year (Pss. 47; 93; 96; 99, cf. also Ps. 24). *Songs of thanksgiving* are difficult to distinguish from hymns because of their theme and form; they are sometimes accompanied by a confession of sin and a somewhat stereotyped list of the times when the person praying has been delivered (these will have had to serve for a number of different occasions). There is also a sacrifice of thanksgiving, and it is probable that the compositions in question are to be connected with its liturgy (Pss. 50.14; 107.22; cf. Joel 2.26). Compositions of this kind are also known from neighbouring countries, cf. the inscription on the sarcophagus of Yehi-milk of Byblos from the fifth century BC, which reads, 'Yehi-milk, because when I cried to my lady, the *ba^calat* of Byblos, she blessed me' (*KAI*, no. 10). This is a prose composition, but the content is identical to that in the biblical compositions, apart, of course, from the deity celebrated; cf. also Isa. 38.9 and Job 33.19–33. The confession can be one of sin, but more often it protests the innocence of the suppliant. Sometimes his misery is described so abjectly that we seem to have the next genre with which we are concerned, the lament. Often the composition ends with a vow, cf. Pss. 66.13–15; 116.14.

The book called Lamentations is only one of a large number of examples of that genre; they have a very close relationship to songs of thanksgiving, to which they often form the introduction. This last literary genre therefore establishes a link between the hymn and the *lament*. Its particular situation should be obvious enough: collective catastrophes like war, pillaging, plague, natural phenomena (drought, famine, earthquakes, etc.); individual cases like illness, persecution, expulsion from society and therefore from the community, outside which the ancient Israelite was unable to live, unjust accusations before judges, and so on. The prophets know the genre and use it frequently, as we shall see in the case of Jeremiah (Part Three, ch. VII). There are also thanksgivings for the community as for the individual, but these presuppose that the suppliant has already escaped danger or tribulation.

There are also other literary genres, even if they are not so abundantly attested: Pss. 15 and 24 list the qualities needed by those who wish to be admitted to the temple precinct; in Pss. 20 and 85 we have the word of a prophet or priest who proclaims the word of God to the listening community. Formulae of blessing or cursing appear in Pss. 1;32; 112; 128 and perhaps also in 134.3. In Pss. 2 and 110 we have the divine reply to a petition of the king on the occasion of his coronation or at the feast on which his enthronment was celebrated: these are evidently ritual demands, the situation and content of which we are now told in a prose passage, II Sam. 7.7–17, cf. also Pss. 89 and 132. While the latter compositions are almost certainly post-exilic, they are rich in earlier material which reflects situations from the period of the monarchy. Finally, Pss. 1; 112; 127 are wisdom psalms: Israel knows wisdom poetry which is attested not only in what we are accustomed to call the wisdom literature, but also in the Psalter. This genre was associated by Israelite tradition with the reign of Solomon, cf. I Kings 4.30ff. We shall meet other details later, see Part Five, ch. II.

§5. *Literary genres in prose*

Hebrew prose, like western Semitic prose in general, has a number of characteristic features which distinguish it not only from classical prose but also from eastern Semitic, Akkadian prose. The sentences tend to be relatively short, except when, as in the case of jurisprudence, the material itself requires more developed forms; this also results from the fact that the grammar and syntax of western Semitic languages in general and Hebrew in particular do not know subordinate clauses and therefore use co-ordination; the verb does not express so much the time of the action as its intensity and its completeness or incompleteness.

The prose contained in the Old Testament can be divided into the

following categories. First of all we have the discourse, as it appears
in prayer, in religious sermons and in public oratory. Throughout the
ancient Near East the word was of the highest account, and one of
the fundamental criteria for judging the capacity of a person was
whether he was able to express himself adequately. A person who was
not gifted in this way could thus easily be judged incapable, although
there are notable exceptions here also: the person of Moses (Exod.
4.10ff.), and that of the prophet Jeremiah (Jer. 1.6). David, on the
other hand, seems to have been a master of the art (I Sam. 16.18).
The two cases of Moses and Jeremiah show how inability to speak well
was considered an insurmountable obstacle to the performance of an
office, an obstacle which was either overcome, as in the case of Jeremiah, or circumvented, as in the case of Moses.

We should not, however, suppose that Hebrew discourse was similar to the Western speech which is derived from the canons of classical
rhetoric. The Greek and Roman speech sets out to convince audience
or adversary by means of arguments, and therefore always has a
marked degree of abstraction, even if it can be accompanied by concrete examples: appeal is thus made to the logic of the audience or the
adversary. As far as we know, Hebrew discourse had a substantially
different effect. We are not in a position to know how the audience
reacted, but its content is symptomatic: rather than convince the
interlocutor by arguments, Hebrew discourse sets out to impress by its
force, by the picturesque character of imagery which we might not
necessarily regard as relevant (cf. II Sam. 17.8). The truth does not
appear as an objective element that the interlocutor is to examine and
evaluate peacefully before making a decision; it is something that has
to be believed and accepted subjectively, through more than argument. Hebrew discourse goes on, bewilders and sometimes, it might be
said, deafens the interlocutor without leaving him a loophole or a
chance to reflect. The speaker who presented his arguments in the
most vivid, indeed violent fashion, in forms which we would restrict
to demagoguery, was to be believed. However, the concept which
underlies this form of discourse is not negative in itself; the Hebrew
is convinced that the truth will make itself felt with its own force,
and that it does not need to be adorned by argument. We have here,
then, a different way of understanding communication which is
not necessarily for that reason erroneous or primitive, much less a
matter of demagoguery. On the contrary, there is no doubt that in the
field of the confession of faith this is a means of proven efficacy and as
such made more impact than Hellenic subtlety. However, its value is
that much less in the world of thought, where it is a question of

doctrine, not faith, and therefore of reasoning, not of confession. In other words, we have two different systems here, each adapted to well-defined situations.

We have political discourses in Judg. 9.7–20, a text which has been considerably revised at a later date; in Josh. 24, in which, however, the religious component now dominates; in I Sam. 22.6ff.; II Sam. 14.1ff.; 17.8ff.; II Kings 18.19ff., 28ff.; cf. also I Macc. 9.8; 13.2–6. We find sermons or other kinds of religious discourses especially in the prophetic books, for example in Isa. 5.1ff.; Jer. 7.1ff.; 26.1ff. These last, however, have also been considerably revised, although every indication is that they go back to original episodes: Deuteronomy and part of Chronicles are presented as religious discourses, the first spoken by Moses. Still, notwithstanding the character of the Old Testament as holy scripture, we find relatively few discourses of a religious type and few cases of real preaching apart from the examples of Isaiah and Jeremiah already given. Some scholars have even been led to suppose that it was only with the reform of Josiah in 622–21 (II Kings 22–23; II Chron. 34–35) that the genre came into current use. Probably, however, this presentation of the facts is an over-simplification of a rather complex situation which we shall examine from time to time in connection with the relevant texts. For now, it is enough to point out in anticipation that from the little we know, the ancient Israelite cult must have had a significant space for preaching or for catechetical instruction given in this form.

Prayers, too, are strangely scarce in the Old Testament: we only have a few examples in Gen. 32.9–12; Judg. 16.28; I Kings 3.6–9; 8.23–52; II Chron. 20.6–12, etc. In all these instances only the prayer of Solomon (I Kings 8) is liturgical and certainly goes back to an original source, even if it has been expanded later. Because of its character, it lends itself to historical verification, but we could hardly suppose that we could verify private and intimate prayers like that of Jacob in Gen. 32. The genre begins to become more frequent in the deutero-canonical and pseudepigraphical books, a phenomenon which coincides in time with the adoption by Israel of certain forms which were well-known in the classical world; in this context they correspond to the public or private discourses given by famous people in circumstances which were considered historically relevant. In this case the prayer is no longer directed by the protagonist to God, but becomes an artificial form of discourse in which the author or redactor puts into the mouth of his hero what he thinks the hero should have said in particular circumstances; his aim is to edify the community or the individual reader, just as happens with classical discourse.

Among the various documents of an administrative nature preserved in the Old Testament we have the texts of contracts in Gen.
21.22–32; 23.17–20; 26.26–31; 31.44–54; Josh.9.15; I Kings 5.10–12
and many others besides. It should be noted, incidentally, that notwithstanding the apparent authenticity of the contracts recorded in
Genesis, it seems somewhat improbable that texts of this kind should
have come down to us or even down to the time of the redaction of
the Pentateuch, that is, centuries after they were made. It is notable
that all these texts belong to the sphere of private contracts, whereas
agreements between states are included only rarely and at a late
date. This is surprising when we think that the ancient Near East
has yielded a rich collection of treaties between nations, especially
from the Hittite, Aramaean and neo-Assyrian worlds (the first two
in the second half of the second millennium BC and the third in the
first half of the first millennium). Only in I Macc.8.22–23 do we have
the text of the alliance concluded with Rome by Judas Maccabaeus in
the first half of the second century BC. It is, however, well known that
relations between God and his people are expressed in juridical categories in the Old Testament (cf. Gen.15.7–20; Exod.19–24; 34;
II Sam.23.1–7; II Kings 23, etc.), and the technical term for this
relationship is the Hebrew *berît*, to which there is only one probable
parallel outside the sphere of the Hebrew language, in a text from
Ugarit which has recently been discovered and published. It is
traditionally rendered 'covenant, alliance', but is probably to be
translated, at least in the semantic field of the Old Testament, as
'obligation' (of God towards the people and of the people towards
God, in the latter case expressed by the 'law').

The Old Testament does, however, provide good information on
letters and epistolary correspondence in general. The earliest letter
known to us is that sent by David to his generals to arrange for the
death of Uriah the Hittite (II Sam.11.14); a similar one is sent by
queen Jezebel to the elders of Jezreel on the occasion of the episode
of Naboth's vineyard (I Kings 21.8–10); in II Kings 5.5f. we have the
letter of an Aramaean king to the king of Israel and, in the same
book, a letter sent to Hezekiah by Sennacherib, king of Assyria
(19.9–14, cf. §2 above). In Jer.29 we have the text (considerably
elaborated at a later date) of a letter sent by Jeremiah to those deported in 597 BC, containing an exhortation not to hope for a speedy
repatriation; there are fragments of two other letters in vv.24–32. In
Ezra 4–6 we have a series of missives which clearly recall the style of
the Persian chancellery, and in the books of Maccabees indications of
the style of Hellenistic chancelleries. Here, too, as in the classical

world, there is no lack of fictitious letters which imitate the genre at a later date (cf. Dan. 4.1ff.; I Macc. 10.22ff.).

Throughout the Old Testament there are countless lists of various kinds: genealogies, cities and boundaries, booty taken in battle, and so on. Some which are clearly authentic are out of context, e.g. Num. 1; 26; 33; Josh. 15–19; 21, etc. We have juridical material in the second part of Exodus, throughout Leviticus, in the first part of Numbers and in the central part of Deuteronomy (chs. 12–26); there is a ritual and juridical programme for the reconstitution of the cult and the community after the exile in Ezek. 40–48.

In all these cases we often have archive material which, if we can argue from the example of neighbouring peoples, will have been handed down by priests.

BIBLIOGRAPHY

§1. For the problem of Israel's origins, see the histories of Israel listed in the general bibliography, §4. For the situation in Canaan at the time of Israel's entry, and the groups of which Israel was formed, cf. S. Moscati, *I predecessori d'Israele*, Rome 1956.

For the reconstruction and textual criticism of the earliest Hebrew poetry along lines suggested by W. F. Albright, cf. his 'The Old Testament and Canaanite Language and Literature', *CBQ* 7, 1945, 5–31, together with the work of his pupils, F. M. Cross, Jr, and D. N. Freedman, *Studies in Ancient Yahwistic Poetry*, Missoula 1975; they have also written articles to which reference will be made from time to time. Although the fundamental basis of this method has been accepted, it is far from producing a unanimous consensus, in view of its inevitable degree of subjectivity, and the uncertainty as to the relation between Canaanite and Israelite poetry. Albright reaffirmed his position in *Yahweh and the Gods of Canaan*, London 1968; it has been criticized by D. W. Goodwin, *Text-Restoration Methods in Contemporary USA Biblical Scholarship*, Naples 1969. A collection of relevant materials is being published by L. R. Fisher (ed.), *Ras Shamra Parallels*, 2 vols., Rome 1972, 1975.

§2. For tradition and literary genres cf. E. Nielsen, *Oral Tradition*, SBT 11, 1954; K.-H. Bernhardt, *Die gattungsgeschichtliche Forschung am Alten Testament als exegetische Methode*, Berlin 1969; K. Koch, *The Growth of the Biblical Tradition*, ET London 1969; G. M. Tucker, *Form-Criticism of the Old Testament*, Philadelphia 1971; and cf. also R. C. Culley, 'An Approach to the Problem of Oral Tradition', *VT* 13, 1963, 113–25, and the works cited in the bibliography to ch. III, §4. In the first edition of his *Introduction* (1934), O. Eissfeldt was the first to include this material and related considerations in his discussion.

For examples of letters which are addressed to the messenger rather than to the eventual recipient, see C. H. Gordon, *Ugaritic Literature*, Rome 1949, 116ff. This material is some centuries earlier than the earliest Old Testament writings. The first scholar after H. Gunkel to indicate in a systematic way the importance of oral tradition was H. S. Nyberg, *Studien zum Hoseabuch*, Uppsala 1935. For the problem of the nature of the relationship between Israel and Yahweh cf. D. J. McCarthy, *Treaty and Covenant*, Rome 1963; id., *Old Testament Covenant*, Oxford 1972 (with bibliography).

§3. For a definition of literary genres cf. H. Gunkel, *ZAW* 42, 1924, 182; M. J. Buss, *The Prophetic Word of Hosea*, BZAW 111, Berlin 1968, 1f. On form criticism, cf. J. H. Hayes (ed.), *Old Testament Form Criticism*, San Antonio 1974. For the Egyptian texts referred to see the translations by J. A. Wilson in *ANET* ³1969, 369ff., 421ff. and 23ff. respectively.

§4. For Hebrew poetry the classic work is H. Gunkel and J. Begrich, *Einleitung in die Psalmen*, Göttingen 1933 (=²1966); cf. more recently L. Alonso-Schökel, *Estudios de poética hebrea*, Barcelona 1963. The possibility of poetry without parallelism has been examined by G. Fohrer, 'Über den Kurzvers', *ZAW* 66, 1954, 199–236. For Hebrew metre see the studies by S. Segert, 'Problems of Hebrew Prosody', *SVT* 7, 1959, 283–91, and H. Kosmala, 'Form and Structure in Ancient Hebrew Poetry', *VT* 14, 1964, 423–44; 16, 1966, 152–80. These views are critically examined by K. Elliger, 'Ein neuer Zugang?' in F. Maass (ed.), *Das Ferne und Nahe Wort, Festschrift L. Rost*, BZAW 105, Berlin 1967, 59–64. For the fourth form of parallelism, see W. F. Albright, *Yahweh and the Gods of Canaan*, ch. 1.

§5. For the epistolary genre in the ancient Near East see the texts translated by Gordon (§2 above), and O. Kaiser, 'Zum Formular der in Ugarit gefundenen Briefe', *ZDPV* 86, 1970, 10–23. For *berit* and its equivalents in languages other than Hebrew, cf. É. Lipiński, 'El-Berit', *Syria* 50, 1973, 50f. This refers to the expression *'el-berit*, which appears in lines 14f. of a Hurrian hymn to Baal; cf. E. Laroche, 'Documents en langue hourite provenante de Ras Shamra', *Ugaritica* 5, 1968, 442–544, cf. 510ff., and F. M. Cross, *Canaanite Myth and Hebrew Epic*, Cambridge, Mass., 1973, 39.

PART TWO

THE PENTATEUCH
AND THE FORMER PROPHETS

II

THE PENTATEUCH

§1. *Introduction*

We have already seen that Jewish tradition considered the first five books of the Bible, commonly designated in the West by the Greek term 'Pentateuch', to be the most important part of scripture. Their Hebrew name is *tōrāh* = 'instruction', and then usually 'law'; this was therefore instruction *par excellence*. In some languages the section has also come to be called 'The Books of Moses', an expression which we already find in the latest strata of the Old Testament itself: II Chron. 30.16; Ezra 10.3; Neh. 8.3. It is only probable, though, and by no means certain that this expression refers to the Pentateuch in its present form. In the New Testament we often find the expression 'the law and the prophets', an evident sign that 'the law', Greek *ho nomos*, had already become synonymous with 'Pentateuch'. For other attributions to Moses which raise identical problems cf. II Chron. 25.4; 35.12; Neh. 13.1. The attribution of the Pentateuch to Moses is generally accepted in the New Testament; cf. Mark 12.26, where Exod. 3.6 is cited, and the passages on divorce, where the quotations from the Old Testament are attributed to Moses (Matt. 19.3–8 par.).

The division into five books is earlier than the LXX translation which takes it over, but we do not know for how long it has existed. From the middle of the last century the term 'Hexateuch' has often been used for the first six books of the Bible, on the grounds that, as some maintain, Joshua continues the Pentateuch and forms its logical epilogue as well as displaying many of its characteristics. Although this term is still used by some authorities, it has been in decline since M. Noth in 1943 proposed a completely new solution: the first four books of the Pentateuch form a separate entity, while Deuteronomy and the 'former prophets' represent an autonomous historical work to be called, as we shall see, the 'Deuteronomistic' history work.

In the course of the present discussion we shall follow the traditional terminology and therefore use the term Pentateuch; we shall also adopt its traditional divisions. The work covers the period from the creation of the universe to the arrival of the Israelites on the threshold of the promised land: its contents have been formed through an extremely complex history of tradition which it will now be our task to examine.

§2. *The tradition of authorship*

(*a*) With very few exceptions, it has always been the view of the synagogue and the church that Moses is the author of the Pentateuch. From our point of view this would seem to be an ancient tradition; however, when we consider the time that elapsed between the earliest writings or even the age of Moses and the time which saw the rise of the tradition in question, we need to recognize that the tradition is relatively recent. In the preceding paragraph we saw that we already find the first traces of an attribution of the Pentateuch to Moses in the work of the Chronicler, that is, towards the end of the fourth century BC, even if it is uncertain whether the attribution refers to the whole of the Pentateuch. However, considering the development of the concept, it is at least probable that it is being stated in these texts as well. The one statement that we can date with certainty is that of Ecclus. 24.22–39, at the beginning of the second century BC; and as we have seen, the view is generally accepted without question by the New Testament. In early Christianity, however, there was a good deal of anti-Christian polemic (from Porphyry and Celsus among others) which put in doubt the Mosaic authenticity of the books in question; similar doubts were shown by heretical and especially gnostic sects, the latter, however, more for dogmatic than for critical reasons. During the Middle Ages there was no lack of claims to this effect by Jewish authors who, in the course of their painstaking analyses, had noticed many inconsistencies between the traditional view and what they read in the text. At the time of the Reformation other doubts were raised by Carlstadt in 1520 and, during the Counter-Reformation, by R. Simon (who has been mentioned in the first chapter) in 1678. It is evident, however, that these are isolated positions, and those who adopted them were soon more or less openly accused of heresy. A discussion of the traditional theory never followed. We must therefore look at the problem a little more closely.

(*b*) In the Pentateuch itself very few passages are attributed to

Moses: Exod. 17.14; 24.4; 34.27; Num. 33.2; Deut. 31.9, 24. In other passages it is said that Moses is speaking, for example throughout Deuteronomy, which is regarded as a series of discourses by Moses. Nothing is said here, however, about the editing of the book. In many other cases it is said that 'God spoke to Moses', but here too nothing is said about the redaction of the writings which we now possess. In the light of more recent investigations it seems almost certain that the pre-exilic prophets knew at least part of the Pentateuch, and this should not surprise us. However, they do not speak of Moses, although this would have given infinitely more authority to their preaching; indeed, apart from a controversial instance in Micah 6.4, Moses is never mentioned. It seems, then, that the attribution of the Pentateuch to Moses took place between the fourth and the second centuries BC, and was then generally accepted from the time of the New Testament on, with the few exceptions that we have mentioned. It should, however, be evident that the deutero-canonical books and the New Testament confine themselves to expressing the common opinion of their time and the world in which they were written, so that their assertions can hardly be considered normative on the level of biblical criticism.

To summarize, then, there is no element which allows us to assert that the attribution of the Pentateuch to Moses was known before the fourth century BC.

(c) It is necessary, however, to make a counter-check, given that much of what we have just said is based on arguments *e silentio*. There are, in fact, passages in the Pentateuch which could not possibly be attributed to Moses, passages which were already noted in part by Celsus and Porphyry (mentioned above) in their anti-Christian polemic, and by the great medieval Jewish exegete Abraham ibn Ezra.

(i) The last chapter of Deuteronomy describes the death of Moses and cannot therefore be his work; this is generally recognized even by those who maintain the traditional opinion, though they do not see that this admission damages the whole theory.

(ii) In a variety of contexts we often find the formula 'until this day' (Deut. 3.14; 34.6, etc.); when, as in the second case mentioned, we have to do with texts contemporaneous with Moses, the formula evidently indicates a later age and marks a contrast between the later time and the time of Moses.

(iii) We twice read, 'At that time the Canaanites were dwelling in the land' (Gen. 12.6; 13.7). This presupposes a period many centuries after Moses, when the Canaanites had either been assimilated or driven out, and consequently no longer lived there. But this was certainly not the situation at the time of Moses' activity.

(iv) In Gen.40.15 Canaan is 'the land of the Hebrews'. This is evidently an anachronism going back to a time not much earlier than that of the Philistines. We find the same phrase elsewhere at this period (I Sam. 13.3ff.): the mention of 'Hebrews' in the traditions of the oppression in Egypt is obviously another matter.

(v) We find anachronisms in geographical references: Gen. 14.14 mentions Dan, which is thus named only from Judg. 18; cf. also Deut. 34.1.

(vi) Gen.36.31 mentions a king in Israel, which takes us to a period not earlier than that of Saul, in the last decades of the second millennium BC.

(vii) Num. 21.14 mentions a source which contains material on the exodus and the march across the desert.

(viii) In Gen.50.10ff.; Num.22.1; 32.32; 35.14; Deut. 1.1, 5; 3.8; 4.46 etc., the territories east of the Jordan, in which, following the traditional itinerary, Israel arrived before its entry into Canaan, are regularly called territories on the *other* bank of the Jordan. This presupposes the point of view of an author or tradent who is living in Palestine. Moses, however, as we know, never entered it.

(ix) Finally, we have a series of parallel passages or contradictions in the Pentateuch which rule out a single author and point, rather, to a somewhat complex redaction. In Gen.1.1–2.4a and 2.4b–25 we evidently have two different accounts of the creation, different both in their fundamental approach and in the order in which the elements are created. Exod.3 and 6 both narrate the revelation of the divine name to Moses. Gen.21.31; 26.33 give two different accounts of the origin of the name of Beer-sheba, meaning respectively 'well of the oath' or the place of 'seven wells'. We now have two recensions of the story of the flood which have been combined: in one the flood lasts for a total of 40+21 days, in the other for 12 months and 10 days; in one there are seven clean animals (or rather seven pairs of animals) and in the other a single pair; in the first recension the flood is the product of a great inundation caused by tremendous rainfall, while in the other it is 'universal', a cosmic phenomenon which reduces the universe to the situation preceding the creation which is described in the terms reported in Gen. 1.2–2.4a. Sinai is called Sinai, but also Horeb (and there is no indication that these are different mountains or peaks); God is sometimes Yahweh and sometimes simply God; in connection with the priesthood there is some discrepancy over such an important question as the age of ordination: 25 or 30 years. Another fact worth noting is that the Pentateuch can use the neo-Babylonian calendar (e.g. Exod. 12.2) when we know that elsewhere it follows the Canaanite calendar (we even know the names of some of the months). It is no accident that the beginning of the year remained in the autumn, thus coinciding with the New Year in Syria and Palestine, whereas the neo-Babylonian New Year began in the spring.

We must therefore conclude that whereas the Pentateuch does not have any internal elements which prove the truth of the tradition which attributes its redaction to Moses, there are many which prove incompatible with such an attribution. The Pentateuch was not composed in a single draft; it is the product of a redactional process which proves to be extremely complex. Thus anyone who wishes nevertheless to maintain the traditional view that it was written by Moses would equally have to postulate a long and intricate work of redaction of such a scope that in the end it would no longer be possible to recognize clearly what did in fact go back to Moses.

§3. History of the literary criticism of the Pentateuch

The problems connected with the redaction of the Pentateuch had been noted, then, by ancient anti-Christian polemicists, by medieval Jewish exegetes and by more or less orthodox Protestants and Catholics. They were not, however, accepted as such and put in focus.

This happened for the first time during the first half of the eighteenth century in the work of the German pastor H. B. Witter (in 1711), and a little later, quite independently, in that of the French Catholic doctor J. Astruc (in 1753), the son of a pastor who went over to Catholicism in the period of the dragonnades, the persecutions directed by Louis XIV. The criterion employed by both was to remain determinative for a long time to come: it was the use made of the divine names in the texts.

(a) *The old documentary hypothesis.* Both Witter and Astruc, quite independently of each other, as we have seen, noted that in Gen. 1.1–2.4 God is called by his title 'elōhīm, whereas in 2.5–3.24 he is called by his title and the name Yahweh: the two passages, moreover, reveal clear differences of style and design. Astruc affirmed that there must have been 'notes' of which Moses would have made use in composing the book of Genesis: in other words, he would have worked with earlier sources. Once this criterion had been established at the beginning of the book, it was easy to extend it throughout Genesis, which is the point from which all scholars, even today, begin their analyses.

Astruc named the source which calls God by his title the 'Elohist' and that which calls him by his name the 'Yahwist', and although the activity denoted by these titles may be understood in different ways, they are still used even today. When, however, Astruc saw that all the material could not be classified as these two sources, he looked for others, and found about ten of them.

As can be seen, he was not yet concerned with the problem of authorship. He sought, rather, to explain how there could be duplications and divergences in the work of a single author. J. G. Eichhorn was the first to pose the problem in the systematic fashion which was necessary.

(b) The *fragmentary hypothesis* was a second attempt to solve the problem. This leaves aside the idea of sources and speaks instead of fragments, which were then collected together by a redactor. Chief among those who put forward this hypothesis was W. M. L. de Wette, to whom we shall return when we consider the book of Deuteronomy (cf. below, ch. III, §2).

(c) The *complementary hypothesis* differed by postulating the existence of a single 'Elohist' source which was then completed by the addition of various texts, for example the Decalogue, the so-called Book of the Covenant and the 'Yahwistic' texts. Its best-known representative was the German H. Ewald. In reality, it is a variant of the documentary hypothesis. A most important contribution towards progress was Ewald's discovery that there are two 'Elohist' sources; this laid the foundation for subsequent studies.

(d) The *new documentary hypothesis* is the most important attempt so far at achieving a synthesis along these lines. It therefore forms the necessary point of departure even for those who reject the hypothesis of the existence of sources.

This admits the existence of a 'Yahwist' and two 'Elohist' sources; the problem of the relationship between the two latter was resolved by the Alsatian scholar E. Reuss: he demonstrated that the 'Yahwist' was the earliest source, followed by the 'Elohist' in the strictest sense of the term. The second 'Elohist', called more appropriately the 'Priestly source', was the latest: it was preceded by Deuteronomy. On the basis of this information the Dutchman A. Kuenen and the Germans K. H. Graf (a pupil of Reuss and his close friend) and J. Wellhausen constructed a system which arranged the sources in chronological order, gathered together the scattered pieces of the other hypotheses and produced a solution which, for those who accept its premises, can still be considered conclusive. It was Wellhausen who gave the documentary hypothesis its definitive form: a brilliant writer and speaker, his influence was immense. He was an acute thinker and his system can be perfected or qualified in detail by those who accept it, or rejected *en bloc*, but it is difficult to ignore it.

§4. *Wellhausen and his school*

The dominant philosophy in German universities in the second half of the last century and at the beginning of this was based in one way or another on the evolutionary dialectic of Hegel. Wellhausen himself had been a pupil of a well-known Hegelian, W. Vatke; Graf's master Reuss, on the other hand, was a Kantian, though he too was profoundly influenced by Hegel. Consequently it is not surprising that those who have rejected the documentary hypothesis as formulated by Wellhausen have sought its weak points in a possible Hegelian derivation, arguing that the system could be explained on the basis of this dependence. In other words, first Vatke and then Graf and Wellhausen would be said to have done no more than apply to the study of the Pentateuch a scheme drawn from Hegelian philosophy. Now the question is not as simple as that. We may begin by pointing out that to postulate philosophical influences on a scholar is not in itself an argument against the validity of the theory which he is putting forward. We are all children of our age and absorb certain of its ideological presuppositions. These presuppositions do not necessarily falsify what we put forward. Again, the 'discovery' that Wellhausen's scheme might be of Hegelian origin not only fails to demonstrate its falsity *per se*; there is a further point. It was only made some decades after the master's death, from the 1930s on. Before that it had not occurred to anyone. Nor is this an *argumentum e silentio*, as some might object: in its reply of 27 June 1906 the Pontifical Biblical Commission gave a negative opinion both on the theory according to which Moses could not be the author of the Pentateuch (only allowing the possibility of later additions) and on the possibility that it could be divided into sources. Here we find anti-modernist polemic in full flood, but there is the significant omission that the document does not give a Hegelian origin as a reason for rejecting the documentary hypothesis. In this historical and ideological context that could easily have been a conclusive argument (for the text see Denzinger, 1997–2000, and Robert-Feuillet's *Introduction*, cited in the bibliography, 98ff., with important clarificatory comments). Again, recent studies have demonstrated without a shadow of doubt that with Vatke only the 'outer frame' was Hegelian, while Wellhausen very quickly freed himself from that.

Thus to speak of the Hegelian character of this school not only fails to demonstrate anything, but is not even exact from a historical point of view, though we obviously cannot exclude the possibility that Wellhausen and his pupils had unconsciously assimilated Hegelian elements as part of the ideological context in which they lived.

It is not surprising that the hypothesis very soon passed from triumph to triumph, being welcomed by anyone who championed the necessity for a scientific-critical Introduction to the Old Testament. The only exceptions were conservative Jewish, Catholic and Protestant circles, which always rejected it.

Wellhausen's system was brilliant in the simplicity of its structure and convincing in the way in which it presented the problems. It can be described briefly along the following lines.

The earliest source is the Yahwist (abbreviated as J by scholars, following the German *Jahwist*), so called because God is always given his name Yahweh, even in the period before the revelation of the name which is made to Moses (Exod. 3; 6). It is now dated between the tenth and the ninth centuries BC, for specific reasons as well as for rather general considerations like the primitive character of its content (whether or not this is the case is another matter) or the immediacy of its expressions – aesthetic and subjective categories which are difficult to evaluate. Relations with the Aramaeans, with whom Israel and, in part, Judah were at war for the greater part of the ninth century, are still at their best. And since the people and places mentioned in J are on the whole to the south of Palestine, it is logical to suppose that the origins of the composition should also be sought there.

The Elohist (usually indicated as E) is about two centuries later, but the material cannot be later than that of J. E is less primitive and immediate: for example, it feels the need to make use of intermediaries between God and man, or at least not to bring about direct encounters. Thus we have angels in the first case and dreams in the second. There is a notable tendency to give the title 'prophet' to men who have a special contact with God, e.g. Abraham and Moses. This suggests a redaction at the time when the prophets were regarded as men of God *par excellence*. The people and localities are predominantly in the north, so that the origin of E is probably to be sought in the territory of the kingdom of Israel; when this was destroyed, the material was probably transferred to the south.

The third source is Deuteronomy (D), which is identical with the greater part of the book of this name. A school which is dependent on D, whether on the ideological or on the linguistic plane, revised the 'former prophets', as we have seen. According to current opinion, the publication of Deuteronomy coincided with the discovery of a 'book of the law' at the beginning of Josiah's reform in 622–21 (II Kings 22; 23), although it is at least probable that there was a second redaction during the exile, in the sixth century. As we shall see, D contains a good deal of earlier material.

The last source is the 'Priestly writing', abbreviated as P, which was published at the end of the Babylonian exile or a little later, and which also forms the final framework of the material collected in the sources J and E. It has little narrative material; the greater part is made up of the ritual laws contained in the second part of Exodus, in Leviticus and in the first part of Numbers. The dates given here clearly refer to the final redaction of each individual source and do not in the least prejudge the possible presence of much older material; moreover, these are approximate dates and have been taken as such. Given the principle, the chronological sequence of the sources is generally accepted today. One important dissenter is the Israeli scholar Y. Kaufmann, who has sought to date P before D. We shall see his reasons later, but by way of anticipation it may be said that his principle has not found supporters outside Jewish circles (cf. also ch. IV, §3 below).

§5. *Developments of the documentary hypothesis*

Once the scholarly world had been presented with a hypothesis which resolved the problems of the Pentateuch, little or nothing seemed to be left to do in this direction. Wellhausen himself turned to other things, to Arabic and New Testament studies, but the many attacks made on him by church circles may have contributed in large part to this decision. Reality was soon to show, however, that although an important principle had been discovered, the documentary hypothesis did not exhaust all the material: it was, rather, the initial phase of research. A first attack was made on the criterion of divine names which had furnished the key for the research of eighteenth-century scholars and which had continued to play an important part. How could this serve as a criterion, it was asked, if an ancient translation like that of the LXX often presupposed 'Yahweh' where the Massoretic text has '*elōhīm*, and vice versa, a phenomenon which could be confirmed by reference to the Samaritan Pentateuch? If the criterion was to be considered normative, the recensions and the ancient translations should have disclosed this with some consistency. However, the criterion is not put in doubt by this method: at the time of the LXX we are already in a period in which the divine name was avoided or replaced with titles like 'Lord', 'God', 'the name' and so on, so that the argument cannot be considered decisive. In the case of the Samaritan Pentateuch the variants in question are only nine in about 300 and therefore do not prove anything.

A second problem soon drew the attention of scholars. The consistency of E is very limited: can one then talk of an independent source? Or does it need simply to be considered as an addition to J, which would bring us back to a kind of complementary hypothesis? Meanwhile, continued discoveries in the field of Orientalia (particularly frequent in the course of the second half of the last century and the beginning of this) have posed problems for every attempt at dating in view of the tendency for the various literary genres to be repeated over a period of time with stereotyped formulae.

But even in the camp of Wellhausen's disciples things did not go as smoothly as might have been expected: the division into only four sources did not seem enough to explain all the questions which continued to arise, and the addition of a fifth element, the redactor, was not enough to remedy the problem. Hence the need to distinguish various strata of tradition within the various individual sources, a problem which had been raised, but not developed, by Kuenen. So at the beginning of this century E, already much reduced, was subdivided into an E^1 and E^2 by O. Procksch, while in the 1930s P. Volz and W. Rudolph denied its existence altogether. Again during the 1930s there was an attempt to divide J into J^1 and J^2 (or S = 'southern' and L = 'lay'), the former with a distinct interest in the cult and the latter without this interest: these divisions are still authoritatively maintained today in the Introductions of Eissfeldt and Fohrer. P too was divided into various sub-codices. Analysis became more and more intricate, taking in even quarter-verses or smaller units. In other words, although the documentary hypothesis had resolved a fundamental problem, it had revealed a multitude of others, capable of unexpected developments.

It is easy now to see the reasons for this development of the theories of Wellhausen and his colleagues: the documentary hypothesis grew out of methodology formed from the study of classical texts, and treated the Pentateuch and the other historical books by the same standard. In reality it was a starting point for a series of investigations and not, as some thought, a goal which had been achieved. The isolation of the principal components of a source in fact produced no decisive results (and in this operation it all too often proved impossible to reach even the minimum degree of unanimity over a number of passages, while, as we have seen, there was an exaggerated tendency to dissect an individual unit to the point of ridiculing a method which was quite valid in itself). There was still no knowledge of how the sources had been formed, what scope the redactors felt they had in selection from the material at their disposal, in what circles the collections developed or to what degree and over what period oral tradition preceded written redaction and continued to exist in parallel to it. The existence of such oral tradition was admitted on all sides as a matter of principle, but no one was particularly concerned to examine its relation to the text which had been transmitted. And while initially the lack of comparative oriental material for comparison could explain this, the abundant discoveries in the course of the second half of the last century and the beginning of this made the existence of a situation of this sort quite unjustifiable.

It was H. Gunkel and his disciples who tackled a great many of these problems, and even if their proposals did not solve them, they contributed in no small degree towards posing the questions in the right form and indicating the way in which they should be solved.

§6. *The study of literary genres*

(*a*) *Precedents*. Foremost among the biblical scholars at the end of the last century and in the first decades of this is the figure of Hermann Gunkel. We have already noted the fact that he was the first to introduce the study of literary genres into Old Testament and oriental studies, a method which is appropriate for the anonymous or even pseudonymous character of the writings. Indeed, in the majority of cases it is the only one applicable, if a method is to be used which is not totally alien to the material studied. Gunkel's commentary on Genesis is fundamental to our theme; in the introduction, which is still a classic and can be considered as setting out a basic programme, he established that: (i) Genesis is a collection of legends and sagas, (ii) originally transmitted orally, (iii) which were already collected into cycles at the oral stage. However, (iv) the sources are more the product of redactional than of creative work, and simply furnished the pre-existent material with a framework and connections; besides, (vi) they are not the works of individuals, whether authors or collectors, but of schools of narrators (scholars now tend to prefer the word 'tradents'). Therefore (vi) the individual material in the collections has its own history and its own setting, quite independently of its later position in the sources, so that (vii) every lesser unit must first be examined by itself, leaving aside its present context. As we shall see, Gunkel and his disciples in Germany considered their method quite compatible with the documentary hypothesis; others, especially in Scandinavia, asserted that the two methods were incompatible and that it was necessary to choose between one and the other.

Meanwhile the documentary hypothesis was subjected to increasing criticism, although it continued to be dominant in the universities. We have already discussed the difficulty caused by the traditional divisions into sources, and shown how the existence of one of these was even denied altogether. We also pointed out that the sub-divisions became increasingly subtle and intricate, sometimes even (if the word may be allowed) impalpable, with the result that the method itself seemed to have been reduced to absurdity and hence implicitly to have been shown to be invalid. Towards the end of the 1930s, Umberto Cassuto, Professor at the University of Rome, demonstrated how the question of the Pentateuch had evolved in parallel to the Homeric question, receiving analogous solutions from different schools in different periods. He also made a rigorous critique of the various theories proposed hitherto in favour of a division into sources, insisting that the data adopted in their support allowed a number of different solutions. This led him to argue that a single redaction took place at the time of David or a little later, on the basis of earlier traditions. In 1934, Cassuto spoke of 'a master of the utmost genius . . .', a figure who was later suppressed in the successive re-elaborations of his work. In Holland, B. D. Eerdmans is a rigorous critic of the documentary hypothesis, but his argument, culminating in a downright rejection of the hypothesis, ends by destroying the credibility of another series of arguments which are valid in themselves. At the beginning of the 1930s the Danish scholar J. Pedersen sought to demonstrate that the Wellhausen school was in fact applying Hegelian categories to the study of the Old Testament, but as we have seen, his argument proved to be without foundation and was not a valid criticism. The arguments used to claim that the documentary hypothesis is invalid are interesting: Pedersen affirmed that the origin of the passover narrative, Exod. 1–15, was not to be sought in a compilation of various sources; the first setting of the passage was an ancient passover liturgy. This origin was, he believed, an excellent explanation for the repetitions and contradictions in the account; consequently it was not only impossible, but completely useless, to look for sources. In 1935, H. S. Nyberg, the Swedish history of religions scholar mentioned above, showed in what was then to be considered a pioneering work how the documentary hypothesis in its classic formulation did not take any account of the primary element, which was oral tradition. Gunkel's best pupil, Hugo Gressmann, had already taken this direction in presenting some critical material. He has the distinction of having isolated a series of complexes of traditions, especially in the Exodus narratives. Meanwhile a school developed in Great Britain during the 1930s known as the 'Myth and Ritual School', to be followed in the 1940s by the so-called 'Uppsala school' in Sweden. The most distinguished representatives of these schools, S. H. Hooke and I. Engnell respectively, underlined the importance of oral tradition and of the location of this tradition in the world of ancient Near Eastern myth. From this setting could be derived all the ideological constants, which were reducible to a more or less coherent pattern. Of course, in a context like this a discussion of sources proved impossible. In due course we shall be turning to these problems in greater detail (cf. §7 below).

In other words, from the middle of the 1930s to the end of the Second World War the documentary hypothesis was attacked at many points and challenged to a considerable degree. This situation did not fail to produce a certain satisfaction in conservative circles associated with the church or the synagogue. The Italian historian G. Ricciotti openly spoke of a triumph of ecclesiastical tradition (and, he might have added, of the synagogue) over literary criticism. In reality the situation was rather more complex: it was not so much a matter of abandoning critical positions in order to return to tradition (besides, it is hard to see how conservative ecclesiastical circles could have accepted the arguments of the Myth and Ritual school or the Uppsala school . . .), as of criticism revolting against a method which was considered partly inadequate and partly erroneous. It is, moreover, typical that none of these scholars ever raised the possibility of attributing the Pentateuch to Moses again. In reality it was an attempt to go beyond the documentary hypothesis, not to retrogress from it.

(b) In Germany in 1938 and in 1940 two pupils of Gunkel, Martin Noth and Gerhard von Rad, having refined the historical and geographical method of Albrecht Alt, sought to reaffirm the documentary hypothesis, but at the same time to go back to the oral tradition which underlay it and to look for the reasons which might have led to the formation of the sources. Von Rad's work of 1938 is still famous (though the outbreak of war a year later prevented it from being widely known until the end of the war); in it he argued that the collection of material, particularly by J, in the Hexateuch (a

term which he continued to accept since he never allowed the existence
of a Deuteronomic history school) followed the pattern of ancient
'confessions of faith' or various editions of an ancient 'creed' to be
found in passages which, while themselves late, he considered to contain early tradition: Deut. 26.5b–6 and 6.20ff.; Josh. 24.2b–13; cf.
Ps. 136, which is a lyric variation of it belonging to the cult. According
to von Rad, these confessions of faith provided, in a nutshell, the
chronological framework for the events which were narrated, from
the time of the patriarchs to the conquest of Palestine, and the
material collected by J began progressively to crystallize around them.
One example of von Rad's working method comes from his examination of Josh. 24, generally considered to be fundamentally an E passage with marked 'Deuteronomistic' revisions. It is a parallel passage
to the Deuteronomistic conclusion to the book of Joshua, ch. 23, and
here, notwithstanding the revisions, reveals its autonomous origin.
The dying leader has summoned representatives of the tribes in time
to pass on to them the words of his spiritual testament and to bind
them to loyalty to the God of Israel. The artificial character of this
situation is obvious: it would never have been possible to summon
such a representative group from the extremities of Israelite territory
to a dying man. If we want to maintain the substantial historicity of
the reunion as a working hypothesis, we would have to argue that the
representatives of the tribes would already have been at the sanctuary
(that of Shechem, to be exact) to celebrate a feast and that among the
passages which were recited liturgically during the proceedings was a
text called 'The last words of Joshua', after which the tribes renewed
their oath of loyalty to God. This would be on the basis of an amplified form of the ancient creed put by tradition into the mouth of
Joshua. Furthermore, it is said that Joshua 'and his house' have
already made their choice; it is now up to the others to make theirs.
This is a sign that originally the formula referred to the foundation of
the sacred league of the twelve tribes of Israel.

Having thus established the importance of the confessions of faith
in the formation of the earliest sources, especially J, it was easy to infer
that in Israel in the pre-monarchical period there was a feast called
the 'feast of the covenant' (we now know that the term b^erit is better
translated 'obligation': of God towards his people, of the people
towards their God, but this is not relevant in the context). This deduc-
tion was made by a number of other authors in the 1950s and 1960s,
and accepted, though with reserve, by von Rad.

This explanation seemed satisfactory to the majority of scholars. It
kept very close to the tradition, took account of the religious character

of the texts, indeed deeming it to be of fundamental importance, and also recognized a creative element in oral tradition. At the same time, it maintained the documentary hypothesis. There were only two problems: in the confessions in question there was no creation narrative (Gen. 1–11) and no account of the events of Sinai. Now while the first omission could be explained on the grounds that this was a preface in terms of universal history, added to the original text at a later time, the question of the absence of the Sinai text was more complex, because in a feast of this kind it should have been of fundamental importance. This is all the more the case since Joshua speaks explicitly of an obligation accepted (or, traditionally, of a covenant celebrated) before Yahweh, an ideal context for the Sinai pericope.

There have been many explanations of this second feature, which is certainly disconcerting. The explanation which began from literary-critical presuppositions was by no means misguided in arguing that the Sinai pericope was in fact interpolated into its present context: Israel arrives in the region of the sanctuary of Kadesh in Exod. 18 and leaves in Num. 11; in the middle is the Sinai block. Those, however, who put the emphasis on comparisons between the alleged biblical 'covenant' and oriental vassal treaties preferred to suppose that just as these treaties were often prefaced by historical introductions setting out to explain how their agreements were arrived at, so the facts narrated in the 'confession of faith' constituted the historical prologue to an agreement which was made in the Sinai pericope. Neither of these explanations is satisfactory; they are merely attempts to explain a situation which is certainly embarrassing for those who accepted the premises which have been set out above. But once these were shown to be invalid, the hypothesis that the confessions of faith formed the framework within which the ancient sources, and especially J, came to be formulated, also collapsed. The wheel came full circle, so to speak, in 1966, when it was established that the confessions of faith, far from representing an early stratum of tradition, in fact constituted a final development, a synthesis arising out of the sources. With this, one of the most successful theories of the past twenty or twenty-five years came to an end.

In 1940, M. Noth subjected the legal texts of the Pentateuch to an analogous examination, reaching much more solid results (not least because of the nature of the material which he examined); they were less spectacular and therefore less discussed.

§7. The compatibility of sources and literary genres

It thus became very evident that the problem of the compatibility of the documentary hypothesis with the method inaugurated by Gunkel could not be resolved through the theory proposed by G. von Rad. Gunkel and A. Alt (another name which we shall often be coming across in this work) and their pupils von Rad and Noth were convinced that these were complementary methods and therefore by no means exclusive. In his other works on the Pentateuch, Noth quietly worked with the presuppositions of the documentary hypothesis at one point and with the study of literary genres at another: I do not remember a case in which this was felt to present any problems. The result was a method which in German is known as *Überlieferungsgeschichte*, and which might be translated 'transmission history'. In the Scandinavian countries, however, authors came forward to whom we have already made passing references, J. Pedersen and H. S. Nyberg among them. Developing the discussion begun by H. Gunkel, they rejected the documentary hypothesis in the terms in which Wellhausen and his followers had presented it, considering it incompatible with traditio-historical methods. They were followed by the founder of the Uppsala school, Ivan Engnell, who introduced a new traditio-historical method called 'tradition history'. The distinction between transmission history (*Überlieferungsgeschichte*) and tradition history (*Traditionsgeschichte*) is difficult to reproduce outside a Germanic context where both a Germanic and a neo-Latin term are often available for the same concept. The former term is conventionally used, then, to describe the work of von Rad and Noth, and the latter to describe the work of the Scandinavians mentioned above.

For Engnell there were never continuous 'sources' in the first four books of the Pentateuch (Deuteronomy was obviously a separate question), or, perhaps better, there were no sources as the documentary hypothesis understood them. The presence of doublets and contradictions as well as repetitions could perfectly well be explained on the one hand by oral tradition and on the other by the specific character of Hebrew and other Semitic literature. Many elements introduced to support the documentary hypothesis were said to be simply a product either of our inadequate Western psychology or – and this is a more serious accusation – of deficiencies on a linguistic and grammatical level. Of course, to sustain this latter accusation it would have been necessary to give a series of proofs, and this never even began to be done. Still, the first of the two accusations remains in all its force. And as the reader will well know, this is not merely an academic question. It is a fundamental methodological choice which is capable of modifying the results of the enquiry quite substantially: once one of the two methods has been allowed, according to Engnell we should automatically exclude the other.

Unfortunately Engnell died prematurely before he was sixty and after only about twenty years of scholarly activity: this prevented him not only from finishing his work but also from making a systematic presentation of what he had already accomplished; nor does he seem to have left pupils able or willing to set in order or continue along similar lines the work which he had undertaken. So we have a series of assertions about principles and methods which, however, fall short of even a purely provisional synthesis. Engnell was very conscious of this when he wrote: 'The traditio-historical method [in the sense of *Traditionsgeschichte*, see above] is still in the first stages of its development.' Such a synthesis could have presented an alternative to the documentary hypothesis, with its highly refined method, and its validity could obviously have been discussed. A particularly interesting feature today is the considerable capacity of those who support the documentary hypothesis for self-criticism, a capacity which among other things has developed from constant preoccupation with early Near Eastern literature.

In the field of transmission history, too, the problem of compatibility with the documentary hypothesis has recently been raised again by R. Rendtorff, a pupil of von Rad. Rendtorff noted the uncritical way in which both von Rad and Noth took for granted the existence of the sources, although this presupposition had not gone beyond a purely conjectural status (a situation which has now lasted for more than a century!). He then criticized the vain search for generally accepted criteria of method, style or content by which a passage might be assigned to J or E (for example, there is a widespread tendency to assign to J anything that cannot be assigned to E or P). Rendtorff accused Noth of inconsistency because he accepted both the sources and the method of transmission history, while arguing that von Rad's theories are valid or invalid quite independently of their connection with the origins of J. In his view, the acceptance of the documentary hypothesis by the supporters of transmission history is a clear sign of inconsistency, and the consequence of a methodological choice. The only reason why this inconsistency has still not been noted properly is the inadequate development of transmission history.

All that the critic can confirm is, rather, first the collection of material into larger literary units, within which we must distinguish various cycles of narratives. This seems clear in the case of the Jacob traditions, but problematical in those about Abraham; only from the cycles can we go back to smaller units. A study of the development from the larger units to our text might possibly also lead to the establishment of the existence of continuous sources, as the supporters of the documentary hypothesis believed, and only in this instance would it be legitimate to talk of 'sources'. Rendtorff, however, thinks it more probable that it will be possible only to establish the existence of 'strata of tradition', with similar style and content; finally, their position in the larger context of the Pentateuch should also be examined. Thus, for example, we would have priestly legal material and a priestly redaction, but not a P source.

It seems, then, that we have here a convergence of transmission history and tradition history, although this is the first attempt in that direction, and it is impossible to forecast any results. However, it does seem legitimate here to go on to review the individual sources, bringing out their details and showing the problems which can arise in each case.

BIBLIOGRAPHY

Commentaries on Genesis
H. Gunkel, HKAT, ⁶1964; O. Procksch, KAT, ³1924; J. Skinner, ICC, ²1930; B. Jacob, *Das Erste Buch der Tora*, 1934; G. von Rad, OTL, ³1972; U. Cassuto, 2 vols., 1961-4; R. de Vaux, JB, ²1958; E. A. Speiser, AB, 1964; and, on Gen. 1-11 only: W. Zimmerli, ZBK, ³1967; F. Festorazzi, *La Bibbia e il problema delle origini*, Brescia ²1967; E. Testa, 1969; C. Westermann, BK, 1974.

Commentaries on Exodus
B. Couroyer, JB, ³1968; E. Galbiati, *La struttura letteraria dell'Esodo*, Alba 1956; M. Noth, OTL, 1962; U. Cassuto, 1968; J. P. Hyatt, NCB, 1971; B. S. Childs, OTL, 1974; W. H. Schmidt, BK, 1974ff.; F. Michaëli, CAT, 1975.

Commentaries on Leviticus
M. Noth, OTL, 1965; K. Elliger, HAT, 1966; N. H. Snaith, NCB, 1967; H. Cazelles, JB, ³1972.

Commentaries on Numbers
H. Cazelles, JB, ³1971; N. H. Snaith, NCB, 1967; M. Noth, OTL, 1968; G. Bernini, Sac Bib, 1972; J. de Vaulx, SB, 1972.

Commentaries on Deuteronomy

C. Steuernagel, HKAT, ²1923; H. Cazelles, JB, ²1958; P. Buis and J. Leclercq, SB, 1963, G. von Rad, OTL, 1966; A. Penna, Sac Bib, 1973.

§1. For the 'Deuteronomic history work' (Dtr) see M. Noth, *Über-lieferungsgeschichtliche Studien*, Halle 1943; for the Pentateuch in general, see M. Noth, *A History of Pentateuchal Traditions*, ET Englewood Cliffs 1972; O. Eissfeldt, *Die Genesis der Genesis*, Tübingen 1961; H. Cazelles and J. P. Bouhot, 'Pentateuque', in *Supplément au Dictionnaire de la Bible*, VII (see general bibliography, sect. 3); Cazelles, 'Positions actuelles dans l'exégèse, du Pentateuque', *EphThLov* 44, 1968, 55–78; id., 'Theological Bulletin on the Pentateuch', *BTB* 2, 1972, 3–24. For the figure of Moses and the problems associated with it, cf. R. J. Thompson, *Moses and the Law in a Century of Criticism since Graf*, *SVT* 19, Leiden 1970.

§2. For the formula 'until this day', cf. B. S. Childs, 'A Study of the Formula "Until this Day"', *JBL* 82, 1963, 279–92.

For the calendar, cf. S. Mowinckel, *Das israelitische Neujahr*, Oslo 1952.

§3. See general bibliography, §6, and R. de Vaux, 'Reflections on the Present State of Pentateuchal Criticism', in *The Bible and the Ancient Near East*, ET London 1972, 31–48.

§4. The two principal works in which Wellhausen presented his theories are *Prolegomena to the History of Israel* (ET 1885; reprinted New York 1957), and the article 'Israel' in *Encyclopaedia Britannica*, 9th edn., Vol. 16, 1883, 86off., which is printed as an appendix to the ET of the *Prolegomena*. On the supposed dependence of Wellhausen and his teacher W. Vatke on Hegel, cf. R. Smend, 'De Wette und das Verhältnis zwischen historischer Bibelkritik und philosophischen System im 19. Jahrhundert', *TZ* 14, 1958, 107–19 (esp. 112); L. Perlitt, *Vatke und Wellhausen*, BZAW 94, 1965.

§5. P. Volz and W. Rudolph, *Der Elohist als Erzähler*, BZAW 63, 1933, and Rudolph, *Der 'Elohist' von Exodus bis Josua*, BZAW 68, 1938, denied the existence of E as an autonomous source. In their Introductions (see general bibliography, §1) Eissfeldt and Pfeiffer divided J into two documents, naming one S (southern) or L (lay) respectively. In each case the element thus isolated shows less interest in theological problems. Eissfeldt reaffirmed and updated his theory in *Die Genesis der Genesis* (§1 above). Fohrer in his Introduction takes a similar view (see general bibliography, §1). G. von Rad, *Die Priesterschrift im Hexateuch*, Stuttgart 1934, divided P into at least two sections; for a criticism of this position, see P. Humbert, 'Die litera-rische Zweiheit des Priester-Codex in der Genesis', *ZAW* 58, 1940/1, 30–57.

§6a. For Gunkel, see his commentary on Genesis (§1 above), and his *Die Israelitische Literatur*, Stuttgart 1925 (reprinted 1963). For his person-ality and academic activity, cf. W. Klatt, *Hermann Gunkel*, FRLANT 100, 1969; K. von Rabenau, 'Hermann Gunkel auf rauhen Pfaden nach Halle', *EvTh* 30, 1970, 433–44; and the memoir by W. Baumgartner included in the sixth edition of Gunkel's commentary on Genesis. There is an evaluation of his programme and methods and their contemporary relevance in R. Lapointe, 'Les genres littéraires après l'ère gunkélienne', *Église et Théologie* 1, Ottawa 1970, 9–38. For U. Cassuto, see his *The Documentary Hypothesis and the Composition of the Pentateuch*, ET London 1961; cf. also the commentaries cited above (§1). The accusation of Hegelianism was made against Wellhausen by J. Pedersen, 'Die Auffassung vom Alten Testament', *ZAW* 49, 1931, 161–81; id., 'Passahfest und Passahlegende', *ZAW* 52, 1934, 161–75; H. S. Nyberg, *Studien zum Hoseabuch*, Uppsala 1935. G. Ricciotti, *History of Israel* I, ET Milwaukee 1958, 103ff., describes the triumph of the ecclesiastical tradition. For the personality of J. Pedersen, see most recently E. Nielsen, 'Johannes Pedersen's Contribution to the Research and Understanding of the Old Testament', *ASTI* 8, 1972, 4–20.

§6b. G. von Rad, 'The Form-Critical Problem of the Hexateuch', in his *The Problem of the Hexateuch and other Essays*, ET Edinburgh 1966, 1–78, accepts the earlier work of M. Noth, *Das System der zwölf Stämme Israels*, Stuttgart 1930; see also Noth's *The Laws in the Pentateuch and other Essays*, ET Edinburgh 1966. For the Exodus and Sinai narratives see W. Beyerlin, *Origins and History of the Oldest Sinaitic Traditions*, ET Oxford 1965, and G. Fohrer, *Überlieferung und Geschichte des Exodus*, BZAW 91, 1964; for J see V. Fritz, *Israel in der Wüste*, Marburg 1970. For the problems associated with the term b^e*rīt* see the article by E. Kutsch, *THAT* 1, 339–52; id., *Verheissung und Gesetz*, BZAW 131, 1973 (both with bibliography); M. Weinfeld, *TWAT* I, 781–808, who wisely maintains a provisional position: there are some occasions when the term can be translated 'pledge', others where it must mean 'pact' or 'alliance'.

§7. For the problems associated with the 'confession of faith' see W. Richter, 'Beobachtungen zur theologischen Systembildung in der alttestamentlichen Literatur anhand des "kleinen geschichtlichen Credo"', *Wahrheit und Verkündigung: Festschrift für M. Schmaus* I, Paderborn 1967, 191–5; B. S. Childs, 'Deuteronomic Formulae of the Exodus Tradition', *SVT* 16, 1967, 30–9; J. P. Hyatt, 'Were there an Ancient Historical Credo in Israel and an independent Sinai Tradition?', in H. T. Frank and W. L. Reed (eds.), *Translating and Understanding the Old Testament; Essays in Honor of H. G. May*, New York and Nashville, 1970, 152–70; N. Lohfink, 'Zum "kleinen geschichtlichen Credo", Deut. 26.5–9', *Theologie und Philosophie* 46, 1971, 19–39; R. de Vaux, *Histoire ancienne d'Israël*, I, Paris 1971, 379f.; E. W. Nicholson, *Exodus and Sinai in History and Tradition*, Oxford 1973.

For I. Engnell see *Gamla Testamentet: en traditions-historisk inledning* I, Stockholm 1945, esp. 189ff. (vol. II was never published). Some of his shorter works have been collected and translated by J. T. Willis: I. Engnell, *Critical Essays on the Old Testament*, London 1970. (The quotation given appears on p. 11.) For the possibility of a convergence of the ideas of 'tradition history' and 'transmission history', cf. R. Rendtorff, 'Traditio-historical Method and the Documentary Hypothesis', *Proceedings of the Fifth World Congress of Jewish Studies 1969*, I, Jerusalem 1971, 5–11.

III

THE INDIVIDUAL SOURCES:
THE 'YAHWIST' AND THE 'ELOHIST'

§1. *Characteristics of the 'Yahwist'*

Both E and J stand out from the other sources through their pre-dominantly narrative character. J differs from E by the relatively few legal texts which it contains, though, as we shall see, the attribution of legal texts to the earlier sources is a problem in itself. God is called by his name 'Yahweh' (hence the name of the source; the letter J is used because of the German spelling of the word, *Jahwist*) before the revelation made to Moses, an episode which E narrates in Exod. 3 and P in Exod. 6. J, too, seeks to fix a date from which this name was used: Gen. 4.26, that is, after the episode of Cain and Abel; however, the name of God and his title are already mentioned in the J narrative of the creation (Gen. 2.4bff.), in the expression 'Yahweh *'elōhīm*', which is never adequately explained. Of course, after the revelation made to Moses, the other sources also use the divine name, and from then on it is no longer a distinctive element. Whereas E and P, in connecting the revelation of the divine name with the beginning of the Mosaic faith, have certainly handed down a fact which seems very likely in the field of the history of religion, J insists on the theological concept of continuity which the other two sources ignore or express in a substantially different way: that is to say, for J there is no break of continuity between the creation narrative and the patriarchal nar-ratives and the story of Moses, whereas E and P prove more interested in underlining the break between the patriarchal era and its revela-tion, and that of Moses.

The divine name is a criterion which is never absolutely valid, and it ends at the beginning of Exodus. In addition, there is a series of other elements which allow us to distinguish between J and E. J calls Sinai by that name, whereas E, followed by Deuteronomy, always uses Horeb. The autochthonous inhabitants of Palestine appear as

'Canaanites' in J and as 'Amorites' in E, which is again followed by Deuteronomy in this respect. The ultimate implications of this term escape us, and in any case it does not seem to be connected with the mention of the race of the same name in the ancient Near East. In J Moses' father-in-law is called Reuel, and in E Jethro. There are other differences on the lexicographical plane, for example the term 'maid-servant': since the reference is often to the same person, it does not seem possible to attribute the terminological difference to different functions. These are arguments which biblical criticism considers to be indicative rather than definitive; it is their number rather than their quality which makes the division between J and E probable. As we saw at the end of the previous chapter, however, this division continues to be hypothetical. There are, though, certain features of content which, leaving aside the inevitable subjectivity in any evaluation, seem to put the scholar on firmer ground. For example, J already has a kind of theology of history which sees the work of God and his true activity developing in the sphere of secular history. In accordance with this criterion J completely transforms the sense of obviously mythical material like the story of the flood (Gen. 6–8), while leaving the component elements formally intact; or it takes over without difficulty material which was originally not Israelite, like the story of Cain and Abel (Gen. 4.1ff.). It finds no difficulty in locating the patriarchs near sanctuaries which were originally quite definitely Canaanite, like Shechem, Bethel, Mamre, etc., the use of which was later condemned by the prophets and the Deuteronomic history writing. These elements probably had nothing to do with the ancestors of Israel to begin with, but came to be connected with them through aetiological legends, for example the statue of salt into which Lot's wife was transformed (Gen. 19.26). All these materials have been put in chronological order following first a dynastic scheme (Abraham–Isaac–Jacob–Joseph), and then the itinerary of the exodus and the conquest, and in this form they are brought together in the confession of faith mentioned in the previous chapter. Once the creation story was put at the beginning, the scheme was complete. The result is a remarkably coherent narrative with an ideological content, even allowing that it is incomplete. The creation is followed by a break in relations between God and man caused by human sin: the creature wishes to become divine. Following this, it proves impossible to maintain relations between man and man, a development which is illustrated in the story of Cain and Abel. Humanity degenerates to such an extent that God decides to destroy it by means of a flood, which only a single clan will escape. However, the new humanity which survives the flood is no better, as is shown by the story of the tower of Babel in Gen. 11.1ff., which was originally an aetiology intended to explain the difference in the languages spoken by men, but is now inserted into a much wider context. God remedies this wholesale fall of man by choosing the head of a western Semitic tribe, Abraham, to be the founder of what will be a new people, cf. his promise to Abraham, 'In you will all the peoples of the earth be blessed' (Gen. 12.1ff.). God enters into solemn obligations (better, as we have seen, than 'a covenant') with Abraham (Gen. 15.17). Notwithstanding the ingenuous and sometimes simplistic character of this vision of history, it cannot be denied that it is a first attempt at a synthesis, at seeing history as the causal and consistent development of interconnected events which are conditioned by one another and lead to a single goal. J thus constitutes the point of departure from a legendary and popular cycle of history to more advanced literary history. With J there comes into being the first nucleus of the Pentateuch as we have it today.

§2. *Reasons for the Yahwistic collection*

Is it possible to establish at this point why J wanted to collect together his material in the way that we have seen? It should be obvious that his intention was not purely historiographical. There is a series of indications which allow us to answer this question in the affirmative, even if the circumstantial character of these elements imposes insurmountable limits on the work of verification.

Noah's curse in Gen. 9.25–27 seems clearly to point to the period of domination by the Philistines, when 'Japheth' lived 'in the tents of Shem', while 'Canaan' was the slave of both; the fact that the curse against Canaan is connected in some precarious form with that against Ham, the real deceiver, only confirms this analysis. In Gen. 49.10ff., a very old text which is now presented as part of the blessing of the dying Jacob, Judah is promised an everlasting sceptre, an element which is taken up in the promise of Nathan to David (II Sam. 7.12ff., 16), where the throne is substituted for the sceptre. The passage Gen. 12.2 (cited above) is more impressive still, because it belongs to the material attributable to J itself and not to its constituent sources (and it does not have the problems inherent in ancient passages of poetry, to which we shall be returning later). Here we find the phrase 'I will make your name great', pronounced by Yahweh to Abraham at the time of his calling. The phrase reappears with slight stylistic variations in II Sam. 7.9b, in Nathan's promise to David, whereas the term *gōy* used in the first passage, which in this context has the meaning of nation in the political sense of the word, can only refer to the empire of David and Solomon, since it insists particularly on its greatness. Again, Gen. 27.40 almost certainly speaks of Edomite attempts to shake the Israelite yoke from their necks, which takes us to the end of Solomon's reign (I Kings 11.14–22). Num. 24.17ff. speaks of David's conquests of Edom and Moab (cf. II Sam. 8.14), but here again we have the problem of ancient Israelite poetry. In any case, there are many indications that the mind of the collector(s) was directed towards the empire of David and Solomon, which they considered to be the logical conclusion of the prehistory of their people and of the ancient oracles (or those oracles which were thought to be ancient).

We may therefore consider the J collection to be something like an apologetic writing intended to justify and legitimate the monarchy in Israel, a form of government which was certainly new and the subject of lively debate, if we consider the sources; this legitimation was achieved by means of an extremely shrewd choice from ancient material enriched by early prophecies which were probably *ex eventu*. In short, J would resolutely be on the side of those who supported the institution of the monarchy, compiling for their benefit a collection of ancient traditions which, with appropriate comment like that to be found for example in Gen. 12.1ff., gave a theological and ideological support to their thesis, namely that the new centralizing institution, conceived of and realized by David, was in full accord with the will of God, already manifested in the past by means of oracles.

§3. *Date, place and composition of J*

The earliest collection of material, then, may go back directly to the time of David; recently there has even been an attempt to date a small part to the time when David was king of Judah in Hebron (II Sam. 1–4); the rest can be dated (hypothetically, but with some degree of probability) to the time of Solomon and a little after, during the first years of the monarchy in Judah. This obviously does not rule out the possibility of later elaboration; it is thought that such elaboration can be seen in the well-known passage Gen. 18.22–33, in which Abraham discusses with Yahweh the influence of the possible presence of righteous men in Sodom and Gomorrah on the fate of the two places. This is a passage which is notably removed from the main theme of J and could reflect later thought on the fate of the righteous and their beneficial influence on their wicked neighbours. The material which we find in J is decisively oriented towards the south, that is, towards what is to be the kingdom of Judah. Not only does its obvious sympathy for the cause of David give it an important slant in this direction; the patriarchs make their home in the south where their sanctuaries are to be found, and turn their attention northwards only to an inevitable zone of transit. There is now a certain consensus to this effect among scholars, with exceptions only here and there.

As far as the composition of J is concerned, we need select only those passages which are generally considered certain, leaving aside controversial sections. It will still be necessary to confine ourselves to Genesis: the situation in Exodus is so complex that it is impossible to assign material to sources with any degree of certainty. Following these criteria we have: Gen. 2.4b–4.26; 6.1–8; 9.18–27; 10.8–19,28–30; 11.1–9,28–30; 12.1ff.; 13.1ff. (each with what is probably a small insertion from P); 18.1ff.; 19.1ff.; 28.13–16; 29.2–14,31–35; 43.1ff.; 44.1ff.; 49.1–27 (a passage which we shall be examining in greater detail shortly); 50.1–11. Chapters 6–8 and 37 are particularly interesting and are used as examples to introduce the principle of division into sources. Some other documents are now traditionally assigned to J which present special problems. Those who maintain the documentary hypothesis in its traditional form see in them some earlier sources which J incorporated into its collection and used for its own ends without substantially modifying the content; others see them as a shining example of the problems posed by the documentary hypothesis in its traditional form (or at least in some parts of it). We shall examine them following the list given by Weiser in his Introduction.

§4. *Autonomous documents in J?*

(*a*) The 'Song of Lamech' (Gen. 4.23ff.). This is a composition by a fierce warrior who does not yet know the *jus talionis*, which limits personal vendetta to the amount of the loss or the wrong suffered. It has no characteristics which would oblige us to assign it to J, but would serve very well to demonstrate J's thesis of the progressive ethical degeneration of mankind after the first sin.

(*b*) The sayings of Noah in Gen. 9.25–27. We have already seen that they in fact refer to the situation in Palestine a little before the institution of the monarchy, but it is possible to date their origin earlier than that, when the Hittites were dominant in the north of

Syria, at the beginning of the second half of the second millennium BC. Here, too, an attribution to J could be challenged: the facts to which it refers are earlier than the time of David, and the appearance of the name of Yahweh in v. 26 seems to be an interpolation: the expression 'Yahweh the God of Shem' is unique in the Old Testament and it would be enough to mention 'God', as happens immediately afterwards in v. 27. It is quite possible that the name Yahweh was added by J, but as we have remarked, this is not necessarily so.

(c) The 'blessing' of Jacob in Gen. 49.1–27 does not refer to tribes in process of formation (as is evidently presupposed by the context), still less to semi-nomadic populations; what we have here are ethnic groups situated in their own territories and known for particular characteristics. In the composition Judah has pride of place; only v. 18, which is an obvious liturgical interpolation, mentions Yahweh; otherwise God is called by other names and titles, all unusual (vv. 24f.). There is a parallel composition in Deut. 33, generally attributed to E, but there as here the problems created by the attribution are more than those which are solved.

(d) The oracles of Balaam in Num. 24.7–9, 15–19, are usually attributed to J and the remaining verses to E; the mention of Agag in v. 7 leads to the episode in I Sam. 15 in the time of Saul, a passage which is certainly late in its present form; it is not possible to determine whether it goes back to an early tradition at this point. Verses 17f. speak of David's war against Edom and Moab, which has already been mentioned. The attribution to J is made in the light of this last element, but it is proper to ask whether arguments of this kind are not involved in a vicious circle.

(e) In Exod. 34.10–26 we have a decalogue or dodecalogue which is often (wrongly) called the 'ritual decalogue' to distinguish it from the other, in Exod. 20.1–17, which is often called (again wrongly) the 'ethical decalogue', and which is attributed to E. In fact this is not a ritual text pure and simple, but a ritual calendar which has parallels in Exod. 23.14–19 (also attributed to E) and Lev. 23 (P); in the latter case we have it in a notably enlarged form. The text is interesting because it gives a series of agricultural feasts which are almost certainly of Canaanite origin, adopted by Israel and adapted to the Israelite liturgy. They do not presuppose a centralized cult and are therefore certainly earlier than the seventh century (cf. also ch. III, §§2ff.) The only reason for attributing it to J is by a process of elimination, but this is a method which was rightly criticized at the end of the preceding chapter.

(f) The Song of the Red Sea (Exod. 15.1–18) is a composition which has notable analogies with Canaanite poetry, of course in its Ugaritic form; it speaks of Zion as the sacred mountain of the gods in terms known in Canaan (cf. above, Part One, ch. V, §1) and has been considered early, perhaps going back even to the eleventh or twelfth centuries. The sole reason for attributing it to J is its frequent use of the name of Yahweh.

We are thus faced with a foregone conclusion: the passages of early poetry and ritual law attributed to J, if only as material incorporated in autonomous form, do not present (except in the last case) any of the characteristics of language and content which make such an attribution probable, apart from one or two elements here and there.

§5. Characteristics of the 'Elohist'

The chief difficulty confronting the scholar in a study of E is the fact, indicated above, that only a few fragments of this source have come down to us. Here, of course, we refer only to those which can be assigned to E with a reasonable degree of certainty. As we have seen, there are many scholars who have denied the existence of E, regarding the material of which it is composed as merely a complement to J. Today criticism generally accepts the existence of E as an autonomous source, but its sparseness remains, and constitutes the principal problem. The 'Uppsala school' would regard E simply as a rather later phase of the redaction of the material contained in J, but this explanation does not seem convincing, because of the clearly contradictory material which is contained in the two sources. We saw in §1 above the lexicographical characteristics which divide E from J; moreover, E has no creation narrative: the term *'elōhīm* attached to Yahweh is not an indication that the two sources are combined, at least in Gen. 2.4b–3.24; there is no trace in the rest of the narrative. E would seem to begin in Gen. 15, which would constitute a parallel to Gen. 12, but the difficulty of dividing this chapter into sources is so great that almost all the modern authors have given it up. In other words, in the present state of research we cannot even say where E begins.

§6. Scope of the Elohistic collection

The few passages which we can assign with a greater or lesser degree of probability to E show characteristic traces of redaction. First of all, there is no trace of any discussion of the kind of historical and political problems that we found in J, and this does not fail to have a positive influence on the manner in which the ancient traditions were handed down: almost all of it is characterized by a greater freshness and an absence of extraneous preoccupations. But the religious situation is different. J did not have any problem in presenting the patriarchs as being in direct contact with Yahweh, but E prefers contacts through intermediaries, by the intervention of angels or through dreams. J occasionally reports miraculous occurrences, whereas E abounds in narratives of this kind for the greater glory of the God of Israel. E's discussion of theological problems is pronounced, whereas this happens only rarely in J (cf. Gen. 18.22ff., a passage which we have already mentioned and which is probably late), cf. Gen. 20.4ff.; 31.5. Its psychological subtlety has been generally recognized: Gen. 22 is sufficient evidence in this respect. Whereas J is indifferent to or equivocal about the Canaanites and their cult (which fits in perfectly with what we know of the policy of David and Solomon towards the non-Israelite population in their empire), E is particularly harsh (cf. Gen. 35.1ff.; Exod. 32; Josh. 24.14ff.). This attitude recalls that of the great prophets from the end of the ninth century to the beginning of the sixth century BC. The title 'prophet' attributed to men who have a particularly close relationship with God is also reminiscent of the prophetic movement (Abraham in Gen. 20.7; Moses in Deut. 34.10, even if, historically speaking, neither of these two were prophets). On the other hand, this criterion is quite untypical, given that a passage like Num. 11.16–30, which speaks of the inspiration of the seventy elders of Israel and which imagines that all the members of the community were divinely inspired, is unanimously assigned to a late phase of J. E shows a greater sensitivity to moral problems: J has no difficulty in recounting the misadventure which befell Abraham and Sarah in Egypt (Gen. 12.10ff.), whereas E tries to show that no irreparable harm was done and that Abraham's lie was not really a lie, since Sarah was his half-sister (Gen. 20.12). Another expression of this sensitivity, which is by no means purely rhetorical, is the remark made by Joseph to his master's wife in Gen. 39.9.

§7. Date, place and composition of E

Here we find ourselves almost certainly at a period in which the prophet had a place of the utmost importance in Israelite religion and in which relations with the indigenous population of Canaan were particularly strained, especially because of religious syncretism.

The struggles of Exod. 32 are not unlike those experienced by Elijah in I Kings 18, an episode which is immediately followed by a pilgrimage to Mount Horeb (ch. 19). Thus everything seems to indicate that we are now certainly in a period after the rupture in the empire of David and Solomon, in the kingdom of Israel (the northern kingdom), some time after the period of Elijah. The *terminus ante quem* is the fall of the kingdom in question in 722–21, since afterwards the material will have been transferred to the south. The places mentioned in E are predominantly in the north, and the cult of the golden calves had its home there (cf. Exod. 32 with I Kings 12). A recently published Samaritan text, the *Memar Marqah*, may confirm this theory; the first book is a paraphrase of the episodes which speak of Moses, from his experience at the burning bush to the crossing of the Red Sea. E episodes predominate, while those of J are sometimes suppressed. Now although the Samaritan narrative texts are late redactions, in every case they reflect northern traditions. This too is not a definitive argument, but there is no doubt that it is a valid addition to the others which are used.

It is usual to argue that E begins with Gen. 15, but we have seen that the difficulty of making a precise distinction of sources in this chapter is too great for us to be sure. Reasonably certain passages are: Gen. 20.1ff.; 21.1–14; 22.1–19; 24.1ff.; 27.1ff. (combined with J); 28.10–12, 17–22; chs. 29–34 (with J elements); 35–37 (with J and P); Exod. 3.1ff. (with J); 11.1–3; 17.1ff.; 18.1ff.; 19.1ff. (with J, but generally doubtful); 20.1–23.33 (but we shall see the difficulties in §8 j below); 32.1ff.; Num. 12.1ff.; Deut. 32.1ff.; 33.1ff.; 34.1ff. (with J).

In E too, however, there are passages which reveal their autonomous origin, as happened in the case of J above (§§3–4). This time, too, the examination of them follows the order adopted by Weiser.

§8. *Autonomous documents in E?*

(*a*) The 'Song of Miriam' (Exod. 15.21), probably going back to the events which it celebrates, is an exact parallel to Exod. 15.1, which was examined in §4f above. But even assuming that Exod. 15.1ff. is truly J, this is not evidently a reason for attributing v. 21 to E.

(*b*) The oath 'by the throne (?) of Yahweh' (Exod. 17.16), normally assigned to E, does not have any of the lexicographical or ideological characteristics which make such an attribution probable.

(*c*) The words spoken as the ark was carried forward in Num.

10.35f. have been marked by the Massoretes with a sign the meaning of which is obscure. This is the inverted *nun*, which is usually meant as an indication that the passage so marked is out of context; the sign is also found as the equivalent to a special punctuation (*niqqūd*), used to prevent a word or a letter finding its way into the wrong place and causing confusion. In either case, the passage would thus be out of context. But we have no features which help us to assign it to one of the sources.

(*d*) In Num. 21.14 we have a quotation from the ancient 'Book of the Wars of Yahweh' (cf. above, Part One, ch. VI, §4,i), the fragment of a description cited here to demonstrate that the river Arnon was originally the boundary between Ammon and Moab. It is impossible to say whether it belongs to one or other of the sources.

(*e*) The 'song of the well-diggers' (Num. 21.17f.) has already been mentioned; here, too, there are no elements for assigning the passage to one or other of the sources.

(*f*) In Num. 21.27–30 we have a taunt song about Sihon, an Amorite king of Transjordania, or an old war song against his country. There are no criteria for assigning it to a source.

(*g*) As we have already seen, the remainder of the oracles of Balaam (Num. 23.7–10,18–24) is assigned to E. They celebrate the particularity of Israel in the religious field (vv. 9,23) and God's rule over it (vv. 21ff.). The use of 'Jacob' to indicate Israel may be a sign of a northern orientation and therefore this passage could be close to E, at least ideologically, though this is difficult to confirm.

(*h*) The 'Blessing of Moses' (Deut. 33) belongs to the literary genre of the 'last words of a great man' and is seen as the E parallel to Gen. 49; the whole passage in fact seems to be later than Gen. 49. Simeon has already lost its autonomy and is no longer mentioned (cf. Gen. 49.5ff.); Levi no longer exists as a tribe but is a priestly caste (vv. 8ff., in contrast to Gen. 49.5ff.); Judah seems to know the division of the kingdom, for which it bears the blame (vv. 7ff.), whereas praise for Joseph is unalloyed. The northern orientation could be a sign at least of its proximity to E. On the other hand, the individual parts of the composition are not homogeneous: some seem older than others, though the main part is to be put in the pre-monarchical period.

(*i*) The 'song of Moses' (Deut. 32) looks back retrospectively at the founder of Israel's religion, whose time is already some way in the past. Until a short time ago it was usual to give the composition a relatively late date, near to the exile or at the earliest towards the middle of the eighth century BC, but Eissfeldt has demonstrated that the composition is probably not later than the eleventh century BC and that perhaps it refers to the events narrated in I Sam. 4–5 (c. 1050 BC), over which it delivers a lament. The song would then have been reworked in the prophetic period, which could well explain the presence of later elements, e.g. vv. 3, 7, 15, 47, etc.

(j) The 'Book of the Covenant' (Exod. 20.22–23.33), which is now traditionally given this name following Exod. 24.7, comes immediately after the Decalogue, but presupposes a situation later than that described in the actual context, cf. Josh. 24.25 and the fact that none of the laws contained in the text refer to situations in nomadic life but only to those of the settlement. We shall be examining its content when speaking of Israelite law in ch. V below, but we can say in anticipation that it is assigned to E for purely conventional reasons, in the same way as Exod. 34.10ff., as we have seen, is assigned to J.

§9. The Decalogue

The Decalogue, contained in Exod. 20.1–17 and Deut. 5.6–18 with some significant variants to which we shall be returning later, should be the eleventh text in the list which was concluded in the previous paragraph. It is discussed in a separate section not only because of its general importance but also because of the special problems which it presents. Here too, the attribution to E is for purely conventional reasons. Two chief problems need to be examined: (a) that of the relation of the two recensions of the Decalogue within the Hebrew Old Testament and the two others outside it; (b) that of its authorship and the date of its composition.

(a) The recensions of the Decalogue. We have seen that the Old Testament presents two parallel recensions of the texts: the two versions are substantially identical, even if there are some important differences. We shall list only the most obvious ones. The commandment on sabbath observance (Exod. 20.8–11 and Deut. 5.12–15) differs completely between the two in motivation and in length of text. The motivation of the first comes from the P version of the creation story (Gen. 1.1–2.4a), while the second, in Deuteronomy, is motivated by the theme of the slavery in Egypt. The length of the text of the commandment about honouring parents (Exod. 20.12 and Deut. 5.16) also differs; in the Exodus version of the commandment against bearing false witness we have the expression 'ēd šāqer, which means false testimony, while in the Deuteronomy version (5.20) we have 'ēd šāw', which is 'vain testimony'. Now whereas the first

expression is juridical, the second, even if its nuances are not completely clear, refers rather to gossip, a particularly destructive form
of conduct within the community, but difficult to detect and to
suppress on a legal level. In the last commandment Deuteronomy
puts the woman at the head of the list, whereas in Exodus she is
simply classified as one of the objects which are not to be coveted,
among animals and goods in general. This element might make the
Deuteronomic version seem more advanced on the social level, whereas in the case of sabbath observance the theme of slavery in Egypt
would certainly belong to the earliest strata of the Pentateuch, which
cannot be said of the P creation story! This analysis, which is based
purely on the content of the two versions, already seems to tend
towards recognizing a greater antiquity in the Decalogue attested by
Deuteronomy. This is reinforced by the fact that the Decalogue in
Exodus occupies an extremely precarious position: there is no doubt
that it is out of context. Exod. 19.25 ends with the words: 'Moses
went down to the people and told them,' after which we would expect
the discourse in question in 20.1ff. Instead, we have, 'And God spoke
all these words saying. .', after which comes the Decalogue. But the
sequel in 20.18ff., with which the so-called Book of the Covenant
begins, also has no relation to the Decalogue. In other words, in
Deuteronomy the Decalogue is in its proper place and contains
elements which suggest an earlier recension from a literary point of
view, even if it is sociologically more advanced.

We have two other recensions of the Decalogue, this time outside
the Hebrew Old Testament: the LXX translation, in which the
commandments appear in a different order, attested in the New
Testament in Luke 18.20; and the Decalogue in the so-called Nash
papyrus, a manuscript from the second century BC (and before the
discovery of the Qumran texts the earliest manuscript of a biblical
text), which follows the Deuteronomic text but shows some variants
from it.

(b) The problem of authorship and date of composition seems
particularly complex in the light of the various recensions of the text:
the Decalogue has undergone a long and eventful history between its
first author and its definitive redaction. The difference in the order of
the commandments, the variants in the text, show that the final
redactors were in doubt for a long time over which form to choose.
The text contained in Deuteronomy is involved in the problems
associated with that book, which we shall be examining in the next
chapter, whereas that of Exodus is, as we have seen, an interpolation.
The question therefore arises whether the Decalogue can be the work

of Moses, and if so, in what form. This problem has been the subject of many recent studies, but nevertheless it cannot be considered to have been resolved even in the smallest degree.

(i) First of all it is certain that no recension of the Decalogue in the form in which we now have it can go back to Moses; moreover, it cannot even go back to a semi-nomadic situation in the desert or in the first stages of the conquest of Palestine. This is not only because the Decalogue in the dimensions in which we now have it could not have been carved on stone tablets that could have been carried with any degree of convenience: this element is obviously legendary and cannot be evaluated in such a way. It is because situations and institutions are attested in the Decalogue which are incompatible with nomadic life. A celebration of the sabbath in the terms described would seem difficult either in the desert or immediately after the entry into Canaan, given that the references to the ox (a typically agricultural animal) and the ass are evidently to be taken in conjunction with agricultural life; moreover, the existence of slavery and the reference to the 'stranger who is within your gates' presuppose the existence of houses and fortified villages. Finally, many commandments have become quite long, as the result of additions made to fulfil the demands of casuistry, homiletic or parenesis.

(ii) This brings us, in passing, to a shorter form in the Decalogue. Some commandments simply consist of the formula 'Do not steal', 'Do not bear false witness', etc. Brief formulations of this kind would lend themselves admirably to being inscribed on tablets and being impressed on the memory of the people. We would then have an original text approximately like this:

Exod. 20.2; Deut. 5.6: 'I am Yahweh, your God, who brought you out of the land of Egypt, out of slavery' (prologue, perhaps late);

Exod. 20.3; Deut. 5.7: 'You shall have no other gods but me' (first commandment);

Exod. 20.4; Deut. 5.8: 'You shall not make a sculpture or any image' (second commandment);

Exod. 20.7; Deut. 5.11: 'You shall not take the name of Yahweh in vain' (third commandment);

Exod. 20.8; Deut. 5.12: 'Remember and keep holy the day of rest' (fourth commandment);

Exod. 20.12; Deut. 5.16: 'Honour your father and mother' (fifth commandment);

Exod. 20.13; Deut. 5.17: 'Do not kill' (sixth commandment);

Exod. 20.14; Deut. 5.18: 'Do not commit adultery' (seventh commandment);

Exod. 20.15; Deut. 5.19: 'Do not steal' (eighth commandment);
Exod. 20.16; Deut. 5.20: 'Do not bear false witness' (ninth commandment);
Exod. 20.17; Deut. 5.21: 'Do not covet' (tenth commandment).

Of course the division or the numbering of the Decalogue made in Israel and in the Christian church is quite unimportant, provided that all the commandments have been reported and introduced by the prologue, without which the Decalogue risks becoming an arid list of commandments and prohibitions without motivation and lacking that evangelical inspiration which alone can serve as a foundation for the divine order: since God has in fact elected and liberated his people, he cannot allow this community which he has constituted to break up or become corrupt because of man's weakness or wickedness. This alone, then, makes the Decalogue different from the fundamental commandments of many other religions whose content is often very much the same.

Once the Decalogue has been reduced to these dimensions, it is possible to accept that it goes back to the nomadic period and that it could be attributed to Moses. Of course we have no proof of this; we have simply indicated that the traditional interpretation does not come up against literary-critical data which make it impossible.

BIBLIOGRAPHY

§ 1. H. W. Wolff, 'The Kerygma of the Yahwist', *Interpretation* 20, 1966, 129–58; W. Brueggemann, 'David and his Theologian', *CBQ* 30, 1968, 156–81.

§ 4c–d. H.-J. Zobel, *Stammesspruch und Geschichte*, BZAW 95, 1965. W. F. Albright, 'Jethro, Hobab and Reuel in Early Hebrew Tradition', *CBQ* 25, 1963, 1–11, is uncertain about the attribution of the 'blessing' of Jacob, but is inclined to attribute the whole of Num. 23–24 to E.

§ 4e. H. Kosmala, 'The so-called Ritual Decalogue', *ASTI* 1, 1962, 31–61; G. Schmitt, *Du sollst keinen Frieden schliessen mit den Bewohnern des Landes*, Stuttgart 1970, esp. 24ff.; H. Horn, 'Traditionsschichten in Ex. 23.10–33 und Ex. 34.10–26', *BZ* 15, 1971, 203–22; B. Chiesa, 'Un Dio di misericordia e di grazia', *BeO* 14, 1972, 107–18.

§ 4f. W. F. Albright, 'The Bible after Twenty Years of Archaeology', *Religion in Life* 21, New York 1952, 537–50; F. M. Cross and D. N. Freedman, 'The Song of Miriam', *JNES* 14, 1955, 237–50; J. Muilenburg, 'A Liturgy on the Triumphs of Yahweh', in W. C. van Unnik and A. S. van der Woude (eds.) *Studia Biblica et Semitica T. C. Vriezen dedicata*, Wageningen 1966, 233–51.

§5–6. H. W. Wolff, 'The Elohistic Fragments in the Pentateuch', *Interpretation* 26, 1972, 158–73. For Gen. 15: H. Cazelles, 'Connexions et structure de Gen. XV', *RB* 69, 1962, 321–49; A. Caquot, 'L'Alliance avec Abram (Genèse 15)', *Semitica* 12, Paris 1962, 51–66; H. Seebass, 'Zu Genesis 15', *Wort und Dienst* 7, Bielefeld 1963, 132–49; N. Lohfink, *Die Landverheissung als Eid*, Stuttgart 1968; S. E. Loewenstamm, 'Zur Traditionsgeschichte des Bundes zwischen den Stücken', *VT* 18, 1968, 500–6; L. Perlitt, *Bundestheologie im Alten Testament*, WMANT 36, 1969, 55ff.

§7. J. Macdonald (ed.), *Memar Marqah*, BZAW 84, 2 vols., 1963.

§8 g, h and i; see the articles listed under 4 c–d above. On 8h, cf. also F. M. Cross and D. N. Freedman, 'The Blessing of Moses', *JBL* 67, 1948, 191–210; and on 8i, R. Tournay, 'Le psaume et les bénédictions de Moise', *RB* 65, 1958, 181–213, suggesting a mid-eighth-century date; and O. Eissfeldt, *Das Lied Moses*, Berlin 1958, suggesting an eleventh-century date (cf. also Eissfeldt's *Introduction*, 227).

§8j. H. Cazelles, *Études sur le Code de l'Alliance*, Paris 1946; S. M. Paul, *Studies in the Book of the Covenant in the Light of Cuneiform and Biblical Law*, *SVT* 18, 1970. For the argument that these texts are not to be attributed to J or E, cf. J. A. Soggin, 'Ancient Israelite Poetry and Ancient "Codes" of Law and the Sources J and E of the Pentateuch', *SVT* 28, 1975, 185–95.

§9. H. H. Rowley, 'Moses and the Decalogue', *BJRL* 34, 1951–2, 81–118 (= his *Men of God*, London 1963, 1–36); J. J. Stamm and M. E. Andrew, *The Ten Commandments in Recent Research*, SBT II 2, 1967; H. Reventlow, *Gebot und Predigt im Dekalog*, Gütersloh 1962; E. Nielsen, *The Ten Commandments in New Perspective*, SBT II 7, 1968; W. Richter, *Recht und Ethos*, Munich 1966, 101ff.; H. Gese, 'Der Dekalog als Ganzheit betrachtet', *ZTK* 64, 1967, 121–38; M. Lestienne, 'Les dix "paroles" et le décalogue', *RB* 79, 1972, 484–510. Modern studies of the decalogue were initiated by S. Mowinckel, *Le Décalogue*, Paris 1927. The text of the Nash papyrus is accessible in E. Würthwein, *The Text of the Old Testament*, Oxford 1957, 24, 92f.; cf. also A. Jepsen, 'Beiträge zur Auslegung und Geschichte des Dekalogs', *ZAW* 79, 1967, 277–304, a useful comparative study of the relation between the two Massoretic recensions and that of LXX. For the history of the transmission of the Decalogue, see W. H. Schmidt, 'Überlieferungsgeschichtliche Erwägungen zur Komposition des Dekalogs', *SVT* 22, 1972, 201–20.

THE INDIVIDUAL SOURCES: DEUTERONOMY

§1. *Characteristics*

The name of the book is derived from that borne by the LXX translation, and means 'second law'. The early translators thus seem to have been perfectly aware of the fact that the fifth book of the Pentateuch constitutes a later phase in the redaction of the whole work, even if they attributed this phase to the last period of the life of Moses. From the standpoint of the documentary hypothesis, D coincides for the most part with the book of Deuteronomy: only the poems Deut. 32 and 33 and the last chapter do not belong to the source.

Deuteronomy has a style which is particularly easy to recognize: there are many stereotyped phrases like 'With all your heart and with all your mind', a formula which describes love towards God; or 'The place which Yahweh has chosen, to make his name dwell there', for the central sanctuary, implicitly the temple at Jerusalem; 'With powerful hand and outstretched arm', as a description of the power of God. The form is almost always homiletical, and in fact the work is presented as a discourse pronounced by Moses to the Israelites on the plains of Moab, in front of the Jordan, before the entry into the promised land. Exhortations in the second person abound, either in the singular or in the plural; there are repetitions typical of direct speech, intended to make it easier for the listeners to remember. There are a number of typical theological concepts: predominant among these is that of reward, in which the sinner goes to ruin and the righteous receives material well-being and spiritual blessings; there are particular humanitarian touches for example in chs. 20; 22; 23, and one may remember the position of the woman in the D version of the Decalogue. Some passages are duplicates of legal texts traditionally attributed to E, and D has some lexicographical characteristics in common with this source (cf. above, ch. II, §1). And although it is easy to divide the work into different sections, its linguistic and ideological characteristics give it a marked uniformity, which is also recognizable in a good translation.

§2. *The problem of origins*

Among the various problems in the higher criticism of the Old Testament, that of the origins of D seems to have been stated best. Some fathers of the church, Athanasius, Jerome, Procopius of Gaza and John Chrysostom, already related the content of the book to the religious reform carried out by Josiah, king of Judah, in the years 622–21 BC, which is noted in II Kings 22 and 23, and also in II Chron. 34 and 35. But the critical presentation of this theory was only made at the beginning of the last century by W. M. L. de Wette (already mentioned above), and soon become one of the axiomatic components of literary criticism. Of course differences continued to exist over the dimensions of the book discovered in the temple and how far this book had in fact become part of Deuteronomy. But there is no doubt that de Wette's theory still dominates the field and that it provides one of the few virtually certain dates in the literary history of the Bible.

De Wette's work, with a somewhat prolix title, thus marks a memorable development not only in connection with the fifth book of the Pentateuch but also in the whole history of the study of the Pentateuch.

In his argument, de Wette began from the fact (which is obvious to those who accept tradition) that the narrative of the Pentateuch refers, or means to refer, to people and events earlier than the conquest of Canaan by Israel or its ancestors. However, a critical examination of this fact shows:

(i) That there is a very close connection between the Deuteronomic legislation and the 'book of the law' discovered in the Jerusalem temple about 622–21 BC in the reign of Josiah, and that it constituted the basis for the religious reform carried out under the auspices of the sovereign.

(ii) That particular features of style and content which are partly attested in the 'former prophets' appear in Deuteronomy.

Only the first of the two questions had been noted by the ancient writers and formulated with a flash of intuition: it was for de Wette to present the whole matter in critical and systematic form, thus providing, as we have seen, the first certain date for literary criticism.

What was the basis on which de Wette presented his arguments? One incontrovertible fact for him was that the threats which appear in II Kings 22.13–17 are to be connected with the curses contained in Deut. 27;28. Furthermore, the implementation of Josiah's reform follows themes which are not only present in Deuteronomy but typical of it: the centralization of the cult in Jerusalem (II Kings 23.5–9// Deut. 12;16, and other minor passages; of course Jerusalem is not mentioned, which would be too gross an anachronism, but there is mention of the 'place which Yahweh will have chosen to make his name to dwell there'); condemnation and extermination of pagan and syncretistic cults, especially astral cults (II Kings 23.4–11// Deut. 17.2ff.); the cults on the so-called 'high places' coupled with sacral objects like the *maṣṣēbōt* (sacred stones) and the *'ăšērîm* (sacred posts or trees) (II Kings 23.4f., 13–19// Deut. 12.2f. and 16.21f.); sacral prostitution (II Kings 23.7// Deut. 23.18f.); the cult of *'molok'*, divination, spiritualism, etc. (II Kings 23.10,24// Deut. 18.10f.); and yet other elements.

There is no doubt that de Wette succeeded in establishing a series of relevant parallels, which were sufficient to prove beyond all question the existence of a relationship between the book and Josiah's reform. But this relationship does not exist in every case; at least once we may note a remarkable discrepancy between the former and the latter. In Deut. 18.6ff. the levites are in all respects equivalent to the priests of the temple, after being concentrated there; in II Kings 23.9, however, they are assigned a markedly subordinate position equivalent to that of the priests from the suppressed sanctuaries, given that this is the interpretation of the passage: it has been authoritatively denied by J. Lindblom in his recent study, which observes with strong arguments that the limitations in question are not imposed on the levites, but on the priests from the dismantled 'high places'. Now if it is true that this discrepancy can be explained in the context of possible struggles and jealousies among the various categories of priests, each one concerned to maintain his vested interests, it would seem very strange that Josiah's reform should be allowed to diverge from what should have been its written programme in a point of such great importance. Furthermore, the two texts which narrate the implementation of the reform differ markedly: II Chron. 34.2–7 makes the reform begin about ten years before the finding of the 'book of the law' and puts it in the context of Josiah's attempts to shake the Assyrian yoke off his neck, and this note is more trustworthy than that in II Kings, which presents the events in perhaps rather a simplistic way, as if it had been the finding of the book which had moved the king's heart towards reform. For this reason the classic theory about the origin of Deuteronomy should be subjected to critical verification, as it presents some elements which are difficult to reconcile.

The matter-of-factness of de Wette's work should certainly be noted. This is a feature which distinguishes it from later studies. The existence of close connections between the 'book of the law' and Deuteronomy might have been established, but he did not accept that the two were identical. It is also interesting that he never spoke about the origins of either the book of the law or Deuteronomy (except to admit the relationship indicated above); he simply raised the possibility that the work had been composed by Hilkiah the priest, a theme which was to reappear constantly during the last century and the beginning of this, sometimes paraphrased in a more or less elegant manner with the expression *pia fraus*. However, he never followed up the hint; he felt that it was enough to have found a kind of critical Archimedean point on which he could hinge all the traditions of the church and the synagogue about Pentateuchal origins, an opinion which they could not but accept.

We shall limit ourselves here to giving some of the salient dates in the development of literary criticism of Deuteronomy, drawing heavily on the works of M. Weinfeld and S. Loersch, which should be consulted for all questions of detail.

For almost a century the question of Deuteronomy remained at the point where de Wette had left it. His theory was generally accepted; Wellhausen established agreements between J and E and Deuteronomy, and between this and the account of Josiah's reform in the books of Kings and Chronicles, but still did not see what Loersch called the 'real problem' of the book, a problem which is expressed in the fact, which should have been obvious after de Wette's discovery, that 'the problems of Deuteronomy are substantially different from those of the other sources of the Pentateuch' (Loersch, 24).

§3. *The revival of Deuteronomic studies*

From the end of the last century to the beginning of the 1930s we witness a revival in studies of Deuteronomy. Among the most important works, the commentary by C. Steuernagel should be singled out. It is a book which cannot be ignored even today by anyone setting out to work on Deuteronomy, and collects together the results of the author's studies from 1894 on. For Steuernagel, chs. 1–4; 5–11 and 28ff. were a later framework for the central body of legislation, chs. 12–26. This situation provided the proof that Deuteronomy could not have been written down all at once, but was rather the product of complex editorial work. It was Steuernagel who drew the critics' attention to the distinction between the passages in the second person singular and those in the second person plural, a criterion by which he thought it possible to establish the original texts in comparison with later redactional additions, with what Loersch has aptly called 'what seems to us a bewildering certainty'. He distinguished four redactional additions. Another extremely important work, because of its advanced character, is that of A. Klostermann. In his second volume, Klostermann showed how Deuteronomy is at the same time both 'law' and a commentary on laws, independent of them and presented as oral instruction. Having established this, he arrived at the important hermeneutical conclusion that Deuteronomy is the product of 'the living practice of public teaching about the law'. As Loersch rightly points out, he was the first to see that an oral tradition of a catechetical type was the basis of Deuteronomy, and with this anticipated by many years the study of literary genres in the book.

In the wake of the Wellhausen school it is not surprising that there were attempts to discover sources or at least sub-sources within Deuteronomy. J. Hempel made an attempt in 1914, but the matter was not followed up, at least along the lines which he indicated. Critics of de Wette's thesis, to that point accepted without further discussion, are also important. In 1922, G. Hölscher argued that Deuteronomy was in fact a post-exilic work about a century later than Josiah's reform; negative arguments of a similar kind were put forward by T. Oestreicher in 1923 and in various studies which came from the pen of A. C. Welch. With marked differences of detail, these authors maintained that Deut. 12.14 and all the similar phrases scattered through the book should *not* be translated 'In the place which Yahweh shall have chosen . . . to make his name dwell there', but 'In every place which Yahweh has chosen, in *each one of* his tribes', arguing from this that the work does not fight for a centralization of the cult, as in Josiah's reform, but, on the contrary, for a plurality of sanctuaries. They also noted that, as we have already seen, the chronology of events given by II Kings 22;23 is qualitatively inferior to that of II Chron. 34;35, insisting on the basis of the latter that Josiah's aim was not so much a reform in the religious field as a political liberation from the Assyrian yoke. Now while the first affirmation will not hold up under criticism, the second seems to be extremely probable, as we have already seen.

§4. *Literary genres and Deuteronomy*

With the progressive application to the Pentateuch of the methods inaugurated by Gunkel, Deuteronomy too began to be analysed in terms of the history of the traditions and the material which it contained and their setting in life, rather than in more narrowly literary terms. The method opened up completely new prospects. Among its precursors we find F. Horst and A. Alt, who has already been mentioned. For Horst, the starting point is the varied terminology which Deuteronomy adopts for the laws which it contains: *ḥuqqīm* and *mišpāṭīm*, terms which refer respectively to sacral law and the norms for everyday life. On the basis of this classification, Horst sought to assemble the former in a decalogue of five pairs of laws, arguing that this decalogue would have constituted the nucleus from which the central section, chs. 12–28, emerged. Its origin is to be sought among levitical circles in the north, cf. Deut. 27, which describes how it was promulgated at Shechem. This, as we have seen, was the site of a most important sanctuary in the pre-monarchical period and certainly continued to maintain a notable importance even after the founding of the Jerusalem sanctuary and the other sanctuaries in the north after the division of the empire of David and Solomon. On the fall of the northern kingdom in the eighth century these norms then, it is argued, passed to the south. Horst did not have a classification to propose for the regulations concerned with everyday life, which in any case consisted of material which was partly parallel to other evidence in the earlier sources (traditionally assigned to E, but, as we have seen, with little cause, see ch. II, §8j). On the other hand, it could be objected against Horst's theory that while such a neat distinction between sacral law and secular law comes readily to the modern Western mind, on the most favourable of hypotheses it seems extremely doubtful in a society which did not recognize distinctions of this kind. Worship and everyday life were an integral and indivisible part of the same reality, and the violation of a ritual regulation was considered by the same standards as that of a secular regulation. The penalties for sacrilege and for homicide were precisely the same, since sacrilege destroyed the stability of the community, and homicide was an offence directed against God, the giver of life! The formal distinction between laws formulated in apodeictic terms and those formulated in casuistic terms, put forward by Alt, was much more apposite; we shall return to it below (ch. V, §4) when speaking of law in Israel and in the ancient Near East.

§5. The studies of von Rad and Noth

On the basis of the premises laid down by Gunkel, Horst and Alt, von Rad and Noth (already mentioned above) constructed an edifice whose foundations – and to a great extent whose structure – must be taken into account even by those who think that they must adopt a negative attitude towards them. This appears clearly in the recent work of L. Perlitt, who is extremely critical of the work done in recent decades and especially over the past ten years, but hardly ever attacks the two authors in question, to whom he declares himself to be much in debt, even if he makes some criticism of details here and there.

Von Rad's first monograph dates from 1929. In it, he applies Gunkel's methods consistently to Deuteronomy, seeking a way out of the vicious circle in which studies seemed to have become inextricably involved. Comparisons between Deuteronomy and Josiah's reform come to an end and so do attempts at dividing up Deuteronomy (apart, of course, from those which arise naturally from the text). The starting-point is, rather, on the one hand the formal characteristics of the text and on the other its content, while von Rad again examines the relationship between the parallel laws in the 'Book of the Covenant' and in Deuteronomy, seeking to establish the modifications in form or substance which were made in the course of transition from one to the other. Von Rad's discovery here is of crucial importance: Deuteronomy is addressed to Israel both as people of God and as a nation in the ethnic and political sense of the term. The people are called the 'am qādōš = 'holy people' or designated with semantically similar phrases; Deuteronomy is addressed to them with a preaching or catechesis which has still not been clearly defined. This discovery explained some of the central concepts in Deuteronomy: the centralization of the cult, the particular sense of responsibility towards neighbours (understood, again, in the ethnic categories which have been indicated), the doctrine of reward, the theology of the divine name which dwells in the temple (a valid way of confessing the divine presence in the sanctuary without binding it to the sanctuary as a complex of buildings). Nor were von Rad's discoveries exhausted by establishing this relationship between God and his people and the key importance that it has in Deuteronomic theology. The significance attached to the concept of the people of God in Catholic theology after the Second Vatican Council in the 1960s and 1970s is well known.

In his work published in 1938 which we have already examined (see ch. I, §6b above) and in which he put forward his theory about ancient confessions of faith (though this, as we have seen, produced extremely doubtful results), von Rad proposed as a working hypothesis the existence of an ancient 'covenant festival' (or better, following the most recent analyses of the term b^erīt, a 'festival of obligation'), originally celebrated in the sanctuary at Shechem and connected with a 'festival of the conquest' celebrated at Gilgal. The earliest part of the Pentateuch would have been formed around these two liturgies. Now according to this theory, Deuteronomy will have been the product of such liturgies, which are thought to be still clearly visible at salient points: in chs. 1–11 we have a summary of the events which took place between the departure from Sinai and the arrival before the Jordan, a summary followed by an exhortation; in 12.1–26.15 we would have the proclamation of the law (or perhaps better, following the etymology of tōrāh, the divine 'instruction'); in 26.16–19 we would have the obligation of the people to obey the divine will, whereas in chs. 27;28 we would have a series of blessings and curses, depending on the attitude of the people towards the obligations undertaken. Moreover, von Rad believed that he could discover some of these elements in the section of the Sinai pericope attributed to E, but we have seen the difficulty created by such an attribution and will be examining other elements below (ch. V, §9). Von Rad therefore concludes that the origins of Deuteronomy are to be sought in the liturgy indicated and in its four constituent parts, supplemented, of course, by successive amplifications; this also explains the substantially unitary character of the composition, despite the sections into which it can obviously be divided. There would be sections which would correspond to the various stages of the liturgy.

In a third work on the question, written in 1948, von Rad brought to light the essentially 'lay' character and orientation of the preaching and instruction in Deuteronomy. In other words, more than being divine 'law', Deuteronomy is preaching to the people on the divine law. In this way von Rad took up again a theme which had earlier been put forward by Klostermann (mentioned above), but which contrasted with elements of Horst's theory.

Von Rad believed that the theme of the centralization of the cult in the sanctuary at Jerusalem, which was identified by the generic phrase 'the place which Yahweh has chosen, to make his name dwell there' and which was usually attributed to the last phase of the Deuteronomistic tradition, that of Josiah's reform, has very old roots. The first central sanctuary of Israel would in fact have been the ark, which takes us back into the pre-monarchical period, to the last two centuries of the second millennium BC; and the ark will have had this function in the sacred tribal league, a concept which, as we have seen, von Rad accepted from Noth. This is therefore probably an element which the reformers of the seventh century wished to restore, together with that of the holy war (with which it was intimately involved) and other ancient institutions which had fallen into disuse or had been distorted. In contrast to Horst, von Rad sees the country levites of the north behind this movement towards restoration. These levites will have been estranged from the cult soon after the division of the kingdom of David and Solomon under Jeroboam I (I Kings 12.31), but will have been supported by the strictly Israelite population against the Canaanites. We also find this population as supporters of orthodoxy in the south during the same period: it is known as the ʿam hāʾāreṣ = 'people of the land', an expression which is not to be confused with the same term in late Judaism, though it is lexically identical. In the later period it is used disparagingly. This last explanation was improved in 1956 by H. W. Wolff and in 1958 by F. Dumermuth, but was not new in itself; it had already been proposed in 1926 by A. Bentzen.

The question of the origin of Deuteronomy at Shechem and more generally in the north has been the subject of a number of studies following the work of Alt in 1953. Authors have included G. E. Wright (who laid special stress on the role of the levites) in 1954, J. L'Hour in 1962, N. Lohfink in 1963, G. Schmitt in 1964. In addition to refining the proposals put forward by von Rad, these works confirmed the theory put forward earlier by Klostermann, according to which Deuteronomy was the product of a homiletical and catechetical public proclamation. Von Rad then confirmed and developed his own position in the first volume of his *Old Testament Theology* in 1957 and his commentary of 1964.

Martin Noth made an important contribution in 1943 to the solution of the problem by putting forward the hypothesis of a continuous 'Deuteronomistic' history work (cf. also ch. VI, §1). As far as Deuteronomy is concerned, he assigned to the history work chs. 1–2 and perhaps also 4, together with 31.1–13, 24–26a and sections of ch. 34. Taking up earlier suggestions, he regards the passages formulated in the second person singular as the earliest, and those in the second person plural as the product of later amplifications, which arose through the need for public reading and explanation, together with interpretation of the law.

§6. *The present generation*

In the course of recent years the discussion thus begun has been effectively carried forward by a series of valuable monographs. Particularly important are the writings of N. Lohfink (1962, 1963 and 1964) on chs. 29–30, chs. 5–11 and the relationship between Deuteronomy and Josiah's reform respectively; of J. C. Plöger (1967) on 1.6–3.29 and on ch. 28; and of R. P. Merendino (1969) on chs. 12–26. Thus as can be seen, virtually the whole book has been re-examined.

Basing his study on the above-mentioned work of Steuernagel, Klostermann and von Rad, Lohfink sees chs. 5–11, on the basis of an analysis which uses techniques drawn from modern linguistics, as a section juxtaposed with the material contained in 12.1–26.16; this last section is in fact a collection of commandments and prohibitions, while the first is centred on the 'great commandment' for which it acts so to speak as a framework, presenting primary and secondary material. The change from the second person singular to the second person plural is not in every case indicative of different strata but is only an important stylistic element which serves to intensify the effect of the discourse. Deut. 5–11 again is neither preaching nor catechesis, but contains liturgical texts intended to be repeated periodically. Their archetypes go back to the earliest period in Israel, probably to the end of the second millennium BC. It is therefore by no means strange that Deuteronomy has been connected with the person of Moses and that from its origins it has consisted of written material. Lohfink summarized his position in the argument again in 1965. Continuing his researches, he showed how the Deuteronomist, to whom we shall return later (ch. VI, §1), built on this basis, introducing the work with Deut. 1–4 and putting it as a prologue to the 'former prophets'. The process of growth will thus have followed more or less these lines: first of all the liturgy of the pre-exilic cult, then, during the exile, the insertion of Deuteronomy into the Deuteronomistic history work, and finally, in the post-exilic period, its addition to the Pentateuch as a conclusion.

To avoid misunderstanding, however, in a study in 1964 Lohfink attempted to make it clear that if the concept of the 'covenant' (or, as we have seen, 'obligation') is central in Deuteronomy (as God's obligation towards the people and the people's obligation towards

God), and this element has its logical consequence in the Deuteronomistic history work, it does not appear without a break. The reasons
for this phenomenon seem to be essentially theological: there is a
danger that the juridical categories in which relations between God
and the people are expressed will end by obscuring Yahweh's special
character; that fulfilling the commandments will create a sense of
personal righteousness, of moral self-sufficiency, with the consequence
of making a claim on God. In the end, given this approach, which
argues in terms of blessing and cursing, fulfilment and violation, the
concepts of grace and pardon will be completely absent. The concept
of *b⁽ᵉ⁾rît* is thus an inadequate category for expressing relationships
between God and the people and therefore must be constantly
brought up to date and even corrected.

The works of Plöger and Merendino are also important, but as
they are very technical, it is enough to give a brief account of them.
Plöger clarifies both the origin of the material contained in the
section 1.6–3.29 and the blessings and curses of ch. 28. He shows how
these last originally belonged to autonomous lists, each one characterized by particular stylistic characteristics (use of the participle,
etc.). Merendino distinguishes in the central section (chs. 12–26) a
pre-Deuteronomic stratum of tradition, a second stratum of Deuteronomic redaction and finally a post-Deuteronomic redaction: the
parallel passages to those contained in the 'Book of the Covenant' do
not depend on it but are the product of an autonomous tradition; nor
are the passages which speak of the centralization of the cult always
unitary and consistent, seeing that they seem to be governed by such
different criteria. This is also indicated by the diversity of the
phraseology used (cf. 12.1ff.; 14.23–27; 15.19–23; 16.1ff.; 17.8–11;
18.6; 26.1ff.).

The approaches of the two most recent works by J. Lindblom and
M. Weinfeld are different again; we have been able to use them only
partially. Both again see the origin of Deuteronomy in terms of a
compilation by scribes or priests during the beginning of the seventh
century (Lindblom insists on the period of persecution under king
Manasseh). The former, however, does not see any affinity between
Deuteronomy and the prophets, a problem which we shall discuss
below (Part Three, ch. III); the latter takes a similar position but
does note the existence of marked affinities with the prophet Hosea.
Weinfeld believes that the compilation by the scribes was influenced
by the wisdom movement and the Assyrian vassal treaties. This would
explain, first, the didactic character of the work and, secondly, the
presence of elements which we shall examine shortly in Excursus 1.

In conclusion, it is possible, then, to assert that although the problem of Deuteronomy is far from being resolved, it is certainly (as has already been said) the best defined of the questions about the Pentateuch. This is all the more the case since it has recently been stressed again that the sources J and E are no more than hypotheses. However, a complete and satisfactory solution to the problem is not to be expected in the near future, seeing that studies proceed with noteworthy circumspection.

BIBLIOGRAPHY

§1. *Bibliographical studies*: M. Weinfeld, 'Deuteronomy – the present State of Inquiry', *JBL* 86, 1967, 249–62; S. Loersch, *Das Deuteronomium und seine Deutungen*, Stuttgart 1967; E. W. Nicholson, *Deuteronomy and Tradition*, Oxford 1967.

§2. W. M. L. de Wette, *Dissertatio critica exegetica qua Deuteronomium a prioribus Pentateuchi libris diversum, alius cuiusdam recentioris auctoris opus esse monstratur*, Halle 1805; for the relation between the 'book of the law' and Josiah's reform on the one hand and Deuteronomy on the other cf. N. Lohfink, 'Die Bundesurkunde des Königs Josias', *Bibl* 44, 1963, 261–88, 461–98; A. Rofé, 'The Strata of the Law about the Centralization of Worship in Deuteronomy and the history of the Deuteronomic Movement', *SVT* 22, 1972, 221–6.

§3. See the commentary by C. Steuernagel, HKAT, ²1923; A. Klostermann, *Der Pentateuch*, two series, Leipzig 1893 and 1907, esp. II, 348ff; J. Hempel, *Die Schichten des Deuteronomiums*, Leipzig 1914; G. Hölscher, 'Komposition und Ursprung des Deuteronomiums', *ZAW* 40, 1922, 161–255; T. Oestreicher, *Das deuteronomische Grundgesetz*, Gütersloh 1923; A. C. Welch, *The Code of Deuteronomy*, London 1924; id., 'When was the Worship of Israel centralized in the Temple?', *ZAW* 43, 1925, 250–5; id., *Deuteronomy, the Framework to the Code*, London 1932.

§4. F. Horst, *Das Privilegrecht Jahwes*, FRLANT 45, 1930 (= *Gottes Recht: Gesammelte Studien*, Munich 1961, 17–154); A. Alt, 'The Origins of Israelite Law', in his *Essays on Old Testament History and Religion*, ET Oxford 1966, 79–132.

§5. The work of L. Perlitt, *Bundestheologie im Alten Testament*, WMANT 36, 1969, is examined in Excursus 1, §4. See G. von Rad, *Das Gottesvolk im Deuteronomium*, Stuttgart 1929; id., 'The Form-Critical Problem of the Hexateuch', in his *The Problem of the Hexateuch and other Essays*, ET Edinburgh 1966, 1–78; id., *Studies in Deuteronomy*, ET, SBT 9, 1953; J. A. Soggin, 'Der judäische *'am hā'āres* und das Königtum in Juda', *VT* 13, 1963, 187–95; H. W. Wolff, 'Hoseas geistige Heimat', *TLZ* 81, 1956, 83–94 (= *Gesammelte Studien*, Munich 1964, 323–50); F. Dumermuth, 'Zur deuteronomischen Kulttheologie', *ZAW* 70, 1958, 59–98; A. Bentzen, *Die josianische Reform und ihre Voraussetzungen*, Copenhagen 1926; A. Alt, 'Die Heimat des Deuteronomiums', *Kleine Schriften* II, Munich [3]1964, 250–75; G. E. Wright, 'The Levites in Deuteronomy', *VT* 4, 1954, 325–30; J. L'Hour, 'L'Alliance de Sichem', *RB* 69, 1962, 5–36, 161–84, 350–68; G. Schmitt, *Der Landtag von Sichem*, Stuttgart 1964; M. Noth, *Überlieferungsgeschichtliche Studien*, Halle 1943; N. Lohfink, *Das Hauptgebot*, Rome 1963; id., 'Die Wandlung des Bundesbegriffes im Buch Deuteronomium', *Festschrift Karl Rahner* I, Freiburg 1964, 423–44; id., *Höre Israel*, Dusseldorf 1965 (a synthesis of his views); J. C. Plöger, *Literarkritische, formgeschichtliche und stilkritische Untersuchungen zum Deuteronomium*, Bonn 1967; R. P. Merendino, *Das deuteronomische Gesetz*, Bonn 1969; J. Lindblom, *Erwägungen zur Herkunft der josianischen Tempelurkunde*, Lund 1971; M. Weinfeld, *Deuteronomy and the Deuteronomic School*, Oxford 1972; G. Seitz, *Redaktionsgeschichtliche Studien zum Deuteronomium*, Stuttgart 1971. For the question of the occurrence of both second person singular and second person plural forms see G. Minette de Tillesse, 'Sections "tu" et sections "vous" dans le Deutéronome', *VT* 12, 1962, 29–87, an attempt to establish criteria on the basis of the usage of the Deuteronomic history work.

EXCURSUS I

'ALLIANCE' OR 'OBLIGATION' IN DEUTERONOMIC THEOLOGY

§1. *A formulary*

We have seen that one of the principal elements in the theology of Deuteronomy, which then went on to be an integral part of Deuteronomistic theology, is that of the *berit*, a word traditionally translated by 'covenant', 'alliance' or similar terms. In recent years the argument has been increasingly put forward that the word really means unilateral obligation (and in this sense it often appears in parallelism with the word 'oath'). This obligation may be of God towards his people or of the people towards God. In the latter case, the expression of obligation is the communication of the divine will, Hebrew *tōrāh*. This was later usually translated 'law', but this rendering can be misleading because of the implications of the term for Christians, who will be used to the sense of the word in Paul. Of course, where we have a reciprocal obligation of the two parties, i.e. of God towards the people and of the people towards God, the term 'covenant' could be admissible, though not 'alliance', since there is obviously no notion of a bilateral agreement because of the qualitative difference between the two contracting parties. Man can only reject what God has promised him; otherwise what remains for him is to accept and act accordingly.

In recent years, an approach to the problem in the bilateral sense implicit in the term 'alliance' has led to a study of political alliances in the ancient Near East, to see if this might not also be the setting for the biblical concept, and the results of these researches have been surprising. The vassal relationship in ancient oriental treaties was grossly unequal when we consider the status of the parties involved, the great king and the vassal, and these treaties have provided an extremely useful collection of material for comparative purposes, even if it is not permissible to draw from it the extreme conclusions sought by some scholars. These treaties range from the second half of the second millennium BC down to the sixth century BC.

The starting point was provided by the young Yugoslav scholar V. Korošec in his work on Hittite treaties in 1931, which was not concerned with possible biblical parallels: E. Bickermann in 1951 and G. E. Mendenhall in 1954 made independent researches in this field. The discussion was then broken off for a few years until in 1960 a young German scholar, K. Baltzer, followed soon after by the American D. J. McCarthy, took it up again with important monographs. The German scholar R. Smend was more critical, but not essentially in opposition. Baltzer concentrated essentially on the biblical material in his study, which soon appeared in a second edition with extended bibliography, while McCarthy collected all the available ancient Eastern parallels, as well as subjecting the biblical material to a new examination. An important series of studies by the South African F. C. Fensham appeared from 1960 on. The bibliography has grown quite terrifyingly and has been recently collected in a critical study by F. Vattioni; it ends provisionally with a book by Perlitt published in 1969 which questions the whole validity of the enterprise, and some studies and a book by E. Kutsch in which the meaning 'obligation' rather than 'covenant' or 'alliance' is established for $b^e r\bar{\imath}t$.

§2. Ancient vassal treaties

The argument put forward by Baltzer, independently of those formulated ten years earlier by Bickermann and five years earlier by Mendenhall, which were verified by McCarthy, may be summarized as follows. The structure of the vassal treaties of the ancient Near East, which begin with the Hittite treaties described by Korošec and go down to the Assyrian and Aramaean treaties from the first half of the first millennium, follows a constant pattern, so that it is legitimate to talk in terms of a 'vassal treaty formulary' or a 'formulary of alliance', depending on whether or not the parties are of equal status. There is substantial agreement over their composition, which follows this pattern:

(a) A preamble which presents the great king who initiates the relationship in vassal treaties, and the two parties in an agreement between equals. In the first case (and this is more interesting in the present context), it can be a true Great King, like the king of the Hittites, of Assyria or Babylon, or a lesser ruler dealing with a still more minor figure or one who is for the moment in an inferior position. The vassal treaty is evidently more an imposition of the stronger on the weaker (though the former voluntarily limits his power) than a bilateral agreement with equal laws and duties for both parties: it is not difficult to see that the more powerful party had almost all the rights, the weaker one almost none.

(b) The preamble is followed by the history of the relationship between the two parties, written for obvious reasons in a way which demonstrates the generosity and the magnanimity of the stronger party.

(c) There follows a basic declaration of the features which will in future determine relationships between the parties, indicating the duties and the rights of each.

(d) This declaration of principle is followed by a detailed listing of the rights and duties of each party, which at first had been expressed only in general terms.

(e) There follows an invocation of one or more deities as witnesses and possibly guarantors of the pledges made.

(f) The document concludes with a series of blessings and curses, the former on those who are faithful to the obligations contracted, the latter on anyone who violates them.

When the treaty has been drawn up, it is notified to the vassal in terms fixed by custom and the relationship is completed. The text is transcribed in duplicate and deposited before the principal deity of each party, i.e. in the temple, and in some cases provision is made for it to be read periodically in public by the vassal. Having established this, Baltzer proceeds to review the Old Testament texts to see if it is possible to find a similar situation. The result of his research is positive, even if it is put in extremely cautious terms. 'On the basis of the texts that have been studied, I think it is possible to say that the covenant formulary, as a literary type, was familiar in Israel' (p. 38). With similar prudence Baltzer demonstrates in a comparison between the vassal treaties and the formulae which govern the relationship between Yahweh and his people in the Old Testament that 'the Israelite covenant is as far removed in content from the international treaties as it is closely related in form' (p. 91). Moreover, the Old Testament does not have any complete version of the 'formulary', whereas it is Deuteronomy and the literature dependent on it which make predominant use of it. Finally, on the basis of Deut. 31.9ff. Baltzer conjectures a public reading of the texts at regular intervals in Israel also.

§3. *Treaties and 'alliance' or 'obligation'*

McCarthy's work, a second completely revised edition of which is in preparation, is much broader in its general approach and in its choice of comparative oriental material: the Near Eastern texts cited run from the third millennium BC to the middle of the first, with special emphasis on western Semitic texts, which are geographically and ideologically nearer to the Old Testament than the others. The results which he achieves are important: 'I believe that, notwithstanding the more or less significant variations in the different manifestations of the treaty, there was in fact a formulary used by international agreements for the greater part of the history of the ancient Near East in the pre-Hellenistic period' (p. 7). For the Old Testament he arrived at similar results to those of Baltzer: the writings of Deuteronomy and the Deuteronomists are those where the best results are to be found, whereas the earlier strata of the Sinai pericope produce more negative results. In Deuteronomy, as has been indicated, we do in fact have an introduction with strong historical elements (chs. 5–11), followed by a collection of laws (chs. 12–26): the work ends with a series of blessings and curses. However, as we have seen, Plöger has demonstrated that the history of this last element contained in chs. 27 and 28 is very complex and that, ruling out a composition at a single point in time, the pattern in question can be attributed to the redactional phase rather than to the original formulation.

§4. *Criticism*

A relationship between Deuteronomy and the 'covenant formulary', if only as variants of the vassal treaty, has not, however, been accepted by all scholars even in the past, and is now of course considered even less probable by those for whom the equation between *berit* and 'covenant', 'alliance', no longer holds on the semantic level. Authoritative criticisms were made of the theory by G. Fohrer in 1964 and by F. Nötscher in 1965; Perlitt's work of 1969 then denied the antiquity of the concept, affirming that it was a theological creation of Deuteronomy, or at best of the period immediately preceding, which came about under the impact of the preaching of the prophets. There are, however, some fundamental objections against this theory: in the first place Perlitt works by post-dating some passages which were considered pre-Deuteronomic, in which the term *berit* is mentioned, doing so on an essentially literary basis and neglecting the whole traditio-historical approach to the problem. His attempts therefore do not always seem convincing. The texts to be taken into consideration as pre-Deuteronomic are: Gen. 15.18; Deut. 33.9; Josh. 24.25; II Sam. 23.5; I Kings 19.10, 14; Hos. 6.7; 8.1; Pss. 44.18; 89.7, 35, 40; 132.12, though for some of these a late date seems likely. In Deut. 33 the mention of *berit* is generally recognized to be late; the possibility of a Deuteronomistic redaction is to be taken seriously into account for Josh. 24 and I Kings 19, and is practically certain for this last passage; Gen. 15 is notoriously a difficult passage throughout and at all levels, while the psalms mentioned present complex problems of dating, as we shall see (Part Five, ch. I, §3). But II Sam. 23 and Hos. 8.1 are dated in the tenth and eighth centuries respectively, the former by a large number of scholars and the latter by almost all. Notwithstanding Perlitt's acute analysis, it is impossible to demonstrate that there is no evidence at all for the term *berit* in the period before Deuteronomy. Rather, the result of the examination suggests that the use of the term is rare in the time before Deuteronomy and that it is only with Deuteronomy that it came to represent a central concept. In other words, it is one of those concepts, like that of the holy war, which Deuteronomy wished to revalue and to restore.

BIBLIOGRAPHY

§1. V. Korošec, *Hethitische Staatsverträge*, Leipzig 1931; E. Bickermann, 'Couper une Alliance', *Archives d'Histoire du Droit Oriental* 5, Brussels 1950–1, 133–56; G. E. Mendenhall, 'Ancient Oriental and Biblical Law' and 'Covenant Forms in Israelite Tradition', *BA* 17, 1954, 26–46, 50–76; (also published separately as *Law and Covenant in the Ancient Near East*, Pittsburgh 1955); K. Baltzer, *The Covenant Formulary*, ET Oxford 1971; D. J. McCarthy, *Treaty and Covenant*, Rome 1963; id., *Old Testament Covenant*, Oxford 1972; R. Smend, *Die Bundesformel*, Zurich 1963; L. Perlitt, *Bundestheologie im Alten Testament*, WMANT 36, 1969; E. Kutsch, opp. citt. (see bibliography to ch. II §6b); M. Weinfeld, 'Covenant Terminology in the Ancient Near East and its Influence upon the West', *JAOS* 93, 1973, 190–9. For a critical bibliography see F. Vattioni, 'Recenti studi nell'alleanza nella Bibbia e nell'Antico Oriente', *AION* 27, 1967, 181–232.

§2. For the neo-Assyrian treaties, cf. R. Frankena, 'The Vassal-Treaties of Esarhaddon and the Dating of Deuteronomy', *OTS* 14, 1965, 122–54.

§3. Cf. G. Fohrer, 'Prophetie und Geschichte', *TLZ* 89, 1964, 481–500 (= *Studien zur alttestamentlichen Prophetie*, BZAW 99, 1967, 265–93) esp. 488ff. (= 274 ff.); F. Nötscher, 'Bundesformular und "Amtschimmel"', *BZ* 9, 1965, 182–214; and L. Perlitt, op. cit.

EXCURSUS II

DEUTERONOMIC OR DEUTERONOMISTIC PASSAGES IN THE OTHER BOOKS OF THE PENTATEUCH

§1. *The problem*

Along with studies of Deuteronomy and the Deuteronomist, the possibility has been seriously considered over recent years that there are Deuteronomic or Deuteronomistic (in this case a distinction between the two is difficult or even impossible) passages in the books from Genesis to Numbers. The starting point for investigations has been another remark by Wellhausen, that in these books there are passages which cannot be assigned to J, E or P, while their style recalls that of Deuteronomy or the Deuteronomist: these passages almost all appear in Exodus. Various authors have returned to this problem from time to time, but without resolving it or reaching any significant results. It was the formation of Noth's hypothesis of the existence of a Deuteronomistic history work, in 1943, which restated the problems in new terms. Denying outright that the books in question could have undergone a Deuteronomistic revision, Noth suggested that in passages like Exod. 23.20ff.; 34.10ff., 'the old text has been elaborated in Deuteronomistic style', whereas Num. 21.33–35 would have been revised secondarily on the basis of Deut. 3.1–3. This remark did not seem to raise problems of any importance, but the question changed once the number of passages involved proved to be greater and their content to be relevant from a historical and religious point of view. In this case we find ourselves confronted with a problem of undeniable importance, which is certainly not marginal and therefore cannot be brushed aside, as Vriezen pointed out in 1961.

Now in the calculation of these passages made by Perlitt, their number seems to have grown to such a point that they no longer represent merely a marginal phenomenon. Perlitt in fact mentions, among others, Exod. 13.5, 11; 19.3–6, 11; 24.3–8; 32.9–14; 33.1 and parts of ch. 34; Num. 11.12; 14.(16), 23; and in addition Gen. 15.7, 18b, 19–21; 26.3b–5; 50.24 and the Decalogue in its two versions, Exod. 20.1–17// Deut. 5.6–21. If this list is correct, we find ourselves confronted with a situation like that of the Deuteronomistic insertions in Joshua and I and II Samuel.

§2. *Criteria of evaluation*

One thing is certain. There are various criteria of evaluation and therefore it is extremely uncertain whether the description 'Deuteronomic' or 'Deuteronomistic' should be applied to some passages in Genesis–Numbers. To avoid this difficulty, the problem has been the subject of several studies. C. H. W. Brekelmans, who has studied the problem more than any other author, and has presented his conclusions in monographs, rightly laments the lack of any objective criteria for recognizing the passages in question, and therefore assigning them to sources. In this respect he cites the perplexity of authors like S. Mowinckel in 1927 and more recently A. Weiser and H. Cazelles. A purely stylistic criterion is evidently not sufficient, given that a Deuteronomistic style could have existed even before the book itself, which we know to have been the product of a complex redaction, continuing the work of E, as the lexicographical affinity shows. For Cazelles, typical elements of Deuteronomistic thought need to be present as well as affinities on a stylistic level; but, he continues, since these elements are absent from the passages in question, these are neither Deuteronomic or Deuteronomistic. The argument is developed by Brekelmans: in addition to stylistic affinity and the presence of elements attested in Deuteronomistic thought, it is also necessary that there should not be elements absent from Deuteronomistic thought, but attested in other Pentateuchal sources. Only when these three features are present can the material be assigned to Deuteronomy or to a kindred source.

Applying these criteria consistently, Brekelmans comes to the conclusion that only Exod. 23.20–23 has contacts with Deut. 7; with Vriezen he then accepts that E, which we have seen to have contacts on an ideological level with the great prophets, and on the lexicographical level with Deuteronomy, had a continuation which we might call 'proto-Deuteronomic'. Other authors have come to similar conclusions with regard to Gen. 50.24 and Exod. 13.3–16. Perlitt, too, accepts these conclusions in principle, though the reader may not succeed in avoiding the impression that he wants all Deuteronomy, even in its earliest strata, to be simply a creation of the seventh century. Here we might follow Childs in asking whether it has not been the Exodus formula which has modified that of Deuteronomy, and not vice versa!

BIBLIOGRAPHY

§1. C. H. W. Brekelmans, 'Éléments deutéronomiques dans le Pentateuque', *Recherches Bibliques* 8, 1967, 77–91; id., 'Die sogenannten deuteronomistischen Elemente in Genesis bis Numeri', *SVT* 15, 1966, 90–6; M. Caloz, 'Exode XIII, 3–16 et son rapport au Deutéronome', *RB* 75, 1968, 5–62; B. S. Childs, 'Deuteronomic Formulae of the Exodus Traditions', *SVT* 16, 1967, 30–9; L. Perlitt, op. cit. (see bibliography to ch. III, §5), 65 ff., 71, 83, 90 f., 169 ff., 193, 197, 205 ff.; J. C. Plöger, op. cit. (see bibliography to ch. III, §5), 69 ff.; T. C. Vriezen, *De Literatuur van Oud-Israël*, The Hague 1961, 131; H. Cazelles, 'Connexions et structure de Gen. XV', *RB* 69, 1962, 321–49, esp. 334 n. 5; W. Fuss, *Die deuteronomistische Pentateuchredaktion in Exodus 3–17*, BZAW 126, 1972.

IV

THE INDIVIDUAL SOURCES:
THE PRIESTLY WRITING

§1. *Characteristics*

Of the sources of the Pentateuch scattered through the first four books of the work, P is the easiest to recognize because of its relatively constant vocabulary, its solemn style tending towards pomposity, its love of elements connected with the cult (liturgy, ritual, institutions) and its genealogies. P's chronology sets out to be very precise ,and it seeks to include a history of the world from its origin. However, we may say in anticipation, the result does not correspond with the intentions, since the chronology in question is clearly artificial, not in the sense that it has been created by the imagination of the redactors, but because it is inspired by criteria which are not really historiographical. We shall return to this argument a little later. P should thus be a unitary source almost by definition, but it also contains contradictory notes and these are in connection with matters which scarcely allow of contradictions. In Lev. 4.4–16 only Aaron and the High Priest are presented as 'anointed ones', whereas in Exod. 28.41 and 29.29 all the priests have this character; in Num. 4.23ff. the service of the levites does not begin before they are thirty, but in 8.24 it begins at the age of twenty-five. Moreover, the offerings required for the sacrifices are not always the same: in Lev. 4.14 the situation is different from that attested in 9.3 and in Num. 15.24. On the subject of altars, in Exod. 27.1ff.; 38.1ff.; 30.29; cf. Lev. 8; 9, we have one for whole burnt-offerings; in Exod. 30.1–10 another appears which is intended for incense. Moreover, some sections seem to have been interpolated in their present context: Lev. 1–7 and 11–15 and 16 clearly interrupt it, while chs. 17–26 are evidently an independent entity with its own vocabulary and stereotyped phraseology. All this is enough to demonstrate that P, too, has experienced an eventful history and a number of centuries of tradition before being accepted as the final source of

the Pentateuch. However, attempts to separate more or less continuous subsidiary sources or strata within P have not been successful:
others have attempted in the past to distinguish between a narrative
P and a legal and ritual P, but here too the legal and ritual sections
have been inserted into the context of a historical narrative, following
the characteristic criterion of the Old Testament, already mentioned,
which is to consider only what has been realized in history as relevant
for faith.

§2. *Chronology*

The chronology of P is one of the most characteristic elements of the
whole source. It begins with creation (Gen. 1.1–2.4a), and the modern
calculation of the Jewish year in use in the synagogue (1976–7 is
5737 'from the foundation of the world') is a direct continuation of it.
The exactness and precision of the figures were a source of certainty
for biblical scholars down to the beginning of scientific biblical criticism, so much so that only towards the middle of the last century,
culminating with the studies of Wellhausen and his school, did it
become possible to demonstrate their artificial character. There is,
however, no justification for the assertion to which we have alluded
briefly that the chronological system of P is fictitious only because it
cannot be reconciled with that of historical or natural science (Charles
Darwin's difficulty, it may be remarked in passing, was that he began
by attempting to confirm the chronology which we know to be that
of P in terms of natural science, and succeeded in proving precisely
the opposite). The figures given in P express theological and ritual
criteria which in some cases are clear and in others have still to be
discovered: for example, that a fundamental divine act in the history
of salvation stands at the beginning of each new period of human
history. Matters of particular importance are accompanied by the
celebration of a b^erît, in which God incurs obligations towards man
and man towards God. This can be verified in two cases. Thus we
have a constant relationship between the division of human history
into periods (which P of course saw and recognized) and its chronology. After the flood we have divine obligations towards Noah (Gen.
9.1–17) followed by a divine command to mankind over food: at the
election of Abraham in P (Gen. 17.1ff.) we have further divine obligations to which Abraham is to respond by adopting circumcision. The
sources J and E did not know such an ancient institution of this rite.
Indeed we find in Exod. 4.24–26 what is apparently a very ancient text

which originally was intended to narrate the institution of circumcision; now it has been harmonized by the redactors so that it has the sense of a repetition. However, what seems to interest P more than anything else is the constitution of the legitimate cult and its priests, and the people among whom the cult is carried on. Thus whether in the case of Noah or in that of Abraham, we have the celebration of a b^{e}rit: in the former we find the first food laws, and in the latter the election of Israel through Abraham and the institution of the rite of circumcision, which was its distinguishing mark over the centuries. Various names for the God of Israel correspond to these periods: until he discloses himself to all humanity he bears the name '^{e}lōhim = God; he presents himself to Abraham as 'el shaddai, a term which has yet to be explained adequately, whereas only with Moses does he receive his true name, Yahweh (Exod.6, a theory which is shared, as we have seen, with E). At the same time, from the creation of the world onwards, there is a degeneration of men's life force: a man's life declines from almost a thousand years (a figure which is never reached, Gen. 5.1ff.) to a little over a century with the patriarchs, then arriving at normal limits, all under a century. In other words, P does not hand down a story on the fall of man as does J (Gen.3), but it does show a very similar belief about his tendency to sin, which is only mitigated by the fact that man can adopt the ritual practices which he has been commanded. For P the climax of history is the theophany on Sinai, to which half Exodus, all Leviticus and a third of Numbers are devoted: in the course of this the basis for later Hebrew worship is established along with some of its details. Anyone who wished to be particularly precise and rational in his observations would be reduced to the absurd conclusion that there was no form of true worship before the theophany on Sinai, with the exception of the laws about food, the sabbath and circumcision, the first and third of which are given to Noah and Abraham respectively.

In a source like P it is not surprising to find an exalted concept of divine transcendence: only Moses is allowed to see God and then only from behind (Exod.24.16ff.; 33.18ff.), and the figure of the mediator between God and man becomes a necessity. J does not seem to be excessively preoccupied with the problem, though in E we already see an inclination in this direction. We no longer find the familiar form in which the patriarchs intercede with their God in J and, with greater limitations, even in E (for this latter source see Gen.22): now we have to do with Yahweh, the God of Israel, in all his majesty, in all his transcendence, and therefore in all his remoteness. Though it may seem paradoxical, this does not exclude the presence of a number of anthropomorphisms and anthropopathisms: P too is concerned to proclaim a personal God, removed but not detached from man and the world, and it tries to indicate this with all the means at its disposal.

§3. Date and place of composition

Once H. Ewald (see ch. I, §3c above) had ascertained that there were two 'Elohist' sources in the Pentateuch and that one was later than the other, discoveries in the material followed with remarkable speed: it was E. Reuss (mentioned above, ch. I, §3d) and his pupil K. H. Graf who placed P at the end of the development of the Pentateuch. The correspondence between the two shows clearly that it was Reuss who first made this discovery, although Graf was the first to make it public. This turned completely upside down the chronology which had been hitherto accepted and, as we have seen, laid the foundations for the definitive construction of the documentary hypothesis.

Over recent decades only a few objections of any weight have been made to what has so far been the dominant theory. In 1929 A. Jepsen argued that the starting point of the chronology of P was the construction of the temple in Jerusalem and that therefore the constitutive elements of the source must necessarily be prior to the exile. This argument was certainly not without its strength, but one would have to ascertain to which temple P referred, whether to the temple of Solomon or to the second, post-exilic temple. In any case, one thing is clear: that the relationship in chronology between P on one side and Deuteronomy and the Deuteronomistic history work on the other would have to be subjected to a thorough examination to discover whether P presupposed the existence of the other two, and if so at what point. We find a similar problem in the case of the Israeli scholar Y. Kaufmann, whose theory we touched on at the beginning of our examination of the sources. He argues for the priority of P over Deuteronomy, a theory which had already been put forward by de Wette. This is because there is no proof that P presupposes Deuteronomy; moreover, for this author P cannot be post-exilic and it therefore has the temple of Solomon in mind. The first theory is only valid if we consider the centralized cult in the single sanctuary which is presented by P not as the consequence but as the presupposition of Josiah's reform, an evaluation in which considerations of a subjective kind have a by no means unimportant role; the second is based on the generally accepted fact that there are certainly important pre-exilic sections in P (a problem to which we shall return), whereas not a few elements of P are incompatible with a post-exilic date. For example, there is constant mention of the ark, but it is unanimously said by tradition to have been made in the desert period, while it disappeared at a date which cannot now be determined, probably in the seventh or the sixth century BC, and certainly not later than the fall of Jerusalem in 587. How could a post-exilic text show so much interest in an object of this kind? The school of Kaufmann has now shaped two generations of Israeli scholars, and his work is highly valued in Jewish circles outside Israel; the fact that the first volumes have not been revised up to the date of more recent biblical studies does not relieve us from an accurate evaluation of his argument, though this enterprise is not helped by the fact that his principal writings exist only in modern Hebrew.

A third theory was developed in 1964 by the American orientalist E. A. Speiser: according to this, P is the work of a school with roots in the earliest history of Israel, which continued to work throughout the history of Israel before and immediately after the exile. Again, Speiser hits the mark when he indicates the complex history of the P tradition or when he demonstrates the existence of what are certainly pre-exilic elements, but there is no proof of a school of this kind.

A fourth theory was presented in the same year by J. Hempel: he discovered in Gen. 17.6 an evident allusion to the monarchy and believed that the roots of P are to be found in the milieu of the ancient sanctuary of Hebron, David's capital when he was king only of Judah (II Sam. 1–4). But what has already been said still holds true: the presence of ancient material does not imply anything about the date of the final redaction of the sources, nor is it evident why this redaction should be dated back to such a remote period, the last years of the second millennium.

It seems that all these arguments, leaving aside those of Kaufmann, do not touch on the fundamental problem: the date of the final redaction of P and its relationship to the other sources of the Pentateuch. They only deal with peripheral elements. All that is shown is that in P, as in all the other sources, there are elements of tradition which are much earlier than the final redaction.

The discussion so far and the objections which have been indicated invite us automatically to consider the problem of the dating of P or of its final redaction, or, finally, that of a possible earlier dating of some of its sections. A *terminus ante quem* here is obviously given by the definitive breach between Jews and Samaritans, at a time when the Pentateuch was evidently complete, since it is common to both; the date of this breach is uncertain, but it is generally put towards the end of the fourth century BC and not later, during the passage from Persian to Macedonian rule.

First, however, it will be necessary to examine the text of P rather more closely. The problem of the relationship between the historical texts and the legal texts, which we have seen to be particularly acute in the J and E sources, seems to be much simpler in P: in the two categories of texts there are lexical, stylistic and ideological constants which make them an undoubted unity, leaving aside some differences of detail and an exception which we shall examine a little later. Now we have seen that the Sinai pericope, with its narrative of the institution of the legitimate cult, indubitably forms the climax of P: the material which follows is essentially connected with the continuation of the journey through the wilderness before the arrival in the Promised Land. Moreover, the Sinai pericope contains the greater part of the material which has been assigned to P. It would not therefore be illogical to argue that the narrative sections also tend towards this high point: the proclamation of the *tōrāh* on Sinai and the foundation of the cult. Paradoxically, however, what would be a climax from the narrative point of view does not constitute the central element of the source on the ideological and theological plane. In this area the centre of the source is to be found in three elements: the institution of the sabbath, of the food laws and of circumcision, which are now to be found respectively at the beginning, a quarter of the way and half way through P. These results have been achieved through laborious examinations which we shall attempt to follow, though only in their main points.

We have already seen in §2 that even at the heart of P we have contradictions, duplicates and interpolations of compositions which clearly show signs of being of autonomous origin. A solution had been sought up to the beginning of the 1930s in the possibility that there were subsidiary sources in P. This had been the case in J and E, and was now being argued for by some in the case of P too. Wellhausen thought of two sources and of a work of a genealogical character (*tōlᵉdōt*); this principle was taken up again in 1934 by von Rad, who sought to divide the fundamental writing (P^g, from the German *Grundschrift*) into two subsidiary sources, P^a and P^b, to which various supplementary elements were then added, indicated by P^s. The hypothesis of the existence of a genealogical source has recently received the authoritative endorsement of O. Eissfeldt, but as early as 1940 the Swiss scholar P. Humbert, followed by Weiser in his Introduction, demolished the theory of two subsidiary sources. In 1948 Noth had proposed the theory that P is an essentially historiographical work,

culminating, as we have seen, in the Sinai narrative. Other materials
of diverse character were then incorporated into this work. This is the
theory which has a majority of adherents today. Of course, if we
allow that P is essentially a historiographical work which has merely
been elaborated with various types of material, it is necessary to study
the nature and the scope of P's historiography.

About twenty years ago an important work on this theme by K.
Elliger was published, while other authors have also been occupied
with it in a more or less direct way. Meanwhile Elliger has produced
a more recent and authoritative commentary on Leviticus in which
his theory has again been subjected to verification. He accepts that P
has a composite character, but sees only the possibility of distinguishing between a Pg (basic document) and Ps (later supplements); many
legal and ritual passages are assigned to Pg because they belong there
without a shadow of doubt; the difficulty in attributions of this kind,
however, rests in the fact that they cannot be made without involving
subjective elements which others can put in doubt simply because they
have a different sensibility. According to Elliger, Pg begins with Gen.
1.1–2.4a, a narrative which concludes with the creation of man but in
reality culminates in the divine institution of the sabbath, one of the
key elements in the theology of P. The first section of the work ends
with the genealogy of the Sethites or antediluvian patriarchs (ch. 5).
The second section begins with the flood and ends with the institution
of the first ritual laws to do with food (Gen. 9.3f.): the prohibition
against eating flesh with blood, which is considered the seat of life.
With the table of peoples we have a transition to the patriarchal
section, chs. 10ff., in which the narrative is distinguished by its dry
and sometimes pedantic style, stripped of all elements of folklore
(with one exception: the dealings over the purchase of the cave of
Machpelah, Gen. 23) and of any narrative which might put the protagonists in a less flattering light. The culminating point is given with
the institution of circumcision (Gen. 17), another key element in the
theology of P which, as we have seen, sets the introduction of the rite
with the ancestors of Israel at a time which is notably earlier than
that attested in J and E. In reality, the account of Sinai which, as we
have seen, constitutes the logical goal of P, only takes up themes
which are already present in the narration: the sabbath, food laws,
circumcision. It is interesting that the regulations seem to presuppose
a public confession of faith, and therefore a situation of contact with
other peoples; in other words, it is a post-exilic situation, even if the
institutions described are obviously much older.

We have already spoken generally about the chronology. It is intended to displace all earlier chronology in the Pentateuch, thus giving rise to interesting discrepancies with the chronology of J and E (cf. Gen. 16; 21).

The intertwining becomes complex in the narrative of the exodus from Egypt and the march across the desert. The revelation of the divine name (Exod. 6) and the liberation from oppression in Egypt re-establish equilibrium between the ancient promises and their fulfilment, which seemed to have been irremediably compromised. For P, however, the revelation of the divine name does not seem to have had the importance which it has, for example in E: P seems to consider the name or title Shaddai more important. This is already attested in the ancient songs, Gen. 49.25 (in a conjecture which is generally accepted, cf. *BHS*); Num. 24.4, 16; from Gen. 17 it becomes a name that is typical of P. During the march through the desert the culminating episode is obviously that of Sinai, where the people receive, through the mediation of Moses, a series of laws which make them a 'holy people' *par excellence*, set aside by Yahweh. The narrative breaks off on the soil of the promised land, to which Moses is not admitted. According to Noth and Elliger, and probably rightly, as we shall see below (ch. VI, §3), P is continued in Joshua only in a number of fragments: Josh. 14.1; 18.1; 19.51a; 22.9–34, and it does not seem that more recent studies, taking up hints made by Wellhausen, have been able to demonstrate the contrary. We shall return to the argument in ch. VI, §1, when we examine the problem of the Deuteronomistic history writing.

It is thus interesting to note that the Sinai pericope for the most part does no more than amplify themes and institutions which are already present in the more strictly narrative section, so much so that Elliger can affirm that various passages in the pericope in question never belonged to Pg: the laws about the altar of incense, the holy oil, the thurible, sacrifices, the ritual calendar and perhaps even the legislation about the levites. It was only later that P felt the need to add this material, which would have been lacking in its original redaction. Sections concerned are especially Lev. 1–7; 8–10; 11–15, a series of codices whose themes are respectively sacrifices, the priesthood and ritual impurity; ch. 16, which deals with the Day of Atonement; and chs. 17–26, already mentioned, a collection usually called the 'Holiness Code' because its regulations are motivated by the holiness of God: the majority of scholars have no difficulty in accepting a pre-exilic origin. A special position is also occupied by Num. 33, an itinerary, and 35, the list of levitical cities and cities of refuge (for these latter see what will be said in connection with the book of

Joshua, ch. VI, §4 below). To what degree these texts can be ascribed to P is debatable: the question, however, is not of great importance. This, then, would be an excellent explanation of the contradictions, inconsistencies and duplications which we have noted so far.

The P Sinai pericope is dominated by a particular kind of theological dialectic: on the one hand God 'lives', 'dwells' in the midst of his own people (root *škn*, whence *miškān* = dwelling, clearly nomadic in origin in that it indicates dwelling in tents and therefore, at least originally, the provisional and precarious character of this dwelling, cf. the analogue *skēnoō* in John 1.14, in the New Testament); on the other hand, he 'meets' with the people in the Tent of Meeting (*'ōhel mō'ēd*), an object also mentioned in J and E and which, like the ark, disappeared in the pre-exilic period. Now in this dialectic the theme of meeting plainly prevails over that of dwelling, however precarious the latter may be, and in this way one of the principal elements of the promises made to Abraham is achieved. This also explains a theory put forward a few years ago according to which the tent of meeting is not so much a projection of the Jerusalem temple into the past as a real, more provisional sanctuary, the importance of which was stressed by opponents of the party which wished for a rebuilding of the temple. Of course the temple was built nevertheless; this, it is argued, is a consequence of a compromise with the priesthood. This theory appears untenable in such a neat form, but if it were toned down more and re-expressed in less extreme terms it could explain the insistence on the tent at a time when there were animated discussions about the rebuilding of the temple, as we shall see in Part Four, ch. III.

There seems no point in calling the attention of the modern reader to the fact that, regardless of the intentions of those who compiled it, this kind of narrative cannot now be considered historical. As Elliger puts it, the primary interest is in the 'truth of faith', to which the redactors testify with due certainty. But, continues Elliger, such a testimony was persuasive to the age of the exile or immediately afterwards, when this kind of certainty tended to recede following the catastrophe that had befallen the nation, in the train of real historical events which theological speculation, however profound, could not change. This chronological situation would explain the contacts which P has with Ezekiel and Deutero–Isaiah: the reference to the temple in Ezek. 40–48 as a prophetic vision, in P as a reference to the tent of earlier times, but in both cases the sign of a totally new beginning. Authors like Noth, Cazelles and Kapelrud, working with different methods, agree in dating Pg at a time not earlier than 562 and not later than about 550.

A very recent work moves on a completely different plane. Its starting-point is Gen. 17, with the institution of circumcision, an element which, as we have seen, is fundamental for P along with the observance of the sabbath and the food laws. It would assign an early date to this chapter on the basis of the vassal treaties mentioned in Excursus I and II above, but since the existence of these treaties is attested right down to the neo-Assyrian period, there are problems in using them to date a passage which could refer to them. Moreover, the work argues that after Gen. 17 other passages speak of circumcision, thus presupposing that it has already been instituted: Gen. 21.4; 34.15; Exod. 12.44; Lev. 12.3; Josh. 5.2–9. This fact had also been noted by Graf, when the documentary hypothesis was taking its first steps, and he had arrived at similar conclusions. However, the situation is already different: all the texts mentioned, with the exception of Gen. 34 and Josh. 5, belong to P and therefore must be ruled out as proof. Nor is it possible to argue that Gen. 34, a passage which presents notable difficulties on the historical level, refers to Gen. 17, even if it knows the practice of circumcision. In Josh. 5, vv. 5–7 are Deuteronomistic, as is the conclusion of v. 2 ('. . . a second time'); only the part which makes a general reference to circumcision is original. Even here, then, given that the passage refers to Egypt and not to Gen. 17, it is more obvious to relate the passage to Exod. 4.18–26. Elliger's theory can thus be defended much better. We therefore have to deal with two strata in P, but not in the sense argued by Wellhausen and by von Rad in 1934: a basic element, P^g, has been supplemented in various ways, P^s, some of which may be earlier than the basic element.

What has so far been lacking is a discussion of Kaufmann's theory: we have seen the importance of the elements which he has adopted; it is no longer possible to ignore them, and we need a new examination of them.

§4. *Composition*

The following passages are usually assigned to P: Gen. 1.1–2.4a; 5.1–27, 30–32; 9.1–7, 28f.; 11.10–27, 31f.; 17.1ff.; 23.1ff.; 25.7–20; 27.46–28.9; 35.9–13, 15, 22–29; 46.6–27; Exod. 1.1–7, 13f.; 6.2–30; 7.1–13, 19f., 23; 8.1–3, 12–15; 11.9–12, 20, 28; 12.40–51; chs. 25–31; 34.29f.; all Leviticus; Num. chs. 1–10; 13; 14; 16.1–19, 20 (in part); 22.1ff.; chs. 28–30(?) and 33–36. It should be noted that the last two sections are traditionally assigned to P, but that this is probably independent geographical material, certainly parallel to Josh. 13–21.

§5. *The final redaction of the Pentateuch*

Those who have followed the discussion so far will have realized how complex the process is which has led to the redaction of the Pentateuch, and what the fundamental points are which remain obscure. We know so little of what has happened to other literature in similar situations that we do not even have the possibility of comparative study. It is possible to note a certain consensus at most on the following points: J and E must have existed in parallel forms for many years until on the fall of the northern kingdom the E material passed to the south, where it was fused with that of J; this would explain why E exists in such a reduced form. Deuteronomy will have taken a similar course, especially if we suppose that it originated with the levites of the north, except that it was hidden, to be discovered and published during the restoration of the temple under Josiah. This would give us a combination of J and E, to which the book discovered in the temple was then added; the earlier traditions of P developed in parallel to this, probably in the Jerusalem sanctuary. At the end of the exile and during the restoration this material will have been collected together again along the chronological and historiographical lines of P. The result was a composition similar to, if not identical with, the Pentateuch as we now have it. This composition must have been finished before the final break with the Samaritans.

We shall be concerned a little later with the problem of a continuation of J, E and P in Joshua (ch. VI, §1), when we study the problem of the Deuteronomistic history work.

BIBLIOGRAPHY

§1. *Bibliographical studies:* J. Roth, 'Thèmes majeurs de la tradition sacerdotale dans le Pentateuque', *NRT* 90, 1958, 696–721; J. G. Vink, 'The Date and Origin of the Priestly Code in the Old Testament', *OTS* 15, 1969, 1–144; cf. also H. Cazelles and J. P. Bouhot, art. cit. (see bibliography to ch. I, §1), 280 ff.; D. Kellermann, *Die Priesterschrift von Numeri 1.1 bis 10.10*, BZAW 120, 1970. On the different sections of Leviticus see the commentary by Elliger (HAT 1966): on chs. 1–7 and 11–15, p. 21 with bibliography; on chs. 17–26, p. 23 with bibliography. Also on Lev. 1–7: A. van den Branden, 'Lévitique 1–7 et le tarif de Marseille, CIS 1, 105', *RSO* 40, 1965, 107–30; A. Capuzzi, 'I sacrifici animali a Cartagine', *Studi Magrebini* 2, Naples 1968, 45–76.

§2. For the possibility of a fall of man as part of the P account, K. von Rabenau in an unpublished communication to the Fifth Congress of the International Organization for the Study of the Old Testament, Geneva 1965.

§3. E. Reuss, *Die Geschichte der heiligen Schriften des alten Testaments*, ²1890; K. H. Graf, 'Die sogenannte Grundschrift des Pentateuchs', *Archiv für wissenschaftliche Erforschung des alten Testaments* I, Halle 1869, 466–77; A. Jepsen, 'Zur Chronologie des Priesterkodex', *ZAW* 47, 1929, 251–5; Y. Kaufmann, 'Probleme der israelitisch-jüdischen Religionsgeschichte', *ZAW* 48, 1930, 23–43, esp. 28–32.; id., *Tôlᵉdôt hā'ᵉmūnāh hayyisrā'ēlit* I.1, Tel Aviv 1937 (English abridgment by M. Greenberg: *The Religion of Israel*, Chicago 1960, 208f.); id., 'Der Kalender und das Alter des Priesterkodex', *VT* 4, 1954, 307–13; S. Mowinckel, *Erwägungen zur Pentateuchquellenfrage*, Oslo 1964, 44–6; J. G. Vink, art. cit. (§1 above), 9f; E. A. Speiser, *Genesis*, AB, xxvi; J. Hempel, *Geschichten und Geschichte im Alten Testament*, Gütersloh 1964, 113ff., 200ff.; G. von Rad, *Die Priesterschrift im Hexateuch*, Stuttgart 1934; O. Eissfeldt, 'Biblos Geneseōs', *Gott und die Götter: Festgabe für E. Fascher*, Berlin 1958, 21–40 (= his *Kleine Schriften* III, Tübingen 1966, 458–70); P. Humbert, 'Die literarische Zweiheit des Priester-Codex in der Genesis', *ZAW* 58, 1940–1, 30–57; A. Weiser, *Introduction to the Old Testament*, ET London 1961, 135–42; M. Noth, *A History of Pentateuchal Traditions*, ET Englewood Cliffs 1972, 8ff.; K. Elliger, 'Sinn und Ursprung der priesterlichen Geschichtserzählung', *ZTK* 49, 1952, 121–43 (= his *Kleine Schriften*, Munich 1966, 174–198; S. R. Külling, *Zur Datierung der 'Genesis-P-Stücke'*, Kampen 1964; cf. also Cazelles and Bouhot, art. cit., 289ff., and Vink, art. cit., 80ff. For the revelation of the divine name in P, cf. N. Lohfink, 'Die priesterschriftliche Abwertung der Tradition von der Offenbarung des Jahwenamens an Mose', *Bibl* 49, 1968, 1–8. For P in Joshua, see J. A. Soggin, *Joshua*, ET OTL, 1972, on individual passages; it does not seem that Vink, art. cit., 63ff, has succeeded in demonstrating the existence of more extended P-passages in Joshua. For the tent-temple polemic, cf. T. E. Fretheim, 'The Priestly Document: Anti-Temple?', *VT* 18, 1968, 313–29; cf. also A. S. Kapelrud, 'The Date of the Priestly Code (P)', *ASTI* 3, 1964, 58–64, and Cazelles and Bouhot, art. cit., 301ff. J. M. Grintz, 'Do not eat of the Blood', *ASTI* 8, 1972, 78–105, has argued in favour of a relatively early date. For the links between P and post-exilic Judaism see W. Brueggemann, 'The Kerygma of the Priestly Writers', *ZAW* 84, 1972, 397–414.

§4. There is a chart setting out a possible outline of the way in which the Pentateuch reached its present form in C. R. North, 'Pentateuchal Criticism', in H. H. Rowley (ed.), *The Old Testament and Modern Study*, Oxford 1951, 81.

ISRAELITE LAW

§1. *Introduction*

The specifically legal parts of the Pentateuch are a particularly important element in it. We have seen that a small section is traditionally attributed to J, a notably larger part to E and most to P; in the first two cases, however, we have indicated various difficulties which arise between the actual configuration of the material in question and its attribution to one of the two sources. It is easier to attribute material to P, though we must allow for later additions and interpolations of material which was probably autonomous in origin. In section 9 of this chapter we shall return to the problem in more detail. It goes without saying that, given the context, legal material in the strict sense is mixed with material which we would tend to regard as liturgical: the world of the ancient Near East did not distinguish between the regulations of the cult and those of civil life.

Whereas the synagogue drew important elements for its cultic and social life from this material, in the context of the Christian church it was usually neglected or at most read in the light of the Epistle to the Hebrews in the New Testament. However, it is of particular importance not only for the study of law in general and that of oriental law in particular, but also to anyone who is interested in the way in which the theological and ethical principles of the Old Testament worked out in practice. This is the case even though it is not always easy to discover whether particular laws were applied in practice and at what point, or whether they were simply programmatic.

After what we have been saying, it will not seem strange that even biblical law belongs in the wider context of the law of the ancient Near East. Thus we find resemblances and sometimes remarkable parallels. For this reason we shall note the points at which the differences in approach are particularly evident.

§2. *Law and faith*

Leaving aside some countries which have Islamic law, today the laws of the various developed countries have an essentially secular perspective: they are not inspired by religious principles and only deal with religious matters in those cases where they have become the object of public or private law. There are, of course, instances of state religion in which we have the acceptance of religious norms in the regulation of certain institutions in the political sphere. For example, in the case of marriage the question whether or not divorce is allowed is influenced by questions which, rightly or wrongly, go back to biblical thought. Again, a church or a religious community can in some cases enjoy considerable privileges compared with ordinary people who have a normal legal status. These instances, however, are fairly rare, and an authoritative current in jurisprudence considers them to be anachronistic survivals, incompatible with the demands and the principles of a modern state, which is regarded as having an essentially secular basis, like the philosophies which underlie it. The state may have an underlying philosophy, but not a theology; with very rare exceptions, modern philosophies are lay, regardless of the personal faith of their major representatives.

Of course, this does not mean that religious law no longer exists: every Christian religious confession, and Judaism too, has its own traditional laws, whether or not they are in codified form. These laws regulate relations within the community in question, whether on a public, personal or cultic level. Thus we have the canon law of the Catholic church, the *hᵃlākāh* of Judaism and certain regulations and constitutions of the Protestant churches. But these are norms which do not have any validity outside the community in which they have been formed, except where a special arrangement has been made with common law (for example the marriage concordat in Italy); therefore the power behind their application is extremely limited. In other words, their value on the practical plane does not transcend that of the statutes and regulations of an ordinary legal party.

If we turn now to the situation in the ancient Near East (and, moreover, to a great degree also that of the classical world), the situation appears to be exactly the opposite. The law is always sacral, whether it refers to the cult or to elements of social life; this is because it has been given either directly by the deity or indirectly with his approval. A dualism between 'church' and state is inconceivable, since religion is one of the principal foundations, if not *the* principal foundation, of the constituted order. As might be expected, the result is a series of extremely conservative societies. In many respects Israel is an exception here, because at least some prophets can visualize a separation between 'church', that is, the believing people, and state, that is, the people in an ethnic and political sense. In a few cases, indeed, they actually proclaim this. Speaking of the prophets, we shall also see how the concept of the 'elect remnant' began to give form to this distinction, though still in a very rudimentary manner.

There were always gods who were competent to mediate the law to man, generally in the person of the monarch, even when this was merely a new compilation of earlier norms. The best-known example is the stele of Hammurabi surmounted by a representation of the sun in the act of delivering the royal insignia to the monarch, his vassal. It should be noted, however, that the situation is not substantially different in the Old Testament. Yahweh delivers the law to Moses on Mount Sinai. However, we now know (and in the case of Israel we were occupied with this question in earlier chapters) that the process was much more complex. The most obvious consequence of this approach to the law is that every law has a sacral character and that all violations are thus automatically sacrilege; this explains in turn the frequency with which the death penalty was inflicted for crimes for which one might expect short periods of imprisonment or even a fine.

In Israel this emphasis on the sacral character of the law is evident from the beginning of the Decalogue: 'I am Yahweh, your God, who brought you out of the land of Egypt, out of slavery' (Exod. 20.1; Deut. 5.6). Considering this sacral character of the law it is likely that, as among so many other peoples in the ancient Near East, it was handed down by priests in the sanctuaries, especially and later exclusively in the sanctuary at Jerusalem. We have seen from Josh. 24 that it is possible that in the pre-monarchical period there were already ceremonies in which the law was proclaimed publicly, though we have no more than pointers in this direction. There is also a less obvious consequence for modern Western man, except perhaps for those who live in the area of Anglo-Saxon law: the state is not the source of the law, since in general the existence of the law is anterior to the formation of the state (and this is particularly apparent in the case of Israel). Even in events like Josiah's reform, religious reform is strictly connected with a series of political acts and indeed is itself a political act, while the king seeks to base his action on the by now well-known 'book of the law' found in the temple, whose complex relationship with the reform we examined in earlier chapters. Thus the state accepted and even sanctioned what already existed, and was not creative in this particular field. It is significant that even the special law about the prerogative of the king, Deut. 17.14–20, is pre-occupied with circumscribing and limiting the power of the monarch. In other countries maintaining the principle that the law comes from the deity, the law finishes in practice by deriving from the person of the monarch or from representatives chosen by him.

Like all the other problems of biblical criticism, the question of the relationship between biblical and Near Eastern law has only been raised in modern times. This, too, is because only from the beginning of this century, with the discovery of the codex of Hammurabi, has such a comparison been possible. As we have seen, this document, which is cut on a stele with phallic form, has a representation on its upper part of the delivery of royal insignia to the king by the sun. One particular reason for its importance is that it is almost complete, unlike the collections discovered in later times which have all been more or less fragmentary; it is also important that these later discoveries, fragmentary though they are, allow us to recognize the composite character of the codex, which thus appears to be the result of complex work with already existing material. The discovery of the Ham-murabi codex was very soon followed by that of early Assyrian, Hittite, Babylonian and Sumerian laws, all, as we have seen, more or less incomplete. This has made it difficult sometimes to understand individual passages or to determine the principles which have shaped the collections. In all these laws we often have striking parallels to laws of the Old Testament, as we shall see in due course; in other cases we have complete independence and sometimes a remarkable contrast. In other words, on the one hand Israel draws on the vast juridical tradition of the ancient Near East; on the other, in some quite significant cases it preserves a remarkable independence.

In the Pentateuch we have the following collections of legal texts which we could call codices if their content had been arranged in a more systematic way. We have already examined most of them:

(i) The 'Book of the Covenant', Exod. 20.22–23.33 and perhaps the beginning of ch. 24;

(ii) The Decalogue, Exod. 20.1–17//Deut. 5.6–21;

(iii) The Decalogue or Dodecalogue of Exod. 34.10–26;

(iv) The twelve curses of Deut. 27.14–26;

(v) The main body of Deuteronomy, chs. 12–26;

(vi) The 'Holiness Code', Lev. 17–26;

(vii) Various codices: on sacrifice, Lev. 1–7; on the priesthood, Lev. 8–10; on ritual purity, Lev. 11–15; on the Day of Atonement, Lev. 16. Other sections seem too fragmentary to allow a classification.

§3. *Characteristics of the biblical collections of laws*

It is impossible here to enter in detail into the problems about the legislation of the cult, of the priesthood and of sacrifice, and the regulations for the ritual calendar and the feasts which it covers. We shall limit ourselves to dealing with those passages which are more concerned with everyday life, those which we would now call secular.

The way in which the laws are distributed over the Pentateuch means that here, too, it is impossible to attribute their range to a single author or redactor; the traditional opinion which derives all law from Moses thus proves to be unfounded. This does not mean, of course, that his person may not be found at the beginning of the work which led to the promulgation of the legal codices in the Old Testament. Here a knowledge of the classical world, and especially of Justinian's collections (sixth century AD), in which it is possible to distinguish the authentic texts from later elaborations, sometimes with remarkable clarity, has provided specific help for studying biblical law. For example, in this way it is possible to recognize law originally intended for nomadic life, and later brought up to date for the new situation of a settled people, a situation in which such norms could apply only with substantial modification; however, this last contingency can hardly ever be verified, given the sacral character of the law. We should also notice at once that the normal distinctions of modern jurisprudence, between public law and private law, between penal, civil and administrative law, are impossible to apply because of the common denominator of sacrality, which makes all the laws qualitatively alike. Here, too, it is only possible to proceed by literary genres and to make inferences from them. Thanks to Alt in 1934, a formal classification has been established once and for all, and has also been accepted as applying to the majority of the laws of the ancient Near East: there are laws framed in apodeictic form and laws framed in casuistic form. We shall begin with the latter, as they present fewer problems.

§4. *Laws in casuistic form*

(*a*) Characteristic of the law formulated casuistically is its attempt to provide for every kind of situation which could arise as the result of an action or an omission, adapting the norm to each one of them. The description of these laws arises from this interest in the specific 'case' in which the law finds its application. In the 'Book of the Covenant', about half the laws are formulated in this fashion. They have a characteristic beginning, always with a conditional formula: 'If . . .' or 'Whenever . . .' or 'Given that . . .', etc. This beginning describes the essential characteristics of the action or omission. An analogous formulation is well known in a Mesopotamian milieu in the formula *šumma awilum* . . . = 'Whenever a man . . .' The description of the fact is then followed by a list of aggravating or mitigating factors or simply points of explanation. The style is normally objective, the discourse is in the third person; in the few cases where the second person appears we probably have explanations or comments on the law given to the community assembled in the sanctuary, sometimes in reply to questions about specific facts. The style is often prolix, as the material requires; it has been said to be 'non-Hebraic' in comparison with other specimens of biblical prose.

(*b*) We do not need to go far for the origins of casuistic law; all the ancient Near East knows norms formulated according to these criteria from the earliest period. Thus Israel did not invent them but took them over from its environment. However, we may notice two peculiarities of the genre in Israel, though they are purely negative.

(i) The casuistic formulation is never used in laws connected with the cult or with ethics. It is therefore at this point that perhaps a distinction between sacral and secular law might begin.

(ii) These laws are therefore neutral in the religious field. A typical example comes from the 'Book of the Covenant', which has already been mentioned. In Exod. 21.6; 22.8 we twice read *'elōhīm* = God (one of the reasons, perhaps, for attributing these passages en bloc to the E source), but it becomes obvious to anyone who sets out to make a translation that, although it would be possible to render the term by 'God', it could also be translated as 'the deity', without any specific reference to the faith of Israel. In other words, the text considers situations relating to a temple, but not typical of Israel.

Alt thought that these laws were taken over by Israel in the process of settling in Canaan, not least because the situations presupposed are typical of agriculture in a village setting. We shall see later how this theory has recently been modified.

§5. *Laws in apodeictic form*

These are the laws which contain a commandment or a prohibition with or without a sanction for the transgressor, and with no provision

for mitigations or special situations. As we have seen, in the Book of
the Covenant they appear mixed in with the others, but in Deut. 27
or in Lev. 17-26 they are collected together exclusively. In Exod.
21.22ff. we have an instance of a law which was originally framed in
apodeictic form and was then attenuated by additions of a casuistic
type.

These laws immediately give the modern legal consciousness the
impression of a primitive harshness, as though they had been made
by a society which was not interested in assessing degrees of culpability, criminal intention or the pressure of circumstances: the commission or omission of the actions seems sufficient reason for the
implementation of the penalty which, when it is provided for, is
almost always a capital one. The shedding of innocent blood (it does
not matter whether the homicide was premeditated, voluntary or
culpable) cries aloud to God (cf. Gen. 4.10, where the blood of Abel
cries out to God) and demands adequate expiation. It might be
concluded that the society which regulates itself by this kind of law is
necessarily a society at the beginning of its development; but it does
seem to be the case that these laws have for the most part been
replaced in the concerns of everyday life by laws formulated casuistically. But an evolutionary valuation of this kind is erroneous: we have,
rather, to do with laws which affect religious and therefore ethical
questions. Homicide is an offence against the God who gives life, and
therefore it can only be expiated by the death of the offender,
regardless of the degree of his culpability. To introduce other elements
of evaluation would be simply to move towards secularization.
Meanwhile, however, when an act which offended God in this way
was discovered within a community, this community had no alternative but to eliminate the guilty one from its midst. This was usually
achieved by executing him; on other occasions he was banished,
which in practice was an equivalent penalty.

Alt's hypothesis, taken up by some of his disciples, was that these
laws reflect the 'primitive' and therefore harsh situation of Israel in
the nomadic period, but from what has been said this is no longer
acceptable. Nor can it be argued, as it could be in the time of Alt, that
law framed in an apodeictic form was a prerogative of Israel, and
was not to be found among other peoples of the Near East. As a
result of such factors, Alt went so far as to suggest that these laws
went back to Moses, and thus formed the beginning of the 'laws of
Moses'.

§6. *Criticisms of Alt's theory and their developments*

We have attempted to indicate that the evolutionary approach of Alt's theory is untenable, but there is yet more to be said. Let us begin by repeating that the criterion of distinction, although essentially formal (it is not completely formal, as we have seen, since the content of the two categories of laws is different), not only remains valid but is the starting point for any investigation of ancient Near Eastern law. What made possible the evolutionary explanation of the two types of law was the fact, to which we drew attention above, that laws formulated apodeictically were not known elsewhere in the Near East. Now the situation is different: laws of this kind have been discovered in Mesopotamia and among the Hittites; the best-known collection is the edict of Ammisaduqa, king of Babylon, of the dynasty of Hammurabi, in the second half of the seventeenth century BC, which was published at the end of the 1950s, cf. *ANET*[3], 526ff.

Even before the publication of this document, however, doubts had already been raised about Alt's distinction by G. E. Mendenhall (see above). He began by indicating that it is impossible to relate Israelite law framed in casuistic terms to Canaanite law: as far as the latter is known from Ugaritic texts, it either reveals a direct Mesopotamian influence and therefore does not constitute an original element or, if it is autochthonous, does not display any parallel features to that of the Old Testament. Moreover, the discovery of laws formulated apodeictically among other peoples in the ancient Near East robs Alt's theory of another of its foundations. But Mendenhall does not limit himself to criticism; he offers his own solution to the problem. The laws formulated apodeictically are only guiding principles, whereas those formulated casuistically reflect judicial practice, the specific decisions of tribunals. Mendenhall finds such a system in Mesopotamia and among the Hittites. He goes on to argue that the system of laws formulated apodeictically, the principles, will have reached Israel through the patriarchs; the earliest collection of Israelite laws will then have developed on this basis. He sees his view supported by the fact that every substantial change of regime feels it necessary to codify the law afresh, citing as examples Hammurabi's accession to the throne of Babylon, the end of the monarchical period in Rome, the Napoleonic era in Europe, etc.; something similar will have happened to Israel on its settlement in Canaan.

Mendenhall's theory represents notable progress, but leaves doubts in at least one point: Alt has rightly observed that the laws in apodeictic form have ethical or religious elements as their content, whereas those formulated casuistically contain secular material. It is therefore difficult to see the progress from the former in the latter, because of the difference in content.

This fundamental gap has now been filled by the studies of E. Gerstenberger and W. Richter, who came to the conclusion, independently of each other, that the laws in apodeictic form did in fact contain principles, directives, but rather as ethical and religious imperatives directed at the ruling class and its instruction. Once this material had been published, it would be supplemented by material drawn from ancient Near Eastern legislation concerned with everyday life. What we have now is simply a synthesis of the two, which has left intact the religious and ethical legacy of Israel.

Two recent studies have meanwhile taken the discussion forward. The first shows that the laws formulated apodeictically can be classified as:

(a) 'Prohibitive' laws (so-called from Akkadian grammar), which in place of the usual imperative negated by 'al use the ordinary imperfect with lō' and relate to matters of principle, generalizing from specific situations;

(b) The counterpart of these is normally a law which commutes the death penalty for the offender;

(c) A third category includes the various laws of retribution, which limit the right of revenge by the victim on the guilty to the loss which has been suffered.

The second seeks, on the basis of these features, to eliminate the distinction between laws formulated casuistically and laws formulated apodeictically, considering it to be purely formal and therefore invalid for distinguishing two literary genres. A legitimate distinction should, it is argued, by the nature of things consider content as well as form. In the present state of research it is difficult to come to a decision on this latter suggestion. The problem is the greater because the distinction has been used with profit, as we have seen, not only in the study of Israelite law but also in the study of ancient Near Eastern laws generally.

§7. *Legal proceedings in the Old Testament*

The best way of seeing how the law functions in practice is to observe the course and conclusion of a trial. To us, the course of such a trial now seems very simple; there is a pragmatic and patriarchal flavour to it, a kind of 'rough justice' of the sort to be found in ancient Anglo-Saxon law. The difference in this case is that the place of meeting was the gate of the village, through which all those going out to work had to pass. The themes are also extremely simple and cover only relatively minor problems of the kind which can arise in an essentially agricultural community, however harmonious it may be: quarrels, woundings, incidents of various kinds, especially involving other people's animals, thefts, runaway slaves and so on. In this sense Hebrew law and legal processes are clearly different from Roman; there is no theory or philosophy of law, simply the most rapid solution possible of conflicts that arise.

Ruth 4 is a relatively late passage and certainly post-exilic, but it does reflect the very old usages preserved in the countryside, which are probably not very different from those of the period we are considering. Here we have the account of what we would now call a civil case; the renunciation of title to a right in a case of redemption and its transference to the party with the nearest claim, Boaz. The plaintiff sits at the only gate of the village, waiting for the arrival of those who constitute the tribunal. When the court is constituted it hears the cases of the parties (here the declaration of the parties) and passes sentence. In Jer. 26 we have a more complex case: this is a criminal trial of the prophet, who is accused of blasphemy, a crime punishable by death. Here we do not have the simple conditions prevailing in the village, but a tribunal constituted with much greater formality. Here too the prosecution and the defence are heard; the latter invokes a 'precedent', that of the prophet Micah, who, about a century earlier, had pronounced a similar phrase (3.12) without being prosecuted. Therefore the prophet is completely acquitted: as we would say, there is no case to answer. The sentence is given: 'This man does not deserve the sentence of death!' (26.16). The tribunal is said to be composed of 'the princes and all the people'. This suggests a kind of jury composed of the elders, and a public debate.

The lack of a basic theory of law does not prevent the Old Testament from formulating its scope with remarkable clarity. Deuteronomy 25.1 asserts that law is concerned with 'acquitting the innocent and condemning the guilty'. This statement has the utmost simplicity, but is an effective guide for the judge.

The death penalty involves the responsibility of all the community in whose name it is pronounced and executed: sometimes the entire community has to take part in the execution, which is carried out by means of stoning. Justice is therefore speedy and public, cheap if not free, and all assume their own responsibility without delegating it to others. Only with the monarchy do we see a new institution arise: appeal to the king (II Sam. 14.1–25; 15.2f.). In this way cases of greater importance are taken to a superior authority, independent of the local situation. Because of the silence of the sources, however, we do not know how this institution developed or what functions it had.

In many ways the older system might seem to have had advantages, but it was too simple to be able to operate effectively in more complex political situations. The relative size of the country, its composite ethnic structure in which the autochthonous Canaanite people were used to the supreme power of the monarch and an assembly with an aristocratic composition, the complication of social relationships in an economic and political structure which was continually tending to evolve, made its functioning difficult and sometimes paralysed it – or worse. We can see, for example, illicit interventions by the court in the local administration of justice and the monarch's unwillingness to submit to decisions of the tribunal. One example is that of Naboth's vineyard (I Kings 21; cf. also the charges against judges made by the prophets), even if this is extreme and therefore uncharacteristic. Here the local tribunal, as a result of court pressure, pronounces an unjust sentence on the basis of testimony which the judges know to be in bad faith. This is the explanation of the law in Deut. 17.8ff. which centralizes all cases of particular importance, and especially those which carry the death penalty, in the central sanctuary. This is to guarantee a debate which is as free as possible from outside interference.

§8. *Israelite law and that of the ancient Near East*

From what has been said, it should be obvious that there are many parallels between Israelite law and that of the ancient Near East. Rather than indicate these, it seems better to highlight the differences between Israelite law and that of the Near East, seeking where possible to elucidate the reasons for them.

Ancient Assyrian law is known for its harshness. The penalties inflicted on the guilty party are extremely cruel: physical mutilation for crimes which today would seem to be far from serious (cf. artt. 4, 5, 7, 8, 15, 18–21, 24, 44, 49, 54, etc.): in contrast, the codex of Hammurabi is more progressive, generally more so even than the Israelite collections of law. In art. 117 we have the institution of slavery for debt, cf. Exod. 21.1–11; Deut. 15.12–18; on the one hand, the codex of Hammurabi is more favourable to the debtor in that it limits his stay in the house to three years; on the other, Israelite law stipulates that the slave shall not be set at liberty without means. In art. 250 we have an important parallel to Exod. 21.28ff. in the case of damage to persons and property caused by a goring ox. For all its progressiveness from a juridical point of view, however, even this collection deliberately accepts a class justice in which the penalty for the same crime varies according to the status of the offender (free or slave, etc.) or the victim (priest, noble, artisan, and so on). Finally, Hittite law seems particularly mild; every misdemeanour committed by a free man can be expiated by a fine, although for slaves the law is as cruel as that of Assyria (cf. I, artt. 5, 7, 79ff.; II, artt. 73–76 etc.).

We have pointed out that Israel does not stand out from its neighbours for the progressive character of its law, and indeed was often retarded in this respect compared with neighbouring peoples; the absence of any physical penalty involving mutilation or torture should, however, be noted, notwithstanding the sometimes greater intrinsic severity: the death penalty for offenders in the religious and moral sphere which among other people can be commuted to a fine. The law of retribution is known in Israel only in a direct form, that is, it applies solely to the guilty party and not to a third person; moreover the death penalty is never exacted for crimes against propery, a concept which still had not been accepted among all the more progressive Western nations at the beginning of the last century! There is no deliberately class justice in Israel: the only difference is that between slave and free, but Exod. 21.20ff., 26ff. know significant limitations to the master's right to dispose of his slaves at his whim. This last element might not seem particularly progressive today, but it is remarkable for its time, especially when we consider the evolution in the institution of slavery in a juridically more progressive area like that of Rome and Greece centuries later. But Israel is also unaware of the exaggerated mildness of Hittite law, another way of devaluing the rights of the human person, this time of the victim.

We have already pointed out that we have no way of verifying how these norms functioned in practice, and this situation is an unavoidable lacuna. But the juridical principles are those that we have been able to see. The question now arises whether there is a way of explaining these notable differences between Israelite law and that of the more advanced neighbouring peoples. One explanation has been proposed by W. Eichrodt and in the present state of research seems to be the most probable: the particular respect for the human person which emerges from a comparison between Israelite law and other laws is the product of a religion which put the human person above every legal norm and therefore rejected every penalty which infringed on his dignity. We have only one case in which this valuation seems to be contradicted: Lev.20.14, where the penalty of burning is provided for a particularly grave and scandalous case of incest. This is probably, however, a very isolated relic of an ancient rule which is perhaps connected with certain very early forms of tabu.

§9. *Israelite law and the sources J and E*

We have seen that it is an integral part of the documentary hypothesis in its traditional form that the legal and ritual passages of the Pentateuch formed part of each individual source along with the narrative sections. For P, as we have seen, this did not present much difficulty, given the relation existing between the narrative passages and the legal and ritual passages, whereas in the body of Deuteronomy the absence of strictly narrative passages made the problem non-existent. However, we have also seen that the situation varies even within the legal sections traditionally attributed to J and E: there is no element here which allows us to assign the passages in question to the two earliest Pentateuchal sources except by a process of elimination, the same problem which is also present in the case of early Hebrew poetry. Starting from a completely different hypothesis, the late R. de Vaux reached similar conclusions in his great work on Israelite origins. We would therefore propose as an alternative to previous practice the study of the legal material in the Pentateuch traditionally assigned to J and E as autonomous forms. This is what happens, for instance, with the various literary genres of poetry, and wisdom or the prophets, leaving aside any documentary hypothesis. As we have seen, the problem of P is rather different in that an attribution of certain material to P takes account of elements which were already present in the source. But we have also seen that considerable narrative sections (the institution of the sabbath, of the food laws and of circumcision) can be classified as P[s]. It is therefore possible that in a relatively short time we might also have surprises over P in this area.

BIBLIOGRAPHY

§ 1. The legal material relevant to the present discussion is collected in a work which, though old, is still valuable: G. Furlani, *Leggi dell'Asia*

Anteriore antica, Rome 1929; cf. also H. A. Brongers, *Oud-oosters en bijbels recht*, Nijkerk 1960. Neither of these works has received the attention they deserve, on account of the language in which they were written. The interdependence between the Old Testament material and that of the ancient Near East has been examined by W. F. Albright, 'The Old Testament and the Archaeology of the Ancient East', in H. H. Rowley (ed.), *The Old Testament and Modern Study*, Oxford 1951, 27–47. For cultic law, cf. H. Reventlow, 'Kultisches Recht im Alten Testament', *ZTK* 60, 1963, 267–304, and R. Hentschke, 'Erwägungen zur israelitischen Rechts- geschichte', *Theologia Viatorum* 10, Berlin 1965–6, 108–33 (a basic study).

§2. For these problems, cf. M. Noth, 'The Laws in the Pentateuch', in his *The Laws in the Pentateuch and Other Essays*, ET Edinburgh 1966, 1–107.

§3. A. Alt, 'The Origins of Israelite Law', in his *Essays on Old Testament History and Religion*, ET Oxford 1966, 79–132.

§4. G. E. Mendenhall, 'Ancient Oriental and Biblical Law', and 'Covenant Forms in Israelite Tradition', *BA* 17, 1954, 26–46, 50–76 (also published separately as *Law and Covenant in the Ancient Near East*, Pittsburgh 1955); R. Kilian, 'Apodiktisches und kasuistisches Recht im Licht ägypti- scher Analogien', *BZ* 7, 1963, 185–202; E. Gerstenberger, *Wesen und Herkunft des 'apodiktischen Rechts'*, WMANT 20, 1965; W. Richter, *Recht und Ethos*, Munich 1966. Some of the apodeictic laws now appear in poetic form; the most obvious example being the *lex talionis* in Gen.9.6, cf. G. Fohrer, 'Über den Kurzvers', *ZAW* 66, 1954, 199–236. For new ways of interpreting the material previously classified as apodeictic, cf. H. Schulz, *Das Todesrecht im Alten Testament*, BZAW 114, 1969. A proposal to abandon Alt's classifications has been made by V. Wagner, *Rechtssätze in gebundener Sprache und Rechtssatzreihen im israelitischen Recht*, BZAW 127, 1972. The legal character of norms formulated apodeictically has recently been denied by G. Fohrer, *Theologische Grundstrukturen des Alten Testaments*, Berlin 1972, 166ff., but without sufficient reason. M. Weinfeld, 'The Origin of the Apodictic Law', *VT* 23, 1973, 63–75, supports Alt's theory, adducing comparisons with other legal material from the ancient Near East which had not previously been cited. See also S. M. Paul, *Studies in the Book of the Covenant in the Light of Cuneiform and Biblical Law*, SVT 18, 1970, 112–24.

§7. L. Köhler, *Hebrew Man*, ET London 1956, 149–75, and G. C. Macholz, 'Zur Geschichte der Justizorganisation in Juda', *ZAW* 84, 1972, 314–40 (important for royal justice in the south and for the legal reform of Jehoshaphat).

§8. W. Eichrodt, *Theology of the Old Testament* I, ET, OTL, 1961, 74–97. For the various oriental laws, cf. T. J. Meek, *ANET*³, 217ff. and 163ff., for Mesopotamian law; A. Goetze, ibid., 188ff., for Hittite law. This is of course a small selection of the vast amount of material which is now at the disposal of scholars, and a comparative study making use of it all would be very useful.

§9. R. de Vaux, *Histoire ancienne d'Israël* I, Paris 1971, 373ff.

VI

JOSHUA

§1. *The Deuteronomistic history work*

We have often referred in earlier chapters to the Deuteronomistic history work (to be abbreviated Dtr). This begins with the first of the 'former prophets'. From what we have seen, its prologue would have been made up of the brief historical summary in Deut. 1–4, while its name derives from the fact that at least two books, Judges and Kings, have been edited in such a way that time after time an early episode or an early notice has been inserted into a context which clearly displays the lexical and ideological features of the fifth book of the Pentateuch. This fact is generally accepted today and can easily be detected by anyone who reads the text in a good translation. The other two books, Joshua and Samuel, have not been subjected to revisions of this kind, but present large sections, often entire chapters, which are the work of the redaction in question and are inserted into the text at key points in such a way as to give an explanation, usually of subsequent and sometimes of previous events. For Noth in his work of 1943 the result of this redaction was a continuous historical text in which the key for understanding was given by the redactors, although they included the ancient sources of which they made use. At the same time, similar results were arrived at independently by A. Jepsen, whose work only saw the light in 1953 because of the war.

Discussion about Dtr does not therefore centre on its existence within the former prophets, which is universally recognized, but on just how much work is involved in it. Is it a matter of scattered interpolations and revisions which only assume a certain organic character here and there (in Judges and Kings), or do we have a history which is unified in scope and ideology, as Noth and Jepsen would prefer?

An answer to this question is far from easy: while it is true that the theories of Noth and Jepsen have found widespread acceptance, we cannot ignore the few voices which deny their validity, particularly as these are the voices of scholars of great prestige: among others we may cite O. Eissfeldt, G. von Rad and G. Fohrer. But whereas Eissfeldt, it should be noted, with due caution keeps the question open, von Rad and Fohrer, having noted that Noth's and Jepsen's observations allow of other interpretations, consider the hypothesis that the sources of the Pentateuch continued in the book of Joshua to be more probable. In other words, they maintain the theory of the existence of a Hexateuch, asking how Deuteronomy could ever have been detached from Dtr had it formed its beginning. The last question can, however, also be turned against those who raise it: however could Joshua have been detached from the Pentateuch if it had formed its conclusion? It is certain that the hypothesis of Dtr, while resolving a series of problems, also explains a certain unitary character in the former prophets and gives a clear reason for the otherwise strange title that is applied to them. Of course we must also allow for the interpolation into Dtr of material which originally had little or nothing to do with it, but it is certain that once the existence of large Deuteronomistic sections has been accepted, whether interpolated among early episodes or as an interpretative framework with which the early episodes were surrounded, it is easier to allow in consequence the existence of a unitary work of revision (which may have taken place in stages) than to stop without drawing what would seem to be the obvious conclusion. Of course it is necessary to recall that this is a working hypothesis and not an established theory.

In this Introduction we, too, accept the hypothesis of a Deuteronomistic history work and will demonstrate in each case what material has been left intact and what material has never belonged to the work in question.

What is the aim of Dtr? The most adequate answer has recently been given by Perlitt in these terms: 'The authors of the Deuteronomistic history work were not moved by a passion for writing history but by the need to give a theological explanation of the fall of the two kingdoms.' Beginning from the Babylonian exile (the last date given in II Kings 25.27–30// Jer. 52.31–34 is that of the pardon given to Jehoiachin about 561 by Evil-Merodach [Amel-Marduk], king of Babylon), the school thus sought to give the people of Israel a series of retrospective historical reasons, beginning from the conquest of Palestine and going down to the exile, to explain how the political destruction of the people was the result not of the weakness but of the power of Yahweh. He had warned the people for many centuries through the prophets, exhorting them to conversion. Failure to respond to this appeal had brought divine judgment upon the people, and oracles announcing judgment through the prophets were strictly fulfilled: the north had fallen between 722 and 720 BC (II Kings 17); the south suffered two exiles, one in 597 and the other, which was definitive, in 587. In other words, Dtr recalls the prophetic preaching, if only implicitly, though we also note in it a tendency to give a legalistic aspect to what the prophets had presented as a possibility.

Dtr tends generally to present its sources in an objective fashion, but the mere fact that it gives them a context which is obviously different from their original setting already includes the possibility, not to say the probability, of significant misrepresentations. Ahab of Israel was certainly not the pious and devoted king that Dtr would have liked, and he is therefore judged harshly (like all the kings of Israel, i.e. the northern kingdom, who were guilty of having caused or continued the breach with Judah, the southern kingdom); but we know that in the political field his work was crowned with success. Praise is heaped upon monarchs who adopted an orthodox religious position like Hezekiah and Josiah, but the attentive reader of the Bible will immediately see that their policies resulted in a series of catastrophes. The position of Dtr is sometimes ambiguous towards other monarchs: it first makes a prophet announce that Jeroboam I of the north will be invested by God with ten tribes, but it then feels constrained to condemn him, as it condemns all the kings of Israel, for theological reasons (cf. I Kings 11 with ch. 12). Perlitt is right, then, in seeing that what we have here is not what he has called a 'passion for writing history', but a history which is clearly written from a theological point of view and which never seeks to disguise its aim. Even here, however, the historiographical element comes in, because the school sets out to explain the present situation (in this case, the political destruction of the people and the exile) as the result of past choices, choices which Dtr obviously considers to have been wrong. But the choices which have brought down the divine judgment on the people are theological; they are not choices in the economic and political field. In this sense, then, Dtr is a history, but the criteria for the choice and collection of its material are substantially different from those that a modern historian would consider suitable for corroborating his theories. We must therefore accept without regret the accusation of tendentiousness, remembering at the same time that every history is tendentious in that it presupposes certain conditioning factors in history writing (no historian starts from an ideological void) and also certain features which it seeks to prove and certain aims which it seeks to achieve.

It is not easy to establish where the Deuteronomists composed their work: whether in Babylon during the exile, which is a minority opinion, or in Palestine, among the survivors of the catastrophe, as most suppose. We tend towards the former of the two alternatives. The inclusion of the unitary narrative of the conquest in Josh. 1–11 and the material relating to the division of the promised land in Josh. 13–21 (even if this is not Deuteronomistic in origin), the concentration on the rule of David, II Sam. 5–12 (though his sins are not glossed over) and other elements, seem to indicate that Dtr is not limited to criticism of the people's past, but also sets out to reinforce ancient traditions. The choice that Dtr makes of some of these is an important indication that it seeks also to strengthen and revive the people. If this theory is admitted, we should also allow that the aim in view was the restoration of the people, as with Ezekiel and later with Deutero-Isaiah.

For Dtr as for Deuteronomy the key point for judgment of people and events is Josiah's reform; the past history of the people is judged on the basis of the degree of faithfulness on the part of kings and people to the precepts of the reform in question. The words of the prophets, fulfilled by the exile, are also seen as pointing towards a conversion of both the community and the individuals who make it up, along the lines sought by the reform. But here too, notwithstanding the obvious tendentiousness of a judgment formulated on a basis of conditions established after the persons or events examined, Dtr is relatively objective: none of the kings, even Josiah, succeeded in fulfilling all the requirements in question. Thus the judgment acquires a relative character which is much to the credit of whoever formulated it. We also know that the problems which found their expression in Josiah's reform were almost certainly debated for centuries, so that a charge of anachronism would not be appropriate to the reality of the situation.

§2. Joshua: divisions and characteristics

We can now go on to examine the first of the 'former prophets' and the first complete book of Dtr, Joshua. We must immediately leave aside the opinion expressed in the Babylonian Talmud (Baba Bathra 14b), according to which Joshua himself was the author of the work, because this is absurd: in that case the author would be describing his own death in ch. 24.

The problem of the authorship of Joshua does not seem to be very different from the problem of the authorship of the Pentateuch which we have just been considering, with the exception that here there is no tradition about the author. Apart from the untenable Talmudic attribution, Joshua is anonymous. The person of Joshua is only the protagonist of the book. The expression 'until this day' appears often (4.9; 5.9, etc), which is the sign of a later revision; we often have cross-references to the Pentateuch, whose promises are 'fulfilled' in Joshua, especially between Deuteronomy and the Deuteronomistic passages, 8.30–35 and ch. 24; moreover, the narrative of the conquest is the obvious conclusion not only of the journey through the wilderness after the exodus, but also of the many indications scattered through the Pentateuch. It is thus quite understandable that in the past, as today, from Wellhausen onwards, the book of Joshua has been seen as the logical conclusion of the Pentateuch, which has thus been expanded into a Hexateuch. However, the situation seems more complex because of the presence of numerous Deuteronomistic texts, whereas in the Pentateuch, outside Deuteronomy, as we have seen, these are reduced to a very small number. Even for those who do not admit the hypothesis of Dtr, the problem of Joshua when examined thoroughly seems substantially different from that of the Pentateuch. In any case, the final Deuteronomistic revision has not completely concealed the presence of sources which could be connected closely with the Pentateuchal sources even by those who accept the Deuteronomistic hypothesis. Chapter 2 (leaving aside some of the dialogues, where we have a good deal of Deuteronomistic material); 6.25; 11.13; 15.13–19, 63; 16.10; 17.12f., 14–18; 19.42, some of which has an obvious parallel in Judg. 1 (see §3 below), appear similar to J (and Noth himself accepts the existence of this kind of material which he attributes to a 'collector', German *Sammler*). The non-Deuteronomistic part of ch. 24 is usually attributed to E, while a few scattered verses, 14.1a; 17.4 and 19.51, seem to belong to P. At all events, the tone of the book is now determined by the Deuteronomistic insertions, chs. 1 and 23, which virtually form the beginning and the end of the book. The second of these chapters is important because it often speaks of divine judgment and of exile, should the people not accept and observe certain obligations towards Yahweh. Here, then, we seem to have the reason why the whole book has been transmitted.

The book of Joshua naturally falls into three parts. The first comprises a unitary account of the conquest by the twelve tribes of Israel under the leadership of Joshua: they cross the Jordan, pitch camp in the region of Gilgal near to Jericho, occupy successively

Jericho and Ai, make a first expedition towards the south and then head north. This narrative leaves many areas unsecured, while others are occupied without our knowing how Israel could have crossed the intervening territory. This is particularly evident in the case of the expedition northwards: how did they arrive there without having occupied the central zone to make the journey possible? We hear that Israel had control of Shechem and its sanctuaries (cf. 8.30ff. and ch. 24), but not how this was obtained: was it by an arrangement with the people of the place, by conquest or in some other manner? All this, of course, presupposes that we start from the actual biblical narrative, according to which all Israel crossed the Jordan near Jericho and succeeded in conquering the greater part of the country under the leadership of Joshua, so that it could be divided. The second parts, chs. 13–21, speaks of this division of the country. Only the tribes west of the Jordan are considered: the others had already received what was promised them before crossing the Jordan. To show solidarity with the others, however, they also shared in the expedition: they are present in ch. 22 but then cross the Jordan to return to their own land. The third and last part relates to the assembly at Shechem, chs. 23 and 24, which has already been mentioned several times; ch. 23 is the purely Deuteronomistic version, while ch. 24 is a version revised by the Deuteronomists.

A last point of interest is the break in continuity between Joshua and Judges: twice we have a note about the leader's dismissal of the tribes, Josh. 24.28 and Judg. 2.6, and twice a note of his death, Josh. 24.29f. and Judg. 2.8–10. It is easy to see that we have the same texts in each case. The explanation is simple. This is the same narrative, which is now interrupted by Judg. 1.1–2.5, a passage which belongs to J or to the source which Noth calls 'the collector'. It is a text which, as we have pointed out and will go on to note in more detail, has remarkable parallels with Josh. 15–27. Here is an almost typical example of texts interpolated into Dtr with which the work itself has nothing to do.

Judges 1 is one of the more important texts for anyone concerned with the study of the 'conquest' of Palestine. Leaving aside the problems of the individual sections, which we cannot examine here, this text gives a picture of the conquest which is markedly different from that attested in Josh. 1–12:

(a) According to this earlier tradition, there was no unitary conquest of Palestine under a single leader. On the contrary, there was a settlement made by individual tribes or the nuclei of tribes or other groups in succession, especially in the wilderness and in mountain country which was thinly populated and therefore particularly suitable for movements of this kind. This text also shows that when the invaders attempted to settle in the fertile plain they were routed.

(*b*) In its initial phases the 'conquest' was an essentially peaceful operation of settlement by semi-nomadic elements in the territories mentioned above. When it came to armed encounters, the technically more advanced Canaanites found no trouble in getting the upper hand. In territories with little or no population, on the other hand, there was no opposition. Gen. 34, a text which is difficult to interpret historically and which is independent of the book of Joshua, clearly shows that the sovereigns of the Canaanite city-states did not see any objection to groups like those of the ancestors of Israel settling in areas of their territory, since they brought with them abundant herds and at the same time populated uninhabited areas.

(*c*) In any case, the conquest was not over with Josh. 12 since 13.1ff. and Judg. 1 list a series of city states and their territory which Israel did not succeed in conquering. On the contrary, Israelites were sometimes forced to become their subjects.

These considerations make extremely unlikely, not to say impossible, the account in Josh. 1–12 according to which the country was conquered by a united Israel under a single commander and composed of a federation of the traditional tribes. This also robs of its foundations the theory according to which the country, when conquered, was divided (cf. chs. 13–21) by drawing lots for the parts which each tribe was to occupy. This immediately raises the question whether the sacral alliance of Israel of which we find evidence in the pre-monarchical period was already in existence at the time when the first immigrants set foot in Canaan. The institution of drawing lots, quite apart from being impossible on the political plane, also appears extremely problematical in purely technical terms: how would it be possible to draw lots for a territory of hundreds of thousands of acres which was for the most part scarcely occupied and in addition almost totally unknown? A division of the land by lot would, however, fit in perfectly with the later pre-monarchical period and the early period of the monarchy (that is, between the end of the eleventh century and the end of the tenth or the beginning of the ninth century BC) as a rotation of tribal lands between the various clans or families, an institution which then began to die out under the impetus of the political and economic situation.

The list of the groups to whom the land is assigned is interesting: we have Caleb, Judah, Ephraim, Manasseh, Benjamin, Asher, Simeon, Zebulon, Issachar, Naphthali and Dan; Levi, the priestly tribe, receives 48 places for its support, six of which are also sanctuaries for the murderer: his blood cannot be shed within their walls. As can be seen, as well as the tribes in the traditional sense of the term, descending from Jacob, we also have other groups which were later absorbed into the tribes, like Caleb. The total number is twelve, but the two Transjordanian tribes of Reuben and Gad are missing, making a total of fourteen (or thirteen if Caleb is considered as a group which receives land but is not a tribe in the strict sense; the figure twelve can only be obtained by counting Ephraim and Manasseh as a single group, that of Joseph). Be this as it may, counting up the twelve tribes of Israel constitutes a separate problem to which we shall return in our discussion of Judg. 5 (cf. ch. VII, §3 below). If we then wanted to add Machir (presented in ch. 16 as 'son' of Manasseh) and the Kenites (Judg. 1.16), a group similar to Caleb, we would have an even larger number. Thus we have a series of ethnic and geographical problems to which we shall return shortly.

Earlier in this chapter we indicated the promises or commandments contained in the Pentateuch which were fulfilled in Joshua. Some of the more important ones have already been noted: Exod. 13.19// Josh. 24.32; Deut. 11.29// Josh. 8.30ff.; among the internal contradictions in the book should be mentioned those of Josh. 15.63 with 18.28; 23.8 with 24.14. Deuteronomistic influence or interpolations can be clearly seen in chs. 1 and 23 and in the speeches in chs. 2, 10 and 24.

§3. Problems

The problems that we have sketched out in the previous paragraph can thus be posed along the following lines: first of all that of the relationship between the unitary narrative of the conquest (Josh. 1–12) and the fragmentary account (Judg. 1); secondly, the question of the territory assigned by lot, although parts of it had not yet been conquered and the rest was scarcely known.

Judges 1 shows clearly, as we have seen, that the 'conquest' took place in a fragmentary way, in stages, and was limited to certain regions in which the autochthonous population had no interest: deserts, steppe, mountains, wooded country. This made the settlement of the new arrivals automatically either a matter of no interest to the city states or in some cases even desirable. The settlement took place, but only in small groups. The same chapter shows how most of the time the efforts of the invaders to occupy better territory (in general in the plains or at any rate in the more densely occupied areas) came up against the resistance of the inhabitants, who almost always proved victorious. In this, Judg. 1 coincides with the parallel passages of Joshua, both probably fragments of J or of the 'collector' (cf. Josh. 15.13–19 with Judg. 1.8; Josh. 16.9 with Judg. 1.29; Josh. 17.11–18 with Judg. 1.27). Josh. 19.47 and Judg. chs. 17–18 belong in the same category, but the two narratives are now too different for us to be able to examine them together.

Now there is a substantial difference between the 'unitary' narrative of the conquest and the fragmentary account, a form of incompatibility which can only be overcome if we admit that we have to do with two different phases of the 'conquest'; but this last possibility is gravely compromised by the fact that the 'unitary' narrative precedes the other. Another difficulty is presented by a feature to which we have drawn attention, that Judg. 1.1–2.5 interrupts the narrative of the final dismissal by Joshua and his death and burial, thus clearly revealing its character as an interpolation into Dtr. But the fact that the same materials are to be found in part in Joshua immediately suggests that here we have a source which the Deuteronomistic narration wanted to replace but which later, in circumstances of which we know nothing, succeeded in finding its way into its Deuteronomistic context. However, it resisted harmonization with this context and was simply ignored. Comparison with patterns of settlement in the ancient Near East certainly make the fragmentary version of the conquest more likely in both geographical and ethnic terms, whereas the other has every appearance of being a later 'official' version.

Credit for having demonstrated this state of affairs goes to A. Alt and his pupils, principally M. Noth. Given the premises, they developed a theory according to which the conquest would originally have been presented in a fragmentary fashion with scattered theological elements: later the new version was superimposed, replacing these elements with a rich unitary version. Continuing the investigation, they established that in Josh. 1.1–10.15 almost all the occupied territories (with very rare exceptions) correspond with those of Benjamin. The sanctuary of Gilgal also belonged to Benjamin up to the beginning of the period of the monarchy (I Sam. 11). The obvious conclusion, though it has still to be universally accepted, is that the version of the conquest which ended by becoming 'canonical' for the whole of Israel was that of Benjamin, handed down through the Gilgal sanctuary, though it is impossible to establish the process by which this happened.

In other words, whereas J or 'the collector' still had the fragmentary account of the conquest which has been preserved in fragments of
Joshua and Judg. 1, the unitary version, which was of considerable
theological importance because it shed light on the great acts of God
of which the conquest was the most miraculous sign, very soon
became the official and canonical version, replacing the other. It is
difficult to say here how that happened and through whose work:
everything seems to indicate that there was a pre-Deuteronomistic
redaction, which immediately makes one think of E, but it is impossible to go beyond conjecture pure and simple.

§4. Geographical texts

Chapters 13–21 are a separate problem. They obviously do not
belong to the Deuteronomistic redaction in either style or content; in
their present position they follow on the whole-hearted acceptance of
the theory of the unitary conquest of the country. Otherwise, their
inclusion in their present context would be obscure. The insertion
into Joshua is thus obviously later than the substitution of the
'unitary' theory for the 'fragmentary' theory: there is no other possibility. They have generally been neglected by Christian theology, but
all the more avidly investigated by students of the geography and
history of the Bible and the ancient Near East, and present such
special problems that it is obviously necessary to devote independent
study to them.

Here too the figure of A. Alt stands in the foreground. In 1925 and
1927, after the most painstaking studies, he reached the conclusion
that in these texts we have two different literary genres: the description of a series of boundary lines between the various tribes obtained
by means of a consecutive listing of places which serve as fixed points
of reference; and a system of provinces essentially connected with
Judah. The first system reflects the situation of the country between
the conquest and the institution of the monarchy and is therefore very
old, still in the last years of the second millennium BC; the second, on
the other hand, relates to the reorganization of Judah under Josiah
after the later conquests and cannot therefore be earlier than the
second half of the seventh century BC. The validity of this distinction
can now be considered to have been generally accepted, and the same
is true for the dating of the lists of boundaries. The situation over the
districts of Judah is rather different: the studies of the Americans
F. M. Cross and G. E. Wright and of the Israelis Y. Aharoni and Z.

Kallai-Kleinmann propose that the dating of these districts should be moved considerably further back in time, in some cases going as far as the tenth century BC.

There is now a certain degree of agreement over the details of the levitical cities in ch. 21 and the cities of refuge in ch. 20. The majority feel that the list in Josh. 21, to which we have parallels in Num. 35 and I Chron. 6, also reflects a historical situation certainly not earlier than the time of David and Solomon, since many of the areas mentioned were conquered under them. However, opinions differ over the dating of the institution. A. Alt again thought of the time of Josiah; W. F. Albright, on the contrary, of the earlier period of the monarchy. The opinion of the Israeli B. Mazar is not very different: he puts it some decades earlier still. The same problem also arises over the cities of refuge, which are all contained in the earlier list. F. Horst, following the lines traced by Alt, also suggested the time of Josiah here: once the sanctuaries in which the guilty party could find refuge had been abolished, it was necessary to institute the cities in question. R. de Vaux, on the other hand, after a thorough examination of Josh. 20.1–9; Num. 35.9–35 and Deut. 4.41–43; 19.1–13, argued that this institution was independent of the tribes and not earlier than the time of Solomon; he was strictly against dating the institution any later. In any case, we know as little about it as about the levitical cities.

§5. Thought

The thought of the book of Joshua is obviously that of successive editors and redactors of the material collected in it, and is thus in a special way that of Dtr. Thus we find a rigid separation of Canaanite elements and a description of the massacre of the autochthonous population with which Israel came into contact. That massacres of the kind described in the book of Joshua never happened (or at most happened in a much reduced form, on a local scale) is sufficiently demonstrated by the presence of a numerous Canaanite population during the whole of the first half of the first millennium BC, especially in the kingdom of Israel. This population several times succeeded in getting the upper hand over Israel. Thus we have a theory typical of Deuteronomy and Dtr, intended to underline the need for the people of God not to accept the customs of these peoples and sometimes to avoid all contact with them. Only once in Joshua do we have the concession of a vassal relationship between the indigenous population and the invaders, that of the Gibeonites in ch. 9 (there is no

doubt as to the essential historicity of this episode, since the theme
reappears in II Sam. 21.1ff., where the house of Saul is punished for
having violated this agreement). Here Dtr constructs a theme in the
narrative according to which Israel had been deceived by the
Gibeonites, who claimed that they had come from a long way away.
No notice is taken of the incongruity of the fact that in that case there
was no reason why they should ask to be vassals, an incongruity
which 'Israel' should have noticed. Jericho (ch. 6), Ai (chs. 7–8),
places in the south (ch. 10) and the north (ch. 11) are thus given over
to extermination. For the crime committed by an Israelite during the
conquest of Jericho, all Israel suffers a defeat before Ai, a place which
Israel succeeds in conquering only after the guilty person has been
identified and punished: this is an interesting narrative variation on
the Deuteronomic and Deuteronomistic doctrine of reward and
punishment. The strength of the combatants has little or nothing to
do with their victories: these are the work of God. Jericho (ch. 6)
falls after a complex cultic act; the narrative about the sending of
spies in ch. 2 suggests that a text now lost spoke of an attack in force
against Jericho, and this is presupposed by a variant attested in LXX
2.18, cf. 24.11; the battle in ch. 10 is won by Israel following the well-
known miracle which caused Galileo Galilei so much difficulty and
which has at least one notable parallel in the Iliad. The events at
Shechem in ch. 24 are centred on the recitation of the confession of
faith and the renewal of the people's obligation, which is just what
Josiah sought to do in his reform. In this way history is simplified and
reduced to a great schematic unity: the conquest of practically all the
country en bloc by 'all Israel' with Joshua at its head, but in reality
led by Yahweh: once occupied, the territory can be easily divided,
and as material Dtr or possibly others afterwards used ancient texts
which speak of frontiers and districts. It is evident that the theological
element, the preaching and the instruction, finished in practice by
having almost absolute dominance over history; and it is the latter
which reappears, almost on the sly, in Judg. 1 and the parallels in
Joshua. Of course, Dtr was not created out of nothing; it made use of
already existing liturgies and tried to historicize them. Instead of
looking for possible agreements between the narrative and the results
of archaeological excavations, it is necessary rather to start from the
principle that Dtr (or possibly others even earlier) historicized pre-
existing liturgical material and used it for its preaching.

BIBLIOGRAPHY

Commentaries:

D. Baldi, SacBib, 1952; M. Noth, HAT, ²1953; H. W. Hertzberg, ATD, 1957; F. M. Abel, JB, ²1958; J. Gray, NCB, 1967; J. A. Soggin, ET, OTL, 1972. For a critical text of LXX (as far as 19.38): M. A. Margolis, *The Book of Joshua in Greek*, Paris 1931–8.

§1. For the Deuteronomistic history work: M. Noth, *Überlieferungs-geschichtliche Studien*, Halle 1943; A. Jepsen, *Die Quellen des Königsbuches*, Halle ²1956; H. W. Wolff, 'Das Kerygma des deuteronomistischen Geschichtswerks', *ZAW* 73, 1961, 171–86 (= his *Gesammelte Studien*, Munich ²1972, 308–24); J. A. Soggin, 'Deuteronomistische Geschichts-auslegung während des babylonischen Exils', in *Oikonomia. Festschrift O. Cullmann*, Hamburg 1967, 11–17; id., *Joshua* (above), 3ff.: J. M. Schmidt, 'Vergegenwärtigung und Überlieferung', *EvTh* 30, 1970, 169–200. For the Deuteronomists' history writing, cf. W. Dietrich, *Prophetie und Geschichte*, FRLANT 108, 1972. For an evaluation of the work of M. Noth, cf. G. Minette de Tillesse, 'Martin Noth et la *Redaktionsgeschichte* des livres de l'Ancien Testament', in C. Hauret (ed.), *Aux grands carrefours de la révélation et de l'exégèse de l'Ancien Testament*, Tournai and Paris 1967, 51–75. For the quotation from Perlitt see his *Bundestheologie im Alten Testament*, WMANT 36, 1969, 7. For a bibliography on the 'former prophets' cf. E. Jenni, 'Zwei Jahrzehnte Forschung an den Büchern Josua bis Könige', *TR* 27, 1961, 1–32, 97–146. For the passages about the prophets within the Deutero-nomic history work cf. W. Dietrich, op. cit. For the view that the last Deuteronomic redaction took place among the exiles in Babylon see J. A. Soggin, 'Der Entstehungsort des deuteronomistischen Geschichtswerkes', *TLZ* 100, 1975, 3–8; cf. E. W. Nicholson, *Preaching to the Exiles*, Oxford 1970. See also the Mainz dissertation by A. N. Radjawane, *Israel zwischen Wüste und Land*, 1972, with numerous critical bibliographies.

§3. A. Alt, 'The Settlement of the Israelites in Palestine', in his *Essays on Old Testament History and Religion*, ET Oxford 1966, 133–69; id., *Erwägungen über die Landnahme der Israeliten in Palästina*, Berlin 1939 (= his *Kleine Schriften* I, Munich ³1963, 126–75). His theories have been contested, especially by archaeologists from the United States: cf. W. F. Albright, 'The Israelite Conquest of Canaan in the Light of Archaeology', *BASOR* 74, 1939, 11–23; J. Bright, *Early Israel in Recent History Writing*, SBT 19, 1956. The whole problem is discussed by M. Weippert, *The Settlement of the Israelite Tribes in Palestine*, ET, SBT II 21, 1971. For the question of the presence of J material in Joshua see S. Mowinckel, *Tetrateuch-Pentateuch-Hexateuch*, BZAW 90, 1964, 17ff., 33ff.; for 'the collector' see M. Noth's commentary (above).

§4. A. Alt, 'Das System des Stammesgrenzen im Buche Josua' (1927), and 'Judas Gaue unter Josia', *PJB* 1925 (= his *Kleine Schriften* I, Munich ³1963, 193–202 and II, Munich ³ 1964, 276–88); F. M. Cross, Jr, and G. E. Wright,

'The Boundary and Province Lists of the Kingdom of Judah', *JBL* 75, 1956, 202–26; Z. Kallai-Kleinmann, 'The Town Lists of Judah, Simeon, Benjamin and Dan', *VT* 8, 1958, 134–60; Y. Aharoni, 'The Province-List of Judah', *VT* 9, 1959, 225–46. For the levitical cities and the cities of refuge, cf. W. F. Albright, 'The List of Levitical Cities', in *L. Ginzberg Jubilee Volume*, New York 1945, 49–73 (a fundamental study); B. Mazar, 'The Cities of the Priests and the Levites', *SVT* 7, 1960, 193–205; F. Horst, 'Recht und Religion im Bereich des Alten Testaments', *EvTh* 16, 1956, 49–75 (= his *Gottes Recht*, Munich 1961), 260–91, esp. 59 = 273f.; R. de Vaux, *Ancient Israel*, ET London 1961, 16off.; id., *Histoire ancienne d'Israël* I, Paris 1971, 493ff.

VII

JUDGES

§1. *Title and content*

The title of the book derives from the figures who are the protagonists in the greater part of it, called in Hebrew *šōpᵉṭīm*, from the root *špt* = normally 'judge'; it is therefore logical that the word has always been translated 'Judges'. However, the root has an archaic sense, well attested in Ugaritic but now also in some Old Testament passages, in which it means 'govern': this sense also appears in Phoenician and Punic, cf. the well-known Carthaginian *suffetes* during the Punic wars. In the Old Testament, this sense is clearly attested, among other passages, in Pss. 96.13 and 98.9, where the rule of Yahweh is mentioned. It is therefore likely that this is the sense to be preferred and that we should not translate the word 'judges' but 'rulers' or something similar. In fact, if we are looking for a negative counter-proof, we never see the 'judges' in the Old Testament exercising any kind of judicial function: the only exception is that of Deborah (Judg. 4.4f.), but here her function precedes her call to be a 'judge'! This is therefore a title assigned to someone who exercised particular powers within the tribal alliance of Israel before the monarchical period.

The 'judges' may be formally divided into 'major' and 'minor' judges; the former are called by Yahweh to deal with situations of especial danger, usually enemy attacks, and are sometimes called 'saviours', which was probably their original title. In the case of the latter, on the other hand, we only have notes of an anecdotal kind, but a particularly detailed chronology. They could, strictly speaking, have been supreme magistrates of the law, even if there is no exact notice about them. We shall return to this problem later.

The book is now divided into three parts: the beginning comprises the section 1.1–2.5 which we discussed in the previous chapter; this speaks of two expeditions, one by the tribes of the south, i.e. Judah, and the other by tribes from the centre and the north, i.e. Israel in the strict sense. We have also seen that the notes recorded here have handed down the echo of the difficulties encountered by individual groups whenever they attempted to occupy territories which were not more or less uninhabited. The second part makes up the body of the book and in it we have notes relating to the judges (2.6–16.31). Here we have an account of the prowess of five or six 'major judges', figures who now appear to be operating on a national scale (this is once again the theme of 'all Israel' with which we are already familiar from Joshua), though a closer examination shows that they work within well-defined territories. We cannot therefore exclude the possibility that, contrary to the theory of the book, which has them acting in chronological succession, they could sometimes also have been active to some degree simultaneously. There is also mention here of the 'minor judges'. Their title was probably extended at a later stage to the 'major' judges, who, as we have seen, were originally called 'saviours'; no important historical narratives about them have been handed down to us. The 'major judges' are: Othniel (3.7–11); Ehud (3.12–30); Deborah and Barak (chs. 4–5); Gideon (chs. 6–8); Samson (chs. 13–16); the 'minor judges' are: Tola and Jair (10.1–5); Ibzan, Elon and Abdon (12.8–15). Jephthah is a figure who seems to combine the characteristics of both (10.6–12.7), while Shamgar ben 'Anat (3.31 and 5.6) and Abimelech (ch. 9) have nothing to do with the 'judges'. The third part of the book, finally, presents two episodes: the conquest of the land in the extreme north by Dan (chs. 17; 18) and a civil war against Benjamin (chs. 19–21). It is, however, the body of the book which presents a series of problems which we shall examine briefly.

§2. The body of the book

The variety of narratives contained in 2.6–16.31 does not prevent the 'body' of the book from having an internal unity which is immediately apparent to the reader. This is disconcerting: it is a quite singular phenomenon, given the diversity of the narratives which the book contains, a diversity which would rather lead one to expect a certain lack of unity in this section. Instead, we have a reduction to schematic categories which stands out clearly: every episode is preceded by an introduction in which it is reported how the people have sinned, how God, to punish them, has sent particular enemies against them (or has delivered them into the hand of particular enemies), how the people have repented and how God has then sent them a 'saviour' in the person of a leader who has guided them to victory and thus liberated them. In this way each of the 'major judges' is dealt with in turn.

This schematic form has every appearance of being artificial, especially when it is repeated a number of times, as happens in this case. It is the product of a later organic rethinking which sets out to use an ancient episode to instruct audience or readers. In this case the instruction is offered in a theological key: sin causes ruin on the historical plane also, and repentance leads to salvation. Such a valuation of events certainly does not arise from the historical experience of the protagonists or their contemporaries. However, these introductions, which are all followed by episodes dealing with individual judges, are appropriate for conferring on the book the unitary aspect of which we have been speaking; thus the redactors allowed the ancient traditions on the heroes in question to be reported almost intact, seeing that the introduction gave the reader the key to their interpretation. Now these introductions prove to be Deuteronomistic in both style and content; among other things, the formulation of the doctrine of reward and punishment also appears typical. The chronology of the 'major judges' is also stereotyped: it always speaks in terms of forty, twenty or eighty years, which does not happen with the 'minor judges'. It would seem, then, that Dtr had at its disposal the ancient narratives about the 'saviours', but that they had no chronology, or the chronology did not fit in with that of Dtr. In the second case apparently the opposite happened: there were no relevant historical narratives, but the chronology was that much more exact; perhaps the redaction, which was not Deuteronomistic, found here notes of an annalistic type which included a precise chronology, as we shall soon discover in the books of Kings. In any case, given that we have no other chronological material available for comparison, this chronology is now of little use.

We have pointed to the fact that the redactors, faithful to their ideal of 'all Israel', wanted to extend the activity of the 'major judges' to the whole nation, but that their theory would not stand verification in geographical terms. And indeed it is not difficult to see that the 'major judges' operate in regions which are geographically limited to the abode of a particular group or the area immediately adjacent to it. Thus, in the very important Song of Deborah (see the next section) only the tribes directly interested take part in the battle, while the rest either prevaricate or do not reply at all. The process is particularly clear in the story of Gideon. It begins with 'all Israel' and finishes with 300 men of Abiezer (7.1ff.), that is, members of Gideon's clan; the inconsistency is obvious from the fact that all Israel is said first to

have been sent home, having been discharged so that the smallness
of the number of combatants can shed a brilliant light on the divine
work (another theme which appears in Joshua): they are then recalled
after a few days or even after a few hours. Samson is another figure
who is active in a limited area: the description of his work is decked
with legendary elements which sometimes come from folklore. It is
limited to the region of the boundary between the Philistines and Dan
which at that time was to the west of Benjamin: the struggle probably
ended in the defeat of Dan, as we see them looking for new territory
in chs. 17–18. Jephthah, on the other hand, works essentially in
Transjordania. Dtr has no chronology for the last two heroes, and it
is possible that to begin with, attempts were made to exclude them
from the work as being ethnically and morally inadequate: they then
will have found their way back into it. The episode of Abimelech in
ch. 9 also stands outside the scheme. It is a text of considerable
historical importance and is basically authentic: it is connected with
the destruction of Shechem, which on the basis of excavations carried
out in the area has been dated at the end of the twelfth century BC.

§3. The 'Song of Deborah' (Judg. 5)

This is considered to be the earliest poetical composition in the Old
Testament: the passage does not show signs of Deuteronomistic revision, but this advantage is almost nullified by the state of the text,
which is like that of the greater part of early Hebrew poetry: whether
the text has been corrupted in transmission or has been composed in
a dialect little known to us, the fact remains that it is generally difficult
and in some cases impossible to understand. In any case, it is full of
Canaanite terminology and shows obvious stylistic as well as lexicographical affinities with Ugaritic poetry.

The theme of the ancient song is how Israel, in the course of a
battle, succeeds in vanquishing a coalition of Canaanite city states
situated around the plain of Jezreel and here assembled under the
leadership of a certain Sisera. This is one of the regions which according to Judg. 1 Israel did not succeed in occupying because it was
tenaciously and skilfully defended by its inhabitants. Yahweh is presented as coming forth from Seir, cf. Deut. 33.2; Ps. 68.8 and Hab. 3.3,
all very ancient or archaizing compositions. Seir is in the region of
Edom, situated in southern Transjordania, and the mention of the
name is often used to attribute to Sinai a location in north-western
Arabia, thus different from the traditional location in the peninsula

which bears its name. Verse 14 shows that the invitation to take up arms was issued to all the tribes, but that only Ephraim, Benjamin, Manasseh or Machir, Zebulon, Issachar and Naphthali joined in the battle. Those who did not take part, probably because they were far removed from the area of operations and consequently were less interested, and who attract taunts from the song, are Reuben, Gilead (the territory inhabited by Gad), Dan and Asher. Levi, Judah, Simeon and Caleb are completely missing, whereas the Kenites appear at the end, in a decisive act of hostility. This suggests an obvious conclusion which we have hinted at earlier: the constitution of the tribal league must have been extremely weak if each of the tribes acted exclusively in its own immediate interests. It is probable that Judah did not yet belong; the absence of Levi can be explained by the fact that it was no longer an ethnic unity but was now exclusively priestly. This would be confirmed by the references in Judg. 17.7 and 19.1, where we find levites of Judah and Ephraim respectively.

The historical basis of this epic is relatively easy to discover. It is one of the attempts to eliminate the Canaanite enclaves which divided the central tribes, Ephraim, Manasseh and Benjamin, from those in the north of the country, by virtue of their domination of the plain of Jezreel. We find that only those tribes are involved in this enterprise whose territories bordered on the plain and who had a direct interest in either eliminating this situation or at least modifying it substantially in their own favour. With good reason, the Israelite victory is felt to be an extraordinary event: up till then Israel had always been defeated in struggles against the Canaanite city-states. It was therefore celebrated in epic style, even if it did not lead to the occupation of the region in question: it was enough that communications had been secured between the northern central area and the north. The miraculous element, testimony to an intervention by Yahweh, was provided by a torrential rainfall which made the battlefield impossible for the horses and chariots of the Canaanite army, whereas the light infantry of the Israelites were not substantially impeded. Now given that fighting tended to take place in the spring and the summer, no rain should have fallen in this season. Rainfall would have been a quite extraordinary event in the eastern Mediterranean, where there is usually no rain from April to September (the last rainfall recorded there in this season was in 1957!). This is the origin of the statement in the poem (vv. 20ff.) that the stars fought on the side of Yahweh: here was a direct intervention by the head of the heavenly armies.

The poem will not date from much after the events described. It is

usually assigned to the twelfth century, towards either the beginning
or the end, depending on what criteria of dating are adopted.

§4. *Chapters 17–21*

Chapters 17–21 are of considerable historical importance, not only
because they have not been subject to Deuteronomistic redaction (at
least there are no traces of this) but because they testify to situations
obtaining at the time of the sacral alliance, that is, before the institution of the monarchy. In general the phrase 'In those days there was
no king in Israel . . .' (17.6; 18.1; 19.1) is seen as a criticism of the
political situation obtaining under the tribal alliance, a situation
which is seen as one of open disorder. The Deuteronomistic history
work, on the other hand, tends to exalt these times and the mode of
government then prevailing; other explanations of the phrase are,
however, quite possible.

(a) Chapters 17–18 narrate some episodes in the migration of Dan
towards its definitive abode in the north of Palestine, after having
left its original place of settlement to the west of Benjamin. Josh. 19.47
also alludes to this migration (Leshem is only a variant of Laish, the
place called Dan by the Danites). This place, treacherously attacked
by the Danites, became their capital and the site of their sanctuary,
whose priests boasted Mosaic descent. In the present redaction of the
story, 18.30 speaks of the conquest of the region and a deportation of
its population under Tiglath-pileser III in the second half of the
eighth century BC (cf. II Kings 15.27); it is obviously later than
the events to which it refers, and the polemical note against the
sanctuary and those who founded it cannot be ignored. The reader
must necessarily receive a totally unfavourable impression, especially
knowing the kind of cult practised in the sanctuary. Thus we have
polemic against the sanctuary from within the northern kingdom or
an argument used by the south to disqualify the north in this field also.

The presence of this polemical element is particularly interesting
in a text which is not prophetic and which, as we have seen, is free
from Deuteronomistic revision.

(b) In chs. 19–21, on the other hand, we have an episode which
narrates the causes and the consequences of a holy war. This institution is also attested outside ancient Israel: we have an example of it
also among the Moabites in the second half of the ninth century BC
on the stele of King Mesha (lines 15f., *KAI* no. 181, *ANET*[3], 320ff.).
At the end of the battle, everything belonging to the vanquished

enemy, people, animals and possessions, is consecrated to the deity in one great barbarous extermination: the victor is not to stain his hands with the spoil. Now those chapters present a situation which at first sight we might consider different: the object of the holy war is not a people hostile to Israel nor are they defeated; they are one of the tribes of Israel, Benjamin. This tribe is accused of having given refuge to the authors of a savage crime, to which we have a partial parallel in Gen. 19, and therefore of complicity in it. Having rebelled against the dictates of the holy law, the tribe is attacked and exterminated, to such effect that to repopulate the region it is necessary to resort to a stratagem which has remarkable parallels in the history of religions and ethnology, among other events in the rape of the Sabine women. The friendship which linked Benjamin with the central and northern region of Transjordania, Gilead, and which so notably helped Saul some time later (cf. I Sam. 11; 31), seems to date from this time. Excavations at Gibeah (present-day Tell el-Fūl, a few miles north of Jerusalem to the east of the main road), later the site of Saul's fortress, have discovered clear evidence of violent destruction towards the end of the twelfth century, which could obviously be connected with the episode recorded here. We would thus seem to have archaeological evidence of the substantial historicity of the facts narrated. But what was the cause of them? Atrocities committed by a people can serve as a pretext for war, but are rarely its cause, especially if, as in this case, the war is a civil war. The historian may find a more prosaic and cynical explanation of the real facts. Both Ephraim and Benjamin were engaged in vigorous expansion. Conditions for the latter were particularly disadvantageous, compressed as it was between its powerful neighbour to the north and the territory of the city-state of Jerusalem and part of Judah to the south. This, rather than failure to observe the laws of the sacral alliance, seems to have been the real reason for the conflict which led to the extermination of Benjamin, even though it can only remain a hypothesis. Judg. 12 also speaks of a civil war, again with Ephraim, but this time against the population of Transjordania, whose friendly relations with Benjamin we already know.

§5. *The origins of the book*

Underlying the book, then, and especially the main body of it, we have narratives which originally told of the deeds of Israelite heroes who had saved their people from distress, heroes working in a limited geographical and ethnic sphere. Dtr has made them heroes of 'all Israel', or perhaps this had already happened in an earlier redaction. It was, however, Dtr which gave the body of the work its present character, with an introduction to each episode containing the doctrine of reward and punishment. The heroes in question were almost certainly originally called 'saviours', and if we leave out of account the Deuteronomistic redactional material it is in fact possible to discover what have been called a 'book of saviours', in which the early traditions were probably collected together before the final Deuteronomistic redaction. Chapter 1 has a history of its own, as we have seen, while chs. 9; 17–18; 19–21, the first of which shows signs of strong Deuteronomistic redaction, give information which is remarkably useful. The same goes for the 'minor judges', whose chronology appears in chs. 10 and 12.

The Hebrew text seems in good condition, but the two versions of the LXX, Codex B (Vaticanus) and Codex A (Alexandrinus) have so many variants that the critical edition by Rahlfs reproduces them both side by side. This allows us to conclude that a much more complex textual tradition underlies the book than the Hebrew text might lead us to suppose.

§6. *Thought*

As in the case of Joshua, the thought of Judges is above all that of the Deuteronomistic redactor, who has revised ancient tradition according to his doctrine of retribution, making use of instances which prove his theory. The original traditions have been well preserved, at least in part, and we can see that much of them is made up of epic material and folklore. This does not mean that we do not have here testimony to quite a mature Yahwistic faith: the problem of religious syncretism is raised by the narratives about Gideon in terms of the alternative Yahweh or Baal, even if the stratification of these traditions is extremely complex. The first redaction cannot be earlier than the eighth century BC; a distinct preference for the theocratic regime over against the monarchy is expressed in 8.22ff., but here too there is already mention of all Israel, a concept which, as we have seen, also belongs to a later stage of redaction, even if it is still pre-Deuteronomistic. Taunts against the institution of the monarchy also appear here and there in ch. 9, especially in Jotham's fable (9.7ff.), though this may have been inserted in the passage at a secondary stage and thus may be no more than an interpolation in the style of wisdom literature

against the abuses of power. But even in the very early Song of
Deborah (ch. 5), as in the narratives about Gideon, the real victor is
Yahweh. God can choose even equivocal people like Jephthah for his
own purposes (11.1f.). Through all the ancient narratives, even those
like e.g. that of Ehud (ch. 3) which seem to have no theological
content at all, there is an expression of faith in the God of Israel
which can even make good all human deficiencies. A particularly lofty
ethic appears in passages like chs. 19–21, when the dishonourable act
against the protégés of the Benjaminites is judged with the words,
'Was ever such a thing seen in Israel?', and followed by the punishment of those responsible and their accomplices, even though this
operation weakens the ranks of the new arrivals. The fact that criticism may show the event to stem from very different motives does not
affect this basic position.

BIBLIOGRAPHY

Commentaries
C. F. Burney, ²1920 (reprinted 1970); H. W. Hertzberg, ATD, ²1959;
A. Vincent, JB, ²1958; A. Penna, Sac Bib, 1963; J. Gray, NCB, 1967;
R. G. Boling, AB, 1975.

§1. E. Täubler, *Biblische Studien*, Tübingen 1958; W. Richter, *Traditions-
geschichtliche Untersuchungen zum Richterbuch*, Bonn 1963; id., *Die Bearbeitungen
des 'Retterbuches' in der deuteronomischen Epoche*, Bonn 1964; id., 'Zu den
"Richtern Israels"', *ZAW* 77, 1965, 40–71. For 1.1–2.5 see G. E. Wright,
'The Literary and Historical Problem of Joshua 10 and Judges 1', *JNES* 5,
1946, 105–14; S. Mowinckel, *Tetrateuch-Pentateuch-Hexateuch*, BZAW 90,
1964, 17ff. For the chronology, cf. G. Sauer, 'Die chronologischen Angaben
in den Büchern Deut. bis 2 Kön', *TZ* 24, 1966, 1–14.
§2. For the Gideon cycle cf. W. Beyerlin, 'Geschichte und heilgeschicht-
liche Traditionsbildung im Alten Testament', *VT* 13, 1963, 1–25; L.
Schmidt, *Menschlicher Erfolg und Jahwes Initiative*, WMANT 38, 1970, ch. 2;
for that of Samson, J. Blenkinsopp, 'Structure and Style in Judges 13–16',
JBL 82, 1963, 65–76.
§3. There is an up-to-date study by D. N. Freedman, 'Early Israelite
History in the Light of Early Israelite Poetry', in H. Goedicke and
J. J. M. Roberts (eds.), *Unity and Diversity*, Baltimore and London 1975,
3–35. Among older studies see W. F. Albright, 'The Song of Deborah in the
Light of Archaeology'? *BASOR* 62, 1936, 26–31; A. Weiser, 'Das Debora-
lied', *ZAW* 71, 1959, 67–97. Albright, 'Jethro, Hobab and Reuel in Early
Hebrew Tradition', *CBQ* 25, 1963, 1–11, esp. 9ff., holds that the song
belongs to the J tradition.

§4. Fo chrs. 17–18 see M. Noth, 'The Background of Judges 17–18' in B. W. Anderson and W. Harrelson (eds.) *Israel's Prophetic Heritage*, London 1962, 68–85. For chs. 19–21, A. Besters, 'Le sanctuaire central dans Jud. XIX–XXI', *EphThLov* 41, 1965, 20–41; J. Muilenburg, 'Mizpah of Benjamin', *StTh* 8, 1954, 25–42. The historical background to the civil war is illustrated by K.-D. Schunck, *Benjamin*, BZAW 86, 1963, 57–79 (with bibliography). For an investigation of the fortress of Gibeah cf. L. A. Sinclair, 'An Archaeological Study of Gibea (Tell el-Fūl)', *AASOR* 34, 1960, 1–52, with Noth's very favourable review in *ZDPV* 78, 1962, 91–4. For the formula 'there was no king . . .' cf. S. Talmon, 'In those days there was no king in Israel', *Proceedings of the Fifth World Congress of Jewish Studies 1969* I, Jerusalem 1971, 135–44 (Hebrew; English summary 242f.): he takes *melek* to stand for *šōpēt*, so that the phrase is simply a reference to a vacancy between the rule of two judges.

§6. For the context of Judges, cf. E. Jenni, 'Vom Zeugnis des Richterbuches', *TZ* 12, 1956, 257–74.

VIII

THE BOOKS OF SAMUEL

§1. *Introduction*

Eusebius of Caesarea (*HE* VI, 25.2), quoting Origen, and Jerome in his *Prologus Galeatus* (his preface to the books of Samuel in the Vulgate) report that originally the two books of Samuel and the two books of Kings were a single work. The division into four books has been attributed by some to the LXX: with written vowels the LXX will have needed more scrolls than the one or two used in Hebrew. And in fact in the LXX the books in question are called I, II, III and IV Kingdoms or Kings, names and divisions which have passed over to the Latin Bibles and which therefore still appear today in some Roman Catholic translations of scripture. In any case, the question is purely one of form: the content remains the same whatever the divisions. These divisions have certainly been made in a quite illogical way, almost haphazardly, which could justify the empirical criterion put forward above. Only I Samuel has a logical conclusion, with the death of Saul and some of his sons; II Samuel should end with the death of David, but his death appears only in I Kings 2. In turn the division between I and II Kings splits at least two episodes between one part and the other, as we shall see in the next chapter.

In the Babylonian Talmud (Baba Bathra 14b) Samuel himself is said to have been the author of I and II Samuel, but there is no foundation to the note: the prophet dies and his death is described twice (I Sam. 25.1 and 28.3), a typical case of parallelism. What we have here, therefore, resembles (though in lesser degree) what we have seen in the case of Joshua: Samuel is the protagonist of the first book (not of the second), but certainly not its author, and his role is sufficient explanation for the book's title.

§2. Content and textual problems

In the 'former prophets' Samuel precedes Kings and follows Judges; Ruth belongs with the Writings (cf. Part Five, ch. V below). It is perhaps possible to connect Judg. 17–21 with the beginning of Samuel, to which it might form an introduction intended to explain why it became necessary to introduce the monarchy in Israel. However, this does not particularly affect the interpretation of the book.

The first seven chapters speak of Samuel's youth: of his birth in circumstances which are at least remarkable, of his service in the temple of the tribal alliance in Shiloh, of the defeat of Israel in its struggle against the Philistines, culminating in the capture of the ark (a kind of container for the law), and of Samuel's activity as judge and prophet. At first sight the narrative has certain unitary and coherent characteristics, but on a closer examination it can immediately be divided into a number of units, though these are connected together in quite a harmonious way. The text presents some irregularities: for example, in 1.20–27 we have a play on words around the verb $šā'al =$ 'ask' and its passive participle $šā'ūl =$ the one who is asked for. This, however, is referred to the person of Samuel, whereas etymologically (and these plays on words are always centred on an aetiological onomastic etymology) it should be connected with Saul and not with Samuel. For that reason, one might suppose that the narrative originally told of the birth of Saul and at a later date was revised in a polemic fashion in such a way as to glorify his opponent Samuel, but there are strong arguments against such a conjecture – for example, the name of Saul's father, which we know to be Kish and not Elkanah. Chapters 8–15 refer to the first phase of relationships between Samuel and Saul, and tell of the institution of the monarchy. We have three versions of this event, which differ in detail although they have many elements in common: (a) ch. 8 + 10.17–27 and ch. 12; (b) 9.1–10.16; 13.5–15; (c) ch. 11; 13.1–4, 16–23 and ch. 14. The first version is very much against the monarchy, though some authors have felt that this tendency is the consequence of a later interpolation. The other two accounts are favourable towards the monarchy, but the description in the last account of the process by which Saul became the first king seems to be much closer to events. The theory has recently been proposed that each of the three narratives was originally the account of how Saul was elected king in three tribal groups; the three narratives would then have been extended to 'all Israel' in the way with which we are familiar from Joshua and Judges. This suggestion should be taken seriously, but it needs to be developed further before it will seem usable. It should also be noted that chs. 7 and 12 have been considerably revised by Dtr, whereas in 13.5–15 and ch. 15 the reasons for the rejection of Saul are rather obscure but apparently connected with the prerogatives which the king will perhaps have to exercise in the cult. The majority of scholars believe that the latter of the two chapters is late, given that it reflects the preaching of the eighth-century prophets, even if it is probably still pre-Deuteronomistic.

Chapters 16–31 describe the conflict between Saul and David, interpreted by the redactors as the consequence of rejection by Yahweh. The narrative shows the progressive decline in the mental health of the first king, while at the same time his general David moves about in circumstances which are more than equivocal. The heroic death in battle of Saul and some of his sons (ch. 31) serves almost to resolve a tension which has become intolerable.

In II Samuel, chs. 1–4 show the difficulties under which the country struggled after the death of Saul. In the south, David, a vassal of the Philistines, had assumed rule over Judah and had a capital of his own, Hebron; in the north Abner, commander of Saul's surviving troops, was *de facto* king, while the institutional figurehead was the weak and insignificant Eshbaal, surviving son of Saul: his name is regularly distorted to Ishbosheth, but it can be reconstructed from Chronicles. In chs. 5–8, David, elected king of Israel after Eshbaal's death, founds a real empire. After conquering the city-state of Jerusalem, which is promptly elevated to become the capital, he defeats the Philistines and occupies or makes vassals of, all Transjordania and Syria. At the same time he establishes the best of relations with the great Phoenician city-states of Tyre and Sidon. Chapters 9–20 speak of the difficulties encountered by the king in his domestic policy, difficulties which involved his own family: he only escaped by a miracle when his son Absalom revolted. Finally, an appendix, chs. 21–24, reports some isolated episodes from the life of the king: 21.1–14 seems to be the basis for ch. 9, which begins with David's question whether any survivors of Saul's family are still alive.

The ordered and coherent appearance of the narrative, especially from a chronological point of view, has already been noted; it does not, however, succeed in concealing some less coherent elements. We noted above the position of the first part of ch. 21, but it is also obvious that chs. 9–20 have their logical continuation and conclusion in I Kings 1–2. Further, we have seen that there are three narratives about the institution of the monarchy, which we may either regard as parallels or take to have arisen successively in three different areas and then to have been extended to 'all Israel'. The anti-monarchical narrative begins in I Sam. 7, in which Samuel achieves a notable victory over the Philistines, and ends in ch. 12, where Samuel takes leave of the people. As we have seen, however, both chapters have clearly been revised by Dtr, which in ch. 7 evidently wanted to demonstrate that the situation was not as grave as the people made it out to be in ch. 8, since Samuel had defeated the Philistines. In fact this note is tendentious, and we now know well that it was the danger from the Philistines which accelerated the institutional move towards monarchy in Israel, even though in any case the time was ripe. This late redaction of the narrative has not disguised the fact that it evidently reflects an ancient dispute about the appropriateness of the institution of the monarchy, while the royal prerogatives listed by Samuel in 8.11ff., which correspond with those of the sovereign in a Canaanite city-state (though they only applied in Israel on exceptional occasions), clearly reflect an ancient document. The narrative in ch. 11 is close to events: Saul was proclaimed king of the people once his longed-for victory over the Ammonites and the liberation of the territory of Jabesh-Gilead in Transjordania had revealed to all that God was with him and that therefore he would from then on be the leader of Israel. This interpretation of the institution of the monarchy is substantially different from the one we know to have existed among neighbouring peoples, and it probably has its origin in the nomadic era of Israel and its ancestors. There are a number of duplicates: in I Sam. 10.11 and 19.24 we have a double explanation of the proverb 'Is Saul also among the prophets'; the first occurrence is probably the earlier and the more authentic. There are also a number of contradictions: in I Sam. 16.23 David comes to court as an expert musician, while in vv. 18ff. he is described as a mighty warrior; however, in the story of his fight with Goliath in ch. 17 he appears as a youth who is presented to Saul for the first time (v. 55). We also have different narratives about David's flight and the change of side in which he becomes a Philistine vassal (21.11–16 and 27.1ff.), while we have two accounts of the death of Goliath (ch. 17 and 11 Sam. 21.19, where he is killed by a different hero, cf. also I Chron. 20.5). The circumstances of Saul's death also differ: in I Sam. 31 he kills himself by falling on his own sword, whereas in II Sam. 1 an Amalekite mercifully kills him so that he does not fall into enemy hands alive, though seriously wounded. As we have seen, the death of Samuel is narrated twice, I Sam. 25.1 and 28.3, whereas chs. 24 and 26 give duplicate versions of the episode in which the fugitive David generously spares the life of Saul. The relationship between the sanctuaries of Mizpah and Gilgal is not clear. Both are mentioned in connection with Saul, provided the theory that makes them regional sanctuaries in which each group of tribes will have elected Saul king will hold.

It is therefore evident that here, too, we have the product of a union of various traditions, though any attempt to distinguish sources, as in the Pentateuch, must be considered unsuccessful. All that can be recognized is a discreet Deuteronomistic redaction; this has affected the text so little that some scholars have been able to deny the existence of a continuous Deuteronomistic history work on the basis of I and II Samuel. The theory is more likely which sees Samuel as a series of different cycles and scattered traditions, assembled by a redactor who was not of the Deuteronomistic group and was certainly earlier than Dtr. He will have followed a scheme which Dtr was able to take over, limiting his revision of the material to minimal interference. Anyone who accepts the hypothesis of a continuous Deuteronomistic history work will therefore have no difficulty in allowing that the final Deuteronomistic redaction accepted en bloc this material which had already been shaped by previous redactions, only adding small retouchings here and there.

§3. Independent units

The units which are certain to have been originally independent and which can be clearly identified in the work are not always very different from those into which the book can be spontaneously divided. They can, however, be classified by distinct criteria, generally by themes.

(a) A first narrative is that about the ark and its vicissitudes, from the time when it falls into the hands of the Philistines up to its triumphal entry to Jerusalem through the work of David (I Sam. 4–6; II Sam. 6). More or less a generation elapsed between its capture and its triumphal return to Israel, during which time it stood for many years in a domestic sanctuary only a few miles away from the future capital. The narrative now appears to have been inserted into the wider context of the struggle between the Israelites and the Philistines. The beginnings of this struggle were narrated in Judg. 13–16, in the story of Samson, and it developed under Saul down to his heroic death. Presumably it came to an end under David (II Sam. 5.17ff.), who defeated the Philistines. The story of the ark has its own stylistic and lexicographical peculiarities (it has some humorous touches, as for example when it relates how the statue of Dagon, god of the

Philistines, was found one morning face downwards before the ark which, though in captivity, is still a sign of the presence of Yahweh; or when it describes the humiliating illness with which the Philistines were afflicted, so that they were persuaded to abandon the ark). Its aim is simply to show how the ark reached Jerusalem under David, having been captured a number of decades earlier by the Philistines. The importance of the ark cannot have been particularly great, since later references are extremely rare (I Kings 8.1, 6, paralleled in Chronicles; Jer. 3.16, a note which it is extremely difficult to evaluate in a historical sense).

(b) Another section is made up of the narratives about relationships between Samuel and Saul (chs. 8–15). We have already seen that these are the result of a remarkable piece of editing with duplicates, contradictions and incongruities. It is not even clear whether or not an attempt at a biography of the first unfortunate king of Israel underlies this collection or up to what point the materials included have been used with a degree of objectivity; it is certain that whoever saw to the redaction of these episodes supported first Samuel and then David against Saul. Another fact indicating the composite character of this material is that we have a neat break at the end of ch. 14. The chapter clearly concludes a literary unit; as we have seen, ch. 15 is a late construction in which we cannot see whether and up to what point ancient traditional material may have been used. The historical value of the material also varies: we have seen that ch. 11 is very old and almost certainly close to the events narrated, and the same also applies for chs. 13 (not vv. 5–15) and 14. The theme of the breach between Samuel and Saul is interesting: in 13.5–15, when Samuel is late for his appointment and the army is about to break up because of its inactivity, the king himself offers a sacrifice; in ch. 15 a variant of the LXX at 15.12f. provides a similar motive, but it is by no means original over against the Massoretic text. In any case, it seems possible to see the reason for the breach between Samuel and Saul in a dispute over the prerogatives of the king in the cult. Be this as it may, although the redactor of the history favours first Samuel and then David, he does not keep silent about the military exploits of Saul and his son Jonathan. He recognizes their considerable achievements in the field and in civil affairs.

(c) Another unit which is directly linked to the preceding section is concerned with the relationship between Saul and David up to the former's death in battle. This is a sometimes ruthless chronicle of the fluctuating relationship between these two heroes of ancient Israel, and there is nothing to prevent our thinking that the same hand is at work here as revised the previous section. This narrative, too, is clearly in favour of David: Saul is now robbed of the divine blessing which had been at the heart of his earlier success. Moreover, he gives signs of mental unbalance with a progressive form of persecution mania. It certainly would not improve the king's mental state to hear the women singing under his window, 'Saul has slain his thousands, but David his ten thousands' (I Sam. 18.17; 21.11; 29.5) but Saul's reaction was clearly pathological. This is confirmed by the homicidal gesture with which he turns against his general in 18.10f. The redactor calls this pathological state 'an evil spirit from Yahweh', a concept which is also attested in classical literature. It remains the fact that, apart from the mental health of the king, his work in the military field was effectively obscured by the deeds of his young general, a situation which evidently put a serious question-mark against the king's future in a milieu in which success in the military field was the incontestable sign that God was with the person who could boast it. The fact that the narrator clearly took the part of David against Saul does not, however, mean that he has defamed the latter, or that he has particularly embellished David's deeds. David is presented here as a man with considerable personal authority, authority which does not even spare Jonathan, the heir to the throne. Forced to flee from Saul, David now becomes leader of a band of outlaws (22.2 describes David's troop as composed of 'people who were in distress and every one who was in debt and every one who was discontented') and collaborates with the Philistines. Indeed, the text does not hesitate to declare that it was quite by chance that David did not take part in the battle in which Saul and his sons were killed (I Sam. 29.1ff.): the Philistines did not trust David and preferred to send him against their and his enemies in the south. And while part of the responsibility would fall on the persecution inflicted by Saul on David, David's position was difficult to justify – so much so that he gave up being a vassal of the Philistines as soon as possible.

In this narrative we also have two quotations from the 'Book of the Upright' which has already been mentioned (cf. above Part One, ch. VI, §4, i): II Sam. 1.19ff. and 3.33; these are compositions which a great many authors do not hesitate to attribute to David himself.

The author or redactor of the history may, then, have been an official at the court of David or Solomon, with a thorough knowledge of events and access to all the available material, well disposed to the ruling house without making partisan judgments on its adversaries or favouring his own side uncritically. The one improvement which might have been made is that perhaps Saul could have been presented in all his greatness: he was, after all, the first king, that is, the first person who succeeded in giving political unity to Israel and in defeating the Philistines and enemies coming from Transjordania, an achievement which he accomplished in an almost desperate situation. And if one can talk of mistakes – here was a man who paid for them himself.

(d) The 'succession narrative', II Sam. 9–20 (perhaps preceded by 21.1–14 and ch. 24, cf. the question in 9.1, which is probably a reference to the episode described in 21.1ff., and the beginning of 24.1ff., the form of which is similar to that of 21.1ff.) and I Kings 1–2, is a historiographical work of remarkable importance. After the classic study by L. Rost, the narrative has often been considered to be one of the earliest history writings in the world, if not the earliest. The author is a supreme storyteller and sees history as a series of interconnected events linked by a chain of cause and effect, and at the same time dominated by the concept of divine recompense. In this sense, then, we have a precursor of Dtr. The narrative begins with a few factual details: David sought to possess the wife of one of his generals, Uriah the Hittite, and did not hesitate to have the latter killed to remove the impediment to his marriage. Now comes retribution: as David has destroyed the family of Uriah, so his own family is to be destroyed by the divine judgment (cf. the speech by the prophet Nathan in II Sam. 12.7–12). The criterion which unifies this historiography is thus the hand of God, who is the real protagonist in the history: he guides it even in its less edifying aspects (cf. also II Sam. 11.27 and 17.14). For the rest, however, we have a secular history and a principle of approach which is fundamental for any scientific history. On the other hand, it has recently been noted that the narrative is rich in elements which by their nature cannot be subjected to historical investigation: not only the concept of divine reward and punishment, an anticipation of Dtr and a feature common to all Near Eastern and Israelite wisdom, which believes in a cosmic order of which Yahweh is the guarantor in Israel, but also other aspects cannot be verified in any way. For example, in v. 9b it is expressly said that there are no witnesses to the conversation between Amnon and his half-sister Tamar (II Sam. 13.10ff.) in the bedroom where the former is pretending to be ill, but the conversation is reported in its entirety. This is a typical example of what we shall be discussing. Thus although the narrative refers to historical events, it is not properly historical, but rather a historical novel which attempts to penetrate into the makeup of the people it describes and which bases its approach on a fundamental theme of wisdom: that no one can escape the laws of the world order which have been laid down by Yahweh. Furthermore, it is a story with an obvious message: that Solomon *is* the legitimate successor to David and willed by Yahweh. Notwithstanding these reservations, however, it is difficult to deny that the account bears witness to the way in which Israel struggled to gain an understanding of history as a world-wide phenomenon, an interest which we do not find among any other people at this time (with the brief exception of the Hittites).

(*e*) This material, then, was collected together on two successive levels: the first comprised the various units which we have described, and involved various redactors each operating in his own field, concerned to combine and co-ordinate the traditions (or complexes of existing traditions) dealing with a particular theme; the second comprised Dtr, the traces of which are, as we have seen, extremely light. On the first level we are probably dealing with court chroniclers, a theory which has already been put forward .They will have had access to all the traditional material and to the existing archives. It was certainly in the course of this work of redaction that the narrative of the ark was divided into two pieces, each of which was inserted in the position in which it now stands: I Sam. 4–6 and II Sam. 6. Other material, however, will have remained outside the general treatment: see II Sam. 21–24, of which we have noted that at least 21.1–14 almost certainly belongs before II Sam. 9.

The result was that the Deuteronomistic historiographers (for those, that is, who accept the hypothesis) found the books of Samuel virtually finished: only I Sam. 7 and 12 were revised, and then the oracle of Nathan in II Sam. 7, a text which certainly contains a historical nucleus, even if in detail it is not always easy to separate the original parts from the revision. However, the general approach of the books was such that the Deuteronomistic historian found he had a predecessor. For those who accept the hypothesis, this explains why his revisions are so scattered and so insignificant ideologically.

(*f*) The text of the LXX also comes under the heading of an independent unit, especially in Codex B (Vaticanus). This is a text which in many cases is not only remarkably different from the Hebrew text, but is almost always considered by critics to be better. Some fragments from Qumran (and we have already alluded to the problem) now confirm at least in part the variants with which it has been customary to emend the Massoretic text; they thus prove that LXX[B] also had a Hebrew archetype and is not therefore a creation of the translators in question. In other cases, however, the same fragments support the variants contained in the text of Chronicles, so that the problem is not limited to the text of I and II Samuel and therefore proves to be more complicated than might appear at first sight. Here once again is a problem of a most technical kind: the extremely fragmentary character of these texts which are indicated by the siglum 4Q Sam^{a–b}; this has made possible the publication of only a few verses in the last twenty years: questions of detail and the bibliography have been discussed in Part One, ch. II, §6.

§4. Thought

The theology which underlies the books of Samuel before their final redaction by Dtr is, given the content of the work, a pre-Deuteronomistic theology of history, but similar to it in many respects. It is customarily called prophetic, since in its later texts, e.g. I Sam. 15, it draws widely on the thought of the prophets of the eighth and probably the seventh century BC. However, this thought is not only indicated in texts like the one mentioned above: it also appears in some questions of detail, which are none the less significant for that. For example, there is the polemical form in which the theophoric names compounded with Baal are reported. In I Chron. 8.33 and 9.30; 8.34 and 9.40, we read of Eshbaal and Meribbaal respectively; in II Sam. 2–4 and 9 these are distorted into Ishbosheth and Mephibosheth, and the polemic is carried on with such consistency that in II Sam. 11.21 the Jerubbaal of Judg. 8–9 has become Jerubbesheth! *Bōšet*, with its orthographical and phonetic variants = 'shame, abomination', is the term often used to replace the Canaanite *ba‛al*, the name of the principal god of Canaan, and also other deities. Now as we have seen in connection with E, anti-Canaanite and anti-syncretistic polemic became acute at the end of the ninth century BC and during the eighth, following the prophetic preaching, while we have clear indications that it was not acute at the beginning of the tenth century. In other words, without at all wishing to cast doubt on what our texts relate, we should remember that their definitive formulation, especially in the realms of ideology and theology, reflects a complex of problems from a time some centuries later, and this complex is also likely to be reflected in the first attempts at history-writing.

One of the fundamental theological problems which appears right through the work is that of the election and the rejection of particular people. Quite apart from any expectation of personal merit, and often choosing men whose morals are at least doubtful (David is the most impressive example of this), God directs human history by making use of individuals whom he elects and whom he endows with particular gifts in view of their vocation. To the modern reader Saul might hardly seem to be a 'sinner', and we might doubt whether his 'sin' made much impression on the reader or hearer of that time. Nor would it interest the reader of some centuries later that at the heart of the conflict between Saul and Samuel there were questions like that of the prerogatives of the monarch in the cult: only decades after Saul, David and Solomon intervened directly in the affairs of the cult, the first bringing the ark to Jerusalem with a solemn procession in which the king officiated and the second building a temple, sacrificing, blessing the people and pronouncing prayers of intercession, with hardly anyone making any objection. Moreover, the religious reforms launched by Hezekiah and then especially by Josiah were praised (with a few reservations) by the Deuteronomistic historian and were not attacked by the prophets, who were often very polemical in their encounters with the monarchy. More than dwelling on facts, then, the redactors were concerned to make an intensely theological presentation of two paradigmatic cases. In the case of Saul we have a man who was elected by God for a specific task but could not surrender his office once that task had been accomplished and could not see that others, more gifted than himself, were ready to succeed him. From this spiritual insensitivity there arose an inner conflict which led the protagonist to pathological forms of mistrust, hypochondria and persecution mania which would have proved suicidal for one who had been (and remained to the end) a prince without fault or fear had not his glorious death on the battlefield (to put it in pious terms) liberated him. In the case of David the situation is substantially different: here we have a most able and somewhat unscrupulous politician (the texts faithfully admit these qualities), a superb leader endowed with a special capacity for dealing with those like himself: so able that even Jonathan, the prince and heir, remains fascinated, although it becomes obvious that David has conspired against his interests. But, again following this description, David is never deaf to the word of God and thus appears to the redactor as a person who is capable of overcoming the many negative elements in his personality. These evaluations, then, are extremely subjective; they are intended to provide examples, and certainly go far beyond any historical investigation. The starting point of such considerations is, of course, the fact that Saul and his house lost the throne while David and his gained it. This fact 'should' have matched some divine intention (and here the interpretation of the facts leaves the sphere of secular history to enter the purely theological sphere) which the explanation given seeks to discover. And this is the weakness of such an approach on the level of history-writing. But it cannot be denied that the authors, whether deliberately or not we do not know, succeeded in presenting at least in the person of Saul a figure who anticipates the protagonists of Greek tragedy; this explains why for centuries, down to a few decades ago (see André Gide's play), the unhappy first king of Israel has been the protagonist of tragedies. He remains the hero, the loyal warrior incapable of taking part in a political game which is both refined and brutal, an art in which David, by contrast, was master. And the fact that David's work was crowned with success while that of Saul ended gloriously, but tragically, on the heights of Gilboa, does not prevent us from considering Saul to be the more sympathetic and the more upright of the two, even if in the intention of the redactors of the texts this is evidently a wrong view.

BIBLIOGRAPHY

Commentaries
S. R. Driver, *Notes on the Hebrew Text of the Books of Samuel*, Oxford ²1913; W. Caspari, KAT, 1926; G. Bressan, SacBib, 1954; H. W. Hertzberg, ET OTL 1964; H.-J. Stoebe, KAT (NS), I, 1973.

§1. For the problems of the origins of the monarchy and of the relations between Saul and Samuel and Saul and David cf. J. A. Soggin, *Das Königtum in Israel: Ursprünge, Spannungen, Entwicklung*, BZAW 104, 1967, I, chs. 1–2.

§2. For the antiquity of the content of I Sam. 8.11ff. cf. I. Mendelssohn, 'Samuel's Denunciation of Kingship in the Light of the Accadian Documents from Ugarit', *BASOR* 143, 1956, 17–22. For the question of the three accounts of the election of Saul see G. Wallis, 'Die Anfänge des Königtums in Israel', *Wiss Z Univ. Halle* 12.3–4, 1963, 239–47, amplified in his *Geschichte und Überlieferung*, Berlin 1968, 45–66, where the theory is put forward that Saul was elected as king by three different groups, each at its own sanctuary. There is a not dissimilar situation for David: he is successively proclaimed king of Judah (II Sam. 2) and of Israel (II Sam. 5), and in II Sam. 3.19 reference is also made to negotiations with Benjamin.

§3b. The figure of Samuel in all its complexity is analysed by J. L. McKenzie, 'The Four Samuels', *BiblRes* 7, 1962, 3–18, and A. Weiser, *Samuel: seine geschichtliche Aufgabe und religiöse Bedeutung*, FRLANT 81, 1962. For the origins of the monarchy see J. Boecker, *Die Beurteilung der Anfänge des Königtums in den deuteronomistischen Abschnitten des I Samuelbuches*, WMANT 31, 1969; L. Schmidt, *Menschlicher Erfolg und Jahwes Initiative*, WMANT 38, 1970, chs. 3–4, 6.

§3c. David's rise to prominence has been analysed by H. U. Nübel, *Davids Aufstieg in der frühe israelitischer Geschichtsschreibung*, Bonn dissertation 1959; L. Schmidt, op. cit., ch. 5.

§3d. For the figure of David cf. R. A. Carlson, *David, the Chosen King*, Stockholm 1964; this illustrates the schematic nature of the Deuteronomic redaction, and shows that the life of David is presented in two clearly defined periods: the king under the blessing and the king under the curse. Although the details cannot always be accepted, this thesis is of interest since the redactors seem to have used similar criteria in regard to Saul and Solomon. The classic study of the history of the succession to David is that of L. Rost, *Die Überlieferung von der Thronnachfolge Davids*, Stuttgart 1926 (= his *Das Kleine Credo*, Heidelberg 1965, 119–53); cf. also W. Brueggemann, 'David and his Theologian', *CBQ* 30, 1968, 156–81; R. N. Whybray, *The Succession Narrative*, SBT II 9, 1968, which emphasizes the novelistic elements in the story and its derivation from a wisdom milieu; J. W. Flanagan, 'Court History or Succession Document? A Study of 2 Samuel 9–20 and 1 Kings 1–2', *JBL* 91, 1972, 172–81. For the nature of doctrinaire narratives, cf. É. Lipiński, *Le poème royal du Psaume LXXXIX 1–5, 20–38*, Paris 1967, 83–6.

§3e. There have been continuing attempts to discover Pentateuchal sources within Samuel, none of them convincing. The most recent is H. Schulte, *Bis auf diesen Tag*, Hamburg 1967.

THE BOOKS OF KINGS

§1. *Introduction*

We have seen that in the Greek Bible the first and second books of Kings are called III and IV Kingdoms, a numbering which is retained in the Latin translations and which has found its way from there into some modern Roman Catholic works. We have also seen that the division between II Samuel and I Kings is artificial: the story of David, the end of which should have constituted the logical point of division, is concluded in I Kings 1–2. However, the division between I and II Kings also leaves much to be desired: the narratives about Ahaziah and Elijah and Elisha respectively are both split in two. The Babylonian Talmud identifies their author as Jeremiah, but here too we have an untenable attribution: the prophet is not named at all. However, the attribution could originate in the Deuteronomistic revision, which dates from the time of the prophet onwards.

The two books can easily be divided into four parts, each distinct from the other:

(*a*) The epilogue to the 'succession narrative' (I Kings 1 and 2);

(*b*) The history of the reign of Solomon (I Kings 3–11);

(*c*) The history of the two divided kingdoms down to the fall of the kingdom of Israel (I Kings 12–II Kings 17);

(*d*) Finally, the history of the kingdom of Judah down to the second fall of Jerusalem and the final deportation (II Kings 18–25).

One of the principal problems of the books is that of their chronology, for the details of which the reader must be referred to the histories of Israel and the monographs devoted to the subject. An eloquent proof of the complexity of the problem is the fact that the authors, whose competence is beyond question, have reached such different results. Sometimes they differ by only a few years, but in almost no case do they reach unanimity except from the time of Josiah on (end of the seventh century BC). The difficulty is that the

chronology of the kings of Israel is calculated on the basis of that of
the kings of Judah and vice versa, without our knowing the starting
date or the criteria used. Were it not for the Assyrian annals and the
mention of phenomena like earthquakes and eclipses, we would have
no firm point at all. Another difficulty arises from the fact that whatever the criterion used to calculate the years of a reign, in at least one
case we find a monarch whose chronology has not been calculated on
the basis of the years in which he effectively reigned, but starts from
the beginning of his co-regency with his father. Therefore the chronology of at least two kings partially overlaps. This happens in the case
of Uzziah/Azariah and Jotham of Judah (II Kings 15.5// II Chron.
26.21), and we cannot exclude the possibility that there are other
cases of this kind which are not properly recorded.

This fundamental difficulty is far from being resolved, but it does
not prevent the books of Kings from disclosing a certain inner unity
and a constant ideology which recalls the pattern in the body of
Judges: the rise and then the decline of the united kingdom under
Solomon, the end of the united monarchy, the alternating political
and religious fates of the two kingdoms up to their fall at the end of
the eighth and the beginning of the sixth centuries BC respectively, are
explained by commentaries which illustrate the religious position
adopted by each individual monarch. The kings who acted as precursors to Josiah, the obvious model for the redactors, are praised and
considered 'just' notwithstanding possible imperfections in their work
which are also mentioned. Those, on the other hand, who followed
syncretistic tendencies in the religious field are severely condemned
and considered 'impious', even though it is obvious that they could
not foresee that they would be judged according to the standard of
persons who lived some centuries after them. The texts are almost
always silent about the political importance of the kings: the redactors
were only concerned with the work of each king in the religious field.
Thus it happens that politically less able kings with 'orthodox'
theologies (according to Deuteronomistic criteria, e.g. Hezekiah and
Josiah) receive unconditional praise, whereas other monarchs, who
were politically very able, but in religious terms failed to keep up
with the requirements of the redactors, are severely censured. Two
instances are Omri, a king so important that the Assyrian annals
continue to call the reigning house of Israel the 'house of Omri'
decades after his fall, and Ahab.

The judgments in question, whether positive or negative, are
formulated in stereotyped phrases which, without being the same as
those that we find prefaced to every narrative in the body of Judges,

certainly recall their content and follow the same criteria: the difference is that in Judges we have a people which sins, whereas here we
have individual kings, even if the results are more or less the same.
Thus, beginning from I Kings 14.21ff., we have a typical formula
with the following structure: the monarch in question is mentioned
with the years of his reign (calculated within the parameters which
we mentioned); then comes the name of his mother and, if it is
important, the name of his wife. Finally there is a judgment on his
reign in accordance with the criteria mentioned above. Thus Dtr has
adapted its criteria to a different subject, while the evaluations remain substantially the same.

The reader may therefore begin from the presupposition that the
criteria by which the person and work of a king are judged are not
political or economic, but theological. This theological criterion is
made up from the standards given by the reform of Josiah: the
rejection or suppression of the syncretistic or Canaanite sanctuaries
(sometimes called 'high places' because they stood above the level of
their surroundings, not because they were necessarily on peaks or in
hill-country), a foreign policy which would be more a testimony of
faith first for the two small kingdoms and then for the one that
remained than a viable form of steering between the great empires
of the age. It is not surprising, therefore, that some have called the
criteria in question anachronistic, because they take as a model the
work of a king who lived at the end of the period of the monarchy.
Others have called them unrealistic because they ignore the existence
of an economic and political situation of which even the king with
deep religious concerns could not fail to take account if he wished to
keep his kingdom alive. The situation is presented in particularly
crude forms in the case of the kingdom of Israel, whose monarchs
without exception are summarily judged to be guilty of the 'sin of
Jeroboam' I, described in I Kings 12.26ff. He set up and maintained
in the sanctuaries of Bethel and Dan a cult separate from that of
Jerusalem, in which Yahweh was celebrated in connection (the nature
of which is obscure) with a golden bull (the so-called 'golden calf').
This was probably the pedestal of the God of Israel who was set
invisibly above it, just as he sat enthroned, equally invisibly, above
the ark in the temple of Jerusalem. According to Exod. 32.1ff., this
form of cult was instituted by Aaron himself. Contrary to the view of
the later redactors, this gave it an obvious claim to orthodoxy. The
relevant passage in Exodus does not condemn the cult in question in
its primary form; the condemnation enters with an evident revision
of the text (cf. Exod. 32.1–6 with 32.7–10).

Thus we have, once again, valuations of a strictly theological character which find their ideological expression, but also their limitation, in this characteristic: on the one hand they in fact tell us precisely how Israel during the exilic period judged its past, but on the other hand they are difficult to sustain on the level of pure historiography, even if the historian can find a mine of historically relevant information in the material they present. For the Deuteronomistic historian, the destruction of Jerusalem and the deportation were important elements of proof that what had been proclaimed was an effective explanation of history, and they became the occasion for announcing that what had happened was not due to the weakness of the God of Israel when confronted first with the gods of Assyria and then with those of Babylon (as non-Israelites of the period might have supposed), but was a product of the judgment of God against the kings and the people of God, who were guilty of not having listened first to the preaching of the prophets and then to the decrees of Josiah's reform. Seen in this context, the message of Kings acquires a new value, though not really from a historiographical point of view; on the other hand, the insistence with which it points to the intervention of Yahweh in human history, instead of making him work in the sphere of myth (battles and victories or defeats of gods, etc), is already a significant fact when we consider the period in question. In short, Dtr preaches, announces, comments on well-known historical facts and seeks to look so to speak behind the scenes.

The homilectic and catechetical character of Dtr would much reduce the value of these texts for the historian did the texts in question not continually contain references to sources which the redactors suppose to be easily accessible, or whose content should have been in the public domain: the 'Chronicles of the Kings of Israel' or 'of Judah', preceded by a 'Book of the Acts of Solomon', works from which a few extracts are cited. It thus seems possible to recognize that it was not the desire or the intention of Dtr to produce history or chronicle so much as to comment on known facts and to 'explain' them in a theological context. What have come down to us are only the commentaries, and sometimes we have none of the original texts on which the commentaries were made. We may think that this is an irreparable loss, but it is in any case not the fault of Dtr, but is attributable to the historical vicissitudes through which the people of God passed. These considerations give a completely different significance to the historical labours of Dtr, and almost automatically refute the criticisms which have been usually directed against the work. Thus the annals mentioned above will certainly have recorded that Omri and Ahab were great kings, even if they appear as impious men in the Deuteronomistic evaluation. We also know from the prophets Elijah, Amos and Hosea that certain social conditions in the north were quite insupportable and that the negative judgment, for strictly theological reasons, was by no means unfounded, even if there seems to be no reason for it on the political plane.

To return to the problem of chronology. The field today is dominated by two rival systems, one of which came out of Germany on the basis of a work by J. Begrich in 1929 which has recently been taken up again by A. Jepsen and is used in the works of A. Alt and M. Noth; the other is that formulated by W. F. Albright in the United States in 1945 and developed by his pupils. For the earlier period the two chronologies show differences of about a decade, but from the time of Josiah on they tend, as we have said, to coincide.

§2. Sources

Three sources are mentioned explicitly by name in the books of Kings, as we have seen:

(a) The 'Book of the Acts of Solomon' (I Kings 11.41);

(b) The 'Book of the Chronicles of the Kings of Judah' (I Kings 14.29 and about fourteen times elsewhere);

(c) The 'Book of the Chronicles of the Kings of Israel' (I Kings 14.19 and about sixteen times elsewhere).

It is obvious that there is no reference here to the book of Chronicles, which the Hebrew Bible places among the Writings, and which the LXX puts after Kings. There is no reason to suppose, as some writers have in the past, that the Pentateuchal sources J and E appear, at least up to I Kings 12; in fact there is no continuous element in the scattered quotations that we have. The one certain thing is that the Deuteronomists, whose work is generally recognized here, even by those who do not accept a continuous Dtr, have worked (as we said in the previous section) on what are almost certainly official sources, on which they have made an interpretative commentary. The only fragment of any length which survives from these ancient sources is I Kings 4.7–19, which describes the administrative system introduced by Solomon (or perhaps already by David) in the north. But the Deuteronomistic revision is substantial as early as chs. 6–8, which narrate how the temple came to be built, even if there is no reason to doubt the historicity of the facts related. In any case, the first part of the narrative is extremely favourable to Solomon, at some points amounting to adulation, while in the second part it is strongly critical. It notes the progressive degeneration and decadence of the kingdom, seeing religious syncretism as the primary cause but not concealing other causes: unpopular fiscal policy and even harsher forms of tyranny.

(d) According to the LXX, the prayer of consecration for the temple, pronounced by Solomon in I Kings 8.12ff. (8.53ff. LXX) has been taken from a certain 'Book of the Song', perhaps the same 'Book of the Upright' which we have already found mentioned in Josh. 10.13ff. and II Sam. 1.19ff. (see Part One, ch. VI, §4 above): this phenomenon could be explained by a metathesis from *yšr* to *šyr*. If the notice given in the LXX is correct (and scholarly opinion is almost unanimous on this point), there is an authentic kernel in the long prayer which was then considerably revised by Dtr.

(e) The epilogue to the 'succession narrative', with which we were concerned in the previous chapter.

(f) The traditions about the prophet Elijah, though they lack a beginning: I Kings 17–19; 21; II Kings 1–2, which are now interpolated with notes on the reign of Ahab of Israel. There are various episodes: the drought (ch. 17); the divine judgment on Carmel, probably the aetiological legend on the end of the Canaanite sanctuary and the substitution of an Israelite sanctuary for it (ch. 18); the theophany on Mount Horeb, in which we note a theological reflection on the relationship between the physical phenomena caused by the presence of Yahweh and Yahweh himself (ch. 19); the episode of Naboth's vineyard, an example of the way in which the monarchy intervened in a destructive way in the popular justice of the villages and of the conflicts which arose in the encounter between Canaanite concepts of landed property and the ancient Israelite tribal tradition which is still attested in Lev. 25.23ff. (ch. 21). From a stylistic point of view these episodes are written in the best Hebrew known to us, so that it is possible to speak with reason of the ninth and eighth centuries as the 'golden age' in the literature of Israel. Discussions of particularly important themes appear: monotheism, the toleration of other cults alongside that of Yahweh, relationships between the citizen and the state, and the conflicts which could arise from different interpretations of the law and the position of the prophet in the context of these relationships. I Kings 17.24; 18.21, 39; 19.1ff., 9ff. etc. give solutions which demonstrate the existence of a remarkable spiritual maturity. The redactional elements from Dtr are very sparse: almost the only appearance is in 19.10, 14. At the beginning of the narrative (17.1), the Massoretic text reads, 'Elijah the Tishbite, one of the inhabitants of Gilead', but the LXX reading, '. . . the Tishbite, from Tishbe in Gilead', seems better: the consonantal spelling of the two terms is practically identical.

(g) The traditions of Elisha (I Kings 19.19–21; II Kings chs. 2; 4–10). These contain some parallel traditions to those of Elijah, whose pupil Elisha was, but are generally considered to be inferior (cf. I Kings 17 with II Kings 4; II Kings 12 with 13.14). In I Kings 19.15ff. Elijah receives the order to anoint king Hazael of Damascus and king Jehu of Israel, and it is Elisha who carries out the charge which he receives from his master (II Kings 8.7; 9.1ff.). These passages, too, are almost completely free of Deuteronomistic redaction; their origin is generally sought in a different setting from that in which the traditions of Elijah grew up. They are thought to be probably more popular because of the miracles they contain, which sometimes have a crude and anecdotal character. The material is also profoundly influenced by the preaching of Elijah. This establishes a *terminus post quem* for their dating. It is interesting to note that less than a century later, Hos. 1.1ff. severely condemns the coup d'état organized by Elijah and Elisha because of the bloodshed which it caused. Only O. Eissfeldt in recent times has argued that the tradition of Elisha is prior to that of Elijah.

(h) The Aramaean wars of Ahab (I Kings 20 and 22) are mixed in with episodes from the life of Elijah and the prophet Micaiah ben Imlah, who is not to be confused with the eighth-century minor prophet of the same name. The narratives are free from Deuteronomistic revisions and are an important historical source, though they only illuminate a few aspects in the life of Ahab, who, as we have seen, was a king of remarkable capability.

(i) Traditions of Isaiah parallel to Isa. 36–39 are to be found in II Kings 18.13–20.19. They are interesting because, like every duplicate text, they provide the occasion for making a synoptic study of the transmission of an identical text by different agents and of the differences which could arise.

(j) We have traditions about various prophets: in I Kings 11.29–39; 14.1–18 and 15.29 on Ahijah of Shiloh; in I Kings 12.21–24 on Shemaiah; in I Kings 12.32–13.32 on an anonymous prophet who comes from the south to curse the sanctuaries of Bethel and Dan, an episode often related to the ministry of the prophet Amos (though in 13.2 we have an explicit reference to Josiah's reform, so that this is probably a *vaticinium ex eventu* interpolated by Dtr). In II Kings 21.10–15 an anonymous prophet attacks Manasseh of Judah, while in 22.14

the prophetess Huldah has an important part in Josiah's reform, even if this is difficult to assess because of the inadequacy of the sources. Deuteronomistic revision is evident in the last three instances.

(k) The Deuteronomistic material seems to have been composed and edited in at least two stages, which can also be distinguished chronologically. There is no complete agreement among scholars: for example, Noth is doubtful about such a double redaction. In any case, the first stratum would be inspired by the precepts of Josiah's reform: centralization of the cult and therefore the elimination of the local sanctuaries (the so-called high places), fundamental hostility to any Canaanite or syncretistic elements. A second and later stratum seeks on the other hand to interpret the tragedy which befell Judah and Jerusalem in 597 and 587, but which had already hit Israel in 722–21. The explanation follows the well-known lines of reward and retribution: the prophets had announced judgment again and again, and look – it had happened. However, Dtr closes on a note of hope: in II Kings 25.27ff. Jehoiachin, the last legitimate king of Judah, is pardoned and admitted to the table of the king of Babylon in 561.

We are thus indebted to Dtr for the fact that although the original sources are lost, at least the commentaries on them have reached us.

§3. Thought

The North American scholar J. A. Bewer has characterized Dtr with the happy phrase 'a philosophy of history'; we would prefer to call it a theology of history, even if at this time theology and philosophy coincided. Its setting is the great struggle between the faith of Israel and the religion of Canaan; we have popular and syncretistic forms of both. The struggle on the religious plane was also accompanied by a hard struggle on the political plane. On the home front the Canaanites had been conquered or otherwise brought into the empire and then into the two states, but especially in the north they in fact maintained a considerable economic and military influence which no king could ignore; in the international field, too, there were struggles first with the Neo-Assyrian empire and then with the Neo-Babylonian empire, not to mention battles with neighbours: the Aramaeans, the Moabites and the Phoenicians. It is difficult to say which had the priority: the struggle on the religious plane, as Dtr would have it, or the struggle on the political plane, as a modern historian would judge. It is probably even better to suppose that the two elements were indissolubly connected. Given a situation that was so overbearing in every field it is not surprising that it was easy to interpret the history of the people in terms like that of divine recompense. Today we may consider it philosophically and historically an inadequate explanation, but we cannot deny that it is a first attempt to do historiography. It may be thought to be primitive, but it *is* historiography.

The Deuteronomistic redactors had some facts which readily served to confirm their theory: the end of the kingdom of Israel and the deportation of some of its inhabitants in the second half of the eighth century; the first fall of Jerusalem and the deportation of some of its inhabitants in 597; and the second, definitive, fall of the capital after the deportation. Moreover, almost all the prophets had proclaimed the end of the people as a divine judgment. Thus verification in the light of facts seemed to confirm the Deuteronomistic valuation completely, and Dtr could solemnly declare that God did not allow himself to be mocked.

Hence Dtr with its critical discussion of the past history of the people became an important link in the chain which led to the postexilic restoration. Even if this restoration succeeded in removing once and for all the dangers of paganism and syncretism, however, it introduced legalistic forms of understanding the faith, sometimes giving the religion of Israel a cold, unbending character, since the Jew was reasonably certain that he was in the right. Judaism was no longer influenced by the animated polemic of the prophets, which was rapidly extinguished in the course of little more than a century of restoration. The place of the prophet was taken by the apocalyptist and the doctor of the law; in the post-exilic theocracy the priests are in charge. The problematical but lively circumstances which preceded the exile were replaced by the tranquillity of a religious orthodoxy. Whether or not this was an advantage, the reader himself will be able to judge.

BIBLIOGRAPHY

Commentaries

C. F. Burney, *Notes on the Hebrew Text of the Books of Kings*, Oxford 1903 (reprinted 1970); S. Garofalo, SacBib, 1951; J. A. Montgomery and H. S. Gehman, ICC, 1951; R. de Vaux, JB, ²1958; M. Noth, BK, 1968 (to I Kings 16 only; following the author's death the work will be completed by R. Smend); J. Gray, OTL, ²1970.

§1. For the chronology of Kings see J. Begrich, *Die Chronologie der Könige von Israel und Judah*, Tübingen 1929 (reprinted 1966); A. Jepsen and

R. Hanhart, *Untersuchungen zur israelitisch-jüdischen Chronologie*, BZAW 88, 1964; D. N. Freedman and E. F. Campbell, 'The Chronology of Israel and the Ancient Near East', in G. E. Wright (ed.), *The Bible and the Ancient Near East: Essays in Honor of W. F. Albright*, New York 1961, 203–28; J. Finegan, *Handbook of Biblical Chronology*, Princeton 1964; E. R. Thiele, *The Mysterious Numbers of the Hebrew Kings*, Grand Rapids ²1965 (an original and independent study); V. Pavlovský and E. Vogt, 'Die Jahre der Könige von Juda und Israel', *Bibl* 45, 1964, 321–47; J. A. Soggin, *Das Königtum in Israel: Ursprünge, Spannungen, Entwicklung*, BZAW 104, 1967, I, chs. 3–5. There is a synopsis of the chronology in the article 'Kronologia' by H. Tadmor, *Encyclopaedia Biblica* IV, 1962, 254–310, esp. 259ff. (in Hebrew). For a history of the neo-Assyrian empire and its relations with Israel and Judah see W. W. Hallo, 'From Qarqar to Carchemish', *BA* 23, 1960, 34–61. The chronological problems of the Deuteronomic history work are dealt with by G. Sauer, 'Die chronologischen Angaben in den Büchern Deut. bis 2 Kön.', *TZ* 24, 1968, 1–14; cf. also pp. 490ff. below.

§2c. For Solomon's districts see F. Pintore, 'I dodici intendenti di Salomone', *RSO* 45, 1970, 177–207; T. N. D. Mettinger, *Solomonic State Officials*, Lund 1971.

§2f–g. For Elijah and Elisha see R. P. Carroll, 'The Elijah-Elisha Sagas', *VT* 19, 1969, 400–15.

§2f. For the traditions about Elijah cf. G. Fohrer, *Elia*, Zurich ²1968; J. J. Stamm, 'Elia am Horeb', in *Studia biblica et semitica T. C. Vriezen dedicata*, Wageningen 1966, 327–34; O. H. Steck, *Überlieferung und Zeitgeschichte in den Elia-Erzählungen*, WMANT 26, 1968, with a comparison between the parallel traditions relating to Elijah and Elisha.

§2g. The priority of the Elisha traditions over those concerning Elijah has been argued by O. Eissfeldt, 'Die Komposition von I Reg. 16.29–II Reg. 13.24', in F. Maass (ed.), *Das Ferne und Nahe Wort. Festschrift L. Rost*, BZAW 105, 1967, 49–58 (= his *Kleine Schriften* V, Tübingen 1973, 21–30). É. Lipiński, 'Le Ben-Hadad II de la Bible et de l'Histoire', in *Proceedings of the Fifth World Congress of Jewish Studies 1969* I, Jerusalem 1971, 157–73, has denied the originality of Ahab in I Kings 22. On Elisha cf. also H. C. Schmitt, *Elisa*, Gütersloh 1972.

§2i. For the parallel accounts II Kings 18–20 and Isaiah 36–39 see B. S. Childs, *Isaiah and the Assyrian Crisis*, SBT II 3, 1967.

PART THREE

THE PRE-EXILIC PROPHETS

I

THE PROPHETS OF ISRAEL

§1. *Etymology*

(*a*) As is well known, our term 'prophet' derives from the Greek *prophētēs*. This is a word attested in classical Greek from the fifth century BC on, with the sense of 'one who announces, makes known, proclaims something'. The accent is thus on the public character of the communication or message. The preposition *pro-* with which the term is compounded thus seems originally to have had a predominantly local sense ('before' the assembly, the group, the individual) and not a temporal sense (before the announcement is fulfilled). On the other hand, from its origins the term has been connected with the proclamation of oracles: the earliest attestation in fact refers to the oracle of Zeus at Dodona in the Epirus. This could have contributed to the understanding of *pro-* in a futuristic sense, notwithstanding the obvious circumstance that the oracle could also announce the present will of the deity. The term was used in Egypt in the Hellenistic and Roman era to designate a religious official called the 'servant of the deity'. It seems that the LXX translators wanted to associate the prophet with this figure. We still note a certain ambivalence in the New Testament: on the one hand, ancient prophecies are 'fulfilled', which presupposes that the people who made them had the capacity to predict events even in the distant future by means of the Holy Spirit; on the other, the presence in the primitive church of 'prophets', that is, of men who announced the word of God for the present, shows that the original sense of the word had not been lost. But with the progressive extinction of prophecy in the primitive church within the space of two or three generations, only the temporal significance remained and the term increasingly acquired the sense which it has today: it denotes the person who has the capacity to predict certain events, of course in the name of the deity. Finally, the Hellenistic world knew yet another meaning of the term: here the prophet appears as a man inspired by the muse, whose herald he becomes among men. Such a sense is attested from Pindar on. This meaning too has passed into modern usage, as when we speak, for example, of inspiration in the artistic field. Thus in the first of the two cases we have a purely religious basis, and in the second a rather more complex phenomenon.

(b) In the LXX translation, as in other Greek translations, the term is always used to translate the Hebrew *nābī'*, and sometimes, though more rarely, renders the terms considered synonymous, *ḥōzēh* and *rō'eh* = 'seer' (the first term accentuates the more particularly visionary character of the phenomenon). It does not seem that there was a particular theological intention behind the choice made in the Greek translations: this was simply the current Greek word which was nearest to the Hebrew original. However, if we consider the difference in character within the religious sphere of oracles and ecstasy, together with inspiration in the Greek and especially the Hellenistic world, in comparison with the work and the message of the biblical prophets, the adequacy of the translation used (not to mention our term, which is phonetically equivalent) is at least doubtful. Thus it is legitimate to suspect that, if only unconsciously, the Greek translation may have distorted the meaning of the original. As is well known, this is an extremely frequent phenomenon in any kind of translation.

(c) The origin of the term *nābī'* is still controversial: W. F. Albright's theory, which had already been put forward by other scholars in a more or less adequate form, increasingly holds the field. This argues that the term is to be related to the Akkadian *nabū* = 'appoint, call', both bearing a vocational sense: the noun *nabī'u(m)* = 'the one who is called', 'the one who has received a vocation, an election, a charge', is derived from this. In Hebrew, moreover, nouns of the *qātīl* type (that is, with the vowel sequence *ā- ī*) usually have a passive meaning. The meaning of the term in Hebrew thus seems to have been 'the one who is called', that is, the one who has received a divine vocation for a particular mission, with a particular task. In this case it is to announce to the people the word of God, usually through preaching, and sometimes also by means of symbolic actions. It is interesting to note that, although the term tends increasingly (and finally exclusively) to indicate a particular category of person, an ancient J tradition has been preserved according to which anyone could and indeed should prophesy when inspired by the spirit (Num. 11.16–25; cf. Amos 3.8). But in the historical era the term is limited to a particular category of person exercising a specific ministry in the community, that of proclaiming the word of God.

(*d*) One of the principal difficulties for the modern scholar in the study of this particular form of ministry is the fact that the Old Testament uses the term *nābī'* and its derivatives to indicate persons and institutions which our way of thinking would differentiate as clearly as possible, but which biblical Hebrew considers all to be capable of being subsumed under this one term. We have seen that Hebrew knew two words to indicate the 'seer', even if they are not completely identical on a semantic level; but they are often in synonymous parallelism with *nābī'*. Phenomena which reappear in the field of ecstasy and soothsaying are also indicated in Hebrew by this term. Thus the verb *nābā'* in the piel can assume the meaning 'fall into ecstasy'. This is a well-known phenomenon in the Old Testament (cf. I Sam. 10.5ff., 10ff.; 19.18ff.); there is the homicidal ecstasy of Saul in which he seeks to kill David (I Sam. 18.10ff.); in I Kings 18.28 the prophets of Baal also seek to fall into ecstasy by means of the use of certain techniques, and this attempt, like the people in question, is denoted by the root *nb'*. In Hos. 9.7, *nābī'* is taken as equivalent to *mešuggā'* = 'fanatic, lunatic', an interesting piece of information about the way in which the *vox populi* reacted to particular forms of ecstasy. Leaving aside the difficulty of the chapter on the historical-critical plane, we have an interesting and typical case of soothsaying on a popular level in I Sam. 9: Saul and his companion, having looked in vain for asses belonging to Kish, Saul's father, decide to ask a 'man of God' living in the vicinity for his advice on the question; and for his services the 'man of God' (whom tradition later identified with Samuel) receives payment. It is interesting that v. 9 explicitly identifies the 'man of God' of that period with the *nābī'* of the period of the redactor. This is not, then, a primitive use of the term so much as a later identification, which is all the more significant in that at the time of this redactor prophecy was at the height of its maturity. We might therefore have expected a greater differentiation between 'prophet' and soothsayer at the popular level.

Seers and ecstatics, some of whom pronounce oracles, are also well-known figures in the history of religion in general and that of the ancient Near East in particular. An early and significant testimony to this effect comes from the account of the travels of the Egyptian official Wen-Amon (*c.* 1060 BC, cf. *ANET³*, 25–29, esp. 26b, and 655b). During his stay at Byblos he assisted at a sacrifice during which the deity took possession of a youth, hurling him to the ground in ecstasy and making him pronounce an oracle. We also find the title *ḥzn* (= *ḥāzīn*?), the Aramaic equivalent to the Hebrew *ḥōzeh* = seer, in the ancient Aramaean world (the first half of the first millennium BC, cf. *KAI*, 202, A 12; *ANET*[3], 655f.), borne by the person through whom Zakir, king of Hamath, receives messages from the deity.

The term *nābî'*, then, could assume the meaning of 'seer' or 'ecstatic' in particular circumstances. This seems to be the reason why we find a reluctance among the classical prophets of the eighth to the sixth centuries to make use of the term and also to appeal to the spirit as the source of their inspiration. This reticence will only be overcome at the beginning of the sixth century, with Ezekiel.

(*e*) The Old Testament does not distinguish on the lexicographical plane between prophets of Yahweh and prophets of other deities (cf. I Kings 18, already cited, and II Kings 10.18). This is another problem not unlike the one we have just discussed about which we would like to have more information. Among the prophets of Yahweh there is a distinction between prophets who announce the truth and those who announce falsehood; the latter group are distinguished in the LXX with the term *pseudoprophētēs*, which we also find in the New Testament. The absence of a distinction in the lexical field for these cases is significant, and certainly does not help any investigation. In any case, there was an important shift of emphasis in the Greek translation: whereas in Hebrew the accent falls on the *message* that is false, in Greek it falls on the *person* of the prophet himself. In other words it makes *him* false, which does not necessarily follow from the Hebrew.

In conclusion, then, we can affirm that whereas the vocational element is clear in the Hebrew term, and is at first independent of a particular category of people, later being in practice limited to them, the word serves to identify prophets of Yahweh and prophets of other divinities, true prophets and false prophets, while also covering seers, ecstatics and other figures who belong more appropriately to piety or to popular superstition.

§2. *Prophecy in Israel and among neighbouring peoples*

(*a*) It is no exaggeration to affirm that with the category of 'true prophets' (a description which obviously also includes a value judgment), Israel created a quite unique category of minister in the sphere of the history of religions. But that is not to say that very similar phenomena were not to be found in the Semitic world.

In the first place, we have what has rightly been called prophecy in the milieu of the western Mesopotamian city-state of Mari between the eighteenth and seventeenth centuries BC.

There are parallel elements here on more than a formal level: the use of the same or similar literary forms and genres, the presence of particular people, the existence of certain relationships between the deity and his emissary, and so on; a number of analogies have also been discovered in matters of greater substance, and these are sometimes impressive. The initiative in the oracle is exclusively divine; techniques of consultation are therefore extremely rare or absent altogether, and there is often no questioning of the deity. The man sent by the divinity is legitimated in his calling by means of signs and wonders; in the messages which have reached us there is often open criticism of the policy pursued by the court or in the state cult; we have promises for the present and the future in either the religious or the political sphere, oracles against the nations and other features. As among the prophets of Israel, in Mari use is rarely made of ecstasy and incomprehensible oracles; the choice falls primarily on the announcement of the divine word to the interested party or parties through the man who is called by the deity.

(b) Unfortunately, the problem of possible relationships between prophecy in the kingdom of Mari and that in the biblical world cannot be resolved in the present state of research: it is only possible to indicate the existence of the fact. We know, and have seen above (Part One, ch.V, §4), that it is possible to encounter remarkable affinities between the people and usages attested among the patriarchs on the one side and the people of Mari and Nuzi on the other. This makes it probable, if not obvious, that there must have been some kind of relationship between the ancestors of Israel and certain peripheral regions of Mesopotamia, especially in regard to the nomads who moved around there. Thus notwithstanding the many centuries which separate prophecy at Mari from biblical prophecy (and which shed no light whatsoever upon the problem), it is possible to suppose, at least as a working hypothesis, that there was some relationship, and the discovery of further sources may contribute towards a solution of the problem in the not too distant future.

(c) We have a very similar phenomenon, though many centuries after biblical prophecy, in the personality of Mohammed.

The discussion on the originality of Mohammed as a prophet, and thus attempts at an evaluation of his ministry, which combined that of a founder of religion with that of a prophet (something which does not happen in the Old Testament, except for the mention made of Moses by E, cf. above Part Two, ch.II, §6) should not in any case put in question his person or his good faith, which are elements beyond all suspicion. The one problem which remains unsolved is that of more or less unconscious conditioning from biblical prophecy, which is a perfectly justifiable hypothesis if one thinks of the close relationship between the prophet and Judaism, at least to begin with. In any case, even those who admit that Mohammed is dependent on biblical prophecy must necessarily recognize the originality of his subsequent development.

Concluding this review, which is regrettably all too brief, we note that although it is impossible to establish assured links between earlier western Semitic prophecy and that of the Bible, and between the prophets of the Old Testament and subsequent Arab prophecy, the prophetic ministry does not develop in an ideological void. It does not start from nothing or end in nothing, as the New Testament and the decades immediately following its composition might make one suppose: it had predecessors and successors. However, the relationships are obvious in the case of ecstatic prophecy and visions, popular forms of soothsaying, etc.

§3. Prophets before the eighth century and from the eighth century to the exile

The first prophet of the Old Testament accessible to the historian is Samuel, who lived in the last decades of the second millennium BC and whose life is developed exclusively in relationship to that of the first king of Israel, Saul. But I Sam. 10.5ff. (which we have seen to be early, above Part Two, ch. VIII, §2) gives evidence of the existence of prophets even before the time of Samuel and Saul, though they are only ecstatic prophets.

(a) At this point there is a distinction to be recognized, even if again it is only a formal one: that between prophets earlier than the eighth century, the protagonists or subjects of particular biblical narratives, and prophets from the eighth century onwards, who have given their names to books of the Bible. In the first category are people like Samuel, Nathan, Elijah and Elisha, and also other figures down to the time of Josiah; we should also include Jonah, although his book appears among the twelve minor prophets. The interest of the narrator is concentrated in this case predominantly on what the prophets in question did, and much less on what they said. In the second category we have the prophets whose names we find on books of the Bible, with the exception, as we have seen, of Jonah:

in their works the redactors sought to present entire discourses or extracts and summaries; they limit their narrative to what was considered essential for putting material in the setting of the prophets' lives. The collections have been made either on chronological and biographical lines or in terms of content, or on other patterns which appear to us to be less logical. As we have said, the difference between the two categories of prophets is thus more one of form than of content, and depends solely on the way in which the accounts of their lives have been transmitted. We know that Samuel, Nathan, Elijah and Elisha were also profoundly interested in politics, and we know of the personal commitment of the second and third figures to the solution of moral problems; all were critical of the predominant form of worship in Israel. Thus independently of the manner in which the material has been transmitted and of the emphasis which it has been given, the prophets earlier than the eighth century and the later prophets whose lives have been reported in the same way have the same interests as the prophets from the eighth century on who have given their names to the prophetic books. There is confirmation of this in Mal.3.23 = 4.5 (cf. Matt.16.14): if the tradition was able to see Elijah over the centuries as the eschatological prophet *par excellence*, one might reasonably suppose that his message had some connection with eschatology, even if it has not been handed down: his ascension alone (II Kings 2.11) does not justify such a position of pre-eminence!

(*b*) If there is, then, no essential difference between the prophets earlier than the eighth century and those who come after this date, the term 'writing prophets', which has been applied to the second category in the past and is still repeated today, can no longer be justified. We have already seen that the allusions to written versions of their message are very rare (cf. above, Part One, ch.VI, §2), and this is not surprising if we remember that they were essentially preachers, just like their predecessors.

(*c*) Some of the earliest prophets (at the time of Samuel, for example, the ecstatics already mentioned) often (but not necessarily) appear in groups and are sometimes connected with a sanctuary. We shall deal with this latter point in §5 below. Elijah had a disciple, Elisha, and he in turn had other disciples (II Kings 4.38ff.); Amos (7.14) on the other hand denies that he has been the disciple of a prophet: his vocation has been a matter between Yahweh and himself. On the other hand, the possibility that even Amos was the disciple of a prophet cannot be rejected *a priori*, and Amos seems to present a somewhat unusual case. We know that Isaiah had disciples (cf. 8.16) and that there was a time when his preaching was limited to this restricted circle instead of being given the greatest possible publicity, which we know to have been his practice at other times: the best-known case is 5.1ff. We can understand, therefore, why many authors have attributed the redaction of Deutero- and Trito-Isaiah to the school of Isaiah. This would be a reasonable explanation why the name of the eighth-century prophet has been given to texts which could not possibly be his, but could easily be attributed to his school. This would imply that the school was in existence throughout the sixth century BC (cf. below, Part Four, ch. II, §5, and ch. V). Allowing a further continuation of the school of Isaiah, we could even see how chs. 24–27, a much later apocalypse, came to be included in the book. Of course these are no more than hypotheses, but they do allow us to take a few steps forward. We know that Jeremiah had a disciple who was at the same time his amanuensis, Baruch.

(d) For the problem of the connection of the prophets with the sanctuaries, which, as we have seen, will concern us later in §5, it is enough to note here that Amos, who came from the south, preached freely at Bethel, the national sanctuary of the north (7.10ff.), and was only expelled when he attacked the person of the monarch Jeroboam II. Isaiah received his famous vision (6.1ff.) in the temple at Jerusalem and in a place where the ordinary believer was not allowed to enter; moreover, he developed, as we shall again see later (ch. IV, §4), a true theology of his own about the election of Zion and its sanctuary. Jeremiah, too, preached freely in the temple (cf. chs. 7;26), and only had difficulty when he announced its destruction, an assertion which according to some was tantamount to blasphemy. The knowledge of the priesthood displayed by Hosea has led some to suspect that he was of priestly stock, and we know this to have been true of Jeremiah and Ezekiel. The result is a close bond on the one hand between the prophets and the sanctuaries and on the other between the prophets and the priesthood, which is the opposite of what might be supposed from a superficial observation of their criticism of these two institutions.

(e) Another distinction, this time real and therefore of considerable importance, should be made within the prophetic movement and is of a historical character: that between the pre-exilic and the post-exilic prophets. As we shall see, the former were concerned in effect with every aspect of life: fidelity to the cult, external and internal politics, social problems, the fate of non-Israelite peoples. This interest in every sphere of life is, however, markedly reduced in the case of the post-exilic prophets: their preaching is increasingly directed to elements within the Jewish community with accents which are sometimes close to legalism: there is mention of the cult, the priesthood and sacrifices, but not so much to challenge the validity of their present forms as to improve them. Ethical problems, too, are seen in a more restricted, we might almost say provincial, perspective. Of course it is easy, indeed all too easy, to pronounce disqualificatory judgments at this point or only to note the lower level of theology and ethics in this prophecy, indicating its essentially introverted character. Its preoccupations often appear to be paltry in comparison with pre-exilic prophecy, and it has a certain chauvinistic tone which was absent earlier. We should, however, remember before giving an over-hasty judgment that the reality of the post-exilic Jewish community in the last quarter of the sixth century BC was that of a laborious economic and political reconstruction on the one hand and a no less laborious reconstruction of a spiritual legacy on the other, which risked being irremediably compromised because of the break in oral tradition which had occurred. We should never forget that everyday reality consisted in harsh confrontations with neighbouring peoples, now no longer held at bay by anyone, and in a political life which was constantly frustrated by foreign domination: first under the Persians, then under the Macedonians, the Diadochi and finally the Romans, with the brief interregnum of the Maccabees (167–63 BC). It is not surprising that in a situation of this kind problems which might seem insignificant to us acquired a crucial importance, perhaps dispropor-tionate to their effective value, and ended by polarizing all the attention of the people upon them. Nevertheless, while rejecting the critical exaggerations of some writers, we should recognize that we do in fact have here a regressive phenomenon on the level of thought and spirituality, with one exception: the development of eschatology and the expectation connected with it, whether or not that was messianic. But even here an element of regression was also to be found: the rise of apocalyptic. Apparently the move from prophecy to apocalyptic took place without a break, and with a logical continuity, whereas in reality these were two substantially different elements. In prophecy we have the struggle for the people of God and its mission, because faith is accompanied by a vision of the breakthrough of a new and more righteous world and of the conversion of nations (cf. Isa.2.2–5// Micah 4.1–5), for which the prophet turns to both individuals and communities, calling on them to be converted. In apocalyptic, which apparently had similar aims, everything happened from the side of God and not from the side of man, by means of phenomena of a miraculous and mythical character, achieved directly by God or the

beings who surrounded him (who unexpectedly acquired an importance which at first they did not have, giving place to a complex
angelology). Man merely experienced these phenomena to a greater
or lesser degree depending on the case, but with the risk of being
totally disengaged from them. It is not, therefore, by chance that in this
way prophecy was progressively extinguished or that, once prophecy
was extinguished, its place was progressively taken by apocalyptic
positions of perhaps a similar scope, like the proclamation of the
establishment of the kingdom of God. There is a substantial difference
in the way in which man is seen in this process, whether as an active
subject or as an object of events greater than himself, coming from a
mythical world which therefore contrasts with that of the traditional
faith of Israel.

§4. *The character of the prophetic ministry and problems still unsolved*

(a) The end of the last century and the beginning of this saw not
only the examination of the Pentateuch but a discussion of the
problem of a new evaluation of prophecy and the prophets. In the
traditional exegesis of the church the prophets had been considered
essentially as heralds of the coming of Christ: their sayings had been
fulfilled in his person, his death and his resurrection. It is also possible
sometimes to find a messianic interpretation of this kind, still of
course directed towards the future, even in the synagogue. This is the
attitude that we still find in some conservative Christian circles or in
some conservative groups within the principal churches. It is not
surprising that, once research was channelled in this direction, it led
to a huge increase in the number of prophecies which were considered
messianic. These were drawn from material which was not properly
prophetic but was interpreted prophetically. The tendency can also
be seen in a number of passages in the New Testament.

Over the centuries, therefore, first the primitive church and then
the later church drew from the Old Testament, and especially the
prophets, an infinity of texts which could apparently be classified as
messianic and which were thought to have been fulfilled in the person
of Jesus of Nazareth, the promised Christ. The procedure was based
(and is still based where it is maintained) on the saying of Jesus
reported in the Fourth Gospel: 'You search the scriptures . . . and it
is they that bear witness to me' (John 5.39).

(b) The extension of historical-critical methods to the prophets
definitively put an end to this kind of research, the character of which

was extremely speculative and therefore irrational. We may add that in the light of a more objective analysis of the text, only a very few passages from the prophets, perhaps five and certainly no more than ten, can be considered messianic: Isa. 8.23–9.6 (EVV 9.1–7); 11.1–9; Micah 5.2–5; Zech. 9.9 and perhaps also, with serious qualifications, Isa. 7.10–17. Furthermore, in all these passages the primary reference is to an imminent if not an immediate future. Only at a later date did they come to be read in an eschatological and messianic key. This approach was an evident violation of the author's intention, though it probably understood the ultimate implications of the proclamation of the message better than the author himself. Had the traditional lines of research been maintained, recognition of this fact would certainly have led to a considerable impoverishment of the prophetic message even for those who saw their work as being historical, religious or even theological, let alone for the rationalists. What would remain of the prophetic message once it was limited to specifically messianic passages? Very little, in fact!

(c) It is therefore understandable that after hundreds, even thousands, of years of impersonal, messianic interpretation, interest and therefore study have been directed in the opposite direction. Investigations have been made into the personality of the prophets and their religious experience, and this experience has been compared with analogous phenomena attested in the history of religions. Studies have been made, for example, of mysticism, their inner conflicts, etc. In other words, an attempt has been made to recover the human dimension of the prophets, which had been neglected for so many centuries. The two most important figures who laid the basis for this research were Bernhard Duhm and Gustav Hölscher, whose works even the modern scholar must take into account, if only because of the questions they ask, even though the answers they give now seem generally to be inadequate. Their positions in fact combine elements of nineteenth-century idealistic philosophy and German Romanticism, the beginnings of scientific psychology, the history of religions and ethnology, nineteenth-century German historicism and other elements typical of the general philosophical and cultural approach of the previous century.

The prophet was thus first examined as an individual and in particular as a religious personality, whose experiences could be considered paradigmatic. The one concession which was made to the idea of community was that he was seen as the head of a school; there was also, of course, the fact that the prophet preached to an assembled people. In a historiography which attributed a fundamental importance in the political, economic and ideological field to the work of the individual genius, disregarding the other factors without which the 'genius' could not have operated and perhaps could not even have existed, an approach to the problem on these lines cannot be surprising; and if on principle we reject it as inadequate, we should at least recognize that it was a valid alternative to the impersonal, disembodied approach by which the prophets had hitherto been studied. Suddenly, in fact, the prophet appeared to his audience as a man of flesh and blood, situated in a particular ideological, social, economic and political context, with all the conflicts which that normally involved. Confronted with a predominantly conservative or conformist people or ruling group, according to this new evaluation the prophet emerged as a spiritual giant, often forced to fight on two fronts: against an audience which was uninterested, if not hostile, and against a God who sometimes did not hesitate to overwhelm the prophet's will. Amos 7.14 in fact affirms that God 'took' (root *lqh*) him; in Jer. 1.4ff. at first the prophet does not know what to do, but is constrained by God who sweeps all his excuses aside. Ezekiel is overwhelmed by a tremendous vision which leaves him no alternative. Where, as in the case of Jeremiah, the theme of direct compulsion appears, we of course have internal insecurity and conflict; the so-called 'confessions' of the prophet bear witness to this (11.18–23; 15.15–21; 17.12–18; 18.18–23; 20.10–13; cf. also 12.1–6; 15.10–12; 20.7–9, 14–18). Conflicts could also arise over certain tasks which were considered to be too hard: in Isa. 6.1ff. (a passage which, as we shall see, was understood only in this particular way, cf. ch. IV, §3a), only a special act of God succeeds in convincing the prophet that he should announce to his people their wholesale destruction. The term 'confessions' applied to these passages of Jeremiah is already itself indicative of the approach to the problem, so much so that it has been rejected in a study of the period by W. Baumgartner, considered a classic, which speaks more soberly of 'laments in poetry', cf. below ch. VII, §2. For the figure of Ezekiel there is no lack in the texts of phenomena which lend themselves to a psychopathological interpretation: abnormal visions (chs. 1,10), aphonia (3.26), catalepsis (4.4–8), while in one case we have an episode which could be put in parapsychological categories: the transportation of the prophet in the spirit from Babylon to Jerusalem (ch. 8).

As individualists, then, whether by nature or vocation, the prophets were said to have rejected the cult of the era in favour of a more spiritual and more personal piety, or at least a piety closer to what was considered piety in the circles of bourgeois Victorian Protestantism.

They were thought sometimes to have foretold the abolition of absolutely every external form of worship in favour of right living by the individual or society; sometimes to have renounced what the authors in question considered an unnecessary superstructure. Typical positions of the 'liberal' or 'pietistic' Protestantism of the period were thus anachronistically projected back by the writers on to the prophetic message: the triumph of the moral law, ethical monotheism (whatever the exact meaning of this expression might have been – it was far from obvious), contempt for any ritual practice, and other elements. Nor can it be affirmed that these positions have been completely superseded today; they still appear, paradoxically, in a theology which some Christian groups would wish to derive from the prophets, rejecting the cult uncritically and substituting for it personal and collective obligations on the ethical level, which are no better, or only vaguely, defined. There are indications of a psychological approach to many problems in the recent, basic work by J. Lindblom.

(d) With few exceptions, contemporary authors agree in rejecting *en bloc* this kind of approach to the problems of prophecy, even if the majority are disposed to recognize that to have suggested it helped considerably in opening up a line of study which had been closed for too long. This rejection has not, however, resolved the innumerable problems nor provided answers to the many questions which have been raised in the course of the last fifty years, except in a very inadequate way, and that holds true both for the synagogue and the church and for oriental studies generally. This is confirmed by a remark of von Rad, who openly declares that the problems raised at the end of the last century and the beginning of this need to be re-examined, though with clearly different presuppositions on both the historical and the theological level. He is followed by M.-L. Henry, who asks how, given the unique character of biblical prophecy in the history of religion, these words which were given in connection with specific facts and situations have survived on the level of tradition, coming down to our own day as authoritative words which are also normative for situations and facts that are evidently very different from those of the age in which they were originally spoken. In other words, criticism directed at a particular form of approach cannot be a reason for not responding to demands which have been raised and problems which have been posed. We shall examine the chief of these in the following sections.

§5. Prophecy and cult

(a) In the pre-exilic prophetic books the following passages refer to the cult, all in a polemical manner: Amos 4.4f.; 5.21–25; Hos. 6.6; 8.11–13; Isa. 1.11–17; Micah 6.6–8; Jer. 7.1–11, 21–23. Only the most important and the most explicit passages are mentioned here. First of all, it should be noted that while none of these texts speaks of the cult in general, all mention some components, often important, of the cult of the period which was practised in the temples of the north (Amos and Hosea) or in the temple of Jerusalem (Isaiah, Micah and Jeremiah). The chief concern is with sacrifices: of the eight principal passages which speak of the cult, six refer to this practice, which must have led to notable abuses in all areas. The other features of the cult are statistically much rarer: there are two mentions, in a general or a detailed form, of festivals, two mentions of different sanctuaries, one each of pilgrimages, altars and prayers.

(b) As we have seen, in the literature of some decades ago one might often read that the prophets sought the abolition of the ritual cult in favour of a more 'spiritual' cult which, in the intention of the authors in question, was to anticipate Jesus' words to the woman of Samaria in John 4.23, understood idealistically. It would be without sacrifices, without ceremonies, without sanctuaries, and composed exclusively of prayers, songs and meditations. As often happens, connections of this kind are possible only at the cost of an excessive simplification of the problems; in the case in point the contrast between the cult on the one hand and spirituality and obligation on the other did not hold in the light of a fundamental study of the message of the prophets. In fact modern scholars are unanimous in recognizing that the point of encounter was the struggle between traditional Israelite faith and Canaanite religion or syncretism, in other words, between two different ways of understanding faith. Elijah had said 'Either Yahweh or Baal'. The situation was in fact as follows. Hebrew worship had apparently remained tied to its traditional content, even if the cruder forms from early times had been refined over the centuries; its essence had not been changed. But this ideological continuity was limited to the *form* of the cult, and it was easy (probably even without the knowledge of those who took part in the cult) for a deity who was much more like Baal and the other Canaanite gods to come to be worshipped under the name of Yahweh and under cover of ancient rites and concepts. Gratitude to Yahweh for benefits received was replaced by a mysticism connected with the fertility of the soil, the flock and the herd, and therefore fully integrated into the seasonal agricultural cycle of Canaan with the basically mythical approach which underlies such a belief. Israelite belief was thus dissociated and alienated from the real problems of everyday life; moreover this other attitude left ethical problems on one side, since cults of this kind obviously tend increasingly to assume the orgiastic forms characteristic of them. The catalogue of objects removed from the Jerusalem temple at the time of Josiah's reform (622–621, cf. II Kings 23.4ff.) is an impressive example of developments in what was to become the central sanctuary of Israel, even allowing that the passage contains considerable exaggerations of a polemical nature. Ezekiel 8.1ff. also testifies to the practice of Canaanite cults at a time later than Josiah's reform.

Once the problem has been posed in this way, it would be relatively simple to solve if we had a full knowledge of Israelite worship in the pre-exilic period or, better still, before the monarchy. That, however, is not the case and we are therefore compelled to reconstruct elements of the cult laboriously and almost always hypothetically on the basis of references to it in the prophets themselves (and since these texts are out of context, we cannot be certain of their significance). We have to rely on the hypothesis that the restoration towards which Josiah's reform was directed reflects beliefs and rites which really were old and were not just believed to be old. Thus it remains extremely difficult to discover whether the prophets proclaimed a message that was substantially new, and if so at what point, although this theory was put forward many times up to the end of the last century and the beginning of this and has recently been advanced again. Nor do we know whether they reminded the people of the ancient content of the cult, in which case they would be not so much against the cult as such as against the form and content which it had assumed. The solution of this problem seems a hopeless undertaking in the present state of research.

However, it is also far from easy to seek to recognize elements of the ancient faith of Israel in the message of the prophets. Thus to affirm for example that the prophets appealed to the ancient concept of the 'covenant' which is originally supposed to have governed relationships between Yahweh and his people is risky, to say the least, not only because of the new sense which has been given to the term $b^e r \bar{\imath} t$ = 'obligation, condition, oath', but also because this word only appears once in the prophets with unquestionably theological connotations, and in a text about which critics are uncertain: Hosea 8.1. The many allusions to the concept which distinguished authors have believed that they could discover in various places in the message of the prophets are no more than allusions, and therefore their identification is the product of judgments which must necessarily be extremely subjective. Nor can we assert that the prophets summoned the people to obey the divine will which had been expressed on Sinai, simply because Isa. 6.1ff. makes an obvious reference to phenomena connected with the Sinai theophany: this proves only that the theme of the theophany was expressed in terms borrowed from the revelation on Sinai (though the contrary might also be the case), and not that the theology in question was the foundation for that of the prophets. As we have seen, the problems of the Sinai pericope are too complex for us to be able to use it to illuminate the message of the prophets.

In any case, it is clear from the polemic of the prophets that the cult practised in Israel and in Judah did not conform to the will of God and that therefore a complex ritual had taken the place of gratitude to God for his past works, gratitude which should have been coherently expressed in everyday life. These two themes, the one the consequence of the other, seem to be all that we can reconstruct of the original faith of Israel. Fertility and 'the good year', the logical aim of the work of every peasant and every herdsman, could not be obtained by rites and beliefs borrowed from Canaan, but were given back as the gifts of God to his people, as Hos. 2 takes pains to point out. Now through Canaanite practices, about which we are relatively well informed by the texts of the city-state of Ugarit which can be dated between the fourteenth and the twelfth centuries BC, the faithful were able up to a certain point to guarantee the happy outcome of the year, whereas everything else remained of secondary importance. Again, these forms of cult offered an abundant system of expiatory rites for faults committed within the sphere of day-to-day life: and it was evidently easier to remedy sins committed in the political and social sphere by ritual than on a practical level. It was against this kind of cult, then, and especially against sacrifices, which more readily lent themselves to abuses of this kind, that the prophets vigorously directed their efforts. They did so in the certainty that they were attacking not only 'heresy' but elements which had a destructive effect on the very concept of the people of God, one of whose chief characteristics should have been a solidarity which bound its members together.

(c) How could matters have reached this point? Taking up the argument of the prophets, we have pointed to syncretism as the principal cause. This is a difficult phenomenon to avoid where populations of different origins first live together and then become assimilated; it is obviously a gradual phenomenon which in time finishes by invading every area of human existence: civilization, culture, language, religion. Typical examples may be found from the sixth century AD onwards, when the non-Christian or Arian 'barbarians' settled in the ruins of the western territories of the Roman empire or when the Spaniards conquered the territories of the old indigenous civilizations of the Americas. We have seen that the tribes of Israel or its ancestors first settled in a more or less peaceful fashion in the thinly populated zones on the periphery of the country, alongside the autochthonous population, with whom they took up commercial relationships and from whom they borrowed language and certain techniques. In at least one case, Gen. 34. 1ff., the Old Testament bears witness to the fact that settlements of this kind could have been considered welcome by the local population because of the richness of the flocks which the nomads brought with them; this advantage certainly far exceeded the disadvantages arising from settlement by a foreign population. But certain techniques, especially in agriculture, the rearing of cattle in a settled situation and building, were closely bound up with the rites which went with them, so that the appropriation of them brought with it the danger that beliefs might be revised and might depart from their original form. No wonder that the more civilized Canaanites, from whom the invaders almost always learnt, also had the better of the raw invaders at a later date, even when the latter had in fact become the masters. However, this sort of syncretism does not seem to have preoccupied the prophets excessively; of course, it could have been that, from the eighth century on, the problem only presented itself in a limited form, and was confined to peripheral areas. What did concern them was what we have defined elsewhere as a 'state syncretism', a phenomenon which appears with David and reaches its climax with the building of the temple in Jerusalem. We know other cases of it elsewhere. As we have seen, David brought the ark to Jerusalem, thus making a pagan city also the religious capital of the united kingdom of Israel and Judah. Solomon then built the temple there, a work which the prophet Nathan had succeeded in preventing during the reign of David. The building was intended not only to offer a worthy dwelling place for the ark; it was also part of a more ambitious plan, that it should be the national sanctuary for all the Israelite empire, that is for Israel, for the Canaanite population which had been subjected or made vassals, and for the territories in Syria and Transjordania which had been made tributary. One god was worshipped in the temple, Yahweh the God of the victors, but this worship had in some way or other to satisfy the other peoples of the empire. Because there was no ethnic unity, there had to be at least religious unity, even if only on a formal level, and this could only be obtained by attributing to Yahweh characteristics of the gods of Canaan and its neighbours. The ease with which the characteristics of one deity could be attributed to another in paganism is well known. These new characteristics revealed themselves not only in the liturgy but in all the theology underlying the temple cult, and the phenomenon in practice lasted down to Josiah's reform. Isaiah, as we shall see, tried to incorporate them in the traditional theology of Israel, but about a century later Jeremiah was extremely perplexed when confronted with them.

(d) The prophets, then, were critical of the cult but did not reject it on principle. This position is confirmed by the fact that, as we have seen, they were able to speak freely in the temple during the cult. And since we have reason to suppose that, as elsewhere, the liturgy of the Israelite cult was regulated down to the last detail, it does not seem rash to argue that, if Amos could preach in the temple of Bethel and Jeremiah in the temple of Jerusalem, the prophets had a position assigned to them in the liturgy, a period of time during which there was a provision that they should speak. We cannot therefore accept that the prophets were far removed from the cult; we would not, however, support the opposite opinion, held by many Scandinavian authors, who would make the prophets functionaries of the state cult. The words pronounced by Amos (7.10ff.) against Amaziah the priest rule out an interpretation of this kind, though there is obviously nothing here to question the existence of this kind of functionary, who may also have been given the title nābī'.

§6. Prophecy and politics

(a) One field in which we see the prophets active from the beginning is that of politics, both domestic and foreign. Samuel and Nathan are advisers, the former to Saul and the latter to David and then, for a brief period, to Solomon; Ahijah of Shiloh promises Jeroboam that he will reign over the ten northern tribes (I Kings 11.31f.); Elijah plots and Elisha organizes a revolution which overthrows the dynasty of Omri in Israel, putting in the place of its last king a general, Jehu (II Kings 9); and one of the first acts of the new sovereign was the extermination not only of the survivors of the despotic dynasty but also of those who were faithful to Baal (II Kings 10.18ff.). The narrative attributes to Elisha a similar operation against Damascus, but the note seems historically improbable on the basis of other Near Eastern sources; the remarkable thing is that the narrator does not find it strange that a prophet should intervene in a revolution not only in his own country but even in that of a foreign state. However, later generations did not accept these actions uncritically: Hos. 1.4 dissociates itself firmly with hard words, especially from the bloodshed which resulted, and notwithstanding the frequent and often harsh criticism directed against particular monarchs by the prophets, they were never ready to back violent actions of this kind with their participation.

(b) Amos and Micah do not take up any position in the political field, unless we want to put the attack against the person of the king in Amos 7.10ff. or some oracles against the nations in this category. Hosea attacks the politicians of the north and especially the monarchy; cf. Hos. 5.13, where there is criticism of attempts at an alliance with Assyria (here, following a generally accepted conjecture, we should read 'to the Great King' in the Hebrew and not 'to King Jareb': the title 'Great King' is frequently attested for the king of Assyria and the correction leaves the consonantal text almost intact); cf. also 7.3 and 8.10. The theme is developed in Isaiah, and we have a real political theology: in 2.12–22 and in 31.1ff. the support given to political alliances is considered a grave lack of faith; in Isa. 7.1ff. two alternatives are considered by the court: to surrender to the coalition of the northern kingdom and Damascus or to call on the help of Assyria against them (which was in fact the policy accepted). The prophet proposes a third possibility: to trust in Yahweh and his promises, since he will not allow the plans of the allies to be realized. Behind the apparent quietism we have here an exhortation to take the divine promises seriously and to act in conformity with them. Throughout his book, but especially in the time of Jehoiakim and Zedekiah, Jeremiah urges the people to submit to Babylon and not to trust in the help of Egypt, and for this stand he is accused of high treason (cf. chs. 32 and 37f.).

(c) In Israel, of course, as with the majority of the peoples of the ancient world, national community and religious community coincided, as we saw when considering the law. Consequently this political involvement of the prophets is at least partially conditioned by particular situations of their time which are different from those of today. The situation has already changed by the time of the New Testament: alongside the people of God in the ethnic and political sense can be found a second people of God, which transcends these limitations. This explains why there are phrases in the message of Jesus and the apostles which can be interpreted in the sense of political disengagement and respect (albeit not unconditional) for established authority. The important thing to note here is that the pre-exilic prophets never grasped problems of this kind, while the post-exilic prophets, who could have grasped them, were never confronted with them. Be this as it may, the fact remains that the pre-exilic prophets always struggled to ensure that politics in every sphere, and therefore the power of decision, should not remain the privilege of the monarchy and of the groups which developed around it, but should be so to speak democratized. Here too they recalled indirectly the ancient institutions of the semi-nomadic tribes. This behaviour, as the case of Jeremiah adequately demonstrates, was not free from danger.

§7. *Prophecy and social problems*

(*a*) Nathan in II Sam. 12 did not hesitate to speak out publicly against David on the occasion of the death of Uriah the Hittite, for which the king was directly responsible. The character of the story, which is full of elements from popular legend, does not disguise the fact that the *vox populi* considered it obvious that even when confronted with the great David a prophet should speak out and publicly accuse the king of an unforgivable crime. We find behaviour of this kind throughout the history of the prophets, even if not in the dramatic form which can be found in this passage. However, the case of Uriah the Hittite, with all the limitations on the historical plane that we noted earlier, does not yet symbolize a fundamentally unjust social structure, but remains within the sphere of the isolated outrage. The fact that the king was forced to yield to the prophetic claim shows that contacts between the monarchy and the populace were still real, that public opinion had an importance which not even the king could ignore. In other words, this was still an essentially healthy society. How far such a picture of the situation is an idyllic and wishful projection back into history and therefore an artificial situation, and how far it corresponds in essentials to reality, is difficult to say. The episode of Naboth's vineyard is similar, but much more complex because of the differences of social structure which underlie it (I Kings 21). Here Elijah accuses Ahab of the assassination, on a pseudo-legal pretext, of a tenant of ancient tribal land, because he refused to yield his land to the crown, despite a more than generous offer. But whereas in the episode of Nathan, Uriah and David, public opinion expressed in the assembly was decisively marshalled against David and David was forced to give way, here the tribunal, made up of the elders of the village (cf. above, Part Two, ch.V, §7), who should have joined forces to a man behind their comrade Naboth against the unjust order of the queen, rejecting evidence which they knew to be false, joins in the game and condemns the defendant to death. Thus while the two episodes are similar in form, there is a basic shift between them, a change in public opinion. In the second instance public opinion does not intervene or is prevented from intervening effectively. In reality it had come about that the Israelite monarchy had been progressively conditioned to an originally Canaanite pattern (sometimes, but wrongly, called feudal), and what was worse, had taken it over from Canaanite civilization in a now decadent phase. The ancient assemblies of the Israelite people had been replaced by absolutist forms of government, a regressive development which the preaching of the prophets from the eighth century on had completely laid bare.

(b) To judge from the social invective of the prophets from the eighth century to the exile, the situation in the social sphere had deteriorated rapidly. We no longer find isolated cases of corruption or suppression which had only to be unmasked for public opinion to take the part of the victim; on the contrary, we must speak of a system so corrupt and repressive that H. Donner could compare it effectively with that of early capitalism, whereas Fohrer spoke of the transition from a closed economy to a commercial economy, underlining at the same time that the prophets did not reject economic progress *per se*, but the distorted situations to which it led in the economic and social spheres. This system gradually took the place of that of the semi-nomadic tribe, in which there was relative equality on the social level. As has been indicated, the origin and the pattern of this transformation was the decadent society of Canaan; we use the word 'decadent' deliberately, because we have noteworthy evidence of good government from Ugarit at the time of its greatest prosperity. There are elements which even in a social situation of a feudal character (as we have seen, the expression 'feudal' is not quite exact, but is used as a convention) guarantee the administration of justice according to certain canons of equity and thus secure the protection of the weakest members. A legendary king like Keret was sternly accused of having omitted through negligence to judge the cause of the widow and to do justice to one who had suffered unjustly, and of not having exiled one who enriched himself at the expense of the poor. Another legendary king, Daniel, 'judged the cause of the widow and did justice to the orphan'. It is not, therefore, the case that justice and equity were unknown in Canaan, but everything suggests that in its state of decadence, Canaanite society made possible a series of abuses and repressions. This was the society with which Israel was involved at the time of David's conquest, when the city-states of the plains were incorporated – we do not know how – into the Israelite empire. Solomon in his turn reconstructed them and refortified them, restoring power to the nobility which fought in his chariotry.

But these remarks are not enough to explain the phenomenon. Furthermore, the tribal structure of Israel, created with a view to a social and economic situation quite different from that of a peasant or bourgeois society, was no longer adequate. It progressively declined, emptied of any effective content, even though it was maintained at a formal level. This process had been accelerated to a considerable degree by the monarchy, which, just as it had favoured syncretism in the religious sphere with the building of the temple, had weakened the tribal structure by dividing the territories into districts created for purely administrative purposes (I Kings 4.7ff.). The new system took no account of the traditional boundaries and thus forced the tribes to integrate themselves rapidly into the milieu of the Canaanite population, at a time when they were not mature enough for such a process. Furthermore, a new and important centre of power was developing around the palace; I Sam. 22.7 already attributes to Saul a discourse which bears witness to the fact that in Israel, too, kings were accustomed to reward their more loyal subjects with land and other benefits, thus favouring the rise of a new class tied to the court instead of to the tribe; in this operation, too, the Canaanite pattern was followed. The class in question had been assigned large pieces of land in competition with tribal property and sometimes in conflict with it, and in those days this amounted to the possession of economic power. In such conditions the tribal structure, quite apart from its intrinsic weakness when faced with a completely different situation, had little chance of survival, and merely sought to adapt itself to the new state of affairs. It was condemned to progressive extinction.

The process was further accelerated by the Aramaean wars which afflicted Israel especially, but also Judah, throughout the ninth century and part of the eighth. During these wars the landed proprietors, while sometimes suffering losses, were at least able to recoup them with plunder from the battlefield, and at least parts of their land, extended as it was, could be saved. On the other hand, owners of tribal property, concentrated in a restricted geographical area and therefore more exposed to pillage and other destruction, without the support of liquid capital, ended by having to resort to loans at a high rate of interest, which tended after a short while to benefit the great landowners. In the face of this new situation, an episode like that of Naboth seems a mere bagatelle.

(c) Prophetic invective in the social field, then, should be seen against the background of this complicated transformation. The principal texts are as follows: Amos 2.6ff.; 3.9ff.; 4.1–3; 5.7,10f.; 6.4f.; 8.4; Isa. 1.10–17 (which we have already examined in connection with the question of the prophets and the cult), 23; 2.7; 3.13–15; 5.11ff., 22ff.; 29.21; Micah 2.1–5; 3.1–4; 6.6–8; cf. also Ezek. 22. The theme is, however, absent in Hosea and is rarely discussed by Jeremiah.

The faults chiefly indicated are, with tragic monotony: the corruption of the courts, which prevented anyone with right on his side or who had suffered a wrong from obtaining what he was owed by law, especially if he was poor; the oppression of those who had no economic means to defend themselves; the plundering of the poor, which usually happened in a way which kept the letter of the law intact (for example, through loans given at high rates of interest); money-making that was illegal or at any rate disproportionate to the capital invested and the risks run, followed by the ostentatious luxury which is typical of the *nouveaux riches*.

We should look in vain, however, among the prophets for an analysis of the economic, historical and political factors by means of which we have attempted to explain the origin of this situation. For them, the problem is an essentially theological one. The people have abandoned belief in Yahweh, so that the criticism of social problems is directly rooted in the criticism of the cult and the syncretistic developments within it. What had happened was only possible because the people abandoned Yahweh. Otherwise, they seem to want to affirm, it should have been possible to find new structures adapted to the different situation in which the people were involved, structures moreover which were outlined in earlier laws.

(d) We also look in vain among the prophets for an integrated plan for reform; still less is there any hint of the possibility of a revolution. The experience of the revolt of Jehu which had been inspired by Elisha must have discouraged the prophets. Although Jehu had deposed the ruling house and had begun with a kind of bloody religious reform, he had left everything worse than it was before. Only the conversion of the people and their rulers could bring about what needed to happen in politics, society and culture. Thus paradoxically the prophets end by proving themselves to be conservatives, in the sense that they remind their audience of the old model of the tribal organization in which the head is the person who combines in himself bravery, wisdom and goodness and whose office was (and among some Bedouin groups until quite recently still has been) elective. The life of the tribal group was characterized by an austere dignity in which the well-to-do were never excessively so and the poor were never indigent. This is still the case among nomadic Arab groups today. Wherever the tribe decided to establish a settled home the land belonged to everyone and was assigned by periodic rotations to the various clans of which it was made up. This reminder of the past is not, however, as conservative as it might seem at first sight: in Israel it was firmly bound up with an eschatological hope which looked to the return of paradise.

The modern reader might perhaps feel the lack of a positive programme in the prophets, but the reasons for this are not difficult to discover: the social structure in Syria and Palestine at that time did not offer valid alternatives, and the prophets, with their eschatological outlook, do not seem to have been capable of suggesting any, while a return pure and simple to the ancient tribal structure was anachronistic and utopian. At the same time, however, we get an answer to the question why the words of the prophets maintained their authority even outside their context: it was not just a question of the sympathy of the Israelite population towards the ancient nomadic structures, as clearly appears from Jer. 35, although they could no longer return to them, but also of the eschatological hope which developed increasingly with time. In the essentially democratic nomadic structures, the prophets gave the people a parameter of judgment in the field of social ethics which produced most remarkable results over the centuries, even if they were not felt immediately.

§8. Prophecy and history

(a) With the biblical prophets we once again come up against an attempt at historical synthesis. To our eyes it might seem to have all kinds of limitations, but it must be given its full value, because along with J and the redactors of the books of Samuel it forms the precursor to the Deuteronomistic movement.

(b) In the prophetic interpretation the past is sometimes assessed in an extremely critical way, even including the nomadic period, though (as we have seen) this was much valued by the prophets from a religious and social point of view. At other times, however, it seems to be idealized. It depends on the message which a particular prophet was announcing. Almost all the extremely rare mentions of the patriarchs outside the Pentateuch fall into the category that we might call 'critical'. One example is Jacob in Hos. 12.3b–5, where the patriarch is severely censured and accused of the same fault as the people: he is their precursor, if not their inspiration. The passage is interesting because it indicates the existence of different traditions from those handed down to us in the Pentateuch. Hosea 9.10f.; 11.1–4; cf. Amos 9.7, give a critical assessment of the exodus. In the second category, however, are passages like Isa. 9.3 (*EVV* 9.4) and Jer. 2.2f., in which the exodus is valued in an extremely positive way, in contrast to the passages we have just mentioned. The description of Saul's reign in Hos. 10.9 seems negative, which is something that we might not expect when we think of the hostility of the north in its encounters with the dynasty of David; there is also a severe judgment on the cult of Bethel and Dan (Hos. 8.5; Amos 4.4; 7.10ff.). Prophetic historiography resembles what we have seen in Dtr, albeit on a smaller scale, in looking for the origin of the situation in which the people now find themselves, and like Dtr, the prophets find this origin in the history of the people. Throughout history there are rare instances in which the people have done their duty, but in general the report is a negative one: on the best showing, the attitude of the people has been inadequate. Sometimes Yahweh has punished them by means of catastrophes which they have incurred through their fault. At the same time, however, prophetic historiography burst through the narrow confines of the people of God to include in its consideration the whole world of nations, especially the neighbouring peoples. In this way there arises a universal historiography; the actions of the people of God are intimately connected with and sometimes conditioned by those of other peoples, who are also instruments in the divine hand.

These concepts are important because they show that by means of the prophets Israel freed itself from the idea that the destiny of the deity is closely bound up with that of the people or peoples who worship him. One can think of the Mesopotamian and Hittite custom of deporting not only the population but also the statues of their gods, to demonstrate what might be called the metaphysical character of their defeat. Thus, when in 597 and 587 the Babylonians did not find any image in the temple, they contented themselves with carrying off the sacred vessels. Cyrus scrupulously restored them in 539. Yahweh existed independently of his people. He could reject them and choose others, and if he decided not to do this definitively, it was only through his goodness. Ezekiel, who was deported in 597 after the first siege of Jerusalem, and who therefore, along with Jeremiah, experienced the drama of his people more deeply than any other, did not hesitate to turn upside down the traditional categories of election which were the inspiration of Israel (cf. chs. 16; 20; 23). When the announcement of the final fall of the capital arrived and all hope of restoration for the exiles had been extinguished (24.1ff.), Ezekiel began to proclaim restoration, and a few years later he was followed by Deutero–Isaiah. These concepts also freed Israel from the idea that there was a fate which held all men in its grasp, in the face of which not only men but even gods were impotent: Yahweh remained the motive force behind history, and everything was subject to him. Within their obvious limitations, these categories took the place of all mythical categories. Everything takes place in the world, among and by the agency of human beings, and this is also the sphere of the divine action.

(c) A particularly disconcerting element appears in the context of this problem: that of the 'false' prophecy which is opposed to true prophecy. This is a disconcerting phenomenon not only for us but certainly even more for the audience of that time, who were often compelled to choose between two substantially different messages, both of which laid claim to being the word of God. The search for an objective criterion by which to distinguish between the two was thus begun at an early stage, and Deut. 18.21f. is the most tangible sign of it: prophecy which is fulfilled is true, and the rest is not. However, it often happens that very simple solutions are simplistic. This one in fact makes a virtue of necessity: normally decisions one way or the other must be made immediately, and cannot be postponed to a time when verification becomes possible.

Two instances are particularly useful for an evaluation of the problem. The first is that of Micaiah ben Imlah towards the middle of the ninth century BC (I Kings 22.6, 16–23). Here the prophet announces that God himself has put a lying spirit in the mouths of the other prophets so that they do *not* tell the truth. They are therefore objectively 'false' prophets, whereas subjectively they are not, since they proclaim what they have received from the spirit! The second case, which is more complicated, is that of the encounter between Jeremiah and Hananiah (Jer. 28: the chronology is in some disorder: 27.1 should be corrected on the basis of the notes given in vv. 3, 12, 16ff., whereas 28.1 should be read, following the LXX: 'In the same year, the fourth year of Zedekiah', that is, in 594 BC, cf. *BHS*). Hananiah prophesies the inviolability of Zion, one of the themes of the message of Isaiah which was, however, put in doubt by Micah 3.12, though there are some who consider the latter passage to be of doubtful authenticity. Yet nothing could seem more correct and orthodox, and the message would therefore have had the marks of 'true' prophecy, to such a degree that Jeremiah himself, not knowing what to say after having announced the opposite, preferred to retreat (28.11b). Soon afterwards, however, having received an explanation from Yahweh, he returned to his charge, pronouncing at the same time a stern indictment against Hananiah, who was guilty of having presented a false message, and against the people who had listened to him. The two cases are a typical illustration of the complexity of the problem and the impossibility of finding a solution to it on the objective level. Here we have one of those cases where the believer is forced to make a choice which will be all the more difficult, the less clear and obvious the dilemma. It has recently been argued that this kind of ambiguity is inevitable in the human proclamation of the word of God, which is also conditioned by contingent factors and the setting in which it is made.

(d) The prophets were not only occupied with the near future, but also with a more distant horizon, though this appears much more rarely in their words. We can already see a second stage in their preaching: after the inevitable judgment, grace is often announced. For some prophets this is limited to an 'elect remnant', who are converted after escaping the judgment. This is an interesting though primitive attempt to distinguish between the people of God as an ethnic unit and the people of God merely as the community of believers. For other prophets the situation has deteriorated to such a degree that God himself will have to intervene, creating in the people 'a new heart and a new spirit' (Ezek.36; 37). Jer.31.31 speaks of a 'new berit' that is going to replace earlier obligations which had no effect because of the prevarication of the people, while Deutero-Isaiah announces the coming of the Servant of Yahweh who will take upon himself in his suffering the weight of the people's sins. Once again, all this is no longer history, but it does show that, in contrast to what happens in the apocalyptic writings, for the prophets even these saving events in the remote future will take place in history and not in myth, through man's conversion (even if this is simply achieved by God) and not through a sudden transformation from on high. We therefore favour the theory which (as we have said above) considers apocalyptic more as a regression than as the final stage in the development of prophecy.

BIBLIOGRAPHY

Commentary on all the prophetic books
J. A. Bewer, *The Prophets*, New York and London, 1949–54.

Select general bibliography

C. H. Cornill, *Der israelitische Prophetismus*, Berlin [13]1920; E. Sellin, *Der israelitische Prophetismus*, Leipzig 1912; G. Hölscher, *Die Profeten*, Leipzig 1914; H. Gunkel, *Die Propheten*, Göttingen 1917; B. Duhm, *Israels Propheten*, Tübingen [2]1922; A. Jepsen, *Nabi*, Munich 1934; P. Volz, *Prophetengestalten des Alten Testaments*, Stuttgart [3]1944; M. Buber, *The Prophetic Faith*, ET New York 1949; T. H. Robinson, *Prophecy and the Prophets in Ancient Israel*, London [2]1953; A. Neher, *The Prophetic Existence*, ET Cranbury and London 1969; C. Kuhl, *The Prophets of Israel*, ET Edinburgh 1960; E. Balla, *Die Botschaft der Propheten*, Tübingen 1958; G. von Rad, *The Message of the Prophets*, ET London 1968 (= the greater part of his *Old Testament Theology* II, ET Edinburgh 1966, reprinted London 1975); J. Lindblom, *Prophecy in Ancient Israel*, Oxford 1962; A. J. Heschel, *The Prophets*, New York 1962; N. K. Gottwald, *All the Kingdoms of the Earth*, New York 1964; J. Scharbert, *Die Propheten Israels*, 2 vols., Cologne 1965–7; W. H. Schmidt, 'Die prophetische "Grundgewissheit"', *EvTh* 31, 1971, 630–50; J. M. Schmidt, 'Probleme der Prophetenforschung', *VuF* 17, 1972, 39–81; cf. also the relevant articles in the encyclopaedias and dictionaries.

§1c. W. F. Albright, *From the Stone Age to Christianity*, Baltimore [2]1957, 303ff., esp. n. 37; H. M. Orlinsky, 'The Seer in Ancient Israel', *OrAnt* 4, 1965, 153–74; A. Jepsen, 'Gottesmann und Prophet', in H. W. Wolff (ed.), *Probleme biblischer Theologie. G. von Rad zum 70. Geburtstag*, Munich 1971, 171–83; K. Koch, 'Die Briefe "prophetischen" Inhalts aus Mari', *UF* 4, 1972, 53–77. For Zakir, see J. F. Ross, 'Prophecy in Hamath, Israel and Mari', *HTR* 63, 1970, 1–28.

§2a. F. Ellermeier, *Prophetie in Mari und Israel*, Herzberg am Harz 1968: a basic work which presents the material available up to the date of publication (some unedited or only partially so) and discusses the bibliography; cf. the review by J. G. Heintz, *RHPR* 51, 1971, 165–8. See also H. B. Huffmon, 'Prophecy in the Mari Letters', *BA* 31, 1968, 101–24; W. L. Moran, 'New Evidence from Mari on the History of Prophecy', *Bibl* 50, 1969, 15–56; J. F. Ross, art. cit.

§2b. For the general problems relating to Mari cf. *inter alios* H. Cazelles, 'Mari et l'Ancien Testament', *XVe Rencontre assyriologique internationale Liège 1966*, Paris 1967, 73–90 and bibliography; A. Petitjean and J. Coppens, 'Mari et l'Ancien Testament', in *De Mari à Qumran: Hommage à Mgr J. Coppens* I, Gembloux 1969, 3–13; A. Malamat, 'Mari', *BA* 34, 1971, 2–22.

§2c. T. Andrae, *Mohammad, the Man and his Faith*, ET London [3]1960, (a classic biography): B. Spuler, 'Muhammed', *RGG* IV [3]1960, 1187–9; G. Widengren, *Religionsphänomenologie*, Berlin 1969, analytical index s.v.

§3. For the relationship between prophecy and apocalyptic a basic study is R. North, 'Prophecy to Apocalyptic via Zechariah', *SVT* 22, 1972, 47–71; cf. also B. Corsani, 'L'apocalittica fra Antico e Nuovo Testamento', *Protestantesimo* 27, Rome 1972, 15–22.

§4a. A complete collection of what have traditionally been regarded as messianic prophecies is found in E. König, *Die messianische Weissagungen des Alten Testaments*, Stuttgart [2-3]1925; for contemporary views, cf. J. A. Soggin, 'mlk', *THAT* I, 1971, 908–20, esp. 913f. For the literary genres of prophecy see C. Westermann, *Basic Forms of Prophetic Speech*, ET Nashville and London 1967.

§4c. W. Baumgartner, *Die Klagedichte des Jeremia*, BZAW 32, 1917.

§4d. G. von Rad, *The Message of the Prophets*, 265 (= *Old Testament Theology* II, 298); J. Muilenburg, 'The "Office" of the Prophet in Ancient Israel', in J. P. Hyatt (ed.), *The Bible in Modern Scholarship*, New York and Nashville 1965, 74–97; M.-L. Henry, *Prophet and Tradition*, BZAW 116, 1969, 3ff.

§5. *Select Bibliography*: R. Hentschke, *Die Stellung der vorexilischen Propheten zum Kultus*, BZAW 75, 1957; E. Würthwein, 'Kultpolemik oder Kultbescheid?', in Würthwein and O. Kaiser (eds.), *Tradition und Situation. Festschrift A. Weiser*, Göttingen 1963, 115–31 (= Würthwein, *Wort und Existenz*, Göttingen 1970, 140–60). For cultic prophecy: G. Quell, 'Der Kultprophet', *TLZ* 81, 1956, 401–4; J. Jeremias, *Kultprophetie und Gerichts-verkündigung in der späten Königszeit*, WMANT 35, 1969; G. Fohrer, 'Priester und Prophet – Amt und Charisma?', *KuD* 17, 1971, 15–27; H. Schüngel-Straumann, *Gottesbild und Kultkritik vorexilischer Propheten*, Stuttgart 1972.

§5b. For the religion of Israel in the pre-monarchical period see G. Fohrer, *History of Israelite Religion*, ET London 1973, esp. 42–65.

§5c. For 'state syncretism' see J. A. Soggin, 'Der offiziell geförderte Synkretismus in Israel während des 10. Jahrhunderts', *ZAW* 78, 1966, 179–204. For the problem of the religion of Canaan and its relationship with that of Israel cf. É. Jacob, 'L'héritage cananéen dans le livre du prophète Osée', *RHPR* 43, 1963, 250–9; O. Eissfeldt, 'Israels Religion und die Religionen seiner Umwelt', *Neue Zeitschrift für systematische Theologie* 9, Berlin 1967, 8–27 (= his *Kleine Schriften* V, Tübingen 1973, 1–20).

§5d. For the view that almost all Israel's prophets were cultic figures see S. Mowinckel, *Psalmenstudien* III, Oslo 1923 (reprinted Amsterdam 1961); A. Haldar, *Associations of Cult Prophets among the Ancient Semites*, Uppsala 1945; for a more qualified view, A. R. Johnson, *The Cultic Prophet in Ancient Israel*, Cardiff [2]1962.

§6. *Select Bibliography*: K. Elliger, 'Prophet und Politik', *ZAW* 53, 1935, 3–22 (= his *Kleine Schriften*, Munich 1966, 118–40); H.-J. Kraus, *Prophetie und Politik*, Munich 1952 (with important bibliography); E. Würthwein, 'Jesaja 7.1–9, Ein Beitrag zu dem Thema: Prophetie und Politik', in *Theologie als Glaubenswagnis. Festschrift Karl Heim*, Hamburg 1954, 47–63 (= Würthwein, *Wort und Existenz*, Göttingen 1970, 127–43); E. Jenni, *Die politischen Voraussagen der Propheten*, Zurich 1956; H. Donner, *Israel unter den Völkern*, Leiden 1964; L. Rost, 'Das Problem der Weltmacht in der Prophetie', *TLZ* 90, 1965, 241–50; R. Martin-Achard, 'Esaïe et Jérémie aux prises avec les problèmes politiques', *RHPR* 47, 1967, 208–24; J. A. Soggin, 'Profezia e rivoluzione nell'Antico Testamento', *Protestantesimo* 25, Rome 1970, 1–14; É. Jacob, 'Prophètes et politique', *Parole et Société* 80,

1972, 3–19; B. Albrektson, 'Prophecy and Politics in the Old Testament', in B. Biezais (ed.), *The Myth of the State*, Stockholm 1972, 45–56. For the attitude of the prophets toward the monarchy in Judah cf. K. Seybold, *Das davidische Königtum im Zeugnis der Propheten*, FRLANT 107, 1972.

§7. *Select Bibliography*: H.-J. Kraus, 'Die prophetische Botschaft gegen das soziale Unrecht Israels', *EvTh* 15, 1955, 295–307 (= his *Biblisch-theologische Aufsätze*, Neukirchen 1972, 120–33); H. Donner, 'Die soziale Botschaft der Propheten im Lichte der Gesellschaftsordnung in Israel', *OrAnt* 2, 1963, 229–45; K. Koch, 'Die Entstehung der sozialen Kritik bei den Propheten', in H. W. Wolff (ed.), *Probleme biblischer Theologie. G. von Rad zum 70. Geburtstag*, Munich 1971, 236–57. For the economic situation cf. G. Pettinato, 'Is. 2.7 e il culto del sole in Giuda nel sec. VIII a. Cr.', *OrAnt* 4, 1965, 1–30; H. Bardtke, 'Die Latifundien in Juda während der zweiten Hälfte des achten Jahrhunderts v. Chr. (zum Verständnis von Jes. 5.8–10)' in *Hommages à A. Dupont-Sommer*, Paris 1971, 235–54; G. Wanke, 'Zur Grundlagen und Absicht prophetischer Sozialkritik', *KuD* 18, 1972, 2–17.

§7b. For the Ugaritic texts referred to cf. the translation in C. H. Gordon, *Ugaritic Literature*, Rome 1949, esp. 82 (translation modified in accordance with E. Hammershaimb, 'On the Ethics of the Old Testament Prophets', *SVT* 7, 1960, 75–101; cf. 89) and 88. For the first see also J. Gray, *The KRT Text in the Literature of Ras Shamra*, Leiden ²1964, 28 and 77; for the second, F. Fronzaroli, *AQHT.Leggenda di Aqhat*, Florence 1955, 38. Gordon lists these texts as 127, line 45 and 2 Aqht V, lines 5ff. respectively. The problem is also discussed by G. Fohrer, *Theologische Grundstrukturen des Alten Testaments*, Berlin 1972, 235ff.

§8. *Select Bibliography*: G. von Rad, 'Les idées sur le temps et l'histoire en Israël et l'eschatologie des prophètes', *Hommage à W. Vischer*, Montpellier 1960, 198–209; S. Herrmann, *Die prophetischen Heilserwartungen im Alten Testament*, Stuttgart 1965; P. Grech, 'Interprophetic Re-Interpretation and Old Testament Eschatology', *Aug* 9, 1969, 235–65; J. Vollmer, *Geschichtliche Rückblicke und Motive in der Prophetie des Amos, Hosea und Jesjaja*, BZAW 119, 1971; K.-H. Bernhardt, 'Prophetie und Geschichte', *SVT* 22, 1972, 20–46.

§8c. *Select Bibliography*: J. Hempel, 'Vom irrenden Glauben', *Zeitschrift für systematische Theologie* 7, Berlin 1930 (= *Apoxysmata*, Berlin 1961, 174–97); G. Quell, *Wahre und falsche Propheten*, Gütersloh 1952 (a basic work); É. Jacob, 'Quelques remarques sur les faux prophètes', *TZ* 13, 1957, 479–81; H.-J. Kraus, *Prophetie in der Krisis*, Neukirchen 1964 (on Jeremiah); T. W. Overholt, 'Jeremiah 27–29: The Question of False Prophecy', *JAAR* 35, 1967, 241–9; R. North, 'Angel-Prophet or Satan-Prophet?', *ZAW* 82, 1970, 31–67; J. L. Crenshaw, *Prophetic Conflict*, BZAW 124, 1971.

§8d. P. Zerafa, 'Il resto di Israele nei profeti preesilici', *Angelicum* 49, Rome 1972, 3–29; G. F. Hasel, *The Remnant*, Berrien Springs 1972. Cf. also below, ch. IV, §4.

III

AMOS

§1. *Personality*

We find some important biographical notes in Amos 7.10ff. Here the prophet appears as a person who originally did not exercise a prophetic ministry and did not belong to an association of prophets, but was involved in some kind of agricultural activity (the term is not clear, v. 14) and in looking after herds. On the basis of the difference between these two occupations it has recently been suggested that the indication is purely conventional and is merely intended to specify self-employment and hence the economic independence of the person engaged in it. There are at least twenty instances to support a theory of this kind. Amos' insistence on his economic independence is also a valid retort to the remarks made by Amaziah the priest in Bethel: 'Go, flee away to the land of Judah and eat bread there', as though Amos practised prophecy in order to live. His story relates how one day Yahweh took him from his everyday work and sent him to the northern kingdom to prophesy. The phrase with which Amos describes his past is not, however, clear. The Hebrew reads *lō' nābī' 'anōkī, we'lō' ben-nābī' 'anōkī*, a statement made up of nouns which could be translated in either the present or the past tense. In fact Hebrew, like other Semitic languages, does not know the verb 'to be' as a copula, so that the sentence is chronologically indeterminate. We can therefore render it either 'I am not a prophet nor do I belong to an association of prophets' or 'I was not a prophet, nor did I belong to an association of prophets.' Those who accept the first possibility often do so to demonstrate that Amos had a polemical attitude towards the title *nābī'*, which he refused to apply to himself. He would thus have been making a distinction, which we have seen to be lacking at a lexicographical level, between the true prophet and other phenomena. But the context, which consists entirely of verbs in the past tense, does not allow a translation in the present tense. A statement formulated with '*Lō' hayītī* . . .', that is, with the verb 'to be' in the perfect, indicating the situation or condition, would have been clearer in purely grammatical terms. Thus Amos is not contrasting his position with other more or less prophetic phenomena of his time. He is stating firmly that he was not a prophet at first, though he is one at the time of his preaching. Here, too, the problem of the distinction between 'true' and 'false' prophecy begins to arise; we were concerned with it briefly in the previous chapter.

According to 1.1 Amos' homeland was the district of Tekoa, south of Jerusalem, towards the desert. According to the superscription, his ministry took place in the time of Uzziah, king of Judah, and Jeroboam II, king of Israel: the latter is mentioned explicitly in 7.10ff. 1.1 also mentions an earthquake, two years before Amos began his ministry. This must have been a very serious one, since it is mentioned again a number of centuries later in Zech. 14.5. We have attempted to establish the exact date, so as to make the reference properly useful in dating the activity of the prophet. Obvious traces of the earthquake have also been found in the excavations at Hazor; archaeologists date it towards the end of the first half of the eighth century. If these considerations are right, we can be reasonably sure that Amos worked a little before the middle of the eighth century, about 760 BC. Economic circumstances were relatively favourable; the Aramaean wars which had devastated the region for more than a century had come to an end because of the pressure exercised by Assyria on the north-eastern Aramaean states, but the Assyrians had not yet appeared on the Palestinian scene. However, as often happens in these cases (and we examined this problem in the preceding chapter), economic prosperity was limited to particular social classes and certain features of public life: it had not raised the living standards of the general population. To judge from what the prophet says, the latter often lived in conditions of abject poverty and oppression.

The calling of Amos is often connected with the visions narrated in 7.1–9; 8.1–3; 9.1–4. In them the figure of the prophet begins to appear for the first time as 'mediator' between Yahweh and his people. The redactors who produced the version we now have split up the visions for reasons which we cannot now discover.

Amos' preaching in the sanctuary of Bethel cannot have lasted long: after his expulsion it is clear that he will have returned to his home in the south, to take up his normal activity – but we do not know more than that about him.

§2. *Divisions and principal problems of the book*

As we saw in the preceding chapter, the criteria which governed the redaction of the prophetic books are not always clear. Whereas we can easily understand a biographical and chronological order (the most obvious to us) and even a systematic order (following the themes discussed and less obvious to our mentality), at other times the criteria seem more disparate: assonance or the use of the same word to facilitate the oral transmission of the text. Sometimes the criteria are so problematical that they give the impression that the whole book is in disorder. In some places insertions of the Deuteronomistic type have been made, and this complicates an already problematical situation still further.

The book of Amos has a relatively well-ordered form. The only problem is that 7.10–17 interrupts the context of the visions, which we would in fact expect at the beginning of the book, if his ministry began with them. There also seems to be no order in chs. 5–6. Moreover, there are texts in the first, second and third persons here: the visions in which the prophet gives an autobiographical account of what he has seen and offers an explanation are in the first person: we have locusts, fire, a plumb line, a basket of ripe fruit (because the people are ripe for their end), the figure of Yahweh in his sanctuary ready to judge. They appear in a certain rhetorical sequence and from the literary and logical point of view constitute a closed unit which has been artificially interrupted by the redactors. The roots of these visions are obviously to be found in the prophet's preaching; he uses them to legitimate what he has to say in the hearing of the whole community.

A collection of oracles against various nations begins with the first chapter (1.3–2.16), culminating in 2.6–16 in an oracle against Israel which has partly been revised by Dtr but which is ancient in its basic elements. As the Danish scholar A. Bentzen has pointed out, the literary genre of the 'oracle against the nations' could have its roots in the Egyptian execration texts: in them the name of an enemy ruler or nation is written on a vessel or a potsherd which is then ritually broken. The symbolic action represents the destruction of the enemy in question. Among the prophets this ritual form will then have been replaced by a form of preaching: given the importance attached to the 'word' in the Old Testament (as throughout the rest of the ancient Near East), its efficacy would not be dissimilar. The validity of this explanation, which is intrinsically fascinating (the 'execration texts' come from the nineteenth century BC, so that the literary genre could be moved many centuries into the past), has recently been challenged by H. W. Wolff and M. Weiss, who feel that the analogies between the rite underlying the execration texts and the oracles against the nations are no more than formal similarities: there is an unbridgeable distance (of more than a thousand years) between the two genres, and there are also considerable differences on a religious and a topographical level.

Before reaching their present form, the prophecies of Amos must have circulated orally, probably in fragmentary form. In ch. 2, as we have seen, there is a passage with Deuteronomistic characteristics; in 9.11–15 we have the interesting oracle about the 'booth of David', an expression unique in the Old Testament, which announces the restoration of the fallen house of David. Until a few years ago the text was usually explained as a late addition, but today there are many authors who argue for its authenticity. In that case we would have a reference to the precarious situation of the house of David after the split in the empire in the tenth century BC and an announcement of its imminent reconstruction. In addition, we then clearly have a polemical position which is taken up against the northern kingdom. Of course, if an oracle of this kind were authentic, it would readily lend itself to amplification at a later date, both at the time of Josiah, when he was effectively regaining from the ruined Assyrian empire the territories which belonged to the kingdom of Israel, and in the post-exilic period, when the passage could be interpreted in terms of a messianic restoration.

§3. Thought

The humble origins of the prophet make him a clear and simple thinker; his thought is not speculative, nor is it original and creative. His life, divided by his calling into two clearly separable periods, bears the marks of a direct and violent divine intervention; we know nothing of a third period, after his expulsion from the north, as we have seen. For him, this personal encounter with the God of Israel became the measure of all things: people, events, attitudes, ethics and cult. All this was judged in accordance with the standard of the sovereign divine will and was usually found wanting. In the visions, which express this judgment in a vivid form, by means of common everyday objects, every element moves towards judgment. In 5.1ff. the prophet intones a funeral lament; the dead person is the 'virgin Israel', which is fallen, never to rise again. The north is already condemned, even if it may be able to survive for a few years; without repentance there is no hope for it. In 5.18ff. the prophet announces the coming of the 'day of Yahweh'; the people apparently expected it as a day of national triumph over their enemies. Amos, however, declares that it will be a day of darkness and not of light, a day in which the people will not only be unable to realize their aspirations but will be overwhelmed.

For Amos, God makes himself felt in every area of Israelite society: this is probably an indirect allusion to the reciprocal obligations which exist between God and his people. Law, morals and politics should all be elements in the area where people bear witness to the lordship of Yahweh, excluding all other forms of lordship. God is not the Canaanite Baal, who could be placated with sacrifices and who only required his followers to observe particular rites which brought fertility to the land and to the herds. As we saw in the previous chapter, it is here that the criticism of the cult begins, since the cult is now thought to be an element which destroys rather than sustains the community and goes on to disrupt a variety of social situations. Thus in 2.10ff.; 3.2; 9.7, we have a strongly polemical attitude against what seems to have been the current concept of the election of Israel: a more or less static privilege, inherent in the people as such. In reality, election is a heavy responsibility: it is made with an end in view, and this end has been stated once and for all in the Old Testament by J in Gen. 12.3b: to be a blessing for all the peoples of the earth.

BIBLIOGRAPHY

Commentaries
On the twelve minor prophets: E. Sellin, KAT, ²·³1929–30; G. Rinaldi, SacBib, I–III, 1953–69; T. H. Robinson and F. Horst, HAT, ²1954; A. Weiser and K. Elliger, ATD, I, ³1956; II, ⁴1959; É. Jacob, C. A. Keller, S. Amsler, R. Vuilleumier, CAT, 3 vols., 1965ff.; W. Rudolph KAT (NS) (Hosea-Jonah only), I–II, 1966–71.

On Amos: E. Osty, JB, ²1958; J. L. Mays, OTL, 1969; H. W. Wolff, BK, 1969; E. Hammershaimb, Oxford 1970.

§1. H. W. Wolff, *Amos the Prophet*, Philadelphia 1973; J. F. Craghan, 'The Prophet Amos in recent Literature', *BTB* 2, 1972, 242–61. On Amos 7.14 the interpretation here given is shared by H. H. Rowley, 'Was Amos a Nabi?', *Festschrift O. Eissfeldt*, Halle 1947, 191–8; H. Reventlow, *Das Amt des Propheten bei Amos*, FRLANT 80, 1962, 7ff. According to H. N. Richardson, 'A Critical Note on Amos 7.14', *JBL* 85, 1966, 89, the *lŏ* should in fact be understood as an emphatic *lamed*, a form attested in Ugaritic. This seems improbable, since such forms are not clearly attested in Hebrew and their meaning would in any case be doubtful. In this case 'Certainly I am a prophet, certainly I belong to an association of prophets' is nonsensical at least for the second half of the statement. Amos was never a member of such a school. For earlier interpretations see the *Introductions* by O. Eissfeldt, 397, and G. Fohrer, 432, with bibliography. For the earthquake, cf. Y. Yadin et al., *Hazor I: An Account of the First Season of Excavations 1955*, Jerusalem 1958, 22ff.; for the date, J. A. Soggin, 'Das Erdbeben von Amos 1.1 und die Chronologie der Könige Ussia und Jotham von Juda', *ZAW* 82, 1970, 117–21; for the historical events of the time of Amos and Jeroboam II, cf. J. García Trapiello, 'Situación histórica del profeta Amós', *Estudios Bíblicos* 26, Madrid 1967, 249–74; C. Sansoni, 'Amos, uomo del suo tempo', *BeO* 10, 1968, 253–65; J. A. Soggin, 'Amos VI, 13–14 und I,3 auf dem Hintergrund der Beziehungen zwischen Israel und Damaskus im 9. und 8. Jahrhundert', in H. Goedicke (ed.), *Near Eastern Studies in Honor of W. F. Albright*, Baltimore 1971, 433–41. Other problems connected with Amos are dealt with by R. Vuilleumier, *La tradition cultuelle dans la prophétie d'Amos et d'Osée*, Neuchâtel 1960; A. S. Kapelrud, *Central Ideas in Amos*, Oslo ²1961; R. Fey, *Amos und Jesaja*, WMANT 12, Neukirchen 1963. For social problems, the economic situation and related issues see L. Randellini, 'Ricchi e poveri nel libro del profeta Amos', *Studii Biblici Franciscani Liber Annuus* 2, Jerusalem 1951–2, 5–86; H. Donner, 'Die soziale Botschaft der Propheten im Lichte der Gesellschaftsordnung in Israel', *OrAnt* 2, 1963, 229–45. Both these articles consider it likely that the economic climate was particularly favourable but that only the well-to-do people benefited. This view is criticized by G. Pettinato, art. cit. (see bibliography to ch. I, §7), who maintains that textual and archaeological evidence supports the view that Israelite society of the time was poor and that very few people achieved some measure of prosperity. For the profession of Amos before his calling, see H.-J. Stoebe, 'Der Prophet Amos und sein bürgerlicher Beruf', *Wort und Dienst* 5, Bielefeld 1957, 160–81: H. Schulte, 'Amos 7.15a und die Legitimation des Aussenseiters', in H. W. Wolff (ed.), *Probleme biblischer Theologie. G. von Rad zum 70. Geburtstag*, Munich 1971, 462–78. For Amos' origins see S. Wagner, 'Überlegungen zur Frage nach den Beziehungen des Propheten Amos zum Südreich', *TLZ* 96, 1971, 653–70. For vocabulary and underlying concepts see V. Maag, *Text, Wortschatz und Begriffswelt des Buches Amos*, Leiden 1951; I. Willi-Plein, *Vorformen der Schriftexegese innerhalb des Alten Testaments*, BZAW 123, 1971 (on Amos, Hosea and Micah).

§2. For the oracles against the nations see A. Bentzen, 'The Ritual Background of Amos 1,2–2,16', *OTS* 8, 1950, 85–99; M. Weiss, 'The Pattern of the "Execration Texts" in the Prophetic Literature', *IEJ* 19, 1969, 150–7; S. M. Paul, 'Amos 1,3–2,3, a Concatenous Literary Pattern', *JBL* 90, 1971, 397–403. The authenticity of the oracles against the nations has recently been defended with strong arguments by W. Rudolph, 'Die angefochtenen Völkerspruche in Amos 1 and 2', in K.-H. Bernhardt (ed.), *Schalom. A. Jepsen zum 70. Geburtstag*, Berlin 1971, 45–9. For 9.11–15 see Kapelrud, op. cit., 53ff., Reventlow, op. cit., 90ff. and Fey, op. cit., 54ff., all of whom support the authenticity of these verses.

III

HOSEA

§1. *The prophet and his age*

'Yahweh helps' is the paradoxical name of a man who must have experienced more misfortune than happiness in his life, more despair than serene faith. The superscription (1.1) presents him as a contemporary of Isaiah, but this note does not seem to correspond to reality. In 1.4 his ministry begins under the last king of Jehu's dynasty, that is, at the latest under Zechariah, son of the Jeroboam II who was mentioned in the previous chapter; but 7.7; 8.4; 10.3, 15 show that he will have been a witness of the disorders which followed Zechariah's assassination. In 5.13; 7.11ff.; 8.8f.; 10.5ff.; 12.2 it seems that he knows of the tribute sent to Tiglath-pileser III of Assyria towards 738 and the relations between his country and Assyria which followed that action. 5.8–6.6 seem to allude to the so-called 'Syro–Ephraimite war' which will concern us when we discuss Isaiah. On another occasion there are mentions of relations with Egypt (7.11; 9.6; 12.2), probably at the time of his namesake (King Hoshea of Israel; although the names are different in English conventional usage, they are the same in Hebrew). However, there is no hint of activity after the fall of the northern kingdom (722–20), so that the period of his ministry is put between the middle of the century and about 725. If Hosea, then, was a contemporary of Isaiah, he was an earlier contemporary, while the names of the later kings will have been added (we do not know why) by the author of the superscription. We shall find that the same thing has happened in Isa. 1.1.

In the proclamation of his message the prophet refers continuously and exclusively to particular situations in the kingdom of Israel, so that it is logical to suppose that he always worked there. His knowledge of the historical and political situation, the effectiveness of his imagery and his elevated language indicate an extensive education, a feature which seems to differentiate him from his contemporary

Amos. A passage like 5.1ff. shows that he was very familiar with the situation of the priesthood; this has led some to suppose that he himself was a priest, but there is no conclusive evidence. On the basis of 9.7, some have wanted to see Hosea as a member of a school of ecstatic prophets, but in this case also, quite apart from the difficulty we have already considered of distinguishing between the various kinds of prophets, all denoted by the same term, we can only admit that the problem of the category of prophecy to which he belonged has yet to be resolved in a satisfactory way.

§2. *Hosea's marriage*

We know little or nothing of the life of the prophet. We have his father's name, which is of little interest to the historian, and we have information about his married life, which must have been very difficult (cf. chs. 1; 3). The question of the prophet's marriage is one of the most obscure matters in the Old Testament. Is it a prophetic and poetic fabrication, an allegory or a parable intended only to symbolize the relationship between Yahweh and his people, or do we have a description of a real experience through which the prophet had to drag himself laboriously for many years in pursuit of his vocation? It is certain that 1.3–9 contains the names of the woman in question and of her children: the latter are clearly symbolic and represent characteristics of the infidelity of Israel or its consequences; the dowry also is mentioned in 3.2. These are elements which make the hypothesis of the symbolic character of the experience improbable: 'It would have been ridiculous if he had presented himself as the fictitious victim of adultery while at the same time living happily in the bosom of his family' (P. Humbert). Be this as it may, the problem remains in all its gravity, and it is no use minimizing it or ignoring it, for example accusing Hosea's wife of 'spiritual fornication', practised, according to the accusation, by all the people before Yahweh, though this has recently been attempted. This would rob the narrative of all its point. Thus we evidently have a real experience. However, the specific meaning of 'prostitute' depends on the translation of the expression *'ešet zᵉnūnīm*, commonly rendered 'prostitute'. Is this a prostitute in our sense of the term, or a sacral prostitute involved in Canaanite or syncretistic cults (thus H. W. Wolff)? Or does the expression simply mean '. . . a person who is disposed to become a harlot, a woman filled with the spirit of whoredom', as A. J. Heschel has recently suggested (*The Prophets*, 52 n.8, with bibliography)? I tend towards this last solution.

There is a second problem in connection with Hosea's marriage. Is it a matter of two marriages with different women, or two marriages with the same woman, who was driven out and then accepted back home again? The character of the symbolic action which the marriage comprised (one of those actions which reproduce in miniature, in a limited sphere, what is happening on a larger scale) seems to suggest that the same woman was always involved, because only in this way would the parallel with Israel be maintained: unfaithful, judged and pardoned, to become unfaithful again. We also find similar imagery in Jer. 3.1ff.; Ezek. 16; 20; the New Testament image of the marriage between the Lord and the church (Eph. 5.21ff.) comes into the same category, but at the opposite end of the scale. The mercy shown by the husband towards his unfaithful wife was, then, for the Israelite the image of the mercy and the love with which God treated his people. In the Old Testament the punishment provided for adultery was in fact without exception the death penalty, carried out by stoning (Lev. 20.10; cf. John 8.3ff.). For this reason also it must have been the same woman, first pardoned and then rescued (3.2) from a situation of slavery about which we have little information; the word used for the redemption from slavery, *nkr*, is attested in an analogous sense in the early passage I Sam. 23.7 and already appears in Ugaritic for the acquisition of a spouse.

On the other hand, if this is the internal logic of the narrative, not all its problems have been resolved: Deut. 24.1–4 explicitly prohibits a man from taking back his wife once he has repudiated her, especially if she belongs to another; however, the text does not mention either a repudiation or a new marriage which the woman may have contracted.

The symbolic names given to the prophet's children are obscure: in 1.9 reference is made to the termination of God's obligations towards his people (i.e. because of the people's sin). The name of his second child is probably meant to be understood in the same sense. The name of the first child has a more incidental reference: it is a judgment on the action of Elisha and Jehu (the house of the latter is mentioned explicitly, 1.4). We also find names of this kind in Isa. 7.3; 8.1. In the case of Hosea, the names in question give bad news: judgment is imminent.

§3. *Divisions and text*

It seems clear that the first three chapters make up an independent unit which has as its theme the matrimonial misadventures of the prophet: ch. 2 then interprets the theme of the unfaithful wife, presupposing the facts narrated in chs. 1 and 3. In chs. 4–14, however, we have a collection of most varied material which seems to have no internal unity and is not always easy to divide. It has, however, recently been shown that there is a break between chs. 4–11 and chs. 12–14. Each group is centred on a particular theme and the two themes seem to be independent of each other. The predominant theme is the religious decadence of the kingdom of Israel and all its effects which, according to the prophet, extend beyond the realm of faith into ethics, law and society: Israel's slide towards cults of a syncretistic type not only had consequences in the sphere of faith but also eliminated the foundations of any form of common life. Thus whereas the economic climate appeared to be favourable, the rich were becoming richer and the poor poorer, and the ancient tribal solidarity of Israel was breaking up completely. The monarchy, which tended to be tossed about between the great powers of the period like an earthen vessel among so many iron ones, does not seem to have been greatly preoccupied with this state of affairs, and for this it is continually attacked by the prophet. However, the details given are not always clear, since we often know nothing about the particular situations which underlie them. This is another difficulty in understanding the work.

Another sorry matter is the state of the text. Everything conspires to persuade us that here we have one of the most difficult texts in the Old Testament because it is corrupt, but we cannot rule out the possibility that it was written originally in a different dialect from the classical dialect of the Old Testament. Thus a linguistic examination on the basis of the new knowledge that we have of western Semitic would be extremely useful. Difficulties are further increased by the presence of plays on words, parallelisms which are sometimes unusual or only approximate, associations based on elements evidently known to the audience but no longer to us, popular etymologies, assonances, and so on. Interpretation of the book will remain at sea until we have a fundamental critical study of all these elements.

In short, there are many passages which we do not know how to translate, and in addition there is the possibility that passages were inserted in Judah after the material was transferred there on the fall of the northern kingdom. However, none of this latter material has been isolated with any degree of certainty.

§4. Message

The message of Hosea can be stated systematically along the following lines. First of all we should note that it has many points of contact with the message that will be announced a century later by Jeremiah, Deuteronomy and the Deuteronomist:

(a) The theme of marriage and forgiveness immediately suggests the love and the depth of feeling which bind Yahweh to Israel. This is evident not only in chs. 1–3 but also in 9.15; 11.1ff.; 14.4ff., and in many other passages. Again, it is this divine love which becomes the criterion for evaluating the past history of the people: Yahweh appears as the father of his son Israel (11.1ff.) and as the husband of his spouse Israel. His judgment does not contrast with this attitude: it is the consequence of disappointed love (cf. 13.7ff.). Hence we can also understand that while judgment is severe, it is never a definitive death sentence: it seeks to educate, not to destroy. In accordance with the pedagogy of the period, it seeks to be the stern but necessary lesson given by a father to a son who has been unwilling to listen to him. The whole aim is simply the re-establishment of the original situation of reciprocal love and affection. A love like this is presented, with bold anthropomorphism, as jealousy: on the other hand it demands total commitment, without hesitation or compromise (cf. 4.1ff.; 6.6). The first passage would seem to indicate that the prophet knew the Decalogue or at least something very close to it; he would also seem to have taken up the ancient ideology of obligation, this time of man towards God.

(b) A second element, which is a consequence of the first, is the unremitting struggle against religious syncretism. Still keeping to the imagery of marriage (cf. especially ch. 2), religious syncretism is adultery of the bride Israel against her husband, Yahweh, and therefore fornication. In view of the penalty attached to this crime, the people should be aware not only of what they deserve but also of the generous offer made on the second occasion. On the other hand, the prophet is too realistic to believe that the present situation of the people is the product of an unpremeditated fall: it has lasted for centuries. In 12.4 the patriarch Jacob is described in far from flattering terms, and this is one of the few mentions of the patriarchs which we have outside the Pentateuch. Some other episodes from the past are described in a critical key: cf. 9.10ff. with Num. 25; 9.15ff. with the story of the sanctuary at Gilgal, the first sanctuary in the conquest (Josh. 3–5) and where the first king, Saul, was acclaimed and crowned

(I Sam. 11). The monarchy, too, is one of the elements which brought about religious decadence and therefore decadence throughout civil life, a process which already began with Saul (10.9ff.; cf. 13.10ff.: in these passages we possibly have a revival of the ancient anti-monarchical thesis which we saw in I Sam. 8.1ff.; 10.17ff.).

(*c*) Hosea's eschatology is characteristic: some of its elements will be taken up a century later by Jeremiah. Only one road is open to the people, that of a return to the desert, the symbol of a new beginning, of starting from nothing (cf. 2.14ff.; 12.10ff.). Hosea does not seem to know the traditions which speak of murmuring in the desert, nor is he interested in them except in the case of Num. 25, and he sees in the journey through the wilderness the ideal time of his people, the time of faithfulness. However, the return to the desert will not come about by human initiative, but will be brought about by God. Thus exile and deportation, which are often mentioned in the text, would seem to be the modern form of this return to the desert, and are seen to be the crucible in which the people will be purified. God is disposed to do even this through love of Israel (cf. 2.1–3 (*EVV* 1.10–2.1); 3.1–5; 5.15–6.5; 11.8–11; 12.7ff.; 14.2–10).

The effectiveness of this element appears clearly from the use which Jeremiah makes of it later. It demonstrates in an impressive manner the realism with which the prophets were capable of seeing the situation of their people, even in the political, social and economic spheres.

BIBLIOGRAPHY

Commentaries
On the twelve minor prophets, see on ch. III above. On Hosea: E. Osty, JB, ²1958; H. W. Wolff, ET, Hermeneia, 1974; W. Rudolph, KAT, 1966; J. L. Mays, OTL, 1969. See also the bibliographical study, J. F. Craghan, 'The Book of Hosea: a Survey of Recent Literature', *BTB* 1, 1971, 81–100, 145–70.

§1. For Hos. 5.8–6.6 see A. Alt, 'Hosea 5.8–6.6. Ein Krieg und seine Folgen in prophetischer Beleuchtung', *Neue kirchliche Zeitschrift* 30, Erlangen 1919, 537–68 (= his *Kleine Schriften* II, Munich ³1964, 163–87), and the opposing view of E. M. Good, 'Hosea 5,8–6,6: an Alternative to Alt', *JBL* 85, 1966, 273–86; id., 'The Composition of Hosea', *SEÅ* 31, 1966, 21–63.

§2. Understandably there is a remarkable bibliography on Hosea's marriage. It includes P. Humbert, 'Les trois premiers chapîtres d'Osée', *RHR* 77, 1918, 157–71; R. Gordis, 'Hosea's Marriage and Message: a new Approach', *HUCA* 25, 1954, 9–35; H. H. Rowley, 'The Marriage of Hosea', *BJRL* 39, 1956–7, 200–33 (= his *Men of God*, London 1963, 66–97).

Pfeiffer, *Introduction*, 569, and J. Coppens, 'L'histoire matrimoniale d'Osée. Un nouvel essai d'interpretation', *Festschrift für F. Nötscher*, Bonn 1950, 38–45, speak in terms of 'spiritual fornication'. The history of the problem and the many solutions proposed have recently been investigated by S. Bitter, *Die Ehe des Propheten Hosea*, Göttingen 1975. For the verb *nkr* in Ugaritic see J. Gray, *The KRT Text in the Literature of Ras Shamra*, Leiden 1964, 13 and 44f.; Rowley, art. cit, 203 n.1.

§3. For the text see the *Introductions* listed in the general bibliography; I. Willi-Plein, op. cit. (see above, ch. II, §1); G. Behler, 'Divini amoris suprema revelatio in antiquo foedere data' (Osee cap. 11)', *Angelicum 20*, Rome 1943, 102–16.

§4. Cf. Behler, art. cit.; H. W. Wolff, ' "Wissen um Gott" bei Hosea als Urform von Theologie', *EvTh* 12, 1952–3, 533–54 (= his *Gesammelte Studien*, Munich 1964, 182–205); E. Baumann, ' "Wissen um Gott" bei Hosea als Urform von Theologie?', *EvTh* 15, 1955, 416–25 (questioning the reduction of Hebrew *ydʿ* to intellectual categories); H. W. Wolff, 'Erkenntnis Gottes im Alten Testament', *EvTh* 15, 1955, 426–31; G. Fohrer, 'Umkehr und Erlösung beim Propheten Hosea', *TZ* 11, 1955, 161–85 (= his *Studien zur alttestamentlichen Prophetie*, BZAW 99, 1967, 222–41); J. M. Ward, 'The Message of the Prophet Hosea', *Interpretation 23*, 1969, 387–407; M. J. Buss, *The Prophetic Word in Hosea*, BZAW 111, 1969 (a basic study).

IV

ISAIAH

§1. *The book and its problems*

Isaiah, with 66 chapters, is the longest of the prophetic books. However, the attentive reader will find it easy enough to see that it is composed of different parts and that there are considerable differences between them. A first part is made up of chs. 1–39, which are clearly distinct from chs. 40ff., as J. G. Eichhorn already noted in the eighteenth century. Chapters 40ff. do not refer to people and events of the eighth century BC, but to those of the sixth century, that is, during and after the Babylonian exile. Even within chs. 1–39, however, there is an erratic block, made up of the apocalyptic section chs. 24–27. Chapters 56–66 again address a different audience: the community of the restoration rather than the community of the exile. They must therefore be assigned for the most part to the last quarter of the sixth century BC. So we have three, if not four, distinct collections, and we shall therefore speak of 'Isaiah' (eighth century), 'Deutero-Isaiah' (flourished from the middle of the sixth century) and 'Trito-Isaiah' (last quarter of the sixth century); the last two will not be examined in any detail until we reach the exilic and post-exilic prophets, and at that point we shall also seek to establish why they bear the name of Isaiah. The first time we have a reference to the whole of Isaiah, that is, with all its 66 chapters, is in the deutero-canonical book of Ecclesiasticus (48.22ff.), at the beginning of the second century BC. Finally, two manuscripts of Isaiah were discovered in Cave I at Qumran, the first practically complete. These are indicated by the sigla 1Q Is^a and 1Q Is^b respectively.

§2. *The prophet and his age*

The biography and hence the person of Isaiah are better known than those of his predecessors Amos and Hosea. We know the name of his father; in the year of the death of king Uzziah/Azariah (6.1ff.) he received a special charge: he was to announce judgment to the people of Judah and Jerusalem in no uncertain terms. The text in question has traditionally been understood to describe the prophet's calling, but in fact it tells how he was given a particular task. This presupposes that by that date the prophet had already been at work for some time. The date of the death of Uzziah is fixed between 742 and 736, depending on the chronology which we adopt. We shall examine the question 'Vocation or charge?' a little later (§§3a, 4). His ministry lasted at least until the Assyrian expedition against Judah and the other allies of southern Syria in 701 (the hypothesis of a second expedition about 688 still seems highly improbable), which brings us down to the lower limit of his activity. Isaiah, too, was married, this time to a respectable woman who bore the title $n^e b\bar{\imath}'\bar{a}$ = 'prophetess'. We do not know whether this reflected her husband's profession or whether she was a prophetess in her own right; in any case, there is no evidence that she acted as one. She was certainly his wife and bore him two sons: in 7.3 we have $\check{s}^{e}\bar{a}r\,y\bar{a}\check{s}\bar{u}b$ = 'a remnant will return (sc. to Yahweh)' or '. . . be converted'; in 8.3 we have $mah\bar{e}r\,\check{s}\bar{a}l\bar{a}l\,h\bar{a}\check{s}\,baz$ = 'speedy spoil, hasty prey'. These are again, as in the case of Hosea, symbolic names which the prophet himself explains in 10.6 and which therefore announce what the people's fate will be: judgment and destruction for the wicked, conversion and salvation for the 'elect remnant'.

If we look for the circles in which the prophet moved, we may infer that he must have belonged to the ruling class, to the aristocracy: he dealt with the king face to face, being admitted to his presence when he wished, even when the king was outside the palace (7.1ff.); in 37.1ff. the king sends for him. He seems to have encountered opposition to his preaching, as did Amos and Jeremiah. It would therefore seem obvious that Isaiah was one of those who were allowed to express their own opinion openly at any time and in any place.

Isaiah's ministry may be said to have taken place essentially in Jerusalem: we have no indication that he travelled elsewhere. The first date given is one that we have already examined, the death of Uzziah/Azariah; there is also mention of the reigns of Jotham, Ahaz and Hezekiah. One tradition reported by the late (first century AD) pseudepigraphical book *The Ascension of Isaiah* (cf. also Heb. 11.37 in the New Testament) states that he met a martyr's death under king Manasseh, whom Dtr considered to be the wicked king *par excellence*, but given the character of the work in question, it is not easy to verify the reliability of the note.

Isaiah's message was given during a particularly troubled period in

the history of Israel, and this is one of the reasons why such a considerable part of it is devoted to political themes. First of all there is
the 'Syro-Ephraimite war' (as it has generally been called from the
time of Luther onwards) of 735–34, during which Israel and the
kingdom of Damascus sought first to persuade and then to constrain
Judah to take part in an anti-Assyrian coalition; when Judah refused,
they moved against Jerusalem to impose the alliance by force. Isaiah
then witnessed the fall of the kingdom of Damascus in 732 and that of
Israel in 722–20. The various rebellions against Assyria in 713–11
and in 705 also took place in his lifetime; the last was overcome by
the expedition of Sennacherib in 701.

Isaiah is a prophet who is distinguished by his matter-of-factness.
Only once is there any account of a symbolic action which seems at
all bizarre: in 20.1ff. he appears naked before the foreign ambassadors
assembled at Jerusalem to show them their potential future as deportees and thus to discourage them from taking part in the anti-Assyrian
rebellion, but we never see him in a situation like that of Hosea's
marriage or committing actions like those attested in Ezekiel. In
Isaiah, the theme of his preaching, common to all the prophets,
appears with much greater clarity than elsewhere. As we indicated
earlier, we know from 8.16 that he had a school, and it will not be
far from the truth to suppose that it is to this school that we owe the
transmission of his words. It is possible that the school collected some
texts of doubtful authenticity under the name of the master. As we
shall see, similar theories have been proposed to explain the use of the
terms Deutero- and Trito-Isaiah. On the other hand, there is the
problem that we do not know for how long after the death of the
prophet this school will have continued to operate. It is not clear
whether 8.16 already presupposes the existence of written material;
it is in any case evident that an oral tradition was developing.

§3. *Divisions and content*

It is the great achievement of the German scholar B. Duhm, professor
at the University of Basle until his death, to have argued for the first
time in his now classic commentary (1898) that Isaiah is composed of
various originally independent units: chs. 1–12; 13–23; 28–33; 34–35.
Chapters 36–39 are a special case, since they present a parallel text to
II Kings 18–20, as we have already seen. Duhm showed a marked
tendency to assign the texts which he examined to a late date, in some
cases going down to the second century BC, the *terminus ante quem*

because of the mention of the book in Ecclesiasticus, but this tendency now seems completely outmoded. The Qumran manuscripts, dating from this period and certainly based on earlier archetypes, include the book in its present form. O. Procksch also put forward similar divisions, but he traced back the individual collections to the prophet himself or to his disciples: chs. 1; 2–6; 9.7 (EVV 8)–10.4; 28–32 were to be attributed to the prophet; 7.1–9.6 (EVV 7); 11.1ff.; 13–23 to the disciples. The suggestion made by K. Budde and S. Mowinckel was on essentially similar lines, but in less detail. According to them the book simply consisted of three parts: chs. 1–12: oracles against Judah and Jerusalem; chs. 13–23: oracles against the nations; chs. 28–33: oracles of salvation. Chapters 24–27 remain outside this scheme because they are obviously later. We shall return to them in due course. In favour of this last division is its extreme simplicity, but sometimes that seems excessive: in 1.1; 2.1; 13.1 we have three superscriptions which were not added to the text before the exile. It follows from them that there was a traditional division between chs. 1 and 2. In 13.1 we have the term *maśśā'* = literally 'burden', hence 'charge, oracle'; this often appears in this sense in Isa. 13–23, but otherwise is a word which is frequently used in post-exilic times. The verb *ḥāzāh* = 'see' and its derivative *ḥāzōn* = 'vision' also seem to belong more to post-exilic language, though the scarcity of the material at our disposal calls for caution in this area.

G. Fohrer has made the most recent division of the book; its extreme complexity makes it tiresome for anyone working with it, whether it is correct or not:

(i) 1.2–28; 1.29–31 (fragments) and 2.2–5 (promises);

(ii) 2.6–4.1 (in 3.25–4.1 fragments) and 4.2–6 (promises);

(iii) 5.1–23; 10.1–4 (5.14–17, 24 fragments);

(iv) 6.1–8.18 (8.19–22 fragments) and 9.1–6 (EVV 2–7) (promises);

(v) 9.7 (EVV 8)–20; 5.25–30; 10.5–15, 27b–32 (fragments); 11.1–9 (promises);

(vi) Chs. 13–23; 28.1–4, 5f. (and 28.17f., promises);

(vii) 28.7–32.14; 32.15–20 (promises).

We shall follow the simpler division begun by Duhm and continued in essentials by other authors; the division proposed by Fohrer is substantially the same, though its form is different. A. Lods, *Histoire*, 277ff., has attempted to give a date for each individual section, but his investigation is too subtle and often is based on imponderable or subjective elements which limit its usefulness.

(a) Oracles against Judah and Jerusalem (chs. 1–12). Here we have a collection of texts which for the most part are authentic; the conclusion, a doxology (ch. 12), justifies the hypothesis that this part has always formed an independent unit from a relatively early date and was used in worship. We have seen that chs. 1 and 2 each begin with a superscription; they will thus have been originally separate. Anyone who considers ch. 6 to be an account of the prophet's calling will rightly be surprised that it does not appear at the beginning of the book; moreover, 6.1–9.6 (7), which form a unit, interrupt a lamentation in three stanzas (5.25–30; 9.7–20 [8–21] and 10.1–4), clearly recognizable from a refrain which keeps reappearing. On the other hand, given the often rather obscure criteria followed by the redactors of the prophetic books, even those who follow the traditional argument that ch. 6 is the account of the prophet's vocation will not necessarily be justified in arguing that the chapter should appear at the beginning. We saw that the visions in the book of Amos probably occurred in the course of the prophet's call, but they not only fail to appear at the beginning of the book, but in two cases are even interrupted. To sum up, in this first part we have the following sections: ch. 1; chs. 2–4; 6.1–9.6 (7); 5.25–30 with 9.7 (8)–10.4; also 5.1–24 and 10.5–11.16. Finally, there is the doxology (ch. 12).

(i) The first chapter presents a collection of various sayings of the prophet dealing with different themes. They date from different times in his ministry. Fohrer put forward the hypothesis that ch. 1 now appears at the beginning of the collection because it amounts to a kind of programme, a summary of the whole of the prophet's preaching. 1.2f. is invective against the people which is impossible to date; it seems to presuppose that the prophet had already encountered difficulties and therefore does not come at the beginning of his ministry. 1.4–9 describes the situation in Judah during or a little after the invasion of Sennacherib in 701; it is impossible to date the other passages, but they probably belong to the earliest period of Isaiah's ministry. 1.10–17, which is only attached to the preceding pericope because of word-play through the words 'Sodom and Gomorrah', is a prophetic oracle in didactic form (*tōrāh*), protesting at the degeneration of the cult in Judah and its consequences on the moral and social plane; it has links with similar passages in Amos and Hosea, though this time the target is the south, where the situation cannot have been much better than in the north. 1.18–20 announces Yahweh's pardon by means of the literary genre of the legal argument (cf. the typical use of the root *yākaḥ* = 'try'); the majority of modern scholars would see the passage as a rhetorical question, in which case a negative reply would be expected. This is an example of the ambiguity of certain texts, which give a great deal of trouble to both exegetes and translators.

1.21–26 is a unit discovered by Duhm; it stands out by ending in the same way as it began, and takes the form of a lament directed against the sin of Jerusalem. In 1.27–31 we have a series of sayings without any logical unity, all on the theme of 'redemption and judgment'. The compiler of this group does, however, seem to have followed a kind of logic in collecting his material, assembling the various oracles by means of similar words which would serve as mnemonics or by similar ideas (1.4–7 follows 1.2f., where the mnemonic is 'sons' and the theme is 'sin'), whereas 1.9 is connected to 1.10, as we have seen, by the mention of the two accursed cities. Thus we have the following order: sin, judgment, discussion of the possibilities open, decisions, possibilities of redemption.

(ii) Chapters 2–4 are a collection of sayings from the prophet's first period: at the beginning we find 2.2–5 (which Fohrer considers to be the conclusion of the preceding collection), a text which is also transmitted (with one extra verse) in Micah 4.1–4. With the information at our disposal it is impossible to establish which of these two versions is the earlier, unless, as seems more plausible, in both cases the text is a quotation of an extract which is independent of these prophets. Fohrer regards it as a text which comes from the post-exilic period, or at the earliest to be dated in the late exilic period, but the arguments which he advances are not conclusive. In 2.6–22 there follows a threat in poetic form and with regular strophes (though there are also later additions). Its theme is the catastrophes which will accompany the 'day of Yahweh'; we have already come across this 'day' in connection with Amos. In 3.1–15 we have threats against the rulers in Jerusalem (vv. 1–9 are perhaps an independent unit) because of their misgovernment. 3.16–24 is directed against the women of the ruling class in Jerusalem, once again in connection with the 'day of Yahweh'. The passage is difficult because of the technical terms used to denote the finery. In 3.25f. we have a terrible vision of coming judgment: the corpses of the fallen lie in the middle of the streets and the women are sold as slaves. 3.27–4.1 is probably an incomplete oracle, whereas 4.2–6 stands out so markedly from its present context that many authors do not consider it to be authentic. Fohrer thinks it was put here as the introduction to the third section, but it is not easy to come to a decision. In any case, the authentic oracles all come from the period before the 'Syro–Ephraimite war', that is, before 735.

(iii) In ch. 5 we have another collection of the prophet's early sayings. 5.1–7 is particularly interesting because it provides an example of his preaching. His method is first to gain the assent of his audience to the condemnation pronounced on his subject (like Nathan with

David in II Sam. 12) and then to identify the audience with the party condemned. In 5.8–24 we have a lament in strophes each of which begins with 'Woe to', a formula which normally introduces invective. The theme is the social situation of the country: it goes on in 9.7–20 (8–21) and 10.1–4, as appears from the refrain which is repeated in 5.25; 9.11, 16 (12, 17) and 10.4: 'For all this his anger is not turned away and his hand is stretched out still.' The structure recalls that of the visions of Amos: perhaps they both follow the same traditional or liturgical pattern, which was in any case an earlier one. There is no positive element, no promise of forgiveness. The passage is early: Fohrer even thinks of the period of the 'Syro-Ephraimite war'. The collection ends with a messianic passage, 11.1–16, only the first part of which, however, can be authentic (vv. 1–9); for Fohrer the whole section is inauthentic because of the gift of the spirit, which is a characteristic of late prophecy. In the introductory chapter on prophecy we saw that this feature only begins to appear in Ezekiel, whereas v. 1 seems to depend on Isa. 65.25 and Hab. 2.14. However, the argument is not conclusive: the gift of the spirit does not appear here in relation to prophecy but as an attribute of the king for good government. The passage may therefore be connected, rather, with a coronation liturgy or something of this kind. Dhorme already noted that the other two passages, in Trito-Isaiah and Habakkuk, are probably quoting this passage and not vice versa; he came to this conclusion after a careful examination of the literary situation. In any case, where we find the use of analogous words and concepts we should prefer to speak in terms of identical literary genres, avoiding the word 'dependence'. Verses 10–16, on the other hand, make explicit mention of 'the dispersed of Judah' (v. 12), an expression which seems to presuppose the exile of 597 or 587; they cannot therefore be authentic.

(iv) The unit 6.1–9.6 (7) now interrupts the previous collection; it is dominated by 6.1–8.18, in which the prophet's vision, traditionally connected with his vocation, has pride of place. There follows ch. 7, an account of a dramatic dialogue between the prophet and king Ahaz about the advisability of the latter's seeking help from Assyria against the coalition of Israel and Damascus at the time of the 'Syro–Ephraimite war'. The enemy was marching on Jerusalem to lay siege to it, and so time was pressing, but Isaiah opposed the king's plan decisively: he argued that the remedy would be worse than the ill, as indeed it was. Isaiah's advice to the king was to have faith (7.9). It is difficult to evaluate this counsel in political terms, but its validity was soon to be confirmed by the facts. No wonder that after an intervention of this kind the prophet was forced to retire to private life among his disciples (8.16). In 8.19–23 (9.1) we have various additions which make it into another messianic passage. Some scholars believe that 9.1–6 (2–7) were spoken to a restricted audience of disciples; others that they are late: from the exile or immediately afterwards (Fohrer). Here again the arguments in favour of a late dating are not decisive.

As we have seen, ch.6 is particularly important, since it is traditionally regarded as the text which describes the prophet's call. The phenomena which accompany the theophany show parallels to the theophany in Exod. 19. However, this interpretation has rightly been put in question in recent years. The prophet has already been called and, rather than describing his vocation, the passage deals with the conferring of a charge which is so portentous that the prophet can only legitimate it by recalling his own vision. The charge is the destruction of the people, and this is presented in such harsh terms that the LXX only gives a weaker version of it which can be obtained without modifying an unvocalized text. The New Testament reproduces this version (Matt. 13.14f.; Acts 28.26f.).

(v) Chapter 12, the final doxology, is composed of two songs and an introduction: in vv. 1f. we have a song of thanksgiving, in vv. 3–6 a psalm of thanksgiving with elements from the hymn, which is in turn concluded with a doxology.

(b) Chapters 13–23 all contain material of the same literary genre: here we have a series of 'oracles against the nations', a form of cursing the history of which we have already considered in connection with Amos. The majority of scholars are now agreed on which passages are authentic and which are not.

(i) The following passages are certainly authentic: 14.24–27, an oracle against Assyria; 14.28–32, an oracle against Philistia dated in the year of the death of king Ahaz (715 or 729/25); 17.1–11, against Damascus, before 732, and thus 'fulfilled' in its conquest by Assyria. Fohrer considers only vv. 1–6 to be authentic, whereas 7f. will be a later addition and 9–11 a second appendix, against idolatry, not composed before 600. 17.12–14, a lament on 'many peoples', is important; some authors would like to connect it with the arrival of Sennacherib's army at the walls of Jerusalem in 701 (cf. II Kings 19). Chapter 18 is probably an oracle directed against Egyptian ambassadors in Judah, a warning against a possible alliance; the allusion is to the Twenty-Fifth 'Nubian' Dynasty, reigning from c. 751 to 656, and the occasion will have arisen when they came in connection with one of the rebellions against Assyria, either that of 713–11 or that of 705, both destined to finish in disaster. Chapter 20 mentions the symbolic action of the prophet to which we have already alluded; it was probably performed round about 713–11 on the occasion of the planning of the anti-Assyrian alliance. Some scholars regard 22.1–14 as an exhortation to the inhabitants of Jerusalem after the liberation of 701, which many people considered to be a miracle, that they should not be led astray by too facile an optimism (v. 13b); in 22.15–25 we have oracles against two important palace officials, Shebna and Eliakim, which were elaborated at a later date. For the first of these see Appendix I, §6; as we have seen, 28.1–4 and the verses immediately following are perhaps additions.

(ii) The following oracles are of doubtful authenticity and some are certainly not authentic: 13.1–14.23 is a taunt song against the king of Babylon with the threat of the final destruction of his kingdom. This includes part of the text of a very early myth about the Titans who wanted to scale heaven and were hurled down into the depths; now the myth serves as an example of the present attitude and the future destiny of the king of Babylon. Its inauthenticity is obvious: at the time of Isaiah Babylon was not an enemy, but rather Judah's ally against Assyria, under whose yoke it also suffered. The Old Testament even records an episode which shows how there were good relationships between Hezekiah of Judah and Merodach-Baladan (= Marduk Apal Iddina II), probably in connection with the coalition of 705 (cf. II Kings 20.12–21//Isa.39.1–8). The Medes are also mentioned, but at that time they had still not appeared on the political scene in the ancient Near East, whereas about a century later they made a decisive contribution to the fall of Assyria, in alliance with Judah and the Babylonians. Babylon only became Judah's enemy towards the end of the seventh century BC, while from 550 to 539 it declined rapidly until its capital was conquered by Cyrus, king of Persia. This oracle, then, announces events from the second half of the sixth century, not from the eighth. Chapters 15 and 16 contain an oracle against Moab divided into three sections: part of it also appears in Jer.48.29; it is probably an early oracle (though not for Fohrer, who puts it in the post-exilic period), but it is not by Isaiah. Chapter 19 records a post-exilic oracle which some scholars want to date back to 550 because it reflects the hope of Deutero-Isaiah. In 21.1–10 we have an oracle which again seems to refer to the fall of Babylon; 21.11f. talks of Edom in terms which seem exilic, while 21.13–15, which also is post-exilic, deal with Dedan, an Arabian tribe. In ch.23 the situation is more complex: there is mention here of the fall of Tyre, but we are not told at whose hands. History records the following successful attacks on Tyre: 1. By Tiglath-pileser III or Shalmaneser

V of Assyria in the second half of the eighth century.; 2. By the hand of Nebuchadnezzar II of Babylon in the second quarter of the sixth century; 3. By Alexander the Great at the end of the fourth century. It is impossible to determine which of these is alluded to here; it is enough to point out that only in the first instance could the author be Isaiah.

(c) Chapters 24–27 are a collection of apocalyptic fragments whose theme is the end of the world. Features which are certainly late are the mention of the resurrection of the dead in 26.19 and the angelology in 24.21. In dating them, critics fluctuate between the fifth and second centuries. In 24.10 there is, further, mention of an unknown city. On the other hand, recent studies on the concept of angelology and resurrection in the Old Testament, most of which are still unpublished, have shown that these elements are certainly earlier than has previously been thought. They cannot therefore be used for dating.

(d) For the most part chs. 28–33 contain authentic words of the prophet: in chs. 28–31 the tone is generally negative. All the sayings are directed against more or less well-known people connected with the rebellions of 713–11 and 705; Fohrer, probably rightly, would put 28.1–4 among the 'oracles against the nations', especially as the style is quite different from the rest of the context. Ch. 33 is a prophetic liturgy with the future as its theme; Fohrer would put it in the post-exilic period and not before.

(e) Chapters 34–35 are a brief apocalypse the theme of which is the destruction of Edom and the liberation of Zion. There are references to the Jewish diaspora here, which only began with the exile, and the exile itself is explicitly mentioned in ch. 35. In any case, there is at least one element in 34.16 which until recently has been considered a sign of late redaction, though different interpretations are now made of it: this is the term *sēper* = 'book', sometimes 'letter'. It does, however, appear in pre-exilic treaties from the area with the sense of 'stele', on which the clauses of treaties were written. Do we have here an originally early text which was then revised and adapted to a later age? The question must remain unanswered.

(f) As has already been mentioned, Isa. 36–39 is parallel to II Kings 18.13–20.18 (cf. above Part Two, ch. IX, §2 i).

These considerations are already complicated enough as they are, but the fact that in no case are the problems presented in these paragraphs the whole story is obvious evidence of the various redactional stages through which the book of Isaiah has passed, beginning with the prophet's preaching in the eighth century and ending with the form of the book as we now have it. The book was probably not completed before the fifth, perhaps even the fourth century, and it is possible that chs. 24–27 were added at an even later date.

However, the addition of material in the course of transmission should not be taken as a sign of inaccurate tradition. Rather, it demonstrates the living character of the tradition, which was ready to be brought up to date over the centuries without anyone raising the problems of literary authenticity as we know them today. This may have damaged the book from the critic's point of view, but it does attest its living, real and topical character.

§4. *Thought*

All through his long scholarly life, K. Budde, who was mentioned above, always argued that there was a certain relationship between Isaiah and Amos, though he did not specify this more precisely nor take the argument further. This has recently been done by R. Fey in an excellent study. He succeeds in demonstrating the existence of a parallel between Amos 6.1–7 and Isa. 5.11–13: the use of technical theological terms like $ṣedāqā$ (= justice) and $mišpāṭ$ (= law) with the same meaning; a common style (e.g. in the construction of individual oracles); similarity of themes and motives (e.g. pride as the root of sin) and also similarity of concepts (e.g. divine holiness). We should not therefore be surprised to rediscover in Isaiah some concepts which we have already examined in Amos. Of course this does not necessarily signify literary dependence: we are concerned not only with particular literary genres, some of which belong to the cult and which each prophet develops in his own way, but also with a common ideological basis, that of the tribal traditions which were felt and lived in the south, in Judah. However, what may seem rather sketchy in Amos, because of the brevity of the text and because it is often presented in rather a crude form, is developed by the cultivated Isaiah: not for nothing is it said that Isaiah is the first Israelite theologian whose name we know.

Isaiah appears in impressive fashion as a theologian in the scene in ch. 6 in which he was an active witness: the famous trisagion is none other than the proclamation of the holiness of God, a theme which recurs with special emphasis right through his preaching. God is even given a special epithet: 'The Holy One of Israel' ($qedōš$ $yiśrā'ēl$), a definition which at the same time underlines the distance which separates God from man (in origin, 'holy' signifies 'separated', 'set apart' for some purpose), and also the tie which binds him to his people and through them to all mankind, through the obligation which he has taken upon himself from earliest times. Confronted with this holiness in a direct encounter, Isaiah can only exclaim in dismay, 'Woe is me, I am lost' (6.1ff.), and wait for God to put him in a position to bear his presence. Confronted with this aspect of God, man's attitude can only be one of trust. Nor is it simply a question of a state of mind; it is a matter of particular decisions, an element which is stressed in a particular way in 7.9; 30.15, etc. Thus it is not a question of the struggle between orthodoxy and heterodoxy or heresy, of some kind of intellectual approach, but of taking up the attitude required by every situation, by each particular moment. The believer is not given norms or abstract rules, but is invited to involve himself actively in a given situation. Chapter 7 is typical in this respect: Isaiah exhorts the king not to seek to play a political game which will be beyond him and in which he will therefore be the loser, but to 'trust' in the Lord. As we have seen, this advice might seem strange on a political level, but it was borne out by the facts and, unlike the attitude of the 'realistic' politicians or those who pretended to be realistic, was shown to be right. Isaiah denies Judah any possibility of trusting in armies or in astuteness (double-crossing policies, and so on); as we have seen, ch. 19 criticizes the foreign policy of Judah harshly and ch. 31 criticizes both foreign policy and recourse to military force. Not only are these sacrilegious attitudes, because they deprive God of his sovereignty in history, but they have no concrete effect on the practical level. Because it is in history that God is at work, as ch. 10.5ff. shows, Assyria is a pawn in his game, which will rapidly be taken as soon as it makes claims. However, Isaiah is neither a fatalist nor a utopian, nor does he expect that things will settle themselves. Man is enjoined to practise justice (1.16ff.); Ahaz is given the alternative of trusting in Yahweh or in himself and the politics of his bureaucracy (ch. 7). Man is always in a position of responsibility, but his actions are assessed by one who knows that he is the one who has thrown the dice.

For Isaiah, sin consists in an unwillingness to recognize this divine sovereignty over all spheres of life. Dishonesty, corruption, immorality, the thirst for riches and luxury, social irresponsibility, syncretistic cults and so on are simply aspects of this fundamental attitude of man's rebellion against the divine will. And confronted with these attitudes God can go to the opposite extreme, that of hardening the heart of his people, making them blind and deaf to the prophetic preaching so that they cannot understand it. An example of this kind of attitude clearly appears in the second part of ch. 6: man is compelled to run the course he has chosen right to the very end (6.9ff.; 29.9ff.); cf. similarly I Kings 22, and the exodus narrative, where the same thing happens to Pharaoh. But this hardening of the heart as part of the divine judgment does not excuse man from his own responsibility; it is part of the punishment, not an alibi by which he can escape. And with his judgment God triumphantly sets himself against anyone who seeks to oppose him or to slow down the realization of his plans (2.12ff.). These are features which evolve and mature with the decades, but in essentials they remain the same. This also happens with the announcement of salvation: the details may change, but the basic question remains the same in its almost incredible magnitude: cf. chs.2.1ff.; 9.1ff.; 11.1ff., that is, allowing their authenticity or at least their place in the prophet's thought.

One of the principal concepts of salvation is that of the 'elect residue' or simply 'the remnant'. This is among the earliest elements in Isaiah's preaching, cf. the name of his first son, who was certainly born before 734 (7.3). After the fall of the kingdom of Israel, Isaiah must have first considered Judah to be the 'remnant': this is attested by a theology of the election of Zion which appears throughout the book from 2.1ff. on. At the end of his ministry, in 701, Jerusalem appeared to be the remnant (and implicitly to be the proof of his theology of Zion, 1.8f.). However, in Isaiah we begin to see the slow progress of the notion that 'the elect remnant' might be something substantially different from the people of God in the ethnic and political sense. Faith could also exist at the heart of the 'remnant' as the believers among the people of God, which was now his people only in name, so that it became impossible to take shelter behind the concept of election and the holy nation. And assuming that the passages in question come from Isaiah or belong to his school, the messianic hope also comes in here, with all the consequences that that brings.

BIBLIOGRAPHY

Commentaries
B. Duhm, HKAT, ⁴1922 (reprinted 1967); O. Procksch, KAT, 1930; V. Herntrich, ATD, 1950 (on 1–12 only and replaced in the series by O. Kaiser); J. Steinmann, Lectio Divina, Paris 1950; A. Penna, SacBib, 1958; E. J. Kissane, Dublin ²1960; G. Fohrer, ZBK, 2 vols., 1960–2; O. Kaiser, ET, OTL, 2 vols., 1972–3; F. Montagnini, Esegesi Biblica, Brescia 1966; H. Wildberger, BK I, 1972 (on chs. 1–12); II, 1974ff. (appearing in separate fascicles); P. Auvray, SB, 1972; P. Auvray and J. Steinmann, JB, ³1972.

§1. For the two Isaiah manuscripts discovered at Qumran see respectively M. Burrows, *The Dead Sea Scrolls of St Mark's Monastery* I, New Haven 1950; E. L. Sukenik, *The Dead Sea Scrolls of the Hebrew University*, Jerusalem 1955. The details of the manuscripts and publications are too extensive for treatment here. The threefold division of the book of Isaiah, argued for by Duhm at the end of the last century, is supported by computer analysis of the vocabulary: cf. Y. T. Radday, 'Vocabulary Eccentricity and the Unity of Isaiah', *Tarbiz* 39, Jerusalem 1969–70, 323–41 (in Hebrew, with an English summary); id., 'Two Computerized Statistical-Linguistic Tests concerning the Unity of Isaiah', *JBL* 89, 1970, 319–24.

§2. For the texts of the *Martyrdom* and *Ascension of Isaiah*, cf. P. P. Riessler, *Altjüdisches Schrifttum ausserhalb der Bibel*, Augsburg 1928 (reprinted 1967), 481–4. For the problems of Sennacherib's campaigns in Palestine, cf. J. Bright, 'Le problème des campagnes de Sennachérib en Palestine', in *Hommage à W. Vischer*, Montpellier 1960, 20–31; id., *A History of Israel*, Philadelphia and London ²1972, 296–308, where he argues for *two* Assyrian campaigns against southern Syria. The principal difficulty lies in the fact that there is no support for this in the Assyrian annals: cf. B. S. Childs, *Isaiah and the Assyrian Crisis*, SBT II 3, 1967. Bright continues to maintain his theory, which would certainly remove many difficulties in II Kings 18–19 (Isa. 36–37), on the basis of its inherent probability.

§3. For the composition of the book cf. G. Fohrer, 'The Origin, Composition and Tradition of Isaiah I–XXXIX', *ALUOS* 3, 1961–2, 3–38, and his *Introduction* (see general bibliography).

§3a(i). G. Fohrer, 'Jesaja 1 als Zusammenfassung der Verkündigung Jesajas', *ZAW* 74, 1962, 251–68 (= his *Studien zur alttestamentliche Prophetie*, BZAW 99, 1967, 148–66). (ii). A. van den Branden, 'I gioielli della donne di Gerusalemme', *BeO* 5, 1963, 87–94. 4. E. Jenni, 'Jesajas Berufung in der neueren Forschung', *TZ* 15, 1959, 321–39; R. Knierim, 'The Vocation of Isaiah', *VT* 18, 1968, 47–68. Scepticism, which seems to me to be justified, over the character of Isa. 6 has been expressed by M. M. Kaplan, 'Isaiah 6.1–11', *JBL* 45, 1926, 251–9; J. Milgrom, 'Did Isaiah prophesy during the Reign of Uzziah?', *VT* 14, 1964, 164–82, esp. 172; O. H. Steck, 'Bemerkungen zu Jesaja 6', *BZ* 16, 1972, 188–206. For Isa. 7 cf. J. Lindblom, *A Study on the Immanuel Section in Isaiah*, Lund 1958; B. Oded, 'The Historical Background of the War between Rezin and Pekah against Ahaz', *Tarbiz* 38, 1969, 205–24 (in Hebrew with an English summary); id., 'The Historical Background of the Syro-Ephraimite War Reconsidered', *CBQ* 34, 1972, 153–65. For 8.23–9.6 (EVV: 9.7) see A. Alt, 'Jesaja 8.23–9,6', in *Festschrift A. Bertholet*, Tübingen 1950, 29–49 (= his *Kleine Schriften II*, Munich ³1964, 206–25); H. Reventlow, 'A Syncretistic Enthronement Hymn in Isa. 9.1–6', *UF* 3, 1971, 321–5: with Alt he argues for the antiquity of this section, which he regards as antedating Isaiah.

§3b. For the 'oracles against the nations' see the bibliography to ch. II, §2. For Isa. 13.2–14.23 cf. S. Erlandsson, *The Burden of Babylon*, Lund 1970.

§3c. G. Fohrer, 'Der Aufbau der Apokalypse des Jesajabuchs (Jesaja

24–27)', *CBQ* 25, 1963, 34–45 (= his *Studien* . . ., 170–81); this dates the section in the fifth century; cf. also M.-L. Henry, *Glaubenskrise und Glaubensbewährung in den Dichtungen der Jesajaapokalypse*, Stuttgart 1967. J. F. A. Sawyer, 'Hebrew Words for the Resurrection of the Dead', *VT* 23, 1973, 218–34, investigates, mainly at the semantic level, the problem of belief in resurrection and on the whole supports the by now traditional view that for the most part terms denoting resurrection appear in late contexts.

§3e. For the term *sēper*, cf. J. A. Soggin, 'Osservazioni a due derivati delle radice *spr* in ebraico', *BeO* 6, 1965, 279–82; ET in id., *Old Testament and Oriental Studies*, Rome 1975, 184–7.

§3f. For the parallel texts Isa. 36–39 and II Kings 18–20 see B. S. Childs, op. cit. (§2 above).

§4. K. Budde, 'Zu Jesaja 1–4', *ZAW* 49, 1931, 16–40, 182–211; T. C. Vriezen, 'Essentials of the Theology of Isaiah', in B. W. Anderson and W. Harrelson (eds.), *Israel's Prophetic Heritage*, New York and London 1962, 128–46; R. Fey, *Amos und Jesaja*, WMANT 12, 1963. On the 'elect remnant' see W. E. Müller, *Die Vorstellungen vom Rest im Alten Testament*, Leipzig 1939 (still a basic work); S. Garofalo, *La nozione profetica del 'Reste d'Israele'*, Rome 1942; P. Zerafa, 'Il resto di Israele nei profeti preesilici', *Angelicum* 49, Rome 1972, 3–29; G. F. Hasel, *The Remnant*, Berrien Springs 1972 (a basic study).

MICAH

§1. *The prophet and his age*

The name, in Hebrew *mikā-yāhū* = 'Who is like Yahweh?', is common enough in the Old Testament. There is at least one other prophet of the same name, Micaiah ben Imlah, whom we considered above (ch. I, §8c), and some other figures; there are also frequent variants. In the book which bears his name, the prophet usually appears under the short form *mikā*. He came from the village of Moresheth-Gath, to the south-west of Jerusalem. According to the superscription he lived under King Jotham, King Ahaz and King Hezekiah (1.1), and was thus a contemporary of Isaiah. His life under the last of these kings is confirmed by Jer. 26.18, a redactional passage, in which Micah 3.12 is presented as a precedent to clear Jeremiah of the accusation of blasphemy. However, the authenticity of the Micah passage is in question. In any case, it is probably because of the greatness of his contemporary Isaiah that Micah has remained in the background as a subsidiary figure. He must also have come from a lower class. This will explain the large proportion of messages dealing with social problems, which are a secondary feature of Isaiah, even if they are not completely absent from his work. It has thus been suggested that Micah may have belonged to the class of free Israelite peasantry who lived on tribal territory, and whose condition became increasingly more wretched as a result of war and the new economic situation, and who were therefore exploited by those who had been able to enrich themselves in the sphere of the court. Thus in some respects Micah would resemble Amos, both in his message and because he passed directly from agricultural work to the prophetic ministry. Micah's ministry seems to have been directed exclusively at Jerusalem, and his geographical and chronological closeness to Isaiah could lie at the root of certain similarities that we can see between the two prophets: both know the oracle in Micah 4.1–4; Isa. 2.2–5 and the idea of the

elect remnant, but there are also real parallels: Micah 2.1–5 is parallel to Isa. 5.8ff.; Micah 5.9–14 to Isa. 2.6ff., and there are others.

The objects of Micah's sallies, in addition to the rich oppressors,
are the priests and prophets who exercise their ministry unworthily,
the syncretism of state religion and the false security which it tends to
create: the feeling that men have done their duty and can therefore
rest easy for the immediate future.

§2. *Content*

The text of Micah can readily be divided into four parts: chs. 1–3,
threats; chs. 4–5, promises; chs. 6.1–7.6, further threats; ch. 7.7–20,
new promises. Here, too, until recently there has been a tendency to
consider the promises inauthentic, since, it is argued, a prophet cannot logically first announce judgment and then contradict himself by
announcing salvation. Today the tendency in these cases is towards
caution: we know that a few lines contain a summary of the preaching
of years, and we are also well aware that the problem of authenticity
or inauthenticity is always difficult and complex: the Uppsala school
rejects the distinction in these terms completely, because it is artificial.

(*a*) Judgment, chs. 1–3. In 1.2–7 we have a threat against the
kingdom of Israel, later adapted to Judah by means of an addition
(v. 5b). We might therefore think of a text which was originally
earlier than 722–21, and was then adapted to a different situation
since Israel no longer existed. In 1.8–16 we have a lament on Judah,
probably on the occasion of the Assyrian invasion under Sennacherib
in 701. Chapters 2–3, which give reasons for the judgment, are more
difficult to date: 2.1–5 are directed against avaricious landowners;
2.6–11 against the prophet's enemies; 2.12f., however, speak of the
assembling of the scattered exiles of Israel and are therefore an
exception in this context, which is entirely one of judgment; 3.1–4 are
against unjust judges; 3.5–8 against false prophets. In 3.9–12 the
priests and prophets are the object of Micah's invective, and for the
first time the threat of the destruction of the Jerusalem temple is
made. As we have seen, this last passage is doubtful: Jer. 26.18 dates
it in the time of Hezekiah. Anyone who accepts its authenticity will
note that the passage must have made a great impression if it could
be quoted a century later in a court as a reason for acquittal in such
an important case.

(*b*) Promises, chs. 4–5. As we have already seen, in 4.1–5 we have
the well-known parallel to Isa. 2.1–4 with one verse more. 4.6f. speaks

of the return of the diaspora and of the establishment of the reign of God in Jerusalem, cf. *inter alia* Ezek. 34; this is therefore certainly later than Micah, and is not to be dated before the exile. 4.8–14 speaks of the destruction of the enemy before Jerusalem and v. 10 is a gloss which identifies the enemies in question with the Babylonians: its character as a gloss appears clearly in the fact that the 'there' in the second half does not refer to Babylon but to the 'fields' which precede the mention of it. If, then, we consider v. 10 to be a gloss, there is nothing against seeing the text as an allusion to the hasty retreat of the Assyrians before Jerusalem in 701; if the gloss however is not a gloss, but an integral part of the text, it is obvious that the text cannot be dated before the exile. In 5.1–5 (EVV 2–6) we have a famous passage, that of the birth of the Messiah in Bethlehem; however, the locality cannot be identified clearly, as the text is uncertain. Most authors in fact suggest that the term *leḥem* should be suppressed and that we should simply read *bēt-eprāt*. In any case, it would seem certain that the author intended Bethlehem and that the gloss, if it really is one, is at least exact. Thanks to the explicit mention of Assyria in vv. 4f. (EVV 5f.), this passage gives the impression of presenting a problem similar to that in Isa. 9.1ff. (EVV 2ff.) and 11.1ff. Micah 5.6–8 (EVV 2–9) is a promise of victory for the remnant of Jacob, perhaps from the exilic period (it is difficult to date it before that), while 5.9–14 (EVV 10–15) speaks of the elimination of the horses, the magic and the syncretistic cult which, as in Isa. 2.7 and 31.1ff., are symbols of human rebellion against God. This, too, is probably an oracle against Judah, adapted at a later time to a new situation and therefore perhaps originally authentic: it is possible that it refers to Hezekiah's reform and was then adapted to that of Josiah.

The difficulty on a chronological level presented by many texts in this group has recently led to the formulation of a hypothesis according to which the whole section should not be dated before the fifth century, thus giving rise to a Deutero-Micah. To chronological reasons may be added reasons of style and lexicography. It should be noted, however, that the text is too brief for us to be able to draw any substantial conclusions on the latter grounds; the chronology is correct in some cases and inaccurate in others. We do not have a late book, but individual texts which are late here and there. The theory thus needs to be reshaped considerably before use can be made of it.

(c) The judgment, 6.1–7.6. 6.1–8 is Yahweh's speech in the course of the trial of his people. Like a great Eastern king, and in a trial quite unlike any modern legal proceeding, Yahweh combines in his person the functions of prosecutor, plaintiff and judge. In the course of the speech, Yahweh argues that the people have shamelessly violated their pledges, while he, Yahweh, has kept them. The term *berit* does not appear, but the concept always seems to be present. Verse 7 could allude to the practice of human sacrifice attested in the time of Manasseh, that is if the question is not intended rhetorically; moreover, it is nowhere said that Micah's ministry lasted into the seventh century. On the other hand, this could be regarded as a sign of inauthenticity. In 6.9–16 we have a tirade against avarice and dishonesty prevalent in Jerusalem, while 7.1–6 laments the decadence of the people of God.

(*d*) Promises, 7.7–20. This passage ends the book with a 'prophetic liturgy'. There are elements here which take us far beyond the time of the prophet: in v. 11 the walls have fallen in ruins, and so the matter is connected with a period after 587. Some scholars even put it in the time of Nehemiah (cf. Neh. 1.1ff.). On the basis of these elements a recent attempt has been made to date chs. 6–7 at the time of the Samaritan schism, so that in this case we would have a 'Trito-Micah'. This theory also needs to be examined carefully.

§3. *Thought*

The complexity of the redaction of this relatively brief work and the difficulty of dating a number of passages, some of which are certainly late and others of which are considered so by some authors, make it difficult to identify a single line of thought. In any case, however, we find directly applied to God the categories of justice which we have already found with Amos and Isaiah. Justice is not understood as a philosophical ideal but as a concrete element in the sphere of personal relationships. Historically it is expressed by the pledge which binds one person to another, even if, as we have seen, the relevant technical term does not appear. However, it has recently been maintained by W. Beyerlin that the themes are present in Micah more than with any other prophet, and his arguments are impressive. An important feature in Micah's eschatology is the promise made to the house of David, so that two different themes come together in his thought. The prophet is able to announce judgment on the basis of the pledge violated by the people.

The social injustice of his period is the most manifest proof of the situation in which the people find themselves, and to them the prophet proclaims the divine justice of which he knows himself to be the representative (3.8). The people delude themselves that they have done their duty and that therefore God is with them (3.11), aided in this by the preaching of the 'false' prophets. But since it should be obvious to anyone that the situation is the opposite of what God desires for his people, the prophet is called to pronounce the only message possible, that of judgment. Confronted with this announcement the only attitude of the people can be that indicated in 6.8.

It is probable that the Assyrian invasion of 701 constituted the proof to the prophet of what he had been proclaiming; a sign had been given that the end was near and that the insights of the prophetic preaching had been correct.

BIBLIOGRAPHY

Commentaries
On the twelve minor prophets see the bibliography to ch. II above. On Micah: A. George, JB, ²1958; J. L. Mays, Micah, OTL, 1976. See also J. T. Willis, 'The Structure of the Book of Micah', *SEÅ* 34, 1969, 5–42.

§2. For the text, cf. I, Willi-Plein, op. cit. (see on ch. II, §1, above). For 'Deutero-Micah' cf. B. Renaud, *Structure et attaches littéraires de Michée IV–V*, Paris 1964. On chs. 6–7 cf. A. S. van der Woude, 'Deutero-Micha: ein Prophet aus Nord-Israel', *Nederlandse Theologisch Tijdschrift*[25], Wageningen 1971, 365–78 (arguing for an early date); T. Lescow, 'Redaktionsgeschichtliche Analyse von Micha 6–7', *ZAW* 84, 1972, 182–212 (arguing for a late date). The expression 'Deutero-Micah' is used in quite different senses by Renaud and van der Woude.

§3. W. Beyerlin, *Die Kulttraditionen in der Verkündigung des Propheten Micha*, FRLANT 72, 1959.

VI

NAHUM, HABAKKUK AND ZEPHANIAH

§1. *Nahum*

(*a*) *The personality of the prophet and the content of his work.* The name Nahum is probably theophoric: *$n^e \dot{h}um$-yah* = 'comforted by Yahweh'; the man is connected with a place called Elkosh, but we do not know where it is nor whether it was his home (1.1). From Hellenistic times on there have been a number of places and tombs connected with the prophet: this is a sign that even at a relatively early date nothing was known about his origins, his life and his death.

The book bears the superscription *maśśā'*, which was examined in ch. IV, §3 above; in the intention of the redactor it is thus a 'charge', an oracle against someone, in fact the city of Nineveh, capital of Assyria. Indeed the whole book contains invective against Assyria, beginning with the acrostic in 1.2–10 which can be followed fairly accurately down to the letter *lamed*. In 1.10–2.3 we seem to have two different positions which are opposed and yet complementary, and have now been combined: an oracle of salvation for Judah (1.12f.; 2.1, 3) and an announcement of judgment on Assyria (1.10f., 14; 2.2). The two compositions are different literary genres, but they fit together, since the liberation of Judah, a vassal of Assyria from the eighth century, was only possible once Assyria had been considerably weakened. The announcement of judgment on Nineveh follows in 2.2–14: the imagery chosen is the scene of an enemy attack against the city. 3.1–7 gives a second threat against Nineveh: the city will be destroyed because of its sins. This attitude is similar to that adopted on more general lines by Isa. 10.5ff. In 3.8–17 a similar fate is prophesied for Nineveh to that of No-amon in Egypt; this last is the current Hebrew term for Thebes, which was conquered and sacked by the Assyrians in 663. The prophecy ends with a funeral lament in an ironic form, a caricature of the city after its destruction, the cause of unrestrained joy for the people who had been oppressed or terrorized by Assyria.

(*b*) *The date and period of the book* are therefore easy to determine: it must be after 663, the year in which the Assyrians sacked Thebes (3.8ff.); on the other hand, while Assyria is decadent, it has not yet fallen, even if it is severely threatened. The situation is such that the prophet may be able to announce the fall of Nineveh at any moment. This puts the book either in 625, when the city was besieged by the Medes, or in 612, when it fell after being besieged by a coalition of Medes and Babylonians.

(*c*) *The text* is particularly fine in chs. 2–3, but falls off in quality and, as we have seen, is interrupted in ch. 1, where the style is also very varied. This is a disconcerting phenomenon in such a short work, and various explanations of it have been given, but none of them commands general approval. Until recently, many scholars challenged the authenticity of the acrostic and in some cases even went as far as dating it in the second century BC (e.g. R. H. Pfeiffer in his *Introduction*). It is possible that the first part was composed before the fall of Nineveh and the second after it. The Scandinavian school has again tried to see the book in terms of an epic and mythical struggle between Yahweh and Tammuz (of course ending in the victory of the former) represented in the cult and constructed on the basis of formulae taken from the liturgy of the two deities. However, an interpretation of this kind, while not excluded by the historical background mentioned above, is not justified given the present state of the sources.

(*d*) *The thought of Nahum* has always been the object of particular interest. Following the studies of P. Humbert, it has been considered almost unanimously as the isolated expression of one of those prophets who proclaimed an optimistic nationalist message and gave so much trouble to their colleagues, who were more critical and therefore more pessimistic about the future of the people. Micah, whom we have already examined, and (as we shall see) Jeremiah and Ezekiel in particular, would fall into the latter category. However, this particular theory shows at least one weakness. In announcing the ruin of Assyria, Nahum takes up an already developed theme, as we have seen in Isa. 10.5ff., which bears witness to the work of God in history. This work embraces the actions of the great powers of the age: Assyria, the Medes and the Babylonians, and of course Egypt are mentioned. In this sense even those who accept the theory that Nahum is nationalistic and optimistic cannot ignore the connection with the message of his predecessors. However, a recent work has changed the lines of enquiry, and comes to diametrically opposed conclusions: only some post-exilic additions to the book have a nationalistic character, while the earliest part of the work clearly announces judgment. Thus the problem of the book cannot be said to be resolved along the lines indicated first, even if we must recognize that the second alternative has not yet been formulated in a definitive fashion, and will not be convincing without further discussions.

§2. *Habakkuk*

(a) *The name of the prophet and the content of the book.* We know nothing either about the prophet or about the origin of this important document. Not even the author's name has been transmitted in a satisfactory way: in Hebrew it appears as *ḥᵃbaqqūq*, in Greek as *Ambakoum*. In any case, he is a visionary who in 2.1–3 gives important information about the circumstances connected with the visionary inspiration of the prophet, whereas in 3.16 there is an account of the physical phenomena which accompany the vision. According to the recent study which we have mentioned in connection with Nahum, Habakkuk will have been the true cultic prophet.

The book can easily be divided into two parts: chs. 1–2 and ch. 3. In 1.2–4 we have a lament by the prophet (according to some, by the community, but this seems improbable) on the power of the wicked; this is the ancient problem of theodicy which we shall examine in detail later in connection with the book of Job. In 1.5–11 it is announced that Yahweh is raising up the Chaldaeans (i.e. the Babylonians), whose irresistible power is described. A second lamentation begins in 1.12–17; notwithstanding his judgment on the wicked, God will allow them to act evilly against the just. In 2.1–3 there is a description of the prophet's preparations to receive the vision, followed by an order to write it down; 2.4–5 contains a new curse against the wicked, followed by the famous phrase which has perhaps been the object of more passionate theological discussion than any other, and is quoted by Paul in Rom. 1.17 and Gal. 3.11. However, while Paul's interpretation is limited to considering faith as the proper attitude towards God, the present text goes further: it also describes the waiting in trust which is prompted by God himself. 2.6–20 contains a threat in five strophes, each introduced by 'woe to', a formula typical of this literary genre: the text concludes with a liturgical expression.

The second part of the book is composed of ch. 3, a hymn which is no different from similar compositions in the Psalter, with strong archaic or archaizing features. The theme of Yahweh's appearing is

presented, and the description recalls such similar compositions as
Deut.33.1ff.; Judg.5.1ff. and Ps.68.1ff. Yahweh is acclaimed as he
comes to the help of his people and destroys the wicked. Like a
number of psalms, the work contains expressions like *selah*, which are
of doubtful meaning. According to W. F. Albright, the work is divided
into four distinctly separate parts: v.2 is a very ancient prayer for
the preservation of life, perhaps that of the king, with an addition in
a Yahwistic sense to adapt it to Israelite faith. This part may be so
old that we might reasonably suppose it to be of Canaanite origin.
We also have examples of compositions of this sort in Sumerian
Mesopotamia, from the Third Dynasty of Ur (the first years of the
second millennium BC) onwards. Verses 3–7 form the second part and
are also a very early text. They speak of the appearance of Yahweh,
who comes from the desert in the south-east, cf. (as we have seen)
Deut.33.2ff.; Judg.5.3ff. The date should probably be put towards
the eleventh century BC. The third part is the Israelite adaptation of
a Canaanite poem which celebrated the victory of Ba'al over the
floods (one of the elements of chaos), the sea (another element of
chaos) and death (which in the summer holds Ba'al in its power and
reigns in his stead). These themes are well known from the mythology
of Ugarit. Now, however, everything seems to be applied to the person of Yahweh, who is also victor over these elements, and there is
no sign that the final redactor was aware of this adaptation. It is
strange that the storm which accompanies Yahweh is not the one
that is usual in the region, coming in the autumn and winter months
from the south-east. This one comes from the north-east, which is at
least an unusual phenomenon. For vv.10ff. cf. Ps.77.17ff. Verse 13
mentions the king as the 'anointed' of David, which shows that the
final redaction comes from a relatively late stage, although it is
certainly earlier than the exile. Finally, from v.14 to the end we
have a composition which recalls that of the pre-exilic prophets and
which therefore has no particularly archaic features. The Norwegian
scholar S. Mowinckel has opposed this division of Hab.3, arguing
that the composition is a unitary one. But although a thorough examination of the text may produce some problems here and there
from the perspective of some of Albright's theories, it also shows that
Albright is essentially right: this is a composite text with a remarkably
complex origin. Of course the motives adopted by Albright for the
dating of the various parts are based to no small degree on subjective valuations and need to be verified on the basis of more objective
grounds.

(b) *The time of Habakkuk.* It is no easy undertaking to date a book like Habakkuk, where even the name of the author is not clearly attested, and there are no specific historical references (as there are, for example, in Nahum). The wickednesses so often mentioned may be those either of Judah (and in that case we would have prophetic invective against the corruption of the time), or of Assyria, which had now come to the end of its power. One explanation does not logically exclude the other. The mention of the Chaldaeans (the first time that Babylon appears on the horizon of Judah after the brief episode of the embassy at the time of Hezekiah) could be a useful element for dating, if it did not give the impression of having been interpolated into its present context (cf. 1.5–11 with 1.2–4, 12–17); besides, there is no reason to suppose that the situation with Habakkuk differs from what we know to be the case with other prophets, namely that many passages are composed of independent units. The vision announced in ch. 2 is meant to describe the destruction of the wicked, but this destruction does not happen. Perhaps Weiser is right when he affirms that ch. 3 could be the conclusive intervention by Yahweh to settle this question. So if the mention of the Chaldaeans may be considered a valid aid towards dating, it would indicate the second half (and probably the last quarter) of the seventh century, and makes it possible that the wicked are in fact the Assyrians. However, we cannot exclude another theory, that the Babylonians are those who are charged to execute judgment on the wicked of Judah, which would put the passage between 612 and 587 as the extreme possibilities. B. Duhm attempted to date the book at the time of Alexander the Great, that is, at the end of the fourth century, but his theory has not met with much favour. First of all it is based on an emendation of *kaśdīm* ('Chaldaeans') to *kittīm* (1.6), and this interference with the text is not only quite arbitrary, but does not resolve anything, anyway. The *kittīm* at the time of Qumran are the Romans, but the name is attested at the end of the seventh century for mercenaries in the pay of Judah, in the ostraca of Tell ʿArad, cf. Appendix I, § 10; they could therefore very well have been a feature of the period to which the prophet is traditionally assigned.

(c) *The thought of Habakkuk* is very like that of Nahum. Here the divine justice appears as the motive force in history and is vividly represented at work in ch. 3. The problem of theodicy appears on the periphery, but without being dealt with very profoundly. The theophany is clearly the central feature of the text. The fact that other peoples are mentioned, but not Judah, could be a nationalistic element, as has been recently argued; in any case, however, this is no chauvinism, nor is there the note of false optimism which we know to have been typical of some of those who were considered 'false' prophets.

§3. *Zephaniah*

(a) *The prophet and his time.* A genealogy at the beginning of the book traces the prophet back over four generations to a certain Hezekiah. Is this the king of the same name, and does it mean that the prophet will have belonged to the royal house of Judah? The question is impossible to answer. In fact a superscription dates the prophet to the time of Josiah. And here a problem arises. The religious situation presented by the book is catastrophic; hence we can either date the book to the time of Josiah but before the reform, or we can assign it a date under his successor Jehoiakim, who, as we know, sought to undo a good deal of Josiah's reform. The choice is not an easy one, and in any case the prophet either comes between Nahum and Jeremiah, or is to be put in the second phase of the latter's ministry.

(b) *Content and composition.* Chapter 1 speaks of the judgment which is coming on Judah because of its sin. We have two narratives about the coming of the 'day of the Lord', which has already been mentioned: 1.7,14–18, a text which forms the foundation for the medieval hymn *Dies irae, dies illa* . . ., to be found in the Roman Catholic liturgy, and 2.1–3, where the just and the humble are exhorted to seek Yahweh, to repent and to be saved 'in that day'. 2.4–15 contains threats and curses against neighbouring peoples, while 3.1–13 is directed against Jerusalem and its leading class, the object of imminent judgment, the instrument of which will be the pagan nations. Only a 'remnant' of the humble will escape, while the haughty will perish. 3.14–20 is an exhortation to Jerusalem and is a hymn of jubilation to Yahweh, the King who restores the exiles of Judah.

The pattern of the book is thus similar to what we have seen (and will continue to see) in other cases: judgment against Judah or Israel, oracles against the nations and announcement of salvation. The schematic character of the work would suggest a redaction, but we have no information about it. In 3.15ff. we have elements which reappear in Ezek. 34; 35 and 37. Here and there we can find traces of revision, but these do not affect the substantial authenticity of the book.

(c) *The thought of Zephaniah* follows the patterns detected in Amos and Isaiah; at its centre is the expectation of the terrible 'day of

Yahweh' (cf. Amos 5.18ff.; Isa.2.7ff.). The doctrine of the 'elect remnant' also has its precedents in Amos, Isaiah and Micah; in this way there comes about a distinction between the people of God as an ethnic and political entity, and the people of God as a group of believers.

BIBLIOGRAPHY

Commentaries

In addition to the commentaries on the twelve minor prophets (see bibliography to ch. II above), see M. Bič, *Trois prophètes dans un temps de ténèbres: Sophonie – Nahum – Habaquq*, Paris 1968.

§1. Commentaries: A. George, JB, ²1958; K. J. Cathcart, Rome 1973. Other studies: P. Humbert, 'Essai d'analyse de Nahoum 1,2–2,3', *ZAW* 44, 1926, 266–80; id., 'La vision de Nahoum 2,4–11', *AfO* 5, 1928–9, 14–19; id., 'Le problème du livre de Nahoum', *RHPR* 12, 1932, 1–15. These articles have been influential in study of the book right down to the present day. Cf. also C. A. Keller, 'Die theologische Bewältigung der geschichtlichen Wirklichkeit in der Prophetie Nahums', *VT* 22, 1972, 399–419. For the myth and ritual interpretation cf. A. Haldar, *Studies in the Book of Nahum*, Oslo 1947. Humbert's interpretation has been challenged by Jörg Jeremias, *Kultprophetie und Gerichtsverkündigung in der späten Königszeit*, WMANT 35, 1969, 11ff., esp. 48ff.

§2. Commentaries: B. Duhm, 1906; J. Trinquet, JB, ²1959. Other studies: P. Humbert, *Problèmes du livre d'Habacuc*, Neuchâtel 1944 (a basic study); J. Jeremias, op. cit., 55ff., esp. 108ff. For the relation of the book to the Qumran text cf. W. H. Brownlee, 'The Composition of Habakkuk', in *Hommages à André Dupont-Sommer*, Paris 1971, 255–75. For ch. 3 cf. W. F. Albright, 'The Psalm of Habakkuk', in H. H. Rowley (ed.), *Studies in Old Testament Prophecy presented to T. H. Robinson*, Edinburgh 1950, 1–18; S. Mowinckel, 'Zum Psalm des Habakuk', *TZ* 9, 1953, 1–23; J. H. Eaton, 'The Origin and Meaning of Habakkuk 3', *ZAW* 76, 1964, 144–71; S. Margulis, 'The Psalm of Habakkuk: a Reconstruction and Interpretation', *ZAW* 82, 1970, 409–42. For the Qumran text cf. M. Burrows, *The Dead Sea Scrolls of St Mark's Monastery*, I, New Haven 1950.

§3. Commentaries: A. George, JB ²1959; L. Sabottka, *Zephanja, Versuch einer Neuübersetzung mit philologischem Kommentar*, Rome 1972. For the date cf. D. L. Williams, 'The Date of Zephaniah', *JBL* 82, 1963, 77–88.

VII

JEREMIAH

§1. *Life and work*

Jeremiah immediately stands out from the other prophets for the number of biographical notes in which his book is so rich. Some of these are autobiographical statements, some are composed of material collected by third parties on his account: the collectors in this latter group will be examined shortly. The notes are also concerned with the inner conflicts to which he was subjected and allow us an unparalleled chance of seeing at close quarters the personal element which accompanied the prophetic ministry and sometimes conditioned it to no small degree. These latter passages are called the prophet's 'confessions', as we have seen, but the material lends itself on more detailed analysis to rather different estimations.

It is easy to distinguish three periods in Jeremiah's life. The first runs its course under King Josiah, in the thirteenth year of whose reign the prophet was called to his ministry. Depending on the chronology followed, this is the year 627–6 or 626–5; this phase of Jeremiah's ministry must have lasted until about the time of the reform, in 622–1. The second period was in the reign of Jehoiakim, and probably at the beginning of it, from 609 onwards. The last period was under Zedekiah, that is, from the first conquest of Jerusalem in 597 to the second in 587, and after a few years was followed by the prophet's deportation to Egypt. He died there; we do not know when, but it will not have been very long afterwards.

The American J. P. Hyatt has put forward a theory which differs substantially from the tradition and from the statements in the superscription to the book. He puts the *birth* and not the calling of the prophet in the thirteenth year of Josiah, and makes his ministry begin only in 615, a few years before the death of the king in battle, and when the reform had already been under way for a number of years. This theory, first put forward in 1942, has been repeated by the author in his commentary. However, as far as I know, it has found only one recent supporter, and for the rest has passed unnoticed. The arguments advanced by Hyatt to support his theory do not seem convincing, and to be presented again validly it would need to be formulated in substantially different terms.

(a) *The first period.* Jeremiah was born into a priestly family living at Anathoth, present-day Anata, about five miles north-north-east of Jerusalem. The date of his birth is conventionally put about the middle of the seventh century, but there is no obvious reason for this. The only information that we have is the prophet's reaction to his call by Yahweh, where we could translate his words either 'I am only a boy' or 'I am too young'. The term used in Hebrew, *na'ar*, can in fact have both meanings and is used to indicate either children or men already capable of bearing arms. In fact Jeremiah's answer does not indicate a particular age, but merely affirms that he has not yet reached a sufficient age to have the authority which seems inseparable from the prophetic ministry. There are evidently a number of possibilities here. We know nothing of his family, but the fact that he belonged to the priests of Anathoth would suggest that he was a descendant of Abiathar and the priests whom Solomon had deported to that area (I Kings 2.26) because they had supported his competitor Adonijah It is not strange, then, that Jeremiah too was originally destined for the priesthood, a function which, as we know, was hereditary and was therefore only connected with particular families. This explains how he was able to speak freely during worship in the temple in Jerusalem. The thirteenth year of Josiah is given as the date of his calling not only in 1.1 but also in 25.3, and thus seems to be fairly well fixed within the tradition. The words addressed to him in the act of his calling are a typical definition of the prophetic ministry: he is 'to pluck up and to break down, to destroy and to overthrow, to build and to plant' (1.10), in other words, principally to announce judgment, as can be seen from the four verbs (even if some writers would like to delete two of them), but also to proclaim an alternative to destruction. Jeremiah's mission thus coincides not only in time but also in content with the theme of Josiah's reform, though his connection with this reform is far from clear. We shall return to the problem in due course.

As in the case of other prophets, the exercise of this kind of ministry must necessarily have made many enemies. But with Jeremiah we certainly find a special case of suffering: twice we hear of conspiracies against him aimed at silencing him for ever (11.18ff. and 18.18ff.), and there are passages which show how there were nests of opposition, even in his own village, which did not hesitate to adopt extreme measures against him. Another time he was handed over to a tribunal on a charge of blasphemy, a crime which carried the death penalty, following his announcement of the destruction of the temple in the course of a sermon given in it (7.1ff.; 26.1ff., 8ff.). The corruption and the superstition which he saw in the country were not limited to it alone, but extended to the cultivated ruling class in the capital. This note is particularly serious when we think that the ruling class served a hard apprenticeship in the wisdom school, as we shall see below (Part Five, ch. II); this evidently aggravated its guilt to no small degree.

In a number of passages, all belonging to the first stage of his ministry, the prophet announces the execution of judgment by means of a people which he does not specify, but which comes from the north: 4.5–31; 5.15–18; 6.1–8, 22–26; 8.14–17; 10.18–22. B. Duhm identified this unknown people with the Scythians, who are reported by Herodotus (I, 103–6) as having reached the borders of Egypt during the last quarter of the seventh century, and who certainly contributed markedly to the weakening of the Assyrian empire, destroying its bases and disrupting the system of communications and administration in the northern and western territories. Interesting though it is, this theory has been generally abandoned today, although it does reappear here and there from time to time.

According to the traditional chronology which we have adopted, Jeremiah seems to have interrupted his ministry during Josiah's reform, taking up his preaching again only after Josiah's death. This is the chief element in favour of Hyatt's theory. We know of no reason for this silence and can only make guesses about it; in any case, it seems sufficiently certain that he approved the work of the reforming king, if we accept as authentic the words of censure directed towards Josiah's successor Jehoiakim in 22.15, where Josiah is praised in comparison with his successor, to the disadvantage of the latter. A number of authors in fact believe that all ch. 31 is quite simply a declaration of support for Josiah's politics, aimed at reconstructing the Davidic empire from the ruins of Assyrian domination. But this is conjecture pure and simple, even if it seems quite probable.

(b) *Under Jehoiakim* both the political situation and the religious situation deteriorated rapidly. Jehoiakim ascended the throne following a crude intervention by Pharaoh Necho II of the Twenty-Sixth Dynasty: the election of Josiah's successor by the assembly of the people in the person of his son Jehoahaz (II Kings 23.30ff.) had been annulled by the Pharaoh, who had installed another son of Josiah,

Eliakim, whose name he changed to Jehoiakim, a typical sign of
vassalage (II Kings 23.34ff.). This situation of dependence on Egypt
must be kept in mind if we are to understand the policy of support for
Egypt maintained by the court, a policy which would inevitably set
Judah against Babylon. If we take the prophet's charges against
Jehoiakim seriously (22.1f.), he must have governed somewhat un-
scrupulously in the political sphere, and in the religious sphere have
followed a syncretistic policy with strong nationalistic features: in the
hands of unscrupulous politicians, Yahweh's ancient promises, his
solemn pledges towards the people and theirs towards him, will have
become a way of preaching a facile, irresponsible faith in God, devoid
of any obligation and certainly far removed from the ancient
promises which were recalled. As always, politics and religion were
inextricably united in Israel, so that the prophet's preaching against
the temple (chs. 7; 26) immediately became a matter of state. On the
other hand, the content of this preaching was portentous for its
audience: what, suggested Jeremiah, was the sense of a cult celebrated not in a 'house of prayer' but what might be called a 'den of
thieves'? Only a recollection of the precedent of Micah, who, about
a century earlier, had also announced the destruction of the temple
(3.12, a passage whose authenticity we have seen to be doubted by
some writers), succeeded in saving the prophet from being condemned to death (26.18).

Jeremiah not only had to endure conspiracies aimed at eliminating
his person physically; he also had to endure prolonged defamation
which threatened his moral destruction (20.10).

However, the real break between him and his people happened as
the result of a symbolic action which appears to be a replica of the
ancient Egyptian ritual of the 'execration texts'. As we have seen, this
ritual has been authoritatively (but not unanimously) connected
with the prophetic oracles against the nations (cf. above ch. II, §2).
In 19.1ff., cf. especially v. 10, Jeremiah breaks a potter's flask, a sign
of the forthcoming ruin of Judah to be brought about by Yahweh.
This act and its implications must have been obvious to everyone, all
the more because the prophet did not make any secret of what was
involved; its significance was heightened by the fact that whereas in
Egypt the 'execration texts' were always used against the enemies of
the country, here the symbolic action was directed against Judah
itself. Jeremiah was imprisoned, put in the stocks and flogged (20.1ff.);
he was forbidden to enter the temple. To the people the prophet
seemed to be a blasphemer and to the politicians a defeatist. It was
better for everyone not to be seen in his company. From that point on

his friends shunned him, leaving him in a solitude which must at times have driven him to despair, cf. the 'confessions', 12.1–3; 15.10ff.; 16.1ff. (where among other things we learn that God had forbidden him to marry, which was a most unusual thing for the Israelite of that time); 18.19ff.; 20.7ff.

However, the king whose vassal Jehoiakim had become did not last long: in 605 the Egyptian troops were defeated in the battle of Carchemish on the Euphrates by the army of Nebuchadnezzar, still heir apparent to the throne of Babylon, who became king a few months later. This is the figure whom the Vulgate called Nabucodonosor, a word which is nearer than the Hebrew to a true rendering of the original. While a victory by Necho II in the summer of 601–600 near the frontier between Egypt and Judah and the Pharaoh's occupation of Gaza might have suggested the possibility of a rapid Egyptian recovery, prudence must have counselled Jehoiakim to adopt a more or less ambivalent position towards the belligerents, remaining undecided in what was still a very confused situation. Jeremiah, however, saw matters clearly: he advised immediate submission to Babylon, denouncing the vassal relationship with Egypt: the 'enemy from the north', the mysterious power in the first period of his preaching, will now have taken historical shape in Nebuchadnezzar II and the Babylonians. In fact Jeremiah was ordered to write down all his sayings spoken up to that date and to have them read before the people and the authorities (ch. 36). The scroll was given to his amanuensis Baruch, whom the prophet sent to the temple a little later, to read it before the people and the authorities on a day of fasting in December 604. The nobility brought the matter to the king's attention, so great was the impression made by the reading, but the king would not listen to reason and cut the scroll to pieces, throwing the fragments on a brazier. At the same time he ordered the arrest of Jeremiah and his secretary. However, the two of them were warned by a court official and succeeded in saving themselves in time. The prophet immediately had a second scroll made to replace the one that had been burnt and added further material: the advantage of oral tradition is the prodigious memory which is developed by it.

(c) *Jeremiah under Zedekiah and down to his death*. In the year 598 the oracles pronounced by Jeremiah against the people seemed to be coming true. Nebuchadnezzar, who could not allow on his southwestern frontier a vassal of an enemy who a short time earlier had defeated him and occupied Gaza, set out on an expedition against Judah and laid siege to Jerusalem. Jehoiakim died during the last months of the siege, leaving the throne and a burdensome legacy to his son Jehoiachin (II Kings 24.6ff.). The city fell, and some of its nobility and the royal family were deported to Babylon, while Nebuchadnezzar replaced Jehoiachin with Mattaniah, a brother of Jehoiakim, whose name he changed to Zedekiah (II Kings 24.17ff.), again to indicate the vassal relationship.

From a constitutional point of view Zedekiah's position was not clear: on the one hand, although the legitimate sovereign had been deported and was in no position to exercise his proper functions, he was still alive, so that Zedekiah was only a regent; on the other hand, he was called upon to exercise fully all the functions connected with royalty. As if this were not enough, he was a weak character, the pliable victim of a number of pressure groups. On the one hand were the priests and prophets who under Jehoiakim had announced that God was with Judah: the fact that Jeremiah's words had been verified historically had made it necessary for them to demonstrate that what had happened was only a temporary set-back, merely intended to be a kind of test to which Yahweh was subjecting his people. On the other hand there were political and military groups who partly relied on Egypt in the hope of a rapid recovery with its help, the extent of which evidently continued to be overestimated. They partly sought to steer a course between the two great powers by means of more or less skilful and disguised forms of double-dealing. All these groups saw Jeremiah as their natural enemy.

The prophet attacks these positions with violence and clarity, advising unconditional surrender to Nebuchadnezzar. Three times the king of Babylon is called 'my servant' in the name of Yahweh (25.9; 27.6 and 43.10), an interpretation of events which repeats exactly that already given by Isaiah about the peoples who would execute judgment on Judah, and anticipates the one to be made later by Deutero-Isaiah about Cyrus, who this time is the instrument of the reconstruction of the people of God. In the course of a rebellion in 594 (for the text and an evaluation of the facts cf. above, ch. I, §8), some prophets exhorted the people to make common cause with the rebels. Chief among them was a certain Hananiah, whose preaching took up Isaiah's favourite theme of the inviolability of Zion (chs. 27–28). Jeremiah had to fight tenaciously against them. Similar voices could be heard among the exiles of 597 (and one echo of their views also reaches us through Ezekiel, who was one of them), but in ch. 29 we have the text of a letter (with considerable Deuteronomistic revisions, though the substance of it will be authentic) in which the prophet struggles to destroy the false hopes of the exiles, exhorting them rather to settle in the new land without being misled by those who promised them liberation too easily.

In 588 Nebuchadnezzar moved against Jerusalem again and laid siege to it a second time. Jeremiah, who was considered a potential traitor and certainly a defeatist, was subjected to all kinds of vexations and was finally accused of communicating with the enemy. He was thrown into an empty cistern where he would certainly have died had the king not given him help in secret (chs. 37–39); the king did not have the courage, or perhaps the physical capability, to help the man under his protection more effectively. The prophet's fortunes changed with the storming of the city: although the conquerors destroyed the greater part of it and deported a large number of its inhabitants, they treated Jeremiah with respect and allowed him to stay, together with the governor Gedaliah, to organize the reconstruction. However, a conspiracy formed by nationalist elements and disbanded soldiers assassinated Gedaliah; the culprits fled to Egypt, taking the prophet with them as a hostage (chs. 42; 43). He died there (ch. 44), but without discontinuing his preaching during his imprisonment. Jeremiah, like Isaiah before him, is said to have died a martyr's death, but again according to a late legend the historicity of which we cannot verify.

§2. The text

Once we take into account the prophet's life, the book of Jeremiah has all the ingredients of a work of remarkable complexity; it in fact seems obvious that neither the prophet himself nor his amanuensis can have succeeded in completing the redaction, given the troubled times in which they lived, the persecutions of which they were the objects and the deportation to Egypt, which were hardly favourable to the creation of literary works. The starting point for the study of the book in its present form is ch. 36, where we have details of the preparation of the two editions of speeches pronounced by the prophet down to December 604; this cannot have been a very large collection of material if it was possible to read the text aloud three times in the course of a day. Of course it is no longer possible to establish even approximately which passages of the book of Jeremiah as we now have it were included in the scroll in question and which were not, though it is clear that all the passages that can be dated after 604 cannot have been included. A recent study has sought to identify chs. 1–6 of the present book as the essential contents of the scroll in question. According to the text of the LXX these chapters are divided into oracles against Judah and Jerusalem, oracles against the nations and oracles of salvation, a scheme which, as we have seen, appears in the redaction of a number of prophets and which in this case will then have been the work of Jeremiah and Baruch. But this question must be verified in some detail before we can reach such a neat conclusion.

Understanding of the personality of the prophet, which until recently seemed irreversibly set on the course of an autobiographical interpretation of the confessions (and we, too, have drawn abundantly on elements of this sort in the preceding section) has over the past few years been put in a new dimension through a book by H. Reventlow. In 1963 Reventlow criticized the personalistic interpretation of these passages, which begins from a characterization of Jeremiah as having been sensitive and fragile, forced against his will to embark on adventures for which he had neither the strength nor the courage. Hence the drama of which the 'confessions' would be the evidence. The reality, however, is different and the problem is infinitely more complex. The 'confessions' come too close to the literary genre of the 'lamentation of the individual', which is well attested in the Psalms and which we have touched upon in passing (in Part One, ch. VI, §4; we shall return to it in due course below, Part Five, ch. I, §5b) for us to be able to consider them simply as personal outbursts. Rather, what we have here are lamentations of a liturgical character which the prophet pronounces in the name of his people, whose mediator he is before God. On the other hand, a re-reading of these texts will show that an autobiographical tone seems unquestionable. It may be that Jeremiah is repeating traditional liturgical material, but it is also obvious that he has chosen passages which correspond very well indeed with his own situation. There are various ways of reciting a liturgical composition; one is in a routine which does not really affect the person who is praying; the other, which is very different, is for the suppliant to identify himself completely with the text which he is reciting. Everything seems to indicate that Jeremiah fell into this latter category. It does not, then, seem to be a matter of alternatives, but of complementary theories which not only illuminate the prophet's personality but also show the origin of the material which he used.

In 1923 the Italian scholar G. Ricciotti defined the book of Jeremiah as a 'miscellany', and this is a very appropriate description. We find a certain systematic character only on a small scale, in particular passages: the whole book gives the impression of having been assembled with almost a complete lack of criteria. This immediately raises the problem of the classification of texts, given that the book is 52 chapters long!

A first classification seemed to be gaining acceptance at the end of the last century and the beginning of this, that of prose passages and verse passages. For B. Duhm in his now classic commentary of 1901, only the verse passages could go back to the prophet; the others were more or less apocryphal additions. However, Duhm himself soon noted that a classification along these lines was too formal and therefore simplistic: in fact there was no reason why the prose material should not be the product of redactional work on the original texts. Duhm therefore proposed a new system of classification which was accepted in 1914 by Mowinckel and re-presented by him in an improved form in 1946, with, among other things, the substitution of 'cycles of tradition' for sources. In this classification we have:

(i) Authentic oracles of Jeremiah (for Duhm, those in poetry);

(ii) The 'biography' of Jeremiah produced by Baruch, though it was impossible to delineate this with any certainty (this, of course, is in prose);

(iii) Finally, secondary revisions to the work by various authors, usually identified with Dtr (W. Rudolph prefers to speak in terms of 'words of Jeremiah, revised by the Deuteronomistic writer').

This threefold classification is generally accepted today, though a recent study has cast doubt on the existence of a biography by Baruch (we have seen that there is no obvious indication of its presence): in fact the writings which are classified in this way do not have a unitary character, and a thorough analysis indicates that they are the product of the fusion of at least three independent complexes of tradition. In any case, Reventlow's warning not to be too much influenced by the distinction between poetry and prose seems to be valid. The latter is certainly the style preferred by preaching of the Deuteronomistic type, the former that preferred by the prophets, and the relationships between Jeremiah and Deuteronomy and the Deuteronomistic school are, as we shall see, so complex that it is inadvisable to keep too closely to purely formal questions.

It is now possible for us to divide the book into five parts: (a) 1.1–25.14; (b) chs.26–36; (c) chs.37–45; (d) 25.15–38 and chs.46–51; (e) ch.52.

(a) In 1.1–25.14 we have a series of oracles arranged according to the three periods of the prophet's life:

(i) chs. 1–6: under Josiah;

(ii) chs. 7–20: under Jehoiakim and

(iii) chs. 21–24: generally belonging to the last period. 25.1–14 is attached to the second section. In this part one may note a tendency to regroup the oracles according to a particular theme: sin, judgment, the temple, laments and invective especially against the prophets. It is here that we find most of the 'confessions'.

(*b*) Chapters 26–36 are generally written in the third person and are a report of the prophet's life. It is interesting to compare two texts which narrate the same episode, chs. 7 and 26. With the exception indicated, this material and especially chs. 37–45 has been considered for the most part the work of Baruch. In chs. 26–29 there is an attempt to follow a chronological order, and in chs. 30–31 and 34–35 a thematic classification appears again.

(*c*) Chapters 37–45 narrate the activity of the prophet during the last years of his ministry, especially during the siege of the city in 588–587. For those who accept the validity of the theory, the hand of Baruch will have been at work here.

(*d*) 25.15–38 and chs. 46–51 are the oracles against the nations which the LXX puts immediately after the second half of ch. 25; the result is a different numbering in the LXX text. Opinions are divided over the authenticity of this material and it is impossible to make a generalized judgment. In any case, we know that the literary genre is attested for the majority of the prophets.

(*e*) Chapter 52 is a historical appendix parallel to II Kings 25; it is therefore another, though shorter, instance of what we have seen in connection with Isa. 36–39 and II Kings 18–20. There is no reason to attribute this passage to the work of Jeremiah or to circles in any way connected with him.

The book may therefore have taken shape more or less in the following way. First of all came the second edition of the scroll dictated by the prophet to Baruch, then a collection of sayings of the prophet and material about him (whether or not the latter was the work of his amanuensis), then Deuteronomistic revisions of various material and finally some additions of different kinds. This work evidently extended over many years.

§3. *The LXX text*

The statements made in the previous paragraph seem to be verified as soon as we turn our attention to the LXX translation. We have already seen that this presents a different division of the material, but here we have only a problem of classification and not one of content. However, there is a problem of content when we compare the text of the LXX with the Massoretic text: the former is notably shorter, by about 2800 words. Now there are cases in which it is clear that the translator will have wished to summarize texts which he considered to be prolix or of little interest to his readers; at other times we have the errors and omissions which are typical of translations and transcriptions. But there are a number of passages of notable importance which the LXX omits: Jer.33.14–26 is a typical case. One of the conclusions we might arrive at is that the LXX will have been translated from a text which was in fact shorter than the Massoretic text, implicit evidence that even after the second century BC the book continued to be expanded with various additions. A Qumran fragment offers partial help in this direction: it is that indicated by the siglum 4Q Jer[b] and gives a fragment of 9.22–10.18. Here the Hebrew follows the order of the LXX, which differs from that in the Massoretic text, and offers at least one reading which is exclusive to the Greek text and is not attested in the Hebrew. Thus the LXX seems to have been derived from a Hebrew archetype which differs in some respects from our Massoretic text. However, the problem of the dimensions of the original text has only been touched on by this discovery and must remain unresolved in the present state of research.

§4. *Jeremiah and contemporary sources*

(*a*) One problem of great importance, though it is far from a satisfactory solution, is that of the relationship between Jeremiah and Josiah's reform, i.e. his relationship with Deuteronomy and Dtr. We have already seen that the book contains texts in a Deuteronomistic redaction, or, to put the problem in a different way, passages which have strong affinities of style and content with the products of this school. The existence of the problem is generally admitted, but there is no agreement among scholars over its implications. For example, ch. 11 is typically Deuteronomistic, but when we say that what do we mean? For H. H. Rowley, passages like Jer.3.1ff.; ch.34; 44.24ff. demonstrate clearly that the prophet knew Deuteronomy. 34.9 in fact shows that women, too, were included in the wholesale liberation of slaves which took place as the end drew near, and this agrees fully with the amplification of Exod.21.2ff. made by Deut.15.1, 17. Jer. 3.1ff. is very closely connected with Deut.24.1ff., while in Jer. 11.5 we seem to have allusions to Deut.8.18 and 6.3. Rowley concludes that Jeremiah must have known the reform and that he restated some of its demands; on the other hand, if this in fact is the case, we do not know how far his support extended. It is no surprise to find a certain similarity in language or the discussion of problems among authors of the same period.

(*b*) In the Lachish letters, with which we shall be concerned in Appendix I, §9, there is an allusion which some writers have wanted to connect with the person of Jeremiah. Letters III, 20 and VI, 4 in fact mention 'the prophet' and 'a man' respectively, who would seem to have much in common with the characterization which the heads of the people made of Jeremiah in 38.4. Some writers would therefore like to identify the figure with him. Attractive though this identification may be (and it would be the only case where a person formerly attested only in the Bible now appeared in extra-biblical sources), it is simply an indication and not a proof, and since we do not know the name of the person mentioned in the letters in question, identification cannot be established.

§5. *Jeremiah the thinker*

We have already seen the personal character of the book of Jeremiah, a feature which has led to different judgments. In any case, this is a factor which gives Jeremiah a special character in comparison with other prophetic books. Jeremiah shares with his predecessors his ministry as a herald of Yahweh to his people, even if he was almost ignored. He seems to have been unwilling to fulfil this function: one has only to compare the bold 'Here am I, send me', with which Isaiah (6.8b) replies to Yahweh's question whether there is anyone prepared to go in his name, with the continual wavering of Jeremiah which is already evident at the moment of his call (1.6); this attitude of perplexity and reticence continued for a good part of his ministry, cf. the 'confessions'. There are many instances in which Jeremiah feels that violence has been done to his own will and that his power of decision has been unjustly nullified; in one case he goes so far as to say that he has been 'seduced', deceived. He is thus anything but a passive instrument in God's hands, a person who goes his own way doing his duty without looking either to right or to left. On the contrary, he struggles to understand; he does not accept anything without being convinced, or at worst being constrained or deceived; where possible he seeks to halt the disaster which he sees pressing in on the future of his people (20.7ff.). There is thus a marked tension between the personality of the prophet and his ministry, between his own inclinations and his vocation. On his own account, he would have been a good citizen by the standards of his age: honest, hardworking, quiet in his everyday life, ready to avoid any excessive emotion or particularly prominent standpoint; in practice he saw himself constrained to act continually against his own character. Even if the 'confessions' are liturgical material and nothing more, they are an excellent expression of his state of mind.

In this spiritual situation the prophet saw himself constrained to face problems like those of theodicy (ch. 12), predestination (1.5) and sin (13.23). But his approach to these problems is always very specific; he does not elaborate theories, but lives by what is proposed to him and what he proposes. And the most adequate solution always seems to him, as to his predecessors, to be obedience to the divine will (15.19). His office as mediator puts him in a difficult situation: on the one hand he feels his solidarity with his people, whom he defends before Yahweh until his God has to prohibit him from interceding for his nation (7.16; 11.14; cf. Isa. 1.15); on the other hand he has to act as a crucible to purify the people in the name of Yahweh (6.27ff.). The drama of a man who seems in this respect to be extraordinarily modern derives from this profound inner conflict.

(a) The testimony about God has remarkable points of contact with that of Hosea, as we indicated in ch. III (above). Like Hosea, Jeremiah proclaimed the divine love and grace, represented by the image of marriage (2.1ff.; 3.1ff.; 31.20ff.; cf. Hosea 1–3 and 11.8). For Jeremiah, too, at the beginning of relationships between God and the people stands the pledge of the former to which the latter responds (11.1ff.). However, this passage has been considerably revised by the Deuteronomist, even if it is not itself Deuteronomistic; the future of these relationships can be seen only in terms of a 'new obligation', 31.31–34 (as has already been said, with Jeremiah the use of $b^e r\bar{\imath}t$ becomes frequent, whereas previously it was limited to Hosea), and is a theme which reappears in different ways in the exilic prophets Ezekiel and Deutero-Isaiah. As for Amos and Isaiah, God is also the Lord of history and makes use of foreign rulers and peoples (remember 'my servant' Nebuchadnezzar) to carry out his plans: so if this is the task of the king of Babylon, all opposition to him becomes opposition to Yahweh's plans and therefore sacrilege. This theological clarity is here united with a political realism to which his contemporaries would have done better to listen. Eschatology does not seem to be very developed in Jeremiah: in addition to the concept of the 'new obligation' which replaced the old one that had been violated (31.31), in 33.14ff. we have a sketch of a messianic figure. As well as presenting textual difficulties, the two passages (and this is especially true of the second) contain obscure concepts and are regarded by some authors as inauthentic.

(*b*) For Jeremiah, too, as we have indicated, man's only possible attitude to God is one of absolute obedience. This takes specific form in love and faithfulness (5.1ff.; ch. 35). The cult is only the expression of an attitude of gratitude and obedience, and not a substitute for them (7.1ff. and 26.1ff.; cf. 6.20). This is especially true in the field of ethics, in which Jeremiah follows the lines marked out by his predecessors, even if, as we have seen (above, ch. I, §7c), the theme is not one of the basic ingredients of his message as it is for other prophets (2.34; 6.7; 7.5ff.; 21.11; 22.3ff.; 34.8ff.). It is true that man's sin is expressed in individual conscious acts, but in Jeremiah more than in any other prophet it appears as something more profound, as the result of a basically wrong attitude, which in fact is now part of human nature (4.22; 5.3 and especially 13.23, where we have the tragic assertion that just as the negro cannot change the colour of his skin nor a leopard that of his coat, a man cannot but be a sinner). This situation cannot serve as a moral excuse for men, so that they can ignore appeals for conversion: chs. 1–6 are full of these appeals, see also 8.4ff. This dialectic, which is part of any authentic theology, expresses the difference which exists between the human situation on the one hand and the power of men to overcome its effects on the other. However, the solution is not found within the context of this dialectic, but in God himself, who pardons men out of his love and takes up again with them the relationships which they have broken off (31.31–34).

BIBLIOGRAPHY

Commentaries
B. Duhm, KHC, 1901; G. Ricciotti, Rome 1923; P. Volz, KAT, ²1928; A. Penna, SacBib, 1952; J. Steinmann, Lectio Divina, 1952; A. Aeschimann, Neuchâtel 1959; A. Gelin, JB, ²1959; A. Weiser, ATD, ⁴1962; J. Bright, AB, 1965; W. Rudolph, HAT, ³1968; O. Loretz, 'Die Sprüche Jeremias in Jer. 1.17–9.25', *UF* 2, 1970, 109–30 (an important philological study).

§1. J. P. Hyatt, 'Jeremiah and Deuteronomy', *JNES* 1, 1942, 156–73; id., in *The Interpreter's Bible* V, 779ff.; C. F. Whitley, 'Carchemish and Jeremiah', *ZAW* 80, 1968, 38–49. These studies put the beginning of Jeremiah's ministry near the end of the seventh century, but the arguments put forward are not strong enough to overthrow the traditional chronology given in the superscription to the book; cf. T. W. Overholt, 'Some Reflections on the Date of Jeremiah's Call', *CBQ* 33, 1971, 165–84. A. C. Welch,

Jeremiah: his Time and his Work, Oxford 1928 (reprinted 1951), is still a basic study of the period.

§1a. On the Scythians cf. H. Cazelles, 'Sophonie, Jérémie et les Scythes en Palestine', *RB* 74, 1967, 24–44.

§1b. For the events of 601–600 cf. É. Lipiński, 'The Egypto–Babylonian War of Winter 601–600', *AION* 32, 1972, 235–41.

§1c. For the problem of false prophecy, cf. T. W. Overholt, *The Threat of Falsehood*, SBT II 16, 1970.

§2. For the 'confessions' the classical study is W. Baumgartner, *Die Klagedichte des Jeremia*, BZAW 32, 1917; cf. also H. Reventlow, *Liturgie und prophetisches Ich bei Jeremias*, Gütersloh 1963 (the liturgical interpretation); H.-J. Stoebe, 'Jeremia, Prophet und Seelsorger', *TZ* 30, 1964, 385–409; id., 'Geprägte Form und geschichtliche, individuelle Erfahrung im Alten Testament', *SVT* 17, 1969, 212–19, an examination of the problem of the relation between fixed literary genres and autobiographical texts which are expressed through them; cf. also J. M. Berridge, *Prophet, People and the Word of Yahweh*, Zurich 1970, an excellent study which rightly argues that Jeremiah has used traditional literary genres to express his life's experience; W. L. Holladay, 'Prototype and Copies: a New Approach to the Poetry-Prose Problem in the Book of Jeremiah', *JBL* 79, 1960, 351–67; id., 'Style, Irony and Authenticity in Jeremiah', *JBL* 81, 1962, 44–54; id., 'The Background of Jeremiah's Self-Understanding: Moses, Samuel and Psalm 22', *JBL* 83, 1964, 153–64; id., 'The Recovery of Poetic Passages of Jeremiah', *JBL* 85, 1966, 401–6; A. H. J. Gunneweg, 'Konfession oder Interpretation im Jeremiahbuch', *ZTK* 67, 1970, 395–416; O. Eissfeldt, 'Unheils- und Heilsweissagungen Jeremias als Vergeltung für ihm erwiesene Weh- und Wohltaten', *WissZ Univ. Halle* 14.3, 1965, 181–6 (= his *Kleine Schriften* IV, Tübingen 1968, 181–92). For the second scroll and its identification with chs. 1–6 cf. C. Rietzschel, *Das Problem der Urrolle*, Gütersloh 1966; for the biographical notes attributed to Baruch cf. G. Wanke, *Untersuchungen zur sogennanten Baruchschrift*, BZAW 122, 1971. Cf. also E. Tov, 'L'incidence de la critique textuelle sur la critique littéraire dans le livre de Jérémie', *RB* 79, 1972, 189–99.

§3. For the special features of the LXX text see the commentaries and J. Ziegler, *Ieremias*, Göttingen 1957; for 4Q Jer^b, F. M. Cross Jr, *The Ancient Library of Qumran*, London 1958, 139, n.38. J. G. Janzen, *Studies in the Text of Jeremiah*, Cambridge, Mass., 1973, has argued that the Massoretic text has been amplified and that therefore more trust should be put in the LXX text.

§4a. H. H. Rowley, 'The Prophet Jeremiah and the Book of Deuteronomy', in *Studies in Old Testament Prophecy presented to T. H. Robinson*, Edinburgh 1950, 157–74; O. Eissfeldt, 'The Prophetic Literature', in H. H. Rowley (ed.), *The Old Testament and Modern Study*, Oxford 1951, 152ff.; S. Herrmann, *Die prophetischen Heilserwartungen im Alten Testament*, Stuttgart 1965, 162–95 (esp. 188ff., where the conclusion is reached that the Deuteronomic-type passages are simply later revisions); E. W. Nicholson,

Preaching to the Exiles, Oxford 1970; W. Thiel, *Die deuteronomistische Redaktion des Buches Jeremia*, Berlin (duplicated dissertation) 1970.

§4b. D. W. Thomas, 'Again "The Prophet" in the Lachish Ostraka', in J. Hempel and L. Rost (eds.), *Von Ugarit nach Qumran. Festschrift für O. Eissfeldt*, Berlin 1958, 244–9.

PART FOUR

THE EXILIC AND
POST-EXILIC PROPHETS

I

EZEKIEL

§1. Name and personality

If Jeremiah can be considered the last of the pre-exilic prophets, although he also suffered the consequences of the political catastrophe which befell his nation, Ezekiel appears as the first of the exilic prophets. He was in fact deported to Babylon after the siege of 597 and exercised the greater part of his ministry in that country. The Hebrew name, *yeḥezqē'l*, means 'God strengthens', and is very appropriate considering the circumstances in which the prophet who bore it had to work; the LXX transcribes it as *Iezekiel* and the Vulgate as *Ezechiel*, hence our Western transcriptions. Like Jeremiah, Ezekiel belonged to the priestly class; we know the name of his father (1.3) and he had a very good knowledge of the temple, its topography and the rituals practised there. There are notes about his deportation in 597 in 1.1; 33.21; 40.1; in Babylon he lived in a place called Tel-Abib (3.15), which was situated near the river Kebar (1.1), not far from the city of Nippur, in the southern part of the country. Like many exiles, he had achieved a reasonable standard of living; among other things, he was the owner of a house in which the elders of Judah were accustomed to meet (3.23; 8.1). In 24.16ff. there is a note that Ezekiel was married, but that his wife had died suddenly. According to the chronology of the book, his call to be a prophet came in the year 593; the beginning of the book (1.1ff.) has a rather obscure text, but the number five in 1.2 seems to be that of the years which have elapsed since the deportation of 597, whereas the enigmatic 'thirty' probably refers to the age of the prophet at the time of his calling. It is certainly not by chance that this was one of the ages established for taking up a levitical ministry (cf. Num.4.23 and above, Part Two, ch.IV, §1). Ezekiel enjoyed a great deal of respect among the exiles (8.1; 14.1). According to A. Bertholet in his commentary of 1936, on the other hand, Ezekiel will have worked in Jerusalem down to the exile of 587 and will then have arrived in Babylon with the second deportation rather than the first: in this way Bertholet tries to explain the large number of notes that we find in the book about the situation in the capital between the two exiles. However, this is an explanation which clearly presupposes the revision of an original text of which we have no knowledge, before it achieved its final form. It would be disconcerting that this work had complicated the contents of the book rather than simplifying them. To explain the presence of Ezekiel in Jerusalem for the period before 587, which would have been clearly attested in the primitive form of the book, the redactors would have had to introduce the theme of the transportation of Ezekiel from Babylon to Jerusalem by the hand of the spirit. It is clear that while this explanation solves the problem of the presence of Ezekiel at Jerusalem at a certain time, it presents considerable problems in other parts of the book.

According to the book, Ezekiel's work falls into two clearly distinct periods: the first extends from his calling to the fall of Jerusalem in 587 (chs. 1–24); the second includes oracles which go from the fall of Jerusalem on. During the first period Ezekiel preached judgment, taking up more or less the lines followed by Jeremiah in 594 (cf. Jer. 27; 28 and the argument of ch. 29): all hope of an imminent return of those who had been deported and thus of a speedy restoration is false. In the second period, on the other hand, Ezekiel preaches God's grace and becomes the herald of the restoration of his people (chs. 33ff.; 40ff.), since the people have accepted the judgment that was announced and have shown themselves ready to be converted. The last oracle that can be dated comes from 571 (29.17), so that Ezekiel's ministry will have lasted at least twenty-five years.

§2. *Visions and symbolic actions*

A first distinctive element of the book of Ezekiel is the quantity and quality of the visionary elements, with a very marked tendency towards excess, indeed towards the bizarre. This is a feature which is virtually absent from the books of Hosea, Micah and Jeremiah, and takes a very sober form in Amos. There is an extraordinary vision only in Isa. 6.1ff., but here it is appropriate because of the importance and the unheard-of character of the message which Isaiah had to pass on and which the vision was meant to justify. In other words, whereas for Ezekiel's predecessors visions were an extraordinary feature, and were often made up of every-day events, in Ezekiel their contents verged on the grotesque and were the forerunners of the kind of vision which would be a feature of the apocalyptic style of certain pseudepigraphical books at the end of the first millennium BC and the beginning of the common era; we find one example in the book of Daniel (cf. below Part Five, ch. VIII).

A second element to note is the ecstatic character that some of his experiences take on: the prophet really is 'outside himself' when the phenomena in question take place. In ecstasy he is transported by the spirit from Babylon to Jerusalem (8.1ff.), as we have already seen; other phenomena can be described as cataleptic (3.15; 4.4; 24.27; 33.22). On the other hand, leaving aside any hasty diagnosis in the medical or the psychiatric fields (and there has been no lack of attempts in this direction in the first half of our century), medical replies to questions in this area have always indicated due reserve towards classifying the phenomena in question under this aspect, and especially towards admitting the existence of pathological phenomena: first of all the material at our disposal is too sparse for us to be able to risk a diagnosis, and secondly these are phenomena which almost by definition cannot be investigated by research of this kind, especially if it is made at such a distance.

A third element is the frequency and the character of Ezekiel's symbolic actions. While these are rare and matter-of-fact among his predecessors (cf. Isa. 20; Jer. 19; 27, where only the first case is at all bizarre) and therefore relatively simple to interpret, they seem to become the rule with Ezekiel, and also show a marked tendency towards the bizarre and the grotesque.

There are no obvious explanations for the transportation in ecstasy from Babylon to Jerusalem: we have seen Bertholet's attempt to set the first part of Ezekiel's ministry in Jerusalem; R. H. Pfeiffer (*Introduction*, 536) makes a similar proposal. He argues that Ezekiel, deported in 597, will have returned home following the order which he received in 3.4 and will have been deported a second time in 587: the redactors will then have attributed his action to the work of the spirit. But although this proposal has better foundations than that of Bertholet, it only avoids the problem and does not overcome it: Ezekiel is and remains an out-of-the-ordinary prophet, often disconcerting, and in any case different in character from his predecessors and also to a great extent from those who came after him.

§3. The book

One particularly striking characteristic of Ezekiel is that the book appears to be in relatively good order – so good, that down to the end of the last century it was presented as a model, apart from a text which in many places is far from easy. It is in fact remarkably simple to make a division: (a) oracles against Judah and Jerusalem in chs. 1–24; (b) oracles against the nations in chs. 25–32; and finally (c) oracles of salvation in chs. 33–48. The last section is subdivided into two parts: the preparation in chs. 33–39 and its programmatic realization in the restoration of the temple and the cult in chs. 40–48. Once again, then, we would seem to have the tripartite scheme which we have also found in other prophetic books, but which we have seen to be almost certainly the work of the redactors. So even in the apparently perfect Ezekiel we have signs of a redaction, and there are in fact many more indications: too often the chronology, which we have seen to be so exact, appears valid essentially for the verses which immediately follow the chronological note, but stops there (and it is worth noting that at this time, from the first tentative indications in Jeremiah, the prophetic oracles begin to be dated, a system left aside by Deutero-Isaiah and then taken up on a large scale by Haggai and Proto-Zechariah); there are a good many contradictions and repetitions, passages edited in the first and the third person, and so on. This has suggested at least two redactions. Others have wanted to make a distinction between passages in poetry and passages in prose, a criterion which, as we have seen, is also followed in the case of Jeremiah, but has been shown to be too simplistic. On the basis of the apocalyptic elements present in the work, yet others have come to view the work as having been written by an anonymous prophet who lived towards the third century BC and who will have projected his work back to the time of the exile in order to make it comply with the criteria established in the first century AD for the place of a book in the canon, namely that it should have been composed at a time earlier than that of Ezra and Nehemiah (cf. above, Part One, ch. II, §1a, b). In reality these attempts are simply the product of a swing of the pendulum in opposite directions: whereas Ezekiel was first cited as an example of systematic redaction (or what was thought to be systematic redaction), at a later stage the truth seemed to be precisely the opposite, and Ezekiel therefore *had to* become an artificial work at a stroke, possibly put together with scissors and paste, with a fictitious order and fictitious chronology. Today, however, as with the other prophets, the tendency is to examine each passage in Ezekiel on its merits, deciding on the authenticity, the inauthenticity or the dubious character of each one of them in turn. Thus it is possible to find some interpolations in 27.2–9a, 25–37; in ch. 38 and in chs. 40–48, and in some further cases. We have seen that this situation also exists for the most part among the prophets who preceded him. It is not possible to establish who has been at work. We do not hear of any disciples whom Ezekiel may have had, but since he regularly received the elders of Judah, a school or at least a circle *could* (this is, of course, only a possibility) have arisen which transmitted his words and meditated on them. In any case, the inauthentic material is difficult to recognize in Ezekiel because we have fewer external points of reference with him than with others.

A theory has been presented very recently which seeks to provide an explanation of the presence of material which does not tally with the prophet's work. It is contained especially in chs. 5; 11; 12; 13; 16; 21; 23; 34, while chs. 20; 33–34 are entirely composed of such material, so that they have been called 'Deutero-Ezekiel'. It is in them that we find the majority of parallels to the 'Holiness Code' in P (cf. above, Part Two, ch. IV, §§1 and 3). Only an initial analysis has been made of the problem, and it is therefore too early to make any form of judgment, but it is certain that the proposed solution would resolve adequately a problem which has always given scholars a great deal to think about, that of the relationship between certain sections of Ezekiel (which then would not come from Ezekiel) and the relevant material in P.

Another problem in Ezekiel is that of the relationship between the Massoretic text and that of the LXX. It is generally recognized that, leaving aside some wrong or tendentious translations, the Greek text goes back to an archetype which is better than the Massoretic text; it is therefore a regular practice to seek to correct the latter on the basis of the former. In particular, it is a fact that even LXX[A], which usually represents an LXX text adapted to the Massoretic text by means of the elimination of some of the material which differs from it (and which is preserved e.g. in LXX[B]), presents remarkable differences from the Massoretic text. However, the extent of the phenomenon is not obvious: no Hebrew document has emerged from Qumran which bears any trace of these recensions, as happened e.g. in the case of the books of Samuel and Jeremiah (only partly, in the latter case), so that we can do no more than note their existence.

§4. *Ezekiel the thinker*

Jeremiah and Ezekiel are the bridge by which we pass from the pre-exilic period to the exile and the post-exilic period. In Ezekiel priest and prophet meet, as clearly appears from the programme of the renewal of the cult in chs. 40–48. A critic of the cult would certainly have been out of work after 587, when it only existed in the most limited form in the ruins of the temple. But in every case in which Ezekiel gives his opinion, he always considers it an essential element of the community, whether past or future. This explains his exceptional task, aimed at a restoration purified of the abuses which his predecessors had pointed out. But Ezekiel is still the theologian, the ecstatic, the organizer of the exiles, beginning with the semi-official meetings in his home. The vision which marked his call almost overwhelmed him, and the divine power excited in him phenomena which were at the same time both mysterious and disconcerting. The originality of his thought is not affected by these elements: Ezekiel has a message of his own to give and it is by no means inferior to the message of those who preceded him. Decades ago he was criticized for a supposed 'coldness' and for particular characteristics which were thought to prove that his writing was only theoretical, and did not therefore have any contact with real life. We may leave aside the aesthetic categories which underlie these evaluations; they are irrelevant, because they have only a very limited bearing on Ezekiel's thought. We may leave aside the criticism that Ezekiel did not have a prophetic 'personality', as this arises from the romanticizing assessment of the prophets which we have seen not to be valid (we may recall what was said in the previous chapter about Jeremiah's 'confessions'). It is obvious that in Ezekiel elements of remarkable complexity existed side by side on the personal level and in the area more closely connected with his ministry. We have seen that attempts have been made to give a psychopathological evaluation of certain aspects of his ministry; the weakness of this approach does not do away with the fact that it has been possible in the case of Ezekiel where it has not worked with his predecessors and his successors, thanks to the presence of certain objective data which cannot be denied. From what we can deduce from the texts, he is a complex personality, who is sometimes contradictory, rich in disconcerting phenomena, deeply tormented but in a very different way from e.g. Jeremiah, and endowed with a remarkable capactiy for organization (we need only think of the circumstances which governed his ministry).

For Ezekiel, too, the axis around which the history of the world and of his people turns is the holiness of God. He refers to this explicitly when he often speaks to his audience with the phrase 'That they may know that I am Yahweh'. For Ezekiel, too, it was the case that what happened to Judah was the consequence of divine judgment. However, once the news of the fall of Jerusalem had arrived, his negative message could immediately be reversed. Since the people had now been freed from all false security, and now seemed ready to listen, the reconstruction could begin, starting first of all with the discouraged figures whom he had in front of him. However, the prophet's fundamental experience always remains that of the divine power which overwhelms him: this is tersely expressed in the form of address which Yahweh most often uses towards him: 'Human being . . .' (lit. 'Son of man'). For the prophet, the recognition of this divine sovereignty is also the basis and the foundation for the message of reconstruction. Since God is sovereign, after judgment and destruction he can rebuild on a completely new basis. Thus the strict censor becomes the pastoral counsellor, if it is permissible to use this modern expression, and in this new guise he visits, exhorts, organizes to such a degree that he is sometimes dubbed 'the father of post-exilic Judaism'. In his teaching he appropriates the doctrine of Deuteronomy and the Deuteronomistic history work on reward, which is the key by which the people are to understand what has happened to them. Here, however, he comes up against individual guilt and responsibility which transcend collective guilt and responsibility (14.12ff.; 18.2–20). In any case, like Jeremiah before him, Ezekiel refutes the easy excuse of collective guilt as a disguise for individual faults: although the responsibility of the individual is closely bound up with that of the community, it is not done away with, and man is presented as completely responsible for his actions.

Concerned as he is to lay the foundations for the reconstruction of his people, Ezekiel does not show any particularly universalistic features, even if the oracles against the nations clearly reveal that he knew that the destiny of the people of God was irrevocably bound up with that of other peoples. It is certain that the temple against which he himself had preached down to 587 now becomes the place for the final gathering of his people, the future centre for the new community (chs. 40–48).

The vision of the final assault of the peoples on Jerusalem, where they meet with destruction, and the visionary character of such a notable part of his own prophetic experience have earned for Ezekiel the title 'father of apocalyptic', a title which until a little while ago was used without any questioning. This is a precise evaluation as long as it is not used as a reproof against the prophet, but as a statement of fact pure and simple: it does seem that the apocalyptic genre is inspired by all kinds of thoughts and expressions begun by Ezekiel. But Ezekiel nevertheless remains a prophet in all that he does and despite everything (for the difference between the prophets and apocalyptic, cf. above Part Three, ch. I, §3e). It is even possible to set the futuristic elements in his preaching alongside the preaching of Deutero-Isaiah: concepts like those of the 'new exodus', the 'new pledge', the 'new people' are common to the two prophets, notwithstanding the fundamental difference on the stylistic level. Like Jeremiah, Ezekiel sees that the ancient exchange of pledges between God and his people and between the people and their Lord has been annulled by the prevarications of Judah. It is therefore necessary for God himself to put this relationship on a new basis (cf. the end of ch. 16 and chs. 34; 36–37). This is the only perspective in which it is possible to look to the future with a certain optimism – otherwise (cf. ch. 13) not. He himself defined his ministry with the appropriate simile of the watchman who warns his people of the coming of the enemy (ch. 33), so that they can be saved, and announces the coming liberation, so that they can make it their own (ch. 37).

BIBLIOGRAPHY

Commentaries
R. Kraetzschmar, HKAT, 1900; J. Herrmann, KAT, 1924; G. A. Cooke, ICC, 1936; A. Bertholet and K. Galling, HAT, 1936; F. Spadafora, SacBib, 1948; G. Fohrer and K. Galling, HAT, 1955; P. Auvray, JB, ²1957; W. Eichrodt, ET, OTL, 1970; W. Zimmerli, BK, 1969; J. W. Wevers, NCB, 1969.

§1. G. Fohrer, *Die Hauptprobleme des Buches Ezechiel*, BZAW 72, 1952; K. von Rabenau, 'Die Entstehung des Buches Ezechiel in formgeschichtlicher Sicht', *WissZ Univ. Halle* 5.4, 1955–6, 659–94; H. Reventlow, *Wächter über Israel*, BZAW 82, 1962; W. Zimmerli, *Gottes Offenbarung*, Munich 1963 (a collection of essays mainly concerned with Ezekiel).

§2. K. Jaspers, 'Der Prophet Ezechiel. Eine pathographische Studie', in *Arbeiten zur Psychiatrie, Neurologie, und ihren Grenzgebieten. Festschrift K. Schneider*, Heidelberg 1947, 77–85, argues against the detection of pathological states in Ezekiel. For prophetic 'symbolic actions' see G. Fohrer, 'Die Gattung der Berichte über symbolische Handlungen der Propheten', *ZAW* 64, 1952, 101–20 (= his *Studien zur alttestamentlichen Prophetie*, BZAW 99, 1967, 92–112).

§3. For chs. 26–28 cf. H. J. van Dijk, *Ezekiel's Prophecy on Tyre*, Rome 1968; for 'Deutero-Ezekiel' cf. H. Schulz, *Das Todesrecht im Alten Testament*, BZAW 114, 1969, 163ff.

§4. W. Zimmerli, 'The Message of the Prophet Ezekiel', *Interpretation* 23, 1969, 131–57. For the relation with Deutero–Isaiah cf. D. Baltzer, *Ezechiel und Deuterojesaja*, BZAW 121, 1971.

III

DEUTERO-ISAIAH

§1. *The prophet and his age*

The second prophet who exercised his ministry among the exiles was an anonymous figure whose words have been collected in Isa. 40–55 and who is therefore often called 'Deutero-Isaiah'. Along with the preaching of Jeremiah, his message is usually classified as one of the culminating points of Old Testament thought. At least, this was the view of the primitive Christian church, which cited it frequently in New Testament texts. A central element of this prophet's thought, the message of the 'servant of Yahweh', very quickly achieved the status of one of the earliest christological formulations in the primitive church.

Today, no scholars, apart from some who belong to conservative circles in Catholicism, Judaism and Protestantism, and who adopt their position because of preconceived dogmatic reasons, attribute Isa. 40–66 to the eighth-century prophet. Although the attribution to Isaiah has been generally accepted over the centuries, the reasons against it are too many. It is enough to list the chief of them.

(*a*) In these chapters the exile is not presented as a threat, as the announcement of judgment in the more or less imminent future, but as an event which has already taken place. The people are in exile and the author addresses the community of those who have been deported, and not the community in Judah. Palestine, however, has remained the prey of the surrounding peoples, who have not hesitated to divide the lands which formerly belonged to Judah (42.22–25; 43.5–7, 28; 44.26–28; 45.13 etc.).

(*b*) The enemy is no longer Assyria, as in the eighth century and at the beginning of the seventh, but Babylon; at the time of Isaiah, on the other hand, Babylon, too, was oppressed and therefore entered into more friendly relations with Judah (II Kings 20.12–19; Isa. 39.1ff.; II Chron. 32.31). Besides, at this time Babylon did not even have the power to invade and to oppress Judah. Moreover, Assyria is not even mentioned in Isa. 40–66.

(c) On the other hand, the people of Judah who live in exile are no longer a prey to discouragement, as we saw in the second period of Ezekiel's preaching, nor in a euphoric state, as Jeremiah and Ezekiel show to have been the case between the two exiles. Deutero-Isaiah begins by announcing that their bondage is over (40.1f.), that the armies of liberation are now on the march and are encircling Babylon (41.2–4; 45.13; 46.11; 48.14–16), and these events are not described in the nebulous form typical of prophetic announcements about the more or less distant future, but with the precision that one would expect from the eyewitness to an event. Babylon is now faced with defeat (41.25–27 and 42.9). But this is evidently the situation at the middle of the sixth century and not in the second half of the eighth.

(d) Cyrus, king of Persia, victor in the year 539 BC, is twice mentioned explicitly in the text (44.28; 45.1–8). This never happens with other prophets in the case of a future figure, even in messianic prophecies.

(e) In many passages the prophet refers to the fulfilment of ancient prophecies against Babylon and in favour of Judah (41.21–29; 42.9; 43.8–13; 44.8; 45.21; 46.8–12). None of these would make any sense to anyone living in the second half of the eighth century or at the beginning of the seventh, but they acquire special significance if, as is said at the beginning of these chapters (40.1ff.), they are intended to console the people of Yahweh between 547–46, the year of Cyrus' victory over Croesus, king of Lydia, and 539, the year of the fall of Babylon.

(f) There is a marked difference of style between the book of Isaiah from the eighth century and the passages under consideration, even in a good translation: Isaiah has been edited according to the pattern and in the style of a prophecy of his time, whereas Deutero-Isaiah is marked by a style which we might call 'epic', with a particularly elevated and flowing manner.

(g) A new vision of history begins with Deutero-Isaiah. There is a clear distinction between the past and the present, which are full of calamity, and the coming era, that of salvation. There is no parallel to this kind of thought in pre-exilic prophecy, but it does appear with Haggai and Zechariah (cf. also below, chs. III and IV).

With few exceptions, virtually all these facts, which are now obvious to anyone with a critical approach, were only noted from the eighteenth century on: and only at the end of the last century did the majority of biblical critics recognize them. A computerized statistical check has recently been carried out at the University of Haifa, and the results obtained have confirmed what critics had said earlier about Isaiah (Part Three, ch. IV, §1). There is still room for doubt and controversy over these results, but they do give scholars the best solution for all their problems. Consequently we too shall begin our investigation by accepting a Deutero-Isaiah whose ministry covered the middle of the sixth century BC.

Once this basic division between chs. 1–39 and 40–66 has been made, a second problem immediately arises: is 40–66 a literary unity, or collections of fragments; and if the latter alternative is accepted, what are these fragments? There are various possible solutions.

(i) Chs. 40–66 are a collection of fragments only connected by key-words or similar systems.

(ii) Chs. 40–66 can be divided into the following units: chs. 40–48, 49–55 and 56–66. The theme of the first unit is the action of Cyrus against Babylon, and it is therefore to be placed between 550 and 539; the second speaks of the new community which arises after the liberation and is therefore dated a little after 539; chs. 56–66 constitute a 'Trito-Isaiah' and need to be studied separately: in fact we have a series of fragments most of which can be dated and located in the Jerusalem community in the last quarter of the sixth century.

(iii) Yet others would see 'Deutero-Isaiah' (chs. 40–55) as a basic unity, the internal breaks within which coincide perfectly with the progress of the author's thought from the period preceding the liberation to that immediately afterwards. Chs. 56–66 then again constitute the 'Trito-Isaiah' of whom we spoke in the preceding section. The discovery of 'Trito-Isaiah' is the result of the work of B. Duhm, who proposed it in the first edition of his commentary on Isaiah (1892). We too shall be discussing Trito-Isaiah among the post-exilic prophets, in ch. V below.

The so-called 'Servant Songs' make up a special category within the sphere of Deutero-Isaiah; we shall deal with them briefly below, in §3.

There is much to be said for the theory according to which Deutero-Isaiah would be essentially a unity, with logical breaks, even if it is possible to divide the text into many smaller units: whether these units come from the author or from redactors is irrelevant to this suggestion.

§2 *Analysis and content*

Deutero-Isaiah can be divided easily into two large units, as we have already seen: chs. 40–48 and 49–55. In the first part the dominant theme is that of Cyrus, king of Persia, whom the anonymous author supports with great enthusiasm, seeing him as the realization of Yahweh's plan in history. The people of Yahweh, who now paid the penalty for their guilt, are on the verge of liberation. This certainly brings us down to the last years before the fall of Babylon, when Cyrus was ably forging the pincers which were soon to squeeze the Babylonian empire on many sides and whose jaws would snap shut in the year 540–39, ending with the fall of the capital, Babylon. As we have seen, it is reasonable to date this unit between 547–46, the year in which Cyrus conquered Lydia, and 539–38. It is perhaps possible to be more exact: a recent study, beginning from the phrase attested in Isa. 40.2, '. . .The time of her servitude (lit. 'of her military service') is fulfilled', and from the fact that such military service lasted forty years, arrives at about 547 BC from a starting point of 587. In the second unit there is none of the epic character which marks the first, and little or nothing is said of political events of any importance. The conquest of Babylon by Cyrus must therefore have taken place, and politically we are now in a static period. However, 40.8 and 55.11 indicate that there is a clear relationship between the two parts.

§3. *The 'Servant Songs'*

The most mysterious part of these chapters consists of the songs of the servant of Yahweh: 42.1–9; 49.1–6; 50.4–9 and 52.13–53.12. They are marked out not only by a special theme, independent from that of the rest of the work, but also by the fact that they have evidently been interpolated in their present context, from which they can be removed without any resultant damage or interruption. They also have their own linguistic characteristics and their own theological content, which is independent of that of the other passages in the work. Collected together in a separate unit, they present a logical progression, culminating in the expiatory death of the servant, and also in his triumph.

We have however recently expressed doubts about this interpretation of the last song; the servant was almost certainly not killed, and in any case he was not raised. The text is unusual for being in the third person, but its hyperbole is familiar from the individual lament.

One obvious question arises: is it possible to identify the servant and to say who he was? The question is an old one: we find it in the New Testament in the mouth of the Ethiopian eunuch of Acts 8.34, directed to the apostle Philip. Philip's reply is well-known, but it is the product of about five hundred years of reflection on the theme. Even within the last century, every possible answer has been given and every conceivable person has been identified with the servant. We too shall therefore attempt to answer the question, with the difference that, in contrast to specialist works or studies, we shall be content to keep to the main headings.

(a) If the author of the songs were Deutero-Isaiah himself, as has been affirmed by Muilenburg and Fohrer, it would be obvious that we should consider the songs in which the servant speaks in the first person as autobiographical (49.1ff.; 50.4ff.). This solution of the problem has received authoritative support in recent years and certainly has much to be said for it, if we leave aside the obvious incongruity of the author's announcement not only of his own expiatory death but also of his glorification. Moreover, to anyone who knows oriental literature it seems fundamentally romantic and unreal, apart from the fact that the prophet could very well have quoted a series of songs in the first person. We would then have a similar problem to that of the 'confessions' of Jeremiah. The solution, then, is improbable and unlikely; it is not only unnecessary, but also by no means the only one that can be put forward.

(b) Another direction in which research has turned has been in that of the great figures of the history of Israel who passed through particularly serious trials, from Moses to Jehoiachin or later Zerubbabel, a figure to whom we shall return in ch. IV below. The attempts and figures have been listed by many commentators, who also give reasons for the choice of one figure rather than another.

(c) The collective interpretation is also important. This theory was particularly acceptable among Jewish scholars, and is based on 49.2–5, where the servant is understood as 'Israel'; the theory was already put forward by the LXX and the Targum, so that it may be based not only on a text but on a very ancient exegetical tradition.

(d) Attention should also be paid to Engnell's theory. He has connected the figure of the servant with that of the king. According to the ritual of the *akitu* festival (the Babylonian day of expiation celebrated during the New Year festival), it appears that on this occasion the monarch took on himself the guilt of his people in a vicarious form, sometimes even suffering death (in this case it seems certain that in Babylon a temporary king was elected and sent to his death

in place of the real king). With this expiatory act the people would
then be freed from their guilt. The ritual of the festival would thus be
an adaptation of the liturgy of the death of the god Tammuz, whose
cult we have seen even to have been practised in the Jerusalem temple
before 587 (Ezek.8). For Engnell there is no doubt that the figure of
the servant was originally a royal figure (and his theory has been
confirmed indirectly by the fact that in the ancient Near East only
royal inscriptions are written in the first person). This would justify
either an individual (the king was obviously an individual) or a
collective interpretation (the king *was* his people according to the
theory of corporate personality elaborated by Wheeler Robinson in
1936). Therefore although the messianic interpretation of the figure
of the servant is not attested in the Jewish writings of the period (with
a single exception which is difficult to evaluate and which we shall be
examining shortly), in the New Testament period it would be completely legitimate, indeed the only truly legitimate interpretation.
The term 'servant' supports this interpretation rather than ruling it
out. The Hebrew *'ebed* is not necessarily a title of humiliation; it has
the same ambivalence as our 'minister', as a word which originally
had clearly servile connotations. The 'King's Servants' are his ministers or at any rate all high officials in I Sam. 16.15ff.; the title is used
for the prophets in Amos 3.7: Yahweh consults with 'his servants the
prophets' before doing anything. The title is thus one of exaltation
rather than of humiliation. In Gen.40.20ff. the ministers and the
other dignitaries at Pharaoh's court bear this title, as does the major-
domo of the patriarchs (Gen.15.1ff.; 24.1ff.), to whom are entrusted
extremely confidential matters, like that of looking for a wife for the
heir. P. Volz in his commentary (p.18) can therefore rightly speak
of a 'favourite minister'. The title is also used of the monarch in his
relationships with Yahweh (cf. Pss.89.21; 132.10, for David), and
while here (but not necessarily elsewhere) it could also indicate the
king's relationship of inferiority with Yahweh, the attribution of the
title to David makes its connection with the monarchy obvious. This
would also explain the universalistic elements which are to be found
in the servant songs, like those that we encounter in the royal psalms 2
and 110. J. Morgenstern has attempted to reconstruct a servant ritual,
but as Muilenburg rightly observes, this is to go too far: too many
links are still missing in a chain of this kind.

It is certain that once we put the problem in these terms, marked
individual elements (cf. the sufferings described in Isa.53, which are
difficult to apply to a collective figure) and collective features (e.g.
'Israel' in 49.2ff.) can alternate without any incongruity.

We remarked earlier that Judaism never knew a messianic inter-pretation of the person of the servant. A variant to Isa. 52.14a to be found in 1Q Is^a (but not in Is^b) shows that the problem was a matter of debate. We read: *kēn mšḥty mē'iš mar'ēhū* (that is, the text has the root *mšḥ*, 'anoint', instead of *šḥt*), giving the translation (the variants from the Massoretic text are in italics): 'As many were astonished at him, so *I have anointed* his face beyond human semblance . . . 15and as many nations are startled *because of him*.' Provided that we do not have a copyist's error here, this shows that in circles a little earlier than or contemporary with the New Testament there was a serious proposal of the alternative of a messianic interpretation, even if we do not know whether and to what degree it was accepted.

§4. *Message*

The prophet presents five principal themes in his primary message:

(*a*) Yahweh is the Lord of history. This is a theme common to all the prophets, but in Deutero-Isaiah it reaches a climax, because the times and the condition of the people had led them to doubt. But the defeat of the people had not been a defeat for Yahweh. And whereas with the prophets who had preceded Deutero-Isaiah it had been a sign of divine judgment announced centuries earlier by other pro-phets and again by Deuteronomy shortly before the exile, it was now to become an impressive testimony to a new creative act by God through which Judah would rise again from its ruins. Now the phase of judgment was terminated, the very people who had first been used to chastise Judah would be the instrument for its rehabilitation. God had rejected his people, but now he re-elected them: a new exodus had brought Judah back to its native land. The warning signs of what was about to happen were given by the slow erosion of the security of the Babylonian empire, which was being undermined by the Per-sians (43.4ff.). Israel is again the elect people of God: the election has never been nullified but only suspended (43.22–28; 48.1–11; 54.10), a theme which the apostle Paul also takes up in Rom. 9–11.

On this basis the people will set out on the march home. They will be liberated, and will be led by the very God who in Ezek. 10.18ff. had abandoned Jerusalem. Things will again be as they were at the time of the exodus (40.3ff.; 42.13ff.; 49.25ff.; 51.9). For this reason some scholars have wanted to see the servant as a kind of Moses of this new exodus. The themes of creation and exodus are key elements in understanding Deutero-Isaiah: this is a *creatio ex nihilo* of a people

who were no longer a people, the exodus of a prostrate people and
their settlement into the promised land.

(*b*) In all this Yahweh shows himself to be the one God. It is not
that Israel had not known monotheism before this period, but rather
that only with Deutero-Isaiah was the faith changed to certainty. Israel
had reckoned with the possibility of the existence of other gods, at
least as far as other nations were concerned, but now they are revealed
for what they really are: non-existent, creations of man's hands in
wood, metal and stone (40.18f.; 41.6f.; 42.17; 44.6; 45.5,15,18;
46.9). In some cases these passages are interpolations, but when they
are authentic, they show for the first time a polemic attitude towards
polytheism even on a theoretical level. In his comparisons Deutero-
Isaiah, followed much later by the deutero-canonical Wisdom of
Solomon (see below, Part Six, ch. IV, §2 d), chs. 13–15, does not
hesitate to use heavy irony and sometimes harsh sarcasm, with obvious
signs that the prophet not only does not understand his opponent
but is not even concerned to understand him. We also find a similar
criticism of the cult of divine images much later, in Western paganism.
It is enough to recall the lines written by Horace, *Satires* I, 8, 1–3:

> *Olim truncus eram ficulnus, inutile lignum;*
> *Cum faber, incertus scamnum faceretne Priapum*
> *Maluit esse Deum.*

We shall take up the argument again when speaking of the Wisdom
of Solomon, whose polemic repeats these texts of Deutero-Isaiah.

(*c*) Another characteristic of the prophet is his universalism: as
Lord of history and creator of the universe, God must necessarily be
the God of all nations, a concept which is expressed in a particularly
clear way in the servant passages (42.1–6; 49.6). A critical reading of
this material, however, leads to a disconcerting conclusion: in this
passage it is not easy to see what the position of the Gentiles will be.
This leads us to the question of:

(*d*) The mission to the Gentiles. The problem, it must be said from
the start, is far from being resolved, and it may be put in the following terms: do we or do we not have in Deutero-Isaiah an exhortation
to his people to begin the mission among the Gentiles? We know that
later the Pharisees had a strong missionary and proselytizing concern, a characteristic of which Jesus reminds them in his polemic in
Matt. 23.15, and it could well be that if the reply to the question is in
the affirmative, they drew from Deutero-Isaiah their inspiration for
what must certainly have been a revolutionary attitude. In general
the reply *is* affirmative, on the basis of passages like 42.1ff.; 49.6,

which are parts of the servant songs, mentioned above. On the other hand, as R. Martin-Achard has recently pointed out with some acuteness, these passages do not mention any kind of mission or proselytism among the Gentiles. 'The Chosen People's business is to exist: its presence in the world furnishes proof of Yahweh's divinity; its life declares what He means for Israel itself and for the universe. The mission of Israel consists in reflecting the glory of God by accepting His gifts and His judgment alike. When they contemplate the singular destiny of the Chosen People, the heavens and the earth find Him who has wrought it.' It is obvious that the idea of mission could be drawn with logical consistency from an interpretation of this kind, but it is another matter to affirm that it was in the intentions of the preaching of the prophet himself.

(e) Another element of considerable importance is one which appears in the servant songs, the new valuation of suffering. While Dtr or Wisdom (as we shall soon see) had unfailingly considered suffering to be a punishment for sins, here it acquired the value of vicarious expiation for the sufferer and those closest to him, and is not the object of mournful laments as happens in certain psalms. There had been in earlier times men who had suffered for their people: Moses, Jeremiah, perhaps Isaiah and perhaps later Zerubbabel, and towards the end of the first millennium BC the 'Teacher of Righteousness' at Qumran; in the New Testament Paul also applied this concept to himself, though in a rather obscure context (Col. 1.24). The depth of thought shows clearly that explanations of an individualistic or a collective type are not sufficient here. This overturning of values in a case like the suffering of the righteous appears to be a fundamental stage in the development of Old Testament thought in general.

§5. *Text*

Notwithstanding the differences from the Isaiah of the eighth century, which were indicated at the beginning of this examination, there are notable analogies: there are many lexicographical elements in common between the two authors, and in both books the designation of Yahweh as 'the Holy One of Israel' is important. In any case, the question arises how these chapters could have been put together as one book; it is certain that the fusion is an early one. Ecclesiasticus 48.23ff. explicitly identifies the Isaiah at work in the time of Hezekiah as the one who 'consoles the afflicted', and he is writing at the beginning of the second century BC. There is a sign between chs. 39 and 40 in 1Q Is^a which some interpret as a sign of separation, but in fact it has not been explained. The situation in the fourth to third centuries BC is confused: II Chron. 36.22f.//Ezra 1.1–3 attribute Isa. 44.28 to Jeremiah, which is perhaps an indication that at this time at least part of the book was attributed to Jeremiah. An explanation deduced from the Babylonian Talmud does not seem satisfactory: arranging the books by size, Isaiah comes after Jeremiah and Ezekiel, which would only be possible if it had less than 48 chapters . . . The argument is too vague for us to be able to draw any conclusions from it.

The solution put forward by the various Scandinavian schools seems more attractive: Bentzen supposes that the school which arose around the prophet of the eighth century had continued to work for a long time afterwards, maintaining certain ideological elements and terminological constants; we have already called attention to these in speaking of Isaiah.

In any case, the difference between Isaiah, Deutero-Isaiah and Trito-Isaiah is now accepted by practically everyone, whatever its explanation may be. The only dissenters are those in very conservative Jewish and Christian circles.

BIBLIOGRAPHY

Commentaries

For commentaries on the whole of Isaiah, see bibliography to Part Three, ch. IV. Commentaries on these chapters: P. Volz, KAT, 1932; E. J. Kissane, Dublin 1943; G. Fohrer, ZBK, 1965; C. R. North, Oxford 1964; G. A. F. Knight, New York and Nashville, 1965; C. Westermann, ET, OTL, 1969; J. L. McKenzie, AB, 1968; K. Elliger, BK, 1970ff. (appearing in separate fascicles); P.-E. Bonnard, EB, 1972; R. N. Whybray, NCB, 1975.

Studies of Deutero–Isaiah in general: L. Köhler, *Deuterojesaja (Jesaja 40–55) stilkritisch untersucht*, BZAW 37, 1923; J. Begrich, *Studien zu Deuterojesaja*, Stuttgart 1938 (reprinted Munich 1963); J. Morgenstern, 'The Message of Deutero–Isaiah in its Sequential Unfolding', *HUCA* 29, 1958, 1–67; ibid. 30, 1959, 1–102; id., 'Isaiah 49–55', *HUCA* 36, 1965, 1–35; M. Haran, 'The Literary Structure and Chronological Framework of the Prophecies in Is. XL–XLVIII', *SVT* 9, 1963, 127–55; A Schoors, *I am God your Saviour*, Leiden 1973.

§1d. On the person of Cyrus and his transformation through eschatological associations cf. K. Koch, 'Die Stellung des Kyros in Geschichtsbild Deuterojesajas und ihre überlieferungsgeschichtliche Verankerung', *ZAW* 84, 1972, 352–6.

§1g. For the division into two eras in Deutero-Isaiah see G. Fohrer, 'Die Struktur der alttestamentlichen Eschatologie', *TLZ* 85, 1960, 401–20 (= his *Studien zur alttestamentlichen Prophetie*, BZAW 99, 1967, 32–58), suggesting that the term eschatology may only be legitimately used where a separation is implied between an evil past and present age and a blessed future age. Cf. also Haran, art. cit.

§2. For the date cf. A. Schreiber, 'Der Zeitpunkt des Auftretens von Deuterojesaja', *ZAW* 84, 1972, 242f.

§3. There is an immense literature on the servant songs. For bibliographical information see H. H. Rowley, 'The Servant of the Lord in the Light of Three Decades of Criticism', in his *The Servant of the Lord and Other Essays*, London ²1965, 1–57; C. R. North, *The Suffering Servant in Deutero–Isaiah*, London ²1956. Among other writings note especially I. Engnell, 'The 'Ebed Yahweh Songs and the Suffering Messiah in "Deutero-Isaiah"', *BJRL* 31, 1948, 54–93; J. Lindblom, *The Servant Songs in Deutero-Isaiah*, Lund 1951; J. Muilenburg, introduction to the commentary in *The Interpreter's Bible* V, 381–415; D. N. Freedman, 'The Slave of Yahweh', *Western Watch* 10, Pittsburgh 1959, 1–19; O. Kaiser, *Der königliche Knecht*, Göttingen 1959; J. Morgenstern, 'The Suffering Servant, a New Solution', *VT* 11, 1961, 292–320, 406–14; G. Kehnscherper, 'Der "Sklave Gottes" bei Deuterojesaja', *Forschungen und Fortschritte* 40, Berlin 1966, 279–82 (a Marxist interpretation of the problem; though its basic thesis is invalid, it is a stimulating viewpoint); G. R. Driver, 'Isaiah 52, 13–53, 12: the Servant of the Lord', in M. Black and G. Fohrer (eds.), *In Memoriam Paul Kahle*, BZAW 103, 1968, 90–105; P. E. Dion, 'Les chants du Serviteur de Yahweh et quelques passages apparentés d' 'Is.40–55', *Bibl* 51, 1970, 17–38; K. Baltzer, 'Zur formgeschichtlichen Bestimmung der Texte vom Gottesknecht im Deuterojesaja-buch', in H. W. Wolff (ed.), *Probleme biblischer Theologie. G. von Rad zum 70. Geburtstag*, Munich 1971, 27–43; G. Fohrer, *Theologische Grundstrukturen des Alten Testaments*, Berlin 1972, 22ff. The theory of parallels from the ancient Near East has recently been questioned by H. M. Kümmel, 'Ersatzkönig und Sündenbock', *ZAW* 80, 1968, 289–318. H. M. Orlinsky, *The so-called 'Suffering Servant' in Isaiah 53*, Cincinnati 1964 (reprinted in *Interpreting the Prophetic Tradition*, New York 1969, 225–73) has argued that the servant is neither a particular individual nor Israel, and that his person is never interpreted in terms of vicarious expiation; vicarious messianic interpretations only arose in circles associated with the New Testament writers. Orlinsky's views have not won general acceptance; they are also set out in Orlinsky and N. H. Snaith, *Studies on the Second Part of the Book of Isaiah*, SVT 14, 1967. An attempt to place the figure of the servant, taken as an individual, within the context of events begun by Cyrus' movements has been made by G. Sauer, 'Deuterojesaja und die Lieder vom Gottesknecht', in G. Fitzer (ed.), *Geschichtsmächtigkeit und Geduld*, Munich 1972, 58–66. P. E. Bonnard in his commentary denies that the servant passages can be detached from their present context; they should be regarded as an integral part of Deutero–Isaiah, and the servant must be considered in terms of the total presentation. Consequently the identification has several dimensions; usually the people as a whole is meant, sometimes the people as an *élite*, at other times the prophet himself or Cyrus.

For the concept of corporate personality cf H. W Robinson, 'The Hebrew Conception of Corporate Personality' in P Volz (ed.), *Werden und Wesen des Alten Testaments*, BZAW 66, 1936, 49–62 (reprinted Philadelphia 1964); R. de Fraine, *Adam et son Lignage*, Louvain and Bruges 1959. For the idea of the king as substitute in Mesopotamia cf. Kümmel, art cit.; J. A. Soggin, 'Tod und Auferstehung des leidendes Gottesknechtes', *ZAW* 87, 1975, 346–55, presents my own view.

For the use of the servant material in Qumran and the New Testament cf. W. H. Brownlee, *The Meaning of the Qumran Scrolls for the Bible*, New York 1964, chs. 9–10; H. W. Wolff, *Jesaja 53 im Urchristentum*, Berlin ²1950.

§4. H. E. von Waldow, 'The Message of Deutero–Isaiah', *Interpretation* 22, 1968, 259–87; O. H. Steck, 'Deuterojesaja als theologischer Denker', *KuD* 15, 1969, 280–93; C. Stuhlmueller, 'Yahweh-king and Deutero–Isaiah', *Bibl Res* 15, 1970, 32–45; D. Baltzer, *Ezechiel und Deuterojesaja*, BZAW 121, 1971.

§4a. S. Porúbčan, *Il Patto nuovo in Is. xl–lxvi*, Rome 1959; W. Zimmerli, 'Le "nouvel exode" dans le message des deux grands prophètes de l'exil', in *Hommage à W. Vischer*, Montpellier 1960 (= 'Das "neue Exodus" in der Verkündigung der beiden grossen Exilspropheten' in his *Gottes Offenbarung*, Munich 1963, 192–204; R. N. Whybray, *The Heavenly Counsellor in Isaiah xl, 13–14*, Cambridge 1971.

§4b.　　　In Days of Yore our Godship stood
　　　　　A very worthless Log of Wood.
　　　　　The Joiner doubting, or to shape Us
　　　　　Into a Stool, or a Priapus,
　　　　　At length resolv'd, for Reasons wise,
　　　　　Into a God to bid me rise.

ET by Philip Francis, *A Poetical Translation of the Works of Horace*, London ⁵1753, III, 125.

§4d. R. Martin-Achard, *A Light to the Nations*, ET Edinburgh 1962, 31; A. Schoors, 'L'eschatologie dans les prophéties du Deutéro–Isaïe', in C. Hauret (ed.), *Aux grands carrefours de la révélation et de l'exégèse de l'Ancien Testament*, Louvain 1967, 107–28; P. E. Dion, 'L'universalisme religieux dans les différentes couches redactionelles d'Isaïe 40–55', *Bibl* 51, 1970, 161–83.

§5. A. Bentzen, *King and Messiah*, ET Oxford 1955; C. Stuhlmueller, *Creative Redemption in Deutero–Isaiah*, Rome 1970.

HAGGAI

§1. *The prophet and his age*

We know little or nothing about the person of this prophet who has given his name to one of the shortest books of the Old Testament. We only know that together with Zechariah he preached to those who had returned from the Babylonian exile, exhorting them to rebuild the temple, since the coming of the Lord was near.

Our basic sources for the reconstruction of the events which underlie this preaching are the books of Ezra and Nehemiah (cf. Part Five, ch. X). As we shall see, these sources are not easy to use because they have been revised extensively; we can, however, discover from them that after the fall of Babylon in 539, Cyrus, king of Persia, allowed all the exiles, including those from Judah, to return to their native lands and to rebuild the sanctuaries which had been destroyed (Ezra 6.3–5; 1.2–4; cf. II Chron. 36.22f.). Acts like this were an integral part of Persian religious policy, tending not only to avoid any unnecessary friction with the peoples incorporated in the empire but also to present the new monarchy as the liberator from Babylonian oppression. Among other things, this policy provided for the granting of complete religious liberty for individual peoples: Cyrus presented himself to his subjects as the great restorer of the religions trampled down by Babylon; in the famous 'Cyrus cylinder' he emphasizes this aspect of the restoration of the cults of oppressed people in a special way. In this fashion he won not only the sympathy of the peoples of the empire but also the support of the priesthood, now the only ruling element which offered some degree of institutional continuity. The last king of Babylon, Nabu-na'id (Nabonidus), incurred the enmity of the priesthood with his attempts to install archaic cults, and this tendency made no small contribution to his fall.

It would thus be reasonable enough to imagine a return of the exiles to Judah *en masse*. On the contrary, however, precisely the opposite happened: most of them had followed the advice given them by Jeremiah (cf. chs. 28; 29) and had established a strong economic position in Babylon; to give up overnight this new position which they had created with so much effort would have seemed absurd. Meanwhile, they contributed generously to the needs of the few who did return. On the other hand, the situation of those who returned very soon proved to be a far cry from the epic descriptions formulated by Deutero-Isaiah. Here was no second exodus! The way was long and difficult, the country had been devastated and had grown wild after having been abandoned for more than half a century. The land lay desolate or, if it were particularly good, had passed into other hands (we may recall the distribution made by Nebuchadnezzar of the land belonging to the deportees, which was given to the lowest classes in the country and in the cities, II Kings 25.12//Jer. 52.16). This had created a complex situation in both legal and human terms: someone who had been given land more than half a century before would not readily be inclined to hand over the fruit of his labour to a family which had once owned it, or had some kind of claim to it. Some bad harvests followed, and the company of the returned exiles soon found themselves in a position of hopelessness and economic restriction, ultimately depending for their survival entirely on money which might reach them from Babylon. No one had imagined that arriving home would be like this; indeed, they had been promised the opposite.

About eighteen years elapsed between the return home and the beginning of the work of rebuilding the temple: Ezra 4.1–5.24 refers to a first attempt in this direction. It was, however, interrupted by the hostility of the neighbouring peoples, who denounced the returned exiles as trouble-makers who were about to re-fortify the city and rebel. Doubts about them were easy to stir up: the temple walls, which today form the south-east corner of the city, were at that time the fortification towards the north-east, and their rebuilding could very well be interpreted as an attempt to reconstruct the defences of the city. Furthermore, the material difficulties which had meanwhile arisen meant that it was too much for the small community to be able to hope and dare to embark on an enterprise of this kind. Judah, incorporated into the Persian empire and therefore deprived of all political autonomy, was a tiny fraction of the old kingdom: the normal calculation is that in a day's march a man could easily walk across from one extreme boundary to another.

As we have said, the legal situation was complicated; the drought, the locusts and the resultant famine did the rest (Haggai 1.5–11;

2.15–19; Ezra 5.1ff.). In the north was the community from which the Samaritans were later to emerge, composed of a mixed population which practised a syncretistic cult, if we accept what II Kings 17.1ff. says. If we make a comparison with the Samaritan traditions themselves, this judgment is probably unfair from a historical and religious point of view, but if nothing else, it at least shows the relationship between the community of those who had returned from exile and the people on their immediate northern borders, a relationship which Ezra 4.1–5 reveals to have been very tense from the beginning. It also seems that there was a lively debate about who was to be considered the 'true Israel', those who had remained after the catastrophe of 587 or those who had returned; it seems that each group regarded themselves as the 'elect remnant' announced by the prophets. There was not only the economic and political factor, but also a breach at the religious level, and all these elements counselled prudence: it was better to face the immediate problems than to embark on more large-scale projects like the rebuilding of the temple. At any rate, the cult continued to exist; indeed, there is reason to suppose that it was never interrupted even during the worst moments of the exile: Jer. 41.4ff. speaks of pilgrims who came from the north to the ruins of the temple, while according to Ezra 3.3 an altar was erected where the temple of Solomon first stood. Things did not therefore seem to be too urgent.

A favourable moment seems suddenly to have arrived. On the death of Cambyses, son of Cyrus, the Persian empire was shaken by a series of grave disorders which threatened to cause its dissolution: this would not have been the first time that an empire of enormous dimensions dissolved into nothing in the course of a few years. Assyria and Babylon are the most impressive examples. Would this not be the warning of the imminent end, of the coming of the 'day of Yahweh' already announced in Amos 5.18? In the person of the prophet Haggai this eschatological hope found its first interpreter. His preaching begins in August 521–20, as he calls on the people to begin the rebuilding of the temple immediately, since the end is near. The Lord is about to come, and where will he find his sanctuary ready to receive him? Ezekiel 43.1ff. had already spoken in these terms (cf. Ezra 4.24–5.1; 6.14ff.): according to Ezekiel, Yahweh himself would come and take up his abode in the midst of his people. Like the prophets of the past, Haggai also interpreted the events of the present and the imminent future in the sense that the present ills of the people were the consequence of their sin and their lack of faith; they had allowed themselves to be diverted from their mission, letting themselves be caught up in immediate needs. These needs were pressing, but not so much as to justify their laziness in the face of the coming kingdom (1.9b–10). For this reason, God was now punishing them through certain reverses which in their turn were harbingers of even more severe judgments. Now the moment had arrived: the reconstruction of the temple was the most urgent matter and had to proceed apace, whatever the economic, political or religious situation. The messianic kingdom was about to be inaugurated, its sovereign was to be the last scion of the house of David, Zerubbabel, grandson of Jehoiachin (note, incidentally his Babylonian name, an all too evident sign of the degree to which the exiles had become assimilated in their new country). At that time he was the governor appointed by the Persian administration. He was designated 'the elect of Yahweh', his 'seal', his 'servant' (1.14; 2.23); enough has been said about the third of these titles in connection with Deutero-Isaiah; for the second, cf. Gen. 41.42.

§2. *Analysis and text*

Unlike the other earlier prophetic books, Haggai has almost no passages in poetry. Moreover, its message is dated in a way which has no precedent in the Old Testament and which is followed only in Zechariah. It runs from 1.VI to 24.IX of the second year of Darius I Hystaspes, that is, from August/September to November/December of 521–20. The third person, which is used right through the text, seems to presuppose the existence of a redactor, and the same thing could be indicated by the note about the effect of Haggai's preaching, the beginning of work (1.12–15). But we cannot exclude the possibility that the prophet wrote in the third person to give the impression of greater objectivity. In any case, the book seems to have been drawn up a little after the events it describes, since (as we shall see in connection with Zechariah) Zerubbabel soon disappeared mysteriously. He is again presented as messiah in 2.23.

The text can be divided into four parts: (*a*) the summons to begin work (1.1–11), followed by the beginning of work (1.12–15); (*b*) an oracle about the building of the temple (2.1–9); (*c*) a series of questions about various matters (2.10–19); and finally (*d*) a messianic oracle about the person of Zerubbabel (2.20–23).

The text of the book is in good condition; only here and there do we find some irregularities in the arrangement of the material. For example, after 1.15 we would expect a date, as the text cannot be related to what has gone before, while in 2.10–19 we have two different themes: that of ritual purity and that of the conditions for being a member of the community; the second was understood until a short while ago as a taking up of positions in the face of the beginnings of the Samaritan schism. It has been suggested that the irregularity should be removed by transposing 2.15–19 after 1.15 and deleting the date in 2.18 as a spurious addition. This new arrangement makes the best sense of the text and only minimally affects the content, but there is no support for it in ancient versions.

§3. Message

Anyone who wants to pass judgment on Haggai by making a comparison with the pre-exilic prophets in terms of content and aesthetics will certainly be misled; like the majority of the post-exilic prophets, Haggai is characterized by a clumsy and heavy style, and anyone accustomed to the themes discussed in the earlier books will find the problems with which he concerns himself often banal. Problems of political and social ethics, of faithfulness to one's calling, and so on, are now replaced by the observance of certain cultic rules and a more or less legalistic approach to life. It has been said of Haggai that he sought to incite his people 'with Utopian dreams of wealth and power as soon as the cornerstone of the Temple was laid' (R. H. Pfeiffer, *Introduction*, 603). Moreover, Pfeiffer continues, although the book is historically interesting for the information that it provides (otherwise we know little or nothing of the period), it has no importance from either a religious or a literary point of view. This is a harsh judgment, which in part is also shared by the introductions of Eissfeldt, 426ff., and Fohrer, 458, who goes so far as to translate *nābī'* in 1.1 as 'cultic prophet'.

Now we can leave aside any criticism which is based on exclusively modern aesthetic criteria: it now seems to be taken for granted that Haggai, like the majority of the post-exilic prophets, does not reach the level of his predecessors in this field. The problem seems more important, however, from a theological perspective; after all, art for art's sake has never been the aim of any prophet, even those who have composed works of notable artistic value. The theological problem of Haggai and then Zechariah derives directly from the political situation: the Persian empire was in decline, and the prophet exhorted his people to look beyond their own difficulties and go beyond their own confines, and consider events on the world scene. To arrive at this position, however, the people needed a leading idea to guide them and courage to dare something apparently far beyond their own weak resources. The rebuilding of the temple in the hope of a messianic future was an act of faith in the unforseeable strength of the divine promises, in the divine rule over the universe and in the kingdom which had been announced and was about to arrive. The rebuilding of the temple in the economic, political and religious situation of the 520s was a blow against present reality with a view to this future.

A faith of this kind is obviously open to a good deal of criticism: that it is removed from reality, that it interprets history almost mechanically, according to pre-established patterns, and that it is not a little reminiscent of the faith of certain zealots and *sicarii* from the time of Jesus and during the two rebellions which led to the destruction of the greater part of the Jewish community in Palestine: it is therefore easily written off. But we cannot deny that it was in effect the preaching first of Haggai and then of Zechariah which aroused the people from their torpor, revived their sense of vocation and enabled them to rise from the nadir which they had reached when the promises of Deutero-Isaiah had not been fulfilled in their literal form. Thus the statement by W. Eichrodt that this position, while being inferior to that assumed by the other prophets, is still a notable testimony to the work of God in history, is a valid one. Instead of being overwhelmed and brutalized by the needs of every-day life, the believer praised the Lord whose coming he awaited, and was concerned not to be found unprepared. This standpoint obviously poses problems which go with any prophetic vocation, even if it is apparently less 'committed' than that of the great pre-exilic prophets.

BIBLIOGRAPHY

Commentaries
On the twelve minor prophets see bibliography to Part Three, ch. II.
On Haggai: A. Gelin, JB, ³1960; T. Chary, *Aggée-Zacharie-Malachie*, SB, 1969.

§1. F. S. North, 'Critical Analysis of the Book of Haggai', *ZAW* 68, 1956, 25–46; P. R. Ackroyd, 'Studies in the Book of Haggai', *JJS* 2, 1951, 163–76; 3, 1952, 1–13; id., 'The Book of Haggai and Zechariah I–VIII', *JJS* 3, 1952, 151–6,; id., *Exile and Restoration*, OTL, London 1968, 153–170; W. A. M. Beuken, *Haggai-Sacharja 1–8*, Assen 1967; O. H. Steck, 'Zu Haggai 1, 2–11', *ZAW* 83, 1971, 355–79. For translations of the 'Cyrus cylinder' cf. A. L. Oppenheim in *ANET*³, 315f.; T. Fish in *Documents from Old Testament Times*, 92–4. For the general history of the period cf. P. R. Ackroyd, 'Two Old Testament Historical Problems in the Early Persian Period', *JNES* 17, 1958, 13–27; K. Galling, 'Die Exilswende in der Sicht des Propheten Sacharja', in his *Studien zur Geschichte Israels im persischen Zeitalter*, Tübingen 1964, 109–26.

§3. Cf. W. Eichrodt, *Theology of the Old Testament* II, ET, OTL, London 1967, 61f.

IV

ZECHARIAH

§1. *The prophet and his age*

As the dates given in the book clearly indicate, Zechariah is contemporaneous with Haggai; thus he too preached to the restored
community at the beginning of the rebuilding of the temple. However, only the first eight chapters refer to the ministry of this prophet;
chs. 9–14, which are generally called Deutero-Zechariah, relate to a
later period and will therefore be examined separately (see ch. VIII
below).

The ministry of Zechariah differed from that of Haggai in lasting
over a number of years, from one month before the last prophecy of
Haggai, at the end of 521–20, to about two years later, 519–18; here
too the principal problem is that of the rebuilding of the temple.

We know very little about the person of Zechariah: Ezra 5.1 and
6.14 mention him alongside Haggai, whereas Neh. 12.16 speaks of a
certain Zechariah, leaving it open to doubt whether the prophet was
the son or the grandson of a certain Iddo. According to Nehemiah,
Zechariah belongs to priestly stock, which would be a good explanation of some tendencies which appear here and there in his book.

The ministry of Zechariah also began during the political up-
heavals which followed the death of Cambyses. Zechariah, too, and
his audience, seem to have believed that these revolutions would be
followed by the end of time and therefore by the inauguration of the
kingdom of God. However, matters turned out differently. Darius I
Hystaspes succeeded in bringing the various centres of rebellion under
control one by one, since they were not co-ordinated, and overcame
the rebels: he soon had the reins of power in his hands. His achievements have been immortalized on the trilingual inscriptions and
immense bas-relief carved on the rock of Behistun in Persia, on the
modern road from Baghdad to Teheran. Apart from its importance in
the historical sphere, the inscription was a help towards the initial

decipherment of Akkadian. Such a rapid conclusion to the events which the people had interpreted, on the basis of the preaching of their prophets, in an eschatological key, was another cause for discouragement and distrust in the community. This appears clearly from Zechariah's cry to the angel (1.12b).

Zechariah's preaching relates to the new situation which has been created following the victory of Darius and the collapse of the messianic dreams of Judah. Its aim is to demonstrate that the unexpected turn of events did not in the least compromise the realization of the divine plans. Despite everything, the end-time was near and the kingdom was at hand. So the work on the rebuilding of the temple continued, through all kinds of difficulties, until one day the Persian governor (satrap) of Syria came to Jerusalem for an inspection. He believed, probably on the basis of tendentious information similar to that which had been received by the Persian authorities some years before, that the messianic hopes of Israel and the rebuilding of the temple posed a danger to the solidarity of the empire (Ezra 5). There are some scholars (cf. Pfeiffer, *Introduction*, 603 n.26) who have thought that hopes to this effect will have been cherished at least among some groups and that 6.9–15 refers to them; moreover, the prophet will have protested against such tendencies in 4.6–10. In any case, the inhabitants of Jerusalem succeeded in demonstrating their innocence, producing as one of their arguments the fact that it had been Cyrus himself who had authorized the rebuilding of the temple. A full authority to proceed was followed by an edict in which Darius I confirmed the validity of the decree of Cyrus, also ordaining that sacrifices were to be offered in the temple for himself and his house (Ezra 5.3–6.18). This is probably the origin of the practice attested in late Judaism before the destruction of the temple of offering a periodic sacrifice for the emperor. To be on the safe side, the Davidic descendant Zerubbabel was removed from the governorship: he disappears from the scene in mysterious circumstances and the last visions of Zechariah no longer mention him. As we shall see later, however, there is a passage that probably shows traces of a revision which removes the mention of Zerubbabel from the text.

§2. Analysis

The visionary style which had become a constitutive element of prophecy with Ezekiel is considerably developed in Zechariah: after an exhortation to conversion in general terms we find eight visions in chs. 1–6, some of them dated (24.XI of the second year of Darius, that is, 8 February 521–20). Each time there is an explanation by an angel because the formulation of the visions is not clear; this element will later be typical of the apocalyptic genre. As we have seen, the purpose of the visions is to console the afflicted people who seemed cheated in their faith when their eschatological hopes failed to be realized.

(*a*) The first vision, 1.7–17, describes a patrol of heavenly horsemen mounted on chargers of various colours. They bring the news that all the earth is now at rest, an alarming piece of information for those who are expecting the cataclysms which should have announced its imminent end. The angel reassures the prophet: Yahweh is still angry with the nations and will not fail to comfort Jerusalem very soon.

(*b*) The second vision, 2.1–4 (1.18–21 in EVV), shows four iron horns representing the nations of the four points of the compass; these are destroyed by four smiths. The action implies a judgment on the nations which are represented.

(*c*) The third vision, 2.5–17 (2.1–13 in EVV) presents a young man, 'a measuring angel', as J. A. Bewer has effectively described him; he proceeds to survey the ruins of Jerusalem with a view to a reconstruction of the city and its repopulation. The city will be inhabited by a multitude so great that it will not even be possible to construct walls within whose perimeter everyone may return. However, there will be no need of walls, since Yahweh himself will protect Jerusalem with a wall of fire.

(*d*) The fourth vision, ch. 3, presents a dramatic scene: the high priest Joshua is accused before the heavenly tribunal presided over by an angel. He is clothed in filthy garments, a visible sign of his sin and that of the people whom he represents; he is accused by a prosecutor who bears the title *haśśāṭān* = 'the Satan', a figure who appears in similar circumstances in the prologue and epilogue of the book of Job (cf. further Part Five, ch. IV). In these two instances, the definite article indicates that what we have here is not a name but a function, and in addition this function is exercised within the heavenly court: evidently 'Satan' is not yet a proper name, much less that of a devil. However, the president of the tribunal interrupts the accuser's speech: God now has pity on his people, a true 'brand plucked from the burning', as the phrase puts it: by a miracle, it has escaped total destruction. And the angel president announces the divine plan to give pardon instead of executing judgment. Then the priest is vested in clean garments, a sign of pardon.

(*e*) In the fifth vision, ch. 4, we find a description of a lampstand. The passage is made difficult by a series of questions of a technical character about the nature, form and function of the artefact which have not yet been resolved. The lampstand is of gold and has seven lamps connected in some obscure manner with two olive trees from which it draws its fuel. The lamps represent the light of the eyes of God and the lampstand the community which mediates it to the world (again there is a clearly universalist note); the two olives from which it draws its fuel are the two 'anointed' of Yahweh: the high priest, Joshua, and the last member of the line of David, Zerubbabel.

(*f*) In the sixth vision, 5.1–4, we see a scroll flying above the earth on which are written divine curses: this is the instrument by means of which Yahweh will exterminate thieves and those who abuse his name by false oaths. There is often talk of the 'magic' character of the scroll, but it is probably better to speak in terms of 'symbolic actions', this time performed by God and not by the prophet. However, the two definitions are not exclusive: all of the ancient Near East believed in the objective value of blessings and curses, and the prophet is interested in what the divine word communicates, not the way in which this is brought about.

(*g*) The seventh vision, 5.5–11, shows a woman, here a symbol of the people's sin, shut up in a measure of volume called an ephah (about nine gallons) and transported to Babylon by two female winged creatures; it is probably from this time on that the woman becomes the very symbol of wickedness; in the New Testament see Rev. 14.8; 18.10, 21.

(*h*) The eighth vision, 6.1–8, shows God giving the heavenly patrol the command to carry out the orders which it has received. Four chariots leave for the four points of the compass: the one with black horses towards the north, that is, to Babylon, the seat of the Persian administration and, as we have seen, of sin, so as to execute judgment.

After the visions we have a prophetic act: Zechariah receives orders to make two crowns from the gold received from Babylon, both for the high priest (6.9–15). As we indicated above, at this point the text seems to be corrupt: the mention of two crowns for one person, the use of a messianic term like 'shoot' which is characteristic of the successor to the throne, and the allusion to the throne and to kingship in vv. 12ff. make it probable that the text originally also contained the name of Zerubbabel, which was eliminated a little later because it seemed inappropriate to introduce a person who was politically suspect and who was, in fact, eliminated from the scene, even if we are in ignorance about the circumstances. The alternative is to read either

'*One* crown for Joshua', or, '*Two* crowns, one for Zerubbabel and the the other for Joshua'. The second is the *lectio difficilior*. In any case, the mention of two crowns for one person should be eliminated, since this is an element which is only attested in Egypt and not in Israel. In Egypt, moreover, it has a special significance: the Pharaoh was the king of Upper Egypt and Lower Egypt, whereas in Israel the use of two crowns would have no significance. A third possibility put forward by Robinson and Horst and by Elliger in their commentaries has also been followed by Chary: we should read '*one* crown', but '*Zerubbabel*' instead of Joshua. In any case, a connection with the now undesirable son of David seems probable. However, we would prefer the second of the readings proposed because it reflects the dualism of 'prince' (*nāśî*) and 'high priest' which is attested in Ezek. 45–48.

These chapters end with a discussion of the problem of fasting, ch. 7, presented in the terms of the pre-exilic prophets; it took place about two years later and the reply to the question about the value of fasting is, 'Mercy is worth more than sacrifice', cf. Micah 6.8.

§3. *Message*

For Zechariah, as for Haggai, the kingdom of God is about to dawn and the sanctuary must therefore be finished. However, whereas the signs under which Haggai's preaching begins raise the hope of an imminent end or at least an imminent upheaval for the world, Zechariah's task is to announce that the people's hope is not vain, even if there are few outward signs to sustain it. God is not bound to signs. In addition, there is a fact which has yet to be mentioned: that the book ends in ch. 8 with a detailed description of the kingdom of God. It is one of those accounts which we might call 'naive' but also 'historical', and is similar to passages like Isa. 9.1ff. (EVV 9.2ff.); 11.1ff.; Ezek. 34;37. Israel's enemies are destroyed (2.4, EVV 1.21); Jerusalem can remain peacefully without walls because God is reckoned to be its protection and no surrounding wall is able to contain its population (2.8ff., EVV 2.5ff.); criminals will be immediately deported (5.1ff.); the scattered remnants of Israel will return (8.7ff.), and many peoples will join them (2.15, EVV 2.11, a theme which we met in Isa. 2.2ff.//Micah 4.1ff. and examined in that context); old men and children will reappear in the squares of Jerusalem, the former sitting quietly and the latter intent on their games (8.4ff.); the fields will give copious crops (8.12), and the divine blessing will be visibly present everywhere (8.13). However, as has been said, this is not a 'bourgeois idyll' in an ancient Near Eastern key; it is the eschatological restoration of true humanity brought about by God, in communion with God and therefore with all men. In other words, it is the transposition of ancient messianic aspirations into everyday life.

As in the case of Haggai, the dates are precise and we have seen how it is possible to date the work.

BIBLIOGRAPHY

Commentaries
On the twelve minor prophets see bibliography to Part Three, ch. II. For Haggai and Zechariah, see on ch. III above; on Zechariah: A. Gelin, JB, ³1960; M.Bič, Berlin 1965.

§1. W. A. M. Beuken, *Haggai-Sacharja 1-8*, Assen 1967; P. R. Ackroyd, *Exile and Restoration*, OTL, 1968, 171–217; S. Amsler, 'Zacharie et l'origine d'apocalyptique', *SVT* 22, 1972, 227–31. For the relief of Behistun, cf. *ANEP²*, 249. For the figure of Zerubbabel, cf. K. Galling, 'Serubbabel und der Wiederaufbau des Tempels in Jerusalem', in A. Kuschke (ed.), *Verbannung und Heimkehr. Beiträge W. Rudolph*, Tübingen 1961, 67–96; id., 'Serubbabel und der Hohepriester beim Wiederaufbau des Tempels in Jerusalem', in his *Studien zur Geschichte Israels im persischen Zeitalter*, Tübingen 1964, 127–48; A. Petitjean, 'La mission de Zorobabel et la reconstruction du Temple', *EphThLov* 42, 1966, 40–71; G. Sauer, 'Serubbabel in der Sicht Haggais und Sacharjas', in F. Maass (ed.), *Das Ferne und Nahe Wort. Festschrift L. Rost*, BZAW 105, 1967, 199–207. Galling argues that Zerubbabel is less likely to have been eliminated by the Persian authorities than rejected by the community in Judah, in which theocratic ideals were increasingly gaining the upper hand, with the person of the monarch excluded. Sauer indirectly confirms this argument by showing how the importance of the person of Zerubbabel is markedly less in Zechariah than in Haggai. Political opportunism may also be involved in this. The textual problem of ch. 6 is unaffected by this argument; Zerubbabel has disappeared from the present form of the text, in which the second crown is unexplained.

§2. L. C. Rignell, *Die Nachtgesichte des Sacharja*, Lund 1950. For New Testament use of these texts cf. F. F. Bruce, 'The Book of Zechariah and the Passion Narrative', *BJRL* 43, 1960–1, 336–53. See also H.-M. Lutz, *Jahwe, Jerusalem und die Völker*, WMANT 27, 1968; A. Petitjean, *Les oracles du Proto-Zacharie*, Louvain 1969. On the horses in chs. 1 and 6 cf. W. D. McHardy, 'The Horses in Zechariah', in *In memoriam Paul Kahle*, BZAW 103, 1968, 174–9; P. Fronzaroli, 'I cavalli del Proto-Zaccaria', in *Rendiconti dell' Accademia nazionale dei Lincei*, VIII, 26, 1971, 593–601. For ch. 4 cf. R. North, 'Zechariah's Seven-Spout Lampstand', *Bibl* 51, 1970, 183–206. For ch. 6 cf. G. Wallis, 'Erwägungen zu Sacharja VI 9–15', *SVT* 22, 1972, 232–7.

V

TRITO-ISAIAH

§1. *Problems*

As has been mentioned several times already, in 1892 B. Duhm suggested in his commentary that Isa. 56–66 should be separated from Deutero-Isaiah. From this time onwards, the independence of Trito-Isaiah from the texts which precede it has been generally accepted, outside conservative theological circles. The difference between chs. 56–66 and those which precede them is too great for the former to be considered as in any way the continuation of the latter. Throughout the greater part of Trito-Isaiah we continually find ourselves in the community of the restoration: there is mention of the temple and of rebuilding it, of sacrifices, of the observance of the sabbath and the regulations of the *tōrāh*, and this observance is considered to be an essential qualification for membership of the community. None of these arguments appears even once in Deutero-Isaiah, and since the setting of Deutero-Isaiah is Babylon, it is difficult to see how that would be possible. However, in a number of places there are notable analogies between Deutero-Isaiah and Trito-Isaiah: we have a similar hope for the imminence of the kingdom of God in 61.1–3, and in 42.1–4 (the latter is a servant passage) we have an almost identical concept of the work of the spirit of God in man. There are also notable affinities of style. The general setting for Trito-Isaiah is Jerusalem and the community described by Haggai and Zechariah, that is, about twenty years after the latest part of Deutero-Isaiah and perhaps even later; in 60.13 the temple has been built and it is only necessary to adorn it. However, the situation in the country has certainly not improved; it remains critical because of the high incidence of crime in some areas and of incompetence in others, the immediate result of which is that the righteous suffer (56.9ff.). For this reason God shows his judgment by continually postponing the fulfilment of his promises (cf. also chs. 59–62), though he will not delay to intervene personally and to achieve justice for the elect. Another figure serves Yahweh in place of Cyrus (63.1–6); foreign nations will not be the object of the divine judgment, which will fall instead on the people of God because of their unfaithfulness (65.11). The walls have still not been rebuilt (60.10), so that if Trito-Isaiah is a little after the time of Haggai and Zechariah, we still have not reached that of Ezra and Nehemiah (but see the theory put forward by Morgenstern, below Part Five, ch. X, §3). Finally, according to Duhm, 66.1f. would refer to Samaritans who were building their own temple. However, this theory seems improbable, seeing that, quite apart from the fact that we know little or nothing about the final separation of the two communities, it is reasonably certain that the break did not come about before the fourth century BC: it seems better to think of criticism directed against the hopes of Haggai and Zechariah, which were perhaps considered in some circles to be rather exaggerated. Duhm also tried to argue for the unity of the book, but hardly anyone has taken up his approach. Trito-Isaiah is a book of a composite kind if ever there was one. The majority of scholars in fact regard it as an anthology containing about twelve passages which are all different either in date or in purpose. Pfeiffer, *Introduction*, 480, seeks to explain the differences between Trito- and Deutero-Isaiah as the result of attempts to apply to the situation of the restoration the great promises formulated by Deutero-Isaiah, which apparently had not been fulfilled. This theory is well worth considering, as it would explain both the analogies and the obvious differences between the two works. It would remain to be seen whether the work were purely redactional or whether Deutero-Isaiah himself, whoever he may have been, continued his activity down to the last decades of the sixth century BC. Here, too, we have a solution proposed by the Scandinavian school: as in the case of Deutero-Isaiah, Trito-Isaiah will have been the product of the 'school of Isaiah' mentioned above, which will have continued its work over the centuries.

§2. *Content*

Taking into account all these elements, let us attempt to classify the various units of which these chapters are composed, using as criteria either dating or connections with particular schools or tendencies.

(*a*) Two passages seem to be earlier than 521–20, when the rebuilding of the temple was put in hand, following the preaching of Haggai and later Zechariah. The first of them is 63.7–64.11 (EVV 12), which

could even be dated to the last period of the exile. It contains a confession of sin followed by a prayer to Yahweh not to sustain his anger
for ever. The second is 66.1–2a, a brief poetic composition on the
theme that God has no need of a temple because heaven is his throne
and earth his footstool. It is impossible to date this passage, but it is
probably an expression of polemic against the rebuilding of the
temple, which was presented by Haggai and Zechariah as the most
urgent task of the moment. Duhm's argument that this is a criticism of
the building of the Samaritan temple certainly cannot be sustained.
Be this as it may, the passage testifies to an interesting fact: even in
the post-exilic period there was at least one line of thought which
was extremely critical of the temple and the official cult, and which
was a worthy continuation of pre-exilic prophecy. Others would see
in the passage a form of consolation addressed to the exiles or perhaps
even to those who had been first to return home and had no sanctuary.
As can be seen, it is difficult to arrive at reasonably certain conclusions.

Next we have passages which come from the same time as the
preaching of Haggai and Zechariah or a little afterwards.

(b) First of all, from the school of Deutero-Isaiah, we have 56.1–8,
which is remarkable for its universalism in laying down conditions for
admission to the community: 58.14–19; chs. 60–62; 66.3–17 are similar passages. They could be attributed without difficulty to the hand
of Deutero-Isaiah if, as was suggested above, it could be thought at all
possible that he was also at work in Palestine among the exiles who
returned. Pfeiffer holds the strange view that 56.1–8 is quite simply
an expedient to swell the somewhat reduced ranks of those who
wanted to return to Jerusalem.

(c) Chs. 58; 59.1–15a recall Haggai and Zechariah because of their
prosaic and moralizing tone.

(d) 56.9–57.13 and ch. 65 recall Ezekiel because of the way in which
they present the internal situation of the community without any
embellishment; in the view of Eissfeldt, 57.1–13 could be much older
because of the way in which it describes the sin of the many, the incompetence of the rulers and the tendency of many groups to paganism; the description would correspond quite well to the situation in
the community before the reforms of Ezra and Nehemiah. In any
case, the importance of these documents is considerable, especially for
the historian: this is a situation about which we otherwise know
almost nothing. Among other things, we see a clear distinction between the 'righteous' and the 'sinners' which foreshadows the categories
into which Judaism was to divide the members of the community

some centuries later and which are reflected in the doctrines of Qumran and in those of the early church. Attempts have recently been made to see the Samaritans or their immediate precursors as the 'sinners', but the whole matter remains on a purely hypothetical level and is hardly probable. In any case, by means of these texts we are given information about the existence of syncretistic groups like those to be found before the exile, groups in quite a close relationship with the priesthood in Jerusalem. There were also contacts between Jerusalem and the syncretistic Jewish community of Elephantine in Egypt; the two parties were in constant correspondence down to the end of the fifth century BC. We shall be occupied with this question further in Appendix II, §§ 1–2.

(e) In 63.1–6 we have a minuscule apocalyptic fragment introduced by 59.15b–20; it is impossible to date either passage.

(f) Finally, 66.18–24 will be redactional. The passage is classified in this way for want of a better solution.

Such a complex composition is certainly difficult for a book as short as the present study to deal with. The situation is complicated by the fact that for the most part we do not know the circumstances which accompanied or led to the composition of the passages in question.

§3. Text

Some textual difficulties must be added to the problems we have already indicated. The most obvious is to be found in 63.1, which reads, 'Who is this who comes from Edom, from Bozrah in crimsoned garments?' The accepted solution is to read: 'Who is this who comes clothed in scarlet ('ādōm for 'ēdōm), with garments more crimson than those of a grape-harvester (mibbōṣēr for mibboṣrā)?' There is no ancient authority for the textual emendation, nor is it absolutely necessary, but it does have the advantage of restoring the parallelism.

BIBLIOGRAPHY

Commentaries
See bibliography to Isaiah (Part Three, ch. IV) and Deutero-Isaiah (ch. II above).

§ 1–2. W. Kessler, 'Zur Auslegung von Jes. 56–66', *TLZ* 81, 1956, 335–8; id., 'Studien zur religiösen Situation im ersten nachexilischen Jahrhundert

und Auslegung von Jes.56–66', *WissZ Univ. Halle* 6.1, 1956–7, 41–74;
H.-J. Kraus, 'Die ausgebliebene Endtheophanie. Eine Studie zu Jes. 56–66',
ZAW 78, 1966, 317–32; K. Pauritsch, *Die neue Gemeinde: Gott sammelt
Ausgestossene und Arme (Jesaja 56–66)*, Rome 1971; E. Sehmsdorf, 'Studien
zur Redaktionsgeschichte von Jesaja 56–66', *ZAW* 84, 1972, 517–76; J. J.
Scullion, 'Some Difficult Texts in Isaiah 56–66 in the Light of Modern
Scholarship', *UF* 4, 1972, 105–28. F. Maass, 'Tritojesaja?', in Maass (ed.),
Das Ferne und Nahe Wort. Festschrift L. Rost, BZAW 105, 1967, 153–63, has
raised doubts about the existence of Trito-Isaiah.

VI

OBADIAH

The critics have written a great deal about this book, which is the shortest in the Old Testament (only 21 verses long). The problem of dating it is particularly complex: many features almost certainly place it in the post-exilic period, but there has been no lack of scholars who would prefer to date at least the first part as early as the ninth century, thus making it the earliest of the prophetic books. Hardly anyone now holds this latter opinion: the events of which the first part of the book speaks cannot be connected with II Kings 8.20, as was earlier supposed.

The book falls into two parts: vv. 1–14, an oracle against Edom, and vv. 15–21, an oracle against the nations in connection with the 'day of Yahweh'. Fohrer suggests a division into five oracles, but the principal break is between vv. 14 and 15.

Given the sparse sources at our disposal, relations between Edom on one side and Israel-Judah on the other do not ever seem to have been particularly tense. The two peoples felt that they shared a common ethnic origin, as is shown by the stories of Jacob and Esau in Genesis and Deut. 2.4–7; 23.7. However, it seems that after the destruction of Jerusalem in 587, refugees from Judah who sought safety in Edom did not receive the welcome that they had expected; it is also possible that the Edomites were allies (or had been forced to become allies) of Nebuchadnezzar, if it is permissible to draw conclusions from the list in II Kings 24.2. Anyway, even without pressing this possibility, which is at least doubtful, we can say that Edom seems to have been cheered by the fall of Jerusalem (Lam. 4.21; Ps. 137.7) and to have profited from it by occupying the southern territories (the Negeb) which were now virtually abandoned (Ezek. 35.10–12; 36.5). Besides, in this case it was not so much a matter of territorial greed as the consequence of an invasion of Edom by Arab groups coming from the south. It seems that from then on Edomite domination of the Negeb steadily increased, to such an extent that from the beginning of the Christian era we find the south simply called Idumaea (see the New Testament and the work of Josephus). Be that as it may, Edom is reproached for having profited from the misfortune of its neighbour.

By contrast, the second part speaks of the 'day of Yahweh', in an oracle against the nations.

The first part makes it quite clear that we are not in the ninth century but in the sixth, at a time later than 587. From vv. 16–18 we know that hostility between north and south was very strong. This feature does not suggest the struggles between the two kingdoms of Israel and Judah so much as the constant disputes between the precursors of the Samaritans and the exiles who had returned to Judah after 539. In v. 20 we have some rather obscure observations which scholars in the past have sought to connect with the wars of the Ptolemies in the third century or of the Maccabees in the second; however, a satisfactory solution does not seem possible, even in hypothetical terms. In a study written some years ago, M. Bič sought to interpret the work as an oracle pronounced on the occasion of the feast of the enthronement of Yahweh at Jerusalem (a feast with which we shall be concerned in Part Five, ch. I, §4 below). He argues that the oracle has been amplified on successive occasions, but his argument is not convincing.

An additional problem in the book is that of the relationship between vv. 1–10 and Jer. 49.7–22, which is also an oracle against Edom. The two passages are certainly parallel, and as usual raise the possibility of the dependence either of one on the other or of both on a common archetype. In any case, Jeremiah has the more ordered text, which might suggest that the text of Obadiah is of a secondary character; however, it is also possible, as we have seen, that both quote an earlier passage, each in its own way.

If v. 19 can really be connected with the migration of the Edomites into the Negeb under pressure from Arab groups coming from the south, it is without question an important note for the historian, since we know almost nothing about the situation in southern Arabia at this time.

Obadiah is of little theological interest and its presence in the canon can easily be explained as a result of the anti-Idumaean polemic which was in full flood at the beginning of the first century AD. The ancient sayings against a neighbouring people provided ready material for polemic against Herod and his house.

BIBLIOGRAPHY

Commentaries
On the twelve minor prophets see bibliography to Part Three, ch. II.
On Obadiah: J. Trinquet, JB, ²1959; J. D. W. Watts, Grand Rapids 1970.

M. Bič, 'Ein verkanntes Thronbesteigungsfestorakel im Alten Testament', *ArOr* 19, 1951, 568–78; id., 'Zur Problematik des Buches Obadjah', *SVT* 1, 1953, 11–25; E. Olávarri, 'Cronología y estructura literaria del oráculo escatológico de Abdías', *EstBibl* 22, 1963, 303–13; G. Fohrer, 'Die Sprüche Obadjas', in *Studia Biblica et Semitica T. C. Vriezen dedicata*, Wageningen 1966, 81–93.

VII

MALACHI

§1. *Authorship and date*

We know absolutely nothing about the author of this book, not even his name. The name given to the book is the result of a misunderstanding. Malachi means 'my messenger' and appears at the beginning of ch. 3, which in fact talks of the arrival of a messenger at God's command. Owing to a confusion, the term then became the title of the book and was taken to be the name of the prophet. A reconstruction of the name as a theophoric name compounded with a Yahwistic element (*mal'ākī-yāhū**) is extremely dubious, quite apart from the fact that such a name is not attested in the Old Testament. J. Pedersen, and the Scandinavian school after him, have very plausibly thought an expected divine messenger, probably identical with the future messianic king or at least very closely connected with him.

Notwithstanding these problems, it is relatively easy to fix the date of the book: it comes from the Persian period. In 1.8 Judah is governed by a satrap (Hebrew *peḥah*) and the temple is now rebuilt (1.10), so that we find ourselves at a time after 516–15; on the other hand, the abuses which the author bewails are those which appear at the time of Ezra and Nehemiah: marriages with foreign women (2.11f.); sacrifices offered with sick animals (1.7ff.). This would seem to bring us to a time before their reforms, probably at the end of the sixth century or the beginning of the fifth.

§2. *Analysis and content*

In the EVV Malachi has four chapters, but in the Hebrew, LXX and Vulgate it only has three, which means that there is a difference over the numbering of the final verses, though their content is identical. The text is usually divided into six oracles and an epilogue.

(*a*) 1.2–5 affirms that Yahweh continues to love Israel despite everything.

(*b*) 1.6–2.9 reproves the faithful for offering sacrifices with blemished animals; for this fault they will be chastised by Yahweh.

(*c*) 2.10–16, which is regarded by some scholars as an interpolation, accuses some men of Judah of having divorced their wives in order to marry foreign women who are pagans. The reasons for actions of this kind are now quite clear, although they are not mentioned here: marriage enabled the Jew to become part of one of the great families of the region, guaranteeing his protection and therefore a certain security on the economic and political level (as we have seen, his situation was very precarious in both areas). A similar procedure has been followed right down to the present day by some Christian Arabs living in the region of Syria: once allied to a powerful Moslem family, the Christian Arab enjoyed its protection and avoided a series of humiliations and sometimes persecutions. However, according to the prophet the end does not justify the means adopted, i.e. to divorce a legitimate wife and to marry a pagan woman. In Judaism even today, it is in fact the mother's religion which determines that of the children: her identity is always secure and she is responsible for the children's education.

(*d*) 2.17–3.5 deals with the 'day of Yahweh', confirming the imminence and the proximity in time of the settling of accounts.

(*e*) 3.6–12 interprets the people's suffering (bad harvests, plagues like locusts, epidemics, etc.) as divine punishment for a failure to pay tithes.

(*f*) 3.13–21 (EVV 3.13–4.3) applies 2.17 to the final judgment.

(*g*) 3.22–24 (EVV 4.4–6) is the epilogue: the prophet Elijah, the precursor of the 'day of Yahweh', is about to come, and the people are exhorted to observe the *tōrāh*. The figure of Elijah the forerunner is well-known in late Judaism; in the New Testament Jesus himself was identified with him in some circles, cf. Matt. 16.14, where one of the replies to his question 'Who do men say that I am?' is '. . . Elijah'; the theme is connected with the announcement in Deut. 18.15.

§3. *Character, style and message*

The religious thought of Malachi is essentially centred on the cult, not to criticize it but to ensure that the execution of it is as orthodox as possible; as A. Lods has rightly observed (*Histoire*, 525), communion between Yahweh and his people is in fact realized here.

However, this is a theory which must not be taken too far. For some scholars this aspect of the prophet's thought is a negative element, especially when it is compared with the position adopted by the pre-exilic prophets towards the cult. However, their evaluation risks remaining on an abstract level, without taking into account the situation of the people involved; when this situation is considered, the prophet's message is quite coherent: the purity of the cult becomes a much more important problem in a Judaism which is now scattered, and surrounded by pagan or syncretistic elements. Even the intransigence of Ezra and Nehemiah (cf. below, Part Five, ch. X) does not fit the hypothesis of racism or nationalism, but is governed by harsh necessity: the believer is moulded by the cult and by the family, so there can be no question of any compromise over the purity of these two elements. Jesus, too, will show a similar intransigence over the question of divorce (though without the motive of preventing marriage with pagan women), allowing it in only one circumstance, the details of which are far from clear.

1.11f. is without parallel in the Old Testament, and presents special difficulties because of its ultimate implications. It has been interpreted in many different terms, ranging from a recognition of the monotheistic longing which extended through all the peoples under Persian rule, an imitation of the ruling power, to a recognition of the fundamental validity of all sincere religious expressions which are directed towards God, even if their intention is not clear. At any rate, the eschatological explanation attempted by some scholars must be excluded: they argue that the past is to be projected into the future. Now since the attitude of all biblical writers to other cults is without exception negative, this passage is remarkable, to say the least, and even more so in the context of a prophet like Malachi, who is completely preoccupied with the purity of the cult. It is not surprising, therefore, that it has been regarded as an interpolation. However, the method of removing difficult texts by declaring them to be interpolations is doubtful at the best of times. Eichrodt has put forward another possibility: this is perhaps polemic against sacrifice understood as a meritorious work and therefore a demolition of the people's defence against the charges made by the prophet. In that case, following the lines of the pre-exilic prophets, Malachi too would be proclaiming that if the cult were only a matter of sacrifice, all religions would have it in abundance and Israel would have no reason to boast that it was its own prerogative.

The last passage in the book speaks of the coming of Elijah, the eschatological prophet who is to introduce the last times. As we have seen, the New Testament not only shows that some people attributed this characteristic to Jesus, but in some passages identifies the mysterious person with John the Baptist (John 1.21; 6.14; 7.40), while orthodox Judaism has continued to await the arrival of Elijah right down to the present day, even leaving an empty place for him at the passover meal. The book therefore rightly comes at the end of the proto-canonical Old Testament, even if it is clearly not its latest book.

The text does not present any difficulties; some authors would prefer to put 3.6–12 after 1.5 so as not to leave it without a context.

BIBLIOGRAPHY

Commentaries
On the twelve minor prophets see bibliography to Part Three, ch. II.

On Malachi: A. Gelin, JB, ²1960; T. Chary (cf. above, ch. III).
G. Wallis, 'Wesen und Struktur der Botschaft Maleachis', in F. Maass (ed.), *Das Ferne und Nahe Wort. Festschrift L. Rost*, BZAW 105, 1967, 229–37. For 1.11 cf. J. Swetnam, 'Malachi 1.11: an Interpretation', *CBQ* 31, 1969, 200–9.

VIII

DEUTERO-ZECHARIAH

§1. *The problem*

It was the English scholar Joseph Mead (or Mede) of Cambridge who was the first to notice, about the end of the sixteenth century, that in the New Testament (in Matt. 27.9) Zech. 11.12f. is attributed to Jeremiah. This observation marks the beginning of studies of Deutero-Zechariah.

These soon made it quite clear that chs. 9–14 have nothing at all to do with chs. 1–8 of the book in question. There is no mention in them either of the rebuilding of the temple or of the political situation at the beginning of the reign of Darius I; neither the high priest Joshua nor Zerubbabel of the house of David appear. Stylistically, they lack the exact dating which we have seen to be a characteristic of both Haggai and Zechariah chs. 1–8; this is replaced by the phrase 'oracle of Yahweh'.

The book can naturally be divided into two units which are more or less independent of each other: chs. 9–11 and chs. 12–14. Finally, Lamarche's study has demonstrated the existence within Deutero-Zechariah of a degree of symmetry in construction, with pronouncements which either correspond exactly with each other schematically or form exact opposites.

§2. *The prophet and his age*

To give some idea of the complexity of the problems connected with the features which we have barely indicated, it is enough to note the various different opinions about the origin of the book.

(*a*) At the end of the last century and the beginning of this, the view that the book was composed in the pre-exilic period enjoyed considerable prestige. In its favour was the fact that, as we have seen,

a tradition reported in the New Testament assigned the work to a
pre-exilic prophet; chs. 9–11 were assigned to the eighth century
because in 10.10 Assyria and Egypt appear as enemies of Israel, while
11.14 was thought still to attest the existence of two states in Palestine,
Israel and Judah. Again, 10.7ff. was supposed to speak of the destruction of the north and the exile of its people, but as a future event,
which would put the chapters in question earlier than 722–21. In this
case the episode of the 'three shepherds' who are destroyed (11.8) and
the description of the precarious situation of the country would have
to be connected with the facts narrated in II Kings 15.8ff., that is,
with the assassination of Zechariah and Shallum, who reigned briefly
after the death of Jeroboam II. The mention of the *terāphīm* in 10.2
would fit well in this context (these were a kind of domestic effigy
sometimes compared with the *penates*; they are also mentioned in
the patriarchal traditions, especially in Gen. 31); so would that of
false prophets. According to some writers of the last century, the
Zechariah from whom the book derives would be Zechariah son of
Jeberechiah mentioned in Isa. 8.2, later confused by the redactor
with the prophet of the same name from the end of the sixth century
and added to his book. On this view, chs. 12–14 would belong to a
rather later date, the seventh century. In fact, only Judah is mentioned in them; the feast of booths is celebrated only in Jerusalem
(14.16–19), an implicit indication that Josiah's reform has taken
place (622–21: II Kings 22;23//II Chron. 34; 35). The suppression of
the false prophets seems to indicate that there are a large number of
them about, while the mention of the earthquake in 14.5 could be
connected directly with the end of the first half of the eighth century,
given that this was the earthquake mentioned in Amos 1.1 (cf. above,
Part Three, ch. II). Of course the mention of these last two elements
is not decisive; they could have been remembered some centuries
later. Finally, the siege and plundering mentioned in ch. 14 would
have been those of 597 and 587.

(b) Later scholars are much more cautious in their valuation of the
data in question and have not accepted the importance which was
previously attached to them. There are too many elements in Deutero-
Zechariah which make him an apocalyptic prophet and put him at a
relatively late date; some have even gone so far as thinking in terms of
Alexander the Great or the struggle between the Diadochi after his
death, which would bring us to the end of the fourth century or the
beginning of the third. Yet others would come down as far as the time
of the Maccabees, in the first half of the second century (cf. below
Part Six, chs. VIII and IX), seeing in the three shepherds who are

killed (11.8) the episode narrated in II Macc. 4.5–13, in which context they would also put the announcement of the 'good shepherd' in Zech. 11.4ff. Now without doubt the general style of the work favours a late date, as does the presence of obvious apocalyptic elements (those at the beginning, as we have seen, have connections with the work of Ezekiel and are developed in Proto-Zechariah). There seems to be no difficulty in construing a relationship of dependence of Deutero-Zechariah upon Ezekiel, cf. 11.4 with Ezek. 34; ch. 14 with Ezek. chs. 38; 39, while 14.8 seems to develop the theme of Ezek. 47.1–10. However, other passages seem to be based more on Deutero-Isaiah: 12.2 on Isa. 51.22; 12.10–13.1 on Isa. 44.3 and 53.5. Moreover, right through the book there is a particular insistence on the cult (cf. 9.7 and 14.16, 21–28). Levi and other priestly groups are mentioned on a level with the house of David (12.12f.), which is the sign of the existence of a theocratic regime; in 9.13 there is a mention of Greeks (Javan, i.e. the 'Ionians'). Finally, 9.1–8 is a passage which some scholars connect with Alexander the Great's conquest of Tyre in 332 by means of the dyke constructed between the mainland and the island on which the city was built. All these are elements which would put the book in the late post-exilic period. Given this dating, 'Assyria' would become the Syria of the Seleucids and Egypt that of the Ptolemies, the two Western kingdoms which developed out of the division of the empire of Alexander the Great. The most that could be allowed would be that in some places the writer made use of earlier traditional material which can be recognized at certain points, following a procedure which is also attested among other authors, especially. in apocalyptic (cf. further on Daniel, below Part Five, ch. VIII).

(c) A third, much more recent, position is that adopted by the Danish scholar B. Otzen, who would see chs. 9–10 as a stratum dating more or less from the time of Josiah, deriving from the traditions of the ʿam hāʾāreṣ ('the people of the land', cf. above Part One, ch. IV, §1), with an anti-monarchical tendency; in chs. 12–13 he believes that we have a selection of texts from the exilic period which are hostile to Jerusalem, while in ch. 14 we have a passage of a late apocalyptic kind. One of the most important arguments in Otzen's theory derives from the fact that the mention of the Greeks does not necessarily indicate the time of Alexander the Great: their presence is attested in Egypt before the sixth century, where they served as mercenaries, and the same thing is true of Judah, where they appear at the same period in the ostraca of Tell ʿArad (cf. also Appendix I, §10), although in Deutero-Zechariah they have more than an episodic, local character and assume the status of a people. This new interpretation of the work threatens to upset the two earlier approaches, of which the later one had the greater degree of probability.

(d) A very recent study by the Norwegian scholar M. Sæbø is less optimistic than its predecessors: he does not see any concrete possibilities of identifying the historical context of the work with any certainty. He is therefore content to study the literary and traditional settings, which prove to be extremely complex. A number of phases of redaction and interpretation follow one upon another, expanding the original texts by what he calls an 'additive procedure'; each unit then displays different characteristics, even if the divisions are usually essentially those of Otzen. He proposes to examine the historical context of the work in a second volume.

In these circumstances it is no wonder that we know nothing about the person of the prophet.

§3. Analysis and transmission of the text

As we have seen, the book can be divided into two parts:

(a) 9.1–11.3: the kingdom of God is about to arrive, the Israelite exiles are on the verge of being brought home and reunited in Palestine, while the powers of this world will fall. The 'peaceful king' will soon reach the capital.

(b) (i) Two important symbolic actions are described in rhythmic prose which is almost poetry (11.4–14, 15–17 and 13.7–9). The details are not always clear.

(ii) The final destiny of Judah and Jerusalem under the final attack and assembling of the hostile nations. They are saved by the miraculous destruction of their attackers (12.1–13.6; 14). Of course, this division presupposes the interpretation of the work in paragraphs (a) and (b) of the preceding section and not that in paragraphs (c) and (d).

The text is in a bad state, and is the most serious obstacle to a proper understanding. Because so much conjecture is needed and reconstructions are consequently open to extremely subjective elements, they tend to be of little help. One valuable aid towards objectivity in the examination of texts is the argument by Lamarche (put forward above) on the symmetrical character of the various units. Even here, however, it has been pointed out that Lamarche is perhaps rather too optimistic about the real condition of the traditional text, transferring the responsibility for the variants which appear to the ancient translations.

§4. *Message*

Eschatology in its apocalyptic forms now tends to hold the field. In the text we have at least two pericopes which were considered messianic, in some degree in late Judaism and always in the primitive church: 9.9ff. and 13.1ff. As we approach the common era, this eschatological messianic hope tends to become increasingly vivid, and finally constitutes the principal characteristic of the thought of Israel at this time.

BIBLIOGRAPHY

Commentaries
On the twelve minor prophets see bibliography to Part Three, ch. II.
On Zechariah, cf. above, ch. IV.

§1. P. Lamarche, *Zacharie IX–XIV*, Paris 1961.

§2. É. Lipiński, 'Recherches sur le livre de Zacharie', *VT* 20, 1970, 25–55.

§2b. K. Elliger, 'Ein Zeugnis aus der jüdischen Gemeinde in Alexanderjahr 332 v. Chr.', *ZAW* 62, 1950, 63–115; M. Delcor, 'Les allusions à Alexandre le Grand dans Zach.ix.1–8', *VT* 1, 1951, 110–24.

§2c–d. B. Otzen, *Studien über Deutero-Zacharia*, Copenhagen 1964; M. Sæbø, *Sacharja 9–14*, WMANT 34, 1969. G. Wallis, 'Pastor bonus', *Kairos* 12, 1970, 220–34, has arrived quite independently at a variant of Otzen's position. He concludes that in content and language Zech.9–11 should really be called 'Trito-Zechariah'.

JOEL

§1. Authorship and analysis

Nothing is said about the authorship of this brief but important prophetic book.

It can be divided into two parts: (*a*) the arrival of the locusts, followed by the 'day of Yahweh' (chs. 1–2, EVV 1.1–2.27); (*b*) the 'day of Yahweh' (chs. 3–4, EVV 2.28–3.21). Here we have two different works combined and co-ordinated at a later date. The book probably became a unity less on a redactional level than on a liturgical level. The studies by A. S. Kapelrud and M. Bič have brought to light the many syncretistic elements of Canaanite origin which underlie the work; it evidently arose in close conjunction with the fertility colts and their problems, a fact which is now generally recognized and accepted by scholars, although the consequences to be drawn from it are somewhat obscure. There is already uncertainty in attempts to date the book. For Bič it is very old, perhaps the oldest of the prophetic books, because it reflects Elijah's struggle; it also has notable parallels to prophetic texts which he considers to be pre-exilic like Isa. 24.7 and Jer. 14.1–15, 19. However, as we have seen above (Part Three, ch. IV, §3c), the first of these passages is certainly late, while the text of Jeremiah is notorious for its 'Deuteronomistic' revisions. There is a more widespread tendency to assign a post-exilic date to Joel, and one of the most recent commentaries on Joel, by H. W. Wolff, takes this position, on the basis both of materials of an apocalyptic kind and of the historical allusions which are to be found in the book. A pre-exilic date (end of the seventh century BC) has recently been proposed by C. A. Keller and W. Rudolph independently of one another, and was first argued for by Kapelrud. In any case, Joel is not to be dated as early as Bič's proposal. Here, too, it is possible that early material has been re-used in new contexts and new situations.

1.1–12 describes the arrival of the 'day of the Lord'; it is represented as an invasion of locusts which brings universal destruction. The prophet warns the people to repent and to show their repentance through prayer and fasting; the 'day' comes in 1.13–20 and is described in detail. In 2.1–11 we again have the scourge of locusts, but this time they have clear characteristics of apocalyptic creatures; from their mysterious and sinister character it is clear that they in fact represent a hostile army coming from the north, whose soldiers race like horses and penetrate everywhere like flames, even if in outward appearance they remain locusts. Yahweh will allow the return of better times at the end of this scourge (2.18–27). Poetically this is one of the finest passages in the Old Testament.

In ch. 3 (EVV 2.28–32) the 'day of Yahweh' arrives, preceded by the pouring forth of the spirit upon all the people of God ('all flesh'); this is a passage which reappears in the quotation in Acts 2.17–21 where the apostolic community proclaims that the prophecy has been fulfilled in the gift of the spirit to its members. Finally, in ch. 4 (EVV ch. 3) we have a description of judgment on the peoples in the valley of Jehoshaphat, followed by favourable times.

These are clearly post-exilic themes. The final attack of the nations on Jerusalem is a typical example; in 2.9 the walls seem to have been rebuilt, although the country has been reduced to Jerusalem and Judah only (4.1ff., EVV 3.1ff.). Because of this, most scholars think of a period a little before the conquest by Alexander the Great in 332. However, the theories of Keller and Rudolph are extremely important, and we must concede to them at least that earlier texts have been used again in a later context. At any rate, the literary genre is that of a collective lament over the catastrophe which has befallen the people, a portent of worse things which are still to come.

§2. *Style and message*

Joel is effective from a poetic point of view and is very well written, but it does not succeed in concealing certain late lexicographical elements. However, this argument should not be pressed to its extreme conclusion: we now know in fact that many words which were at first considered Aramaisms and were therefore used as evidence for a late date for the text in which they appeared are sometimes western Semitic words and attested as such in non-biblical texts of undoubted antiquity, like those of Ugarit. Thus in 2.8 we have the term *šelaḥ* = 'javelin', which is attested in Ugaritic and therefore cannot be considered late in itself, even if it only appears in the Bible in late texts. The fact remains that the language of Joel is classical, inspired by that of the eighth-century prophets, which is not surprising, seeing that the text must have been used from time immemorial in the liturgy. Only the eschatological adaptation, then, would seem to be later.

As things are, the prophet's thought seems totally directed towards the God who is coming, awaited at the same time with hope and fear. Only at his coming will the restoration of Israel take place, while the 'day of Yahweh' (and here we notice a remarkable difference from the pre-exilic prophets) tends to become a day of judgment not so much for Israel as for the Gentiles. Before the exile, this type of religious feeling is connected more with popular religion on a nationalistic and syncretistic basis, against which all the prophets protested vigorously. We must seriously consider the hypothesis that post-exilic eschatology had its roots at least partly in popular religious feeling and the prophets who gave it expression (prophets whom the Old Testament does not hesitate on occasion to describe as false prophets), rather than in the message of the 'great' prophets. As we have seen, such elements appear to a considerable degree in the book of Joel.

However, the presence of elements of this kind does not indicate that Israel had renounced its traditions in this area. In 2.12f. we see clearly that the people of God do not in the least exclude divine judgment on themselves, and by means of this element Joel too transcends the ethnic limitations of the faith of his time.

BIBLIOGRAPHY

Commentaries
On the twelve minor prophets see bibliography to Part Three, ch. II.
On Joel: M. Bič, Berlin 1960; H. W. Wolff, BK, 1963; C. A. Keller, CAT, 1965; W. Rudolph, KAT, 1971.

§1. A. S. Kapelrud, *Joel Studies*, Uppsala 1948; W. Rudolph, 'Wann wirkte Joel?', in F. Maass (ed.), *Das Ferne und Nahe Wort. Festschrift L. Rost*, BZAW 105, 1967, 193–8 (cf. also Rudolph's commentary). For the origins of the work cf. G. Rinaldi, 'Gioele e il Salmo 65', *BeO* 10, 1968, 113–22, claiming that the book is a meditation on Ps.65 and therefore to be dated in the fourth century BC. A rather earlier date is supported by G. W. Ahlström, *Joel and the Temple Cult of Jerusalem*, SVT 21, 1971.

JONAH

§1. *Analysis*

Jonah contains not so much sayings and messages pronounced by the prophet as a narrative of his activities. It is a work which belongs to the literary genre of 'prophetic novel', as may be clearly seen from the fact that it has no historical basis.

The content of the book enjoys more notoriety than it deserves because of the miraculous elements which make up a large part of it. Yahweh calls the prophet Jonah to go and preach judgement on Nineveh, the capital of Assyria. However, the prophet is unwilling to assume a certainly burdensome and perhaps even dangerous task, and escapes in the opposite direction, taking a ship directly westwards, to Tarshish. During a severe storm the crew connect his presence on board ship with the danger to the voyage and finally, to placate the deity of the sea, throw Jonah into the waves. Devoured by a great fish, within which he remains for three days, he is then cast up by the monster on the eastern coast of the Mediterranean. This time Jonah prefers to obey and goes to Nineveh, where he preaches judgment, so that the inhabitants are converted. In these circumstances God decides to suspend judgment, and this irritates the prophet, who fears that he has cut a bad figure. He sits under a gourd which has miraculously sprung up as a shade from the sun, but God unexpectedly makes the tree shrivel. Still more annoyed, Jonah remonstrates with God, but is given the reply: 'You pity the plant . . . which came into being in a night, and perished in a night. And should not I pity Nineveh, that great city?' With this thought the book ends.

§2. *The prophet*

There is mention in II Kings 14.25, in the time of Jeroboam II, of a

Jonah ben Amittai who is said to have announced forthcoming triumphs. According to this note he will therefore have been an earlier contemporary of Amos, and this would fit perfectly with the mention of Nineveh as the capital of Assyria. Thus there may well in fact be an ancient tradition underlying the narrative, and this seems all the more likely since in the course of the reign of Adad-Nirari III, son of Semiramis, there seems to have been an attempt at religious reform in Assyria with tendencies which might be considered monotheistic, in that they put the god Nabu in a place of prominence. However, this is only a question of appearances: even if we allow that the book used traditional material, it is obvious from the way in which it is presented that in fact we are dealing with the product of a later period, in the sense that, like Ruth, it has an 'open' atittude towards the pagan world (cf. below, Part Five, ch. V). Moreover, the book is full of vague and even improbable remarks; there is no proof that the eighth-century Jonah was ever in Nineveh or that the protagonist of the book is to be identified with him.

§3. *The problem*

We have suggested one of the aims of the book, which is to proclaim openness towards the pagans: God does not want any human being to perish without having had at least the opportunity of being converted. The theme that salvation comes to those who hear and receive the word of God and not to an ethnic entity, however consecrated it may be, is directed against the tendency of groups in Palestinian Judaism to segregate themselves at all costs from their neighbours. However, this theme does not exhaust the content of the book, which also seeks to demonstrate to Israel that God is not necessarily bound to all his promises and his threats, and that in any case they are not fulfilled in a legalistic way; if the circumstances which produced the divine promise or threat change, its fulfilment can change or even be annulled.

If this is the ideological context of the book, there are also other elements which indicate a relatively late date:

(*a*) Problems connected with its historicity:

(i) Nineveh is not described as a city contemporaneous with the author, but seems to be set in remote times; the whole account is more reminiscent of the Hellenistic legend of Semiramis than of the testimony of a contemporary (cf. 3.3 and 4.11).

(ii) Miracle appears in the book as an obvious and customary event

in the life of the believer, and occasions none of the surprise which
would be the normal reaction of anyone who witnessed a happening
that in his opinion transcended the natural course of events. The
story of the great fish, which is certainly best known, is not unique in
this context: the waters subside after the crew has thrown Jonah into
the sea, the gourd grows and dies in the space of twenty-four hours,
and thousands of inhabitants of the Assyrian capital are converted
following preaching which we cannot even be sure was in Assyrian.
Titles and descriptions are vague and sometimes even absurd: as
Pfeiffer remarks (p. 588), to speak of the 'king of Nineveh' as in 3.6
is tantamount to calling the king of England the 'king of London'.

(b) This brings us back to the problem of the character of the work.
We have seen that it is not just a legend but a prophetic novel, though
unlike the stories of Elisha, we are uncertain whether the protagonist
is a historical figure. Some scholars have wanted to see the work as an
allegory or a parable. The English scholar T. C. Cheyne saw it as an
allegory: Jonah represents the elect people with a mission to convert
the pagans. The people prefer to renounce their mission by leaving
on a sea-going ship; the fish is the exile, which devours Israel like a
monstrous dragon (cf. Jer. 51.34–44). This explanation is attractive,
not least because it eliminates at a stroke the difficulties on the
historical and scientific level. However, it should be remembered that
when the Old Testament makes use of literary genres of this type, e.g.
in Judg. 9.7ff. or Isa. 5.1ff., it says so explicitly – and the fish helps
Jonah instead of punishing him. By contrast, in 1907 H. Schmidt
argued that Jerusalem was represented under the image of Nineveh,
while the book sought to give an affirmative answer to the question
whether God would suspend his judgment if it were converted, an
argument which is also touched on in Ezek. 33.11ff. Here too, however, quite apart from the objection already made against allegorical
interpretations, the prophetic theme does not leave any room for
doubt: in the message of the prophets, conversion is always a sufficient
reason for divine pardon.

It therefore seems better to consider the book of Jonah as a parable
elaborated with novelistic elements. The author, at any rate, means
it to be historical, and his purpose was either to remind a people with
introverted tendencies of the fulfilment of their mission according to
the ancient phrase in Gen. 12.3 (J), or to proclaim that God is not
legally bound to his pronouncements, especially those of judgment,
and that he remains free to modify them or cancel them at will, as new
circumstances arise. As one can see, these positions are not mutually
exclusive.

§4. *Chapter 2*

Chapter 2 is immediately distinguishable from its context by being
composed in poetry: moreover, it gives the only words which are said
to have been pronounced by the prophet. On the other hand, it is not
a prophetic discourse but a psalm edited in the style of the earliest
compositions in the Old Testament, the theme of which is thanksgiving for escape from danger. Canaanite elements abound. The
suppliant is now dead and has gone to Sheol, the Hebrew Hades
(v.3); in v.7 this concept is expressed by means of the word *'ereṣ*,
which normally means 'earth' or 'region': in Ugaritic, however, the
meaning 'lower regions' is attested; cf. also the expression, 'The
waters have gone over my neck', where the term *nepeš*, which normally
means 'life principle', here has the archaic sense of neck which is well
attested in Akkadian and Ugaritic. It is from the nether regions that
Jonah returns after his descent. Given the premises, we can easily
understand how in the New Testament Jesus speaks of his own death
and descent to hell as the 'sign of Jonah' (Matt. 12.38ff. par.), a proof
that even in the first century AD the implications of the psalm were
perfectly clear. The question of the fish also takes on quite new
dimensions in this context: Jonah, thrown into the sea, has now
become the prey of death and descends to Hades, which is symbolized
by the sea monster; God rescues him from this desperate situation, for
which the prophet gives thanks.

§5. *Date and text*

It is impossible to assign a date to the text, even hypothetically; at
most we might allow that ch.2 could be ancient. However, the problems dealt with in the book are clearly post-exilic. Some lexicographical elements also point in this direction: in 1.7 the expression *bešellemī*
= 'by means of whom' is clearly an Aramaism; in 3.2 *qerī'ā* =
'announcement' is a late term, although it is not really an Aramaism,
as was supposed until recently. Even here, however, we must be
careful: there is evidence of the term, albeit in a slightly different
form, in Ugaritic. Furthermore, the author seems to know Joel (cf.
3.9a with Joel 2.14ff.; 4.2 with Joel 2.13b). Expressions and customs
are connected with the Persian period: the expression 'God of heaven'
in 1.9, the extension of mourning even to animals in 3.7f., a usage
which is attested in Herodotus IX, 24. However, the book is already

cited in Tobit 14.4–8 and Ecclus. 49.10, so that it would be wise not to bring the date down beyond the end of the fifth or the beginning of the fourth century BC.

The prose section, chs. 1 and 3, has some special features: there are various expressions to indicate the same people (the sailors) and the same object (the ship). We cannot, however, talk of sources here. For the rest, the style is lively and the argument sometimes subtlc, and the language is correct.

BIBLIOGRAPHY

Commentaries
On the twelve minor prophets see bibliography to Part Three, ch. II. On Jonah: A. Feuillet, JB, ²1960; W. Rudolph, KAT, 1971.

§1. For Tarshish cf. G. Garbini, 'Tarsis e Gen. 10.4', *BeO* 7, 1965, 12–19.

§2. E. Bickermann, 'Les deux erreurs du prophète Jonas', *RHPR* 45, 1965, 232–64; H. W. Wolff, *Studien zum Jonabuch*, Neukirchen 1965; G. M. Landes, 'The Kerygma of the Book of Jonah', *Interpretation* 21, 1967, 3–31; M. Burrows, 'The Literary Category of the Book of Jonah', in H. T. Frank and W. L. Reed (eds.), *Translating and Understanding the Old Testament. Essays in Honor of H. G. May*, Nashville and New York 1970, 80–107; E. G. Kraeling, 'The Evolution of the Book of Jonah', in *Hommages à A. Dupont-Sommer*, Paris 1971, 305–18.

§4. A. R. Johnson, 'Jonah II, 3–10: a Study in Cultic Phantasy', in H. H. Rowley (ed.), *Studies in Old Testament Prophecy presented to T. H. Robinson*, Edinburgh 1950, 82–102.

§5. For the Aramaisms cf. M. Wagner, *Die lexikalischen und grammatikalischen Aramaismen im alttestamentlichen Hebräisch*, BZAW 96, 1966, n. 238.

PART FIVE

THE WRITINGS

I

THE PSALMS

§1. *Introduction*

Few books of the Old Testament have been read more than the Psalms, because, whether it be through Jewish and Christian liturgy or through personal piety, they seem to come closest to the heart of believers. Many compositions contained in the Psalter also have special importance on a linguistic and philological level.

In the Christian church we often find the Psalms as an appendix to editions of the New Testament, in as much as they give a kind of compendium of the whole of the Old Testament: some monastic orders rule that certain psalms are to be read every day. This is a complex situation, conditioned as it is by historical and ritual elements, and makes a critical examination all the more necessary.

The term 'psalm' and the title 'psalter' for the whole book come from the Greek: *psaltērion* is a stringed instrument and *psalmos* is a song accompanied by the instrument in question. The New Testament already speaks of the book of Psalms (Luke 20.42; Acts 1.20), and from here the expression has passed into the Christian church. In Hebrew the designation *tehillīm* = hymns is attested only at a relatively late period, but a study of literary genres immediately shows that hymns in the strict sense only make up part of the Psalter. Psalm 72.20 speaks of the 'prayers of David', which is evidently a designation for some parts of it. On the other hand, not all Hebrew poetry is to be found in the book of Psalms; some of this poetry consists of real psalms, e.g. Gen.49; Exod. 15.1–18; Deut.32; 33; Judg.5; I Sam. 2.1–10; II Sam. 1.19ff.; 3.33; 22.2ff.; Isa.38.10–20; Jonah 2.3–10 and other lesser passages. We also have two real psalms in the New Testament, in Luke 1.46–55, 67–79, although they have of course been preserved only in Greek. There are also many compositions which should be classified as psalms in the deutero-canonical books and the pseudepigrapha and among the Qumran sect.

The canonical psalter contains 150 psalms; in some cases different compositions have been combined to form a whole, e.g. Pss. 19, 24, 27, etc.; at other times a single composition has been sub-divided into two parts, e.g. Pss. 9 + 10; 42 + 43. In the case of Pss. 9 + 10, LXX and the Vulgate have kept the original unity, dividing Ps. 147 into two instead; this means that the two translations employ a different numbering from the Hebrew, though the content is exactly the same. Some modern Catholic Bibles still follow the numbering of the LXX and the Vulgate, but there is an increasing tendency to follow the Hebrew numbering, putting the other in parentheses. The Syriac translation (cf. above, Part One, ch. II, §8b) has preserved the text of Ps. 151, the Hebrew original of which has recently been discovered in Cave 11 at Qumran together with other similar compositions in an incomplete manuscript which contains the Psalter; these writings have never had canonical status, and we do not know to what degree they ever belonged to any collection of psalms before the problem of the canon arose.

The Psalter is now divided into five books: I. Pss. 1–41; II. Pss. 42–72; III. Pss. 73–89; IV. Pss. 90–106; V. Pss. 107–50. We know nothing of the criteria by which this division was made; however, it does not seem to have any historical or exegetical value.

The Psalter is a unique book in the Old Testament, not least because it accompanied Israel throughout its history, from the early period of the monarchy and perhaps even earlier (some scholars think that some psalms were of Canaanite origin), probably down to the time of the Maccabees. The setting of the psalms makes the study of them particularly interesting, while the scarcity of specific historical references makes them difficult to interpret. Because of the substantial differences in the material, it is impossible to give an overall explanation of the psalms; we must study the origin of each individual psalm, its setting, its literary genre and the possible transformations which it has undergone over the centuries, one by one. We can only look for general solutions where we have similar literary genres. In any case, the genres represented in the psalms are extremely old, notwithstanding the date of individual compositions. Moreover, the late datings which were so frequently proposed a few decades ago (Pfeiffer, *Introduction*, 620, regarded the Psalter as the 'great manifesto of the Pious' in the post-exilic period, while in his commentary B. Duhm wanted to date the majority of the psalms in the Maccabean period, that is, towards the end of the second century BC) can now be considered obsolete: for example, how could we put a 'royal psalm' in the post-exilic period unless there had been a possible messianic revision? However, the more obvious dating would be one prior to 587.

§2. *The use of the psalms*

(*a*) Direct biblical testimony. Jer. 33.11 (cf. Pss. 118; 136); I Chron. 16.8ff. (cf. Ps. 105.1–15; 96.1–13; 106.1, 47–49); Ezra 3.10ff. provide interesting information on the use of some parts of the Psalter. The Chronicles passage is especially interesting, as it gives us first-hand information about the use of some of the compositions in temple worship. They were sung by choirs, and the community responded 'Amen', 'Hallelujah'. Earlier in this book we saw that the superscriptions at the beginning of the psalms are late, but they do give us information about the worship in which the psalms were used, at least at the time when the superscriptions in question came into being: that to Ps. 30 speaks of the feast of the dedication of the temple (cf. below Part Six, ch. IX, §2); that in Ps. 100 of the sacrifice of acts of praise; in Ps. 92 of the sabbath; in Ps. 24 (LXX) of Sunday; in Ps. 93 (LXX) of Wednesday; in Ps. 81 (Old Latin and Armenian) of Thursday. Thus it is evident that at some time, certainly before AD 70, the date of the destruction of the temple, these psalms were connected with the morning sacrifice which was the beginning of each day's liturgy and which was called the *tāmīd*: moreover, this name appears in the superscription of some psalms. The Talmud knows the practice of singing some psalms (or parts of them) before prayer, and Pss. 113–18 before the celebration of the passover; there is also independent evidence of this latter practice in Matt. 26.30, and it has lasted down to today. There is therefore striking evidence of the use of the psalms in temple worship in Jerusalem, even if it is relatively late, though for the most part it is not possible to go back in time, still less to other sanctuaries than that of Jerusalem.

(*b*) In addition to the material already examined, the superscriptions offer other elements for determining the use of certain psalms. These are the psalms known as the 'Hallelujah' psalms (Pss. 106; 111; 112; 113; 146–50), probably because the community replied with this formula at the end of each stanza; this element, too, goes back to the cult. However, other expressions which recur in the superscriptions are not clear: we find *lammᵉnāṣēᵃḥ* = literally 'for the director' (of the choir?) 55 times; the term *selah*, which is also attested in Hab. 3, 78 times. It is sometimes understood as 'pause', but its meaning is uncertain and it should perhaps be translated 'for ever' (a kind of *per omnia saecula saeculorum*, Kraus). *mizmōr* appears 57 times: it is translated *psalmos* by LXX which means simply 'song', like the Akkadian *zamāru*; sometimes it is similar to *šīr* = 'song', though in a more specific form. Other terms like *miktām*, *maśkīl* and *šiggāyōn* are less clear: the second can be connected with the root *śkl* = 'understand', and perhaps means 'instruction'; if we can connect the third with the Akkadian *šegū*, it perhaps means 'lament'. Other expressions are even less clear: Ps. 22.1, 'the hind of the dawn' or 'a hind is the dawn'. Perhaps this is the title of the tune to which the composition was sung; we cannot rule out the possibility that this melody was of Canaanite origin, as there is explicit evidence of a deity *šḥr* = Aurora in Ugarit. As we saw at the beginning of this book, the superscriptions often attempt to set the psalms to which they refer in the context of particular events in the history of Israel.

As a result, we see that there is decisive evidence of the use of the Psalter at the time of the second temple. However, this does not mean that many of the compositions in it are not much older. In other words, this is a *terminus ante quem*, not *a quo*.

§3. *The formation of the Psalter*

The few lines above are enough to show that when we study the origin of the Psalter we are embarking on a particularly complex problem. There is a notable difference between the compositions which it contains, in terms of chronology, aim and authorship. So it is not surprising that until a few decades ago there have been scholars who thought that the Psalter grew in size right down to the time of the Maccabees, i.e. to the second century BC. Today the situation has changed considerably: we have the Qumran psalms, the so-called *hōdāyōt*, and the manuscript of the Psalter discovered in Cave 11a, even if it is incomplete. We can see from these writings not only that the Psalter must have been complete by the second century BC, but also that the compositions outside the Psalter which can be dated to this period are substantially different from those in the Psalter itself. This last point is particularly interesting: although the Qumran psalms often echo themes and phrases from the canonical Psalter, they are somehow substantially different. To this impossibility of a late dating of the whole Psalter we must add the fact, already noted, that many compositions (e.g. the royal psalms) clearly presuppose a pre-exilic situation.

Another problem is presented by the artificial character of some of the collections of psalms; this emerges clearly from the presence of obvious duplicates, cf. Pss. 14 and 53; 40.14–18 and 70.1ff.; 57.8–12 with 60.7–14 and 108.1ff. (Here and elsewhere the verse numbers are those of the Hebrew and LXX, which number the title, when there is one, as v. 1.) However, we should not rule out the possibility that in some cases this is the result of the use of the same literary genre or of analogous formulae. Moreover, in Pss. 42–89 we find that the name Yahweh has been replaced almost constantly with the title *'elōhīm* = God, a substitution which seems to be entirely artificial. Consequently the term 'Elohist psalter' is regularly used; the designation does not, of course, have anything to do with the Elohist in the Pentateuch. Perhaps we have here an example of the tendency of late Judaism to substitute one of the titles of God for the divine name, which was being used less and less. On the other hand, this might be a special collection, since otherwise it would be impossible to explain why this work was not carried out consistently throughout the Psalter.

On this basis we can now try to isolate some of the collections which are immediately recognizable:

(*a*) The 'Davidic' psalter, which is so-called because the superscriptions connect the compositions in question in some obscure way with king David. It includes Pss. 3–41 and chronologically is probably the earliest collection. The relationship with David is expressed by the formula *leadāwīd* = literally 'for David'; in ancient times it was believed that this indicated the authorship and so there was talk of a *lamed auctoris*; hence the attribution of a large part of the Psalter to David. Like so many other attributions in the Old Testament, however, this seems extremely problematical, cf. the attribution of the Pentateuch to Moses. It arises from the account in I Chron. 22.2–29.5, which describes how David reorganized worship in view of the imminent building of the temple of Jerusalem entrusted to his son Solomon; it finds its ultimate support in the tradition which makes David a skilful singer (cf. I Sam. 16; II Sam. 1.19ff.; 3.33), a tradition still related in Amos 6.5. Put in explicit terms, the tradition which makes David the author of particular psalms only appears in the Babylonian Talmud, Pesahim 117a, where it is attributed to R. Meir, a disciple of R. Akiba (first half of the second century AD); it is therefore quite late, even if there are evident traces of it in the New Testament. On the other hand, in the 'Davidic' psalter also there are too many cases which presuppose not only the existence of the temple built by Solomon but also the exile and the destruction of Jerusalem, so that with the best will in the world it is impossible to connect these compositions with David. The formula *leX* is also attested in Ugaritic, and in some contexts which quite rule out the possibility that the person mentioned could be the author of the composition: *lkrt, l'qht, lb'l*. While the first two of these terms give the names of legendary kings and it would not

be intrinsically impossible that the compositions should be ascribed
to them, the last is the name of a deity, Ba'al, who is hard to envisage
as the author of a psalm. Thus the most logical explanation in the case
of the mention of David remains that it means 'belonging to the
Davidic collection', or something of this kind.

(b) The 'Elohistic psalter', Pss. 42–89, to which we have already
referred above, is characterized by the fact that in about two hundred
cases the name Yahweh is replaced by the title '^{e}lōhīm; Yahweh is left
in only about forty cases. In addition to a second edition of the compositions in question, in which this substitution was made, there are
traces which indicate that this collection was added to the first. In it
we can distinguish:

(i) The psalms of the Korahites, 42–49; 84; 85; 87; 88. The people
in question appear in II Chron. 20.19, but we do not know the circumstances in which they came to undertake the role of temple singers.
Similar to these are:

(ii) The psalms of Asaph, 50; 73–83, probably a collection for
another group of singers attested in Ezra 2.41; I Chron. 15.19; II
Chron. 35.15, though we cannot establish the origins or the antiquity
of the group.

(iii) We have a second 'Davidic Psalter' in Pss. 51–65; 68–70; its
conclusion has almost certainly been preserved in Ps. 72.20. It is possible that before its revision it formed part of the collection which was
mentioned in section (a) above.

These are observations which relate particularly to the redaction
and the later use of the compositions in question: as we shall see,
some of them are basically much older.

(c) Pss. 90–150 do not present any elements which allow us to
identify them on the historical and traditional level. Pss. 120–34 are
distinguished by a superscription which in a literal translation means
'Songs of ascent'; it is possible that they were used as songs on a
pilgrimage to Jerusalem, since the verb 'ālā, 'go up', was used for this
act. However, the hypothesis has not been proved, and there is not
a single reference to pilgrimages within the individual texts. Another
possibility is that the word might refer to the liturgical ascent of the
stairway of the temple, but we have no precise knowledge here.

(d) Ps. 1 seems to have a special setting. First of all it is a wisdom
composition (we shall examine the significance of this statement in
the next chapter). Moreover, there are traditions attested in the
Talmud and the New Testament (Acts 13.33 in the 'Western text'
of cod. D) in which it appears prefixed to Ps. 2. There is no connection
between the content of the two psalms, but Ps. 2 sometimes appears as

Ps. 1. It is not easy to assess the significance of this discovery on the critical level; however, it does not seem probable that the Psalter once began with Ps. 2 and that Ps. 1 was added at some point as a kind of prologue.

Finally, another theory should be mentioned which has been put forward by M. Bič. According to this, the whole of the first book of the Psalter will originally have been a liturgy for the feast of the enthronement of Yahweh, a feast with which we shall be concerned shortly. In this case at least, we would have an explanation of the division of the text into books, but the theory seems extremely improbable.

§4. *The setting of the psalms*

While the Hebrew and Christian tradition tended to attribute the greater part of the Psalter to the pen of David, critical Introduction from the end of the last century and the first decades of this has taken the opposite course: in his commentary, B. Duhm argued that it was no longer a question of asking whether there were any psalms from the Maccabaean period, but rather of asking whether there were any earlier than this period, and the authority which his opinion enjoyed is amply demonstrated by the support given to it by R. H. Pfeiffer's *Introduction* and by the indecision of that of A. Lods. However, we have already seen that it is impossible to put the question in these terms, not only because of the recent discoveries from Qumran but also because of the studies made in the 1920s by S. Mowinckel, H. Gunkel and H. Schmidt. The second in particular advanced a more moderate argument, pointing out the absence of any convincing proof for such a late date and showing at the same time that there could be no question of 'dating' pure and simple or of the 'origin' of a given psalm. The task was, rather, to establish in as exact a form as possible the literary genre of each composition, and within the field of the literary genre, the use which was made of it. As we saw above (Part One, ch. VI, §3), this is not so much a matter of a new method of removing problems; here, in fact, is the only approach that really fits the material under consideration, which is largely anonymous and therefore difficult to date. A similar situation arises over other compositions which are virtually psalms: Gen. 49; Exod. 15; Deut. 32; 33; Judg. 5, etc. There was first a desire to attribute them to the two earliest sources of the Pentateuch, but we saw (above Part Two, ch. II, §§4 and 8) that they presented problems of their own: they have obvious affinities with certain compositions in the Psalter which today are generally recognized to be quite old, and sometimes have the characteristics which mark the transition from Canaanite to Israelite poetry (Pss. 29; 68; 110).

In any case, however late the dating of a particular psalm, there is no doubt that the psalms generally represent the development of a literary genre (or rather genres), the roots of which lie far back in the pre-Israelite past, though this does not rule out an independent development or a use substantially different from that of the literary genre from which they descended.

In this context, we must also take account of another element which has also been mentioned above (Part One, ch. VI, §2), that of oral tradition. This is the vehicle by means of which material of a literary and liturgical nature was transmitted throughout the ancient Near East. In this context the remembrance of the person of the author tends to become secondary, while elements which would enable us to date the material cannot be established by comparing them with information known to us (the content is normally expressed in very general terms). The only guide is given by particular linguistic characteristics which enable us to establish a rough dating, with a great deal of room for manoeuvre. For example, the abundance or prevalence of Canaanite lexicographical elements which tend later to disappear in Hebrew would obviously suggest an early date, but we must remember two factors: first, that all poetry preserves a series of archaic elements much longer than everyday language, and secondly, that what we have may be artificial archaisms which are not really old. This feature is well attested in the ancient Near East, where a composition may display characteristics from centuries earlier. As we have seen, historical information is rarely to be found in the psalms, but it is obvious that the royal psalms cannot have arisen after the destruction of the monarchy, even if it is more than likely that they were used again in connection with the messianic hope. Furthermore, the prayer for the speedy rebuilding of the walls of Jerusalem which comes at the end of Ps. 51 at least presupposes their destruction in 587 and cannot be reconciled with the superscription which attributes the psalms to David. This observation, though, does not allow us to draw conclusions about the rest of the composition.

§5. *Literary genres represented in the psalms*

(*a*) We have already discussed literary genres above (Part One, ch. VI, §3). At this point we must examine them in rather more detail.

One of the most frequent genres in the Psalter is the hymn or song of praise to Yahweh; sometimes the praise can be given through a sanctuary, e.g. Zion (Pss. 48; 74; 102, etc.); at other times through a special form of hymn commonly called the 'enthronement psalm'. This designation was given to it by S. Mowinckel and continued through the British 'myth and ritual' school and the Uppsala school in Sweden, because they postulate the existence of a festival during which, on New Year's Day, Yahweh is believed to have been solemnly enthroned in his sanctuary after having been solemnly led in procession (perhaps by means of the ark). Pss. 24; 47; 93; 96–99 are hymns which fall into this category, and fragments are scattered here and there throughout the Psalter. However, there is a certain amount of disagreement among scholars over the festival: some, like the Germans A. Weiser and H.-J. Kraus, suggest rather the existence of a 'feast of the covenant', though this is equally problematical. In any case, these are hymns which praise Yahweh in particular forms. Psalms 2; 18; 20; 21; 45; 72; 89; 101; 110; 132; 144.1–11 etc. praise Yahweh through the person of the king, his anointed, and marked features of this genre are also scattered throughout the Psalter.

The predominant themes of the hymn are: the history of the acts of Yahweh, in which the community is exhorted to give thanks and praise; creation (and in this context, as among some of the prophets, interesting mythical elements appear which have now been eliminated from the Genesis narratives); the preservation of the world against the perils of chaos (Pss. 8 and 19a praise creation on this basis); and episodes in the history of Israel as the history of salvation. This element, which we have seen to be predominant in the faith of Israel, also makes up a large part of the Psalter: the hymn is certainly one of the forms of composition best represented not only in the Psalter but also in the poetical compositions outside it, from earliest times to the New Testament. Sometimes (Pss. 98; 150) we have indications of the musical instruments which accompanied the hymn, and at other times we have an indication of the place where it was sung (Ps. 100, at the temple gate). Predominant indications are of public use, but this clearly does not exclude private use also, in the worship of the individual and the family. Almost by definition, the hymn is characterized by its enthusiasm, expressed in a language which is full of adjectives and laudatory superlatives; there is a tendency to exaggeration and hyperbole. These are factors which anyone who is studying Israelite belief must take into account, if he wants to evaluate it properly.

The structure of the hymn is not very complex. It begins with an invitation or invocation to a cultic action: 'Sing . . .', or 'I will sing . . .', or even, 'Praise/bless, my soul . . .'. The invocation in the second person predominates. There follows the reason for the invitation or invocation: there are particular reasons which make it right and proper for the community and the believer to celebrate the praises of Yahweh. In general these reasons are introduced by 'Because . . .', and less frequently by a relative preposition, 'Who has', or 'It is he who'; the latter is especially used if the preceding phrase ends with 'Yahweh'. These reasons are then followed by what we may call the 'body' of the hymn, which is composed of a selection of divine acts which are the reason for the exhortation to worship God. The genre recalls what we saw in the Pentateuch when studying the confessions of faith, though it is not possible to conjecture any kind of relationship between the two genres.

Of the royal psalms, Pss. 2 and 110, the details of which are not always clear, probably refer to the coronation of the monarch (cf. also Pss. 21; 72; 101); Ps. 20 probably refers to the departure of the king for war, an occasion on which the divine blessing was called down upon him. Ps. 144.1–11 seems to be similar, but it also has features which recall the lament. Ps. 18 seems to be a hymn of thanksgiving by the victorious king, while Ps. 45 is probably an epithalamium on the occasion of his wedding. In v. 5 the king is called by the title *'elōhīm*, 'god' (though this is not clear from some English versions [cf v. 6]). This is the only instance in the Old Testament in which the divinity of the monarch is supposed. In Pss. 2.7–9; 20.7; 21.5; 110.1–5; 132.11f. we have a word of Yahweh directed towards the monarch, probably in the form of an oracle from a priest or prophet; or it may be a stereotyped phrase, now fixed as a ritual formula.

(b) Another very frequent literary genre is the lament. First of all we may distinguish between public laments and private laments. In the first case, the people are assembled in the sanctuary on the occasion of some national or local disaster, an occasion which is foreseen with an abundance of detail in Solomon's prayer at the inauguration of the temple (I Kings 8.23–53, esp. vv. 33–40); there is a special instance in Joel 1–2. In the Psalter we have Pss. 44; 60; 74; 79; 80, centred upon the theme of the injustices committed by others on Israel, and on one occasion Ps. 44, accompanied by a passionate prayer. There is frequent mention of the blessings which the people have experienced in the past, with which the present misery makes a sad contrast – again a connection, albeit remote, with the ancient confessions of faith; in Ps. 79 the lament is probably accompanied by a vow. In Ps. 60.8–10, we have a divine response, again communicated by means of an oracle from priest or prophet. The literary genre is

already attested in Sumerian Babylon; the use made of this genre by
the prophets from the eighth century onwards clearly demonstrates
that the situation was similar in Israel (Amos 5.2ff.; Hos. 6.1–6; 14.3–
9; Jer. 3.22b–4.2; 14.7–10 etc.). In some cases the genre is parodied,
as with Amos.

The funeral lament has one of the few metres which we are able to
identify with some certainty; it is a quintuple metre in two lines, one
of three and the other of two beats, if it is permissible to use classical
terms in this context. However, paradoxically this metre also appears
in Isa. 40.1ff. to announce freedom to the captives; is this perhaps a
kind of proclamation which in form is *sub contraria specie*? The earliest
of the public laments attested in the Old Testament is, according to
more recent studies, Deut. 32, a composition which is probably not
later than the eleventh century and which according to Eissfeldt's
convincing theory is to be connected with the events narrated in I
Sam. 4. The well-known book of Lamentations is composed exclusively
of laments (for the two compositions see above Part Two, ch. II,
§8i and ch. V, §2 below). Here too, then, a possible late dating
presents problems, though we cannot exclude the possibility that
ancient laments have been used again during the Maccabaean period
and have been suitably revised.

The individual lament can be distinguished by the use of the first
person singular, a sign that it was recited by the individual suppliant.
However, in Ps. 129.1f., the first person singular is identified explicitly
with Israel, though there are no signs that a collective interpretation
of the first person is known elsewhere in the Psalter (it is also attested
as a possibility in the 'servant songs', cf. above Part Four, ch. II, §3c).

The argument of the individual lament is carried on through
prayers and protests of innocence from the suppliant, who feels that
he is unjustly the victim of the divine anger (with arguments which
sometimes sound strange to modern ears, cf. Ps. 6.6, a verse which
until recently was interpreted as a kind of blackmailing of Yahweh by
the suppliant). The lament also normally has a 'body' in which the
theme is expressed, followed at least by protests of innocence and a
declaration which confirms the certainty of a hearing; in this last case
the certainty is the product either of the faith of the suppliant, an
assurance that it is enough for him to turn to Yahweh, who will surely
hear the prayer, or of the declaration of an oracle, now inserted to a
greater or lesser degree into the liturgy, by means of which Yahweh
himself responds (Mowinckel and Gunkel). According to H. Schmidt,
a special category of lament is one which he calls the 'prayer of the
accused', brought before the court which is to try him (cf. I Kings

8.31ff.; Jer.26.1ff.). Pss.7; 35; 57; 59 would fit this situation well. Once his case has been placed in the hands of Yahweh, the accused can rest assured: his adversary will have dug his grave with his own hands.

(c) Psalms of trust, among which the well-known Ps.23 holds pride of place, are often considered as being the same as the 'certainty of being heard' which we have seen to have been added to many laments. In other words, the 'body' of the lament is thought to have disappeared, leaving only the certainty.

(d) Finally, there are not many instances of wisdom psalms in the Psalter: they are all connected with the exaltation of the *tōrāh* (Pss.1; 19b; 119 and some others).

§6. *Conclusions*

The Psalter, then, offers a cross-section of the cultic life of Israel from earliest times, in which Hebrew poetry was still to a large extent under the influence of Canaanite poetry (e.g. Pss.29; 68). These 150 compositions thus make up a collection presenting the story of the faith of Israel. Studies of the question prove to be extremely complex, and we cannot exclude the possibility that at some time in the not too distant future, excavations at Ugarit will reveal the existence of similar compositions, of real parallels to the psalms, which would make their study very much easier. Thus the tendency of Christian faith to attribute a special importance to the psalms is fully justified, though some of the compositions which have been handed down to us are extremely difficult to interpret because of notorious textual difficulties. As we have seen, Qumran Cave 11 has produced a scroll containing some canonical psalms and others which lie outside the canon.

BIBLIOGRAPHY

Commentaries
B. Duhm, KHC, ²1922; H. Gunkel, HKAT, ⁴1926; H. Schmidt, HAT, 1934; W. O. E. Oesterley, London 1939; E. J. Kissane, Dublin ²1964; G. R. Castellino, SacBib, 1955; H.-J. Kraus, BK, ²1961; R. Tournay et al., JB, ³1964; A. Weiser, ET OTL, 1962; A. González, Barcelona 1966; M. J. Dahood, AB, 1966–70; A. A. Anderson, NCB, 1972; L. Sabouria, New York ²1974.

General Introduction and Bibliography: J. J. Stamm, 'Ein Vierteljahrhundert Psalmenforschung', *TR* 23, 1955, 1–68 (a sequel, though announced several times, has not yet appeared); R. de Langhe (ed.), *Le Psautier*, Louvain 1962; R. Martin-Achard, *Approche des Psaumes*, Neuchâtel 1969; E. Gerstenberger, 'Literatur-zu den Psalmen', *VF* 17, 1972, 82–99.

§1. For recurring historical themes in the Psalms cf. A. Lauha, *Die Geschichtsmotive in den alttestamentlichen Psalmen*, Helsinki 1945; F. H. Jasper, 'Early Israelite Traditions and the Psalter', *VT* 17, 1967, 50–9. For style cf. N. H. Ridderbos, *Die Psalmen*, BZAW 117, 1972.

§2. For the superscriptions cf. B. S. Childs, 'Psalm Titles and Midrashic Exegesis', *JSS* 16, 1971, 137–50.

§3. C. C. Keet, *A Study of the Psalms of Ascents*, London 1969.

§3d. M. Bič, 'Das erste Buch des Psalters, eine Thronbesteigungsfest-liturgie', *Numen* Suppl. 4, Leiden 1958, 316–32.

§4. S. Mowinckel, *Psalmenstudien*, 6 vols., Oslo 1921–4 (reprinted 1961); id., *The Psalms in Israel's Worship*, 2 vols., ET Oxford 1962; H. Gunkel and J. Begrich, *Einleitung in die Psalmen*, Göttingen 1932 (reprinted 1966); É. Lipiński, *La royauté de Yahwé dans la poésie et le culte de l'ancien Israel*, Brussels 1965. Fohrer's *Introduction*, 285–93, gives a useful table of dates assigned to individual psalms. For the problem of the relation of some psalms to Canaanite poetry cf. J. H. Patton, *Canaanite Parallels to the Book of Psalms*, Baltimore 1944; J. Coppens, 'Les Parallèles du Psautier avec les textes de Ras Shamra-Ougarit', *Muséon* 59, Louvain 1946, 113–42; R. T. O'Callaghan, 'Echoes of Canaanite Literature in the Psalms', *VT* 4, 1954, 164–76; H. Donner, 'Ugaritismen in der Psalmenforschung', *ZAW* 79, 1967, 322–50. This last counsels caution in the use of Ugaritic to explain biblical texts and shows some examples where such use is held to be legitimate.

For the problems of individual psalms see: Ps. 1: J. A. Soggin, 'Zum ersten Psalm', *TZ* 23, 1967, 81–96; Ps. 2: id., 'Zum zweiten Psalm', in *Wort – Gebot – Glaube: Festschrift W. Eichrodt*, Zurich 1970, 191–207; Ps. 8: id., 'Textkritische Untersuchung von Psalm VIII vv. 2–3 und 6', *VT* 21, 1971, 565–71; id., 'Zum achten Psalm', *ASTI* 8, 1972, 106–22; Ps. 29: F. M. Cross, Jr, 'Notes on a Canaanite Psalm in the Old Testament', *BASOR* 117, 1950, 19–21; Ps. 45: O. Loretz, *Das althebräische Liebeslied*, Neukirchen 1971, 67ff.; Ps. 51: E. R. Dalglish, *Psalm 51 in the Light of Ancient Near Eastern Patternism*, Leiden 1962; Ps. 68: W. F. Albright, 'A Catalogue of Early Hebrew Lyric Poems: Psalm 68', *HUCA* 23, 1950, 1–39; S. Iwry, 'Notes on Psalm 68', *JBL* 71, 1952, 161–5. Albright argues that Ps. 68 is an index of ancient Israelite-Canaanite compositions listed by the initial line of each. Ps. 73: A. Caquot, 'Le Psaume 73', *Semitica* 21, 1971, 29–55; Ps. 82: O. Loretz, 'Eine kanaanäische *short story*'; Ps. 82', *UF* 3, 1971, 113–15; Ps. 89: G. W. Ahlström, *Psalm 89*, Lund 1959; É. Lipiński, *Le poème royal du Psaume LXXXIX 1–5, 20–38*, Paris 1967. For enthrone-ment psalms cf. É. Lipiński, *La royauté* . . . (cf. above); J. A. Soggin, 'Gott als König in der biblischen Dichtung', *Proceedings of the Fifth World Congress of Jewish Studies 1969* I, Jerusalem 1971, 126–33.

§5. Cf. H. Gunkel and J. Begrich, *Einleitung*; the *Introductions* by Eissfeldt and Fohrer; É. Lipiński, 'Psaumes: Formes et genres littéraires', *Supplément au Dictionnaire de la Bible* 9, 1–125.

§5a. For the 'Uppsala School' cf. I. Engnell, *Studies in Divine Kingship in the Ancient Near East*, Oxford ²1967; A. Bentzen, *King and Messiah*, ET London 1955; J. Coppens, 'Les Psaumes de l'intronisation de Yahvé', *EphThLov* 42, 1966, 225–31. The possibility of a 'covenant festival' on Zion during the autumn celebrations has been examined by H.-J. Kraus, *Die Königsherrschaft Gottes im Alten Testament*, Tübingen 1951; cf. also his commentary, 197ff., and that of Weiser, 27ff., where the emphasis is different.

§5b. G. R. Castellino, *Le lamentazioni individuali e gli inni in Babilonia e in Israele*, Turin 1939; C. Westermann, 'Struktur und Geschichte der Klage im Alten Testament', *ZAW* 66, 1954, 44–80; J. W. Wevers, 'A Study in the Form-criticism of Individual Complaint Psalms', *VT* 6, 1956, 80–96. For detailed points cf. H. Schmidt, *Das Gebet des Angeklagten im Alten Testament*, BZAW 49, 1928; G. Sauer, 'I nemici nei Salmi', *Protestantesimo* 13, 1958, 201–7.

§6. For the Qumran text (11Q Psᵃ) cf. J. A. Sanders, *The Psalms Scroll of Qumran Cave 11*, Oxford 1965; Y. Yadin, 'Another Fragment (E) of the Psalms Scroll from Qumran, Cave 11', *Textus* 5, Jerusalem 1966, 1–10; J. van der Ploeg, 'Fragments d'un manuscrit de Psaumes de Qumran (11 Q Psᵃ)', *RB* 74, 1967, 408–12.

III

INTRODUCTION TO WISDOM

§1. *The wisdom books in Israel*

The wisdom books make up an important part of the thought of the Old Testament, not only because they are so many but because we continually find their influence in other books. For all the differences in detail, they have a fundamental element in common, which is their principal characteristic and is not to be found in other books: faith in a divine cosmic wisdom which rules and governs the universe with rational and immutable norms. The wise man is the one who adapts himself to these norms and discovers the way in which they work, perhaps even their essence; the fool or even the wicked man is the one who fails to do this and is quite unconcerned. Each man receives his deserts in accordance with his wisdom or his foolishness: the wise man is given wisdom and through it a serene and fruitful life, while the fool and the wicked man have a life full of troubles.

This divine cosmic wisdom for which all men must search with every means at their disposal is called *ḥokmāh* in Hebrew, but the concept can also be expressed by means of derivatives of the root *ṣdq* = 'justice'.

Now a glance at the thought of the ancient Near East will immediately show that the worlds of Mesopotamia and Egypt were also aware of a cosmic wisdom, Egyptian *ma'at*, which governed the world justly and to which the wise man therefore had to try to adapt himself. We have to do here with the insertion into Yahwistic belief of a typically non-Hebraic, unhistorical element, so it is no surprise to find throughout the wisdom books a contrast with the essentially historical approach which is characteristic of the other books of the Old Testament. There is no religious, social and political criticism here such as we find in the prophets; here we only have wise men and fools, the former intent on living in accordance with a cosmic principle, guaranteed by Yahweh, the latter without this concern and therefore, at least in theory, destined to perish.

The wisdom books of the Old Testament are Proverbs, Job, Ecclesiastes in the Palestinian canon and the Wisdom of Solomon and Ecclesiasticus in the Alexandrian collection; we may also note strong influence from wisdom in some prophets and psalmists, in the Song of Songs, the book of Tobit and perhaps even in Deuteronomy and Dtr. It is beyond the scope of a work like the present volume to deal with the complex problem of relationships between Israelite wisdom and that of the Near East; anyone who wishes to pursue matters more deeply will have to make use of the books listed in the bibliography. However, we can offer the reader some basic information for a critical reading of the wisdom literature, so that he may understand the range of problems involved, and the means and ends of wisdom.

We have considered the feature which is common not only to the wisdom literature of the Old Testament but also to that of the ancient Near East. It has two more obvious and to some degree disconcerting consequences, if we think of the strong polemical note which pervades the whole of the Old Testament where it touches on the problems of Yahwistic belief and its relationship with the religions of the pagan world. In the first place, while we may note the due differences between the cosmic wisdom of Yahweh in the Old Testament and the theologically neutral wisdom of Egypt and Mesopotamia (neutral only up to a certain point, since it tends to assume characteristics which come increasingly close to those of a fate or destiny), we also discover a fundamental affinity at the level of content or effect. Moreover, affinities of form have been noted for some decades, and in at least one case it is easy to see the existence of a real dependence of quite an extensive Hebrew text on an Egyptian text. This affinity even extends to the crisis in wisdom which developed at a relatively late and more critical phase of thought, a phase in which the naive idea of reward and punishment outlined above proved untenable when put to the test. In the second place, the more typical themes which characterize the faith of Israel, like the proclamation of the acts of God in historically verifiable events, the election of Israel, promises about the people and the land, and so on, are almost completely absent in the wisdom literature. The scholar cannot avoid the impression that this is a matter more of a complete lack of interest than of ignorance: the wise man is preoccupied with the cosmic order; the rest seems irrelevant. It is therefore not surprising that biblical theology passed a harsh judgment on the wisdom literature, regarding its thought as an element alien to Israelite faith, an erratic block of material, a theologically false vein; and this valuation seemed to be supported by the obvious parallels with Near Eastern wisdom. Only in the last few years have these characteristic elements of wisdom been examined in a coherent fashion. Moreover, the problem of its insertion into the message of the Bible seems to have been obscured, if not deliberately avoided.

Today the situation may be said to be very different. From the middle of the 1960s onwards, Israelite wisdom has been the object of many studies primarily concerned to deal with the reality of the phenomenon; apart from discovering the presence of wisdom features in other sections of the Old Testament, these studies are concerned to examine the position and the limits of wisdom within the message of the Bible generally.

§2. *Proverbial wisdom and wisdom literature*

A first distinction which the student of wisdom, whether Israelite or Near Eastern, is led to make is a formal one, though closer consideration shows that it is also valid in terms of content. This is a distinction between proverbial wisdom and wisdom tractates. The former is expressed in brief sentences which are either of universal validity or conditioned by particular situations; it provides brief affirmations or negations, and gives practical advice. It makes use of maxims which are usually composed of a single verse in two lines, sometimes of a rather larger unit, and is essentially to be found in the books of Proverbs and Ecclesiasticus, and (in part) in Ecclesiastes and the Wisdom of Solomon. Its aim is principally to offer the hearer or reader observations on day-to-day life, and therefore practical rules for behaviour in particular circumstances. If he follows these instructions, a man will fit in with the social order which is a reflection of the cosmic order. He will behave wisely, and live a social life which is harmonious, integrated and free from conflict. This form of wisdom is not concerned with the ultimate realities of existence, and does not conceal its pragmatic character or the complete lack of criticism of the society within which it is developed: that society is seen, rather, as a fact which the wise man must not seek to change. He must attempt to fit in with it by discovering the rules of the game. As can be seen, this is an attitude which differs profoundly and in essentials from that assumed by the prophets towards society. On the other hand, it is not an attitude which is completely lacking in faith: Prov. 1.7 solemnly affirms that 'the fear of Yahweh is the beginning of all knowledge'. However, the attentive reader who is versed in the history of religion will not miss the fact that the mention of the God of Israel is made more in the form of a concession to the dominant faith than as a personal confession: we could easily substitute the more general phrase 'fear of God' or even 'of the deity' for the expression 'fear of Yahweh', without facing the problem of the identity of the deity to which reference was made. The expression could very well be considered as equivalent to the popular modern saying that a bit of religion never does anyone any harm. It is only with the wisdom psalms and then with Ecclus. 24.23ff. that the identification of wisdom with the *tōrāh* is made, thus bringing Israelite wisdom so to speak into the bosom of orthodoxy.

The content of the wisdom tractates is different. Sometimes, as with Job, they take the form of a dialogue and sometimes, as with Ecclesiastes, they are a confession in the form of a monologue. They rarely speak of minor questions and instead tackle the fundamental problems of human existence. The two best-known examples are certainly those of Job and Ecclesiastes and the solution which they put forward is submission to the divine plan. This is typically Israelite, although it does not have the historical approach which we find outside the wisdom literature.

§3. *The setting of wisdom*

In Israel, as throughout the surrounding nations, wisdom was taught and practised in wisdom schools. Jesus ben Sirach, the author of Ecclesiasticus, was the head of one of these schools, as we shall see shortly. These schools cannot be compared with the philosophical schools of Greece and the Hellenistic world; in Israel and the surrounding countries their aim seems to have been eminently practical: to educate state officials, especially among the ruling classes. The existence of such officials in Israel is explicitly attested from the time of David onwards. It is also a quite indisputable fact, supported as it is by irrefutable evidence, especially of an onomastic kind, that the ancient Israelite bureaucracy (if it is permissible to use the term for this period), not only was organized along Egyptian lines but also made use of Egyptian officials, whose names appear in the Old Testament, sometimes in a distorted form (II Sam. 20.25; I Kings 4.3; I Chron. 18.16). This is sufficient explanation for the conservative sociological orientation of the proverbs. The way to behave at court, the good name which the wise man must guard jealously, and other elements of this kind, were either outside the horizons of the common man or were evaluated by him in a substantially different way. They were, however, extremely important subjects for anyone who found himself in an elevated social position. We can also see the explanation for the favourable attitude towards society as it was, if we accept that proverbial wisdom was essentially directed towards high officials. It is therefore substantially correct to see the ethics of Proverbs as a 'group ethic' or even a 'class ethic', as W. Richter has put it. It is the ethic of the class of leading officials, educated for the post which they will be occupying. But since, leaving aside differences in structure, the needs of a state tend to be essentially the same in the same historical and sociological situations, it is not surprising that this type of wisdom has an essentially international form: behaviour at the Babylonian court will not after all have been very different from that required at the court of Judah or even at the court of Egypt. Material thus circulated from one nation to another with the greatest of ease, notwithstanding the relatively closed character of the society of the time. One example which we might consider typical is that of the romance of Ahikar: it was written in Assyria not before the eighth century and circulated throughout the ancient Near East; we find one copy in the archives of the Jewish colony at Elephantine (cf. Appendix II) in southern Egypt at the end of the fifth century BC.

Of course, the more speculative aspects of wisdom go beyond this approach, which is at the same time didactic and pragmatic, aimed at an adequate professional training. This does not, however, mean that the officials did not continue to be occupied with wisdom during the years when they were at work. Thus in the ancient Near East (and indeed until a few decades ago) the figure of the wise man has never been a rarity, not to mention the figure of the wise monarch, of which there are many examples, from Solomon to Saladin.

BIBLIOGRAPHY

J. Fichtner, *Die altorientalische Weisheit in ihrer israelitisch-jüdischen Ausprägung*, BZAW 62, 1933 (a pioneer work); J. C. Rylaarsdam, *Revelation in Jewish Wisdom Literature*, Chicago 1946; *Les sagesses du Proche-Orient ancien* (Colloque de Strasbourg, 17–19 May 1962) [by various authors], Paris 1963; W. Zimmerli, 'The Place and Limit of the Wisdom in the Framework of the Old Testament Theology', *Scottish Journal of Theology* 17, Edinburgh 1964, 146–58; H. H. Schmid, *Wesen und Geschichte der Weisheit*, BZAW 101, 1966; W. Richter, *Recht und Ethos*, Munich 1966; J. L. McKenzie, 'Reflections on Wisdom', *JBL* 86, 1967, 1–9; F. Festorazzi, 'La sapienza e la storia della salvezza', *RBibl* 15, 1967, 151–62; R. E. Murphy, 'Assumptions and Problems in Old Testament Wisdom Research', *CBQ* 29, 1967, 407–18; A. M. Dubarle, 'Où en est l'étude de la littérature sapientielle?', *EphThLov* 44, 1968, 407–19 (with valuable bibliography); H. J. Hermisson, *Studien zur israelitischen Spruchweisheit*, WMANT 28, 1968; H. H. Schmid, *Gerechtigkeit als Weltordnung*, Tübingen 1968; J. L. Crenshaw, 'Method in Determining Wisdom Influence upon "Historical" Literature', *JBL* 88, 1969, 128–42; R. E. Murphy, 'The Interpretation of Old Testament Wisdom Literature', *Interpretation* 23, 1969, 289–301; A. Barucq, 'Israele e Umanesimo', *BeO* 11, 1969, 97–107; G. von Rad, *Wisdom in Israel*, ET London 1972 (a basic introduction to the material and its understanding, which should be read in conjunction with the review of the original German edition by W. Zimmerli, *EvTh* 31, 1971, 680–95); W. Brueggemann, 'Scripture and an Ecumenical Life-Style: a Study of Wisdom Literature', *Interpretation* 24, 1970, 3–19; R. B. Y. Scott, 'The Study of the Wisdom Literature', ib., 20–45; B. L. Mack, 'Wisdom, Myth and Mythology', ib., 46–60; F. C. Fensham, 'The Change in the Situation of a Person in Ancient Near Eastern and Biblical Wisdom Literature', *AION* 31, 1971, 155–64; H. J. Hermisson, 'Weisheit und Geschichte', in H. W. Wolff (ed.), *Probleme biblischer Theologie. G. von Rad zum 70. Geburtstag*, Munich 1971, 136–54; O. Plöger, 'Zur Auslegung der Sentenzensammlungen des Proverbienbuches', ib., 402–16; J. Harvey, 'Wisdom Literature and Biblical Theology', *BTB* 1, 1971, 308–19; G. von Rad, 'Christliche Weisheit', *EvTh* 31, 1971, 151–4.

§3. For the development of a class of officials in Israel cf. T. N. D. Mettinger, *Solomonic State Officials*, Lund 1971, which includes an extensive bibliography and an analysis, on 25ff., of the Egyptian names of the officials discussed.

PROVERBS

§1. *Author and title*

At the beginning of the book we find a superscription which makes king Solomon, famed for his wisdom, the author of the work. True, it could also be translated, 'The proverbs of Solomon serve to make known wisdom . . .' and so on, but with this approach the problem is only shelved, and has to be dealt with later on another level. What would be the proverbs mentioned here? Thus it seems evident that the editors wanted to attribute the work to king Solomon. However, this note cannot be verified in any way, and like the attribution of the Pentateuch to Moses and the Psalms to David, it seems highly improbable, even if it is true that the origins of wisdom in Israel are to be connected with the king in question. The passages which speak of the wisdom of Solomon are I Kings 5.9–14 (EVV 4.29ff.) and 10.1ff. The former is particularly important because it lists the areas with which Solomon was concerned: the king is credited with 'three thousand proverbs, and his songs were a thousand and five. He spoke of trees, from the cedar that is in Lebanon to the hyssop that grows out of the wall; he spoke also of beasts, and of birds, and of reptiles, and of fish' (5.12f., EVV 4.32f.). However, this precise description cannot be applied in any way to Proverbs: themes like those described do appear in other passages of the Old Testament like Judg. 9.7ff.; II Kings 14.9, but they are not to be found in Proverbs!

The book as we have it is made up of seven collections: 1.1ff.; 10.1ff.; 22.17ff.; 24.23ff.; 25.1ff.; 30.1ff.; 31.1ff. We find the same material in LXX, but it is arranged differently, which is evident proof of redactional work. As a further check we can detect numerous duplicates and variants. The Israeli scholar Y. M. Grintz has made an important investigation which now suggests that: I. Every collection has its own typical vocabulary; II. The first, third and fourth collections have enough elements in common to suggest the same scholastic basis; III. The first and second collections have many elements in common on a lexicographical level, notwithstanding their different themes; IV. There are notable differences between the first and the fifth collections. He concludes that the first collection had access to the second collection but not to the fifth; the third and fifth collections had a common 'heredity'; finally, 1.1–6 matches the characteristics of the first collection perfectly. Chapters 30 and 31 are considered separately.

§2. Date

The date of the composition of Proverbs is as difficult to determine as that of the Psalms and all the non-prophetic Israelite poetic literature. The first collection (chs. 1–9) seems to be the latest part of the book, and this impression is confirmed both by the fact that wisdom is personified here (1.20; 9.1ff.), and by the presence in 7.16 of the term *'ēṭūn* = flax, equivalent to the Greek *othonē*, which would put the passage in the Hellenistic period. The dimensions of a number of passages, which are too long for classical Hebrew style, should also be noted. However, these arguments are not definitive.

On the other hand, the second section (10.1–22.16) seems to be much older: 16.12ff.; 21.1; 22.11 presuppose the existence of the monarchy, and while it would not be impossible in theory for this to be a mention of a king in general terms, it seems more logical to think of the kings of Judah and Israel. This last possibility would be logical if it could be proved or at least be shown to be probable that the passage in question came from the north. The customs described also go back to the eighth century BC rather than to another period, and it is possible that in this case we have material which, if it does not come from the time of Solomon or even earlier (taken over from Canaan?), is at least of considerable antiquity. Another section of great interest is the third (22.17–23.12). In the 1920s, it was discovered to be dependent on a text by the Egyptian sage Amenemope (in Greek Amenophis), who lived during the second half of the second millennium BC (we cannot determine the date exactly). A. Lods, *Histoire*, 657, gives an interesting synopsis of the two texts, but the most recent comparison has been made by Richter, who has demonstrated the composite character of the two entities, the Egyptian text and the Hebrew text. He argues that the latter goes down to 24.22 and will have given a literal translation of material from Amenophis. Be this as it may, it seems that in this case, too, the Hebrew text has to be dated in the pre-exilic period.

In the fifth section (25.1ff.) we have words of Solomon which according to the superscription were collected by the men of king Hezekiah's time (second half of the eighth century). We should therefore reckon with quite a long oral tradition down to the redaction in writing (that is, if the superscription is to be trusted). A large part of ch. 25, specifically vv. 2–27, has recently been connected with the work of the Egyptian Seḥetepibrēʿ of the second half of the nineteenth century BC in the Twelfth Dynasty, but the studies on this complex subject are still in process.

In 30.1 (emended text, the Hebrew has *maśśāʾ* = oracle) and 31.1 we have a mention of the North Arabian tribe of *maśśāʾ* of which there is also evidence in Gen. 25.14 and I Chron. 1.30. The wise man who spoke the words in question will have been its king. It is difficult to find any kind of indication of date here except for that ch. 30, where there are obvious lexicographical affinities with Ugaritic literature. Unless we wish to argue for artificial archaisms, this would suggest an early date for the text in question.

BIBLIOGRAPHY

Commentaries
H. H. Duesberg and P. Auvray, JB, ²1956; B. Gemser, HAT, ²1963; A. Barucq, SB, 1964; R. B. Y. Scott, AB, 1965; W. McKane, OTL, 1970. For the text cf. W. A. van der Weiden, *Le livre des Proverbes*, Rome 1970. For bibliographical material cf. F. Vattioni, 'Studi sul libro dei Proverbi', *Aug* 12, 1972, 121–68.

§1. C. Kayatz, *Studien zu Proverbien 1–9*, WMANT 22, 1966; Y. M. Grintz, 'The "Proverbs" of Solomon', *Lešōnēnū* 33, 1968–9, 243–69 (Hebrew; English summary); O. Plöger, art. cit. (see on ch. II, §2 above); D. Michel, 'Weisheit als Urform von Humanität', in H. Foerster (ed.), *Humanität heute*, Berlin 1970, 11–21.

§2. M. V. Fox, 'Aspects of the Religion of the Book of Proverbs', *HUCA* 39, 1968, 55–69. For the Wisdom of Amenemope, cf. *ANET*³, 421ff., for the text, and for problems relating to it cf. P. Humbert, *Recherches sur les sources égyptiennes de la littérature sapientale d'Israel*, Neuchâtel 1929; W. Baumgartner, *Israelitische und altorientalische Weisheit*, Tübingen 1933; W. Richter, *Recht und Ethos*, Munich 1966; I. Grumach, *Untersuchungen zur Lehenslehre des Amenope*, Munich 1972. For Seḥetepibrēʿ, cf. *ANET*³, 331 for the text (part only); for the problems raised cf. G. E. Bryce, 'Another Wisdom "Book" in Proverbs', *JBL* 91, 1972, 145–57. For the Instruction of ʿOnḥšešonqy, with numerous parallels to Proverbs, cf. B. Gemser, 'The Instructions of ʿOnchsheshonqy and Biblical Wisdom Literature', *SVT* 7,

1960, 102–8; see also his commentary (above). (The text is not in *ANET*.) For Prov. 30 cf. G. Sauer, *Die Sprüche Agurs*, Stuttgart 1953. For the origins of wisdom and its Canaanite links cf. W. F. Albright, 'Some Canaanite-Phoenician Sources of Hebrew Wisdom', *SVT* 3, 1955, 1–15; M. J. Dahood, *Proverbs and North-west Semitic Philology*, Rome 1963. For a general survey of the problems in this section cf. R. N. Whybray, *Wisdom in Proverbs*, SBT 45, 1965.

JOB

§1. *Character, division and content*

The Hebrew name of the book is 'Iyōb, hence the Greek and Latin name *Iob* and the English Job. The book is a wisdom tractate which discusses the problems of theodicy and of the suffering of the righteous, which is intimately connected with it. However, other problems are discussed in the work: how the righteous sufferer must behave when faced with obviously undeserved sufferings, or how it is possible to continue to be a believer in a world made in a particular manner, i.e. an evil world. In this last question, what is considered is not so much belief in the God of Israel as the validity of the axiom of wisdom that the world is governed in a rational manner by the divine wisdom. And as always happens in these cases when the faith of Israel is being discussed, the final reply may seem inadequate from a philosophical point of view, in that none of the tormented questions put by the protagonist is given a logical and systematic reply; rather, they are resolved in the sphere of faith, that is, in a sphere where ultimate reality transcends the possibility of a rational and intellectual analysis. Thus the only thing to come out the worse for wear is Hebrew wisdom, the principles of which are challenged by the reality of the facts. The problem as such appears among all the people of the ancient Near East, and there are some Mesopotamian writings which are rightly compared with Job; however, the solution put forward here is only acceptable to those who, like Job, abandon the idea of an ordered and harmonious universe of wisdom and enter into the sometimes hard and irrational world of faith, accepting its paradoxical categories of thought.

The book can easily be divided. First of all we have a prose prologue (chs. 1–2), which describes the felicity and the patriarchal life of the righteous Job, an upright and pious man. However, this idyllic picture is disturbed by a meeting of the celestial court. Here the Satan (as in Zech. 3 the figure indicates a function, not a name, and is therefore the title of a functionary, not the name of a 'devil'), who, as the prosecutor, is always in search of culprits over whom to pursue his office, enters into discussion with God about the virtue of the righteous Job: is his virtue authentic or is his much-vaunted justice simply part of an astute calculation aimed at winning the divine favour? The result of the discussion is that Yahweh allows a series of tests to be imposed on Job, designed to bring out his righteousness even more. A series of catastrophes deprives him in succession of his family (apart from his hyper-critical wife), his goods, and finally his health, so that Job, who is at first honoured and respected by all, finds himself at the end of the trials sitting on a heap of rubbish, with only his life to call his own. This too is threatened, since he has been smitten with a foul disease. The second part (3.1–42.6) makes up the main body of the book. First of all, three of Job's friends, Eliphaz, Bildad and Zophar, arrive. In chs. 3–14 we have a first series of disputes between Job and his friends, in chs. 15–21 a second series and in chs. 22–27 a third series, from which only Zophar is missing. Job replies to each series of discourses. The argument of Job's friends can be reduced to the following point: if Job is being punished in this way, something must have happened, otherwise he would be blaspheming, accusing God of injustice and denying his just and wise ordering of the world. But Job replies that he does not know what fault he can have committed, and that if God is dissatisfied with him, it is enough for him to indicate what is wrong and the reason for it. There is an interpolation in ch. 28, a short poem about the inscrutable character of the divine wisdom, which has nothing to do with the context in which it appears. Chapters 29–31 contain Job's self-defence and a challenge to God to explain the reasons for his attitude. This reply by Job has led the Swedish scholar J. Lindblom to compare him with the figure of Prometheus, but the fundamental difference between the two narratives lies in the fact that in the case of Prometheus it is Zeus who has unjustly punished the man out of envy, while in this case, even if Job is finally won over, God has simply put him to the test and recognizes his righteousness. A fourth person, Elihu, enters the scene in chs. 32–37. He is a friend who was not mentioned to begin with and does not appear later; he, too, delivers some speeches, which have a different content from the rest. In chs. 38–39 we have the first discourse by Yahweh, to which Job replies in 40.3–5; in this reply he submits to the majesty and the will of God, which he is incapable of understanding. In 40.6–41.26 we have Yahweh's second discourse, to which Job replies in 42.1–6, in words which show his complete

submission. Finally, to conclude the book we have an epilogue edited
in the same style as the prologue, but which continues the body of
the book. God judges the first three friends severely (42.7–9), while
in 42.10–17 we have a final scene in which Job is completely restored to the social and economic position which he enjoyed to begin
with.

The construction of the book is quite complex, but has its own
internal logic; it justifies the assertion by Westermann that, as well as
being a piece of wisdom literature, the book of Job is a dramatic
representation of the literary genre of the 'individual lament' in a
dramatic form. We have already come across this genre in our
discussion of the psalms. This also explains the affinity of many
passages with the Psalter.

One difference between the various parts of the work which
immediately strikes the eye is that between the prologue and the
epilogue on the one hand and the body of the book on the other,
although, as we have seen, there is a connection between them. The
difference is first of all one of form: the prologue and epilogue are
presented in prose in a clear narrative style, while the body of the
work is in poetry. However, there are notable differences in terms of
content, too. In the prologue Job is resigned; he is ready to receive
evil from the Lord just as hitherto he has received good (cf. 1.21b;
2.10). In the body of the book, on the other hand, he struggles to
defend his righteousness either towards his friends or – and this is
much more important – towards God, whose wisdom must be the
guarantee of the cosmic order, even if it seems to be absent at the
moment of trial. In 16.11 the concept of suffering is markedly different from that contained in the prologue, and in the body of the work
we have a whole series of wisdom features which are completely
lacking in both prologue and epilogue. Notwithstanding the obvious
fact that the three parts of the book are for the most part inter-
dependent, in other ways than being connected with the same
protagonist, we can discover at least two different traditions, without
counting independent parts like ch. 28, even if they have now been
skilfully joined so as to show a consistent pattern of thought. For this
reason it is customary to call the prologue and the epilogue the
'framework' of the work. This framework relates the legend of a just
man called Job, a wise man and a patriarch who, although afflicted
by God in many ways, still bears the suffering imposed on him with
courage, in the certain belief that God himself will sooner or later
secure justice for him. And this in fact is what happens. This legend
could be placed towards the end of the pre-exilic period. Moreover,

there is evidence of a person with this name in two Old Testament texts (Ezek. 14.14, 20). He is mentioned along with Noah and a certain Daniel, obviously not the protagonist of the book of this name, since at that time he could not be put alongside Noah (he has been identified as probably being connected with the legendary Ugaritic king known under the name *dn'il*; in Ezekiel, too, the name is written in a defective form without a *yod* after the second consonant). This is an indication that we can connect Job with the heroes of prehistory (the Ugaritic text comes from the fourteenth century, but it obviously refers to an earlier figure). The problem of the historicity of the person of Job as it has been handed down in the framework of the book thus arises almost automatically, and a negative response is already given in the Talmud (Baba Bathra 15a) and by rabbinic exegesis (Beresit Rabba 57), notwithstanding their tendency to attribute a historical character to the most improbable episodes. We shall return to this question later.

As we have seen, some passages in the book do not seem to fit well into their present context. We have already mentioned ch. 28 (the theme of which would nullify the words of Yahweh in chs. 38; 39). To this should be added the discourses of Elihu (chs. 32–37), which interrupt the context in which they are set. Job challenges God to show himself, but what happens is the appearance of Elihu. The divine response which ought to follow the challenge only appears in ch. 38, after Elihu's discourses. Elihu's argument, that suffering serves to purify a man, has an eminently pedagogical function, but it is substantially different both from that of the three friends and from that of Yahweh (chs. 38ff.). These are features which have been known for some time. Gregory the Great already expressed grave doubts about the legitimacy of the present position of such passages in the book.

What we have here, then, are interpolations, inserted into the book because (at least in the case of the discourses of Elihu) they deal with an analogous theme. The descriptions of exotic animals in 40.15ff., 25ff. (EVV 41.1ff.) and of the various animals throughout chs. 38–41 are also an independent element: the first animal bears the name *behēmōt*, usually translated 'hippopotamus' by analogy with a hypothetical Egyptian term which is not attested, *p-ehe-mau* = 'water-oxen'; others render it 'crocodile'. In the second instance the animal is called *lewyātān*, a name which appears in Ugaritic as *ltn* and which there is a mythical monster; it is usually translated 'crocodile'. It is possible that these were originally mythological monsters which have now been depotentiated to become the hippopotamus and the crocodile. Effective as the mention of them is from an aesthetic point of view, along with the other animals, it disturbs the development of the theme in its present context, which is the acceptance by Job of his lot.

The structure of the book thus seems to be very complex in every respect, and this complexity is increased by the fact that almost all the literary genres in the Old Testament are represented in the work.

§2. *Date, place and problems of composition*

As can easily be seen, the information at our disposal is very uncertain. There is no direct or indirect mention of any events which can be identified in the context of history, and the geography of the book is a mystery. When we come to consider the date, it does not seem wise to put the 'framework' further back than the late pre-exilic period; a post-exilic dating seems advisable for the body of the book. The problems are seen in an individualistic key, and we know that this approach is sometimes to be found during the exile (cf. Deut. 24.16; Jer. 31.29ff.; Ezek. 18.1ff.); the basic issue discussed in the book is that of the legalistic application of the understanding of the cosmic order put forward by wisdom, an understanding which also underlies the idea of reward and punishment proclaimed by Deuteronomy and Dtr. The problem of the language of the book has yet to be resolved; in this respect the book is one of the most complex in the Old Testament. In fact it contains the largest number of *hapax legomena*, and there is an abundance of Aramaisms (though now these might also be interpreted as common Semitic roots); to such a degree, that N. H. Tur-Sinai has been able to suggest that we have the translation of an Aramaic original into Hebrew. Other scholars have thought that they have discovered a large number of Arabisms in the book (Guillaume counted 41 of them), but Fohrer in his commentary is very sceptical. On the other hand, the extraordinary richness of the vocabulary of Job should not surprise us excessively, once we accept its character as a wisdom tractate and the complexity of the theme with which it is concerned; it is much more a matter of our inadequate linguistic knowledge. In any case, it will not do to speak of a particularly corrupt text, as was the custom until a few years ago. Of course, the ancient translations also found themselves up against similar problems and they provide little help in solving them. The recent publication of the Targum on Job discovered in Qumran Cave 11 might perhaps help to resolve some problems.

At the end of the book, in 42.17b, the LXX identified the person
of Job with that of Jobab, a king of Edom in Gen. 36.33. This
identification is linguistically possible, but there is no concrete
evidence to support it. Job is said to have lived in the East, in a
country called Uz which Lam. 4.21 connects with Edom; the very
frequent use of 'ĕlōᵃh instead of 'ĕlōhīm for God (a title which the
ancient psalm in Hab. 3 connects with Teman, a region probably
situated either in north-western Arabia or in present-day Yemen),
also points in this direction: in the first case we would have another
pointer towards Edom. However, many elements in the book do
not fit in with this locality: the mention of reeds in 8.11, of papyrus
in 9.26 and of the animals in 40.15,25 (EVV 41.1) suggests swamps
or the broad deltas of rivers, and certainly not the desert of north-
western Arabia. But in this case we could have interpolations, or
notes that could have been made by any cultured person (and we
have seen that the language of Job is of such a kind that we may
suppose elements of high culture in the redaction of the book). For
the rest, the problem of suffering is resolved in typically Israelite
categories, even if the problem was posed throughout the ancient
Near East. The very character of the work as a wisdom book makes
it difficult to put it in any geographical and historical setting, given
the international and cosmopolitan character of wisdom, even in
Israel.

Thus for the prologue and the epilogue we come near to the time
of the exile: Satan is still a title, and not a proper name; the mention
of the Chaldaeans in 1.17, however, seems to be old; it takes us back
to the end of the second millennium or the beginning of the first
millennium BC.

§3. *The problem and the message of Job*

The ancient traditional narrative of the suffering of the righteous and
pious Job, whose loved ones and possessions are later restored, thus
seems to have been used as a starting point for the redaction of the
body of the book and as a vehicle for discussing problems like those of
theodicy and the behaviour of the righteous in a world which concrete
reality has shown to be very different from that presupposed by
wisdom. The problems dealt with in the book, then, are typically
those of wisdom, but with the difference that, as among neighbouring
peoples, Israelite wisdom also disputed the fundamental thesis of
wisdom elsewhere, displaying a remarkable degree of scepticism over

the existence of a universe governed by cosmic wisdom. But whereas among other peoples a practical solution could not be found, in Israel it was discovered in submission to the divine will, many aspects of which could not be understood by man, however hard he tried (contrary to the argument of wisdom). Nor could he always adapt himself to this will (as wisdom argued). In other words, the approach made by wisdom to the problem of the government of the world proved to be too simplistic. However, whereas among other peoples this discovery led men to cynicism or despair, the Old Testament made it an occasion for proclaiming its faith. According to the solution which God himself proposes to Job, it is not for man to ask God to give an account of his works, seeing that he has neither the competence nor the right; God has sovereign freedom, and this freedom cannot be comprehended in any categories of thought, whether theological or philosophical. God reveals to a Job who has not asked for material or spiritual goods, but simply for what is his due, that his plans are not man's plans, and his wisdom is not man's wisdom. This declaration satisfies Job. God has taken him seriously, and at the same time has recognized that the way in which the problem has been posed by Job's friends is not a serious one – though this approach is in fact that of wisdom. Precisely in his acceptance of the irrationality of Yahweh, Job rediscovers his peace and escapes from the vicious circle into which he had been led by a presentation of the problem according to the categories of wisdom. There is a New Testament parallel in Paul's discussion of the divine wisdom as opposed to human wisdom (I Cor. 1.17–25), as there probably is also in the total reversal of values contained in the Sermon on the Mount.

BIBLIOGRAPHY

Commentaries
G. Ricciotti, Turin 1924; É. Dhorme, ET London 1966; C. Larcher, JB, [2]1957; G. Hölscher, HAT, [2]1952; A. Weiser, ATD, [5]1968; N. H. Tur-Sinai, Jerusalem 1957; G. Fohrer, KAT, 1963; M. H. Pope, AB, [3]1974; F. Horst, BK, 1968 (on chs. 1–18 only; following the death of the author, the work is to be completed by E. Kutsch); H. H. Rowley, NCB, 1970; P. Fedrizzi, SacBib, 1972.

Monographs
H. Richter, *Studien zu Hiob*, Berlin 1959; R. Gordis, *The Book of God and Man. A Study of Job*, Chicago 1965; N. H. Snaith, *The Book of Job*, SBT II 11, 1968; J. Lévêque, *Job et son Dieu*, Paris 1970.

§1. J. Lindblom, 'Job and Prometheus, a Comparative Study', in *Dragma*, *M. P. Nilsson dicatum*, Lund 1939, 280–7; W. A. Irwin, 'Job and Prometheus', *Journal of Religion* 30, Chicago 1950, 90–108; C. Westermann, *Der Aufbau des Buches Hiob*, Tübingen 1956; H. H. Rowley, 'The Book of Job and its Meaning', *BJRL* 41, 1958, 167–207 (= his *From Moses to Qumran*, London 1963, 141–83); D. N. Freedman, 'The Elihu Speeches in the Book of Job', *HTR* 61, 1968, 51–9; D. Michel, 'Hiob – oder der inhumane Gott', in H. Foerster (ed.), *Humanität heute*, Berlin 1970, 37–50; J. Barr, 'The Book of Job and its Modern Interpreters', *BJRL* 54, 1971–2, 28–46; H. McKeating, 'The Central Issue in the Book of Job', *ExpT* 82, 1970–1, 244–7.

§2. M. J. Dahood, 'North-west Semitic Philology and Job', in *A. Gruenthaner Memorial Volume*, New York 1962, 55–74; A. Guillaume, 'The Arabic Background of the Book of Job', in F. F. Bruce (ed.), *Promise and Fulfilment: Essays for S. H. Hooke*, Edinburgh 1963, 106–27; A. C. M. Blommerde, *Northwest Semitic Grammar and Job*, Rome 1969; A. Guillaume, *Studies in the Book of Job*, Leiden 1968. For Babylonian and other ancient Near Eastern parallels cf. J. J. Stamm, *Das Leiden des Unschuldigen in Babylon und Israel*, Zurich 1946; A. Kuschke, 'Altbabylonische Texte zum Thema "Der leidende Gerechte"', *TLZ* 81, 1956, 69–75; J. Lévêque, op. cit., 13ff. For the Job targum from Qumran cf. J. P. M. van der Ploeg and A. S. van der Woude, *Le Targum de Job de la Grotte XI de Qumran*, Leiden 1917; recently, N. Sokoloff, *The Targum to Job from Qumran Cave XI*, Ramet Gan 1974.

V

RUTH – LAMENTATIONS

§1. *Ruth*

This superb short story deals with events which took place in the time
of the judges (and therefore LXX and the Vulgate, followed by
modern translations, insert it after that book); in the Hebrew Bible,
however, it appears in the third part of the canon.

The content is simple: its purpose is to establish the genealogy of
king David, showing that he is descended from, among others, a
Moabite woman called Ruth. A couple from Judah with their two
sons migrate to Moab and settle there, and the sons take Moabite
wives. All the males die, and Ruth returns to Judah with her mother-
in-law, thus renouncing her own people and joining that of her
husband, at the same time accepting their faith. In Judah she meets
Boaz, a close relation of her dead husband, to whom she is married by
means of a somewhat obscure combination of levirate marriage and
the law of redemption.

As a literary genre, the narrative belongs to the class of popular
legends, with features of the *Novelle*. It should probably be dated
after the exile, but this does not exclude the use of earlier material.
The names seem to be symbolic: Ruth means 'companion'; Orpah,
Ruth's Moabite sister-in-law who is in the same position but chooses
to remain in Moab, means 'disloyal'; Naomi, the mother of the two
dead men of Judah, is 'peaceful'; Boaz, 'strength', and so on. The
practice prescribed in Deut. 25.9 is quoted in 4.7 as a feature of past
times; the attitude of the book to non-Israelite peoples is positive and
is reminiscent of that of Jonah. Here, too, there seems to be a polemical
note against the tendency of post-exilic Judaism to be shut in on
itself, while the book maintains the argument, later to be taken up by
the Pharisees in particular, that no one should be excluded from
joining the people of God if they so wish. Maybe there is also a
polemical note against the injunctions of Ezra and Nehemiah that

foreign wives are to be expelled (Ezra 9; Neh. 13). Here, however, we are already on less solid ground. In any case, the book maintains the argument that nationality is a secondary element: what really counts is the choice of faith.

The language of the book contains a series of Aramaisms, and despite the simplicity of the argument, it is not always easy. Nor is the text in the best of condition; indeed Ruth is a book which has one of the highest numbers of Massoretic notes. In any case, it is not possible to date the book back beyond the fifth or fourth centuries BC. That does not mean that it has not preserved the memory of much earlier customs: for example, the village tribunal meets at the gate, and we have been able to use the way in which it assembles, following the study by L. Köhler, in our reconstruction of trials in Israelite law (see above, Part Two, ch. V, §7). The book does not show any signs of disruption, and there are no omissions or additions of any substance. It may be that the genealogy, which is the feature which gave the book its place in the canon, is an addition. It is interesting that the work maintains its argument by making David the descendant of a converted foreigner.

The atmosphere which the reader finds is that of a trusting abandonment to divine providence, without any limitations.

§2. *Lamentations*

While LXX and the Vulgate, followed by modern translations, put this book after Jeremiah, in the Hebrew Bible it appears in the third part of the canon. The Hebrew title, that is, the first words of the text, is *'ēkāh* = 'Alas, how . . .', which introduces a lament, Hebrew *qīnāh*. The superscription in LXX[B] connects the work with Jeremiah, and perhaps that is why it occupies its present position in the LXX: its origin should probably be sought in II Chron. 35.25, which speaks of a funeral lament by Jeremiah on the death of Josiah; however, four-fifths of the book speaks of the destruction of Jerusalem, and cannot have anything to do with this lamentation.

The work is composed of five laments, one for each chapter. However, they are not all composed in the same way. Chapters 1–4 are acrostics; but in terms of content, chs. 2;4;5 describe the situation of Jerusalem after the destruction of 587, while ch. 3 belongs to a different literary genre. It is an individual lament, and it has nothing to do with the exile. The despair expressed in 1–2; 4–5 is a fairly certain sign that the work is not far removed in time from the events which it narrates, so that an attribution to Jeremiah would not be impossible from a historical point of view. The author was not in fact deported, but is one of the survivors left behind by Nebuchadnezzar in the ruins of the capital: the details of the description in chs. 2;4 indicate this. It would also be impossible to understand 2.9 on the lips of the exiles among whom Ezekiel worked.

With the exception of ch. 3, the lamentations seem to have been recited on the occasion of the commemoration of the fall of the capital, which Zech. 7.1–5; 8.18f. show to have taken place among the first groups of those who returned from Babylon.

The historical interest of the book lies in the fact that it is the only document which originated from among those who were left behind in Judah after the catastrophe of 587. Among them we find seriousness, composure, feelings of penitence and readiness to accept the lesson which they had been given; all this differs markedly from what we know to have been the dominant attitude only a few years earlier.

BIBLIOGRAPHY TO RUTH

Commentaries
G. Gerleman, BK, 1965; P. Joüon, Rome ²1953; A. Vincent, JB, ²1958; E. Würthwein, HAT, 1969; J. Gray, NCB, 1967; E. F. Campbell, AB, 1975.

§1. D. R. Ap-Thomas, 'The Book of Ruth', *ExpT* 79, 1967–8, 369–73; J. L. Vesco, 'La date du livre de Ruth', *RB* 74, 1967, 235–47; O. Eissfeldt, *Stammessage und Menschheiterzählung in der Genesis. Wahrheit und Dichtung in der Ruth-Erzählung*, Berlin 1965.

BIBLIOGRAPHY TO LAMENTATIONS

Commentaries
A. Weiser, ATD, 1958; H.-J. Kraus, BK, ²1960; O. Plöger, HAT, 1969; D. R. Hillers, AB, 1972.

§2. T. F. McDaniel, 'Philological Studies in Lamentations', *Bibl* 49, 1968, 27–53, 199–220. G. Brunet, *Les Lamentations contre Jérémie*, Paris 1968, has argued that the first four laments are directed *against* Jeremiah, but the theory has gained little support.

VI

ECCLESIASTES – THE SONG OF SONGS

§1. *Ecclesiastes*

The very name of this book, in Hebrew *qōhelet*, presents a problem: in
1.1,12 the person who is given this name is called 'son of David, king
in Jerusalem', a designation which could only be applied to Solomon.
But the gender of the noun is feminine, which would suggest rather a
title or a description of function; this explains why in many languages
it is sometimes translated 'preacher', from the etymology of the word,
which seems to be connected with the term *qāhāl* = 'cultic assembly'.
Be this as it may, the note which seeks to make Solomon the author
of the book is similar to the one which attributes the book of Proverbs
to him or the one which makes David the author of various psalms,
and will not stand critical examination.

Ecclesiastes has a distinctive content, which is quite unique in the
Old Testament: for good reason the work has always perplexed
scholars. It takes the form of reflection, confessions, maxims and
meditations of various kinds, almost always put in autobiographical
form; in them the author seeks to attract the attention of his readers
to the problem of the scope of human existence, a problem which is
characteristic of wisdom. He knows that human existence inevitably
leads to death (and in this sense, after the Second World War he was
seen as a precursor of existentialism). For him, everything, however
noble and lofty, is 'nothing but vanity', the famous *vanitas vanitatum*
of the Vulgate. Even the wisdom of which the wise men are so proud,
believing that they can acquire adequate knowledge of the mech-
anism which rules the universe, so that they can adapt themselves to
it, seems to the author to be a vain and futile thing, and he looks at
man's cherished values in the same way. Thus Ecclesiastes is a sceptic
and comes to conclusions which we can see to be disastrous for
wisdom; this characteristic of his is in contrast to the attitude of the
Old Testament: both traditional theology and wisdom there are

usually optimistic. This pessimism is to be explained not so much from the context of a crisis of faith as from a crisis of wisdom, of which the book of Job is another expression, as we have seen. And in any case, for a biblical author to come to the conclusion that 'a living dog is better than a dead lion' is quite sensational (9.4b).

The fact that only one problem is discussed, and its characteristic language, make the book a unified composition, although there have been some scholars who have seen it as a collection of different fragments. However, even if this latter theory were correct, it would be necessary to recognize that the fragments have been reconstructed as an organic unity with a marked artistic and logical sense, so that in practice it is impossible to isolate the units in question or sometimes even to see what the argument is about.

The language of the book is a particular problem. Pfeiffer in his *Introduction* (729) gives a substantial list of Aramaisms and expressions taken from the Greek, and on the basis of this he assigns a late date to the work; this is the most commonly held opinion and is also supported by the content of the work. However, the theory has recently been put forward that the forms supposed to be Aramaisms are in fact western Semitic elements which are well attested from Ugaritic onwards; this might be an indication of the 'northern' origin of the work. It is not easy to see what value these observations have for a dating of Ecclesiastes, though for some scholars they are the sign of an earlier dating than that usually assigned to the book. On the other hand, in 9.7–10 we have parallels to Mesopotamian and Egyptian texts, and in 8.1f. to the romance of Ahikar which, as we shall see (Part Six, ch.I), was also well known by the deutero-canonical book of Tobit. Despite everything, the problems with which the book is concerned seem to be those of a late date; above all it reflects the crisis of wisdom which was attested throughout the ancient Near East and which in Israel was aggravated by contacts with Hellenistic philosophy from the end of the fourth century onwards. Elements came into Israelite belief like resignation, which is otherwise unknown in the Old Testament; one unique element is a valuation of time as a cyclical entity, whereas the rest of the Old Testament sees it only in linear and historical terms. In the other wisdom books, regardless of their thought, the problem is carefully avoided; there is still no hope for the future. Nevertheless, the author never goes so far as practical or theoretical atheism; he continually insists on the power of God and the weakness of man, although some writers have seen these affirmations as indications of insecurity, of a lack of personal communion, of a more rationalistic faith from which encounter and dialogue are absent. On the other hand, considering the general tone of the book the conclusion is extremely positive: 'The sayings of the wise are like goads, and like nails firmly fixed are the collected sayings . . .' (in other words, the author does not deny the validity of wisdom, but assigns it a determinate position beyond which it should not enquire); 'Fear God and keep his commandments, for this is the whole duty of man' (12.13). If wisdom fails as a human attempt to dominate existence, faith remains, and we return to the more particularly Israelite element of thought. From the point of view of wisdom, Israel might have been inferior not only to the Greeks, as will be obvious, but also to its neighbours, yet in the realm of faith its insecurity vanishes to leave room for unconditional faith. What we said at the end of our discussion of Job therefore also applies here, and the reader is referred again to the passage.

In other words, Ecclesiastes concludes the work of limiting wisdom which Job had begun; it deprives man of the vain hope of being able to recognize the supposed order of the universe. He only knows one thing, that we must all die and that here the wise man and the fool are on the same level. Ecclesiastes thus puts all human sentiments in a new perspective, however noble they may be, by showing the vanity even of what seems unshakable, indicating that this is not the way for Israel. Only in this way can it truly prepare Israel for the new difficulties and the new tasks which lie ahead.

§2. The Song of Songs

The traditional translation of the title of this book is questionable: it can be translated either 'The best song' or 'The song *par excellence*', an alternative which is well-known to anyone familiar with Hebrew grammar (cf. the *vanitas vanitatum* in §1). This work, too, is traditionally attributed to Solomon, who was a great singer as well as the possessor of a harem of notable dimensions. However, Solomon is mentioned only in general terms (3.7, 9, 11; 8.11f.) and there is not the slightest indication that he might in any way be the author. Scholars have always been divided over the character of the book, whether it is fragmentary or a unity. Origen was already in favour of the former alternative. Here, too, the linguistic question complicates matters considerably: Aramaisms abound (which could also be understood as western Semitisms), but so do terms of Persian and Greek origin.

The most probable explanation of the book seems to be that it is a collection of various songs on similar themes, if not the same theme; this would also explain the linguistic variations which can be found in the work. Firm ground has been discovered since J. G. Wetzstein, Prussian consul in Damascus, made an investigation into the practices and customs of Arab peasants in the area which he completed in 1873. Among other things, he established that during the long marriage festivals the married couple bore the title of king and queen of the festival; they sat at a special table which was called the 'throne' for the occasion, while the public sang special hymns, essentially in honour of the wife. Meanwhile available material has been increased considerably, to such a degree that we have now virtually reached certainty. The identity of the king and the Shulamite of the book has thus unexpectedly become clear: they were the bride and bridegroom during the feast in their honour.

In Scandinavia, however, an attempt has been made to go back to an earlier phase of the question. It is argued that before the Song of Songs was 'democratized' and applied to a wedding feast, it was a series of liturgical songs in the sphere of the cult which celebrated the sacred marriage of Ishtar and Tammuz and was transplanted to Judah, perhaps at the time of the 'impious' Manasseh, during the first half of the seventh century BC. This was a time when the surviving Israelite state was a vassal of Assyria, and it may well have accepted, among other things, elements of the victor's cult. Research here was carried out before the recent work of O. Loretz, which confirms these two phases in the use of the composition.

The book did not become part of the canon without discussion. The collection was still controversial in the first century AD, and we have an echo of the discussion in the Mishnah (Yad. 3, 5, cf. Taan. 4, 8). As an image of the marriage between Yahweh and his people (a concept which is already present in Hosea), and then as an image of the marriage between Christ and his church, the book enjoyed canonical status only thanks to an allegorical interpretation which falsified the content, besides making it useless: both Israel and the church have always accepted marriage with all its implications, and it is quite consistent with this acceptance that marriage songs like those in the Song of Songs should have found a place in scripture alongside the history of religion and ethnology.

BIBLIOGRAPHY TO ECCLESIASTES

Commentaries
K. Galling, HAT, 1969; R. Pautrel, JB, 1948; H. W. Hertzberg, KAT, 1963; L. di Fonzo, SacBib, 1967; P. Ellermeier, Herzberg 1967–8; R. B. Y. Scott, AB, 1965.

§1. J. Pedersen, 'Scepticisme Israélite', *RHPR* 10, 1930, 317–70; M. J. Dahood, 'Canaanite-Phoenician Influence in Qoheleth', *Bibl* 33, 1952, 30–52; A. G. Wright, 'The Riddle of the Sphinx: the Structure of the Book of Qohelet', *CBQ* 30, 1968, 313–34; P. Magnanini, 'Sull'origine dell'Ecclesiaste', *AION* 28, 1968, 363–84; D. Michel, 'Humanität angesichts des Absurden', in H. Foerster (ed.), *Humanität heute*, Berlin 1970, 22–36; E. Horton, 'Koheleth's Concept of Opposites', *Numen* 19, 1972, 1–21 (which is concerned with the relationship between Greek philosophy and the thought of the ancient Near East and the Far East). For a Christian evaluation cf. W. Vischer, 'L'Ecclesiaste, testimone di Cristo Gesù', *Protestantesimo* 9, 1954, 1–19; M. A. Klopfenstein, 'Die Skepsis des Qohelet', *TZ* 28, 1972, 97–109.

BIBLIOGRAPHY TO THE SONG OF SONGS

Commentaries
G. Ricciotti, 1928; M. Haller, HAT, 1940; A. Robert, JB, ²1958; H. Ringgren, ATD, ⁵1962; W. Rudolph, KAT, ²1962; G. Gerleman, BK, 1965; R. Gordis, New York ³1968; E. Würthwein, HAT, 1969; O. Loretz, *Das althebräische Liebeslied, Studien zur althebräischen Poesie* I, Neukirchen 1971.

§2. H. Schmökel, *Heilige Hochzeit und Hohelied*, Wiesbaden 1956; A. Robert, R. Tournay and A. Feuillet, *Le Cantique des Cantiques*, Études Bibliques, Paris 1963; A. M. Dubarle, 'Le Cantique des Cantiques dans l'exégèse récente', *RechBibl* 9, 1967, 139–52; E. Würthwein, 'Zum Verständnis des Hohenliedes', *TR* 32, 1967, 177–212; D. Lys, *Le plus beau chant de la création*, Paris 1968; J. Angénieux, 'Le Cantique des Cantiques en huits chants à refrains alternants', *EphThLov* 44, 1968, 87–140 (= H. Cazelles (ed.), *De Mari à Qumran, Hommage à J. Coppens*, Gembloux 1969, 192–245); C. Carniti, 'L'unità letteraria del Cantico dei Cantici', *BeO* 13, 1971, 97–106. For a study of allegorical and spiritualizing exegesis of the work cf. S. Grill, *Die Symbolsprache des Hohenliedes*, Heiligenkreuz ²1970; for the figure of Wetzstein cf. H.-J. Zobel, 'J. G. Wetzsteins Schrifttum', *ZDPV* 82, 1966, 233–8; for an extra-biblical parallel which may throw light on the origin of the form of the Song cf. S. N. Kramer, 'Sumerian Sacred Marriage Songs and the Biblical "Song of Songs"', *MIO* 15, 1969, 262–74; O. Loretz, op. cit.

VII

ESTHER

The story of Esther is well known and has been the subject of numerous literary and artistic works. She is said to have been queen of Persia after the deposition of Vashti, the queen who refused to appear at the banquet of king Ahasuerus (Xerxes I), and she thwarted a plot arranged by some Persian nobles against the Jewish community in the country (probably the first indication of an antisemitic persecution that we have, leaving aside the Pharaoh of the exodus). The book is now presented as the aetiological legend of the feast of *pūrîm*, which the Jews still celebrate today as a kind of carnival; the word is interpreted in the text as the plural of *pūr* = 'lot', from the method by which the date of the massacre was fixed. The work is quite familiar with the customs of the Persian court of the fifth century BC, but it also contains some puzzling notes. In 2.5ff. Mordecai is described as one of the people deported under Jehoiachin, i.e. in 597, whereas the term *pūr*, the origin and etymology of which were unknown until recently, is Akkadian rather than Persian or Hebrew, and seems to be unknown to the readers of the text, for whom it has to be translated (3.7; 9.24). Furthermore, the relationship between the word and the narrative is obscure, and it could be removed altogether without the narrative being any the worse. The idea that the word is given an artificial explanation by means of a tradition which described the difficulties encountered by the Jewish community in Persia at the time of Xerxes I (and the same goes for the feast) is therefore very probable. Others have noted that the names of the characters belong to Mesopotamia rather than to Persia: Esther is a phonetic variant of Ishtar, Mordecai of Marduk, both important Babylonian gods; indeed the second was the patron deity of the city. Thus the question arises almost of its own accord whether we are not dealing with fragments of an ancient myth which has now been secularized and connected with the feast in question, in which two of the supreme deities of Babylonia are contrasted with other gods. On the other hand, there is no reason to exclude a more prosaic explanation; namely, that these are simply theophoric names of Babylonian origin given to Jews living in Babylon or Persia: Zerubbabel is a similar case.

There is mention in the book of the 'chronicles of the kings of the Medes and Persians', but we do not know whether this is an official document, a chronicle of the life of the Jews resident in the region, or even a literary fiction; no form of literature of this kind is to be found on the Persian side.

Some scholars have sought to see in the story echoes of an event which in fact took place and is described by Herodotus (III, 68–79): on the death of Cambyses a magus made himself out to be the dead man's brother, the legitimate heir to the throne, though Cambyses had earlier had this man killed. He was, however, unmasked by a certain Othanes with the help of his daughter, who was a member of the royal harem. The people then killed all those who had taken part in the plot, an event which was commemorated in a 'feast of the killing of the magi'. The attempt, but not the feast, is also attested in Persian sources; it seems to have been connected with the New Year festival. If there is any relationship between this narrative and that of Esther, the historical basis of the book is even more complex than it already seems to be.

The book has strongly nationalistic accents, a characteristic that can easily be explained from the frustration of a people constantly under foreign domination, which contrasted greatly with the mission with which they had been entrusted. It is characteristic that the name of Yahweh does not appear once in the book; this negative element was recognized some centuries later in the deutero-canonical additions to the book, which among other things try to make up this lack (cf. below Part Six, ch. III, §1). Judaism at the beginning of the common era took account of this anomalous situation, as is shown by the discussions which preceded the admission of Esther to the canon. In the end, it only found a place because the book explains the institution of an annual feast which was very popular among Jews, and not because of its intrinsic content.

Historically the book is interesting because it is evidence of the voice of nationalism, which is rarely heard in the Old Testament. However, this theme should not be exaggerated: the connection between the book and a carnival tends to show the absurd, ridiculous and humorous side of events rather than their cruelty. On the other hand, the history of the people of Israel shows that often the distance between tragedy and humour is not great.

BIBLIOGRAPHY

Commentaries
A. Barucq, JB, ²1959; H. Ringgren, ATD, ²1962; H. Bardtke, KAT, 1963;
E. Würthwein, HAT, 1969; C. A. Moore, AB, 1971; G. Gerleman, BK,
1973; L. H. Brockington, NCB, 1969.
W. Dommershausen, *Die Esterrolle*, Stuttgart 1968; H. Bardtke, 'Neuere
Arbeiten zum Estherbuch', *Ex Oriente Lux* VI, 19, 1965–6, 519–49 (with
full bibliography).

DANIEL

§1. *Character and content*

We have seen that in the Hebrew Bible the book of Daniel is to be found among the Writings; the LXX puts it after Ezekiel, thus making it one of the prophets. In fact Daniel is an apocalyptic work, but the error could easily arise at a time when prophecy and apocalyptic tended increasingly to coincide.

The book can readily be divided into two parts: chs. 1–6, in the third person, which tell the story of Daniel and his three companions at the court of Babylon; and chs. 7–12, which contain four visions, narrated in the first person and explained by an angel. The situation here is similar to the one that we found in the case of proto-Zechariah.

In ch. 1 we have a description of the hero of the book: he was deported to Babylon in the third year of Jehoiakim, that is, in 607 BC, together with his three friends, and educated at the court of Nebuchadnezzar II, where he kept the food regulations of the *tōrāh* with exemplary zeal, even though this meant being restricted to an exclusively vegetarian diet. However, this had no bad physical effects on the four, who in fact prospered. In ch. 2 Daniel interprets to Nebuchadnezzar a dream which had baffled the wise men of Babylon and receives a rich reward from the king. In ch. 3 the three have to undergo a harsh test; after refusing to pay divine homage to a statue which has been erected by the king, they are thrown into a fiery furnace; the heat is such that none of their escorts can survive in the vicinity, but the heroes are miraculously saved, to the king's understandable astonishment. In ch. 4 we have another of Nebuchadnezzar's dreams, the content of which is very soon realized in the person of the king: he remains mad for seven years until he is finally cured by Daniel and praises Yahweh. In ch. 5 we have the famous account of Belshazzar's feast with the mysterious writing on the wall which is interpreted by Daniel and soon fulfilled. In ch. 6 Daniel is accused of having violated a law of Darius the Mede through his mode of prayer and is thrown into a den of lions; however, he miraculously escapes from it unharmed, thus achieving recognition of the cult of Yahweh from the king by means of an edict.

In the second half of the book, first of all, in ch. 7, we have four beasts who nowadays are unanimously interpreted as symbols for Babylon, Media, Persia and Macedon: ten horns grow out of the last beast, one of which is particularly violent in language and action and is generally understood as a symbol for Antiochus IV Epiphanes (the horns represent the 'Diadochi' who succeeded Alexander the Great). In ch. 8 we have a struggle between two more symbolic beasts, a ram and a he-goat, which symbolize the kingdoms of Persia and Macedonia respectively (8.20); in ch. 9 the angel Gabriel reveals to Daniel the meaning of the prophecy in Jer. 25.11, cf. 29.10, where the duration of the Babylonian exile is reckoned at seventy years, a round figure to indicate two or three generations (i.e. a long time, not to be understood in a literal sense). This is said really to be seventy weeks of years, 490 years in all. This calculation evidently brings us down to the time of the Maccabees and the period immediately following, the end of the second and beginning of the first century BC: the peace will be followed by the inauguration of the kingdom of God. In these chapters the sea often appears as an element of chaos, which is a widespread theme in the Old Testament, just as the horns and the beasts described are symbols of force. In ch. 11 an angel reveals to Daniel the course of history from Cyrus to Antiochus IV, while in 11.40–12.3 we have details of the events which will follow the death of the oppressor. The nations will fall, the kingdom of God will dawn, the dead will rise: the pagans to eternal death and the just to eternal life (12.2; cf. Isa. 26.19). In 12.5–13, by way of conclusion, there is mention of a date by which these things will have happened: between 1290 and 1335 days respectively (12.11f.).

§2. *Authorship and origin*

The text is silent about the origin and authorship of the book. The tradition of the synagogue and the church takes the author to be Daniel, the protagonist of the work, but he is a person who is otherwise unknown: in fact we saw when considering Job that the Daniel of Ezek. 14.14,20 cannot be identical with the exilic Daniel. The question of authorship cannot therefore be resolved.

The first difficulties in the historical classification of the book begin with the deportation of Daniel and his companions. We do not in fact know anything of a deportation which took place in the third year of Jehoiakim, i.e. in 607 BC. If we allow its basic historicity, the event might be connected with the conquest of Syria and Palestine by Nebuchadnezzar II a little later, after the battle of Carchemish in 605–4 and the victory over Egypt; it was on this occasion that Jehoiakim moved out of the sphere of Egyptian influence and into that of Babylon (cf. II Chron. 36.5). Complex problems of foreign policy followed, to which we alluded in our discussion of Jeremiah. Until recently the note in Chronicles was considered spurious, since there was no point of comparison, but discoveries during the 1950s of various unedited fragments of the Babylonian Chronicle have unexpectedly made sense of both this passage and II Kings 24.1ff. But even admitting the substantial historicity of the events narrated, there remains the problem of chronology, which is evidently some years out. Other elements are no less perplexing: in 5.11 Belshazzar is implicitly called the son of Nebuchadnezzar and in 7.1 he appears as king of Babylon. However, he was neither one nor the other, but the son of Nabonidus, one of Nebuchadnezzar's successors who came to the throne as the result of a plot. (The only other possibility is that 'son of . . .' is intended in a generic sense, as 'descendant of . . .', a usage which is attested in Akkadian.) On the other hand, the statement that Belshazzar was king may simply be imprecise wording: towards 553 he was resident in Babylon as a kind of lieutenant-general for the king during his numerous absences, and could therefore have been called king, at least by the people. Again, in 5.31, as we have seen, a certain Darius the Mede appears, who is considered to be king of Persia after the fall of Babylon. In 9.1 he appears as son of Xerxes, whereas in 6.29 Cyrus succeeds a Darius. If we are to be precise, the question arises what Daniel is doing at the court of the Medes before the Babylonian empire has fallen, always assuming that we take the term 'Mede' seriously. This question has never been answered. We must therefore accept that Media is in reality Persia. But the genealogy of the kings of Persia is well known: Cyrus, Cambyses, Darius I Hystaspes, Xerxes. If the Darius mentioned here was Darius I from the last quarter of the sixth century, how old would Daniel be? These are features which were already pointed out by the anti-Christian polemicist Celsus at the end of the second century AD.

Although the chronology of the work thus seems to be somewhat confused, at least in the first part, elements of considerable historical value also appear: Herodotus (I, 191) and Xenophon, *Cyropaedia* (VII, v, 15), report that Babylon was in fact conquered during a feast and that its inhabitants had no idea of what was about to happen. Eusebius of Caesarea, *Praeparatio Evangelica* IX, 41, confirms the note about Nebuchadnezzar's madness through a tradition which is independent of that of the Bible. It is thus evident that here we have traditions which, quite independently of their intrinsic value, are certainly not the product of the imagination of the person who wrote the book.

The language of Daniel is certainly post-exilic, and terms of Greek and Persian origin abound. Whole passages are written in imperial Aramaic, whereas logically we would expect early Aramaic. Some of the concepts expressed in the book are also late: the development of the food laws in a legalistic sense, prayer with the body turned towards Jerusalem, angelology, the doctrine of the resurrection (12.2), which we know still to have been the subject of lively debate at the time of Jesus (Matt. 22.23ff.) and which was never defined in Judaism. In the first part of the book, we thus find ourselves at some remove from the exile and certainly not at its beginning. The second part, however, is an apocalyptic writing pure and simple, and is to be assigned a late date.

On the other hand, in recent times there has been a tendency not to date the book too late: it is true that Daniel is not mentioned in Ecclesiasticus, but it is equally true that many fragments of it have been found among the writings of the Qumran sect, which is an evident sign that the book had acquired considerable importance at the earliest in the third century and certainly in the second. This position is confirmed by an analysis of the historical information given in the second part of the work; it becomes exact in describing the time of Antiochus IV and the Maccabees, i.e. the first half of the second century, while the earlier account of the Babylonian and Persian period is rather inaccurate. The book is quite familiar with Antiochus IV's two campaigns against Egypt in 170 and 169 BC respectively, and with the repression of Hebrew worship down to the introduction of the 'abomination of desolation' into the temple in 167 (cf. 7.1ff.; 11.21–39); in 8.14 we probably have an indication of the purification of the temple by Judas Maccabaeus which took place in 165. The question becomes more complex when we reach 11.40, where there is an announcement of the death of the oppressor in the course of an attack against Jerusalem. This is evidently a variant on the theme of the attack of the nations on Jerusalem at the end time. In fact, Antiochus died on an expedition to the East in 163. Thus it is clear that Daniel is quite familiar with events connected with the life of Antiochus IV, but does not know of his death, which is presented only as an event in the future. We shall not go far wrong in dating the book between 168 and 164; this theory was already put forward by the neo-Platonist Porphyry in his anti-Christian polemic.

The book is not a unity in either content or language: from 2.4b to 7.28 it is composed in Aramaic – as we have seen, in imperial Aramaic. The change of language from Hebrew to Aramaic has still not been explained adequately, but Rowley is probably right in affirming that the author seems to be using Aramaic material of the Maccabaean period for chs. 2–6; ch. 7, also in the same language, was added a little later. On the other hand, the author himself wrote in Hebrew the visions of chs. 8–12, which are directed to a wider audience than the humbler section of the population, i.e. to all educated people. As far as content is concerned, we have a clear break between narrative and apocalyptic passages (chs. 7–12). In the first part, feelings towards the Gentiles are only moderately hostile, whereas in the second part the hostility is obvious; we might conclude that the first part is made up of elements which circulated in the eastern Jewish diaspora, whereas the second part refers to events of the time of the Maccabees and was intended to strengthen the Jewish population in the homeland for the struggle.

The LXX gives a text of Daniel with some additions which, as in the case of Esther, we shall study below (Part Six, ch.III, §2). In any case, its text is in extremely bad condition, so much so that Theodotion's version was soon used instead; the original was forgotten until it was rediscovered in modern times in the Chester Beatty papyri; according to a recent theory, what is thought to be Theodotion's text is really that of Symmachus. However, the important fact is that here we have a unique example of one of the minor Greek translations of the Old Testament at some length.

§3. *Purpose and message*

From time immemorial the book of Daniel has been the favourite text among sectarian elements for using the dates in it to calculate the end of the world, for condemning certain political regimes often rightly considered to be demoniacal, and for other speculative exercises. It is therefore perhaps even more necessary than with the other books of the Bible to be particularly careful in reading it and to avoid making the text say things which it cannot say. The four kingdoms symbolized by the four beasts represent those which we have seen, and cannot in any way be applied to persons and institutions from our own time.

The horn is Antiochus IV Epiphanes and not say, Hitler, Stalin or any other ill-omened figure of our time. Even if attempts of this kind often arouse strong feelings, they are to be rejected by anyone, believer or unbeliever, who means to read the Bible seriously.

Once it has been established that the work is concerned with Palestinian Judaism in the time of distress during the first half of the second century BC, we must surmount a second barrier: we must overcome the obstacle presented to modern man by the pseudonymity which is so markedly represented in the apocalyptic books. Its sole aim seems to have been to lend greater authority to the books, and the idea that this might be a fraudulent proceeding never entered the heads of the writers. On the other hand, according to the criteria governing admission to the canon, the book only found a place because it was attributed to the Daniel of the exile. In other words, without the phenomenon of pseudonymity, Daniel would never have entered the canon.

Thus the book of Daniel is an authoritative representative of the thought of Palestinian Judaism in the first half of the second century. It could be that it took up pious legends which were in circulation about the faith of individuals and groups of deportees during the sixth century; it is certain that it was directed at contemporaries, using these traditions as a comparison. If it was possible *then* to resist the guiles and the threats of the enemy, how much more was it possible *now*, when the people were united in their own country and the enemy was much less powerful! If he wished, a pious Jew could continue to observe the ritual prescriptions by which he made public confession of his faith to the pagan world. The first part of the book also seeks to show that relationships with Gentiles need not necessarily be as bad as they were at the time; and if they were, this was due to the intolerance of the pagans and not to any fault of Israel in this sphere. Moreover, with the help of God Israel could survive all tests: consider Daniel and his friends, first in the furnace and then in the lions' den.

On the other hand, the second part of the work reacts to a paganism which had unexpectedly become intolerant and irrationally aggressive, contrary to its principles of rationality and tolerance. Here there could only be war, whether on an ideological level or, where restrictions had taken forms which were physically or morally intolerable, even on the level of an armed struggle. Otherwise that would have been the end of Israel, which like all the peoples of the ancient Near East would have been absorbed into the Hellenistic world. By taking up this intransigent position, Israel, by contrast hand, succeeded in resisting guile and threats, persecution and war, and emerged victor from the conflict.

The apocalyptic compositions in the second part have a variety of features. On the one hand we have a genuinely prophetic interest in the future development of history, and on the other a purely speculative approach (one has only to think of the 'exegesis' of the seventy years in Jeremiah), and an expectation of divine intervention with strong mythical elements which leave man completely outside their perspective. These concepts in fact seem to be a form of escapism, of a flight from the historical reality in which the prophets lived so intensely, into metaphysics and myth. This refusal to face history and to live in it was a mark of regression in Israel, an adaptation to the ruling mentality in the Hellenistic world, and in the last analysis one of the involuntary causes of the catastrophes of AD 70 and 134–5.

BIBLIOGRAPHY

Commentaries
J. A. Montgomery, ICC, ²1949; G. Rinaldi, SacBib, 1947; A. Bentzen, HAT, ²1952; J. de Menasce, JB, ²1958; N. W. Porteous, OTL, 1965; O. Plöger, KAT, 1965; M. Delcor, SB, 1971.

§1. W. Baumgartner, *Das Buch Daniel*, Giessen 1926; H. H. Rowley, 'The Bilingual Problem of Daniel', *ZAW* 50, 1932, 256–68; id., *Darius the Mede and the Four World Empires in the Book of Daniel*, Cardiff ²1959.

§2. E. Gross, 'Weltreich und Gottesvolk', *EvTh* 16, 1956, 241–51; O. Eissfeldt, 'Daniels und seiner drei Gefährten Laufbahn im babylonischen, medischen und persischen Dienst', *ZAW* 72, 1960, 134–48 (= his *Kleine Schriften* III, Tübingen 1966, 513–25). For II Chron. 36.5 cf. D. J. Wiseman, *Chronicles of Chaldean Kings*, London 1956, 26f., 46f.; E. Vogt, 'Die neubabylonische Chronik über die Schlacht bei Karkemisch und die Einnahme von Jerusalem', *SVT* 4, 1957, 67–96. For Belshazzar see K. Galling, 'Politische Wandlungen in der Zeit zwischen Nabonid und Darius', in his *Studien zur Geschichte Israels im persischen Zeitalter*, Tübingen 1964, 1–60, esp. 12ff. For Dan. 7 cf. E. Dhanis, 'De Filio hominis in Vetere Testamento et in Judaismo', *Greg* 45, 1964, 5–59; J. Coppens and L. Dequeker, *Le Fils de l'Homme et les Saints du Très-Haut en Daniel VII*, Louvain 1961; M. Delcor, 'Les sources du chapitre VII de Daniel', *VT* 18, 1968, 290–312. For the language of the book cf. H. H. Rowley, *The Aramaic of the Old Testament*, London 1929; id., 'The Meaning of Daniel for Today', *Interpretation* 15, 1961, 387–97. For the Greek text cf. P. Grelot, 'Les versions grecques de Daniel', *Bibl* 47, 1966, 381–402; A. Schmitt, *Stammt der sogenannte ' Θ'-Text bei Daniel wirklich aus Theodotion?*, Göttingen 1966. He thinks Symmachus is a more likely source.

§3. On apocalyptic in general see above on Part Three, ch. I, §8. See also R. Martin-Achard, 'L'apocalyptique d'après trois travaux récents', *RTP* 103, 1970, 310–18; P. D. Hanson, 'Old Testament Apocalyptic re-examined', *Interpretation* 25, 1971, 454–79; B. Corsani, 'L'apocalittica fra Antico e Nuovo Testamento', *Protestantesimo* 27, 1972, 15–22.

CHRONICLES

§1. *Character, analysis and date*

'Chronicles' is a literal translation of the Hebrew title *dibrē hayyāmīm* = lit. 'facts of the day'; the Greek, followed by the Vulgate, has *paraleipomenōn*, as though Chronicles were a kind of complement to the books of Samuel and Kings. In reality, along with Ezra and Nehemiah, it is a large independent historical work, although it sometimes draws on the same sources as the 'former prophets' and thus appears so to speak in a parallel form to them. It was Jerome who proposed the title *Chronicon totius divinae historiae*, a title which corresponds well with the intentions of the compiler.

The content can easily be divided into four parts: I Chron. 1–9, the genealogies from Adam to David, with interesting variants and new notes in comparison with the books of the Pentateuch and the 'former prophets' (however, in 3.17ff. the genealogies have six stages after Zerubbabel [cf. pp.325, 332 above], which gives an important *terminus a quo* for the dating of the book); I Chron. 10–29, the life of David; II Chron. 1–9, the life of Solomon; II Chron. 10–36, from the schism to the exile. From the death of Saul onwards we have an obvious parallel narrative to Samuel and Kings, though this parallel does not detract from the originality of Chronicles in both choice of sources and ultimate intention. In the earlier part, however, the parallel appears only on the onomastic level, since (as we have seen) Chronicles here gives only genealogies and lists of places.

For Chronicles, the centre of the history of Israel is to be found in the temple and its worship, its priesthood and even in less elevated personnel. History before that of David, the history of the kingdom of Israel after the separation of the two kingdoms, and all forms of worship earlier than and then parallel to that of the temple, are thought to be devoid of interest and can therefore be ignored. David appears essentially as the spiritual father of the temple; although he was not allowed to build it, he organized all its worship and prepared the material for its construction (I Chron. 22; compare with this I Kings 5). On his death he hands over to Solomon to continue the work thus begun and to bring it to a conclusion. David is also seen to have reorganized the cult, and especially its music; this is within the context of the tradition which makes him a singer and a psalmist. His spiritual successors are Solomon, Jehoshaphat (the pious king who was zealous for the law), and of course Hezekiah and Josiah. These people appear as the embodiment of a synthesis of national saints and heroes, thus taking to an absurd degree a tendency which is already present in Dtr. Almost every feature which does not fit in with the hagiographical character of their biographies disappears from the life of these kings: the story of David's family, certain aspects of the life of Solomon and so on. The direct intervention of Yahweh is often the decisive element in the victorious solution of a conflict: we have a particularly clear instance of this approach in II Chron. 20.1–30. Thus Chronicles is deliberately sacred history, perfecting historiographical tendencies which were earlier represented by Dtr and the prophets. Chronicles accepts the approach to certain historical problems in terms of reward and punishment which is well attested in earlier history writing, but it now takes this to excess. For example, the authors raise the problem how a king like Manasseh, who was considered the embodiment of the wicked ruler, could have reigned for so long a time; the explanation of the fact, which contradicts the theory in question, is sought along the following lines: the king, who was deported to Assyria, was converted there (II Chron. 33.10ff.), which explains the divine favour towards him. In reality, Manasseh, a vassal of Assyria, arrived in Asshurbanipal's capital along with other vassals, in 667, to pay tribute and supply military contingents (cf. the Assyrian chronicle on the so-called C cylinder I, lines 24ff., ANET[3], 294). There can therefore be no question of a spiritual crisis, much less of a conversion.

As well as being particularly interested in worship, the priesthood and the levites, the Chronicler is very familiar with the Pentateuch, especially the Deuteronomic legislation, the application of which is presupposed even in cases where the parallel passages of Samuel and Kings know nothing of it (cf. e.g. I Chron. 14.2 with II Sam. 5.11).

§2. Sources

We saw above that the Chronicler knew the Pentateuch and quotes people and places from it. He probably also knew Dtr, or at least its sources, since he agrees with it in many passages. He also cites the 'Book of the kings of Israel' (I Chron. 9.1; II Chron. 20.34) and knows the 'Chronicles of the kings of Israel' (II Chron. 33.18). It is difficult to know whether these are the works cited in Kings (cf. above Part Two, ch. IX, §2bc), different works, or literary fictions to give the work greater credibility. A midrash (= commentary) on the book of Kings is mentioned in II Chron. 24.27, but we know nothing about it.

Until recently the work of the Chronicler was held in low esteem by biblical scholars: its crude interpretation in terms of reward and punishment, the episodes in Israelite history interpreted in a mythical and miraculous fashion, and other elements of this kind, give the critical reader too many reasons for discrediting the work. Recently, however, it has been recognized that in Chronicles we have a series of notes from a reliable source, perhaps even at first hand, which complement what we know only partially from the books of Samuel and Kings. For example, the chronological notes about Josiah's reform in II Chron. 34.3–7 are certainly authentic and better than those in II Kings 22; 23; we saw above that the reform in fact began about ten years before the discovery of the 'book of the law' during the restoration of the temple, while II Kings 22; 23 makes the two events coincide, as though it were the discovery of the book which prompted Josiah to the reform. Here Chronicles offers the most comprehensive account of events: Josiah begins the reform in the eighth year of his reign, probably in the context of a progressive disengagement from the Assyrian empire, which was now in decline, whereas the 'book of the law' was found in the eighteenth year, a date on which Kings and Chronicles agree. It is also II Chron. 35.20ff. which gives detailed information about the death of Josiah in the battle of Megiddo against Necho II of Egypt, an element which is absent from Kings. In II Chron. 32.30 we have a note that Hezekiah developed the aqueduct and the water system of the capital with a view to a long siege: this aqueduct was rediscovered and explored in the second half of the last century. The lists of fortresses in II Chron. 11.5–10; 16.1–6 and various notes about conspiracies and rebellions contained throughout the work are also authentic and early. There are a number of cases where Chronicles gives the exact names of particular people, which have been distorted for polemical reasons in Dtr: Ishbaal in I Chron. 8.33; 9.39 for Ishbosheth; Meribbaal in I Chron. 8.34 for Mephibosheth; and so on. It is also Chronicles which gives the correct interpretation of the delegation from the king of Babylon to Hezekiah in terms of 'treaties', according to the probable translation suggested by H. Cazelles for II Chron. 32.31. This detail does not emerge from the parallel passages in II Kings 20.12f.//Isa.39.1f. We must be very cautious over these notes given by Chronicles which do not reflect the theology of the book in any particular way, and remember that in cases of this kind the burden of proof is always with the prosecution, and not with the defence.

At other times, however, the theology of Chronicles is actively at work in the revision of information that we can verify through other sources available to us. We have examined the cases of I Chron. 14.2 and II Chron. 33.10ff.; another similar case can be found in I Chron. 21.1ff.: the parallel passage II Sam. 24.1 relates, 'The anger of Yahweh was kindled against . . .', whereas I Chron. reads 'Satan stood up against Israel . . .' (incidentally, this is the only instance in the Old Testament in which Satan appears as the proper name of a person and therefore as a demon). It is clear what has happened between the two versions: in II Sam. God himself acts to punish David; in I Chron. hagiography already has the king in its grip and therefore he cannot be punished; instead the king is 'tempted' by Satan, who has now taken over the role assigned to the Tempter, a role which he will have in later Judaism, the New Testament and Islam.

§3. Thought

In Dtr the theological interpretation served as an interpretative key for explaining the events which were reported; they were considered, if we may put it this way, as 'proof texts' for certain theories, for a particular theology of history. The texts did not emerge substantially transformed, but were simply cited outside their original context. Paradoxically, in Chronicles we may say that the theological theory existed first and that the facts came second and were often forcibly made to fit it: the case of Manasseh's conversion may be considered typical. That does not mean that the Chronicler was deceiving the reader or the hearer: terms like 'pious fraud' have often been applied to him in the past, but they do not get to the heart of the phenomenon. In any case we cannot disregard the utter good faith of the author: in fact the Chronicler saw events from the creation of the world to the time of Ezra and Nehemiah and beyond – as the genealogies show – as having taken place in the way in which he describes them. It is, however, difficult to call this process 'historiography'. The modern reader continually has the impression that, given the theory, having established the premises, the results can only be what the Chronicler wants them to be, and the impression which this situation makes on his understanding is not a favourable one: without insisting on an impossible degree of objectivity in his history, he asks that at least he shall not be asked to know *a priori* the result to which his investigations are leading him.

In other words, instead of selecting examples for his preaching from history, like Dtr, the Chronicler adapts history to his preaching, taking to absurd lengths doctrines like that of reward and punishment, well-known to the prophets and the Deuteronomistic writers, not to mention wisdom.

As Noth has rightly recognized, there are probably other reasons for the implicit protest against the attitude of the northern kingdom of Israel which is contained in the fact that there is not a single favourable mention of it (we may note a fundamental difference from Dtr, which condemns 'the sin of Jeroboam' but does not conceal the reasons which led to the separation). Here we have incipient anti-Samaritan polemic, and the Samaritans considered themselves, quite rightly, as the legitimate heirs of the kingdom of Israel. In other words, the Chronicler takes up an ancient condemnation to renew the present condemnation of a movement which was considered schismatic or even heretical, whose members were involved in the guilt of their fathers. The reduction of the Pentateuch to genealogies and lists of places could also be explained as a desire not to give the hated neighbours material which they might use in self-defence.

The danger inherent in the approach made by Chronicles to theological and ethical problems, not to mention the obvious tendentiousness in its account of the greater part of the past history of Israel, should be evident: the legalistic application of the doctrine of rewards and punishments; the distortion or the invention of facts to fit the theory; belief in the correctness of the cult, which is even enough to win battles – all these indicate that the theology of the Chronicler is something of a regression from that of his predecessors. However, we must be particularly careful here, and in any case we should avoid crude and dogmatic judgments: we know too little of the time at which Chronicles was written, nor do we know the need in response to which it was written. Just as a degree of tendentiousness in Dtr can be explained from the need to give a theological explanation to the catastrophe of the exile, so some of the elements which we may rightly criticize in Chronicles may perhaps be explained when we know the need to which they are a response. This might also resolve much of our obvious perplexity.

In any case, we can see one thing from Chronicles. The preaching of the prophet and Dtr have had a salutary effect on post-exilic piety: the various forms of syncretism or idolatry have either disappeared or have been absorbed in such a way as no longer to be recognizable. The government of Israel is theocratic and the great social injustices seem to have been overcome within the community, the centre of which is now the cult at Jerusalem. To some the price paid for this will seem to be high: orthodoxy and spiritual tranquility have been obtained through the introduction of certain forms of legalism which were developing while Israel was becoming a diaspora. Here too, however, a healthy balance between the two things is easier to look for than to obtain.

BIBLIOGRAPHY

Commentaries
W. Rothstein and J. Hänel, KAT, 1927 (I Chron. only); W. Rudolph, HAT, 1955; K. Galling, ATD, 1958; H. Cazelles, JB, ³1961; J. M. Myers, AB, 1965; L. Randellini, SacBib, 1966; F. Michaeli, CAT, 1967; P. R. Ackroyd, TBC, 1973.

Monographs and synopses
M. Noth, *Überlieferungsgeschichtliche Studien* I, Halle ²1957; P. Vannutelli, *Libri Synoptici Veteris Testamenti*, Rome 1931–4 (for a comparison with Samuel and Kings, LXX and Vulgate); T. Willi, *Die Chronik als Auslegung*, FRLANT 106, 1972 (for the interpretative principles underlying the parallels with Samuel-Kings).

§1. S. Japhet, 'The Supposed Common Authorship of Chronicles and Ezra-Nehemiah Investigated Anew, *VT* 18, 1968, 330–71 (which produces significant arguments for the view that Chronicles and Ezra-Nehemiah cannot have had the same author).

X

EZRA AND NEHEMIAH

§1. *Character and content*

The conclusion of II Chron. 36 is identical with the beginning of Ezra; this fact is usually interpreted as a sign of the continuity between the two works, in spite of the fact that Ezra and Nehemiah precede Chronicles in the Hebrew Bible. In the LXX they are combined to form II Esdras. In the Vulgate, which has four books of Ezra, these books are called I and II Ezra (the LXX I Esdras becomes III Ezra, see pp.471f. below).

The division is very simple, as in Chronicles. In Ezra 1–6 we have the account of the restoration down to the rebuilding of the temple, events to which Haggai and Zechariah also refer, as we have seen. In Ezra 7 – Neh. 13 we have an account of the two persons in question from their arrival from Persia: the reforms they introduced, the difficulties they encountered, the religious and moral situation prevailing in Judah, and so on. In language, content and theology the two works are usually thought to belong to the tradition of the Chronicler, though they have also drawn on sources contemporaneous with the events, which we shall be examining in due course. One exception to this theory was given in the bibliography to the previous chapter, but it has not found a following. Ezra and Nehemiah share with Chronicles an interest in the cult, the priesthood, genealogy, the levitical families and so on.

§2. *Sources*

What material formed the basis for the composition of the present text of the two books? This is one of the most complex questions in Old Testament Introduction. At the very beginning, Ezra 1.1–4.5, it is impossible to establish with the slightest degree of certainty how far we have authentic material, (e.g. the lists of the first people to return to Judaea from exile, Ezra 2//Neh. 7; the catalogue of the sacred vessels of the temple, removed by the Babylonians and restored by the Persian administration, 1.7–10; the problem of the edict of Cyrus, II Chron. 36.22f.//Ezra 1.1–4, etc.), or whether we have here no more than an editorial compilation pure and simple. This last possibility comes to mind when we consider the figures, which are inflated and therefore out of touch with reality. It does not in fact appear possible that in 538 and in the years immediately following, a little after the edict of liberation promulgated by Cyrus concerning the deported populations, such a vast movement of population could have taken place, before there had been time to reorganize the civil administration, at least in Palestine, if not throughout the empire. On the other hand, the list of the sacred vessels of the temple restored by Cyrus could well have been compiled at the moment of liberation and delivered to the rightful owners, on the basis of the inventory existing in the Babylonian administration, without this implying in the least that they were transported to Palestine. One solution to the first problem might be that the list of those returning does not refer to 539–38, but to 520, when another group moved from Babylon to Judah, as Zech. 6.9 informs us, and began the rebuilding of the temple.

5.6–6.18 are written in Aramaic; as in the case of Daniel, this is imperial Aramaic. For a long time the text has been thought to be a memorandum sent by the Jews in their defence to Artaxerxes I Longimanus, to reaffirm their loyalty to their new imperial lord and to defend themselves against the opportunist calumnies which were being circulated by the neighbouring peoples on their account; this would have been produced on the basis of material dating from the time of Cyrus onwards. However, this theory finds no support in the facts: there are contradictions in the supposed 'defence' (e.g. 4.24 with 5.16). Noth thought that there were two original documents here, which were fused together at a later stage: one from the time of Artaxerxes, mentioned above, concerned with the rebuilding of Jerusalem, and the other from the time of Darius I Hystaspes, concerned with the rebuilding of the temple. The Chronicler is supposed to have combined them and confused them, because of the affinity of the material and because three kings of Persia each bore the names of Darius and Artaxerxes.

7.12–9.15 contain what have been called the 'memoirs of Ezra'; the Chronicler has drawn on these abundantly, but has left the first person; perhaps ch. 10, which has been rewritten in the third person, originally formed part of them also.

Neh. 1–7 are the 'memoirs of Nehemiah'; we should probably add to them chs. 10; 12.27–43; 13. It is possible that the lists to which we have referred were preserved in these memoirs (which would explain the duplication of Ezra 2//Neh. 7), while Neh. 3 gives a list of the names of the workers involved in rebuilding the walls of Jerusalem.

§3. Chronology

The problem of the chronology of the protagonists of the two books is also one of the most complex in the Old Testament, this time in a historical context. A satisfactory solution has yet to be found, and here we can only move in the realm of hypothesis.

According to the two books, Ezra arrived at Jerusalem before Nehemiah in the seventh year of Artaxerxes I, that is in 458, whereas Nehemiah will have arrived in the twentieth year of the same king, that is, in 445 (cf. Ezra 7.7; Neh. 2.1). This theory has traditionally been maintained down the centuries and apparently presents no difficulties; it was put in doubt for the first time with arguments of considerable weight by the Belgian scholar A. van Hoonacker in 1880 and in the years up to the end of the last century. Its starting point is the fact mentioned in Ezra 10.6; Ezra is accompanied by a certain Jehohanan ben Eliashib; but Eliashib, whether father or grandfather of Ezra's contemporary, is clearly connected with Nehemiah and his ministry, which would suggest that Nehemiah, and not Ezra, was the first to come to Jerusalem, and indeed half a century earlier. In other words, in fact the two will always have worked separately and not together, as in the traditional scheme; they were only made contemporaries on the redactional level and this never happened in reality.

This theory immediately enjoyed considerable success among scholars, though from the moment it was presented it inevitably caused a great dispute. There were also other elements in its favour which can be listed briefly:

(a) Nehemiah never mentions Ezra's work, a strange omission, even if it is only an argument from silence.

(b) When Nehemiah arrives, the city seems to be sparsely populated and the walls have not yet been rebuilt, details which conflict with the account in Ezra 7–10.

(c) In Neh. 5.15 Nehemiah's predecessors are blamed for the disorder reigning in the city; this is somewhat strange, to say the least, if we put Ezra among these predecessors, and if the critical situation is the result of a full thirteen years of his rule.

(*d*) In Ezra 9.9 it is affirmed that God allows the people to rebuild the ruined temple and that he gives the people a wall; but we know that the walls of Jerusalem (and this is what must be meant here) were rebuilt under Nehemiah. A spiritual interpretation of 'the wall' is not convincing, since it has an artificial character and does not conform to the Hebrew spirit, nor can we invoke Zech. 2.9, since this passage announces the situation in Jerusalem in an eschatological age.

(*e*) Under Nehemiah, the country is dominated by some local noblemen, a feature which does not appear in the texts dealing with Ezra.

(*f*) Neh. 12.22 mentions a series of high priests, and it is here that the problem of Jehohanan ben Eliashib arises, which was mentioned above. In 10.6 he was a contemporary of Ezra, while according to the Elephantine papyri (cf. Appendix II below) he would be dated towards 410 BC.

Of course, taken individually, none of these arguments is particularly strong and those who would maintain the tradition can obviously call attention to the following points: (*a*) and (*e*) are arguments from silence and do not prove anything; (*b*) does not prove anything, because even so sparsely populated a city could succeed in bringing together an assembly of a considerable size if the population was disposed to collaborate; (*c*) can be explained by the fact that Ezra simply did not succeed in eliminating all the abuses, while (*d*) has recently been explained by J. Morgenstern with the hypothesis of a second destruction of the city following a second rebellion. Such a situation would seem to underlie the conversation reported in Neh. 1.3;2.3, where there is a reference to the precarious situation of Jerusalem, which is in ruins with its gates consumed by fire. Now if this were a description of the city as it had remained from the time of the rebuilding of the temple, there would be nothing sensational about the news, which is the case if we suppose a new destruction. Finally, (*f*) proves little or nothing, since there could have been different priests of the same name.

For this reason scholars are still divided: G. Ricciotti, J. Pedersen, H. H. Rowley, N. H. Snaith, M. Noth and W. Rudolph favour the arrival of Ezra after Nehemiah (and the seventh year of Artaxerxes would then refer not to Artaxerxes I but to Artaxerxes II, which would bring us down to the beginning of the fourth century); a few, including Y. Aharoni and U. Kellermann, are in favour of the traditional sequence, finding the alternative date assigned to Ezra too low. A third solution has been proposed and has some elements in its favour. The celebrations mentioned in Neh. 1–7 seem to be an integral part of a sabbatical year and its liturgy. We know the dates of at least two of these, 164–3 (cf. I Macc. 6.49) and 38–7 (cf. Josephus, *Antiquities* XII, 9.5 = §378; XV, 1.1 = §7). It is thus relatively easy, by calculating backwards, to arrive at a sabbatical year celebrated in the time of Artaxerxes I Longimanus; this date falls in 430–29, that is, in the thirty-seventh year of the monarch's reign. It is then necessary to suppose an error in the dating: instead of reading 'In the seventh year of Artaxerxes' we should read 'In the thirty-seventh year of Artaxerxes'. In this case Ezra would indeed have come after Nehemiah, but not so late as a connection with Artaxerxes II might suggest. The greatest defect of this theory is obviously the fact that it not only requires a textual emendation at a vital point, but also is based on the celebration of the sabbatical year, a festival the origins and celebrations of which are still shrouded in mystery. In fact we have no proof that it was ever celebrated before the time of the Maccabees.

§4. *The legal status of Ezra and Nehemiah in the Persian administration*

Another disputed problem which is far from being solved is that of the legal status of the two protagonists of the book in the Persian administration, with which they obviously had contact. Without going into details, which are of little value in understanding the book, we may cite the conclusions reached by R. North and which seem to take the discussion a good deal further forward.

(*a*) Nehemiah was never governor, since the text of Neh. 5.14 on which the theory is based is corrupt. The term *peḥah* = 'satrap' is not to be found in the Massoretic text, and has been reconstructed only on the basis of LXX[B–A] and the Vulgate; it is also completely isolated in the two books.

(*b*) Nor was his adversary Sanballat governor, although he was an important official.

(*c*) Nehemiah was only a page at the Persian court, and in Judah he exercised the functions of a master-builder.

(*d*) Ezra was only a priest and a scribe, with functions which were exclusively religious and never political.

(*e*) Neither Ezra nor those involved in rebuilding the temple had unlimited financial resources at their disposal.

(*f*) Ezra was never given any form of authority; he was an ordinary subject who enjoyed special favours from his sovereign.

BIBLIOGRAPHY

Commentaries
W. Rudolph, HAT, 1949; A. Gelin, JB, ²1960; B. M. Pelaia, SacBib, 1957; K. Galling, ATD, 1954; J. M. Myers, AB, 1965; F. Michaeli, CAT, 1967; L. H. Brockington, NCB, 1969; P. R. Ackroyd, TBC, 1973.

§1–2. M. Noth, *Überlieferungsgeschichtliche Studien*, Halle ²1957, 110–79; A. S. Kapelrud, *The Question of Authorship in the Ezra-Narrative*, Oslo 1944; H. Cazelles, 'La mission d'Esdras', *VT* 4, 1954, 113–40. On Nehemiah see U. Kellermann, *Nehemia: Quellen, Überlieferung und Geschichte*, BZAW 102, 1967.

§4. J. Morgenstern, 'Jerusalem – 485 BC', *HUCA* 27, 1956, 101–79; 28, 1957, 15–47; 31, 1960, 1–29; id., 'Further Light from the Book of Isaiah upon the Catastrophe of 485 BC', *HUCA* 37, 1966, 1–28. For the third suggestion concerning the dating see A. Pavlovský, 'Die Chronologie der Tätigkeit Esdras. Versuch einer neuen Lösung', *Bibl* 38, 1957, 273–305, 428–56. Y. Aharoni, *The Land of the Bible*, London 1957, 358, and U. Kellermann, 'Erwägungen zum Problem der Esradatierung', *ZAW* 80, 1968, 55–87, both support the traditional chronology with solid arguments. Cf. also K. Galling, *Studien zur Geschichte Israels im persischen Zeitalter*, Tübingen 1964, chs. 2, 3, 4, 6, 7.

§4. R. North, 'Civil Authority in Ezra', in *Studi in onore di E. Volterra*, Milan 1971, 377–404.

PART SIX

THE DEUTERO-CANONICAL BOOKS

GENERAL BIBLIOGRAPHY FOR THE
DEUTERO-CANONICAL BOOKS
(THE APOCRYPHA)

R. H. Charles (ed.), *Apocrypha and Pseudepigrapha of the Old Testament*, 2 vols, Oxford 1913 (text and commentary on all the relevant works)
R. H. Pfeiffer, *History of New Testament Times*, New York 1949
L. H. Brockington, *A Critical Introduction to the Apocrypha*, London 1961
L. Rost, *Einleitung in die alttestamentlichen Apokryphen und Pseudepigraphen*, Heidelberg 1971
See also the Catholic *Introductions* listed in the general bibliography, together with that of Eissfeldt.

I

TOBIT

§1. *Character and content*

Apart from a few fragments discovered at Qumran and not yet published, the book has been transmitted only in Greek. It bears the
title 'Book of the Words of Tobit', which is an exact translation of the
Hebrew *sēper dibrē ṭōbīt*; the phrase could also be rendered 'Acts of
Tobit', which would be an apt title, considering that the work is
largely narrative. The Vulgate has simply *Liber Tobiae*. It contains a
series of narratives centred on the person of Tobit and his son Tobias.
The Vulgate uses the same name for father and son, and in this is
followed by many modern translations; both figures are said to have
been deported from the northern kingdom in 734.

We have three recensions of the text:

(*a*) That attested by codex ℵ (or Sinaiticus) of the LXX, compiled in the fourth or fifth century AD and probably the best; it has
been confirmed by the surviving fragments of the Old Latin. It served
as a basis for the Vulgate translation and for retrotranslations into
Hebrew and Aramaic;

(*b*) That attested by codex B (or Vaticanus) and A (or Alexandrinus)
of the LXX before the discovery of Sinaiticus. The Syriac, Coptic,
Ethiopian and Armenian translations are dependent on this, as is
another retrotranslation into Hebrew. There are some scholars who
continue to regard it as better than Sinaiticus;

(*c*) A third recension is attested by some fragments of a Syriac
translation and some papyri from Oxyrhynchus; it is certainly later
than the two preceding texts, from which it seems to have been
compiled. We cannot go into the complex problem of the variants
here, for which we refer the reader to the critical text.

Tobit is naturally divided into four parts (or into seven if we divide
the second part into two and the third part into three):

(i) The prologue (1.3–3.17) tells of the vicissitudes of Tobit and his family during the exile, where he remains faithful to the law, the faith and the customs of his people; leaving aside life at court, this is a theme which is reminiscent of that of Daniel and his three companions. Even before deportation to Assyria, however, the group had been opposed to the laxity of their compatriots in the religious and ethical sphere, and were thinking of the possibility of moving to Judah where the spiritual situation seemed better. However, the deportation made these plans fruitless.

One night Tobit, after having buried the body of one of his compatriots who had been assassinated in the street, had to remain outside because of the ritual impurity which he had contracted. While he was sleeping in the open, the droppings of some birds fell in his eyes, making him completely blind. The doctors did not know how to cure the illness and Tobit was soon reduced from prosperity to complete destitution.

Without warning, the scene of the narrative shifts to Ecbatana in Media, where a pious Hebrew woman by the name of Sarah was living. She had been married seven times, but each time had been made a widow before the marriage could be consummated, because of a demon called Asmodeus who regularly broke in and killed her husbands on the first night. Public opinion made the woman responsible for this situation and almost drove her to suicide. Tobit on the one hand and Sarah on the other turned to God in prayer and he sent the angel Raphael to them, to cure Tobit and to free Sarah, who in due course became Tobias's wife.

(ii) Chapters 4–9 show Tobias' journey to Media, where he had been sent by his father to recover a sum of money which had been deposited there. In ch. 4 Tobit gives Tobias some advice and in ch. 5 he entrusts him with the documents relating to the deposit. Tobias leaves, and on the way meets the angel Raphael in Hebrew dress. The young man takes him into service and the two go on their way together. While Tobias is washing in the Tigris a fish tries to devour him (LXX^{B-A} and Vulgate, whole; LXX$^{\aleph}$, only a leg), but the young man succeeds in catching it; on the advice of the angel he keeps the heart, the liver and the gall of the creature, which may be useful as medicine. When they arrive at Ecbatana they spend the night in Sarah's house and Raphael begins negotiations with a view to a marriage between the pair (ch. 6). They are married, chase the demon away by means of the smell of the liver and heart of the fish, which they burn, and finally Sarah's marriage is consummated without incident. Meanwhile Raphael recovers the sum of money to save time (ch. 9).

(iii) Chapters 10–13 describe the return of the young couple to Nineveh. Tobias applies the gall from the fish (a medicine which is also known elsewhere in antiquity) to his father's eyes and cures him, and after that Raphael takes his leave without revealing his true identity and ascends to heaven. In ch. 13 Tobit utters a psalm and praises God for his great works.

(iv) An epilogue (ch. 14) shows Tobit dying at the ripe age of 99 or 127 years, depending on the recension, having given instructions to his son Tobias.

§2. *History and literature*

To speak of the historicity or even of the legendary character of what is evidently a pious *Novelle* seems out of place: Raphael himself in 12.19 reveals to Tobit that his presence is only a vision. On the other hand, the author of the book is concerned to establish some historical synchronisms which are an attempt to add verisimilitude to the narrative: in 1.1 we have a reference to the deportation of Naphthali during 734 (II Kings 15.29), but this in fact took place under Tiglath-pileser III and not under Shalmaneser V, as the author supposes. Here we have a confusion of dates: 734, if we accept that the deportation happened under the first of the two kings, 722–21, if we suppose that it happened under the second. The last note contained in the work is that about the fall of Nineveh at the hands of Cyaxares, king of Media, in 612 (two variants have Nabopolassar and Ahasuerus, i.e. Xerxes I, respectively), 14.15. Thus notwithstanding the preoccupations of the author or redactor, the chronology is far from precise and presupposes, among other things, a much longer life for Tobit than that indicated in 14.1. The supernatural and visionary element is another factor of historical uncertainty, but to rob the book of it would be to deprive it of its point, namely, faith in divine providence which intervenes directly whenever it is needed and which brings everything to a good end, despite difficulties of every kind.

The author is familiar with the scriptures, which he calls 'the law and the prophets', a terminology which is well attested in the New Testament; it thus seems that he presupposes the existence of something like a canon, which puts him at a relatively late date, not much earlier than that of the Maccabees. The Pentateuch appears as the 'law of Moses' (7.13) or the 'book of Moses' (7.12), designations which, as we saw at the beginning of Part Two of this book (above, p.79), are attested from Chronicles onwards. The 'golden rule', which is found in the New Testament (Matt. 7.12), is presented in its negative form in 4.15. Throughout the work we find features classified as 'the tradition of the elders', sometimes Hebrew traditions which were first communicated orally and then codified in the Mishnah in the second century BC; however, there is no lack of heterodox customs or even customs prohibited in scripture: in 4.17 we have an offering on a grave, a practice expressly forbidden in Deut. 26.14 (cf. Hos. 9.4; Isa. 8.19; Jer. 16.3) and later in Ecclus. 30.18. Of course this kind of practice continued for many years in popular piety, but it is surprising to see it praised here rather than condemned. In 5.16 Tobias and Raphael are accompanied by a dog which then follows them in 11.4; but in Deut. 23.18 and Ecclus. 13.18 the animal was considered impure, and still is today by Muslims in the Near East, where the word is a serious insult. It is not surprising, therefore, to find the mention of the animal omitted in the Aramaic version. On the other hand, the author draws on the moral precepts of the Pentateuch and the prophets: in 2.6 he cites Amos 8.10 with remarkable exactitude; in 14.4 he cites Nahum 3.7 and Zeph. 2.13f. with reference to the imminent fall of Nineveh (LXX[B-A] wrongly has Jonah instead). Moreover, throughout the book the author shows himself to be quite familiar with the content of the prophetic books. Again, in 1.21f.; 2.10; 11.18 and 14.10 there is mention of the oriental sage Ahikar, to whom we have already referred several times. This is an oriental wisdom *Novelle* about Sennacherib; the *terminus post quem* of the work is thus the end of the eighth and beginning of the seventh century, and a complete copy of it has been found in Elephantine, as we shall see in Appendix II below. Finally, the narrative of Tobit is interwoven with features from folklore and from fairy tales. It is therefore easy to come to the conclusion that the work is dependent on the Pentateuch and the prophets for its theological formation, while the rest of the material belongs to the world of wisdom, of folklore and popular piety. It would be more precise to call the book a historical novel, in the sense that its characters may very well have existed in reality; however, the narrative seeks not so much to recount their fortunes as to edify the reader by their example. It may be said that this aim is fully achieved, since the narrative abounds in original touches, often very attractive, and is a unique instance of its kind, even if the traditional themes of Jewish faith tend to become secondary and to be replaced by the observance of the law and the prophets (not too strict in the case of the popular piety which we have examined).

§3. *Problems of language and origin*

(*a*) Origen did not know of the existence of a Hebrew text of Tobit, and affirmed that the book was not used among the Jews (*Epist. ad Africanum*, Migne, PG 11, 80); in his prologue to the work, Jerome knows of an Aramaic version from which he translates (perhaps belonging to the same tradition as the unpublished fragments from Qumran), but his information cannot now be verified and we cannot exclude the possibility of a retrotranslation from the Greek. While we are waiting for the publication of the Qumran fragments, only the Greek text (with the problem of its various recensions) seems relatively certain. On the other hand, scholars agree that Tobit had a Semitic archetype, in either Hebrew or Aramaic; in fact we have a series of Semitisms, the presence of which would be impossible if the work had originally been composed in Greek. In 1.11 we have the expression 'my soul' for 'I'; in 3.8 'someone . . . not' for 'no one'; in 3.10 'I am the only one of my father . . .' for 'I am his only daughter'; in 3.6 (ℵ.) 'the face of the earth' for 'the (surface of the) earth'; in 13.13 the 'sons of the just' to indicate individuals belonging in this category; in 12.15 (LXX^ℵ) 'stand in the presence of' for 'serve', and so on. Of course one might think of a diaspora Jew writing in a Semitic-type Greek or deliberately adopting a style of this kind to confer greater authority on his words; however, the theory that we have a more or less literal translation into Greek of a Hebrew or Aramaic text seems more probable. Scholars are in general inclined to accept the last possibility.

(*b*) When we look for the place of origin and date of the book, an examination shows that we must immediately rule out the two countries mentioned in it, Assyria and Persia. Information about them is either vague or inaccurate; the Assyrian people and dates mentioned in 1.1 and in 14.15 present problems in the different variants which are attested, and the corrections which we find in some cases seem to have been made with the aim of remedying these difficulties. They are therefore of no value for the historian since they contradict the critical principle of the *lectio difficilior* (cf. above Part One, ch. III, §3). The geography of the book also presents problems: the journey from Assyria to Media and Persia evidently reflects situations more appropriate to the Persian period and perhaps even the Macedonian era; they certainly do not come from the eighth and seventh centuries BC. The date cannot therefore be earlier than the fourth century and probably should be brought down to the end of the third century or even to the second. It is debatable whether the origin of the book is to be sought in oriental Judaism of the diaspora in Babylon and adjoining countries (and the geographical information, for all its problems, points in this direction) or in western Palestinian Judaism, as is suggested by the insistence on the temple and the elements connected with the canon. However, no definitive statement can be made to resolve this argument.

§4. *Message*

Pfeiffer has defined the message of Tobit in succinct terms (*History of New Testament Times*, 278): 'By example and by precept the Book of Tobit inculcates the noble religious and moral principles of Judaism in the first third of the second century BC.' The variants attested throughout the work do not detract in any way from this definition. At the centre of Tobit's religious thought stands the temple (1.4; cf. 13.10f.; 14.5 etc.). The problem of the observance of the food laws, which has already occupied us in the book of Daniel, is typical of the Judaism of the Hellenistic period, which was in contact with a paganism that was somewhat intolerant in this sphere; this was particularly the case with diaspora Judaism. The book is also distinguished by a firm personal piety (4.5) and a universalistic vision (13.13; 14.6); the law has marked ethical dimensions (2.11–14 etc.). There are a large number of prayers, contrary to what we find in the other books of the Old Testament (3.1–6, 16; 12.25, etc.).

BIBLIOGRAPHY

Commentaries
G. Priero, SacBib, 1953; R. Pautrel, JB, ²1957.
See also J. Gamberoni, *Die Auslegung des Buches Tobias*, Munich 1969; F. Vattioni, 'Studi e note sul libro di Tobia', *Aug* 10, 1970, 241–84.

§3b. J. T. Milik, 'La patrie de Tobie', *RB* 73, 1966, 522–30.

III

JUDITH

§1. *Character and content*

Judith is the name of the heroine of this book; by means of a violent act, which proves to be the only way out, she succeeds in saving her city from capture. Given such a theme, we shall not be surprised to find in the work nationalistic tendencies of the kind that we have already met in the book of Esther.

The book can be divided into three parts: (*a*) chs. 1–7; (*b*) 8.1–16.20; (*c*) 16.21–25.

(*a*) To begin with, we have a confused historical note: Nebuchadnezzar, king of Assyria (sic!), and Arphaxad, king of Media (1.1), are at war (1.5). Neither figure can be dated in any particular period, so we shall have to make a special study of their historicity in due course. Nebuchadnezzar occupies Media and then turns westwards, conquering a series of places which are for the most part unknown to us; only Israel puts up any resistance (chs. 4–7), having recently returned from captivity (4.3; 5.19). Holofernes, commander of the Assyrian troops, then attacks Israel with the aid of Edom and Moab and lays siege to Bethulia, succeeding in cutting off its water supply.

(*b*) Judith, a descendant of Jacob, chides her fellow-citizens for their lack of faith and their readiness to be sold into slavery to save themselves from the imminent danger (8.11–24). She has been a widow for three years, and is beautiful, pious and rich. She then prepares a plan to seduce Holofernes and goes to the camp of the besiegers accompanied by a servant girl who carries a basket containing ritually pure food, so as to avoid all contact with pagan fare. The general (ch. 12) is bewitched by the woman and holds a banquet for her; at the end, when they are alone, Judith succeeds in cutting his head off. She gives it to the servant girl, who carries it to Bethulia in the basket. The inhabitants then hang the head on the walls and attack the Assyrians, who are disconcerted by the disappearance of their commander and are defeated. Judith sings a hymn of praise for the victory.

(c) In the last part of the book Judith lives the life of a pious widow faithful to the memory of her dead husband.

§2. *Text, date and historicity*

Contemporary Catholic authors have no hesitation in admitting the obvious historical and geographical difficulties presented by the work, limiting themselves in general to giving more or less probable reasons for this disconcerting phenomenon. Some suggest textual corruption. On the other hand, we have other parallels in the Old Testament, even if they are not so obvious, in Esther, Daniel and Tobit (though, as we have seen, this last work makes no claim to historicity), which bear witness to an equally approximate or sometimes inaccurate knowledge of the events of a remote past. Jerome already supposed that this was a similar instance. The author evidently wants to describe events which he puts between the eighth and the sixth century in terms of his own time, presenting the whole affair as an allegory of the triumph of Israel, with God's help, over the assaults of the pagans.

The most obvious inaccuracies and inconsistencies in the historical sphere seem to be as follows (we indicate them following the basic study made by A.-M. Dubarle). First of all, there is the question of Nebuchadnezzar of Assyria and Arphaxad of Media in 1.1, then the presentation of the Babylonian exile as a past event in 4.3 and 5.19; the claims to divine honours made by these monarchs in 3.8 and 6.2 bring down the date of the work quite considerably, so that it cannot be before the time of the Diadochi (end of the fourth century). One explanation has been sought in a little-known episode of Persian history: towards 521, during the disorders which followed the death of Cambyses, a certain Arakha seized the throne of Babylon and on occupying it took the name of Nebuchadnezzar; for a short time he sought to reconquer the territories which belonged to the Babylonian empire, but was then swept away, along with many others, by Darius I Hystaspes. However, to associate the book with these somewhat obscure facts is a feeble basis for affirming its historicity. The Israeli scholar Y. M. Grintz has pointed out the parallels between the theme of the book and an episode which took place during the siege of Lindus, on the island of Rhodes, but here again the comparison is extremely weak. A more probable theory is that according to which the generals Holofernes and Bagoas are to be identified with the two generals sent against Phoenicia, Palestine and Egypt by Artaxerxes III towards 350. The names are certainly Persian, and are attested frequently, but there are many difficulties, unless we accept that Judith is a fictional account of one of the episodes in this campaign. Holofernes' itinerary in ch. 2 also seems impossible: he covers almost 300 miles in three days, passing through places which are either unknown, or absurd when they are known. No account is taken of the fact that an average of 100 miles a day is in any case excessive for an army consisting of infantry as well as cavalry. As we have seen, the identity of Bethulia is also unknown.

Until recently we had only a Greek LXX text known through B,A, ℵ, a codex connected with the Old Latin and the Syriac, and another independent codex. However, Jerome asserts that he translated from an Aramaic text, and this is not surprising, since the Greek text shows evident syntactical and stylistic characteristics of Hebrew and Aramaic, even if the biblical quotations are taken from LXX. Moreover, more or less extensive fragments of the Hebrew text of the work are in existence, and lesser fragments contained in quotations, commentaries, etc., which remained partially unknown until Dubarle's study. In his work he collected them together in a systematic form, succeeding in reconstructing the greater part of the Hebrew text. From this he demonstrated that the Hebrew was original in comparison with the translation. This was clearly an important step forward in textual criticism, even if it was of no consequence for the historical and geographical problems presented by the book.

§3. Message

It is impossible to reduce the message of Judith to purely nationalist categories, even if this feature is recognized to play a dominant part. For example, important elements of a religious and ethical character make an appearance, and they are by no means limited to the sphere of food regulations. God is presented in the book as omnipotent and omniscient, to such a degree that he knows of events before they take place (9.5f., where the Greek text, but not the others, uses the term *prognōsis*). He is just (5.15), but also full of compassion (7.20; 9.14). On the other hand, his help to Israel is not unconditional: in 8.25–27 he does not hesitate to present precise conditions to his people; the way in which he exercises judgment on his people is the traditional one of making their enemies triumph (5.18–20; 11.10–15).

Although the book is very interesting for the spiritual practices and problems of Israel at the time of the Maccabees, its historical and geographical inaccuracies and its novelistic character fully justify the perplexity which there has been over its status. It was never admitted to the Hebrew canon, and in the Catholic Church the discussion over its place in the Christian canon lasted in effect down to the Council of Trent.

BIBLIOGRAPHY

Commentary
A. Barucq, JB, [2]1959.

§1. Y. M. Grintz, *The Book of Judith. A Reconstruction of the Original Hebrew Text*, Jerusalem 1957 (Hebrew, English summary); A.-M. Dubarle, *Judith*, Rome 1966; id., 'L'authenticité des textes hébreux de Judith', *Bibl* 50, 1969, 187–221.

ADDITIONS TO PROTO-CANONICAL BOOKS

§1. *Additions to Esther*

The Alexandrian canon provides additions to the books of Esther and Daniel. We shall begin with the former.

(*a*) *Character and content.* In this case also the textual situation is complicated by the presence of several recensions. The LXX in its various uncial and minuscule codices, the fragments of Origen's Hexapla, the versions of Hesychius and Lucian, and the text of Josephus, *Antt.* XI, 6.1ff. = §§ 184ff., between them offer at least five different recensions, all of which however agree in presenting a total of about 107 verses more than the Hebrew text. In the Greek text they appear in their proper context: before 1.1; after 3.13; 4.17; 8.12; 10.3; and at the end of the book. However, Jerome put them all in an appendix to the book because he considered them controversial in terms of the canon; the modern Catholic Bibles tend to follow the LXX order and the numbering of the Massoretic text.

We have the following passages:

(i) Mordecai's dream (11.2–12.6), through which he discovers a plot against the king of Persia by the eunuchs. He denounces them and receives a reward, but incurs the enmity of high Persian officials.

(ii) The edict of Artaxerxes (13.1–7), for the extermination of Jews accused of disturbing the peace of the realm.

(iii) Mordecai's (13.8–18) and Esther's prayer (14.1–19);

(iv) Esther appears before the king (15.1–16; Vulgate, vv. 4–19);

(v) Decree for the rehabilitation of Israel (ch. 16);

(vi) Mordecai recognizes that his aim has been achieved (10.4–13), followed by a colophon which ends the work (11.1).

(*b*) *Literary problems.* Without going into the problem posed by the variants of the Greek text, we must note that of the relationship between the Greek and the Hebrew text: it is immediately evident that we have two substantially different narratives about the same event. The purpose of the additions seems evident: in a context in which Esther ran the risk of not being accepted in the canon because of its nationalistic approach and its lack of theological elements, the additions seek to remedy the situation by supplying what is absent from the work: prayers, a theological approach to particular problems, and so on. Furthermore, they set out to demonstrate the historicity of the narrative by attaching documents to the text which are meant to enhance the positive impression caused by the addition of theological elements.

The scholar is faced with three principal problems:

1. Were the additions originally composed in a Semitic language, Hebrew or Aramaic, and if so, to what extent?

2. Are they contemporary with or later than the proto-canonical text?

3. Finally, do they have any relationship, other than that described, with the original text, or are they completely independent of it?

Until about a century ago, the most widespread view among Protestant scholars was that the additions were originally composed in Greek and were therefore later than the Hebrew text. However, according to the studies by Wellhausen, Nöldeke, Cheyne and Torrey, the sections referred to above as (i), (iii), (iv) and (vi) are certainly translations of a Hebrew or Aramaic original, while (ii) and (v), that is, the edicts, were originally composed in Greek, the diplomatic language of the time. Authors are still divided over the antiquity of the additions: among Catholic scholars it is commonly argued that the additions are more or less contemporaneous with the proto-canonical text, whereas Torrey sees the Massoretic text as no more than the summary of what was originally a much more extensive original Greek text, some of which has been preserved in the deutero-canonical additions; this Greek text would in turn have been the translation of a Semitic original which had also been lost. The position over the additions, then, is quite complicated, and is difficult to resolve in the present state of research. In any case, the most widespread opinion continues to be that the additions are later than the proto-canonical text.

(c) *The aim of the additions is also their message.* As we have seen, the proto-canonical book does not mention the name of God once, nor is it very concerned with Jewish belief; these elements appear continually in the additions. It is therefore easy for those who defend the need to read Esther with the additions to show that without them the book would be theologically void and its presence within the canon incongruous, to say the least. But notwithstanding the presence of these theological elements, the additions, like the Hebrew text, have a strongly nationalistic attitude which is also projected on to almost a cosmic plane, in this way far transcending the original dispute between Mordecai and Haman. They thus become a kind of anti-Gentile manifesto, carrying on a discourse which we have seen to be extremely problematical in itself. This is probably the reason why they were not admitted into the Hebrew canon, despite the theological element, which admirably completes what is lacking in the proto-canonical Esther.

§2. *Additions to Daniel*

(*a*) *Introduction and content.* Like Esther, in the Alexandrian canon Daniel has some additions which have been transmitted in the LXX and the translation of Theodotion (or Symmachus, according to the recent theory mentioned above) which supplanted the LXX. There are three additions, but they give five different compositions, depending on the Greek text which we use; unlike the additions to Esther, they have no theological value of their own. They are: (*a*) The Prayer of Azariah (3.24–45, EVV vv. 1–22); (*b*) The Song of the Three Young Men in the Furnace (3.52–90, EVV vv. 29–68); (*c*) The stories of Susanna and Bel and the Dragon (chs. 13;14). In Theodotion (or Symmachus) Susanna precedes the text, and the variants between the two Greek versions are remarkable.

(*b*) *Content.* The Prayer of Azariah is preceded by an introduction which shows how the three young men are placed in the furnace and then how Azariah, one of the three, sings a hymn in which he praises God for his justice, confesses his sin and that of his people, and ends by expressing trust in the Lord. The Song of the Three Young Men, which appears in the same context, is also preceded by an introduction, which describes how the king's servants continually fed the flames; in their midst, however, the young men sang a song which later entered Christian liturgy as the Benedicite, a liturgical invitation to all creation to praise and bless God. The story of Susanna has different connotations depending on the recension of the text. In Theodotion we have Joachim, a rich Jew living in Babylon, married to the pious and chaste Susanna. During a feast two young Jews come to her husband's house and, after seeing her walking in the garden, become infatuated with her. One day while she is bathing in the pool in the garden, they surprise her and try to seduce her under the threat that if she refuses she will be charged with adultery. The woman prefers to be accused of adultery, and the court, in view of the social position of her accusers, believes them and not her. However, Daniel intervenes under divine inspiration, interrogates the accusers and succeeds in confounding them. According to the law recorded in Deut. 19.18ff., in the rigorist interpretation of the first century BC, the two are condemned to death, while the family praises God who has made justice triumph through Daniel. Daniel comes out of the affair with his prestige markedly enhanced by the position he has adopted. As we have indicated, the variants in the LXX text are remarkable: the two elders had been elected judges and regularly frequented Joachim's house where they became infatuated with his wife. One night they sought to rape her, but she resisted them, preferring their threats to dishonour. Brought before the assembly of the synagogue she was humiliated and would certainly have been condemned had not Daniel intervened; from this point on, the narrative continues more or less as in Theodotion.

In the story of Bel and the Dragon in Theodotion we in fact find two narratives: in one Daniel is asked by Cyrus, Astyages' successor (cf. Herodotus I, 130, but there is a good deal of uncertainty here) to prostrate himself before the god Bel. Naturally, Daniel refuses, since, as he explains to the king, it is an image of clay. When the king objects that the deity eats and that therefore Daniel's explanation cannot be true, Daniel lays a trap in the temple where the statue is, and by this means is able to prove to the king that the offerings are being consumed by the priests, not by the deity. The sanctuary is destroyed and the priests are put to death. In the second story the Babylonians worship a dragon, but Daniel refuses to join them. He kills it, but as a penalty for his misdeed he is thrown into a lions' den where the lions have been deliberately starved for seven days. However, God sends a certain Habakkuk to bring them food. The lions do not touch Daniel and the king praises God for the miracle. In the LXX the content is the same, but in the first episode Daniel is a priest and is accompanied by the king of Babylon.

(c) *Text, problems and date.* In his preface to Daniel, Jerome (Migne, PL 28, 1291) affirms that the LXX departed considerably from the 'Hebrew truth', praising the church for having preferred Theodotion's version. We are also made aware of this preference of the early church by the fact that Theodotion seems to be used at the end of the first century AD by Clement of Rome.

The Song of the Three Young Men belongs in the same literary genres as those represented in the Psalter, and the general opinion is that it is a translation of a Hebrew or Aramaic original. The story of Susanna, which R. H. Pfeiffer somewhat irreverently but aptly compared with a detective story, in all probability echoes the content of a popular tale, adapted by Israel to its beliefs and used to celebrate divine omniscience and conjugal virtue. Julius Africanus (Migne, PG 11, 44f.) already expressed his doubts on the Hebrew origin of the story in a letter to Origen, since it is full of word-plays which are only possible in Greek. However, the question has yet to be resolved. Of course it is futile to discuss its historicity, given the novelistic character of the narratives and the liturgical character of the poetical compositions, or to consider its relationship with the proto-canonical book of Daniel.

The story of Bel and the dragon tends to ridicule paganism, showing that pagan worship primarily served particular well-determined interests. In the second story, we have no evidence of any cult of this kind, while the narrative fits in well with the novelistic theme of the brave young man who kills a monster and which is already attested in Sumeria (one variant has a damsel who is threatened by the monster, cf. the story of St George).

BIBLIOGRAPHY

The Catholic commentaries on Esther and Daniel include sections dealing with the additions.

§2. J. Schüpphaus, 'Das Verhältnis von LXX- und Theodotion-Text in den apokryphen Zusätzen zum Danielbuch', ZAW 83, 1971, 49–73.

IV

THE WISDOM OF SOLOMON

§1. *Character and content*

The book which bears this title (in Latin simply *Sapientia*) belongs to Hebrew wisdom literature, as the title itself indicates, although no Semitic original has come down to us. The principal argument of the book is that there is no wisdom without justice, which only comes from God. Therefore the work is presented as an exhortation directed by 'Solomon' to pagans, first of all to seek wisdom, and to seek where it is to be found. They will receive great benefits from it because (*a*) it brings salvation to pious Jews (chs. 1–5); (*b*) it is divine in essence, so that kings cannot do better than to follow it (chs. 6–9). Finally, (*c*) the history of Israel shows sufficiently that wisdom brings blessings to Israel and calamities to the Gentiles (chs. 10–19). The attribution of the work to Solomon indicates that it is a pseudonymous book.

§2. *Principal problems*

The principal problems presented by the book are: (*a*) the original language in which it was written; (*b*) its authorship, or at least the circle from which it comes; (*c*) the place and date of composition; (*d*) its aim and therefore its ideological content. We shall examine each of these in turn.

(*a*) At least in the view of those who attributed the work to Solomon (who certainly did not write in Greek), the original language of Wisdom would seem to have been the Hebrew of the classical period. On the other hand, traditions handed down by the Muratorian canon and by Origen, Jerome and Augustine among the church fathers, contrast with the theory of an original Hebrew text. Jerome in particular insisted on the Hellenistic character of the work, especially as regards the book's oratory. In passing, we might point out that this is probably the first case of the application to a biblical book of the method of the history of literary genres. Practically all scholars, even in conservative circles, agree that the book should not be attributed to Solomon, while a linguistic examination of the work also rules out with a reasonable margin of certainty that its original language might have been Hebrew or Aramaic. There are too many technical terms and expressions typical of the world of Hellenistic philosophy for one to be able to conjecture that Wisdom was originally written in a Semitic language. It might be conceded that in ch. 1 we still have the relics of a translation of some kind, but the treatment has been so free that the final result is very far removed from the archetype.

(b) *Authorship and division of the book*. The divisions indicated at the beginning of this chapter are the most logical ones, although it is also possible to put forward others. However, the book presents a literary and ideological continuity which indicates a single author or redactor; this theory is confirmed by a remarkable uniformity of style. It is perhaps possible to reconstruct Palestinian characteristics in chs. 1–5 and more Alexandrian characteristics in chs. 6–19, with nationalistic elements in the first half and universalistic elements in the second, but if this statement can be supported, it may be explained by the fact that the first part is directed to Israelites and the second to Gentiles. Such a unitary character is certainly rare in Hebrew wisdom, and it recalls, rather, a Western philosophical tractate. We therefore have here a feature which indicates that Wisdom may derive from 'the Hellenistic Jewish diaspora. Of course, the author may have been a Jew who was assimilated to his environment but familiar with the Jewish wisdom tradition and the mentality and the customs of the surrounding peoples, and also driven by a strong desire to convert his non-Jewish audience to Judaism.

(c) *The place and date of composition* are thus indicated almost automatically. If the original language is Greek, it is improbable, though not impossible, that the work was composed in Palestine. (The LXX fragments discovered at Qumran and part of the correspondence of Bar Cochba from the first half of the second century AD bear witness to the use of Greek in the Holy Land, even in quite nationalistic groups, but the content, style and thought of the work do not suggest Palestinian Jewish circles.) Rather, everything indicates that the place of origin of Wisdom is Alexandrian Judaism, which was so well assimilated in languages and ideas to its setting (the most famous example is Philo of Alexandria, who lived in the first half of the first century AD; Wisdom does not show knowledge of his work). We may thus date the book about the first half of the first century BC.

(d) *Ideology*. We have drawn attention to the fact that the author makes use of terms and expressions which recur in Hellenistic philosophy at the end of the first millennium BC. We find them in 7.22, 24; 11.17; 14.3; 16.21; 17.2; 19.2, and in other passages where they are less obvious. The orientation of the book reveals strong Platonic, neo-Platonic and Stoic influences. On the other hand, an examination of it shows that although the author took over philosophical concepts typical of his time, he was not a philosopher and did not have a creative mind; rather, he seems to have been a brilliant popularizer of philosophical concepts, which are expressed in affirmations taken from the proto-canonical Old Testament. This is another feature which is typical of the educated diaspora Jew, especially in our case, where the aim of the book is the conversion of Gentiles. In 7.22–30 we have a description of wisdom in terms which we might feel to reflect a form of primitive gnosticism; in 8.7, on the other hand, we have a presentation of the four cardinal virtues.

When the author discusses scientific or philosophical themes, he seems to opt for poetic forms rather than for a precise terminology, and here we find a limit to what was said above about the use of technical terms; these are also used in an often uncritical and indiscriminate way. This is another feature which indicates that the author is not a philosopher. Sometimes we find omissions, as in 7.1–6 when he speaks only of the human body; at other times he takes over Neo-Platonic concepts in an uncritical way: in 8.19f. that of the pre-existence of the soul, in 9.15 the idea that the body 'weighs down' the soul. In 2.23 we have an interpretation of Gen. 1.26 which does not accord completely with the original; in LXX ᴮᴬℵ, we have here 'an image of his own nature' (*idiotētos*), and elsewhere 'of his own eternity' (*aidiotētos*), which comes very close to Philo's doctrine in *De opificio mundi* 13. Hebrew Sheol has now simply become Hades, and exists only to punish the wicked (2.1ff.).

The points described in § 1 above in fact serve three aims: (i) They confirm Jewish believers in their faith and make it more profound. (ii) They restore to these Jews what they have lost. (iii) Finally, they convert the Gentiles by showing them the absurdity of their religion.

To begin with the first aim: it seems that the author is addressing Jews whose hopes have been shattered. They have lived much of their lives in an oppressive and difficult environment, sometimes leading to open persecution; they have often been saddened and sometimes dismayed by the prosperity in which the Gentiles or the wicked have been living, a prosperity which has cast doubt on the reality of divine justice. The author deals with these problems on either an individual or an ethnic and collective level, by examining the past and the present, to develop a theory which he takes up in 1.13–16, based essentially on the argument that God, whose sovereignty over the world is beyond question, is also just and merciful (11.23 and 12.15–18). This is a line of argument with which we are also familiar from the proto-canonical Old Testament. The author does not seem to take account of the hypothesis of a conflict between divine omnipotence and divine justice, at this point proving himself to have a less developed sensibility than that of Job. In this context suffering can appear as a trial (3.4–6), with the aim of purification and spiritual progress, a kind of divine education of the believer (12.2 and 16.5–13). Basically (the author's argument runs), Israel has been punished relatively little compared e.g. with Egypt (11.6ff.; 12.20–22), and moreover (as is shown by a series of examples from Adam to Moses), goodness and right conduct in this life unfailingly receive their reward, while wickedness is punished (ch. 10). Here, too, the range of problems considered by the author is much less developed than that in the book of Job: almost as if the book of Job had never existed, he returns to the wisdom concept of a just and right order of the universe, without taking into account either the possibility that this concept may not prove capable of validation from the facts, or the irrational element which lies at the root of relationships between God and man. Moreover, what are material goods like riches, a long life, children, and so on, compared with virtue and wisdom (4.1–9)? The author also does not seem to be aware of the problems considered in Ecclesiastes.

Finally, one typical feature of Israelite wisdom elsewhere is a lack of interest in the hope of Israel and the great themes of its past history: as we have seen, these themes are absent from the wisdom which is directed essentially to Israel; think of it here, where those to whom the message is addressed are Gentiles!

As for retribution, this befalls the individual rather than the community, as in Joel (cf. 4.20–5.1); no direct statement is made about the resurrection, but 4.18ff. seem to exclude it for the wicked.

The second aim of the work is, as we saw, to restore the faith of apostate or indifferent Israelites. The author begins by posing the question 'What must I do to obtain eternal life?' There seems to be an answer to the question in 15.3: a man can gain immortality only if he knows God and does his will. Here, too, the argument adopted is of a philosophical kind: it has an ontological character in 13.1ff., cf. Plato, *Timaeus* 27d, where we find the theme of the builder who, being immortal, is also the source of immortality (12.1; cf. 6.19 and again Plato, *Timaeus* 29e–30b). Of course, it is not possible to claim that Wisdom is dependent on the *Timaeus*, but in any case it seems to know the *Timaeus* well, including its cosmogony. On the other hand, the author of Wisdom differs from Plato (and comes close to Philo's position) when he admits as a good Israelite that miracle can change the natural order of things, even if, again in the wake of Plato, he knows the concept of the harmony of creation (19.18). Wisdom, too, poses the problem of evil and its origin, but it not only fails to provide a solution, but even arrives at a contradictory position: on the one hand it accepts the Platonic concept of the evil of matter (9.15), and on the other a variant of the traditional Hebrew view (Gen. 3) that evil came into the world 'through the envy of the devil' (2.24). This is the earliest attempt known to us to explain the origin of the serpent in demonic terms, a theory which is later taken up by the New Testament.

Finally, the author seeks to convert the pagans. Deutero-Isaiah (40.17–20; 41.6f.; 44.9–20) had directed all his irony towards the cult of idols, interpreting the effigies, in a crudely materialistic way, as identical with the person of the deity worshipped. Few pagans would have recognized themselves in this form of worship, which in any case is so easy to demolish; all the more so, since many ancient thinkers showed all their scorn for what they considered to be the product of superstitious popular piety. Wisdom discusses the problem in chs. 13–15, beginning with the general question of worship of this kind and ending in 13.11–19 with the grosser forms of idolatry (following Isa. 44). We have already commented on this kind of argument above (cf. Part Four, ch. II, §4a). In 14.15ff. the author attributes this idolatrous worship to a twofold love, that of a father towards his dead son and that of the people for a distant king. This theory is reminiscent of the views put forward by Euhemerus of Messene (a place in the Peloponnese, or Messina in Sicily) in his *Hiera anagraphē*: Euhemerus in fact argued that the origin of the worship of the gods was to be sought in the veneration of rulers or deceased wise men. The argument, which despite its rationalistic and psychologizing features is obviously simplistic, was also used in the early Christian church by the Apostolic Fathers of the second century in their polemic against the pagans, probably on the basis of Wisdom. However, it has no foundation in the history of religion. The worst taunts are directed against theriomorphic Egyptian polytheism in 15.14–19, but here again many educated pagans would have taken the side of the author, among them Plutarch, Cicero and Horace.

However, the comparison with Deutero-Isaiah is only formal. The author is not interested in the *berît* on which Israel still based its relationship with Yahweh in the post-exilic period; he is more interested in wisdom, which is defined in 7.22ff. by a list of twenty-one characteristics in a form which is as prolix as it is systematically inadequate.

BIBLIOGRAPHY

Commentaries
J. Fichtner, HAT, 1938; E. Osty, JB, ²1957; J. Reider, New York 1957. Cf. also C. Larcher, *Études sur le livre de la Sagesse*, Paris 1969.

§2a. For the view that the translator of Ecclesiasticus was also the author of Wisdom cf. C. Romaniuk, 'Le traducteur du livre de Jésus ben Sira n'est-il pas l'auteur du livre de la Sagesse?', *RBibl* 15, 1967, 163–70; G. Scarpat, 'Ancora sull'autore del Libro della Sapienza', *RBibl* 15, 1967, 171–89; C. Romaniuk, 'More about the Author of the Book of Wisdom – an Answer to G. Scarpat', *RBibl* 15, 1967, 543–54.

§2d. For the relation with Greek and Hellenistic philosophy see S. Lange, 'The Wisdom of Solomon and Plato', *JBL* 55, 1936, 293–302; J. M. Reese, *Hellenistic Influences upon the Book of Wisdom and its Consequences*, Rome 1970. For faith as understood in the book cf. C. A. Keller, 'Glaube in der "Weisheit Salomos"', in H.-J. Stoebe et al. (ed.), *Wort – Gebot – Glaube. W. Eichrodt zum 80. Geburtstag*, Zurich 1970, 11–20.

V

ECCLESIASTICUS, OR THE WISDOM OF JESUS BEN SIRACH

§1. *Character and content*

Ecclesiasticus is the only book of the Old Testament about whose author we can be certain, although his name has not been handed down clearly. There are variant forms of the title: Simeon, son of Jesus called *ben Sīrā'*; or Simeon, son of Jesus, son of Eleazar *ben Sīrā'*; or also, in the Talmud, the book or instruction of *Ben Sīrā'*. Another feature of the work is that we have a good deal of it in the original Hebrew: fragments were found principally in 1896, then in 1931, in 1955 at Qumran and in 1964 at Masada, the fortified palace on the western side of the Dead Sea. This solves the problem of the original language of the work: it is a late form of Hebrew, the forms of which are particularly interesting for the study of Hebrew grammar.

The book presents a series of sayings composed in the style of proto-canonical Proverbs, with which in many cases it shows a marked relationship; unlike the Wisdom of Solomon, it thus has a fragmentary character and does not allow obvious classifications. The book itself gives its date as the beginning of the second century BC, and the preface dates its translation into Greek about fifty years later. In a recent and painstaking piece of textual criticism, H. P. Rüger has argued for the existence of a first Hebrew recension written in late Hebrew and very close in content to the Greek translation of the work, made in Alexandria towards 130 BC; and of a second Hebrew recension written in a language close to that of the Mishnah, connected with the Syriac translation and forming the basis of a number of later Greek variants attested for the first time in Clement of Alexandria. The Syriac translation was made later on the basis of these two texts. It is interesting to note that the text resulting from this last operation in some cases resembles that of the Targum.

The present text is thus the product of rather a complex literary process and is certainly removed from the original intentions of the author.

We find many quotations from or allusions to Ecclesiasticus in the New Testament, especially in the Epistle of James.

The work can be divided into two parts. In the first (chs. 1–23), we find to begin with a celebration of wisdom, which in all cases is given by God (1.11, cf. 1.16). In 2.1–4.10 there is praise of the virtues connected with it: patience, humility, mercy, trust in God and obedience to his commandments, filial piety, solidarity with the poor, and so on; in 4.11–6.17 we have a series of instructions from a wise man or from wisdom itself, the promise of reward after trials have been undergone, and various pieces of practical advice. 6.18–8.7 describes the best way of finding wisdom, by avoiding wickedness and following some advice on the company to keep (advice which is also important from a social point of view). 9.17–11.19 is directed to the rich and powerful, exhorting them to use the power which they derive from their social position justly, and to make good use of their money. 14.20–15.20 delivers a eulogy on wisdom, while 16.1–18.14 presents the doctrine of God the Creator with some examples drawn from biblical history. In 18.15–20.26 we have a series of counsels on love, foresight and self-control. 20.27–23.28 contrasts the wise man and the fool, the righteous and the sinner.

The second part (chs. 24–50) begins with an account of wisdom by herself (24.1ff.); she is identified with the 'law of Moses' (24.22). Chapters 25–26 deal with the theme of marriage, and in 26.29–29.28. we have an exhortation to honesty and prudence in word and deed. 30.1–32.13 discusses the education of children, health and manners, especially at banquets; 32.14–33.18 gives advice about how to find wisdom. 33.19–36.17 instructs heads of families about various themes: the administration of a patrimony, true piety (cf. 34.18–25, etc.). 36.18–38.23 deals with some difficulties in which a man might find himself; in such cases, however, he is aided by wife, children, friends, the counsellor, the wise man, the doctor and so on. 38.1–15 discusses the interesting theological problem of the relationship between the doctor's cure and faith in God: which of the two is it better to trust? The reply is similar to that given by James 5.14 in the New Testament: the divine wisdom enlightens the doctor and gives him his gifts; therefore the two positions are complementary. 38.24–39.35 praises the scribe, whose profession is the most noble of all, whereas 40.1–41.33 considers suffering and death. In 41.14–42.14 we have considerations on shame, whether it is justified or not, a text which ends in 42.15ff. with a song of praise to God for the virtue of which the fathers have given proof. We have a list of the fathers in 44.1ff., followed by a mention of the last legitimate high priest, Simeon II son of Jonathan (50.1). The book ends with praise to God (ch.51).

§2. Authorship

Jesus, son or grandson of *Sīrā'* (also written *Sīrāḥ*), lived in Jerusalem at the beginning of the second century BC and composed his book towards 180 BC. We can infer this from the praise of Simeon II mentioned above. Simeon seems to have died before the work was finished, though in LXX 50.1ff. he still seems to be alive. Flavius Josephus, *Antt.*XII, 2.5 = §43, cf. XII, 4.1 = §157, mentions a Simeon I, 'the Just', who lived about 300 BC, while in *Antt.*XII, 4.10 = §227 and 5.1 = §238 he mentions a Simeon II whose son, Onias III, was deposed by Antiochus IV Epiphanes at the beginning of the anti-Jewish persecution which led to the Maccabaean revolt (cf. II Macc.3;4). Simeon II lived some time after 200 BC and also bore the title 'the Just', cf. Mishnah, *Aboth* 1, 2; Eusebius of Caesarea, *Dem.Ev.*VIII, 2.71; Jerome, *Comm.in.Dan.* 9. (Migue, PL 25, 545). For the identification of Simeon with Simeon II the information given by the Greek translator of the work, the grandson of the author, is decisive. He is writing towards 132 BC (the thirty-eighth year 'of king Euergetes', who is almost certainly Ptolemy VII Euergetes), which obviously rules out a date earlier than the end of the third or the beginning of the second century BC, and obliges us to take the Simeon whom it mentions as the second of that name. Antiochus IV and his persecutions are not yet mentioned in the work, so that its composition can certainly be put in the time before his ascent of the throne.

Ben Sirach also gives some information about his identity and his work. In 51.23 he makes propaganda for his school, inviting the ignorant to join it; it is in fact possible to acquire wisdom 'without money' (51.25); on the other hand, the charges of the school seem to have been quite high. According to 51.28, the author can say, 'Get instruction with a large sum of silver, and you will gain by it much gold'. In other words, the price is high, but it's worth it! In 51.29 we have an interesting variation between the Greek and Hebrew texts; whereas the former read: 'And your spirit will delight in his (viz. God's) help', the Hebrew has, 'And I will rejoice *byšybty'*, a term which can be translated 'in my *yešibāh'*, a term which from then on has been used to denote the seminary-school of pious Jews. Given the nature of the terms, it is not unreasonable to suppose that the members of the school belonged to the ruling class in Jerusalem, the only ones who would be able to pay. This confirms what we have already seen in connection with wisdom in general (above Part Five, ch. II, §3).

The definition of wisdom which the author gives throughout the work is interesting: in the words of R. Smend Sr, the first editor of the Hebrew fragments, 'subjectively wisdom is the fear of God, and objectively the law of Moses'.

In 51.13ff. we have a somewhat confused account of the author's past life of study. For Ben Sirach, the ideal of life is expressed in 38.24–39.11: to be a scribe and to have enough to be able to devote oneself full-time to that work without being preoccupied and without having to work elsewhere. The traditional rabbinic ideal is rather different: every wise man has to work, to carry on a trade or a profession, as well as being occupied with wisdom. This is still attested in Paul's remarks in I Cor. 4.12 and in the early church (cf. Didache 12.3, where the maxim holds, 'Those who do not work do not eat'). At heart the ideal put forward by Ben Sirach is Hellenistic rather than Jewish (and this explains the difficulties encountered by Paul when living in a Hellenistic community). In Jewish belief, manual labour and work of other kinds has always been held in high honour, in contrast to the views of the surrounding world.

Be that as it may, Ben Sirach succeeds in remaining faithful to his ideal. Moreover, he shows a good knowledge of traditional wisdom, both Hebrew and Near Eastern, and perhaps also of the Greek language. This is so much the case that some scholars have thought to detect echoes of quotations of Euripides and Theognis in the text; if this is the case, their value is not so much cultural as proverbial, in that they constitute material known by all.

In 1.22–24 we have what is perhaps a polemical phrase directed against the Hellenizers in Jerusalem, whose attitude was probably one of the reasons why Antiochus IV believed that he could import Hellenism into Israel; in 30.18f. the author attacks idolatry, and in 34.1–8 prophecy and the interpretation of dreams. Here too, then, he is completely within the milieu of the orthodox Judaism of his time.

§3. Message

(a) *Faith.* Jesus ben Sirach knows of salvation on both the individual and the collective level, and follows the terminology introduced by Deuteronomy and Deutero-Isaiah; moreover, this will be the basis of Jewish resistance to Hellenistic attempts at spiritual and cultural assimilation. 17.17 attests both his patriotism and his universalism, which he bases on Deut. 32.8; however, he does not quote this according to the Massoretic text, but according to the important LXX variant which is also attested in a Qumran text. This has 'sons of God' instead of 'sons of Israel'; the latter reading does not make any sense. The Gentiles are often condemned (50.25), especially when they oppress Israel (36.1–10; cf. 35.18–20); the author's love of Jerusalem and of the land of his ancestors also appears throughout the work (24.10ff.; 36.14).

Whether or not Ben Sirach knew of the synagogue is a disputed question: it is perhaps mentioned in 39.6, while the term in Greek in 24.23 probably refers to the assembly generally.

There is strong interest in the temple and its worship, and here the author is notably different from his predecessors (cf. 24.10–15; 36.12–17). In the description of Simeon the Just, there is probably a mention of the Day of Atonement (cf. 50.11); the priests are called 'sons of Aaron' in ch. 51. Notwithstanding these references, it seems that worship and ritual are a secondary element for the author, who sees their importance as being in the realm of tradition. Sacrifice offered by the wicked is openly condemned (34.18–26; 35.11–20); observance of the law and the demands of mercy, moreover, are as good as sacrifice (35.1–3; cf. 17.11–27). Prayer appears as the expression of the author's mind (23.1–6; 36.1ff., etc.). The fulfilment of the law occupies a central place in Ben Sirach's piety. He seems to know a concept of resurrection, but often speaks of Sheol (14.16; 17.27; 28.21). The doctrine of divine rewards and punishments, which the author knows well, is nicely oriented on the life to come, according to the best Hebrew tradition, whether on an individual or a collective level (11.14; 16.6; cf. 1.11–13, etc.).

Monotheism is now accepted as a given fact in Israel, but at the same time it is proclaimed with vigour, perhaps in polemic against the Hellenistic world. Israel is the elect people of Yahweh (45.19ff. and chs. 48;49, where the concept is expressed in praise of the fathers of old); the power and majesty of God are proclaimed in 16.26–18.14.

(b) *The law.* We have already made several references to the importance of the *tōrāh* (traditionally translated 'law') in Ben Sirach's message. He does not yet know it in the rabbinic sense of the term as a written and oral revelation of God's teaching and will, though it often has a sense which goes beyond the bounds of the Pentateuch. In 39.1f. he mentions the law, the prophets and wisdom, cited in parallel form, but as a technical term he speaks of 'the Law which Moses commanded us' (24.23; cf. 45.5). As in Chronicles, there is no definite proof that in these instances the author meant to refer to the Pentateuch, but this does seem probable. Ben Sirach is also a witness to the tendency to attach to scripture the oral tradition which was later to be codified in the Mishnah; this is one of the elements which appear in New Testament polemic against the Judaism of the time. This tendency has only just begun to appear with him, and for want of a systematic study of the theme it is enough to cite an example. One of the earliest traditional prohibitions was against pronouncing the divine name of Yahweh; the only exception to this was the high priest during the blessing in the temple on the Day of Atonement (cf. Mishnah, Yoma 6,2; Sotah 7,6). There is also provision for other instances in which the divine name can be pronounced, but there is no definition of blasphemy here or elsewhere. Now in 50.22 we have a blessing which is very clear in Hebrew: ʿattā bārᵉkūnā' 'et Y. . . . (cf. the abbreviation of the name), whereas in the Greek text we simply have *toi theoi*, a translation of the name by a title. In 23.9 the author criticizes the misuse of the name, especially in oaths, a tendency which returns in the New Testament.

Thus in the application and the fulfilment of the law the accent is more on the ethical element than on the ritual element, cf. 17.17ff., a passage in which we have a kind of summary of the law like those which will later be given by Jesus and some masters of late Judaism like Hillel and Akiba.

(c) As in the rest of Hebrew wisdom literature, wisdom is essentially directed towards everyday life, with the qualification discussed above, that *tōrāh* and wisdom coincide (24.23f.). Such a convergence did not come about in other wisdom literature, and we have had occasion to show how, in these works, Hebrew wisdom moved more in the milieu of international wisdom than in a specifically Israelite context. We may therefore attribute to Ben Sirach an attempt at synthesis, intended to bring Hebrew wisdom into the sphere of orthodoxy instead of leaving it on the periphery of Israelite faith.

The author asks his pupils and hearers not to seek to investigate too far; despite this, he shows remarkable openness towards the problems of the universe (3.23ff.). His anthropology is expressed in a strange tension between optimism and pessimism as regards human nature, a tension which is never resolved: man is 'dust' (33.10), his life is 'flesh and blood' (i.e. humanity, without any participation in the divine nature, 17.31), and death makes him 'dust and ashes' (10.9–17). Man's life goes quickly and is soon over (18.7; 17.2), that is, apart from some privileged figures like Enoch and Elijah. Survival in Sheol is terrible, according to the best traditions not only of Judaism but of the ancient Near East (14.16; 17.27ff.), even if it has its good side for the infirm and the afflicted. An optimistic note appears in the affirmation that God has created man in his own image, giving him power and lordship over creation (17.1ff.) and a free judgment (15.11ff.); on the other hand, the world is fundamentally good (39.16ff.). Throughout the work we hear an exhortation to man to be content with what he has.

This is the starting point for the practical advice about order, the family, honesty, mercy, a sense of responsibility, which appear throughout the work. As throughout the ancient Near East and also in Israel, the perspective is typically masculine (cf. Prov. 31.1ff.); the view is that of a man understood as the patriarchal master of his family. The utilitarian theme which we have seen to be so important in the author's thought underlies his social ethics (cf. 16.1–6; 30.1–6; 11.29). There are a number of egotistic themes in the discussion of the problem of money; as well as knowing its value, the author throughout the work gives advice about the way to become rich, but at the same time exhorts his readers not to take too much account of riches. Health, for example, is better than riches (30.14ff.), while the wise man can attain a good social position even without being rich himself (10.30–11.1); the love of money can also cause ruin (11.10–13; 31.5ff.). On the other hand, an unregulated life can soon destroy a considerable inheritance (9.6; 18.32–19.1). These are questions which do not have a particular theological or ethical value, but which are simply a matter of common sense.

(d) For Ben Sirach ethical norms derive from the divine will, a principle by which he puts himself in the tradition of prophetic preaching (2.15–17; 15.11–13; 32.14; 35.3–5). This will is revealed to man by means of the tōrāh (2.16); thus to love and honour God is the same as to observe the commandments (cf. 10.19; 17.14).

We have seen that Ben Sirach accepts man's free will (15.15–17) and stresses his responsibility. On the other hand, as we have seen, man is also dust and ashes (17.27). All men are sinners and therefore guilty (8.5); they are 'flesh and blood' (17.26), but they are also free. As in many biblical writers, the tension between free will and determination is not resolved. Similarly, there is no solution to the problems of theodicy and the nature of man. Sin appears as voluntary transgression; involuntary sin is deemed irrelevant to the author's ethical scheme. He too knows the doctrine of reward and punishment, as we have already seen (35.12ff.).

§4. *Text and style*

In the first section we examined the character of the Hebrew text and saw what an advantage it was to us to have a considerable part of it. The complexity of its transmission is an indication that the work was not considered canonical in Israel, a reason why when studying the text it is necessary to keep an eye on the Hebrew, the Greek and the Syriac.

The theme of the work is within the sphere of the thought of the proto-canonical books but is original; one new element is to be found in the negative evaluation of work, which (as we have seen) is a feature of Hellenistic origin. Had it not been for the chronological limits imposed on the Palestinian canon, it is probable that Sirach would have found a place there, given its extremely high theological and ethical level.

BIBLIOGRAPHY

On the Hebrew text
R. Smend, *Die Weisheit des Jesus Sirach*, Berlin 1906; M. Z. Segal, *Sēfer ben-Sirā' haššālēm*, Jerusalem ²1959; F. Vattioni, *Ecclesiastico*, Naples 1968 (the extant Hebrew, together with Greek, Latin and Syriac versions).

Commentaries (in addition to the above):
H. Duesberg and P. Auvray, JB, ²1958; H. Duesberg and I. Fransen, SacBib, 1966.

§1. For textual criticism see H. P. Rüger, *Text und Textform im hebräischen Sirach*, BZAW 112, 1970.
§2. There is dispute over the identification of the high priest here mentioned with the Simeon the Just of Aboth 1.2: cf. the statements in G. Beer, ' 'Abot', *Die Mischna* IV.9, Giessen 1927, ad loc. The importance of the problem is lessened by the availability of other factors for dating.
§3. G. von Rad, 'Die Weisheit des Jesus Sirach', *EvTh* 29, 1969, 113–33; J. Marbock, *Weisheit in Israel. Untersuchungen zur Weisheitstheologie bei Ben Sira*, Rome 1971.

VI

BARUCH AND THE EPISTLE OF JEREMIAH

§1. *Introduction to Baruch and its contents*

As we saw when studying Jeremiah, Baruch the son of Neriah was the prophet's amanuensis who, in 606 BC, wrote two editions of prophecies at Jeremiah's dictation, the first of which was destroyed by king Jehoiakim after he had read it (Jer. 36). The work with which we are concerned was presented as a writing of similar origin, read after the destruction of Jerusalem. 1.1–3.8 is in prose; 3.9–5.9 in poetry. In the first part we find a confession of faith composed in the fifth year of the exile and read to the exiles and to king Jehoiachin in prison; in some respects the style recalls that of Jeremiah (cf. 2.23 with Jer. 7.34), but it is even more like that of Daniel (cf. Dan. 9.4–19). The second part contains first of all a writing in honour of wisdom, which is considered the source of all good things (3.9–4.4); in 4.1ff., as in Ecclesiasticus, wisdom is identified with the law of Moses. 4.5–5.9 announces the consolation of Jerusalem, while in ch. 6 we have the 'text' of the letter which Jeremiah addresses to the exiles (Jer. 29).

§2. *Authorship and date*

The mention of Jehoiachin and the fact that temple worship appears to be functioning (2.26) has suggested to some scholars that the exile mentioned is that of 597, so that the fifth year would be 593, and therefore a little while after the events narrated in Jer. 27;28. Difficulties begin when we try to see whether, and when, Baruch was in Babylon; there is nothing to support this, and the information that we have tells against this theory. In Jer. 43.5f. Baruch still appears at his master's side, even after the fall of Jerusalem in 587, and it seems most probable that he was deported with Jeremiah to Egypt. A rabbinic tradition, *Seder 'olām rabbā'* 26, reports that after conquering Egypt, Nebuchadnezzar freed Jeremiah and Baruch and brought them back to their native land, but this is a legendary element and therefore has no bearing on our narrative. Another strange feature is the note contained in 1.6–11, that some of the sacred vessels were handed back in Babylon and were sent to Jerusalem: this happened to the bulk of the material brought back in the second half of the sixth century, but that was a result of the edict of Cyrus and the liberation of Judah. In 1.1 Belshazzar again appears as son of Nebuchadnezzar, an error which we already find in Dan. 5.2 (unless we understand the word in the widest sense possible, as 'successor'). There are also other elements than the two indicated which show links with Daniel (cf. 1.15–20; 2.1–3, 7–14, 16–19 and Dan. 9.7–11.18). Now since Baruch is clearly fragmentary, whereas Daniel is relatively a unity apart from the dichotomy between 1–6 and 7–12 and the difference in language, it is logical to suppose that the former is dependent on the latter and that at least the first part of Baruch is to be connected with Daniel rather than with Jeremiah and his Baruch.

It is difficult to date the book and to identify the author; it is certain that they both belong to a late date. The original language in which the writing was composed was almost certainly Hebrew; this is indicated by the marked Semitisms, which are difficult for anyone to understand who does not have a certain acquaintance with Hebrew. This also applies to the first part.

On the other hand, the second part is made up of two unrelated writings which do not have any connection even with the fictitious framework of the book. They, too, are late and were originally composed in Hebrew, even if this is not so obvious as in the first part: the text often presents strange expressions which can only be explained if we admit errors in orthography or reading which are only possible in Hebrew. 4.5–5.9 is radically different from the preceding sections and seems to be inspired by Deutero-Isaiah. Liberation from exile is expected in the immediate future, and the destruction of Babylon is imminent (4.22); there will be a return to Zion in miraculous circumstances (5.5–9). The alternative is therefore clear: either what we have here is ancient material which was used again at a later date, as may have happened in the case of Daniel, or we have yet another example of pseudonymity. We have no idea at all of the date at which this section of the book was composed.

§3. Message

There is nothing original about the message of Baruch. It assumes a form borrowed from Daniel and Deutero-Isaiah, but it lacks precision and its affirmations are generic and without force. The God of Israel is the creator (4.35), and wisdom is identical with the *tōrāh*; 4.37 seems to refer to the election of Israel. God is merciful to his people, but they respond to his attitude with sin.

§4. The Epistle of Jeremiah

Chapter 6 sets out to give the text of the writing sent by Jeremiah to the exiles (Jer. 29). Israel must remain in exile for seven generations, which brings us down to the end of the fourth century BC, counting forty years for each generation; however, this is much earlier if we reduce a generation to thirty years. At the end of this time God will be pleased to free his people, but in the meantime they will do well not to allow themselves to be led astray by idolatry, which seems very easy in their present surroundings; to this end they are strengthened with useful advice.

The book is not a letter, nor can it be derived from Jeremiah. In the preface to his commentary on Jeremiah (Migne, PL 24, 706), Jerome already called the work 'pseudepigraphical'. It is impossible to establish the date and the circumstances of composition exactly, but the calculation of generations brings us down to the fourth century, while other elements in the text suggest an even later date. The problem to which the question about the generations seeks to give an answer is the same as in Daniel. How is it that the divine curse continues for so long after the exile? Here, too, no reply is given.

This work, too, may have been originally composed in a Semitic language, but in this case the fact is not so certain.

Compared with other late writings, whether proto- or deutero-canonical, the present book raises one marked difficulty: it gives evidence not only of a good writer, but also of one who is well informed about the situation of the people in Babylon. Verses 1f. are typical of the style of Jeremiah, but the rest of the work lacks any features which might connect it with the prophet; for example, there is no trace of his tenderness, his despair and his hope, or the profoundly evangelical character of his message. Marduk is called by his late name of Bel, a corruption of Baal, as he is in the additions to Daniel; the writing's admiration of the stars contrasts strangely with the polemic against astral worship in Deutero-Isaiah and P. In general the work is directed against paganism; at a time of persecution it can be a good tactic for the oppressed to go over to the attack, and the author adopts this course. We probably have here a Jew of the Babylonian diaspora, well informed about the situation and the history of that part of the world.

BIBLIOGRAPHY

Commentary
A. Gelin, JB, ²1959.

§2. B. N. Wambacq, 'Les prières de Baruch (1.15–2.19) et de Daniel (9.5–19)', *Bibl* 40, 1959, 463–75.

VII

THE PRAYER OF MANASSEH

As we saw earlier, in II Chron. 33.11–13 we read that the wicked King Manasseh was deported to Assyria and there converted. We examined the historical value of this note, and therefore the occasion on which the prayer given here is thought to have been pronounced. It came to form part of the LXX, but did not find a way into the Catholic canon and can only be found in some Catholic Bibles. We do not know how it came to be part of the canon; at all events, there is no mention of it by Origen or Jerome.

The text seems to be studded with Hebraic and Hellenistic expressions, so it is difficult to establish which was the original language: here, too, we probably have a translation from a Hebrew original. The prayer has no relevance to theology, but from a literary point of view it is an interesting example of a lament.

BIBLIOGRAPHY

H. Volz, 'Zur Überlieferung des Gebetes Manasses', *Zeitschrift für Kirchengeschichte* 70, 1959, 293–307.

VIII

I MACCABEES

§1. *Introduction*

'Maccabee' is the nickname borne by Judas, son of Mattathias, the priest who began the revolt against the Syrians of Antiochus IV Epiphanes in 167 BC. As the years went by, the nickname gathered such associations that it turned into a kind of surname for the whole family. Etymologically it is connected with the Aramaic *maqqābā'* = hammer, and thus means 'the hammerer'. However, the term does not refer to a weapon used in war but to a tool; for this reason other etymologies have been proposed, or none at all. The first two books of Maccabees are recognized as deutero-canonical in the Catholic church; the other two are not recognized.

I and II Maccabees are particularly important for the historian. I Maccabees begins with the year 175, the date of the coronation of Antiochus IV Epiphanes, and goes down to the death of Simon Maccabaeus in 134; II Maccabees extends from 176 to 161. Consequently I Macc. 1–7 is more or less parallel to II Macc. 4–15. III and IV Maccabees have nothing to do with the Maccabees: III Maccabees (with which we shall be concerned in due course, because it is in the Alexandrian canon) reports events which took place at the end of the third century under Ptolemy IV Philopator; IV Maccabees, which did not find a place in the Alexandrian canon, is a sermon with Stoic tendencies on reason as the mistress of the emotions. There is even a V Maccabees in Syriac, which in fact is a version of the six books of Josephus' *Jewish War*. The reasons against the canonicity of III–V Maccabees are obvious even to those who accept the Alexandrian canon.

§2. Content

The content can be divided into the following sections: an introduction (1.1–9), which refers to Alexander the Great and the struggles among the Diadochi after his death. The first part (1.10–2.70) describes the origins of the revolt: first of all the manifest hostility of the Syrians (who in 198 succeeded the Ptolemies of Egypt as rulers of Palestine) against Israel and its cult (1.10–64), then the rebellion of Mattathias (ch. 2). The second part (3.1–9.22) celebrates the work of Judas Maccabaeus in his struggles against the Syrians (3.1–4.61) and in his conflicts with other people, including the Idumaeans and Ammonites (chs. 5; 6); also in his battle against Demetrius I Soter, successor to the more reasonable Antiochus V Eupator, who was disposed to let the matter drop (7.1–9.22). In the third part, Jonathan Maccabaeus first fights against Bacchides (9.23–73); there follows his alliance with Alexander Balas who, as alleged son of Antiochus IV, laid claim to the throne (10.1–11.19); finally, there is the relationship between Jonathan and Demetrius II (11.20–12.53). Simon Maccabaeus appears in the fourth part, which describes his relations with Trypho and Demetrius II (13.1–14.3); his rule (14.4–49); his relations with Antiochus VII Sidetes (chs. 15; 16) and his death.

The book thus presents the following sequence of Maccabaean commanders, all brothers: Judas, died 160; Jonathan, died 142; Simon, died 134.

§3. Relationship between I and II Maccabees

A comparison between the two books which, as we have seen, for part of the time cover the same period, reveals common features, features which appear in I Maccabees and not in II Maccabees, and vice versa. This suggests that the two books are independent of each other. It could be that I Maccabees made use of the work of a certain Jason of Cyrene who is mentioned in II Macc. 2.23 and whom we shall meet in the next chapter. This theory was put forward by O. Eissfeldt some years ago, but there is no evidence for it, and in fact he has abandoned the argument in the last edition of his *Introduction*. Be this as it may, the period treated by both works extends for about fourteen years.

From a historical point of view I Maccabees seems to be the more trustworthy source, even if it does not succeed in making all the chronology agree. For this problem we would refer the reader to the study of Hanhart. The same problem arises in an examination of the statistics given, the number of troops involved, and so on. It might be possible to solve the problem of chronology by accepting two different systems of calculation, but here too we cannot go beyond the realm of hypothesis.

The theology of the two works also differs. I Maccabees has a patriotic and nationalistic approach, as we shall shortly see in detail, while II Maccabees places more stress on divine power and retribution in the world to come. Furthermore, as we shall again see, I Maccabees is of Palestinian origin while II Maccabees is Hellenistic.

§4. *Literary problems*

(a) The first problem to arise is that of the original Hebrew text. The LXX version which has come down to us is obviously the translation of a Semitic original which was still known to Origen and Jerome, though the Hebrew tradition is unaware of it. But Flavius Josephus already quoted the Greek text when he used I Macc. 1–13, including some points which are clearly erroneous; he seems to be unaware of the existence of a Hebrew original. Thus we can be sure that I Maccabees is the translation of a Hebrew or Aramaic text, though we cannot establish what the text was or what it looked like. Notwithstanding his evident Hebraisms, the author is obviously an effective writer even in the Greek translation. His model seems to have been the historical work of the Chronicler; like him he reports official documents (cf. especially Ezra and Nehemiah), genealogies and dates. Rather than being a reflection of reality, the speeches and prayers are recollections constructed in a polished rhetorical form, following a custom which is well-attested elsewhere. It is interesting to note that in the epic narratives the accent is more on human bravery than on divine intervention. Military pride and trust in God are strangely combined within the book, and there are a number of comparisons with figures from antiquity: the judges and the first kings (cf. I Macc. 9.73).

I Maccabees abounds in copies of contemporary documents, accounts of missions accomplished or the results of conversations with important people of the time. In this sense it almost seems as if the authors wished to continue the work of the Chronicler by bringing it down to the second century. However, it is not clear whether the copies are authentic, and if so up to what point, or whether they are revisions of authentic material, or simply apocryphal. One thing is certain: the material is an integral part of the text, and the remarkable degree of historicity shown by the text is also an element in favour of the historicity of the material included.

(b) The author of the work is not mentioned once. Whoever he was, he must have composed his text in the last years of John Hyrcanus, and in any case before the occupation of Jerusalem by Pompey, that is, about the end of the second or the beginning of the first century BC. He was a Palestinian Jew who knew Hebrew and Aramaic well; we do not know whether he also knew Greek. He was an ardent patriot, for whom religion and nation were identical. The celebration of the action of the Maccabees stands out here against the modesty of the last chapters of proto-canonical Daniel. The author does not seem to have had any close contact with the sect of the Pharisees, since he never speaks of resurrection or of the messianic hope; it is possible that he wanted to write a kind of unofficial history of his time glorifying the Maccabees. However, he does not conceal some of the misdeeds of Simon, the founder of the dynasty: 14.4–48; 15.15–24 are the only texts which give him unqualified praise. In reality the author admires those who have made a substantial contribution towards liberating his country from Syrian oppression, but he also tries to show that they were subordinate to an institution which is historically obscure but mentioned on a number of occasions, which he calls 'the Great Synagogue' (3.44; 14.26–28): in the last analysis this decides policy and confirms Simon in his position.

Like the Chronicler, the author of I Maccabees sees the people as a religious community, a feature which is absent from II Maccabees; however, those who do not observe the law are excluded from this group (2.67 and other passages). Like Daniel, the author is well aware of the danger presented by militant paganism to those who observe the law.

(c) The LXX Greek text is all that is left after the loss of the original Hebrew. We have it in codices ℵ and A, but it is lacking in B. Sometimes it seems as if the translator knew Greek well and was less familiar with Hebrew: in 1.28 he says 'Against its inhabitants . . .' in Greek, instead of 'For its . . .'; in 2.34 we have an obscure text which can, however, be reconstructed by someone who knows Hebrew as 'We do not wish to violate the sabbath'; 4.24 has the translation 'heaven' for 'God' or 'Yahweh'; according to some, this is a way of not mentioning the divine name, but more probably it is an erroneous quotation of Pss. 118 and 136 with a confusion between *šēm* = 'name' and *šāmayim* = 'heaven'; in the same passage the phrase 'For good and everlasting is his mercy' should obviously read 'For he is good and his mercy is everlasting' (Semitic languages do not use the verb 'to be' as a copula); in 6.1 (cf. Tobit 2.10) the Hebrew must certainly have been something like 'the province of Elam', but the translator, who did not know the double meaning of the Hebrew *medīnā*, invented a non-existent Elimais! In Cod. A the quotations from the LXX are recognizable and the Greek is better.

For bibliography see after ch. IX.

IX

II MACCABEES

§1. Content

The introduction presents the reader with two letters written to the Jews of Alexandria; the first speaks of the restoration of the temple and the second of events a little earlier, with a legend about how the sacred fire was kept alive during the exile in Persia (sic!) and a reference to archives of Nehemiah in which were deposited books about the kings and the prophets, works of David, royal letters and so on. It ends by saying that the author, a certain Jason of Cyrene, wrote the deeds of the Maccabees in a work made up of five books, which have been condensed into one. There follow three parts and an epilogue. The first begins with the prelude to the rebellion (chs. 3–7): the intrigues between the Israelite high priests and the Syrian kings (chs. 3; 4), and the persecution by Antiochus IV (chs. 5–7, with the famous episode of the martyrdom of the mother and her seven sons in ch. 7). The second part (8.1–10.9) describes the rebellion: the first victories (ch. 8), the death of the tyrant (ch. 9) and the purification and dedication of the temple (10.1–9; cf. I Macc. 4.36–61). The third part (10.10–15.36) describes the campaigns of Judas Maccabaeus. The work ends with an epilogue (15.37–39).

§2. Authorship

Although we do not know much about the person who wrote the book, there can be no serious doubt as to who he was. The two introductory letters seem to have been added at a later stage and prefixed to the work, as has the preface which says that the five original books have been compressed into one (2.19–32); the epilogue also seems to fall into this category (15.37–39). However, the original text certainly goes back to Jason of Cyrene, mentioned above, and there is no reason to doubt that the summary was in fact made on the basis of his work. Still, we know nothing at all about this Jason; we do not even know whether his work continued after the events of the year 161.

The drama of this book revolves around the temple in Jerusalem. It is threatened, profaned, liberated and rededicated at what is to become an annual feast in Israel, the feast of dedication, Hebrew *ḥᵃnukkāh*, which is still observed today and which normally falls round about Christmas. Indeed, in the course of time it has even taken over popular elements and folklore from Christmas.

The book abounds in explanations of the law, either for the use of the pagans or for Israel (cf. 6.5 and 5.17–20; 6.12–17 respectively). In fact II Maccabees has a much greater interest in theology than I Maccabees, although it is expressed in a somewhat rough form of reward and punishment. The pagans are defined as 'blasphemous and barbarous nations' in 10.4, but there are also severe censures of apostate Jews, of whom there must therefore have been considerable numbers. We find a series of theological features in II Maccabees which were absent from I Maccabees: for example, the resurrection of the body in 7.11; 14.46, a feature which is quite a contrast first to Wisdom and then to Philo, both of whom, following Neo-Platonic lines, tend rather to teach the immortality of the soul. In 7.28 there appears for the first time in Hebrew thought the doctrine which will later be called *creatio ex nihilo*, though not in the absolute form in which it has sometimes been presented: the Greek is *ouk ex ontōn epoiēsen auta ho theos*, that is, 'God made the world not from things which were', which is not identical with 'nothing' in the philosophical sense of the term. In 7.9, 14 (cf. 14.46; 12.43) we have concepts of eternal life and death, and in 12.43 the intercession of the living for the dead, an element on which the Catholic church has sometimes sought to found the doctrine of Purgatory. We have drawn attention to a well-developed angelology (3.24–28; 5.2–4; 10.29ff.; 11.8, etc.). As Pfeiffer has well observed, the fact is that II Maccabees is more a work of edification than of history. The author, Jason of Cyrene (in Cyrenaica), seems to have been a diaspora Jew who lived at Alexandria about 100 BC.

From a literary point of view the book does not seem to have known I Maccabees in either its Hebrew or its Greek form; it seems rather to have used a history of the Seleucids in Greek, i.e. a history of the dynasty of Antiochus IV, which seems also to have been known by Josephus, though he in turn does not know II Maccabees. The use of this non-Hebraic source probably explains the references to the cult of Dionysus in 6.7; 14.33 and some copying errors in 11.5 and 12.17.

Hence it comes about that the author of II Maccabees can give an opposite version of the facts to that in I Maccabees: cf. I Macc. 5 with II Macc. 10.15, etc.

Following a method which is well-attested in this period, the author confines himself to summarizing the work of Jason of Cyrene, leaving him with the responsibility for his statements; the summary is justified by the excessive length of the original (2.24).

Finally, the book also seems to take some liberties both with chronology, often disagreeing with that of I Maccabees, and with doctrine, which is stressed or not depending on the view of the epitomizer. To this extent the original thought of Jason has been distorted, and it cannot of course be established, since we do not even have fragments of the text.

BIBLIOGRAPHY

Commentaries
F. M. Abel, EB, 1949; A. Penna, SacBib, 1953; F. M. Abel-J. Starcky, JB, ³1961.

VIII §4. A. Jepsen and R. Hanhart, *Untersuchungen zur israelitisch-jüdischen Chronologie*, Berlin 1964; H. Sahlin, 'Antiochus IV Epiphanes und Judas Mackabäus' (sic!), *St Th* 23, 1969, 41–68; W. Wirgin, 'Judah Maccabee's Embassy to Rome and the Jewish-Roman Treaty', *PEQ* 101, 1969, 15-20.

X

III MACCABEES AND III EZRA

§1. *III Maccabees*

The book appears in the Alexandrian canon, but it has not been accepted into the Catholic canon; as we saw above, it has nothing to do with the Maccabees. It tells how after his victory at Raphia over Antiochus III at the end of the third century, Ptolemy IV Philopator of Egypt (last quarter of the century) sought unsuccessfully to enter the temple at Jerusalem. He then tried to outwit the Jews of Alexandria, but did not succeed in his attempt. In the face of such determined opposition, a violent persecution broke out against the Jews, but three times they were miraculously saved. The king was converted and granted them letters of protection which at the same time authorized them to exterminate the apostates. The affair ends with a feast of thanksgiving and thus seems to be a kind of Alexandrian parallel to the feast of Purim.

Historical features in the narrative are: Ptolemy's victory, the celebration of the feast, and the anti-Jewish sentiments prevailing in certain circles in Alexandria. The rest, however, seems to be a romance centred on these features. Finally, the account is insignificant from an ideological standpoint.

There are no elements here which allow us to suppose the existence of a Semitic original; the original language is almost certainly Greek, and the work has been handed down in that language.

§2. *III Ezra*

This is the title given to the work in the Vulgate, in which, as we have seen, Ezra and Nehemiah are called respectively I and II Ezra; it is more often called I Esdras (sometimes also the Greek Ezra), following the LXX, in which Ezra and Nehemiah together make up II Esdras.

In the Vulgate it appears after the New Testament and is not canonical in the Catholic church. It sets out to give the history of Israel from the passover celebrated under Josiah in 622–21 to the proclamation of the law under Ezra, and in fact runs parallel to Chronicles, Ezra and Nehemiah, with some differences of order and of detail. Ezra 4.7–24 precedes 2.1; Ezra 4.6 and Neh. 1.1–7.5 and 8.1–13.31 are missing; instead, it has the story of the three young men at the court of Darius. A contest is won by Zerubbabel who, as a reward, receives permission to rebuild the temple (III Ezra 3.1–5.6, cf. Josephus, *Antt.* XI, 3.2ff. = §§33ff.). The Greek of the texts which are parallel to the work of the Chronicler has remarkable style, whether as a translation or as an original. It always keeps its independence from the LXX and is much closer to the Hebrew text; sometimes the translation is very free, but at other times it offers readings which are superior to the Massoretic text. In other words, it is an extremely useful work for textual criticism.

There are, however, also chronological differences which Pfeiffer lists in a table (*History*, 242). In any case it would not be strange if what we had here was a revision of the work of the Chronicler which, for reasons that we cannot explain, remained outside the present canon. As we have indicated, it is interesting that Josephus followed the text of III Ezra rather than the Chronicler.

One section without parallels is the account of the adventures of the three young men at the court of Darius. Some scholars have seriously considered the possibility that it is a lost chapter of Chronicles, but in that case we would have to read 'Cyrus' instead of 'Darius'. However, there are considerable difficulties here: e.g. in Ezra and in III Ezra it is Sheshbazzar who, under Cyrus, brings back the temple vessels which had been carried away by the Babylonians, whereas III Ezra puts Zerubbabel under Darius without any possibility of a confusion. That is, unless, as Eissfeldt has suggested in his *Introduction*, the name of Zerubbabel was simply added at a later stage.

Although the text is written in the best Greek, it equally seems to presuppose a Semitic archetype, perhaps in Aramaic. Its relationship with Hebrew and international wisdom is also clear; as in the case of the book of Tobit, the latter is essentially represented by the story of Ahikar. However, we also find Persian features in the narrative: the exaltation of the truth at the expense of lies as the supreme virtue, as can be seen in 4.34–40, a hymn of praise to truth in which some scholars have found the echo of an ancient Persian hymn with a similar content. However, since it does not appear in Avesta, ultimate certainty is impossible.

Another feature characteristic of wisdom is the subtlety of the work on a psychological as well as a literary level. It is impossible to assign a date to it or to indicate the circumstances in which it was composed.

BIBLIOGRAPHY

§1. M. Hadas, 'III Maccabees and Greek Romance', *Review of Religion* 13, New York 1949, 155–62; I. Levi, 'Ptolémée Lathyre et les Juifs', *HUCA* 23, 1950–1, 127–36; F. Jesi, 'Notes sur l'édit Dionysiaque de Ptolémée IV Philopator', *JNES* 15, 1956, 236–40.

§2. *Commentary:* W. Rudolph, HAT, 1949.
A. L. Allrik, 'I Esdras according to Codex B and Codex A as appearing in Zerubbabel's List in I Esdras 5, 8–23', *ZAW* 66, 1954, 272–92; A. Shalit, 'Koile-Syria from mid-Fourth Century to the Beginning of the Third Century BC', *Scripta Hierosolymitana* 1, Jerusalem 1954, 64–77; W. T. in der Smitten, 'Zur Pagenerzählung im 3 Ezra (3 Ezra III 1–V 6)', *VT* 22, 1972, 492–5; K. F. Pohlmann, *Studien zum dritten Ezra*, FRLANT 104, 1970.

APPENDIX I

PALESTINIAN INSCRIPTIONS FROM THE FIRST HALF OF THE FIRST MILLENNIUM

§1. *Introduction*

Once we leave aside the discoveries at Ugarit relating to the second half of the second millennium BC and those at Qumran in the period immediately preceding the end of the first millennium, the region of Syria and Palestine is notoriously poor in finds of inscriptions and manuscripts. Thus the few texts that have been found over about the last century are all the more interesting to us; of course we shall be examining essentially those which belong to Israel or to peoples of particular interest for the biblical narrative.

Among the most important evidence we have the so-called agricultural 'calendar' of Gezer; the stele of Mesha, king of Moab; the Samaria ostraca; the inscription on the Siloam aqueduct; the epitaph of a high royal official; a funeral inscription found near Lachish; the ostracon of Yabneh-Yam; the ostracon of Ophel; the Lachish ostraca; and finally the ostraca of Tell-'Arad. Of these we must leave aside the ostracon of Ophel because it is too badly damaged and is therefore illegible; we must also refrain from examining the large amount of important material preserved on seals or as stamps on jars: this material is very important evidence for names, but is composed of only a few words, usually the name, patronym and sometimes the functions exercised by the owner through the seals, so we never have a proper literary text. The ancient Aramaic material will also be left out of account: it is easily accessible in a number of collections of texts.

§2. *The agricultural 'calendar' of Gezer*

The small tablet which was soon given this name was discovered at Gezer in 1908 during excavations carried out there. The archaic form of writing and the archaeological stratum in which the tablet was discovered allow us to date it in the second half of the tenth century BC at the latest, probably towards 925; some scholars would prefer to put this dating a few decades further back. In any case, it is the earliest Hebrew text that we have outside the Bible; some scholars date it before the Israelite occupation of the area and others immediately afterwards (I Kings 9.15–17). The text has some marked peculiarities of grammar, syntax and orthography in comparison with classical Hebrew; as in Ugaritic and ancient Phoenician, there is no article and it has final endings in *w*, the exact significance of which has yet to be explained. Some scholars would understand this as an archaic ending for the dual (W. F. Albright), which then fell into disuse and was kept only for proper names. The translation of this ending as a dual would give a working cycle of twelve months, hence the title agricultural 'calendar'. The text would be as follows: 'There are two months of ingathering, two months of sowing, (2) two months of late sowing, (3) one month of pulling flax, (4) one month of barley harvest, (5) one month of harvesting (grain) and counting (?), (6) two months of vine-tending, (7) one month of summer fruit.' However, another translation made by Garbini and recently taken up by Gibson, which does not consider the endings in *w* as duals, runs: 'Months of vintage and olive harvest; months of (2) sowing; months of spring pasture; (3) month of flax pulling; (4) month of barley harvest, (5) month of wheat harvest and measuring (?), (6) months of pruning; (7) month of summer fruit.' In the margin we also read '*by* . . .', which Albright has understood, probably rightly, as '*byhw* = '*Abiyāhū*, i.e. the name of the writer. The theophoric name ending with Yahweh would of course be a feature in favour of dating the writing later than the occupation of the place by Solomon.

The writing is generally understood today as being a school exercise by a pupil whose name is indicated in a mutilated form in the margin; this would explain the rather clumsy look of the writing. Others would see it as a tablet deposited in the local sanctuary, with the aim of seeking a favourable harvest throughout the year. The two are not mutually exclusive.

§3. *The stele of Mesha, king of Moab*

On the stele of king Mesha we have the longest text of the series, amounting to 34 lines. It is particularly important as an essentially historical text, because it gives the Moabite version of the facts narrated in II Kings 1.1ff.; 3.4ff., 24ff. The text agrees with that of, the Old Testament in the note that Israel had to abandon Moab. For the Moabites this was an understandable triumph. We then learn how the king had to reorganize his territory after he had won it back. The language of the text is very similar to biblical Hebrew, though it has some important grammatical peculiarities: for example, verbal forms with an inserted *t* which are limited in Hebrew to verbs beginning with a sibilant; we also have the pronominal suffix of the third person singular masculine in *h*, the plural in *n* instead of in *m*. These elements, however, seem more a matter of dialect in comparison with biblical Hebrew and may reflect northern Israelite dialect; it has therefore been supposed that the author of the inscriptions was a Hebrew. In lines 11f. we have an interesting parallel to the institution of the ban, well-known in the context of the Holy War in Israel: the vanquished are massacred in honour of the national god Chemosh, to whom they have been consecrated. The stele can be dated not later than the second half of the ninth century BC.

§4. *The Samaria ostraca*

The Samaria ostraca offer material of another kind: they are invoices and delivery notes for jars of wine and precious oil sent to the royal palace of Samaria. Almost all of them were discovered during the course of excavations in 1910; a last one was discovered in the excavations of 1932. They give us not only important information about nomenclature and topography, but also valuable details about the administrative situation in the kingdom of Israel under Jeroboam II (first half of the eighth century), the time of Amos and the beginning of Hosea's ministry. The system initiated by Solomon to get supplies for his palace, which was one of the reasons why the north separated from the south (I Kings 12), remained in force throughout the eighth century. The dates which appear in the ostraca point to the years between about 778 and 770.

§5. *The Siloam inscription*

During the reign of Hezekiah, in the second half of the eighth century, the water system of the capital was extended and in part renewed by order of the king (II Chron. 32.30; Ecclus. 48.17); it brought water from the spring of Gihon, in the bottom of the valley, to within the city, and is still partially working today. An inscription describes the last phases of the work; it is on the lower part of a surface which was dressed for the purpose; no inscription has been put on the upper part.

Some of the text has been damaged, but the rest is quite legible: '. . . . the piercing through. And this is the way (in which) the piercing through (was done): (2) While (the stone-cutters were swinging their) axes, each towards his fellow, and while there were still three cubits to be pierced through, (there was heard) the voice of a man (3) calling to his fellow, for there was a *zdh* (?) in the rock to the right (and to the left). When the (4) piercing through was complete, the stone-cutters struck through each to meet his fellow, axe against axe. And the water ran from the spring to the pool for 1200 cubits, and 100 cubits was the height of the rock (6) above the head of the stone-cutters . . .'

The inscription was discovered in 1880 and is generally dated towards the end of the eighth century, a little before the arrival of Sennacherib in 701; it is also most probable that the improvement of the aqueduct was made with a view to a siege. There is an incomprehensible term in line 3.

§6. *The epitaph of a high royal official*

Discovered in 1870 in present-day Silwan, on the east slope of the Kidron valley, this contains an important text, though slightly damaged, from the end of the eighth century BC. Restored, it reads: 'This is [the sepulchre of . . .] *yahu* who is over the palace. There is no silver and no gold here (2) but [his bones] and the bones of his concubine with him. Cursed be the man (3) who opens this!' The style is that customary for this literary genre.

Overseers of the palace appear often in the Old Testament, and are also to be found on many of the seals which have been discovered. However, we do not know of anyone whose name ends in *-yāhū* and who was buried in Jerusalem. Y. Yadin has suggested that this is Shebna, object of the invective in Isa. 22.15, written in its full form as *Šᵉbān -yāhū*, abbreviated in Isaiah to Shebna, since it is said that he had a tomb constructed in Jerusalem (22.16).

§7. *The inscription in the burial cave near Lachish*

This was discovered in 1961 in a cave used for burial from ancient times, about 5 miles north-north-east of Lachish. The inscriptions are graffiti, not engraved, and part of their importance lies in the fact that they are the only ones with a religious subject. Their date can be fixed at the end of the eighth or the beginning of the seventh century BC on the basis of palaeographical and historical elements. Among the lesser ones we have the inscription at the entrance to the mortuary room, the reconstruction of which reads: 'Cursed be he who robs this room'; among the major ones, the reconstructed texts read: 'Yahweh (is) the God of the whole earth [cf. Gen. 24.3 and Isa. 54.5]; the mountains of Judah belong to him, to the God of Jerusalem'; another is, 'The (Mount of) Moriah thou hast favoured, the dwelling of Yah, Yahweh', cf. II Chron. 3.1; this is the earliest identification of Moriah, a name which we find in Gen. 22.2 for a country, with the temple mount. A last inscription reads, '[Ya]hweh deliver (us)!'

§8. *The ostracon of Yabneh-yam*

The text in question was discovered along with two other obscure ones during the excavations carried out in 1960 on the perimeter of the ancient fortress in the area, in the neighbourhood of the gate. On the basis of palaeographical features, the text has been dated in the last decades of the seventh century.

(*a*) The text, as translated by Amusin and Heltzer, reads: (1) 'Let my lord the governor hear (2) the word of his servant. Thy servant, (3) reaping was thy servant in Ha-(4)ṣar Asam. And reaped thy servant (5) and finished, and gathered as usual before Sabbath. (6) When thy servant had finished his reaping and gath(7)ered, as usual, there came Ḥashavhayu, the son of Shova(8)i and took thy servant's clothes. When I had finished (9) my reaping (in) these (postulated) days, he took away thy servant's garment. (10) And all my brethren will bear witness in my favour, (all who) were reaping with me when hot was (11) [the sun. And all] my brethren will bear witness in my favour. Verily, I am free of gu(12)[ilt. Please, return] my garment. And I appeal to the governor that he retur(13)[n the garment of thy servant and sho]w him mer(14)[cy . . . s]ervant of thine, and do not be speechless.'

(*b*) Another suggestion has been made for lines 5–6: 'I harvested, (5) gathered in and wanted to put it in store while it was still the middle of the day before the sabbath. (6) After your servant had gathered his share and wanted to put it in store while it was still the middle of the day, there came . . .' and for line 9: '. . . . When I had gathered my share, while it was still the day which . . .' etc. On the basis of this interpretation an attempt has been made to see the writing as the text of a petition sent to the governor by someone who had violated (or was thought to have violated) the sabbath. However, he denies his guilt and puts the blame on the one who made the distraint, certainly a levite, to judge from the name: we also know from Neh. 13.22, though this is some centuries later, that the levites were charged with supervising sabbath observance. The term 'put in store' used in the translation is certainly wrong, since when the harvest was gathered it was not put in store, but left to dry before threshing.

(*c*) A third interpretation has been proposed recently: '. . . (3) Your servant stood harvesting (4) in the area of his share of the grain; he reaped (5) and measured, and the quota of the grain accorded with the daily quota before the day of rest. (6) After your servant had measured the harvest and the daily (7) quota of grain was in accordance with the daily quota, H. son of Š. came (8) and took the cloak of your servant after he had measured (9) my harvest, exactly the daily quota . . .'

The three possibilities considered show clearly that we are still far from an accepted reading of the text, though the subject matter is intelligible. It speaks of a band of harvesters each of whom is assigned a quota, a contract; a harvester is accused of not having done his proper work and is fined; to guarantee that he will pay he has to leave his cloak. He appeals to the governor for the garment to be restored to him, a case which is expressly provided for in Exod. 22.25–27; Deut. 24.10–13, cf. also Amos 2.8; Prov. 20.16; 27.13; in the case of a pledge of this kind the law provides that it shall be handed back before dusk. This injunction does not seem to have been respected by those who took the pledge, hence the appeal. From Amos' invective we can conclude that cases of this kind must have happened quite frequently. The theory about a failure to observe the sabbath, cf. Jer. 17.19–27, seems improbable. As can be seen even in translation, the language is very poor and full of repetitions; perhaps the petition was dictated to a scribe, who provided the introductory formula.

§9. The Lachish ostraca

The Lachish ostraca are another piece of written evidence the importance of which cannot be put too highly. The first eighteen were discovered during the excavations of 1934–5, and nos. 19–21 during those of 1938. The letters belong to the last years preceding the fall of Jerusalem, probably the period between 590 and 587; in Jer. 34.7 we read that only Lachish and Azekah were still resisting Babylonian pressure; the enemy tactics were to isolate Jerusalem progressively from all the surrounding strongpoints, so as to be able to lay siege to it on all sides, a tactic which had already been used by Sennacherib in 701 and was repeated much later, in AD 67–70, by Titus. In letter IV, line 12, we read: 'We no longer see (the signals of) Azekah', while those of Lachish are still visible from other strongpoints (for the system of signals see Jer. 6.1b). In XI, line 4 there appears the son of a certain Jeremiah, but not the prophet, because we know that he was not married (Jer. 16.2). III, line 20, talks of an anonymous 'prophet' and VI, line 4, of a defeatist (cf. Jer. 38.4), but it does not seem possible to identify this figure with the prophet Jeremiah.

§10. The ostraca of Tell-ʿArad

The ostraca of Tell-ʿArad, which number about ten, were found during the excavations carried out in the area in 1962 and 1963. Those published so far (autumn 1972) can be dated in 598–7 and thus fall shortly before the first siege of Jerusalem; for the most part they are administrative texts: they speak of rations given to mercenaries and similar matters. Among the mercenaries we have the *kittīm*, a term to which we drew attention when discussing Deutero-Zechariah, a name which at the time of Qumran was to be used for the Romans or for Westerners in general. Here it probably refers to mercenaries originating from Greece or the islands, though we cannot identify them more precisely.

§11. The texts of Deir-ʿAlla

In the spring of 1967 a Dutch expedition under the leadership of H. J. Franken discovered a series of fragments belonging to different texts in the course of excavations on Tell Deir-ʿAlla (in Transjordania, a few miles north of the mouth of the Jabbok, the present-day Wadi Zerqa, a tributary on the left bank of the Jordan). The writing has been done on plaster, which probably comes from a cultic object, perhaps a stele, rather than from a wall. It fell and was thrown outside the building in the course of an earthquake. This feature, along with the condition of the material, which was very fragile to begin with, makes the work of deciphering the texts extremely difficult. So far it seems possible to divide the fragments into twelve combinations, two of which are particularly important. These are two texts written in Aramaic: the language can be dated back to about 700 BC. The words still appear without *matres lectiones*, as we would expect, except at the end of a word, where a rudimentary system seems to have been in use for the personal pronominal suffixes.

The first combination contains a prophecy of Balaam son of Beor, apparently the same figure as the one who appears in Num. 22–24; Deut. 23.5f. and in other texts, where he is a Moabite prophet. Here too he has nothing to do with the faith and the worship of Israel: he is a 'divinely inspired clairvoyant' who announces destruction to his hearers according to orders received from a goddess. It is possible that the text, the end of which is badly damaged, calls for repentance. In the second combination we have a series of curses of the kind which we find attested in the Old Testament and in the ancient Near East, probably from the mouth of the same person.

These brief foretastes indicate that the texts are very important for the history of religions, for language and for philology. We therefore eagerly await even a provisional publication of them.

BIBLIOGRAPHY

§1. *Texts*: D. Diringer, *Le inscrizioni antico-ebraiche palestinesi*, Florence 1934; S. Moscati, *L'epigrafia ebraica antica 1935–50*, Rome 1951; T. C. Vriezen and J. Hospers, *Palestine Inscriptions*, Leiden 1951; H. Donner and W. Röllig, *Kanaanäische und aramäische Inschriften* (3 vols.), Wiesbaden ²1966–70; J. C. L. Gibson, *Textbook of Syrian Semitic Inscriptions* I, Oxford 1971.

Translations: D. W. Thomas (ed.), *Documents from Old Testament Times*, London 1958 (reprinted New York 1961), 195ff.; K. Galling (ed.), *Textbuch zur Geschichte Israels*, Tübingen ²1968, 51ff.; *ANET* ³1969, 320ff.

For a general introduction cf. H. Michaud, *Sur la pierre et l'argile*, Neuchâtel 1958; there is a philological and linguistic study in F. M. Cross, Jr, and D. N. Freedman, *Early Hebrew Orthography*, New Haven 1952.

§2. W. F. Albright, 'The Gezer Calendar', *BASOR* 92, 1943, 16–26;

J. G. Février, 'Remarques sur le calendrier de Gézer', *Semitica* 1 1948, 33–41; A. M. Honeyman, 'The Syntax of the Gezer Calendar', *Journal of the Royal Asiatic Society*, 1953, 53–8; G. Garbini, 'Note sul "calendario" di Gezer', *AION* 16, 1956, 123–30; W. Wirgin, 'The Calendar Tablet from Gezer', *Eretz Israel* 6, 1960, 9*–12*; J. B. Segal, '"Yrh" in the Gezer Calendar', *JSS* 7, 1962, 212–21; S. Talmon, 'The Gezer Calendar and the Seasonal Cycle of Ancient Canaan', *JAOS* 83, 1963, 177–87. Garbini suggests 'put in store' at the end of line 9 instead of the more usual but improbable 'count'. He also argues that the language of the calendar is a dialect related to Hebrew and with archaic elements: the final *w* is not a dual but a nominative plural construct to be read as *ū*. He takes the text to be not a calendar but simply a list of agricultural tasks to be carried out, some of which take one month, some two.

§3. S. Segert, 'Die Sprache der moabitischen Königsinschrift', *ArOr* 29, 1961, 197–267. For the syntax see F. I. Andersen, 'Moabite Syntax', *Or* 35, 1966, 81–120; for the historical problems see J. Liver, 'The Wars of Mesha, King of Moab', *PEQ* 99, 1967, 14–31, with bibliography of earlier work. A second, very fragmentary, inscription found in 1963 now allows Mesha's patronymic to be established: cf. W. L. Reed and F. V. Winnett, 'A Fragment of an Early Moabite Inscription from Kerak', *BASOR* 172, 1963, 1–9; D. N. Freedman, 'A Second Mesha Inscription', *BASOR* 175, 1964, 50f.; I. Schiffmann, 'Eine neue moabitische Inschrift aus Karcha', *ZAW* 77, 1965, 324f.; cf. also the archaeological surveys by M. Weippert, *ZDPV* 80, 1964, 150–93; 82, 1966, 274–330. For the chronology of the events described cf. G. Wallis, 'Die vierzig Jahre der achten Zeile der Mesa-Inschrift', *ZDPV* 81, 1965, 180–6; B. Bonder, 'Mesha's Rebellion against Israel', *Journal of the Ancient Near Eastern Society of the University of Columbia* 3, 1970–1, 82–8 (taking the view that 'forty years' means 'a generation'): É. Lipiński, 'Etymological and Exegetical Notes on the Meša' Inscription', *Orientalia* 40, 1971, 325–40.

§4. B. Maisler (Mazar), 'The Historical Background of the Samaria Ostraca', *JPOS* 21, 1948, 117–33; Y. Yadin, 'Ancient Judaean Weights and the Date of the Samaria Ostraca', *Scripta Hierosolymitana* 8, 1960, 9–25; A. F. Rainey, 'Administration in Ugarit and the Samaria Ostraka', *IEJ* 12, 1962, 62f.; id., 'The Samaria Ostraka in the Light of Fresh Evidence', *PEQ* 99, 1967, 32–41; A. Lemaire, 'L'ostracon C 1101 de Samarie – nouvel essai', *RB* 79, 1972, 565–70.

§5. H.-J. Stoebe, 'Überlegungen zur Siloahinschrift', *ZDPV* 71, 1955, 124–40; G. Levi della Vida, 'The Shiloah Inscription Reconsidered', in *In Memoriam Paul Kahle*, BZAW 103, 1968, 162–6, where he takes up and develops themes expressed in a review of Donner and Röllig, op. cit., in *RSO* 39, 1964, 311f.; G. Garbini, 'L'iscrizione di Siloe e gli "Annali dei re di Giuda"', *AION* 29, 1969, 261–3. These scholars argue that the lack of stylistic parallels in analogous contemporary inscriptions is explained by regarding this inscription as an extract from the court-annals of Judah (cf. above Part Two, ch. IX, §2).

§6. A. Reifenberg, 'A Newly Discovered Hebrew Inscription of the Pre-exilic Period', *JPOS* 21, 1948, 134–7; N. Avigad, 'The Epitaph of a Royal Steward', *IEJ* 3, 1953, 137–52.

§7. J. Naveh, 'Old Hebrew Inscriptions in a Burial Cave', *IEJ* 13, 1963, 74–92; F. M. Cross, Jr, 'The Cave Inscriptions from Khirbet Beit Lei', in J. A. Sanders (ed.), *Near Eastern Archaeology in the Twentieth Century*, New York 1970, 299–306 (reading the first inscription differently and proposing 587 as a date).

§8a. J. Naveh, 'A Hebrew Letter from the Seventh Century BC', *IEJ* 10, 1960, 129–39; S. Yeivin, 'The Judicial Petition of Mezad Hashavyahu', *BO* 19, 1962, 3–10; J. D. Amusin and M. L. Heltzer, 'The Inscription from Meṣad Ḥashavyahu: Complaint of a Reaper of the Seventh Century BC', *IEJ* 14, 1964, 148–57; S. Talmon, 'The New Hebrew Letter from the Seventh Century BC in Historical Perspective', *BASOR* 176, 1964, 148–57.

§8b. L. Delekat, 'Ein Bittschriftentwurf eines Sabbatsschänders', *Bibl* 51, 1970, 453–71; A. Lemaire, 'L'ostracon de Mesad Hashavyahu replacé dans son contexte', *Semitica* 21, 1971, 57–79.

§8c. G. Garbini, 'L'ostrakon ebraico di Yavne-Yam', *AION* 32, 1972, 98–102.

§9. H. Torczyner, *Lachish I*, Oxford 1938 (nos. 1–18); O. Tufnell, *Lachish III*, Oxford 1953; W. F. Albright, 'The Lachish Letters after Five Years', *BASOR* 82, 1941, 18–24; H. Michaud, 'Les ostraca de Lakiš conservés à Londres', *Syria* 34, 1957, 39–60. N. R. Ganor, 'The Lachish Letters', *PEQ* 99, 1967, 74–7, has proposed a late tenth-century dating of the ostracka, the occasion being the expedition of Pharaoh Shishak, cf. I Kings 14.25–28; II Chron.12.9–11, with reference to Rehoboam's fortifications described in II Chron. 11.5–11; this theory has not won general acceptance.

§10. Y. Aharoni, 'Hebrew Ostraka from Tell Arad', *IEJ* 16, 1966, 1–7; id., 'Arad, its Inscriptions and Temple', *BA* 31, 1968, 2–32; id., 'Three Hebrew Ostraca from Arad', *Eretz Israel* 9, 1969, 10–21 (= *BASOR* 197, 1970, 16–42); A. F. Rainey, 'A Hebrew "Receipt" from Arad', *BASOR* 202, 1971, 23–9.

§11. H. J. Franken, 'Texts from the Persian Period from Deir 'Alla', *VT* 17, 1967, 480–1 (the datings proposed are sometimes obsolete, as has been indicated); G. Sauer, 'Die Tafeln von Deir 'Alla', *ZAW* 81, 1967, 145–56; J. Hoftijzer, 'De ontcijfering van Deir-'Alla-texten', *Oosters genootschap in Nederland* 5, 1973, 115–34.

(NB. An unusually full bibliography has been provided for this Appendix, since this material is often not examined in Introductions to the Old Testament.)

APPENDIX II

PAPYRI FROM THE FIRST CENTURIES
AFTER THE EXILE

§1. *The Elephantine papyri*

The island of Elephantine is on the border between Egypt and Nubia
at the level of the first cataract, where the Aswan dam has now been
built; at the end of the fifth century BC it housed a Jewish military
colony in the service of the Persian occupation. Traces of it disappear
with the end of Persian domination, at the beginning of the fourth
century BC. The colony is already attested in the pre-Persian period,
before 525, the year in which Cambyses occupied Egypt. It is therefore probable that it was stationed in the region at the end of the
seventh and the beginning of the sixth century BC, under Pharaoh
Psammetichus I or Amasis.

Some of the archives of this Jewish military colony were discovered
towards the end of the last century, probably about 1890, containing
papyri composed in imperial Aramaic, very close to that of Ezra and
Nehemiah; they refer to people and events at the end of the fifth
century BC.

The archive is composed for the most part of contracts, transactions
of various kinds and other documents in the realm of private law
which shed important light on the practices and customs to be found
in a setting and during a period about which we know almost nothing.
The correspondence between the authorities of the colony and the
religious authorities in Jerusalem is particularly interesting for the
Old Testament scholar: from it we learn that at Elephantine there
was a temple built by members of the colony in honour of Yahu (an
abbreviated form of Yahweh) which had been destroyed about 410,
so it seems, at the instigation of the priests of the local Egyptian god
Khnum. Either they were afraid of the competition, or they were
scandalized by the sacrifice of sheep and goats, which was sacrilegious
to them: in fact the Egyptian god was represented with the head of a

he-goat. The destruction took place with the connivance of the local authorities. Among other things, the correspondence deals with the reconstruction of the ruined temple and is addressed to the local governor and to the religious authorities in Jerusalem. Names appear in it which are also attested in the books of Ezra and Nehemiah, as we have seen; since the letters themselves are dated, the dates of these figures can be established objectively.

When the colonists received no reply to their initial protests, they renewed their requests towards 408, and this time it seems that their efforts were crowned with success; it proved possible for the temple to be rebuilt very soon.

Among the writings discovered in the archive we also have a copy of the story of Ahikar, the importance of which we saw during the course of our study of Israelite wisdom.

§2. *The religion of the Jews of Elephantine*

The religion of the Jews of the colony is a problem of notorious complexity. First of all we have the question of the temple. How was it possible that the construction of another sanctuary was authorized after Josiah's reform, not only outside Jerusalem but even outside the Holy Land, in Egypt, without giving rise to endless polemic? At this point we are shortly before the period when the schism between Jews and Samaritans finally came to a head, and one of the reasons for the disagreement was the construction of a sanctuary by the Samaritans on Mount Gerizim, near Shechem. Furthermore, two other deities appear alongside the figure of Yahweh, Anath-bethel and Asham-bethel. It is beyond question that these were gods worshipped along with Yahweh; their names are mentioned on lists of offerings and tithes together with that of Yahweh, and these are lists which refer only to the Jewish inhabitants of the region. A temple outside Jerusalem and a cult which was at best syncretistic: these are two facts whose origin and implications are still a matter of controversy.

First of all, it seems obvious that the reforms of Ezra and Nehemiah did not reach as far as Elephantine. Many scholars would prefer to go further back: the group, they claim, was formed even before Josiah's reform and maintained practices and religious traditions earlier than the last quarter of the seventh century BC. The relationship of the two deities with Bethel seems to indicate a northern origin for this cult, but the term might also be a divine designation, which is also attested. For Kraeling, 83ff., it would simply be a matter of compromise: the colonists worshipped their God, Yahweh, but to be on the safe side they did not overlook the other deities of their homeland, who were considered as his vassals or subordinates. However, there is no proof for this theory. In any case, it seems strange that dealings with the religious authorities of Jerusalem, who were otherwise so jealous in their defence of orthodoxy, were frequent and normally cordial, without there being any trace of a conflict. The problem is destined to remain unsolved.

The so-called 'passover papyrus' (no. 21 in Cowley's collection) is of particular interest to the reader of the Bible. It was studied fully by Grelot, and we follow his reconstruction here:

'(To) my (brethren (2) Ye)doniah and his colleagues (the J)ewish gar(rison), your brother Hanan(iah). The welfare of my brethren may the gods (seek . . .) (3) Now this year, the fifth year of King Darius, an order was sent from the king to Arsames (a third of a line is missing) (4) (a third of a line is missing). Now therefore do you count four(teen days from the first day of Nisan) (5). . . . (another lacuna) and keep (the passover). And from the fifteenth day until the twenty-first day of Ni(san) will be a feast of unleavened bread: (6) for seven days eat unleavened bread. Be ritually clean and take heed, (do not do any) work (on the fifteenth and the twenty-first day). 7 . . . (another lacuna) . . . For the rest, do not drink (beer) and do not eat anything (in) which the(re is) leaven . . . (another lacuna) . . . (8) (Eat unleavened bread after the fourteenth day of Nisan at) the setting of the sun, until the twenty-first day of Nisa(n at the setting of the sun. For seven days, (9) let not leaven be found among you and do not intro)duce it into your houses, and keep it far from you during (those) days (a third of a line missing) . . . (10) . . . (a third of a line is missing). (Address): '(To) my brothers Yedoniah and his colleagues, the Jewish garrison, your brother Hanan(iah).'

It will be obvious, even to the reader who is unfamiliar with this material, that the papyrus is badly damaged and therefore mutilated in the key passages, so that it is far from clear to read and understand, notwithstanding the brilliant work of reconstruction carried out by Grelot. For example, Kraeling rejects the introduction of the term 'passover' into the lacuna in lines 4f., and this objection was already put forward by Cowley and Vincent. But if this conjecture were correct, we would also have here the distinction between the passover and the feast of unleavened bread attested in P in the Pentateuch (Exod. 12 and Lev. 11–15, against Deut. 16.8 which tries to make the two feasts into one). Line 7 has been restored on the basis of the practice attested in the Mishnah, Pesahim 3, 1, of not drinking any kind of drink fermented on a cereal base (in this case beer made from barley) during the week of the passover. It is interesting that the passage is dated in the fifth year of Darius II, i.e. 419; it also bears witness to a direct intervention by the king in internal matters of worship.

§3. The Samaria papyri

About twenty fragments of papyri were found during 1962 and 1963 in a cave near the *wādī dāliye* in the Jordan valley, at about the thirty-second parallel, none of which has so far been fully reconstructed; they are documents of a legal and administrative character. The latest date attested in the papyri is 18 March 335 BC; the earliest papyrus comes between the thirtieth and fortieth year of Artaxerxes II, i.e. between 375 and 365, though the figure is not exact because of a lacuna which has destroyed one part of the number.

While waiting for a fundamental study and for the definitive publication of the documents, we can expect that they will be of considerable interest to the historian, either because they give information about the Persian administration and features of public and private laws connected with it, or because they give a complete list of five governors of Samaria, thus filling a gap left by Flavius Josephus, *Antt.* XI, 7.2` = §§302f.

BIBLIOGRAPHY

Texts
A. E. Cowley, *Aramaic Papyri of the Fifth Century BC*, Oxford 1923 (= 1967); E. G. Kraeling, *The Brooklyn Museum Aramaic Papyri*, New York 1953; G. R. Driver, *Aramaic Documents from the Fifth Century BC*, Oxford 1957 (a useful edition of selected texts; B. Porter, *Archives from Elephantine*, Berkeley-Los Angeles 1972; M. Greenberg, *Jews of Elephantine and Aramaeans from Syene*, Jerusalem 1974).
Translation: ANET³, 222f., 491f.

On the juridical questions cf. A. Verger, *Ricerche giuridiche sui papiri aramaici d'Elefantina*, Rome 1965 (with full bibliography); Y. Muffs, *Studies in the Aramaic Legal Papyri from Elephantine*, Leiden 1969; P. Grelot, *Documents araméens d'Égypte*, Paris 1972. K. Galling, 'Der Gott Karmel und die Ächtung fremden Götter', in *Geschichte und Altes Testament: Festschrift A. Alt*, Tübingen 1953, 105–25, has argued for the northern origin of the colony; cf. also E. Volterra, ' "Yhwdy" e " 'rmy" nei papiri armaici del

V secolo provenienti dall'Egitto', *Atti dell' Accademia dei Lincei*, Rendiconti VIII, 18, 1963, 131–73. For the date of the rebuilding of the temple see P. Grelot, 'La réconstruction du temple juif d'Éléphantine', *Or* 36, 1967, 173–7.

§2. A. Vincent, *La religion des judéo-araméens d'Éléphantine*, Paris 1937 (a classic study). For the 'passover papyrus' cf. P. Grelot, 'Études sur le "papyrus pascal" d'Éléphantine', *VT* 4, 1954, 349–84; id., 'Le papyrus pascal d'Éléphantine et le problème du Pentateuque', *VT* 5, 1955, 250–65; id., 'Le papyrus pascal d'Éléphantine: nouvel essai', *VT* 17, 1967, 114–17; id., 'Le papyrus pascal d'Éléphantine', *VT* 17, 1967, 201–7 (on which the text reproduced here is based); id., 'Le papyrus pascal d'Éléphantine et les lettres d'Hermopolis', *VT* 17, 1967, 481–3.

§3. F. M. Cross, Jr, 'The Discovery of the Samaria Papyri', *BA* 26, 1963, 110–21; K. Galling, 'Die Liste der Statthalter von Samaria im 5/4. Jahrhundert', in his *Studien zur Geschichte Israels im persischen Zeitalter*, Tübingen 1964, 209f.

CHRONOLOGICAL SYNOPSIS

The aim of the following tables is to set the people and events presented in the Old Testament, some of which are mentioned in this *Introduction*, in the context of the ancient Near East and the classical Western world of Greece and Rome.

It has, of course, been necessary to make a selection of the most important people and events. In the case of the ancient Near East, this selection has been based on the figures who are mentioned in the Old Testament or are of particular importance for it. The names always appear in the form in which they are given in the Bible, and not in their original language (e.g. those of the kings of Assyria and Babylon). For the classical world we have indicated events and figures most of which will already be well known, especially to those who have studied classics.

As in the earlier edition of this book, the table is based on the chronology worked out by W. F. Albright and the American Schools of Oriental Research (cf. above, Part Two, ch. IX, § 1). In some instances, however, later investigations have shown that at times the chronology of J. Begrich and A. Jepsen is more credible: this has been shown in parentheses. For a careful examination of all the chronologies proposed for the Old Testament see H. Tadmor, 'Kronologia', *Encyclopaedia Biblica* IV, Jerusalem 1962, 245–310 (in Hebrew).

For Assyrian and Babylonian chronology we have made use of W. W. Hallo, 'From Qarqar to Carchemish', *BA* 23, 1960, 34–61, and J. A. Brinkman, 'Mesopotamian Chronology of the Historical Period', in A. L. Oppenheim, *Ancient Mesopotamia*, Chicago 1964, 335–52, which brings down the figures given here by about a year. The kings of Babylon are indicated by an asterisk (*).

For Aramaean chronology cf. recently F. M. Cross, Jr, 'The Stele dedicated to Melcarth by Ben-Hadad of Damascus', *BASOR* 205, 1972, 36–42. This chronology is not, however, accepted by all scholars and therefore will have to be verified again.

The important and recent book by K. A. Kitchen, *The Third Intermediate Period in Egypt (1100–650)*, Warminster 1973, proposes substantial modifications to Egyptian chronology. These are indicated in parentheses; on the other hand, we have not felt able to adopt the chronology of E. R. Thiele (cf. above, Part Two, ch. IX, §1), which Kitchen proposes for the period of the kings of Judah and Israel.

Century BC	ISRAEL		EGYPT	PHOENICIA AND SYRIA
	History	Texts, people and events of importance		
XIII	Beginning of 13th century: Exodus	Moses	*c.* 1290–24: Rameses II	
		Joshua	*c.* 1223–11: Merneptah	
XII	End of 13th century, beginning of 12th: Conquest of Palestine	Judges Beginning of 12th century: Philistine occupation		
XI		*c.* 1050: Battle reported in Judg. 5		
X	*c.* 1020–1000 (1012–04): Saul *c.* 1000–961 (1004–965): David *c.* 961–22 (965–26): Solomon	J	*c.* 964–46 (978–59) Siamun *c.* 935–14 (945–24) Shishak I	*c.* 970–36 (973–42) Hiram of Tyre
	c. 922 (926): Dissolution of the united kingdom			

	Kingdom of Israel	Kingdom of Judah			
IX	*c.* 922–01 (926–07): Jeroboam I *c.* 901–900 (907–06) Nadab *c.* 900–877 (906–883): Baasha *c.* 877–76 (883–82) Elah	*c.* 922–15 (926–10): Rehoboam *c.* 915–13 (910–08): Abijah *c.* 913–873 (908–868): Asa	9th century: Aramaean Wars		*c.* 891–59 (873–42): Ittobaal of Tyre *c.* 885–70: Benhadad I of Damascus
	c. 876 (882): Zimri *c.* 876–73 (882–78): Tibni				

MESO-POTAMIA	PERSIA	GREECE	ROME	Century BC
				XIII
		12th century: Trojan war (?)		XII
				XI
				X
				IX

Century BC	ISRAEL			EGYPT	PHOENICIA AND SYRIA
	History		Texts, people and events of importance		
	Kingdom of Israel	Kingdom of Judah			
	c. 873–69 (878–71): Omri *c.* 869–50 (871–52): Ahab *c.* 850–49 (852–51): Ahaziah	*c.* 873–49 (868–47): Jehoshaphat	Elijah 853: Battle of Qarqar		*c.* 870–42: Benhadad II = Hadadezer of Damascus
	c. 849–42 (851–45): Jehoram *c.* 842–15 (845–18): Jehu *c.* 815–01 (818–02): Jehoahaz	*c.* 849–42 (847–45): Joram *c.* 842–37 (845–40): Athaliah *c.* 837–800 (840–01): Jehoash	Elisha E		*c.* 845–42: Benhadad III of Damascus *c.* 841–06: Hazael of Damascus 814/13: Foundation of Carthage
VIII	*c.* 801–786: (802–787) Joash *c.* 786–46 (787–47): Jeroboam II *c.* 746–45 (747): Zechariah	*c.* 800–783 (801–787): Amaziah *c.* 783–42 (787–36): Uzziah/ Azariah *c.* 750–35 (759–44: regent): Jotham	Amos Hosea Isaiah		806–?: Benhadad IV of Damascus
	c. 745 (747): Shallum *c.* 745–38 (747–38): Menahem *c.* 738–37 (737–36): Pekahiah *c.* 737–32 (735–32): Pekah *c.* 732–24: Hoshea	*c.* 735–15 (736–29/25): Jehoahaz	Micah 734: 'Syro-Ephraimite' War		?: Rezin of Damascus *c.* 732: Fall of Damascus

MESO-POTAMIA	PERSIA	GREECE	ROME	Century BC
c. 859–25 (858–28) Shalmaneser III				
c. 811–784 (810–783) Adad-nirari III				VIII
c. 783–74 (783–72) Shalmaneser IV		776: First Olympiad		
c. 755–46 (754–45) Assur-Nirari V		754–53: Third year, Sixth Olympiad	753: Foundation of Rome	
c. 745–28 (744–27) Tiglath-Pileser III		8th century: Homer (?)	753–509: The seven kings of Rome	
c. 727–23 (726–22) Shalmaneser V				

Century BC	ISRAEL			EGYPT	PHOENICIA AND SYRIA
	Kingdom of Israel	Kingdom of Judah	Texts, people and events of importance		
VII	723–22: Fall of Samaria 720: End of resistance Province of Assyria	c. 715–687 (728–700): Hezekiah c. 687–42: Manasseh			
		c. 642–40: Amon	Nahum Zephaniah Habakkuk	663: Conquest of Thebes by Assyria c. 690–63: Tirhaka 663–09: Psammeti-chus I	
	End of 7th century: Reconquest by Josiah	c. 640–09 (639–09): Josiah	Jeremiah 622–21: Josiah's reform		
		609: Jehoahaz 609–598: Jehoiakim	609: Battle of Megiddo 605: Battle of Carchemish 601–600: Necho II recaptures Gaza	609–594: Necho II	
VI	Beginning of 6th century: Babylonian province	597: Jehoiachin: pardoned in in 562 597–87: Zedekiah 587–39: Babylonian exile	597: First fall of Jerusalem Ezekiel 587: Second fall of Jerusalem P II Isaiah 539: Edict of Cyrus Haggai Zechariah III Isaiah	568–26: Amasis 525: Cambyses occupies Egypt	
		c. 538–21: Zerubbabel governor	516: Rebuild-ing of the temple		

MESO-POTAMIA	PERSIA	GREECE	ROME	Century BC
c.722–06 (721–05) Sargon II c. 705–682 (704–681): Sennacherib c. 703: Merodach Baladan* c. 681–70 (680–69): Esarhaddon				VII
		7th century: Hesiod		
c. 669–33 (668–32) Asshur-banipal 625: First fall of Nineveh 612: Second fall of Nineveh	625–585: Cyaxares	c. 640: Solon End of 7th century: Thales		
611–09: Asshur-uballit II 605–561: Nebuchadnezzar II*				
		6th century: Anaximander Anaximenes Xenophanes		VI
561–60: Evil-Merodach* 555–39: Nabonidus*	559–30: Cyrus II 530–22: Cambyses II			
	522–486: Darius I		509: Republic of Rome	

Century BC	ISRAEL		EGYPT	PERSIA
	Judah	Texts, people and events of importance		
V				486–64: Xerxes I
		Malachi		464–23: Artaxerxes I
		Mission of Ezra and Nehemiah		423–04: Darius II
IV		Chronicles Ezra Nehemiah		404–360: Artaxerxes II 360–38: Artaxerxes III 338–35: Arsebes 335–32: Darius III
	332: Alexander the Great conquers Syria and Palestine			
III	c. 300: Simeon I High Priest	323–198: Sovereignty of the Ptolemies of Egypt	285–46: Ptolemy II Philadelphus	
II	c. 200: Simeon II High Priest	198 ff.: Sovereignty of the Seleucids of Syria c. 190: Jesus ben Sirach		
	174–71: Jason High Priest			
	171–62: Menelaus High Priest	167: Abomination of desolation: revolt of Mattathias Daniel		
	162: Alcimus High Priest 165–60: Judas Maccabaeus	164: Re-consecration of the temple		

MACEDONIA	SYRIA	GREECE	ROME	Century BC
		500/497–428/27 Anaxagoras 492–90: First and second Persian expeditions (Marathon) 480–78: Third Persian expedition (Thermopylae, Salamis, Plataea) Middle of 5th century: Herodotus 431–04: Peloponnesian war		V
		c. 469–399: Socrates c. 428–348: Plato 384–22: Aristotle		IV
356–23: Alexander the Great 333: Battle of Issus	334: Alexander the Great attacks Syria 332: Conquered by Alexander 312–198: Struggle of Diadochi			
	223–187: Antiochus III		281–72: Pyrrhic wars 264–41: First Punic War 218–01: Second Punic War	III
	187–75: Seleucus IV		200–197: Second Macedonian War	II
	175–64: Antiochus IV Epiphanes 164–61: Antiochus V		192–87: War against Antiochus III of Syria	

Century BC	ISRAEL		EGYPT	PERSIA
	Judah	Texts, people and events of importance		
II	160–42: Jonathan Maccabaeus 142–34: Simeon Maccabaeus 134–04: John Hyrcanus	*c.* 125: Qumran monastery founded		
I	104–76: Juda and Alexander Jannaeus 37–4: Herod the Great	63: Pompey conquers Palestine		

MACEDONIA	SYRIA	GREECE	ROME	Century BC
	161–50: Demetrius I		171–68: Third Macedonian War 149–46: Third Punic War 133–21: The Gracchi 118–100: C. Marius 91–88: Civil war 60–53: First triumvirate	II I

INDEX OF MODERN AUTHORS